THIRD EDITION

Working with Older Adults

Group Process and Techniques

Edited by

Irene Burnside, RN, PhD, FAAN

Mary Gwynne Schmidt, MSW, PhD, LCSW

JONES AND BARTLETT PUBLISHERS
Boston   London

Editorial, Sales, and Customer Service Offices

Jones and Bartlett Publishers
One Exeter Plaza
Boston, MA 02116
1-617-859-3900
1-800-832-0034

Jones and Bartlett Publishers International
P.O. Box 1498
London W6 7R5
England

Library of Congress Cataloging-in-Publication Data

Burnside, Irene Mortenson.
      Working with older adults : group process and techniques / Irene Burnside, Mary Gwynne Schmidt. — 3rd ed.
          p.   cm.
      Rev. ed. of: Working with the elderly / Irene Burnside. 2nd ed.   © 1984.
      Includes bibliographical references and index.
      ISBN 0-86720-679-9
          1. Social work with the aged.   2. Social group work.   I. Schmidt, Mary
Gwynne.   II. Burnside, Irene Mortenson.   Working with the elderly.   III. Title.
HV1451.B88   1994   94-3105
362.6--dc20   CIP

Acquisitions Editor: Jan Wall
Production Coordinator: Joan M. Flaherty
Manufacturing Buyer: Dana L. Cerrito
Production: Ocean Publication Services
Interior Design: Katherine Harvey
Cover Design: Rafael Millán
Typesetting: Ruth Maassen
Printing and Binding: Malloy Lithographing, Inc.
Cover Photo: Marianne Gontarz

Photo Credits: Part Opener photos on pages 1, 39, 107, 225, 291, and 333 by
Marianne Gontarz.

Printed in the United States of America
98 97 96 95 94   10 9 8 7 6 5 4 3 2 1

Contents

Preface

When the first edition of *Working with the Elderly: Group Process and Techniques* appeared in 1978, it was the only book written exclusively about group work with older persons. Since then, several books have been published on group work with older adults, which indicates the continued need for this special modality.

This third edition, *Working with Older Adults: Group Process and Techniques,* has been changed in an obvious way by the addition of a co-editor to broaden the view from the social worker's viewpoint. Because nurses and social workers are the two largest groups of professionals who do group work with older adults, it seems beneficial to all readers to have both disciplines involved in presenting content for the third edition.

Twelve new chapters have been added to reflect changes in this field since the second edition. One important change at the governmental level is the Omnibus Budget Reconciliation Act of 1987 (OBRA '87), which mandates psychosocial intervention and treatment and makes it unlawful to mask behavior problems and unhappiness with psychotropic medications. But at the same time, few facilities provide the educated, qualified professional staff required to deliver group services. This book has always had as its goal improving the quality of life and the psychosocial care for older persons.

One important reason for revision of this book is the increased community care of older persons and the rapid changes in the health care system that impose new demands and standards on the agencies, facilities, and caregivers that serve older people.

While few innovative groups have been designed for older adults since the last edition, we are pleased to add one important new group—the guided autobiography group originated by Dr. James E. Birren.

As with the second edition, we do not focus exclusively on group dynamics; our purpose is to delineate the modifications and the special types of groups implemented with older adults in a variety of settings. We have placed increased emphasis on settings in this revision because the setting has a great impact on the group.

This text is meant to be used by beginning group leaders; instructors teaching group work with older adults; and experienced practitioners, who will use the book as a resource, a reference, and a refresher. The second editor knows this well, as betokened by her own well-worn copies of the two earlier editions. The greater attention to settings and the new emphasis imparted by the Nursing Home Reform Act and other changing regulatory and work requirements make this third edition a valuable addition to the field and a good book to have at hand.

Part 1 includes demographic data about older persons and an introduction to group work with the aged. The book begins with an overview of the types of groups currently being conducted and the types of professional people needed to lead them both now and in the future.

Part 2 briefly discusses theoretical concepts that are particularly applicable to the older adult population. Education, contracts, group membership, leadership, and maintenance of groups are all covered in Part 3.

Part 4 is the "how to"—the nuts and bolts of the book. Many of the suggestions included here may seem obvious to those who have had group experience with older adults, but it is good to remember that a myriad of details and complex arrangements precede the smooth running of a group. The logistics cannot be overemphasized, because no matter how simple conducting a group may seem, in actuality it is a complex intervention.

Part 5 describes the various settings and the implementation of groups in those settings. The new demands of the population and new regulations have expanded the range of settings now seeking to offer groups to their participants, patients, residents, clients, staff, and families.

Part 6 presents the perspectives of three disciplines—the social worker, the nurse, and the recreational therapist.

Part 7 discusses curricular changes to promote group work and innovative approaches to teaching. It also deals with consultation and responsibilities of preceptors.

Controversy often erupts about the question of who should be doing group work with older adults. Professionals tend to guard their territories jealously and to feel that nonprofessionals will unleash strong feelings and emotions with which they cannot deal. This attitude sells the aged short; they are a tough lot. Moreover, group experiences help dilute feelings in a way that one-to-one relationships do not, and peer support and feedback are valuable assets to the group members. The danger is not in conducting groups, but rather in not providing them at all and thereby fostering the prevalent attitude of "therapeutic nihilism." It is better to take a risk than to sit by and watch apathy, fear, sensory deprivation, loneliness, helplessness continue in the aged.

Professional caregivers are not and will not be carrying the whole load in group work with older people. The tremendous need for leaders of all types of groups will continue and increase with the "graying of America." Much responsibility contin-

ues to fall on persons who have not been trained adequately for work in long-term care facilities.

We have made a clear distinction in *Working with Older Adults: Group Process and Techniques* between group work and formal group psychotherapy. Instructors will have to do the same with their students. This third edition follows the same format as the second edition to make it useful to students, instructors, and clinicians.

To the Student

You do not have to read or study all the chapters in this book (unless, of course, your instructor assigns them); you can pick and choose those that interest you the most. Each chapter is independent of the other chapters. Key words, learning objectives, student projects, and resources are included to facilitate learning. It will help if you also know the basics of group dynamics.

To the Instructor

We recommend that you select the chapters most germane to your discipline and to your objectives if there is limited time for teaching the content. However, the book is easy reading, and some instructors have assigned the entire book for a quarter or semester class.

To facilitate teaching, key words, learning objectives, student exercises, and resources are included in each chapter; and in this third edition, new student projects have been suggested. We did not delete any of the projects included in the second edition, however, because some of them may be helpful for teaching purposes.

To the Clinician

The book has clinical content and "how to" materials in all chapters except Chapter 1. To increase your knowledge and skills, you might want to try doing some of the creative projects at the end of the chapters. Extensive references, bibliographies, and resources enable tailoring your curriculum to meet particular needs.

For both of us, working with older adults has been a humbling experience. We have learned how much they know, and how much they can teach us if we remain open.

Acknowledgments

We warmly and gratefully acknowledge the people who helped improve the quality of the book and made revision much easier for us. First of all, we thank the contributors who offered suggestions; wrote with short deadlines facing them; coped with earthquake, copious snow, and bitter cold; and added breadth and depth to this edition.

E. Percil Stanford, Sofia Clemente, Barbara Reuer, Joan Roberts, Alicia Vallejo of the San Diego State University Center on Aging, offered support in many ways during the work on this book. Their warmth and friendliness were constant.

The excellent critique by Ellen Janosik helped us improve the original plan for the book; we incorporated many of her suggestions.

Pearl Bladek, who also typed her way through the earlier editions, once again provided word processing help when needed. Gail Mazzola-Gerard was a valuable research assistant.

Jan Wall, our editor and guide from Jones and Bartlett, offered support to keep us on track and helped with many of the details that go with revising a book, as did Joan Flaherty.

It is the families who pay a high price when writers are in the throes of producing a book. We are grateful for the understanding and the patience and the myriad types of help that we received from our significant others.

For Sally, Chad, Zoë, and Zachary,
one of my very favorite groups

IB

For Albert Schmidt, my husband,
and Fredrick Nels Schmidt, my son

MGS

and for
Mary Jane Hennessey, who
did not live to revise her chapter.

Contributors

Judith A.S. Altholz, PhD
Private Practice in Psychotherapy
Consultation and Training
Tallahassee, Florida

E. Frederick Anderson, MSW, PhD
Chair, Department of Social Work
California State University
Los Angeles, California

James E. Birren, PhD
Associate Director
UCLA Center on Aging
University of California
Los Angeles, California

Janet E. Black, LCSW
Professor
Associate Director/Director of Field Education
Department of Social Work
California State University
Long Beach, California

Elissa Brown, RN, MSN, CS
Assistant Clinical Professor
University of California

Clinical Nurse Specialist
Department of Veterans' Affairs Medical Center
Sepulveda, California

Irene Burnside, RN, PhD, FAAN
Adjunct Professor
School of Nursing
San Diego State University
San Diego, California

Roger Delgado, MSW, PhD
Professor
Department of Social Work
California State University
Los Angeles, California

Helen Dennis, MA
Project Director and Lecturer
Ethel Percy Andrus Gerontology Center
University of Southern California
Los Angeles, California

Donna E. Deutchman
Associate Director for Development
Borun Center for Gerontological Research
UCLA School of Medicine and Jewish Home
    for the Aged
Los Angeles, California

Jean Kittredge Duchesneau, RN, BSN, GNP
Director
Redwood Elderlink Day Care Center
Escondido, California

Sally A. Friedlob, LCSW, OTR
Clinical Coordinator
University of California
Neuropsychiatric Institute
After Care Unit
Los Angeles, California

Mary Jean Hennessey, RN, MS
Formerly, Violinist, Monterey County Symphony
Formerly, Health Educator, Gerontology
    Geriatric Patient Care and Music
Carmel, California (deceased)

Joann Ivry, MSW, PhD
Assistant Professor
Aging Specialist
School of Social Work
Hunter College of the City University
    of New York
New York, New York

James J. Kelly, PhD
Professor
Director, Department of Social Work
California State University
Long Beach, California

Joan K. Parry, LCSW, DSW
Profesor Emerita
College of Social Work
San Jose State University
San Jose, California

Susan Rice, DSW
Department of Social Work
California State University
Long Beach, California

Florence Safford, DSW
Associate Professor
Department of Social Work
Florida International University
Miami, Florida

Mary Gwynne Schmidt, MSW, PhD
Professor Emerita
School of Social Work
San Diego State University
San Diego, California

Research Associate
Center on Aging
San Diego State University
San Diego, California

Florence S. Schwartz, MSW, EdD
Professor Emerita
School of Social Work
Hunter College of the City University
    of New York
New York, New York

Bernita M. Steffl, RN, MPH
Professor Emerita
College of Nursing
Arizona State University
Tempe, Arizona

Karin Mueck Vecchione, MEd, CTRS
Administrator
Senior Network, Inc.
Crescent Cities Adult Medical
    Day Center
Oxon Hill, Maryland

Elizabeth M. Williams, RN, MSN, GNP, C
Head Nurse
Nursing Home Care Unit
Department of Veterans' Affairs Medical Center
Denver, Colorado

PART 1

Overview

The third edition of this textbook opens with an introduction that reflects the philosophy of the editors about group work with older persons.

Chapter 1 introduces the reader to some of the rapid changes that have occurred in care of older persons.

Chapter 2 offers demographic data about older Americans and specifically notes the preponderance of older women and the projections for the 85 plus population. The second half of the chapter is about physical changes in normal aging and discusses psychosocial theories that may help the new group leader.

Chapter 3 is an overview of group work and gives a brief history of group work and group psychotherapy with older adults in the United States.

These three chapters set the stage for the remainder of the book, which moves from the theoretical positions presented in Part 2 into the general knowledge needed to start and maintain groups and on to the practical aspects of leading groups of all types. The final part of the book has chapters about less common issues regarding group work with older persons.

CHAPTER 1

Introduction

Mary Gwynne Schmidt

KEY WORDS

- Adult day health care centers
- Assisted living
- Board-and-care facilities
- Informalization
- OBRA '87
- Senior centers
- Social day care centers
- Special care units

LEARNING OBJECTIVES

- Describe five programs that serve older adults and are congregate in character.
- Differentiate among social day care centers, adult day health care centers, and Alzheimer's day care centers.
- Describe three trends that are increasing the demand for group services.
- List living arrangements on a continuum from retirement communities to nursing facilities and the older adult populations appropriate to each.
- Explain how the Omnibus Budget Reconciliation Act of 1987 (OBRA '87) has increased the demand for group activities in the nursing facility.

In the last decade, rapid changes in the eldercare system have placed new demands and set new standards for the institutions, agencies, and individuals that comprise it. The formal system is receiving older and frailer persons than it served previously. In the interests of cost containment, more care has been "pushed back" to families and community agencies (Binney, Estes & Humphries 1993). Regulations call for more emphasis on the psychosocial aspects of care and the involvement of a wider array of professions. The law mandates greater sensitivity to the rights and potential of residents, patients, and clients. One result of these changes is an accelerating demand for group work with older adults.

The changes can be observed in a variety of settings.

Senior Centers

Senior centers and nutrition sites are serving more needful persons and doing so with fewer resources and a shifting sense of mission. In his seven-year follow-up of a national sample of 424 senior centers, Krout (1990) found that participants in 1989 were more numerous than in 1982 and that a greater proportion were older and frailer as well. During the decade, federal funding dropped, and centers were compelled to turn more to hard-pressed state and local governments. Most of the centers were struggling to provide as much program as before, often with less staff. Although they were often viewed as serving the well elderly, more than 35 percent of the centers in

Krout's study reported a decline in the health status of participants.

In addition to congregate meals, senior centers provide services such as screening, referral, emergency assistance, counseling, advocacy, and home-delivered meals. Their educational and recreational activities include classes, current events, and reminiscence groups. Many of the seniors attending the centers live alone, and for them, attendance at the sites not only guarantees nutritional benefits but also helps to reduce the isolation in their lives.

With increasing demands for the health care dollar, the centers face another challenge: To get the resources to serve the persons who need them most, they must emphasize their supportive and maintenance functions so that they will be recognized as part of the continuum of eldercare. This is less of a problem for the day health care centers that are recognized by Medicaid.

Day Care Centers

Day health care centers and social day care centers are being joined by the more specialized Alzheimer's family centers. Day care centers serve a mix of physically frail and mild-to-moderately impaired older adults, while the Alzheimer's centers provide respite for caregivers and social stimulation for the more seriously cognitively disabled. From 1974, when there were 18 day care centers in the United States, they have grown to an estimated 1700 (Conrad, Hughes, Hanrahan & Wang 1993). Kane and Kane (1987) define *day care* as a long-term care service provided in an outpatient setting and offered for a limited time during the day. In their attempt to classify day care centers, Conrad and his associates (1993) identify two kinds of specialized programs, the Alzheimer's family centers and the rehabilitation programs for the physically impaired. Between lies a mix of centers that differ mainly in the resources they bring to care, including the most numerous group, the general purpose programs.

The more usual division is between health and social day care centers. The boundaries between the more medically oriented day health care programs and social day care become more precise when Medicaid is paying the bill. The day health care centers are required to provide active rehabilitation and richer staffing. Chapter 22 describes day care centers and their use of group activities.

During the decade since the previous edition of this book, the number of special day care programs for persons with Alzheimer's disease and related disorders increased. These programs provide not only respite for family caregivers but also social stimulation for the participants. Their purpose is to slow decline and preserve social functioning. Many, but not all, are sponsored by local chapters of the Association for Alzheimer's Disease and Related Disorders. These centers have an endless need for group activities designed specifically for this population.

The more impaired the population the center serves, the more likely it is to offer support groups for family caregivers. There is a reason for this: What Binney, Estes, and Humphries (1993) refer to as *informalization* has been used to transfer services from the formal system to the informal sector—that is, from nursing facilities and hospitals to families and friends. This, plus the rising cost of care, is resulting in untrained persons struggling to care for individuals who previously would have been in nursing homes and state hospitals. These caregivers are heavily burdened and in need of both respite and group support.

Board-and-Care Facilities

Board-and-care facilities for the many, and assisted living for the more affluent, are serving a wider range of persons and, in some instances, expanding their services. A variety of living arrangements fills the gap between fully independent living in the community and nursing facilities. Described under different categories, these have in common the fact that their residents are not supposed to be in need of nursing care. Many persons prefer them because they are less institutional. Because regulatory standards are lower, they are also much cheaper.

The House Select Committee on Aging has charged that states, "in an effort to cut costs," have contributed to the unchecked growth of board-and-care facilities (U.S. House of Representatives 1992, 79). The Committee expressed the view that since the federal government was "funneling about $3.5 billion a year, through Supplemental Security Income (SSI) and Social Security programs" into these settings, Congress had a responsibility to see that their residents got good care (p. 77). In general, they are poorly regulated. There are an estimated 41,000 licensed facilities and at least as many unlicensed ones (U.S. Senate and House of Representatives 1989). Many are six-bed enterprises; some proprietors own more than one. Others are large facilities. In some states, some facilities are allowed to have secure perimeters so their supposedly "independent" residents will not wander and get lost.

There are a growing number of corporate and privately owned facilities aimed at a more affluent class of residents. Some offer assisted living with personal care, including help with bathing and dressing. Nursing care can be provided as a home-health service. Large enterprises offer a closed system with independent cottages or apartments, sheltered care, assisted living, and skilled nursing facilities. A resident can move through different care and cost levels without ever leaving the grounds.

For the middle class as well as the poor, two features are driving the industry: costs and a distaste for the status of nursing-home patient. The higher-priced settings often offer activities programs. At the midpoint in the spectrum, owners of board-and-cares might well contract with professionals for group services as a selling point with relatives. In his manual for board-and-care administrators, Schwartz (1991) tells the untrained facilitator how to lead groups.

In Chapter 21, Black, Kelly, and Rice discuss group work in retirement communities, and in Chapter 23, Black, Friedlob, and Kelly deal with reminiscence groups in board-and-care homes.

Nursing Facilities

Nursing facilities also have experienced a changing clientele, but, unlike the others, they have been given clear orders to provide their traditional services within a different framework. As discussed in the next chapter, nursing facilities are now serving two distinct populations: ill older adults, arriving sicker because of earlier hospital discharge, and frail people, entering later because of rising residential-care costs and the availability of more community supports for staying home (Shaughnessy & Kramer 1990).

Ill older adults tend to be depressed and fearful of being institutionalized. Generally, they are younger and more alert than the very old and, unlike them, they can look forward to returning home. Their convalescent care is covered by Medicare. Most of the physically frail are very old, and sometimes they are mentally frail as well. They re-

main, and sooner or later, the expenses of most of them are paid by Medicaid.

When they first enter, both the ill and the very old struggle to come to terms with their changed status and living arrangements (Schmidt 1990). Resident and family groups help. In addition, the mentally alert need groups to help them find their peers within the setting. Otherwise they cocoon in their rooms, depressed by the sight of so much senility. The less alert need groups for stimulation, companionship, and pleasure. Their family members can use group support to cope with guilt and unhappiness about having had to place a relative in a nursing facility. From other people's relatives, they learn ways to meet their older kinspersons' changing needs.

These needs of residents and their families always existed and therefore were not the main lever pushing facilities to provide group services. Those needs were brought into sharper focus by the Nursing Home Reform Amendments of 1987 (OBRA '87) and the increased attention to psychosocial issues they introduced. The character of the changes is indicated by the new terminology that came with OBRA '87. The place itself is now called a *nursing facility* instead of a *nursing home,* it being conceded that there was little homelike about these institutions. The persons served in them are now *residents,* instead of *patients.* So ingrained is the old vocabulary, however, that readers will find both terminologies used in this book and in professional journals.

More to the point, the reform amendments and the regulations flowing from them require that residents be afforded care that will help them "attain or maintain the highest practicable physical, mental, and psychosocial well-being" (OBRA '87; U.S. Department of Health and Human Services 1991). In exceptionally concrete terms, the regulations mandate psychosocial intervention and rehabilitation based on individual care plans. Physical and chemical restraints cannot be used to solve management problems before behavioral interventions have been tried. Residents' rights are spelled out. The regulations also demand multidisciplinary approaches to patient care planning and broaden the team to include social workers; dietitians; communicative disorders specialists; physical, occupational, and recreational therapists; and other rehabilitation specialists. Unfortunately, few professionals have received the special education that would make multidisciplinary collaboration, much less interprofessional teamwork, effective.

At the same time, new pressures on staff have led to the need for more knowledge about group processes occurring in team meetings and support groups, as well as in resident and family groups.

Special Care Units

Special care units for residents with dementia in nursing facilities multiplied rapidly and were aggressively marketed, but with little standardization.

European countries such as Germany, Sweden, and England had long segregated their mentally impaired elderly residents, but in the United States, the decade since the last edition of this book saw a burst of interest in special dementia care units. A few units were freestanding, but more often they were distinct parts of existing nursing facilities. Usually, they had more private-pay residents. Higher rates of reimbursement appeared to be a factor in their proliferation.

The Ohtas (1988, 804) noted their "rapid expansion and heavy marketing" and questioned the appropriateness of so much promotion of a product whose efficacy had yet to be established. Other researchers also commented on the diversity of stated aims, staffing, physical structure, and assumptions (Gold, Sloane, Mathew, Bledsoe & Konanc 1991; Cairl, Kosberg, Henderson & Pfeiffer n.d.). Consumer pressure is beginning to press states to set standards (Mace 1988).

Although it would seem that these units could be used as laboratories for studying behavior and its management, the differences in their admission criteria are so great as to preclude generalization (Gold et al. 1991; Ohta & Ohta 1988). Many of the facilities themselves make little effort to evaluate the effect of their programs in a systematic way (Cairl et al. n.d.).

One commonality does exist: the extensive use of group approaches. As in Alzheimer's day care centers, group activities for patients are a staple. In addition, because of concern about burnout, both training and support groups are employed for staff (Robinson & Spencer 1991). Family members are often assertive about their desire to be a part of the team, and family meetings and sometimes family involvement in programming for patients is encouraged (Hansen, Patterson & Wilson 1988). Cleary, Clamson, Price, and Shullaw (1988) describe a reduced stimulation unit that let residents wander, eat, and rest as they wished. The consistent part of the daily routine was provided by scheduled rest and small-group activity periods.

SUMMARY

Although they represent a continuum of care, the five programs described above have in common their congregate character. The unfolding changes in each present both an opportunity and a challenge—the opportunity provided by an increasing demand for group work and a challenge to develop the techniques that will make it a more effective instrument. The purpose of this book is to support its readers in taking advantage of that opportunity and meeting that challenge.

EXERCISE 1

Interview one person who has worked in a nursing facility since 1986 and ask about the changes that have occurred since the implementation of OBRA '87. With two colleagues, prepare a short role play illustrating "now and then."

EXERCISE 2

A hearing on the need for respite care: The issue is whether Medicaid should pay for respite care. Role play the taxpayer ("The patient's not going to get any better anyway and his wife's got nothing to do but stay home and take care of him"); the wife of a man with dementia ("I'm afraid to leave him alone"); the day care worker—nurse or social worker

("They need the stimulation, and the caregiver needs time out"). Appoint one class member the hearing chairperson. All can question the witnesses.

REFERENCES

Binney EA, Estes CL, Humphries SE. 1993. Informalization and community care. In CL Estes, JH Swan (eds.), *The long-term care crisis: Elders trapped in the no-care zone* (pp. 155-170). Newbury Park, CA: Sage.

Cairl R, Kosberg J, Henderson N, Pfeiffer E. n.d. *Special care for Alzheimer's disease patients: An exploratory study of dementia special care units*. National Resource Center on Alzheimer's Disease, Suncoast Gerontology Center, University of South Florida.

Cleary TA, Clamson C, Price M, Shullaw G. 1988. A reduced stimulation unit: Effects on patients with Alzheimer's disease and related disorders. *Gerontologist* 28(4):511-514.

Conrad KJ, Hughes SL, Hanrahan P, Wang S. 1993. Classification of adult day care: A cluster analysis of services and activities. *J Gerontol Soc Sci* 48(3):S112-122.

Gold D, Sloan PD, Mathew LJ, Bledsoe MM, Konanc DK. 1991. Special care units: A typology of care settings for memory-impaired older adults. *Gerontologist* 31(4): 467-475.

Hansen SS, Patterson MA, Wilson RW. 1988. Family involvement on a dementia unit: The resident enrichment and activity program. *Gerontologist* 28(4):508-510.

Kane RA, Kane RL. 1987. *Long-term care: Principles, programs, and policies*. New York: Springer.

Krout JA. 1990. *The organization, operation and programming of senior centers in America: A seven year follow-up*. Final report to the AARP Andrus Foundation. Fredonia, NY: State University of New York, Department of Sociology and Anthropology (June).

Mace N. 1988. *Commonalities in international dementia care*. Paper presented at the 40th Annual Scientific Meeting of the Gerontological Society of America, San Francisco (November 18-22).

Ohta RJ, Ohta BM. 1988. Special units for Alzheimer's disease patients: A critical look. *Gerontologist* 28(6):803-808.

Omnibus Budget Reconciliation Act of 1987 (OBRA '87). Amendments to Title XIX of the Social Security Act, Sections 1819 & 1919, b.4.

Robinson A, Spencer B. 1991. Reducing staff burnout in the dementia care unit. In DH Coons (ed.), *Specialized dementia care units* (pp. 144-160). Baltimore: Johns Hopkins University Press.

Schmidt MG. 1990. *Negotiating a good old age: Challenges of residential living in late life*. San Francisco: Jossey-Bass.

Schwartz R. 1991. *The residential care handbook: A practical guide to caring and staying in business*. Durham, NC: Carolina Academic Press.

Shaughnessy PV, Kramer AM. 1990. The increased needs of patients in nursing homes and patients receiving home care. *N Engl J Med* 322(1):21-27.

U.S. Department of Health and Human Services, Health Care Financing Administration. 1991. Medicare and Medicaid: Requirements for long-term care facilities. *Federal Register* 56(187):48826-48865 (September 26).

U.S. House of Representatives, Select Committee on Aging, Subcommittee on Health and Long-term Care. 1992. *Drug abuse and misuse in America's board and care homes: Failure in public policy*. Comm. Pub. No. 102-856. Washington, DC: U.S. Government Printing Office (March).

U.S. Senate, Special Committee on Aging, & U.S. House of Representatives, Select Committee on Aging. 1989. *Board and care: A failure in public policy*. Senate Special Committee, Serial No. 101-1; House Select Committee Pub. No. 101-714. Report on Joint Hearing. Washington, DC: U.S. Government Printing Office (March 9).

BIBLIOGRAPHY

Edelson JS, Lyons WR. 1985. *Institutional care of the mentally impaired elderly*. New York: Van Nostrand Reinhold.

Estes CL, Swan JH, et al. 1993. *The long-term care crisis: Elders trapped in the no-care zone*. Newbury Park, CA: Sage.

Kane RA, Wilson KB. 1993. Assisted living in the United States: A new paradigm for residential care for frail older persons? Washington, DC: National Association for Retired Persons.

Programs need to match individual needs: Activities should be consistent with the participant's life story. 1993. *Respite Report* (Winter):4-5. Winston-Salem, NC: Bowman Grey School of Medicine of Wake Forest University.

Regnier V. 1992. Assisted living: Promoting independence, choice and autonomy. *Supportive Housing Options* 1(1):1, 4. National Eldercare Institute on Housing and Supportive Services. From Regnier's book, *New concepts in assisted living: Design innovation from the United States and Northern Europe*. New York: Van Nostrand Reinhold.

CHAPTER 2

Demographic and Psychosocial Aspects of Aging

Mary Gwynne Schmidt and Irene Burnside

KEY WORDS

- Age cohort
- Ageism
- Confabulation
- Continuity theory
- Dementia, multi-infarct type
- Dementia, Alzheimer's type
- Developmental tasks
- Disengagement theory
- Identity evolution
- Old
- Oldest-old
- Senescence
- Personhood
- Self-concept
- Self-perception
- Successful ager

LEARNING OBJECTIVES

- Tell three ways the oldest-old as a group differ from people in their sixties and seventies.
- Describe three characteristics of today's nursing-home residents that group program leaders should take into account.
- List 10 normal age changes a group leader needs to consider in planning a group.
- List three developmental tasks of late life that group members may be dealing with.

This chapter provides a background for group work with older people by telling who they are, describing the normal processes of aging, mentioning some psychosocial theories of aging, and sketching physical and psychosocial variables often found in the later years. Some terms, such as *median age* and *ageism*, are defined in a glossary in Appendix 1 of this chapter, in order not to impede readers already familiar with them.

WHO ARE THE OLDER ADULTS?

Age grading is a social process influenced by such factors as gender, occupation, class, and place. In Western industrialized society today, old age is defined principally by sanctioned withdrawal from the work force.

Historically, people have been described as "old" when they have reached pensionable age, usually 65. (The exception to this is teenagers describing their 39-year-old parents!) In the 1970s, Neugarten (1974) extended this definition downward. Because many persons were leaving the work force before 65, she set 55 as a "meaningful lower limit" and spoke of persons 55 to 74 as the young-old. She viewed the rising generation of young-old as better educated, better off economically, and more vigorous and therefore as a potentially more assertive group that would get its needs met. Succeeding decades have borne her out, as demonstrated by their fierce defense of their Social Security and their rising presence on college campuses. Neugarten defined persons 75 and older as the old-old because of their increased vulnerability in health, income, and male survivorship.

Oldest-Old

More recently, attention has shifted to the oldest-old, those 85 and older (Bould, Sanborn & Reif 1989; Longino 1988; Suzman & Riley 1985). Just as Neugarten found the young-old identifiably different from those 75 and above, Rosenwaike (1985) compared the oldest-old to other older adults and showed them to be a distinctive group: The male-to-female ratio drops from 80 men for every 100 women at 65 to 69 to 44 men for each 100 women at age 85 and over; they are more likely to be living alone or in group settings; they use hospitals more; and they tend to be poorer. The National Medical Expenditure Survey of 1987, a household survey of persons 65 and over, shows a jump beginning at age 85 in the percentage of persons needing help with at least one activity of daily living (Leon & Lair 1990). (See Table 2-1.)

They differ also in increasing more rapidly than other age groups, both among older adults and within the population as a whole. Between 1980 and 1990, they grew from 1 percent of the total population to 1.7 percent (U.S. Senate, Special Committee on Aging 1991). While they represent a small proportion of older adults, they constitute 40 percent of nursing-home patients (Hing 1989a). Their rapid growth and their higher rates of nursing-home and hospital utilization make them a source of lively interest to health care planners, especially when those planners look ahead to 2020, when the numbers of oldest-old are expected to more than double.

TABLE 2-1 Persons needing help with activities of daily living

Age	Percentage
65-69	5.9
70-74	13.2
75-79	11.5
80-84	18.6
85 and older	34.5

SOURCE: Agency for Health Care Policy and Research: National Medical Expenditure Survey—Household Survey, round 1, as reported in Leon and Lair (1990).

Cohorts Growing Old Together

Although the median age of the population crept from 27.9 years in 1970 to 32.9 years in 1990, the distribution of growth among generations has been uneven. It is popular to attribute population greying to greater survival, but this is only part of the story. More important than increased longevity has been the effect of cohort size. All age cohorts have not been advancing at the same rate. The number of persons in any cohort reaching old age depends in part on its size at the start.

Today's oldest-old were born before the United States entered World War I, when immigration and large families were the rule. Therefore, more of the very old in groups are likely to have been foreign born or to have had parents who were. After World War I, immigration quotas slowed the flow. More important, the oldest-old are a "fat" cohort, drawn from a big base, because theirs was a generation that grew up in large families. The size of succeeding cohorts was limited by the Depression and World War II, which reduced the birthrate. The rate of growth of the oldest-old will slow during the next two decades when the "skinny" cohort of Depression and wartime babies moves up. Growth will accelerate again as the baby boom cohort reaches old age (U.S. Senate, Special Committee 1991, 3-8). Figure 2-1 indicates the relative distribution of age groups within the older-adult population.

The cogwheeling of these cohorts affects caregiver burden. The group leader will often find adult children dealing with their own retirement and aging and also with concerns about their parents. Close to three quarters of disabled older

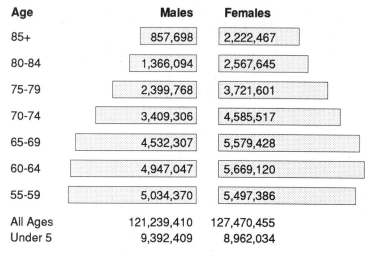

Age	Males	Females
85+	857,698	2,222,467
80-84	1,366,094	2,567,645
75-79	2,399,768	3,721,601
70-74	3,409,306	4,585,517
65-69	4,532,307	5,579,428
60-64	4,947,047	5,669,120
55-59	5,034,370	5,497,386
All Ages	121,239,410	127,470,455
Under 5	9,392,409	8,962,034

FIGURE 2-1 *The U.S. population pyramid in late life*

SOURCE: Based on 1990 U.S. Census.

adults have either a spouse or an adult child as the primary caregiver. Seventy-two percent of the caregivers are wives or daughters. About 63 percent of the adult child caregivers are between 45 and 64, but 12.5 percent are 65 or older (Stone, Cafferata & Sangl 1987).

Within cohorts, the probability of having a living brother or sister will vary. According to Cicirelli and Nussbaum (1989), at least three quarters of older persons have a living sibling. This is a circumstance that waxes and wanes as we move through fat and skinny cohorts.

When we speak about the percentage of older adults, more than the size of a particular cohort is involved. The percentage reflects the proportion of the elderly in a total population that includes the young and middle aged. In 1900, there were fewer old people in relation to a very large number of infants and children: They were just 4 percent of the population. In 1990, the 31 million Americans over age 65 constituted 12.56 percent of the population. The size of the younger cohort groups had gotten smaller: There were fewer babies and children to balance the proportion. Middle-range projections predict 52 million older Americans, about 17.7 percent of the whole, by 2020.

Remember the limitations of projections. These projections assume that current conditions will continue. They cannot fully take into account the effect on specific cohorts of epidemics like Acquired Immune Deficiency Syndrome (AIDS) or socioeconomic factors that may alter the birthrate, such as economic depressions.

The Older Adults in Your Group Today

A closer look at today's older adults is less speculative. They are living longer and staying healthier. Life expectancy at birth has advanced from 47 years in 1900 to 75 in 1987, a comparison misleading because it reflects more the drop in infant and child mortality during the first half of the century than the declining deaths of adults from acute illnesses after 1970 (U.S. Senate, Special Committee 1991). The significant gain is real but smaller. This is the gain in old age itself. In 1900, persons who arrived at 65 could expect to make 77; by 1991 those who were 65 had a good chance of reaching 82.4 years and life expectancy at birth had risen to 75.5 (*New York Times* 1993). Even these extra years are distributed differentially according to sex, race, and ethnicity. At the beginning of the century, the gap was greatest between African Americans and Caucasians. As the century neared its end, the greatest difference was between men and women. At age 65, women could expect to live more than four years longer than men.

This greater longevity of women plus the tendency of men to marry younger women has meant that almost half of the women over 65 are widowed, in contrast to 14 percent of the men. The old widower is eight times more likely than the widow to remarry. The discrepancy grows, and among the oldest-old, 82 percent of the women and 42 percent of the men are widowed. According to the 1985 National Nursing Home survey, 73 percent of the female residents were widowed, but only 33 percent of the males. Seventy-two percent of nursing-facility residents were women (Hing 1989a). Table 2-2 illustrates the increasing imbalance between men and women in the later years.

About 54 percent of older people live with their spouses, another 15 percent with friends or

TABLE 2-2 Women after 55, the lonely majority: Distribution of males and females in each age group

	Males	*Females*
Under 18	51%	49%
55-59	48%	52%
60-64	47%	53%
65-69	45%	55%
70-74	43%	57%
75-79	39%	61%
80-84	35%	65%
85+	29%	72%
Total Population	121,239,410 49%	127,470,455 51%

SOURCE: Based on 1990 U.S. Census.

relatives, and about one third (30.5 percent) live alone. Almost half (47 percent) of the oldest-old live by themselves (U.S. Senate, Special Committee 1991). Most older adults are widows. Of all old people living alone, 43 percent are poor or just above the poverty line (Kasper 1988).

Whether you work in the community or in residential settings, you can expect a large number of very old persons and a disproportionate number of women, especially among the very old. You will encounter centenarians. According to a study of U.S. centenarians, there were 15,000 in 1980, and the odds of reaching that age were falling (Spencer, Goldstein & Taeuber 1987). You will also encounter persons whose lives have been affected by mental retardation or dementia.

The Retarded and Their Parents

Individuals with mental retardation are living longer than they did in the past but aging faster than the general population. Averaging findings of three large population studies, Walz, Harper, and Wilson (1986) have estimated that about 12.5 percent of persons with retardation are reaching age 65. Because the studies included only individuals receiving agency services, actual numbers would be greater.

Persons with Down syndrome, epilepsy, and cerebral palsy have slightly shorter life expectancies than many other categories of developmentally disabled persons, but they, too, are living longer than they did before. A major study found that individuals with Down syndrome now have

excellent survival rates up through age 54 and poor survival rates thereafter (Eyman, Call & White 1989). Because the aging process starts sooner for them, the retarded are described as old at 55. Some authorities would push the onset of old age for them even lower (Sisson & Cotton 1989).

As a group worker, you may be planning groups for the retarded when they have "retired" from sheltered workshops, are confronted with the death of a parent (McDaniel 1989), or have moved into a group home. You may be working with parents who thought they would always be able to watch over disabled children and now find that they may not survive them.

Dementia and Functional Impairment

Some of your participants will have problems with dementia, either their own or that of a parent or a spouse. Estimates of the prevalence of Alzheimer's disease and other dementias vary, with an authoritative estimate being that 4 to 6 percent of persons over 65 are severely incapacitated, and another 10 percent are moderately impaired (Katzman 1986). A Swedish study found that almost 30 percent of the oldest-old had some dementia—mild in 8.3 percent, moderate in 10.3 percent, and severe in 11 percent of the cases (Skoog, Nilsson, Palmertz, Andreasson & Svanborg 1993). For nursing-facility residents, estimates run higher. According to the 1985 National Nursing Home survey, 46.9 percent of all residents over 65 and 52.8 percent of those 85 and over manifested some organic brain syndrome (Hing 1989a).

Functional impairment may arise from physical or cognitive causes or a combination of both. The National Health Interview Survey found that 62.5 percent of older Americans living in the community had no limitation of activity because of chronic conditions. For those 70 and over, the figure was 61.7 percent (Adams & Benson 1991). In contrast to this, most nursing-facility residents needed help with one or more of the activities of daily living.

Nursing-Facility Residents

The 1985 National Nursing Home Survey found residents entering older, frailer, and more dependent in activities of daily living than they had been during the 1977 survey (Hing 1989a; Hing 1989b). Three factors appeared to be contributing to this trend. First, prospective payments were leading hospitals to discharge patients earlier, and some of these persons were going to Medicare-certified facilities for convalescence and rehabilitation. Many of these were relatively younger and more alert. Second, rising costs and more careful screening by many states of their Medicaid clients were leading to later entry by older persons chiefly in need of personal care. Third, in many places there were more community resources to help frail older persons stay at home. Between 1973 and 1985, the rate of nursing-home entry for persons 65 to 84 dropped, and the rate of entry for those 85 and older remained steady. In response, nursing homes are evolving into two types of facilities: traditional homes, offering personal care, and Medicare facilities that are becoming more like mini-hospitals (Shaughnessy & Kramer 1990).

There were other changes as well. Older persons with schizophrenia were formerly "deinstitutionalized" to nursing homes. In the same period, nursing facilities were viewed as suitable settings for older individuals with mental retardation. The mandated preadmission screening and annual resident review (PASARR) provisions of the Nursing Home Reform Amendments to the Omnibus Reconciliation Act of 1987 (OBRA '87) stopped this by precluding both groups unless they truly needed skilled nursing care (U.S. Department of Health and Human Services 1992). By the 1985 survey, African Americans and Latinos, long underserved, were entering nursing facilities in larger numbers (Hing 1989b).

Summary

In short, changing demographics and social provisions are altering the populations of older persons you will encounter in the community and in residential care. The age range is wider. Many of the community aged are healthier, better educated, and better off economically than an earlier generation, but some are frail and would have been in residential care in the early 1980s. There are two distinct groups in nursing facilities: younger residents coming to recuperate after hospitalization and the oldest-old with functional impairment. Those most likely to be living alone are poor older women.

BIOPSYCHOSOCIAL ASPECTS OF AGING
Normal Aging

A knowledge of some of the variables in the patterns of normal and abnormal aging is useful to the group leader. The important variables fall into the triad used by most gerontologists: social, psychological, and physical/physiological. These variables ultimately have a great influence on the type of group chosen, the knowledge needed by the leader, and the adaptations that will have to be made.

Normal aging, according to Atchley (1989), "refers to usual, commonly encountered problems of aging" (p. 183). Normal aging is different from culture to culture because of the sociocultural overlay. Pathological aging means there is physical or mental disease. A successful ager can meet needs—for example, income, housing, health care, nutrition, clothing, and recreation. Atchley contends these positive outcomes occur because older people use "continuity strategies" to help them adapt to the changes that occur with normal aging.

Aging and Physical Changes

The physical changes that occur during aging require that a group leader maintain a constant health orientation. The leader needs to be aware of physical changes (or mental changes that may indicate a physical problem) because such changes may require adaptations in the group structure and format. Illness that precludes a member's attendance at a meeting may be a reason for the leader to see or call the individual outside of the group.

Group leaders must be aware of the common disorders that occur in later life, both because they may cause absenteeism or loss of members through death, and also so that the leader can encourage prevention or early detection of diseases.

Table 2-3 contains a detailed list of aging changes. Remember that oldness is not to be equated with illness. Chapter 12 presents common diseases that occur in later life and suggests how the disease process may affect a group member's participation. Regarding normal aging, the changes in vision and hearing will have a great impact on the group communication. Leaders should be prepared to handle them. Leaders should also encourage healthy aging at every opportunity. Table 2-4 may be helpful when teaching healthier habits to older members of a group.

Psychosocial Theories of Aging

Disengagement Theory. One of the best known and most controversial theories in gerontology is the disengagement theory, which emerged in 1960 in a study commonly referred to as the Kansas City Study. For a fairly complete bibliography on disengagement theory, the reader is referred to Hochschild (1975). The four premises of the theory are as follows:

- Disengagement is a gradual process.
- Disengagement is inevitable.
- Disengagement is a mutually satisfying process for both the society and the individual.
- Disengagement is the norm.

The research has stimulated a great deal of response, including differing positions by theorists who do not see disengagement as an intrinsic or inevitable part of the aging process.

Activity Theory. Some theorists who do not agree with the disengagement theory use the activity theory to describe normal aging. This theory advances the idea that development of a high level of physical, mental, and social activities is needed by the individual. If roles in society are given up, then new roles must be found to take their place. The major criticism of activity theory is that activity may not ensure high morale. Not all older people want high activity; they are happy to reduce their activity and enjoy a more relaxed schedule. There have been relatively few empirical attempts to test activity theory.

Erikson's Stages of Man. Another popular framework is Erik Erikson's eight stages of man. Erikson believes that an individual must successfully complete each stage before passing into the next. The eighth stage, which Erikson (1959) calls "ego integrity versus despair," is the least developed in his writings. Some authors who criticize the Eriksonian model feel that it is "idealistic and... seen from a middle class perspective" (Riegel 1977, 83). Riegel also states that detailed studies of the intrinsic changes and the outer sociological conditions that affect the aging individual are needed to better explain the movement from one stage to another. In fairness to Erikson, however, one must admit that beginning students take to this model, and it seems to give them an understanding of the life span approach and the concept of developmental tasks across the life span.

Peck's Contribution. Erikson's work provided a basis for later work by Robert Peck (1968), who formulated psychological developments for the second half of life. Peck suggests that the eighth stage of man seems to represent in a global and nonspecific way all of the psychological crises, and also the solutions to those of the latter half of the life span. Peck divides the development into two categories:

Middle Age
1. Valuing wisdom versus valuing physical powers.
2. Socializing versus sexuality in human relationships.
3. Cathectic flexibility versus cathectic impoverishment.

Old Age
1. Ego differentiation versus work-role preoccupation.
2. Body transcendence versus body preoccupation.
3. Ego transcendence versus ego preoccupation.

Peck's interpretations are well described in a chapter in the fine book *Middle Age and Aging* by B. L. Neugarten (1968).

Clark and Anderson Framework. One other framework should be mentioned: that of Clark and Anderson (1967), who described five adaptive tasks of the aged. These delineations may help a new group leader better understand group dynamics among the elderly:

1. Perception of aging and definition of instrumental limitations.
2. Redefinition of the physical and social life space.
3. Identification of sources of need satisfaction and substitutes for these.
4. Reassessment of the criteria of self.
5. Reintegration of life values and goals.

Developmental Tasks in Later Maturity. R. Havighurst (1972) calls later maturity the "examination stage," and his developmental tasks are well known and widely used:

1. Decide where and how to live our remaining years.
2. Continue supportive, close relationships with spouse or significant other (including sex).

TABLE 2-3 Normal age-related changes

Understanding normal age-related changes is the foundation to understanding health and disease in older people. The following section highlights changes within each organ system that are known to decline with age.

Skin and connective tissue

- Loss of dermal thickness produces transparent, thin skin appearance.
- In the epidermis, melanocytes' (pigment-producing cells) number and activity decrease, making skin more sensitive to ultraviolet sunlight.
- Progressive loss of melanocytes in hair bulbs and decreased number of hair follicles result in greying and thinning of hair.
- Decrease in epidermis turnover contributes to slower wound healing.
- Sebaceous and sweat glands decrease in number, size, and function, therefore producing less oil and sweat.
- Decreased vascular bed and responsiveness (and sweating) predispose older people to hypothermia and hyperthermia.
- Decreased vitamin D3 production and decreased exposure to sunlight may contribute to osteoporosis and osteomalacia.

Nervous system

- Moderate cortical atrophy.
- Loss of neurons in the neocortex, substantia nigra, and limbic system.
- Lipofuscin pigment accumulates primarily in glial tissues.
- Certain neurotransmitters decline.
- Binding sites for dopamine and serotonin decrease.
- Peripheral nerve fibers decrease in number and size.
  - Motor and sensory nerve conduction decreases.
  - A decrease in vibratory sensation in feet and ankles may occur.

Special senses

Vision
- Atrophy of periorbital tissue may cause upper and lower lids to droop.
- Visual activity may decrease due to changes in the retina or neural components.
- Loss of accommodation causes hyperopia.
- Nuclear sclerosis causes myopia.
- Decreased tear secretion may cause dryness of eyes.

Hearing
- Pure tone loss is greater at high frequencies than at low frequencies.
- Pitch discrimination declines primarily at very high and low frequencies.
- Speech discrimination declines and is worsened with background noise.

Smell
- Olfaction declines, causing poor detection and discrimination by the eighth decade.

Oral

- A reduction in the integrity of epithelial and connective tissue causes a thinning of the oral mucosa and affects bone pulpal tissues.
  - Blood supply is decreased.
  - Nerve innervation is compromised.
  - Tissue quality is modified.
  - Calcifitic tissue changes occur.
- A compositional change in the nature of saliva.
  - Altered sodium levels.
  - Increase in potassium.
  - Decrease in secretory proteins.
- A reduction in taste perception.
  - Increase in threshold potentials for salt and bitter tastes.
- Structural changes to the teeth.
  - Erosion.
  - Abrasion.
  - Attrition.

- Gingival recession.
  - Alveolar dehiscence.
  - Compromised spatial position of teeth.

Cardiovascular

- Conducting system loses cells and fibers and becomes infiltrated with fat.
- Heart rate at rest and achievable maximum declines [maximum HR = (220-age)].
- Increase in stroke volume (S.V.) compensates for lower heart rate (H.R.) and maintaining cardiac output (C.O.) [C.O. = H.R. $\times$ S.V.].
- Intrinsic contractile function declines.
- Vascular compliance decreases due to changes in the vessel walls with intima cellular proliferation and fibrosis and media elastin fragmentation and calcification.
- In Western and developed countries, systolic blood pressure increases with lower rate of increase in diastolic pressure.

Respiratory

- Lung elastic recoil decreases as a result of collagen and elastin changes.
- Chest wall compliance decreases due to stiffening of the chest wall.
- Respiratory muscle strength decreases.
- Lung volumes change as a consequence of the above changes.
  - Increase in residual volume and functional residual capacity.
  - Decrease in vital capacity and expiratory flow rates.
- Gas exchange.
  - Decrease in arterial po2, due to ventilation-perfusion mismatch.

Gastrointestinal

- Esophageal motility decreases due to lower amplitude contractions after swallowing (presbyesophages).
- Gastric mucosa thins, acid-producing parietal cells atrophy, and gastric acid secretion decreases.
- Small and large intestinal mucosa atrophies, reducing absorptive surface area and decreasing the ability to absorb sugars, calcium, vitamin B12, and iron.
- Liver decreases in size but maintains function; however, the microsomal enzyme function declines.

Renal

- Renal mass decreases with primarily cortical losses of nephrons, glomeruli, and capillaries.
- Renal plasma flow decreases.
- Glomerula filtration rate (GFR) falls.
- Creatinine clearance progressively declines 1 percent per year after age 40 with no change in serum creatinine level, because creatinine generation also decreases.
- Ability to retain sodium (Na) declines.
- Ability to concentrate urine declines.

Musculoskeletal

- Decrease in muscle weight compared to total body weight.
- Decreased muscular strength and endurance associated with decrease in number of muscle fibers.
- Hyaline cartilage water content declines.
- Bone loss is universal, but rate is highly variable; loss is more rapid in women after menopause than in men.

Hematopoietic

- Overall red cells, hemoglobin, hematocrit, white cells, and platelets maintain normal values and functions.
- Active bone marrow decreases and marrow fat increases but remains adequate for hematopoiesis.

Immune system

- Thymic involution begins about age of puberty.
- Number of T- and B-lymphocytes does not change.
- T-lymphocyte function declines.
  - Decreased response to skin tests.
  - Production of interleukin-2 is reduced.

Continued

TABLE 2-3 *Continued*

- B-lymphocyte function is not as clear.
  - Immunoglobulins IgM and perhaps IgG levels decline.
  - Immunoglobulin production to a challenge (vaccine or antigen) is lower response and shortened duration.

Endocrine

- Progressive decline in carbohydrate tolerance.
  - Primary defect in insulin resistance as post-receptor defect.
- Metabolic clearance rate of thyroid hormone decreases but thyroxine (T4) levels are normal.

Genital/Sexual Function

Women
- With menopause, rapid decline of estrogen and progesterone.
- Hormonal changes cause atrophic changes of uterus, vagina, external genitalia, and breasts.
- Sexual activity decreases, but exact roles of biologic changes and sociocultural factors are unknown.

Men
- Testosterone levels remain level.
- Prostate gland increases in size due to hyperplasia.
- Erectile and ejaculatory function declines; postejaculatory refractory period increases.
- Sexual response is delayed due to reduced penile sensitivity and increased threshold for tactile stimulation.

SOURCE: Stanford EP, Schmidt MG. 1991. *Guidelines for education: Geriatric health care professionals* (pp. 18-20). Used with permission. Diane L. Schneider, MD, U.C.S.D. School of Medicine, prepared this for the San Diego Geriatric Education Center publication.

TABLE 2-4 Ten tips for healthy aging

1. Eat a balanced diet.
2. Exercise regularly and wisely.
3. Get regular medical check-ups.
4. Don't smoke. It's never too late to quit.
5. Practice safety habits at home to prevent falls and fractures. Always wear your seatbelt when traveling by car.
6. Maintain contacts with family and friends, and stay active through work, recreation, and community activities.
7. Avoid overexposure to the sun and the cold.
8. If you drink, moderation is the key. When you drink, let someone else drive.
9. Keep personal and financial records in order to simplify budgeting and investing. Plan long-term housing and financial needs.
10. Keep a positive attitude toward life. Do things that make you happy.

SOURCE: National Institute on Aging, National Institutes of Health, Bethesda, MD.

3. Find a satisfactory, safe living place.
4. Adjust living standards.
5. Maintain maximum level of health.
6. Maintain contact with children, grandchildren, and other relatives.
7. Maintain interest in people, civic affairs, and so forth.
8. Pursue new interests; maintain former ones.
9. Find meaning in life after retirement.
10. Work out philosophy.
11. Adjust to death of spouse and other loved ones.

The Self in Later Life

The aging person's task is to preserve an acceptable self in the face of change and impending death.

Lieberman and Tobin (1983) hold that older adults invest their energies in maintaining the "self-continuity, self-integrity, and self-identity" essential to their psychological survival (p. 348). They become myth makers,

- Transforming situations so they can feel they are really controlling their own destinies.
- Turning to the past for the self-affirmation that the present denies them.
- Reconstructing their personal histories to support the self-image they would like to keep.

Lieberman and Tobin (1983) call for a psychology of aging that takes into account distance from death instead of time from birth. They believe that individual distances from death account for the great variability in the functioning of the aged.

Their studies show that even before physical changes become evident, there are psychological forerunners of death:

- A relative drop in cognitive functioning.
- Psychological withdrawal.
- Increasing difficulty in integrating stimuli.
- More death symbols in the person's talk.

These changes differ from the transitory instability that occurs with acute illness; they are a more enduring response to failing biological competence, the person's last fight against entropy. They are most apparent when the demand for adaptation is high and the perception of personal control is low, as, for example, in forced relocation. Most old persons manage their deaths well, but they have difficulty when they must deal with externally imposed stress at the same time.

Kaufman (1986) concluded that older individuals continually reconstruct their personal histories so they can interpret their current experience in a way that supports a continuing and ageless self. They are willing to admit even unflattering details in the interests of continuity—"I was always…"

Atchley's Continuity Theory

One theory relevant for group work with older adults is Atchley's theory of continuity (1989). He states that "a dynamic view of continuity starts with the idea of a basic structure which persists over time, but it allows for a variety of changes to occur within the context provided by the basic structure" (p. 183). Continuity theory assumes evolution rather than homeostasis and allows changes to be incorporated into the older person's prior history. This is particularly relevant for reminiscence and life review therapies.

According to Atchley's (1989) framework for continuity theory, old people can meet late life challenges better when they are supported by what is familiar: predictable persons, known settings, and customary strategies.

Change is stimulating but easiest to flow with if it occurs within a familiar domain, such as the person's worldview or vocation, and if it is linked to experience or learning that has gone before. Whether something feels familiar is a personal judgment, affected in part by cultural expectations. Only the individual knows what feels familiar and right to him or her.

Mentally healthy older people have strategies for the preservation of an acceptable self, such as reinterpretation, selective avoidance, and the abandonment of some of the psychic baggage that served them in the past.

Robert Atchley says his continuity theory does not apply to the pathological aging but only to the alert. Those lacking memory do not have the remembered inner structure needed to define identity. Without memory, everything is strange to them, and their world is unpredictable. For him, internal continuity arises from the ability to relate inner change to one's past and use it in supporting the new self. External continuity depends on familiar environments, the practice of familiar skills, and interaction with familiar people.

With too little continuity, life becomes unpredictable; with too much, life is in a rut. Optimal continuity means that the pace of change is comfortable and social demands are within the individual's coping capacity.

In early life, the self is built with feedback from others. Successes and failures are integrated into self-image. This identity crystalizes and is relatively impervious to subsequent change. Thereafter the individual tends to interact with persons who support this self view and to avoid or discount those who do not. "Identity evolution is thus an active, cumulative, and lifelong process of restructuring ideas to fit current realities" (Atchley 1989, 187).

EXERCISE 1

Give a brief definition of ageism; then write a two-page account of an incident in which an individual displayed ageism. The expression of or behavioral cues indicating ageism can be either overt or covert. (If the cues are subtle, provide enough detail to identify them.)

EXERCISE 2

Select as an example an older person (a member of a group you are leading or a past or present client) and choose a developmental task from one of the theorists in this chapter. State the task and explain how the person successfully (or unsuccessfully) fulfilled it. (It usually is better not to use relatives in writing assignments, for obvious reasons.)

EXERCISE 3

Interview one older person to find out if he or she has incorporated negative views of aging (for example, old people cannot learn new things, or old people are not interested in sex) into the self-system. What is the belief? How does it affect the person? Has the aged person passed the belief on to others?

EXERCISE 4

You have been engaged to organize three groups at Sunnyvale Nursing Facility. In view of today's demographic trends, what sex and age distributions would you expect to find among residents? What age groups would you be likely to find attending meetings of the family council? Sunnyvale is a Medicare-certified facility; describe three groups of residents you might expect to find there and tell how their needs might differ.

EXERCISE 5

On the blackboard, draw four parallel lines. Write 1900 above one end and the current year above the other, with the intervening years at 10-year intervals in between. Indicate major events that would affect ordinary people's lives, such as World War I, autos becoming common, the Great Depression, World War II, TV becoming common, the baby boom beginning and ending, and the like. On the four lines indicate the birth and overlapping life spans of four generations: mother, daughter, granddaughter, and great-granddaughter, or father, son, grandson, and great-grandson. Discuss how their lives and outlooks might differ because of the years in which they were born.

EXERCISE 6

Take the quiz in Appendix 2, "What's Your Aging I.Q.?" Study the questions you missed by reading the explanation for the answers. Then select three of the quiz questions and explain how they might be relevant to a group you plan to lead.

REFERENCES

Adams PF, Benson V. 1991. *Current estimates from the National Health Interview Survey, 1990*. National Center for Health Statistics. *Vital Health Stat* 10(181). Washington, DC: U.S. Government Printing Office.

Atchley RC. 1989. A continuity theory of normal aging. *Gerontologist* 29(2):183-190.

Bould S, Sanborn B, Reif L. 1989. *Eighty-five plus: The oldest old*. Belmont, CA: Wadsworth.

Burgraf KV, Stanley M. 1989. *Nursing the elderly: A care plan approach*. Philadelphia: Lippincott.

Cicirelli VG, Nussbaum JF. 1989. Relationships with siblings in later life. In JF Nussbaum (ed.), *Life-span communication: Normative processes* (pp. 283-299). Hillsdale, NJ: Erlbaum.

Clark M, Anderson B. 1967. *Culture and aging*. Springfield, IL: Thomas.

Erikson E. 1959. Identity and the life cycle. In *Psychological issues*, Monograph 1 (p. 166). New York: International Universities Press.

Eyman RK, Call TL, White JF. 1989. Mortality of elderly retarded persons in California. *J Appl Gerontol* 8(2):203-215.

Havighurst R. 1972. *Developmental tasks and education*, 3d ed. New York: David McKay.

Hing E. 1989a. Nursing home utilization by current residents: United States, 1985. National Center for Health Statistics. *Vital Health Stat* 13(102), DHHS Pub. No. 89-1783. Washington, DC: U.S. Government Printing Office.

————. 1989b. Effects of the prospective payment system on nursing homes. National Center for Health Statistics. *Vital Health Stat* 13(98), DHHS Pub. No. 89-1759. Washington, DC: U.S. Government Printing Office.

Hochschild AR. 1975. Disengagement theory: A critique and proposal. *Am Soc Rev* 40(5):553-569.

Kasper JD. 1988. *Aging alone: Profiles and projections*. A report of the Commonwealth Commission on elderly people living alone. Baltimore: Commonwealth Fund.

Katzman R. 1986. Alzheimer's disease. *N Engl J Med* 314 (15):964-971.

Kaufman SR. 1986. *The ageless self: Sources of meaning in late life*. Madison, WI: University of Wisconsin Press.

Leon J, Lair T. 1990. Functional status of the noninstitutionalized elderly: Estimates of the ADL and IADL difficulties. *National Medical Expenditure Survey Research Findings* 4 (Agency for Health Care Policy and Research), DHHS Pub. No. PHS-90-3462. Rockville, MD: U.S. Public Health Service.

Lieberman MA, Tobin SS. 1983. *The experience of old age: Stress, coping, and survival*. New York: Basic Books.

Longino CF Jr. 1988. Who are the oldest Americans? *Gerontologist* 28(4):515-523.

McDaniel BA. 1989. A group work experience with mentally retarded adults on issues of death and dying. *J Gerontol Soc Work* 13(4/5):187-191.

Neugarten BL (ed.). 1968. *Middle aging and aging*. Chicago: University of Chicago Press.

————. 1974. Age groups in American society and the rise of the young-old. *Ann Am Acad Poli Soc Sci* 415:187-198.

New York Times. 1993. Life expectancy of '91 newborn American rises to 75.5 years (September 1).

Peck RC. 1968. Psychological developments in the second half of life. In BL Neugarten (ed.), *Middle aging and aging* (pp. 88-92). Chicago: University of Chicago Press.

Riegel K. 1977. History of psychological gerontology. In J Birren, KW Schaie (eds.), *Handbook of the psychology of aging* (pp. 70-102). New York: Van Nostrand Reinhold.

Rosenwaike I. 1985. A demographic portrait of the oldest old. *Milbank Q* 63 (2):187-205.

Ryff CD. 1993. The self in later life. *Gerontol News* 2 (March):11.

Shaughnessy PV, Kramer AM. 1990. The increased needs of patients in nursing homes and patients receiving home care. *N Engl J Med* 322(1):21-27.

Sisson GFP Jr., Cotton PD. 1989. The elderly mentally retarded person: Current perspectives and future directions. *J Appl Gerontol* 8(2):151-167.

Skoog I, Nilsson L, Palmertz B, Andreasson L, Svanborg A. 1993. A population-based study of dementia in 85-year-olds. *N Engl J Med* 328(3):153-158.

Social Security Act (OBRA '87). 1987. Amendments to Title XIX (Medicaid), b.(3) F and Sec. 1819 (Medicare).

Spencer G, Goldstein AA, Taeuber CM. 1987. America's centenarians: Data from the 1980 census. National Institute on Aging, U.S. Bureau of the Census. Washington, DC: U.S. Government Printing Office.

Stanford EP, Schmidt MG (eds.). 1991. *Guidelines for education: Geriatric health care professionals*. San Diego: San Diego Geriatric Education Center, University Center on Aging, San Diego State University.

Stone RI, Kemper P. 1990. Spouses and children of disabled elders: How large a constituency for long-term care reform? *Milbank Q* 67(3-4):485-506.

Stone R, Cafferata GL, Sangl J. 1987. Caregivers of the frail elderly: A national profile. *Gerontologist* 27(5):616-626.

Suzman R, Riley MW. 1985. Introducing the oldest old. *Milbank Q* 63(2):177-186.

Tobin SS. 1991. *Personhood in advanced old age: Implications for practice*. New York: Springer.

U.S. Department of Health and Human Services, Health Care Financing Administration. 1992. Medicare and Medicaid programs, preadmission screening and annual resident review. *Federal Register* 57(230):56450-56513 (November 30).

U.S. Senate, Special Committee on Aging, the American Association of Retired Persons (AARP), the Federal Council on the Aging, and the U.S. Administration on Aging. 1991. *Aging America: Trends and projections*, DHHS Pub. No. FCoA-91-28001. Washington, DC: U.S. Government Printing Office.

Walz T, Harper D, Wilson J. 1986. The aging developmentally disabled person: A review. *Gerontologist* 26(6): 622-629.

BIBLIOGRAPHY

Brody E. 1985. Parent care as a normative family stress. *Gerontologist* 25(1):19-29.

Curb J, Guralin J, LaCroix A, Korpen S, Doeg D, Miles T, White L. 1990. Effective aging: Meeting the challenge of growing older. *J Am Soc Aging* 38(7):827-828.

Katz S, Green DS, Beck JC, Branch LG, Spector WD. 1985. Active life expectancy: Societal implications. In Committee on an Aging Society, Institute of Medicine and the National Research Council, *America's aging: Health in an older society* (pp. 57-72). Washington, DC: National Academy Press.

Kemper P, Murtaugh CM. 1991. Lifetime use of nursing home care. *N Engl J Med* 324(9):595-600.

National Institute on Aging. 1991. *Physical frailty: A reducible barrier to independence for older Americans*, NIH Pub. No. 91-397. Bethesda, MD: NIH.

Pastorino C, Hickey T. 1990. Health promotion for the elderly: Issues and program planning. *Orthop Nurs* 9(6): 319-334

Stanford EP, Torres-Gil FM (eds.). 1991. Diversity: New approaches to ethnic minority aging. *Generations* 15(4).

U.S. Department of Health and Human Services. 1990. *Healthy people 2000*. Boston: Jones and Bartlett.

RESOURCES

Publications

Aged to Perfection: Your Guide to Healthy Aging. 1990. A prevention program of the California Department of Mental Health by RW Lutz, RJ Pasick, KR Pelletier, and NL Klehr (monograph and a relaxation exercise audiotape).

American Association for Retired Persons (AARP, 601 E Street, NW, Fifth Floor B, Washington, DC 20047):

——— . 1990. *Healthy aging: Making health promotion work for minority elders.*

——— . n.d. *Healthy older adults: Health promotion articles for your newsletter.*

Federal Interagency Forum on Aging—Related Statistics. 1992. *Interagency forum on age-related statistics.*

National Center for Health Statistics. 1989. *Health of an aging America* (see bibliography).

National Eldercare on Health Promotion. 1991. *Health promotion for older adults.*

National Institute on Aging. A free list of publications on aging is available; phone: 800-222-2225.

Films

Aging. This film challenges the common stereotype that old people are one homogeneous group. The film emphasizes the individuality of older people and the breadth of their needs and desires. It focuses on their life styles. James Branch Cabell Library, Virginia Commonwealth University, Richmond, VA 23284; phone: 804-257-1098.

The Art of Silence (color, 8 minutes). This pantomime by Marcel Marceau reveals how mime can condense time. In four minutes Marceau symbolically presents the cycle of life. Film Library, University of Minnesota, Minneapolis, MN.

Growing Old: Something to Live For (color, 15 minutes). This film is informative and optimistic in its treatment of aging, focusing on successful adaptations to growing old. There are interviews with enthusiastic older persons as well as learned advocates. CRM McGraw-Hill Films, 110 Fifteenth Street, Del Mar, CA 92014.

The Third Age: The New Generation (color, 15 minutes) 1975. This film pictures aging as a normal, natural process of life and is a positive statement about creative roles of older persons. Vignettes are woven into the narrative. Useful for motivation and for discussion of transmission of values. NBA AV Library, P.O. Box 1986, Indianapolis, IN 46202; phone: 800-251-4091.

And When You Grow Old (16 mm, color, 30 minutes). In this positive and unpretentious portrayal, older adults share their ideas about old age and their attitudes toward life. They discuss sickness, death, limited income, and housing arrangements. Department of Mental Health, James Madison Building, 109 Governor Street, 13th Floor, Richmond, VA 23219; phone: 804-786-1332.

APPENDIX 1

Glossary

Activities of daily living (ADLs) Skills necessary for self-care, usually listed as bathing, dressing, feeding oneself, toileting, and transferring oneself between bed and chair.

Age cohort A group of people born at about the same time and therefore likely to share some experiences and values because they have passed through the same period of history.

Ageism Generalizing about persons on the basis of a single common characteristic, their age; a form of negative stereotyping. Rarely acknowledged but expressed through various subtle—and not so subtle—forms of discrimination such as planning *for* rather than *with* older persons.

Average age All the ages added together and divided by the number of persons. The average can be skewed by extremes: The average age of Latinos is low, for example, because the high birthrate means there are many children.

Developmental tasks These are responses to normal life stressors that occur throughout life, including the aging process.

Disengagement theory is a debatable theory that contends that there is a mutual withdrawal of the elderly and society from one another.

Instrumental activities of daily living (IADLS) include meal preparation, housecleaning, handling money, shopping, and getting around in the community.

Median age The point in the age distribution at which there are an equal number of persons above and below.

Modal age The mode, the most common age, may fail to express the range.

Omnibus Budget Reconciliation Act of 1987 (OBRA '87) This is also referred to as the Nursing Home Reform Amendments. These are amendments to Title XIX of the Social Security Act. They spell out the rights of residents and their families, require multidisciplinary assessments and individually tailored care plans, limit the use of physical and chemical restraints, and require that psychosocial approaches to problem behavior be tried before recourse to either. They emphasize activities programs, which would include group work (Social Security Act 1987).

Personhood Sheldon S. Tobin (1991) defines this as "the qualities that confer distinct individuality to each person," but then expands it for use in his book. This is the self that individuals strive to keep through the vicissitudes of loss and institutionalization in old age.

Prospective payment Medicare payments to hospitals predicated on the average cost of caring for patients in each Diagnosis-Related Group (DRG). Although it was intended that length of stay average out among patients who recuperated quickly and those needing extra hospital days, hospitals tend to use this mean as the ceiling.

Self-concept A person's total sense of self; how the older individual feels about himself or herself and the person's attitudes, values, and all of life's experiences.

Self-perception The process of questioning the image that one has of oneself. This questioning may present conflict, which might include dependency on others, devaluation of one's contributions, and a multitude of losses. Such factors can create fear, a sense of powerlessness, and an overall diminished quality of life (Burgraf & Stanley 1989).

APPENDIX 2

WHAT'S YOUR AGING I.Q.?

	True	False
1. Baby boomers are the fastest growing segment of the population.	❑	❑
2. Families don't bother with their older relatives.	❑	❑
3. Everyone becomes confused or forgetful if they live long enough.	❑	❑
4. You can be too old to exercise.	❑	❑
5. Heart disease is a much bigger problem for older men than for older women.	❑	❑
6. The older you get, the less you sleep.	❑	❑
7. People should watch their weight as they age.	❑	❑
8. Most older people are depressed. Why shouldn't they be?	❑	❑
9. There's no point in screening older people for cancer because they can't be treated.	❑	❑
10. Older people take more medications than younger people.	❑	❑
11. People begin to lose interest in sex around age 55.	❑	❑
12. If your parents had Alzheimer's disease, you will inevitably get it.	❑	❑
13. Diet and exercise reduce the risk of osteoporosis.	❑	❑
14. As your body changes with age, so does your personality.	❑	❑
15. Older people might as well accept urinary accidents as a fact of life.	❑	❑
16. Suicide is mainly a problem for teenagers.	❑	❑
17. Falls and injuries "just happen" to older people.	❑	❑
18. Everybody gets cataracts.	❑	❑
19. Extremes of heat and cold can be especially dangerous for older people.	❑	❑
20. "You can't teach an old dog new tricks."	❑	❑

Answers

1. **False**—There are more than 3 million Americans over the age of 85. That number is expected to quadruple by the year 2040, when there will be more than 12 million people in that age group. The population age 85 and older is the fastest growing age group in the United States.

2. **False**—Most older people live close to their children and see them often. Many live with their spouses. An estimated 80 percent of men and 60 percent of women live in family settings. Only 5 percent of the older population lives in nursing homes.

3. **False**—Confusion and serious forgetfulness in old age can be caused by Alzheimer's disease or other conditions that result in irreversible damage to the brain. But at least 100 other problems can bring on the same symptoms. A minor head injury, high fever, poor nutrition, adverse drug reactions, and depression also can lead to confusion. These conditions are treatable, however, and the confusion they cause can be eliminated.

4. **False**—Exercise at any age can help strengthen the heart and lungs and lower blood pressure. It also can improve muscle strength and, if carefully chosen, lessen bone loss with age. See a physician before beginning a new exercise program.

5. **False**—The rise of heart disease increases dramatically for women after menopause. By age

65, both men and women have a one in three chance of showing symptoms. But risks can be significantly reduced by following a healthy diet and exercising.

6. **False**—In later life, it's the quality of sleep that declines, not total sleep time. Researchers have found that sleep tends to become more fragmented as people age. A number of reports suggest that older people are less likely than younger people to stay awake throughout the day and that older people tend to take more naps than younger people.

7. **True**—Most people gain weight as they age. Because of changes in the body and decreasing physical activity, older people usually need fewer calories. Still, a balanced diet is important. Older people require essential nutrients just like younger adults. You should be concerned about your weight if there has been an involuntary gain or loss of 10 pounds in the past 6 months.

8. **False**—Most older people are not depressed. When it does occur, depression is treatable throughout the life cycle using a variety of approaches, such as family support, psychotherapy, or antidepressant medications. A physician can determine whether the depression is caused by medication an older person might be taking, by physical illness, stress, or other factors.

9. **False**—Many older people can beat cancer, especially if it's found early. Over half of all cancers occur in people 65 and older, which means that screening for cancer in this age group is especially important.

10. **True**—Older people often have a combination of conditions that require drugs. They consume 25 percent of all medications and can have many more problems with adverse reactions. Check with your doctor to make sure all drugs and dosages are appropriate.

11. **False**—Most older people can lead an active, satisfying sex life.

12. **False**—The overwhelming number of people with Alzheimer's disease have not inherited the disorder. In a few families, scientists have seen an extremely high incidence of the disease and have identified genes in these families which they think may be responsible.

13. **True**—Women are at particular risk for osteoporosis. They can help prevent bone loss by eating foods rich in calcium and exercising regularly throughout life. Foods such as milk and other dairy products, dark green leafy vegetables, salmon, sardines, and tofu promote new bone growth. Activities such as walking, biking, and simple exercises to strength the upper body also can be effective.

14. **False**—Research has found that, except for the changes than can result from Alzheimer's disease and other forms of dementia, personality is one of the few constants of life. That is, you are likely to age much as you've lived.

15. **False**—Urinary incontinence is a symptom, not a disease. Usually, it is caused by specific changes in body function that can result from infection, diseases, pregnancy, or the use of certain medications. A variety of treatment options are available for people who seek medical attention.

16. **False**—Suicide is most prevalent among people age 65 and older. An older person's concern with suicide should be taken very seriously and professional help should be sought quickly.

17. **False**—Falls are the most common cause of injuries among people over age 65. But many of these falls, which result in broken bones, can be avoided. Regular vision and hearing tests and good safety habits can help prevent accidents. Knowing whether your medications affect balance and coordination also is a good idea.

18. **False**—Not everyone gets cataracts, although a great many older people do. Some 18 percent of people between the ages of 65 and 74 have cataracts, while more than 40 percent of those between 75 and 85 have the problem. Cataracts can be treated successfully with surgery; more than 90 percent of people say they can see better after the procedure.

19. **True**—The body's thermostat tends to function less efficiently with age, making the older person's body less able to adapt to heat or cold.

20. **False**—People at any age can learn new information and skills. Research indicates that older people can obtain new skills and improve old ones, including how to use a computer.

SOURCE: National Institute on Aging, Bethesda, MD.

CHAPTER 3

History and Overview of Group Work

Irene Burnside

KEY WORDS
- Age-specific
- Member-specific
- Psychotherapy
- Social-emotional area
- Topic-specific groups

LEARNING OBJECTIVES
- Describe the origin of group work in the United States.
- Discuss the work of the pioneers in group work with older adults.
- Discuss three principles of group work with the aged.
- Describe four levels of group work with older adults.
- Describe two member-specific groups.
- Discuss age-specific groups.

...understanding is obtained by explaining what we know.

ROBERT L. CAUSEY (1969, 24)

This chapter provides a brief history of group work with older adults and an overview of current group work. The following sections introduce students, health care workers and volunteers, and instructors to some principles of group work and to the most common types of groups and group methods used with older clients or patients.

The psychosocial care of older adults in the United States needs improvement. Group work is one form of treatment that is effective and that should be considered in prevention and maintenance aspects of the health care of older persons. In this book, *group work* covers a wide range of groups of older people that could be conducted by nonprofessionals. *Group psychotherapy,* as used in this book, designates only groups that are conducted with older people who have psychiatric problems and that are led by professionals with psychology or psychiatry training.

HISTORICAL BACKGROUND

The originator of group psychotherapy was Joseph Henry Pratt, an internist. In 1905 in Boston, Dr. Pratt developed a plan for the treatment of tuberculosis in poor patients. At that time, the disease was often called consumption; however, he called the group meetings "tuberculosis classes." The group consisted of 15 to 20 patients who met with him once a week. Although aimed at fostering an understanding of tuberculosis, the classes also showed positive results in the mental health of the group members; unfortunately, other physicians who tried to emulate his classes were not nearly as successful. Some writers feel that Pratt's personality had a great deal to do with the success of his group and that he tended to conduct the group work intuitively. It was the improvement of the emotional status of the tuberculosis patients in these groups that led to the use of the treatment modality for patients who suffered from mental illness.

Elwood Worchester, director of the Emmanuel Church in Boston, advanced money to Pratt to assist him in launching the tuberculosis classes. At a later date, Dr. Worchester, assisted by Isidore Coriat (one of the first members of the American Psychoanalytic Association), began seeing patients in group meetings to assist them with health problems; these groups were not restricted to tuberculosis patients.

Pratt continued to work in the group modality but switched his attention to patients who had emotional problems. At that time, no theoretical basis for group psychoanalytic therapy existed for teaching the method. Also, no worthwhile research had yet appeared. Pratt then applied the ideas of Joseph Deperine, who emphasized persuasion and reeducation, Pratt continued his work as a group psychotherapist into the 1950s.

In 1909, L. Cody Marsh worked with psychotics in classes and lectures. Psychiatric patients were treated by group psychotherapy as early as 1921. Although Marsh's groups probably would not be recognized as psychotherapy, he did realize the therapeutic value of group treatment for psychotics. He also applied such techniques as formal lectures, art classes, and dance classes (Ruitenbeck 1970).

In the 1920s and 1930s, Louis Wender worked with institutionalized borderline cases. He thought of his groups as psychoanalytic rather than educational or orientational, his view of the other groups of that time. Wender saw groups of six to eight patients two or three times a week. Group members were of the same sex; each group meeting lasted for one hour. He also combined individual and group psychotherapy and suggested that the group might represent the family to its members. In 1934, Paul Schilder, who was at Bellevue, also worked with groups in the psychoanalytic framework (Pinney 1970).

J. L. Moreno came to the United States from Germany in 1930. He introduced the concept of sociometry and diagramming the interactions that occur in groups (Hardy & Conway 1978).

It is said that the term *group psychotherapy* originated with Moreno, a fact that Moreno confirms (Ruitenbeck 1970). He is the leading exponent of a treatment technique called *psychodrama.* Since Moreno's death, the teaching of psychodrama has been carried on by his widow.

Samuel Slavson, a civil engineer, practiced group psychotherapy with children for the Jewish Board of Guardians in the 1930s. In 1943, he published *An Introduction to Group Therapy.* Later he was instrumental in the formation and development of the American Group Psychotherapy Association. He became the first editor of the *International Journal of Group Psychotherapy* in 1951 and was an active force in the advancement of group psychotherapy for both social work and psychiatry.

During World War II, group psychotherapy began to be used extensively as a treatment modality in military hospitals. The army psychiatrists then returned to civilian practice and applied group therapy in their own settings.

REVIEW OF THE LITERATURE

Group work with older persons in the United States, according to Toseland (1990), developed in three distinct settings and occurred in settlement houses and community centers, homes for the aged, and state mental hospitals.

Since World War II group work has become an increasingly popular form of treatment in the care of the aged—partly because it is economical. The efficacy of group treatments can be noted in the savings of the therapist's time. Toseland and Siporin (1986) noted reports of savings of between 15 percent and 40 percent of therapist time. In this economic crunch, with cutting back noted across the health care system, these figures become important. Moreover, according to Leonard Gottesman, Carole Quarterman, and Gordon Cohn (1973, 422), "Small-group treatment can be used in both contrived settings like psychotherapy and naturalistic ones like families or communities of aged persons. This technique is valuable because it can be more naturalistic and more long lasting than individual therapy."

The literature is beginning to include more about both the benefits and the limitations of such work, but book chapters and journal articles on the topic are still widely scattered. Irvin Yalom's (1975) excellent book on group psychotherapy, for instance, does not discuss psychotherapy with the aged at all, while Gwen Marram's (1973) book on the group approach in nursing only briefly describes some of the aspects of working with the aged.

Nevertheless, the available literature does indicate that such work with older adults is conducted by a diverse occupational group, including psychiatrists; recreational, occupational, and physical therapists; social workers; psychologists; nurses; and administrators of skilled nursing facilities (Burnside 1970a). For example, Maurice Linden (1953), a psychiatrist, pioneered group work with the aged when he co-led a group of 40 to 51 regressed women in a state hospital. (See Chapter 4.) In the same year, Susan Kubie and Gertrude Landau published a book about their nine years of group work experience in a recreation center for the aged. Jerome Kaplan (1953) was one of the first social workers to write about group work with older adults, and Eugenia Shere (1964), a psychologist, wrote a classic article on group work with the very old.

The trend for nurses to publish reports about their group work with the aged came later. The first collection of papers appeared in *Psychosocial Nursing Care of the Aged* (Burnside 1973). Most were written by nurses in graduate nursing programs (Blake 1973; Burnside 1973; Gillin 1973; Holland 1973; Holtzen 1973; Janosik & Miller 1982; Morrison 1973; Stange 1973).

Unfortunately, at international meetings on gerontology, reports on group work with the aged are still scarce. After combing three thick volumes of abstracts published following the International Congress of Gerontology held in Kiev, in 1972, I could locate only four papers pertaining to group work with older adults: Three were from the United States (Bloom 1972; Finkel & Fillmore 1971; Weinstock & Weiner 1972), and one was from the Netherlands (ter Haar 1972). During the International Congress of Gerontology held in Jerusalem three years later, two papers were given dealing specifically with group work and older adults (Burnside 1975; Kahana 1975). Other papers merely alluded to group work (Gaitz 1975; Kennedy 1975). At the 1978 International Conference, one paper on the subject was listed in the abstracts (Stevens &

Wimmers 1979). Three years later at the conference in Hamburg, Germany, two papers were presented, one about music therapy and one about group work with the confused aged (Bright 1981; Burnside, Baumler & Weaverdyck 1981).

During the 1970s and 1980s, types of groups for older persons included short-term educational groups, skills-building groups, reminiscence and life-review groups, self-help, support, and advocacy groups (Toseland 1990).

GENERAL GROUP PROCESSES

Space limitations preclude all but a few comments on interaction in groups generally. Kurt Lewin (1948) organized and developed *field theory*, which he saw as "a method of analyzing causal relations and building scientific constructs." His work at the University of Iowa in the 1930s and later at the Massachusetts Institute of Technology established the field of group dynamics. *Group dynamics* refers to the study of individuals who are interacting in small groups. *Dynamics* means "the motive and controlling forces,... also the study of such forces" (*Webster's* 1976). Other terms used are *group processes, group interaction, group psychology,* and *human relations.*

The reader who feels deficient in group process theory is referred to *Groups: Facilitating Individual Growth and Societal Change*, by Walter Lifton (1972); *Group Processes: An Introduction to Group Dynamics*, by Joseph Luft (1963); *The Small Group*, by Michael Olmsted (1959); *The Process of Group Communication*, by Ronald Applbaum et al. (1974); and *Groups in Social Work*, by Margaret Hartford (1972). These works deal with groups in general but do not include group work with older adults. For those interested or engaged in group psychotherapy, Yalom's *The Theory and Practice of Group Psychotherapy* (1985) and Chapter 19 in this book are recommended.

SOME PRINCIPLES OF GROUP WORK

The differences between group work with older adults and work with other age groups should be mentioned. In general, group work with the aged involves a more directive approach (Corey & Corey 1992; Rustin & Wolk 1963), and leaders must take a more active role in giving information, answering questions, and sharing themselves with the group members.

Group leaders need to provide much support, encouragement, and empathy, because the aged often have special problems that must be recognized and dealt with. On the emotional level, older people may be preoccupied with loss and death and may refer to these topics again and again (Burnside 1970b). A major objective in group work is to alleviate this general anxiety by helping group members solve immediate problems. Thus, psychotherapy groups for the aged stress this aspect of mental health more than insight or personality changes (Rustin & Wolk 1963).

Group leaders also must contend with the physical problems of the aged. Sensory defects, for example, require special techniques. Speaking slowly and clearly, sitting close to the members, and keeping the groups and circles small are all helpful. Assessing the energy level of each member is another important aspect of group work with older adults.

Psychological support from the leader increases group members' confidence and promotes cohesiveness. For example, group members may use their advancing age and/or illness as defenses against attending group sessions (Rustin & Wolk 1963). But making meticulous *contracts* (agreements between leaders and members) (see Chapter 8), attending to physical complaints, and personally visiting or telephoning members outside the group may help reduce the need for such defensive behavior. Of course, maintaining such groups is a demanding task for the leaders, especially since they must feel comfortable with the dependency on them that may develop among their group members.

Group leadership can be much easier if a leader emerges from the group itself. Even with mentally impaired aged persons diagnosed as organic brain syndrome, I have had a member become a "helper" and try to assist me, although in institutions the frailty of members seems to have an impact on their leadership potential, and their own dependency needs preclude leadership roles for them. Nonetheless, leaders need to praise and encourage a member who demonstrates an inclination toward group leadership; this reward in itself can help raise the low self-esteem that so many of the aged experience.

All these principles of group work with older adults presuppose carefully handled communication between leaders and members, leaders and staffs, leaders and families. Poor communication creates problems, confusion, ill feelings, and lack of interest. With forgetful, confused, or disoriented aged especially, it is crucial to communicate clearly and consistently.

Toseland (1990) makes the important point that "groups will take on quite different dynamics if members are energetic and healthy, or if they are cognitively or physically impaired" (p. 9). This is one of the basic reasons for carefully screening all potential group members and for the leader having the group purpose and objectives clearly in mind before beginning a group.

COMMON GROUPS AND GROUP METHODS

The possibilities for group work with the aged are varied, which makes it a challenging and exciting form of treatment. Some of the current groups and group methods are described here briefly and in detail in subsequent chapters. Although avant garde groups are increasing in popularity, they are not covered in this book.

The following list shows the possible levels of group work and of the group member. The levels will indicate the knowledge base, skill, and practice needed by the leader. The four levels are

1. Reality orientation.
2. Remotivation.
3. Reminiscing; music (creative movement), art, and poetry; bibliotherapy; scribotherapy; current events; family therapy.
4. Health teaching/educational.
5. Group psychotherapy.

The levels of group work and some general information about each can be seen in Table 3-1.

Reality Orientation

Reality orientation (RO) groups are currently very popular, especially for regressed older persons who are affected with dementia. These groups were first started at the Veterans Administration Hospital in Tuscaloosa, Alabama, by a nurse and a psychologist (Taulbee & Folsom 1966).

TABLE 3-1 Levels of group work with older adults

Group modality	Number of members	Type of leader	Length of meeting	Props useful	Refreshments
Reality orientation	4	Nurses' aide with special training	As tolerated: 15 or 30 minutes to 1 hour	Yes	Yes
Remotivation	12-14	Student, nurses' aide, or psychiatric technician with special training	1 hour	Yes	No (according to founder of remotivation therapy)
Reminiscence	6-8	Activity director, psychologist, nurses' aide, bibliotherapist, nurse, occupational therapist, social worker, or student volunteer	1-1½ hours	Yes	Yes
Art	4-6	Artist or art major	1 hour	Yes	Optional
Music	6-8 (or a very large group)	Musician or a person who is musically talented	1 hour	Yes	Optional
Poetry	6-8	Poet or teacher of poetry	1 hour	Yes	Optional
Bibliotherapy	6-8 (if frail aged); otherwise 10-12	Librarian, volunteer	1 hour	Yes	Optional
Health teaching	Variable	Health-related professional, nurse, health educator	1 hour	Optional	Optional
Psychotherapy	6-8	Psychiatric nurse, psychiatric social worker, psychologist, psychiatrist, certified counselor	1 hour or 2 times weekly	No	Usually no

Reality orientation groups are designed for confused, disoriented older adults. Meetings are half an hour long, held usually Monday through Friday, and led by a nursing assistant, a volunteer, or an activities coordinator. (Although meetings are regularly scheduled, the reality orienting process should be continued around the clock.) A group should not have more than four members because of the tremendous demands such a group places on the leader. A large reality orientation board is kept in the meeting room. Posted on it daily is such common information as the weather, the date, and the next meal.

Reality testing is an important aspect of reality orientation groups, and correct information must be constantly given to the confused, disoriented older person. It is sometimes important to reduce disorientation in the three spheres of time, place, and person. Misperceptions of the environment are commonplace among confused aged, especially those with poor vision. This area is often neglected in reorienting older adults; staff members often do not clarify or reality test for visual illusions (Burnside 1977).

Reality orientation groups are often mistakenly called reality therapy groups Reality therapy is a specific type of psychotherapy begun by William Glasser (1965) for delinquent adolescents. See also Chapter 13.

Two glaring problems are frequently seen after RO is introduced in an institution. One problem is that reality testing is not continued around the clock by all shifts, so it is not as effective as it might be. The other problem is that the instructor (or responsible shift) does not keep the all-important reality orientation board up to date. I have been in a skilled nursing facility where the board read, "The weather is sunny today," and I had just come in from a rainstorm! Because RO has been immensely popular and garnered its share of publications, the concept is presented in detail in Chapter 13.

Remotivation Therapy

Remotivation groups, the next level in group work, are also popular. The focus of remotivation therapy is on simple, objective aspects of day-to-day living.

The leader arranges a very structured classroom setting, with props, and tries to get the patients to discuss their experiences in regard to a specific topic.

Generally, patients in remotivation groups are helped toward resocialization. For example, Mary Ann Miller (1975) studied different types of group therapy and selected a remotivation group to conduct in a nursing home. She reached all levels of confused individuals and described the experience as successful. Miller observed that many of the members began to converse and ask questions after not having spoken for several years. They began to ambulate and feed themselves, and they asked for bathroom assistance after long periods of incontinence. (See Chapter 14 for Helen Dennis's review of other research findings and a report on her own.)

The model of the remotivation technique and its application to the mentally ill originated with Dorothy Hoskins Smith, an English literature teacher from Claremont College, Claremont, California. She trained a large group of personnel at the Philadelphia State Hospital in 1956. Because this treatment method was developed in a state hospital for use with mental patients, adaptations are necessary if it is to be used with older persons in other settings.

Although many remotivation groups seem to have been successful, such groups do have drawbacks. There are several reasons that remotivation groups may lack appeal and challenge for the leader: They do not (1) explore feelings; (2) permit the leader to touch the members; (3) focus on leisure, but rather are based on the "work world" (which is fine for young institutionalized persons but is unrealistic for very old persons who are in extended care or intermediate care facilities or even boarding homes); (4) allow for much spontaneity or originality in leadership; or (5) permit refreshments to be served. All of these characteristics violate the principles and philosophy so vital to group work with the aged. It seems especially inappropriate for an older group to have the work world as part of its focus. That implies being a producer. To old people who can no longer work, it is a reminder that they not only cannot produce but may also be in a quite dependent role. That remotivation groups were launched in a state hospital has influenced the model. We need new and different models for individuals in extended care facilities and perhaps for community residents as well.

Reminiscence Groups

Therapists have long recognized the power of the here-and-now (Slife & Lanyon 1991). The power and the typology of the there-and-then are also emerging as reminiscence therapy enters its third decade as a treatment modality. The reminiscence therapy group is one of the most widely used therapeutic modalities for older persons, and the literature is on the increase. One of the differences in reminiscence groups and traditional group therapy models is that reminiscence groups are more theme-oriented than traditional models. Also, props may be adjuncts to the use of themes.

Because reminiscence therapy (RT) is so important as a treatment modality with the aged population, a long chapter in this text is devoted to RT (see Chapter 15). Reminiscence groups are designed to explore memories with a group of six or eight older persons and can meet in either an institutional or a noninstitutional setting. Meetings are held once or twice weekly, according to the leader's and the group's wishes, for approximately one hour. The leader encourages the sharing of memories that run the gamut from happy to sad, carefree to somber, and include all stages of life. Many subjects can be discussed in a reminiscence group—holidays, birthdays, major events, families, geographical places, travel, modes of transportation.

Hamilton (1992) offers reminiscence therapy as an intervention for 19 nursing diagnoses. In 1985, she designed it for 11 nursing diagnoses; it is clearly an intervention popular with nurses, in both the group and the one-to-one modality. Social workers also implement reminiscence in their clinical practice (Beaver & Miller 1992) at all levels of intervention: primary, secondary, and tertiary. Research on the phenomenon continues by all disciplines. Watt and Wang (1991) sum up very well the present state of reminiscence research. Their words also could apply to reminiscence group therapy. "However, in spite of the recent surge of interest in reminiscence, many of its effects on our lives remain a mystery that awaits further investigation" (p. 37). See Chapter 15 for more on reminiscence therapy groups.

Topic-Specific Groups

Music Groups. Music groups can accommodate a large number of members and can be led by a registered music therapist or a musically talented person with leadership skills. A solid base in gerontology is needed. Some leaders also incorporate creative movement into their music groups. Groups with other foci often incorporate appropriate music into some of the group meetings.

The type of music group—whether sing-along, listening group, instrumental group, or any other—will depend on several factors: available space for meetings; available musical instruments; talent of the leader, members, staff personnel, and family members; and budget for sheet music, rental or purchase of instruments, and so on.

It is not the goal of music groups to teach music per se. The goal can vary; common ones are to improve the quality and enjoyment of daily living, to increase body movement, to reach withdrawn members, to provide props in group work, to increase or enhance reminiscing within the group through music, and to increase feelings of relatedness to cohorts through familiar music.

Mary Jane Hennessey (1976a, 1976b), nurse and concert violinist, experimented with a variety of music groups. She worked with large and small groups of older people and always used the central theme of music. She observed a gradual but varied effect among group members: increased socialization and sensory stimulation, increased reminiscing, enhanced self-esteem, decreased hostility and loneliness, lessened incontinence. (See Chapter 17 on methods for establishing music groups with older adults.)

Art Therapy and Poetry Groups. Art therapy and poetry groups are highly recommended, but they are not commonly used in the care of the aged. This book does not include a chapter on poetry groups; the reader is referred to an excellent book by Kenneth Koch entitled *I Never Told Anybody* (1977). Space does not permit a lengthy description of that poet's warm and human approach to old people in a nursing home. His book is based on weekly meetings in a nursing home in New York City with residents in their seventies, eighties, and nineties. He offers guidelines for leaders of poetry groups.

Most art and poetry groups are therapy groups conducted with children or young adults. Simple drawings can be incorporated into group meetings at any level for discussion and exploration. The use of drawing is further described and illustrated in Chapter 11, "Group Work with the Cognitively Impaired." Weber (1981) describes her group work in art therapy with members ranging in age from the sixties through the nineties. Hers was a practicum placement at a nutrition site. She perceived isolation and boredom in the members. She responded to the women's interest in cloth and quilting and assisted the group in making a cloth mural, which she describes (p. 52) as "concrete evidence of the strength, vitality, and creativity of a group of largely disadvantaged old people."

Bibliotherapy. Bibliotherapy is a special form of therapy that can be done individually or in a group. It uses reading aloud as a therapeutic approach to problems and problem solving.

Scribotherapy. Another type of group, called scribotherapy, was the subject of a paper presented at the Twenty-Ninth Annual Scientific Meeting of the Gerontological Society (Stewart 1976). Scribotherapy, derived from the Latin *scribo*, which means to write, is "writing therapy."

For more than a year Janice Stewart, an activities therapist at Philadelphia Geriatric Center, conducted scribotherapy with 32 severely mentally impaired and behaviorally disturbed residents from a wing of the center. The group wrote material to publish in their own newspaper, which was distributed to staff, families, administrators, and other residents. The benefits of scribotherapy include a chance for self-expression, the enhancement of self-esteem, the encouragement of reminiscence, and an increase in social interaction.

Health-Related Groups. Health-related groups are currently often conducted at nutrition centers. A variety of disciplines could lead them. A podiatrist might teach foot care, a dentist might teach dental care, a cardiologist might teach about heart problems; a nurse or health educator could coordinate the group. Older people do need more information about such things as glaucoma, cataracts, hearing problems, diabetes, arthritis, strokes, organic brain syndrome, and sexuality and aging. One effort to provide family members with information was handled through a stroke club.

These groups can be organized as large, formal classes with a lecture approach, or they can be small and informal discussion groups. Few kinds of groups for the aged lend themselves to large size; health-related groups can be larger than most other groups because of their educational nature. However, regardless of size or subject matter, it goes without saying that prevention should be a recurring theme in any health-related group.

Health-related groups can have a wide range of goals. For example, Johnston (1965) used group reading of a stroke victim's experiences as a therapeutic approach to treatment with elderly cerebrovascular accident (CVA) patients. Murphy (1969) and Valentine (1970) conducted health-teaching groups. Anderson and Andrew (1973) describe health conferences for groups of older people. Other health-related groups described in the literature include those in which all of the members struggle with the same affliction (Conte, Brandzel & Whitehead 1974; Heller 1970; Holland 1973).

In other research, Schwartz and Papas (1968) stated that group therapy minimized the anxiety of older patients with medical problems. Group therapy techniques were adopted to improve communication. Through identification in the small group (see Yalom's "curative factors" in Chapter 5) and association with members of a small group, aged persons with diabetes and heart problems coped with many of their symptoms.

Liederman and Liederman (1967) described a group of 11 persons, ranging in age from 62 to 86, who were referred to outpatient therapy because of maladjustment in day-to-day living situations. These people had consulted from two to seven physicians in a period of one and a half to two years before being referred to group therapy. The group helped them resolve crises and reduced feelings of isolation.

Member-Specific Groups

Groups for Grievers. Some groups use grief as the common denominator for membership. Such groups can be especially beneficial for older widows, many of whom may have little or no preparation for the widow role, by helping them adjust to widowhood and preventing subsequent problems. Statistics reveal that most older men are married; in Chapter 1 (p. 10) it is noted that half of women over 65 are widows in contrast to 14 percent of the men. For women 85 and older, 82.3 percent are widowed (U.S. Senate, Special Committee on Aging 1991). This neglected group of older women has not been extensively studied or adequately considered in our policies or in medical and nursing care planning. Widow groups can be conducted in high-cost or low-cost housing units, senior citizen centers, extended care facilities, day care centers, and in the community.

Loneliness, the most pervasive complaint of widows, occurs especially during the first six months of widowhood (Silverman 1969). Groups of grievers can be conducted during the early stages of grief—say, the first few weeks or months—or even later.

Patience and empathy are required of a leader who chooses to conduct a group of recently widowed older women. The leader also must be able to listen without consoling, should discourage verbalizations of "I can top that" (that is, descriptions of the most tragic suffering or demise), and must be aware of the pacing necessary for widow groups and not attempt to accelerate the process of grief work. Decision making should be held to a minimum. Here other members as well as the leader can be helpful. Before initiating such a group, the leader should have a good understanding of the research and results of Helen Lopata (1975), C. Murray Parkes (1965), and Phyllis Silverman (1976).

Groups for Family Members. Group work with family members may be initiated for a variety of reasons: to reduce hostility, anxiety, and guilt feelings of the family; to orient the family to nursing home life; to educate the family about the aging process or the pathological processes occurring; to encourage family interest in the progress of the relative; and to reduce family conflicts detrimental to the aged person. Such family groups can be conducted by administrators of nursing homes, chaplains, nurses, social workers, or psychologists.

The interaction of the family with their older member frequently reflects unrealistic expectations (Herr 1976), and this incongruence between "significant other" expectations and the aged individual's capabilities leads to discomfort and the possibility of behavioral disturbances (Gottesman, Quarterman & Cohn 1973). Establishing a group experience for family members can provide an opportunity for catharsis and can help them identify incongruencies, realign their expectations with the aged member's present level of functioning, and focus on the future potential for rehabilitation and/or change.

Also, group work with families of newly institutionalized older members can be therapeutic in the expression of guilt feelings and anticipatory grief.

Such groups can be particularly helpful when family members are old too. Parent and child may both be aged, but we are not accustomed to thinking of old children. I am reminded of an incident that occurred on the back ward of a state hospital. A very confused old man kept saying that he was going on pass for the weekend with his mother. Since he was so old, the staff did not believe him until Friday afternoon, when a spry old lady in her nineties drove up to take her son home.

Age-Specific Groups.   In age-specific groups, age is a criterion for membership. Although some writers believe that topics in a group of exclusively aged people center mainly on illness, death, loneliness, and family conflict, thus increasing the sense of isolation among the members (Butler & Lewis 1982), others feel that age-specific groups can contribute to the mental health of the members. Eugenia Shere (1964), a psychologist who conducted a group of 90-year-olds, observed the following improvements in the members: increased self-respect, diminished feelings of loneliness and depression, reactivated desires for social exchange, reawakened intellectual interest, and increased capabilities to resume community life. It is worth noting that Shere's colleagues made fun of her for choosing such a group.

As life experiences are shared, empathic listening increases both the cohesion and the desirability of the group. I once grouped six nonagenarians for an evening meal each week. The frailties of the group made it a difficult one to lead. However, one day a woman wheeled herself into the office and stated, "Today I'm 90! Where is that group that I'm now eligible to join?" The eliteness of the group had not dawned on many of us until she asked to join it.

Leaders who choose to work with an intergenerational group will need to have a solid knowledge base in developmental tasks across the life span. Leaders of such groups must understand changes in puberty, young adulthood, midlife, and later years. Always when there are older persons in a group, the leader must be sensitive to the developmental tasks of later life. Handling sensory loss,

sad themes of personal loss, and increasing illness or frailty will be a few of the responsibilities inherent in the leadership role.

Leaders of intergenerational groups might be from the disciplines of nursing, psychiatry, psychology, social work, or theology. Group methodology would depend on the leader's style, philosophy, training, and experience; the ages of the group members; and the size and disabilities of the group.

Psychotherapy Groups

Group psychotherapy is often the preferred treatment for older psychotic patients because it makes the most of the therapist's time and is economical. There are benefits for the aged person too. Adrian Verwoerdt (1976, 138) states that "supportive psychotherapy with aged patients is best carried out in a group context. The experience in the group enhances a sense of belonging, also an appreciation for the value of external sources of satisfaction, and the effectiveness of reality testing." Reality testing in a group context is an important component in therapy, as was mentioned earlier in this chapter in regard to reality orientation groups. Rationales for group therapy with older adults can be found in Table 3-2.

S. Finkel (1982, 167) writes:

In my experience, *group therapy* is the treatment of choice for the nonpsychotic elderly who are experiencing difficulty in adjusting to loss(es). Groups offer a number of advantages for the older person: They decrease the sense of isolation, facilitate the development of new roles or the reestablishment of familiar roles, provide information on a variety of topics from other group members, and afford group support for effecting change or enhancing self-esteem.

Group therapy for the elderly differs from group therapy for younger groups in the following ways:

1. Therapists share more personal information.
2. There is more physical contact—hugging, touching, kissing.
3. There is more tolerance of silent group members.
4. There is usually a predominance of female members.

TABLE 3-2 Rationales for group therapy for older adults

1. Frequent later-life presenting problems.
2. Reduce social isolation, depression, loneliness.
3. Reduce feelings of inadequacy.
4. Change sense of anonymity.
5. Opportunity for camaraderie.
6. Opportunity for social exercise.
7. Opportunity for meaningful interpersonal interactions.
8. Forum for personal feedback.
9. Work through unresolved conflicts.
10. Transference is "divided"; not as intense as in standard psychotherapy.
11. Offer cognitive stimulation.
12. Offer emotional responsivity.
13. Reduce feeling of being rejected by family.
14. Offer almost immediate relief.

SOURCE: Based on Tross S, Blum JE (1988, 3) and Grotjahn M (1983).

5. Common themes are loss (physical, social, economic), intergenerational conflicts, and struggle to adapt.
6. There is a greater emphasis on reminiscence and life review.

My attempts to mix demented patients with patients with other diagnoses have proved unsuccessful. In general, nondemented patients become anxious, fearful, and sometimes hostile in such circumstances; especially early in therapy, these "threatened" patients tend not to return to group sessions—it is as if dementia were an infectious illness.

There are two major obstacles to outpatient group therapy: transportation (particularly during the winter), and economics. Paradoxically, though group therapy is less costly than individual psychotherapy, its longer-term nature means additional cost as well as additional benefit. Medicare limitations act as a particular deterrent for those of modest means.

A. Verwoerdt (1976) discusses the value of psychodrama, which can be used by a group therapist. The therapist assigns a specific role for the aged person to play. Portraying the role is therapeutic because it involves the expression of specific emotions and ideas; a spin-off is the catharsis experienced without feeling guilty or unduly inhibited. I recall a psychiatrist who asked a depressed, guilt-ridden man to play the role of a judge and mete out a punishment. The man's guilt feelings subsided and his feeling of self-worth improved when he realized how self-castigating he had been.

Psychotherapy groups for the aged should have a professional leader well educated in psychiatric theory and group dynamics. Clergy, nurses, psychiatrists, psychologists, and social workers all conduct such groups. Since there are as yet no geropsychiatric nurses, the leaders are usually psychiatric nurses. A new group therapist should be familiar with the writings of Butler and Lewis (1974, 1982), Goldfarb (1971), Linden (1953), and Shere (1964). Yalom's *The Theory and Practice of Group Psychotherapy* (1985) is recommended for the basic principles in group therapy. A. I. Goldfarb's article "Group Therapy with the Old and Aged," in *Comprehensive Group Psychotherapy* (1971), is suggested for all beginning group psychotherapists. Chapter 19 describes in detail a psychotherapy group co-led by a male psychiatrist and a female social worker.

CONTRAINDICATIONS FOR GROUP WORK

While group work may be therapeutic for many older clients, it must be remembered that it is "not appropriate for everyone and also involves some possibility of risk" (Waters 1984, 67). It is especially inappropriate, according to Waters, for persons who "are so preoccupied with and overwhelmed by their own problems that they are unable to listen, or respond, to other people" (Waters, 67). Some people are so concerned about their privacy that they will not be able to discuss personal matters in a group meeting. Extremely disoriented people may be detrimental in the functioning of a group. It is important to consider the mix of the group members as well as the goal of the group (Waters 1984).

A very skillful leader will be able to handle some categories that might overwhelm a neophyte group leader. Some of the categories are: disturbed or very active wandering persons, incontinent adults, those with psychotic depression, members recommended solely by the staff, bipolar individuals, very deaf persons, and hypochondriacal persons. Pronounced hostility due to paranoia or schizophrenia can be detrimental to a group.

Waters (1984) stated that most older people who are inappropriate for groups do know that about themselves. Waters was the only one to make this important point about potential members. If an older person adamantly refuses to join a group, it is a point worth remembering.

Toseland (1990) presents three broad categories of contraindications for group participation. These are: practical barriers, certain personality attributes, and particular therapeutic needs. He makes the point that if there is severe pathology and a low frustration level, it may create too much stress for the older person to be in groups. This is especially true if there is an expectation regarding responses, interactions, relationships, or competition for the time of the leader.

For further information about groups with older persons, the reader is referred to excellent overviews of the literature by Tross and Blum (1988) and Rose (1991).

SUMMARY

This chapter presents a brief history of group work with the aged and an overview of current group work. In this book *group work* covers a wide variety of groups led by nonprofessionals; *group psychotherapy* designates group work by professionals with psychology or psychiatry training with people who have psychiatric problems.

Since World War II, group work with older adults has become increasingly popular—partly because it is economical.

Group work with the aged is more directive than work with other age groups. Because older adults often have special emotional and physical problems, leaders need to provide much encouragement and empathy. Groups will provide psychological support for their members and focus on ego enhancement rather than confrontation. A cardinal principle of such group work is careful communication between leaders and members, leaders and staffs, and leaders and families.

There are a variety of levels of group work: reality orientation, remotivation, reminiscence (which may include art, poetry, and music), and group psychotherapy. These levels also indicate the knowledge, skill, and experience needed by the leader. See Table 3-1 for a more detailed explanation of the levels of groups.

The research to date indicates that a variety of disciplines conduct groups. The techniques and approaches are of a wide range—from the very basic reality orientation group work to sophisticated psychotherapy. However, gaps in knowledge do remain regarding groups and their effectiveness.

EXERCISE 1

Prepare a list of types of group work with the aged, indicating the important publications pertaining to each type.

List chronologically the important articles about group work you have read. Study the list, and write on e thoughtful page on each of the following:

1. A classic book or article that influenced subsequent group work with older clients. Your answer should include:
   a. Complete documentation of the book or article.
   b. Whether it was a pioneering effort.
   c. How you think it influenced subsequent group work.
   d. A description of the leadership style.
2. A discipline that has influenced group work (selected from your readings of the literature). Give reasons why.
3. The aspects of group work that are not covered in the literature. Select one or two readings and state the missing aspect in each. This missing aspect can be based upon your own group work with older adults, or it can be an omission you have discerned in your reading of the literature.

EXERCISE 2

To test your understanding of the cognitive ability and the physical and emotional requirements necessary for group participation, write a one-paragraph description of a person you would place in each of the following groups. For each individual, state cognitive level, physical abilities, and emotional requirements.

- Reality orientation group.
- Remotivation group.
- Reminiscence group.
- Music group.
- Art therapy or poetry group.
- Health-related group.
- Member-specific group.
- Psychotherapy group.

EXERCISE 3

You are about to implement an age-specific group for centenarians. Write your goals and objectives for the group.

REFERENCES

Anderson E, Andrew A. 1973. Senior citizens health conferences. *Nurs Outlook* 21(September):580-582.

Applbaum R, Bodaken E, Sereno K, Anatol K. 1974. *The process of group communication.* Chicago: Science Research Associates.

Beaver ML, Miller DA. 1992. *Clinical social work practice with the elderly: Primary, secondary and tertiary intervention,* 2d ed. Belmont, CA: Wadsworth.

Blake D. 1973. Group work with the institutionalized elderly. In IM Burnside (ed.), *Psychosocial nursing care of the aged,* 1st ed. (pp. 153-160). New York: McGraw-Hill.

Bloom S. 1972. Sensitivity training with elderly. Paper presented at Ninth International Congress of Gerontology, Kiev, USSR (July 2-7).

Bright R. 1981. Music therapy as a socializing and reorienting influence for the aged. *Programme, Twelfth International Congress of Gerontology.* Hamburg, Germany.

Burnside IM. 1970a. Group work with the aged: Selected literature. Part 1. *Gerontologist* 10(3):241-246.

———. 1970b. Loss: A constant theme in group work with the aged. *Hosp Comm Psych* 21(6):173-177.

———. 1973. Long-term group work with hospitalized aged. In IM Burnside (ed.), *Psychosocial nursing care of the aged,* 1st ed. (pp. 202-214). New York: McGraw-Hill.

———. 1975. Overview of group work with the elderly. Paper presented at Nursing Symposium, Tenth International Congress of Gerontology, Jerusalem, Israel (June 24).

———. 1977. Reality testing—An important concept. *ARN J* 11(3):3-9.

Burnside IM, Baumler J, Weaverdyck S. 1981. A model for group work with confused elderly in a day care center. *Programme, Twelfth International Congress of Gerontology.* Hamburg, Germany.

Butler R, Lewis M. 1974. Life-review therapy: Putting memories to work in individual and group psychotherapy. *Geriatrics* 29(11):165-173.

———. 1992. *Aging and mental health,* 3d ed. St. Louis: Mosby.

Causey R. 1969. *Scientific Progress Texas Engineering and Science Magazine* (October):24.

Conte A, Brandzel M, Whitehead S. 1974. Group work with hypertensive patients. *Am J Nurs* 74(5):910-912

Corey G, Corey M. 1992. Groups for the elderly. In G Corey, M Corey (eds.) *Groups: Process and practice* (pp. 399-430). Monterey, CA: Brooks/Cole.

Finkel SI. 1982. Experiences of a private practice psychiatrist working with the elderly in the community. *Int J Ment Health* 8(3-4):147-172.

Finkel S, Fillmore W. 1971. Experiences with an older adult in a private psychiatric hospital. *J Geriat Psychiatr* (4)2:188-199.

Furukawa C, Shomaker D. 1982. *Community health services for the aged.* Rockville MD: Aspen.

Gaitz C. 1975. Rehabilitation of the elderly: Mental health aspects. Paper presented at the Tenth International Congress of Gerontology, Jerusalem, Israel (June 22-27).

Gillin L. 1973. Factors affecting process and content in older adult groups. In IM Burnside (ed.), *Psychosocial nursing care of the aged*, 1st ed. (pp. 137-147). New York: McGraw-Hill.

Glasser W. 1965. *Reality therapy: A new approach to psychiatry.* New York: Harper & Row.

Goldfarb A. 1971. Group therapy to the old and aged. In H Kaplan, B Sadock (eds.), *Comprehensive group therapy* (pp. 623-642). Baltimore: Williams & Wilkins.

Gotestam KG. 1980. Behavioral and dynamic psychotherapy with the elderly. In J Birren, B Sloane (eds.), *Handbook of mental health and aging* (pp. 775-805). Englewood Cliffs, NJ: Prentice-Hall.

Gottesman K, Quarterman C, Cohn G. 1973. Psychosocial treatment of the aged. In C Eisdorfer, M Lawton (eds.), *The psychology of adult development and aging*. Washington, DC: American Psychological Association.

Grotjahn M. 1983. Group communication and group therapy with the aged. In M Grotjahn, FM Kline, CTH Friedman (eds.), *Handbook of group therapy* (pp. 149-158). New York: Van Nostrand Reinhold.

Hamilton DB. 1985. Reminiscence therapy. In GM Bulechek, JC McCloskey (eds.), *Nursing interventions: Treatments for nursing diagnosis* (pp. 139-151). Philadelphia: Saunders.

———. 1992. Reminiscence therapy. In GM Bulechek, JC McCloskey (eds.), *Nursing interventions: Essential nursing treatments*, 2d ed. (pp. 292-303). Philadelphia: Saunders.

Harbert A, Ginsberg L. 1979. *Human services for older adults*. Belmont, CA: Wadsworth.

Hardy M, Conway M. 1978. *Role theory.* New York: Appleton-Century-Crofts.

Hartford M. 1972. *Groups in social-work.* New York: Columbia University Press.

Heller V. 1970. Handicapped patients together. *Am J Nurs* 70(2):332-335.

Hennessey M. 1976a. Group work with economically independent aged. In IM Burnside (ed.), *Nursing and the aged*, 1st ed. (pp. 231-244). New York: McGraw-Hill.

———. 1976b. Music and group work with the aged. In IM Burnside (ed.), *Nursing and the aged*, 1st ed. (pp. 255-269). New York: McGraw-Hill.

Herr J. 1976. Psychology of aging: An overview. In IM Burnside (ed.), *Nursing and the aged*, 1st ed. (pp. 30-44). New York: McGraw-Hill.

Holland D. 1973. Co-leadership with a group of stroke patients. In IM Burnside (ed.), *Psychosocial nursing care of the aged*, 1st ed. (pp. 187-201). New York: McGraw-Hill.

Holtzen V. 1973. Short-term group work in a rehabilitation hospital. In IM Burnside (ed.), *Psychosocial nursing care of the aged*, 1st ed. (pp. 161-173). New York: McGraw-Hill.

Janosik E, Miller J. 1982. Group work with the elderly. In E Janosik, L Phipps (eds.), *Life cycle group work in nursing*. Belmont, CA: Wadsworth.

Johnston N. 1965. Group reading as a treatment tool with geriatrics. *Am J Occup Therapy* 19(4):192-195.

Kahana B. 1975. Training the aged for "competent coping"—A psychotherapeutic strategy. Paper presented at Tenth International Congress of Gerontology, Jerusalem, Israel (June 22-27).

Kaplan J. 1953. *A social program for older people*. Minneapolis: University of Minnesota Press.

Kennedy B. 1975. The rehabilitation of the elderly: The role of the therapist. Speech given at Tenth International Congress of Gerontology, Jerusalem, Israel (June 22-27).

Koch K. 1977. *I never told anybody*. New York: Random House.

Kubie S, Landau G. 1953. *Group work with the aged.* New York: International Universities Press.

Lewin K. 1948. *Resolving social conflicts: Selected papers on group dynamics*. New York: Harper & Row.

Liederman P, Liederman V. 1967. Group therapy: An approach to problems of geriatric outpatients. *Cur Psychiatr Ther* 7:179-185.

Lifton W. 1972. *Groups: Facilitating individual growth and societal change*. New York: Wiley.

Linden M. 1953. Group psychotherapy with institutionalized senile women: Study in gerontological human relations. *Int J Group Psychother* 3:150-170.

Lopata H. 1975. On widowhood: Grief work and identity reconstruction. *J Geriatr Psychiatr* 8(1):41-56.

Lowy L. 1979. *Social work with the aging*. New York: Harper & Row.

Luft J. 1963. *Group process: An introduction to group dynamics*. Palo Alto, CA: National Press.

Marram G. 1973. *The group approach in nursing practice*. St. Louis: Mosby.

Miller M. 1975. Remotivation therapy: A way to reach the confused elderly patient. *J Gerontol Nurs* 1(2):28-31.

Morrison J. 1973. Group therapy for high utilizers of clinic facilities. In IM Burnside (ed.), *Psychosocial nursing care of the aged*, 1st ed. (pp. 142-150). New York: McGraw-Hill.

Murphy L. 1969. A health discussion group for the elderly. In *ANA clinical conferences*. Atlanta, GA: Appleton-Century-Crofts.

Olmsted M. 1959. *The small group*. New York: Random House.

Parkes C. 1965. Bereavement and mental illness: A clinical study of the grief of bereaved psychiatric patients. *Br J Med Psychol* 38(1):1-26.

Pinney E. 1970. *A first group psychotherapy book*. Springfield, IL: Thomas.

Rose SR. 1991. Small group processes and interventions with the elderly. In PKH Kim (ed.), *Serving the elderly: Skills for practice* (pp. 167-186). New York: Aldine de Gruyter.

Ruitenbeck H. 1970. *The new group therapies.* New York: Avon.

Rustin S, Wolk R. 1963. The use of specialized group psychotherapy techniques in a home for the aged. *Group Psychother* 16(1-2):25-29.

Schwartz W, Papas A. 1968. Verbal communication in therapy. *Psychomatics* 9 (March/April):71-74.

Shere E. 1964. Group therapy with the very old. In R Kastenbaum (ed.), *New thoughts on old age* (pp. 140-160). New York: Springer.

Silverman P. 1969. The widow-to-widow program: An experiment in preventive intervention. *Ment Hyg* 53(3):333-337.

———. 1976. *If you will lift the load . . . I will lift it too: A guide to the creation of a widowed to widowed service in your community.* Hackensack, NJ: Gutterman-Musicant-Krietzman (P.O. Box 648).

Slife B, Lanyon J. 1991. Accounting for the power of the here-and-now: A theoretical revolution. *Int J Group Psychother* 41(2):145-146.

Stange A. 1973. Around the kitchen table: Group work on a back ward. In IM Burnside (ed.), *Psychosocial nursing care of the aged,* 1st ed. (pp. 174-186). New York: McGraw-Hill.

Stevens N, Wimmers M. 1979. Encounter groups from a life cycle perspective. In *Recent advances in gerontology,* 622. Tokyo, Japan: International Congress of Gerontology.

Stewart J. 1976. Scribo-therapy: Meaningful words from the mentally-impaired. Paper presented at the Twenty-Ninth Annual Scientific Meeting of the Gerontological Society, New York (October 13-17).

Taulbee L, Folsom J. 1966. Reality orientation for geriatric patients. *Hosp Comm Psych* 175:133-135.

ter Haar H. 1972. Adaptation therapy for psychogeriatric patients. Paper presented at Ninth International Congress of Gerontology, Kiev, USSR (July 2-7).

Toseland R. 1990. *Group work with older adults.* New York: New York University Press.

Toseland R, Siporin M. 1986. When to recommend group treatment: A review of the clinical and research literature. *Int J Group Psychother* 36(2):171-201.

Tross S, Blum JE. 1988. A review of group therapy with the older adult: Practice and research. In BW Maclennan, S Saul, MB Weiner (eds.), *Group psychotherapies for the elderly* (pp. 3-29). Madison, CT: International Universities Press.

U.S. Senate Special Committee on Aging. 1991. *Aging America: Trends and projections.* Washington, DC.

Valentine L. 1970. Self-care through group learning. *Am J Nurs* 70(10):2140-2142.

Verwoerdt A. 1976. *Clinical geropsychiatry.* Baltimore: Williams & Wilkins.

Waters EB. 1984. Building on what you know: Techniques for individual and group counseling for older people. *Counsel Psych* 12(2):63-74.

Watt LM, Wong PTP. 1991. A taxonomy of reminiscence and therapeutic implications. *J Gerontol Soc Work* 126(1/2):35-57.

Weber B. 1981. Folk art as therapy. *Am J Art Ther* 20(2):47-52.

Webster's new twentieth century dictionary. 1976. New York: Collins & World.

Weinstock C, Weiner M. 1972. Community aged in problem-solving groups. Paper presented at Ninth International Congress of Gerontology, Kiev, USSR (July 2-7).

Yalom ID. 1975. *The theory and practice of group psychotherapy,* 2d ed. New York: Basic Books.

BIBLIOGRAPHY

Burnside IM. 1969a. Group work among the aged. *Nurs Outlook* 17(6):68-72.

———. 1969b. Sensory stimulation: An adjunct to group work with the disabled aged. *Ment Hyg* 33(3):331-388.

———. 1971. Long-term group work with the hospitalized aged. Part 1. *Gerontologist* 11(3):213-218.

———. 1976. Overview of group work with the aged. *J Gerontol Nurs* 2(6):14-17.

D'Afflitti J, Weitz G. 1974. Rehabilitating the stroke patient through patient-family groups. *J Group Psychother* 24 (3):323-332.

Foster JR, Foster RP. 1983. Group psychotherapy with the old and the aged. In HI Kaplan, BJ Sadock (eds.), *Comprehensive group psychotherapy* (pp. 269-278). Baltimore: Williams & Wilkins.

Getzel CS. 1983. Poetry writing groups and the elderly: A reconsideration of art and social group work. *Soc Work with Groups* 6:65-76.

Godbole A, Verinis J. 1974. Brief psychotherapy in the treatment of emotional disorders in physically ill geriatric patients. *Gerontologist* 14(2):143-148.

Guarino S, Knowlton C. 1980. Planning and implementing a group health program on sexuality for the elderly. *J Gerontol Nurs* 6(10):600-603.

Hayter J. 1983. Modifying the environment to help older persons. *Nurs Health Care* 4(5):265-269.

Johnson E. 1975. Health education and the elderly. *Midwife Health Visit Comm Nurs* 11(3):71-73.

Levine B, Poston M. 1980. A modified group treatment for elderly narcissistic patients. *Int J Group Psychother* 30(2):153-167.

Mayadas N, Link D. 1974. Group work with the aging: An issue for social work education. Part 1. *Gerontologist* 14 (5):440-445.

Morrin J. 1988. Art therapy groups in geriatric institutional settings. In BW Maclennan, S Saul, MB Weiner (eds.), *Group psychotherapies for the elderly* (pp. 245-256). Madison, CT: International Universities Press.

Mummah H. 1975. Group work with the aged blind Japanese in the nursing home and in the community. *New Outlook for the Blind* 69(4):160-164.

———. 1976. Fingers to see. *Am J Nurs* 76(10):1608-1610.

Nevruz N, Hruskha M. 1969. The influence of unstructured and structured group psychotherapy with geriatric patients on their decision to leave the hospital. *Int J Group Psychother* 19:72-79.

Nolter M. 1973. Drama for the elderly: They can do it. *Gerontologist* 13(2):153-156.

Nordin SR. 1987. Psychodrama with the elderly. *Group Psychother/Psychodrama Sociometry* 40:51-61.

Petrov I, Vlahijska L. 1972. Cultural therapy in the old people's home. *Gerontologist* 12(4):429-434.

Petty B, Tamerra J, Moeller P, Campbell R. 1976. Support groups for elderly persons in the community. *Gerontologist* 16(6):522-528.

Rosin A. 1975. Group discussions: A therapeutic tool in a chronic disease hospital. *Geriatrics* 30(August):45-48.

Sobel E. 1980. Countertransference issues with the later life patient. *Contemp Psychoanal* 16(2):211-222.

Sorenson MH. 1986. Narcissism and loss in the elderly: Strategies for an inpatient older adults group. *Int J Group Psychother* 36:533-547.

Weisberg N, Wilder R. 1985. *Creative arts with older adults: A sourcebook*. New York: Human Sciences Press.

Zgliczynski SM. 1982. Multimodel behavior therapy with groups of aged. *Small Group Behav* 13:53-62.

PART 2
Theoretical Frameworks

Part 2 offers the reader a brief description of theoretical frameworks applicable to groups of older persons. The focus of the book is not on concepts or theories, but their inclusion will help the neophyte leader better understand the dynamics of group work with older adults.

Chapter 4 focuses on Linden's group psychotherapy research. Although his writings about group work with institutionalized women were written long ago, they have become classics and remain as fresh and applicable as when they were first published in the 1950s.

Chapter 5 is an extrapolation of theory from Yalom's excellent book, *The Theory and Practice of Group Psychotherapy.* Roles of the leader and the curative factors based on Yalom's research are emphasized.

Schutz's theoretical framework for group therapy is called Fundamental Interpersonal Orientation (often shortened to FIRO). Chapter 6 covers inclusion, control, and affection as they apply to older group members.

All the theorists in this section have several things in common: strong theoretical bases; an inquisitive, observing approach to behavior in groups; and the practical, humanistic attitude essential in group work. The importance of such an attitude in group work with the aged cannot be overstressed; unfortunately, it is sometimes obscured by overemphasis on theory and/or research.

CHAPTER 4

Principles of Linden

Irene Burnside

KEY WORDS

- A good reality
- Catalytic
- Contract
- Co-therapist
- Co-therapy
- Dual leadership
- Group psychotherapy
- Psychotic
- Regressed

LEARNING OBJECTIVES

- Discuss Maurice Linden's pioneer research in group psychotherapy.
- List five outcomes of therapeutic intervention in group.
- Compare and contrast the group led by Burnside with the one led by Linden.
- Define *dual leadership*.
- Discuss five considerations in the development of a contract between co-therapists.
- List four indicators that a group leader may need supervision.
- Write six questions co-leaders might ask one another before beginning co-therapy.

> *The therapist's mode of managing...is to create out of himself, out of the treatment situation, and out of the group a "good" reality.*
> MAURICE E. LINDEN (1955, 64)

Maurice Linden was one of the early presidents of the American Group Psychotherapy Association and pioneered the use of group therapy with older mentally ill patients. Dr. Linden died in 1984, but he left a rich legacy to group leaders who work with older clients.

Beginning leaders of groups of older adults often think that they have discovered new principles of group work. However, a thorough search of the literature in different disciplines would reveal

that many of the dynamics of group work have already been discovered, refined, and published. Maurice Linden's three articles (1953, 1954, 1955) on his group psychotherapy with older women on the back ward of a state hospital in the early 1950s are classic examples.

Although Linden wrote the articles many years ago, his words are still marvelously fresh. All that dates the articles is his frequent use of the term *senile,* which most group workers are determined to banish from their vocabularies. (Indeed, Linden himself cautioned against promiscuous use of the term in his 1955 paper.) The articles are still recommended reading for group psychotherapists working with regressed and/or psychotic aged individuals. This chapter discusses a number of principles derived from Linden's articles that are applicable to group work with the aged in extended care facilities or day care centers.

PRINCIPLES OF GROUP PSYCHOTHERAPY

Linden's first article, "Group Psychotherapy with Institutionalized Senile Women: Study in Gerontologic Human Relations," contains several statements that are relevant to group work with the aged.

1.   Modification of behavior does occur in group work with the aged (p. 152). Because modification of behavior in the aged may be slight or slow in appearing or both, leaders may fail to realize the impact of their leadership and the catalytic quality of the group.

2.   In state hospitals an interested, alert resident staff makes therapies available to younger hospital patients; old patients receive little more than custodial care (p. 152). During my own group work in a state hospital, I learned from the staff during coffee breaks that working on the geriatric ward was used as a punitive measure; if staff members—at any level—got out of line, they were immediately assigned to the geriatric unit. I have observed this managerial tactic throughout my years of nursing and have seen it occur in the acute care hospitals too. The geriatric ward is apparently considered the Siberia of the medical continent. According to Linden, the staff's attitude is "why disturb their natural decline by intervention?" (p. 153). This attitude, which is often encountered today, is a license to do nothing at all. Sometimes staff members and administrators are less than enthusiastic about reality orientation or other programs because "they [the residents] seem so happy in their confused state" (p. 153).

3.   The atmosphere of state hospitals can be one of "resignation, futility, and decadence. Traditionally admission to a senile building has been a prelude to a morgue. The depressing inactivity of the typical senile ward completed the disillusionment, melancholy, and hopelessness of the aged and furnished the additional impetus toward abject regression" (p. 153). Today this statement applies particularly to extended care facilities, which abound with former state hospital patients.

An additional burden for such patients is the stress of environmental change. Many U.S. state hospitals are located in pastoral settings, with trees, birds, and space. Contemporary extended care facilities are usually in the inner city or in noisy suburbs.

4.   "Hospital discharges alone do not reflect the actual degree of response to therapy" (p. 153). This point is especially important to remember during group work with regressed residents, because the leader may become discouraged by the seemingly insignificant changes.

5.   Four important areas to evaluate in such a group are mood, alertness, memory, and orientation (p. 154). The leader who has not carefully assessed mood, alertness, memory, and orientation can describe some of the consequences. (See Chapter 9 on group membership and also Chapter 8 on contracts.) I recall one lovely older woman with many social graces and much poise who never remembered who I was from one meeting to another. The fluctuation in these four areas from meeting to meeting does seem to keep the leader more alert.

6.   Therapeutic intervention assists in the "resolution of depressive affects, increases alertness, diminishes confusion, improves orientation, and replenishes memory hiati, all this being reflected in bettering of the many minute factors inherent in ward socialization" (p. 154). Chapter 11 discusses in depth the change in mood I saw in a group of six regressed old people even within a couple of months after launching the group.

7.   Senility "is the logical culmination of the combined social rejection of the late mature person and the senescent person's self rejection" (p. 154). How little we have done thus far to banish the pejorative word *senility* and to raise the self-esteem of the aged!

All of these statements are as relevant for group work today in extended care facilities or day care centers as they were for Linden's state hospital residents. I compared and contrasted Linden's group of aged women and a group I led alone for 14 months in a light mental facility. (Light mental facilities are unique to the state of California. They provide locked quarters for persons who are deemed unmanageable—for example, suicidal persons, arsonists, wanderers—in the nursing home.)

TABLE 4-1 Positive and negative criteria used by Linden and Burnside for admittance to groups

Positive criteria used by Linden (after Slavson)	Positive criteria used by Burnside (compared with Linden's)
Expressed desire to join the group	Given choice; could attend and leave later if wanted to
Appearance of relative alertness	No
A fair degree of good personal hygiene	Not considered
Ability to understand English	Same
Ability to walk or to be wheeled to the meeting	Same
At least a minimal range of emotions	No
Evidence of some degree of adult adjustment prior to entrance into senile state	Unable to secure data to assess
Capacity for evoking interest and affection from nursing and attendant personnel	Not considered
Sardonic hostility	Not considered

Negative criteria used by Linden	Negative criteria used by Burnside
Dementia	All diagnosed chronic brain syndrome or "senile"
Advanced physical debility	Accepted many
Systematized and chronic paranoia throughout life	Did not apply
Manic behavior	Did not apply
Intense chronic hostility with assaultiveness	Same
Unremitting bowel and bladder incontinence	Same
Advanced deafness	Accepted one very deaf woman
Monothematic hypochondriasis	Did not apply
Undirected restlessness with inability to sit still	Same
Unwillingness to participate	Same
Inability to understand English	Same

My group was comprised of six persons, three men and three women, all of whom were diagnosed as chronic brain syndrome. Tables 4-1 through 4-4 show the results of my analysis. Although Linden's group was large (40 to 51) and mine small, the similarities are obvious.

I have certainly benefited, as have many others, from Linden's writings and philosophy about older adults. His courage in leading groups of demented women on a back ward in a state hospital inspired me to work with such individuals. I do not believe, however, that I could have led a group of 40 women (even with the best of co-leaders). For that alone, one must admire Linden.

What I learned from studying Linden's works about the groups he led was that there were things I simply could not do, so I made adaptations. I think this is the crux of group work with the aged. One does have to make refinements and adaptations. There is probably no model that will perfectly fit a setting different from the one in which that group work was done.

I also found that I could not employ the deft, good-humored sarcasm that Linden used—gentle teasing, yes, but not sarcasm.

DUAL LEADERSHIP

Linden's second article is entitled "The Significance of Dual Leadership in Gerontologic Group Psychotherapy: Studies in Gerontologic Human Relations III." In that article, he uses the term *dual leadership* to describe what is currently called co-leadership or co-therapy, although his definition refers to male and female leaders. The female leader in this instance was a registered nurse, and one can only wish that she too had written about her co-leadership experience. The nurse's role was somewhat serendipitous; she was supposed to be there when the male therapist "found it necessary to leave the therapy room occasionally to answer urgent telephone calls and attend emergencies" (p. 265). (In those days there was no outcry from the women's movement, and liberated nurses were few.)

However, we can still empathize with Linden. Of his experience during the first six months of the group work, before the nurse became his co-leader, he wrote, "The temptation to give up the group as an unsuccessful experiment was very strong" (p. 265). That strikes me as a really important

TABLE 4-2 Characteristics of Linden's and Burnside's group members

Linden	Burnside
Mean age 70 (mode = 69). Three persons younger than 60; one member aged 89 at beginning of group.	Mean age 79 (mode = 79). Ages 64-82. No member younger than 60; one man aged 90 at end of group.
All were women.	Both men and women.
All were institutionalized.	All had been confined to nursing homes or light mental facilities from 2 weeks to 10 years.
All had needs inherent in pathological later maturity.	Severe physical disabilities plus mental problems, mostly depression.
All had virtually the same kind of care and daily experiences, since environmental factors could be fairly well controlled.	Same.
Diagnoses	Diagnoses
Psychosis with cerebral arteriosclerosis: 12 Involutional psychosis: 8 Schizophrenia: 6	Male, 68: postfracture, right hip; ASCVD;[1] alcoholism with secondary OBS.[2]
Senile psychosis: 5 Paranoid condition: 4 Senile dementia: 3 Character neurosis: 2	Female, 82: ASCVD with CBS;[3] postfracture, right hip, with prosthesis; neurofibroma of scalp.
Psychosis with intracranial neoplasm: 2 (operated)	Male, 64: CBS associated with arteriosclerosis; secondary polyneuritis.
Psychoneurosis: 1 Huntington's chorea: 1	Female, 79: ASCVD with associated CBS.
	Female, 81: ASCVD with associated CBS.
	Male, 80: CBS due to arteriosclerosis; CNS[4] lues; blindness; anemia.

[1] Arteriosclerotic cardiovascular disease.
[2] Organic brain syndrome.
[3] Chronic brain syndrome.
[4] Central nervous system disorder (syphilis).

sentence, especially since he ultimately wrote three articles about the experiment. New leaders, particularly young ones, are impatient and may be tempted to give up their group as an unsuccessful venture. They can learn from Linden's perseverance and leadership skill.

Seating of Co-Leaders

Another point of interest in the 1954 article is the seating of the co-therapists during meetings. They sat side by side at a central table. (See Chapter 10, Figure 10-2a for an example of this type of seating.) Although the older women in the group certainly must have been impressed with the importance of the nurse because she sat so close to the authority figure on that ward, the arrangement leaves one wondering about communication between the leaders. Most group leaders find that sitting across from each other is most effective for continual group assessment, eye contact, and nonverbal messages. Also, in such a seating arrangement four group mem-

bers can sit next to a leader. This advantage is important because it allows each leader to lessen the anxiety of members, to support grieving members, and to reach out and touch members. (There is no reference to the use of touch by either leader in any of the three articles by Linden.) The patient sitting next to the therapists can also be more easily and quickly assessed for mood, group participation, anxiety, and nonverbal cues than those seated further away. Students in a group work class agreed that sitting next to the monopolizer in a group of aged people was helpful in decreasing the verbal flow of that member (Group Work with the Elderly 1976).

The advantage of co-leadership in groups of the aged is that there is someone to take over during the times when one feels bogged down, bored, or unable to fulfill the commitments of the original contract with the group. Linden (1954, 266, 267) states:

It is a common experience among organizers of gerontologic groups, formed for whatever purpose, that it is difficult to obtain a group *esprit* with aged people. . . . The elements characteristic of senility of

TABLE 4-3 Type of groups led by Linden and Burnside

Group characteristics	Linden	Burnside
Physical setting	Day hall	Half of dining room (folding door shut)
Number asked to join	25	6
Number later attending	40	6
Type of group	Open	Closed
Time of meetings	Twice weekly (1 hour)	Once weekly (45 minutes to 1 hour)
Duration of group	2 years	14 months
Group arrangement	Semicircles before table in tastefully decorated day room	Close circle; round table
Visitors welcomed (catalytic effect on group)	Yes	Yes
Staff in other disciplines visited	Yes	Never, although invited; group used as a teaching group for classes of 3 years; many disciplines represented among students
Group leader	Male ward psychiatrist	Psychiatric nurse (a volunteer)
Co-leader	In 6 months, ward nurse	None
Auxiliary leaders emerged	Yes	No
Formal approach	Yes	No
Rules	No violence or physical acting out; confidentiality	Basically none

TABLE 4-4 Progress in Linden's and Burnside's groups

Areas of progress	Linden	Burnside
In the beginning, group quiet	Yes	Yes
Gripe sessions	Yes	No
Deft, good-humored sarcasm	Yes	Never used; leader's role supportive; always took ego-enhancing stance (staff provided sarcasm)
Leaders patient and persevering	Yes	Yes
Welcomed any amount of complaining	Yes	Members rarely complained; often denied problems
Change in morale throughout building	Yes	Did not occur; interest in classes, groups began; reminiscence groups started later by licensed vocational nurse and activity directors
Strong affectional ties between group members	Yes	Yes
Group identity evolved	Yes	Yes
Cliques of patients formed	Yes	No
Saving things to tell the leader	Yes	Rarely
Improved personal appearances	Yes	Yes (perhaps partly due to the fierce pride the aides had in their assigned residents)
Both leaders complimented	Yes	Leader always responded
Method of group approach at one time or another "opportunistic group therapy"	Yes	Yes
Every opportunity for fun and laughter exploited to the fullest	Yes	Yes
Mutual support and protectiveness	Yes	Yes
Benefits through group dynamics other than verbal participation	Yes	Yes

vacillating amnesia, capricious disorientation, and variable confusion which may have presented an insurmountable obstacle to therapy were partially overcome by two factors: the spacing and frequency of the sessions and dual leadership. The first gave the group a predictable, routinized, serial continuity generating a rhythmic expectation in the participants. This allowed them to bind other realities as well to space-time guideposts.

Linden's second factor, dual leadership, tended to reinforce the first factor. The male therapist frequently had to miss meetings; then the nurse led the group. She was a benevolent authority on the ward, so she was a supportive and therapeutic factor in the interim between meetings. However, Linden's dual leadership evolved out of necessity rather than pre-planning. See Chapter 10 for more on co-leadership.

SUMMARY

This chapter discusses salient points made by Maurice Linden, one of the pioneers in group psychotherapy with older adults. His writings are now classic and should be read by all those who intend to work with regressed older adults. According to Linden, the emphasis in gerontological group psychotherapy should be on resocializing the individual and should promote tranquillity, a chance for happiness, and a return to some self-sufficiency. An intelligent system of care and group management can help to decrease defenses and stimulate the return of object interest.

Co-leadership is termed *dual leadership* by Linden (1954). The nurse co-leader played an important role in his research study. The reader is referred to Figures 10-1 and 10-2 to contrast usual seating arrangements with that of Linden and his co-leader.

Linden "introduced directive techniques into analytic practice, an innovation necessitated by the functional capacity of patients" (Tross & Blum 1988, 5). It seems appropriate to end a chapter about Linden's work with a repetition of his excellent admonition for all group leaders working with the aged: The leader's focus should be to "create a 'good' reality" for and from the group.

EXERCISE 1

Describe how you think Linden or the nurse co-leader went about accomplishing a good reality out of themselves and the treatment situation in the groups they led. Discuss how Linden might have used sarcasm.

EXERCISE 2

This exercise has two parts:

- Define "directive techniques" (Tross & Blum 1988, 5).
- List "directive techniques" Linden introduced into his group work with members in a state hospital.

EXERCISE 3

Write a two-page paper describing what you think were Linden's greatest contributions to group therapy with older persons.

REFERENCES

Linden ME. 1953. Group psychotherapy with institutionalized senile women: Study in gerontologic human relations. *Int J Group Psychother* 3:150-170.

———. 1954. The significance of dual leadership in gerontologic group psychotherapy: Studies in gerontologic human relations III, *Int J Group Psychother* 4:262-273.

———. 1955. Transference in gerontologic group psychotherapy: Studies in gerontologic human relations IV. *Int J Group Psychother* 5:61-79.

Tross S, Blum J. 1983. Review of group therapy with the older adult: Practice and research. In BW Maclennan, S Saul, MB Weiner (eds.), *Group psychotherapies for the elderly* (pp. 3-29). Madison, CT: International Universities Press.

BIBLIOGRAPHY

Dick B, Lesser K, Whiteside J. 1980. A developmental framework in co-therapy. *Int J Group Psychother* 30 (3):273-285.

Getty C, Shannon AM. 1969. Co-therapy as an egalitarian relationship. *Am J Nurs* 69(April):1482-1485.

Goldfarb AI. 1971. Group therapy with the old and aged. In HJ Kaplan, B Sadock (eds.), *Comprehensive group psychotherapy* (pp. 623-642). Baltimore: Williams & Wilkins.

Linden ME, Courtney D. 1953. The human life cycle and its interruptions: Studies in gerontologic human relations 1. *Am J Psychiatr* 109(12):906-915.

———. 1963. The aging and the community. *Geriatrics* 18:404-410.

Maizler JS, Solomon JR. 1976. Therapeutic group process with the institutionalized elderly. *J Am Geriatr Soc* 24:542-546.

Msyzka MA, Josefiak D. 1973. Development of the co-therapy relationship. *J Psychiatr Nurs* 11(May-June):27-31.

Rustin SL, Wolk RL. 1963. The use of specialized group psychotherapy techniques in a home for the aged. *Group Psychother* 16(1-2):25-29.

CHAPTER 5

Principles of Yalom

Irene Burnside

KEY WORDS

- Altruism
- Catharsis
- Culture building
- Fractionalization
- Group cohesiveness
- Guidance
- Identification
- Instillation of hope
- Interpersonal learning
- Social reinforcement
- Subgrouping
- Universality

LEARNING OBJECTIVES

- Discuss subgrouping.
- Describe crises in aged group members.
- State an important area of expertise of the group therapist.
- Discuss culture building of a group.
- Describe two roles of the group leader.
- Discuss six of the curative factors developed by Yalom.

Irwin Yalom, in his excellent book *The Theory and Practice of Group Psychotherapy* (1985), does not specifically discuss group psychotherapy with the aged. However, students, health care workers and administrators, and instructors can profitably adapt his ideas for group work with older people. Although Yalom does not direct his book to group therapy with older adults, one has to realize that "group counseling, goals of problems resolution, improved coping skills, and personal growth are not unrealistic for many older adults" (Tappen & Touhy 1983, 44). As these writers state, "Group psychotherapy is still seldom offered to older adults in comparison to other age groups" (p. 44). This chapter discusses a number of Yalom's principles in relation to group work with the aged, including the maintenance of stable groups, subgrouping, crises in group life, the group leader as a transitional object, roles of the group leader, social reinforcement, and curative factors in group work.

Yalom's book is extremely comprehensive. It is also technical; he uses psychiatric jargon freely. The reader will have to be very selective about reading the portions deemed most relevant to work with the aged but may ferret out appropriate sections other than those described here.

THE MAINTENANCE OF STABLE GROUPS

According to Yalom, an important function of leaders is the maintenance of stable groups. He states, "Stability of membership seems to be a sine qua non of successful therapy" (1975, 84). This is most certainly true in group work with older adults. If members do leave the group, they should be replaced. However, dropouts may be an advantage for students in group work with the aged. New group leaders often select too many members when they begin a new group. Thus, if one or two members leave and are not replaced, the size of the group becomes more manageable.

In my own work, I naturally have made wrong choices for group membership. Usually the person who did not tolerate the group or disrupted the meetings left before I had a chance to discuss the separation. Such dropouts do help the leader become more careful in selecting future group members. In other cases, aged people may be placed in groups against their will but remain passive in the beginning. Later they may state their own views and leave. Such actions can be one way of retaining some control over their own constricted lives, for some old people are allowed to make few decisions.

Death is, of course, a much more common cause of attrition among aged groups than younger age groups. After a death occurs, leaders are immediately faced with three tasks: (1) dealing with their personal feelings of loss for that member, (2) helping the group deal with the death of the peer, and (3) finding a replacement to join the group. In institutions, there is often a waiting list for entry into the group, so someone is ready to move into the group immediately. Well-established groups soon become a topic of interest and concern to nongroup patients, and if these patients do not request to be in the group, very often their relatives will request it for them.

Such interest in a group may not occur as readily with psychotherapy groups. For one thing, the present generation of older people are not particularly impressed by psychiatric interventions, and many of them still prefer pastoral counseling. It may also be difficult to replace a member in a noninstitutional group because of transportation problems. Finally, the group may be known to only a few employees in an agency—for example, those who work in an outpatient clinic. At this writing, I know of no psychiatrist doing group work with old people in nursing homes, although I have heard several speak on their consulting roles. Psychiatrists in nursing homes are usually counseling staff members and doing groups with them.

In spite of all these problems, stable groups do frequently occur among the aged, especially if the leader is conscientious about dealing with tardy and absent members. The effect of day-to-day crises on attendance can be minimized if the leader is alert for them (Burnside 1970a). Another reason for tardiness and absenteeism in elderly groups in institutions is staff apathy, neglect, or lack of information about group schedules. If the patients need staff help to manage the activities of daily living, they may be in the bathtub at meeting time, be in the process of being dressed, or lack the necessary help to get to the meeting.

SUBGROUPING

Subgrouping, or "fractionalization—the splitting off of subunits" as Yalom (1985, 333) describes it, may be transient or enduring, but it is inevitable. Yalom finds that it is usually disruptive. I have found it quite the opposite in group work with older adults. Perhaps the need for friendship, mutual support, and a confidant makes it less threatening than in other groups. It probably should even be encouraged at times.

Margaret Hartford (1972, 267) states that "as people become involved in subgroups of two, three, and four, they may acquiesce to the dominant or influential partners, or to the more aggressive initiators to the extent that the relationships between or among them have particular meaning." However, leaders strive for increased relationships and "particular meanings" in groups of old persons. Perhaps subgroups are not so deleterious to the group process.

Subgrouping does not seem to be as common among the institutionalized aged as it is in other groups. These persons tend to avoid one another in a search for privacy. One member of a group I led always sat in a corner of the patio when the weather permitted. His reasons were "to get away from the old folks," "to read in peace and quiet," and "to be outdoors." Yet group meetings had great meaning for him, and eventually he made friends with another man in the group and asked to be transferred to his room. They got along well as roommates.

Groups can provide a much-needed mechanism for the development of friends in either an institution or an outpatient setting. One is reminded of Toffler's comments in *Future Shock* (1970) about the importance of groups in helping to increase stability in our fast-changing world; his words surely apply particularly to the elderly, who face so much duress, loss, and change in late life.

Leaders may choose to encourage subgrouping outside the group meetings. Meeting outside the group need not be detrimental to the group process. Until more research has been conducted on groups of older people and adverse effects have been delineated, it is safe to say that many friendships begin and increased socialization occurs when group members gather outside regular meetings.

I have not had group experience in settings such as senior citizen centers or nutrition sites. Therefore, I cannot comment on subgroupings as they occur in these places.

CRISES IN GROUP LIFE

Many large and small crises plague old people and can be the reasons for absenteeism. We should redefine the term *crisis* in group work with the aged. Crises usually mean deaths, suicides, holocausts, and other tragic happenings, but I have worked with institutionalized patients whose behavior and functioning changed during such episodes as fires, employee strikes, serious illnesses, losses of pets, high staff turnovers, and rejections by family (Burnside 1970a). The cumulative effect of small crises also needs to be considered. What seems to be a simple, easily solved problem may not be one in the eyes of the older person experiencing the problem. Small crises can include losing one's glasses, teeth, or hearing aid or being constipated and consequently functioning poorly. Even slight falls can rattle the aged considerably and tip them into a state of functioning less well.

For example, a small fraternity pin was stolen from a member of a group I led in a nursing home. He had had the pin for more than 50 years, and his wife had worn it for much of that time. I thought it was the value of the small diamond in the pin that concerned him, but it was the sentimental value of the pin. As he said, "I can always buy another dia-

mond." He never got the pin back even though he offered a $50 reward for it, and he mentioned the loss to me frequently both in and outside the group. Another man's watch was stolen while he was in the same group. These were both sharp, alert men who might misplace their canes occasionally but who always managed to find them. This man said bitterly in a group meeting, "They'd steal the eye out of a snake here!" (Burnside 1970b).

Much group time can be spent discussing the losses experienced by the members. I think it is very important to allow these expressions of grief. Younger people are so much more geared toward "let's replace it." We need to learn what losses cause the aged to grieve. Restitution may be more difficult than we realize.

TASKS OF THE GROUP PSYCHOTHERAPIST

According to Yalom, the two basic tasks of the group psychotherapist are group maintenance and culture building. The leader has the sole responsibility for creating and carrying the group. "A considerable part of the maintenance task is performed before the first meeting…the leader's expertise in the selection and the preparation of members will greatly influence the group's fate" (Yalom 1985, 113). The members are strangers as the group begins, so the therapist serves as a "transitional object" and is the group's primary unifying force. This is especially true in working with older adults. The members may ignore one another and relate to, and sometimes speak only to, the group leader in meetings. This sort of behavior seems to be particularly characteristic of depressed, withdrawn, or repressed individuals. Group maintenance also includes gatekeeping functions to prevent absenteeism and member attrition. Continued tardiness, absences, disruptive socializing, subgrouping, and scapegoating are all factors that can be harmful to a group; the leader must constantly watch for them and intervene.

Culture building is assisting the group to develop therapeutic norms. The group will turn to the leader for direction, and the leader must help the group establish norms consistent with the goals of therapy. The leader must, however, remember that norms "are created relatively early in the life of a group and once established are difficult to change" (Yalom 1985, 118).

The following anecdote from my group experience is an illustration of a norm set by a member of a group of 80-year-olds who met weekly in a nursing home. One group member was a man of 85 who attended the meetings regularly each week. He admitted that the intellectual stimulation and the camaraderie meant a great deal to him, and even when he did not feel up to par he came to the meetings. On several occasions when he was not feeling well, he arrived at the meeting in his bathrobe and pajamas. The leader hesitated to comment on his attire, since the man's energy level was low and he was making the effort to attend. After he had come to his second or third meeting in his nightclothes, one of the women in the group eyed him and said tartly that she thought he could dress up a little bit for the meetings and have enough respect not to come in a robe and pajamas. Her statement had a marked effect; thereafter the man's grooming improved, and he never again came to the meetings in his robe and pajamas.

TWO ROLES OF THE GROUP LEADER

According to Yalom, group leaders use two roles to accomplish their basic tasks and to influence the group: the technical expert and the model-setting participant. The technical expert role involves using all the leader's technical knowledge and skill. One important task is to develop a pattern of communication that will help the group move toward a "social microcosm" and enhance subsequent learning among members.

The role of model setter and participant in the group is concurrent with the role of technical expert. The leader role models behavior to help the group members develop therapeutic norms. For a group to be maximally effective, the members should interact with one another "in a confrontive, forthright, nondefensive, nonjudgmental manner." For many older people who were taught to be seen and not heard, this is obviously new and unaccustomed behavior. The safety of the group can be enhanced as the members see the therapist interacting freely without adverse effects.

The leader who offers nonjudgmental acceptance and who can appreciate the strengths of the aged as well as their frailties and problems can help to shape a group to a health orientation. Yalom,

incidentally, discourages being a "detective of psychopathology."

Yalom discusses monitoring the amount of affect (mood) in neurotic and psychotic groups, but the opposite has been true in my experience as a group leader of the aged. one does not always monitor the affect; just waiting to see what happens may be more useful. Patience is an important attribute in a leader. Apathy in the institutionalized aged may be overpowering at times. New leaders must always keep in mind that such apathy may be a mask for depression (Levin 1967) and be on guard against it for the members' sakes and their own.

SOCIAL REINFORCEMENT

Social reinforcement in group psychotherapy may be subtle or nondeliberate. More often, in group therapy with the aged, it is very deliberate, as in the use of touch in group meetings.

Touch is important in working with the aged (Burnside 1975). Its use—a quick hug, a pat on the hand or shoulder—can be a simple, positive reinforcement. Sheer enjoyment of older adults is another positive and powerful kind of reinforcing—a hearty laugh by the leader may go a long way to convince old people that they still have a sense of humor and that they are appreciated.

Listening is important in all therapy situations with the aged. Again, the leader must role model for attentive listening, because many old people are impatient with one another. In the effort to make someone listen to them, they may not be able to listen to others effectively. Such behavior is often due to high anxiety and diminishes after a few meetings.

CURATIVE FACTORS IN GROUP WORK

Yalom developed 12 general categories of curative factors from the data he received from patients in group therapy:

1. Altruism.
2. Group cohesiveness.
3. Universality.
4. Interpersonal learning: "input."
5. Interpersonal learning: "output."
6. Guidance.
7. Catharsis.

8. Identification.
9. Family reenactment.
10. Insight.
11. Instillation of hope.
12. Existential factors.

Yalom does not state the ages of the patients who reported, but seven of the categories seem especially important in elderly groups: group cohesiveness, universality, interpersonal learning (input), interpersonal learning (output), catharsis, identification, and instillation of hope.

Group Cohesiveness

One way of defining group cohesiveness is the togetherness feeling that a group develops over time. The relationships among members become very meaningful. This is terribly important for the aged, who are slowly being stripped of such relationships. Even after the group disbands, the members will remember the basic acceptance they had in the group and again feel that they belong.

Numerous writers have discussed group identity, although they have referred to it by different names. Charles Cooley (1909), the first to note this phenomenon, described it as "we-feeling." Grace Coyle (1930) also described it. It is of utmost importance for the leader to strive for the "we" feeling. This can be most difficult when working with several egocentric elders. The leader should listen carefully for the pronouns and for any changes in substance or timing during group meetings. Group cohesion, according to Leon Festinger, Stanley Schachter, and Kurt Back (1930), can be seen by how much the members want to be a part of the group. Hartford (1972) states that evidence of cohesion appears when the members refer to themselves and the group as "we" and when they begin to take hold of an idea or a problem and go to work on it. (The reader is referred to Hartford's book for a discussion of changes in cohesion and their effects.)

Universality

Learning that others have had many of the same feelings and experiences can be very reassuring to old people. Stroke patients, for example, will often share in group meetings what it was like when they had their stroke (Holland 1973). In one of my groups with frail elders, three patients with vision problems used to compare their loss of vision in group meetings and their methods of handling it. Adroit leaders can maximize the universality aspect of groups.

Groups also give older people the chance to discuss the problems of aging, so that the members begin to feel that they are not so different after all. Sometimes listening to how others have coped with their losses, illnesses, and tragedies can inspire a group member toward better adjustment. Moreover, a nursing background is a special advantage in work with the disabled older adult: The group leader can do health teaching during group work. Encouraging nurses to take on this task may be fruitful. One health maintenance clinic, for example, conducted weekly programs on sight conservation (Storz 1972). Problems with vision can vary in degree but tend to be pervasive among older clientele. Impaired hearing is another common sensory defect that would be an appropriate topic for such group work.

Interpersonal Input and Output

Many older people suffer from what I call conversation deprivation. The need to talk and share is very important for these people, and finding persons who will listen and take them seriously is a problem. This need for human interaction occurs not only in institutions but also in private homes. Old people as a rule get very little feedback. They need to know what relatives, peers, and staff members think about them and also how they are coming across.

Group membership gives such people a chance to learn about their own habits and their ability to communicate with others. Although membership can be one means of working out difficulties with peers—or of communicating dislike—the personal closeness generated by group meetings may be one of their most important contributions. In my own group work, I often have the residents hold hands as we sit in the circle to say a nonverbal goodbye. Blind people still hold the hand of the person next to them long after the others have dropped one another's hands.

Catharsis

The importance of catharsis in groups becomes apparent early in the meetings. Once aged individuals find that the leader is not going to write down their every word, they feel free to express many feelings, especially hostile ones. With no fear of retribution, older people are quick to use the group as a sounding board.

Catharsis is especially important for groups in nursing homes. Group meetings give members a place to rant and rave about the coffee, the food, the bathing procedures, the pills, the night nurse, and so forth—usually in that order. I recommend the book *As We Are Now* (1973), by May Sarton, as one example of the tremendous need for patients who feel downtrodden to have a place to air their feelings. For the aged in community settings, day-to-day living problems, discouragement about living conditions, high prices, and problems with agencies or personnel are fertile ground for group digging.

Identification

Upon first glance, identification seems closely related to interpersonal learning, both input and output. This curative area largely involves honest feedback and improvement of skills in getting along with people, especially group members (no small feat, with feisty, cantankerous old ones in a group). Identification of self increases self-esteem in the older person because the individual can identify with others in the group or even admire and behave like the therapist. Here again, the importance of role modeling by the leader is stressed. Its effect is most noticeable when the aged emulate the leader's communication. Increased articulateness is one result of an aged member's identification with the therapist. The leader of old people must, however, also encourage expression of self—of the importance and uniqueness of each old person in the group.

Identification is commonly seen in groups of regressed older persons. In such instances, the members may emulate the leader. Since one strives to promote individuality in the aged, this curative factor plays an important part in groups of mentally impaired older adults. Identification with other members in a group is a positive force in

group work. In my own experience, I was struck with how well a group of aged persons—all of whom were over 90 years old—identified with one another. Identification may be one very important rationale for leading cohort groups. Eugenia Shere (1964) also found that to be true.

Instillation of Hope

Many institutionalized aged have little hope left in their lives. The group meeting each week offers hope and something to look forward to. They can be inspired by other persons in the group. The leader also can inspire them by helping them discover that they still have power over their own lives. These people can also learn that their autonomy exists outside group meetings and that they can meet on their own. Instilling hope and working on a future are important goals for group leaders.

SUMMARY

This chapter describes various extrapolations from Irvin Yalom's *The Theory and Practice of Group Psychotherapy* (1985) and their application to group psychotherapy with the aged. The focus is on how the leader can maintain stable groups and underlines the importance of that aspect of leadership. Subgrouping, or fractionalization of groups, is usually considered deleterious, but it may have benefits for long-term residents.

Crises both large and small can occur during group life. Large crises include loss of loved ones (including pets), suicide, employee strikes, staff turnover, and rejections by family. Little crises are day-to-day problems that may tip the functioning level of the elderly person.

Two tasks of group therapists are group maintenance and culture building. The leader must use considerable technical expertise to prevent absenteeism, tardiness, and attrition. The therapist serves as a transitional object during the time the members do not relate to one another but rather to the leader. Culture building is accomplished through development of therapeutic group norms.

Two roles of the group leader are being both a technical expert and a model-setting participant. The group has to be helped to move toward a social microcosm, but growth and learning also need to occur in the group. Social reinforcement is a powerful shaper of behavior and may be used knowingly or unknowingly by a leader. A wise leader is generous with the use of touch as a social reinforcer with the aged group member.

Curative factors selected for discussion from Yalom's book are cohesion, universality, interper-

sonal learning (input and output), catharsis, identification, and hope. Each curative factor has an application and ramifications in older groups.

The depth and breadth of Yalom's book cannot easily be indicated in one chapter. The group therapist who is leading psychotic or neurotic persons should read the entire book.

EXERCISE 1

Understanding shades of meaning, innuendoes, and the importance of definitions and semantics is necessary in group theory. To test your own meanings and thoughts, take one of the seven curative factors described in this chapter and write an in-depth analysis of what that term means to you and of instances in your life when you felt that curative factor was operating.

EXERCISE 2

Imagine yourself as an aged person. Select an age you think is really old. Take the same curative factor chosen in Exercise 1 and describe an ideal group you would like to be a member of so that the quality you described could flourish.

EXERCISE 3

Make a list of behaviors occurring in a group that would indicate group cohesiveness.

EXERCISE 4

Norms are created early in a group. What would be some of the norms that you might help establish in a group of older people?

REFERENCES

Burnside IM. 1970a. Crisis intervention with geriatric hospitalized patients. *J Psychiatr Nurs* 8(March-April): 17-20.

———. 1970b. Loss: A constant theme in group work with the aged. *Hosp Comm Psych* 21(June):173-177.

———. 1975. The therapeutic use of touch. Paper presented at conference entitled Sensory Processes and Aging, Dallas, TX (December 3).

Cooley CH. 1909. *Social organization: A study of the larger mind*. New York: Scribner's.

Coyle GL. 1930. *Social process in organized groups*. New York: Smith.

Festinger L, Schachter S, Back K. 1950. *Social pressures in informal groups: A study of human factors in housing*. Stanford, CA: Stanford University Press.

Hartford ME. 1972. *Groups in social work*. New York: Columbia University Press.

Holland DL. 1973. Co-leadership with a group of stroke patients. In IM Burnside (ed.), *Psychosocial nursing care of the aged*, 1st ed. (pp. 187-201). New York: McGraw-Hill.

Levin S. 1965. Depression in the aged. In M Berezin, S Cath (eds.), *Geriatric psychiatry: Grief, loss and emotional disorders in the aging process* (pp. 203-225). New York: International Universities Press.

Sarton M. 1973. *As we are now.* New York: Norton.

Shere E. 1964. Group therapy with the very old. In R Kastenbaum (ed.), *New thoughts on old age* (pp. 146-160). New York: Springer.

Storz RR. 1972. The role of a professional nurse in a health maintenance program. *Nurs Clin North Am* 7(June): 207-223.

Tappen R, Touhy T. 1983. Group leader—Are you a controller? *J Gerontol Nurs* 9(1):44.

Toffler A. 1970. *Future shock.* New York: Random House.

Yalom ID. 1985. *The theory and practice of group psychotherapy*, 3d ed. New York: Basic Books.

BIBLIOGRAPHY

Yalom ID. 1966. Problems of neophyte group therapists. *Int J Soc Psychiatr* 12:29-52.

——— . 1975. *The theory and practice of group psychotherapy*. New York: Basic Books.

Yalom ID, Houts PS, Newell G, Rand KH. 1967. Preparation of patients for group therapy: A controlled study. *Arch Gen Psychiatr* 17:416-427.

Yalom ID, Houts PS, Zimberg SM, Rand KH. 1967. Prediction of improvement in group therapy. *Arch Gen Ther* 13:267-276.

Yalom ID, Terrazas F. 1968. Group therapy for psychotic elderly patients. *Am J Nurs* 68(August):1690-1694.

RESOURCE

Videotape by Irvin Yalom, Volume 2. *Inpatients* consists of two 50-minute tapes that are part of the series *Understanding Group Psychotherapy*. Contact: Brooks/Cole Publishing, Pacific Grove, CA 93950-5098.

CHAPTER 6

Principles of Fundamental Interpersonal Orientation

Irene Burnside

KEY WORDS

- Affection
- Control
- Inclusion
- Underinclusion
- Underpersonal
- Undersocial

LEARNING OBJECTIVES

- List eight interpersonal problems in group work.
- Select three interpersonal problems that are particularly applicable to groups of aged members.
- Define Schutz's interpretations of *inclusion, control,* and *affection.*
- Analyze the leader's role in promoting inclusion in the group.

> *To help is to enter the existence that is the other's.*
> J. H. VAN DEN BERG (1955)

William Schutz (1958) has written about several important aspects of group leadership that can be applied to work with older adults. This chapter briefly discusses interpersonal problems in groups and then examines three interpersonal needs—inclusion, control, and affection (intimacy)—in more detail.

INTERPERSONAL PROBLEMS IN GROUPS

Schutz describes a variety of interpersonal problems that spell difficulties for a leader. Although he is not referring to groups of older persons, the following list is certainly applicable:

- Withdrawing members.
- Personal hostilities between members.
- Members who are either inactive and unintegrated or overactive and destructive.
- Power struggles between group members.
- Members battling for attention.
- Dissatisfaction with the leadership in the group.
- Dissatisfaction with the amount of acknowledgment that an individual's contributions receive.
- Dissatisfaction with the amount of affection and warmth in the group.

Of the eight interpersonal problems, three deserve special mention: (1) the withdrawing member, (2) power struggles between group members, and (3) dissatisfaction with the amount of affection and warmth. The withdrawing member is ever a challenge to a group leader. Reasons for withdrawal by a group member need to be fully explored. Is it illness or pain? Is it grief? Is it lack of inclusion? Is it a communication problem, such as a language barrier? I encourage power struggles between members. Sometimes they are the first indication of spark in the individuals. The tremendous effect of members' constant losses may mean that the leader has to step up the amount of affection proffered in a group.

Formality has to go out the window when one is struggling with these problems. Leaders need to concentrate on their own style and, particularly, on how adroit they are in including each member in each meeting.

INTERPERSONAL NEEDS IN GROUPS

Schutz describes inclusion, control, and affection (intimacy) as interpersonal needs of a group. If the group has been cohesive (that is, has maintained a high level of closeness) and if a process of control has been in effect, decisions can be made and the group has made a healthy adaptation.

The Need for Inclusion

Inclusion of all members in each meeting is vital in working with the aged. Inclusion can be either verbal or nonverbal. The impact of the nonverbal behavior of group leaders has not yet been studied, but it is a very important factor, as I learned after I had not been conscientious about including two very quiet women in my first group of old people. They dropped out of the group and returned only after I had seen them on a one-to-one basis for several weeks (Burnside 1969). Group members, even the less alert ones, often watch the leader intently. Such watchfulness may be one way of compensating for hearing loss.

It is easy to ignore the quiet, shy ones or those with difficulty in speaking, especially if there is a monopolizer in the group. Monopolizers increase the difficulties of the leader; hence careful selection of group membership is important. Underinclusion may also occur when the anxiety of the leader is high. When new group leaders begin a group, they have many variables to consider, and they tend to ignore one or two members. Absenteeism should be carefully studied to rule out underinclusion as a cause.

Leaders need to maintain satisfactory relationships with the staff, family members, friends, and peers in order to assess group members' interaction or belongingness needs. Some people are very gregarious, while others want much less personal contact. They prefer to stay out of groups and to maintain their own privacy.

The FIRO theory attempts to explain interpersonal behavior in terms of orientations to others in the group. This theory holds that people behave toward others in certain characteristic patterns; these patterns are the major determinants of interpersonal behaviors.

Remember the acronym ICA in group work. *ICA* stands for inclusion, control, and affections. These are important points to remember.

Some specific methods of inclusion that work well with aged group members follow.

1. A personal hello and goodbye to each member is a basic way to make everyone feel included. In the early meetings, a handshake is appropriate; in later meetings, when everyone is better acquainted, more affection is often displayed by both the leader and the members.

2. Another common method of verbal inclusion is frequently calling the members by name.

3. The leader should keep track of who has not spoken and gently draw them into the discussion. An analogy is playing a game of bridge: One always keeps the number of trumps in mind as the hand is played.

4. Sometimes it is helpful for the leader to go around the circle to be sure that everyone is included. New group leaders might try using this method until they are able to balance the contributions of the members in each meeting so that all are included.

5. Eye contact is one form of nonverbal inclusion. Since members may have serious vision problems or may not be wearing their glasses, such members should be seated where they can see the leader. If the leader sits in front of a window or bright lights, for example, vision difficulties are increased. Group meetings should not be held in dimly lit rooms, for the same reason.

6. Sitting close to an individual may help satisfy the need for inclusion. Physical closeness is also a way to support shy, withdrawn, or anxious individuals.

7. In group work with regressed members, nonverbal communication is very important. For

example, in a demonstration of a group for teaching purposes, a 90-year-old regressed man was very anxious and kept noisily stamping his feet on the wheelchair footrests. I was talking to another member, so I reached over and placed my hand on his knee. His agitation decreased. Try to touch two members simultaneously; frequently the two members will interact with each other. Holding a member's hand can also serve as a means of inclusion.

New leaders who are trying to strengthen the inclusion aspects in their group leadership should remember a Spanish proverb, "Habits are first cobwebs, then cables." As new leaders refine their skills, the cobwebs may develop into cables.

The Need for Control

This chapter focuses on the importance of control to the members of the group. However, there is another aspect of control, which is described so well by Tappen and Touhy (1983). They state that a purpose of group work with institutionalized older adults is to increase their feelings of satisfaction and well-being and to raise their self-esteem. However, Tappen and Touhy add that there are numerous examples of control and condescension in group approaches designed for older adults. This is an important component of group work that is not fully explored in the literature at this time.

Young students often balk at the use of the word *control* in discussing one-to-one relationships and group work (Burnside 1976). However, after observing or trying to lead a group that is out of control, students better understand the crucial balance of inclusion, control, and affection in a group.

We all need to maintain a satisfactory balance of power and influence in our relationships with other people. One reason is that we need to make our environment predictable to some degree. Keeping it predictable often amounts to controlling other people, because they are the main agents creating unpredictable and uncontrollable situations. The degree of predictability needed varies widely. Some individuals want to control their entire environment, while others do not want to control anyone in any situation, no matter how appropriate controlling them would be.

Older people who have lived alone and made their own decisions for a long while are accustomed to being in control. However, the institu-

tionalized aged lose so much control over their lives that a group meeting provides one area where the individual can say an adamant "no" or vie for control. New group leaders need to be helped with feelings of rejection when such occasions arise in group meetings, for students often do not realize the great need of the older adult to maintain an inner locus of control.

Despite this need, lack of exertion to secure control is common in institutionalized groups. Some of the reasons may be lack of energy, institutional neurosis, depression, boredom, or lack of finesse in groups. I have frequently had to encourage older persons to exert more control in group meetings as well as over their own lives. Student leaders have had similar experiences (Blake 1973; Holland 1973; Holtzen 1973).

Student leaders need to be guided into encouraging aged members in institutions to take more initiative and control. In my own experience, the overcontrolling group member is usually less of a leadership problem than the passive, submissive member. The dependency and helplessness of the groups can often frustrate and/or depress a new group leader. One example of such a group is a reality orientation group.

New leaders often feel a loss of control of the group when a member leaves abruptly. Although older members generally do not leave their groups as abruptly as some younger persons do because they are physically slowed down for one reason or another, older persons may leave the group before it is dismissed if their anxiety is high. Anxiety in new group members and the leader may result in especially tight control of the group by the leader. Overcontrolling may be demonstrated by the leader's making all the decisions alone, by impatience with tardiness or absenteeism, or by ignoring the needs of the members.

Old people who are not accustomed to groups may take some time to warm up to the group. Or they may try the forms of control they used in their own families. Many of the present generation of older persons came from extremely large families, and the place they had in the family constellation may influence their actions in the group—thus, the mother (she was the oldest girl in the family) or the father (he was the oldest boy) or the baby of the family, the clown, the teaser, and so forth.

In general, the style of leadership and control for group work with the aged is different from that for other age groups. In groups of aged people the leaders are more often "completers," the ones who enable the group to accomplish any task the group is not doing for itself, either by having it done or by doing it themselves.

The Need for Affection

We all need to maintain a balance between ourselves and others regarding love and affection. In essence, affection is a relationship between two people only. At one extreme, some people like very close, very personal relationships with each individual they meet. At the other extreme are those who like their relationships to be quite impersonal and distant, friendly perhaps, but not close and intimate. Arthur Schopenhauer (Freud 1922) once compared people to porcupines in winter. He said that the problem is to find positions close enough together for them to enjoy each other's warmth but far enough apart so that their quills will not prick.

The affectional (or intimacy) needs of the members are an important component of group work with the aged (Table 6-1). According to Amitai Etzioni (1971), the withdrawal of affection is one of the forces that push an aged person into "senility." Older people may need much more affection than younger ones because they have lost so many peers and significant others. How the leader demonstrates and uses affection may also be different. The easy flow of affection between the leader and a group of aged people would not be seen if the same leader were working with schizophrenic young people.

Lack of affection and warmth in a group is to be expected in the beginning meetings if all the members are strangers, but that should change as the group continues to meet. Expression of affection may occur soon if the group members have known one another before.

The responses of aged persons in group meetings mirror the way they are treated in the facility or in their homes. If they receive affection, they tend to give affection in the group. If they live in a hostile or punitive environment, they are guarded, shy, or draw away from affectionate gestures offered them.

Groups offer student leaders a chance to understand better the sexuality needs of the aged members. The importance of body image, self-esteem, and sexual drives may all appear to some degree in group work with older adults. As leaders display interest and affection (both verbally and nonverbally), they role model behavior that can be emulated by the group. The leader's touching the very obese person, the jaundiced patient, or the unattractive aged, for example, may make a great impression on all involved in the care of and interaction with that person (Figure 6-1).

SUMMARY

Several important aspects of group leadership that are applicable to the elderly can be extrapolated from William Schutz's theory of fundamental interpersonal orientation. Three of the interpersonal problems discussed by Schutz can be especially significant in group work with the aged: withdrawing members, power struggles between members, and dissatisfaction with the amount of affection and warmth in the group.

Some applicable interpersonal needs of a group are inclusion, control, and affection. Carefully balanced fulfillment of these needs helps to keep individuals in the group and helps them flourish as group members.

Inclusion can consist of either verbal or nonverbal acknowledgment of individual members. Underinclusion of a member by the leader may lead to absenteeism. Some suggestions for inclusion are personal attention before and after the meeting, frequent use of names, allowing every member a chance to speak, frequent touching, sitting close to an individual, and eye contact.

FIGURE 6-1 *Role modeling affection*

TABLE 6-1 Affection in groups of older people

Occasions for expression of affection to aged group members

1. During hellos	5. Assuage guilt	8. Spontaneous reaction of leader
2. During goodbyes	6. Ease forgetful moments, memory	9. Alleviate grief
3. Congratulate over accomplishment	loss	10. Share happiness of leader or
4. Assuage embarrassment	7. Intervene in loneliness	member

Problems in giving affection

Leader	Group member	Staff or agency
1. Professional, reserved stance	1. Too lonely	1. Lack of role models in agency
2. Embarrassed by affectionate ges-	2. Grieving	2. Philosophy of agency inhibited
tures	3. Lifestyle; not used to it	3. Hurried atmosphere; everyone
3. Lifestyle; not used to it	4. Cultural background	always busy
4. Cultural background	5. Depressed	4. Task-oriented physical care takes
5. Aged person dirty; has bad odor,	6. Embarrassed	priority over psychosocial care
jaundiced, and so on	7. Lack of significant others	5. Rapid turnover of staff precludes
	8. Apathy	close relationships
	9. Dying	
	10. In pain	
	11. Angry	
	12. Paranoid state	
	13. Low energy level	

Problems in receiving affection

1. Embarrassed by affectionate gestures	1. Embarrassed by affection	1. Embarrassed by affectionate overtures:
	2. Barricades: bed rails, wheelchairs, walkers	(a) staff/staff
		(b) staff/patient
		(c) patient/patient
		2. Need to maintain a professional stance; discomfort in role

Encouraging older people to seize more control over their day-to-day situations and their lives in general is a difficult leadership task. Yet it is important for the institutionalized aged especially, who seem to have lost or given up the locus of control. Group members can be important in increasing control.

Affection is lacking in initial meetings, when everyone is a stranger. Affection for the leader and between members usually increases as the group continues. The intimacy should not overwhelm the group member. The group leader can be a role model for giving and receiving affection.

EXERCISE 1

Schutz describes inclusion, control, and affection as components of a group. In the following case study of a group meeting, describe at least one example of inclusion, one example of control, and one example of affectional needs.

This is the twentieth meeting of a long-term, closed group that meets weekly in a retirement home. The group was begun by a baccalaureate student from a nearby college who was interested in reminiscence groups. After the student completed the semester, the activity director continued the group. The group had been discussing important people in their childhood and had brought photograph albums to share with one another. One rather quiet lady had no photographs with her. The leader noticed and made a special effort to draw her out and to get her to describe some of the people in her early life for the rest of the group. As she described them, she quietly explained that the family possessions had been lost when their home burned to the ground. She started to cry. The leader said, "Oh, let's be brave now," and quickly changed the subject. A woman sitting next to the crying woman reached over and took her hand. At that point, an older man stated that no one had listened to him when he talked about being a fireman in the 1906 earthquake in San Francisco. The leader ignored him and asked what the group would like to see in next month's activity programs.

EXERCISE 2

From the list of eight interpersonal problems Schutz describes, select one problem that you think could be related to the situation depicted in Figure 6-2. Describe why, and then list several ways you would try to get each of the members back into the group.

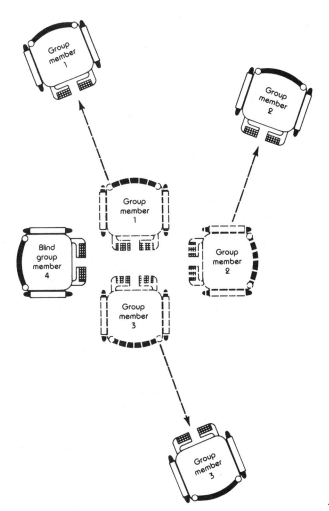

FIGURE 6-2 *An example of difficulties with inclusion and control that occurred during an initial meeting of a group of aged persons in a skilled nursing facility.*

EXERCISE 3

Select two interventions each for inclusion, control, and affection. Write only interventions that you as a leader would be comfortable implementing.

EXERCISE 4

Of these interpersonal problems, write one intervention you think might be effective:

Problem
1. Withdrawing member.
2. Personal hostility between members.
3. Members who are inactive.
4. Member who is overactive.
5. Member who is battling for the leader's attention.
6. Dissatisfaction with the leadership of the group.
7. Dissatisfaction with the amount of acknowledgment that members' contributions are receiving.

REFERENCES

Blake D. 1973. Group work with the institutionalized elderly. In IM Burnside (ed.), *Psychosocial nursing care of the aged*, 1st ed. (pp. 153-160). New York: McGraw-Hill.

Burnside IM. 1969. Group work among the aged. *Nurs Outlook* 17(6): 68-72.

———. 1976. One-to-one relationship therapy with the aged. In IM Burnside (ed.), *Nursing and the aged*, 1st ed. (pp. 126-135). New York: McGraw-Hill.

Etzioni A. 1971. Home—A Buberian play. *Psychother Soc Sci Rev* 5(10):26-27.

Freud S. 1922. *Group psychology and the analysis of the ego*. Trans. J. Strachey. London: Hogarth.

Holland DL. 1973. Co-leadership with a group of stroke patients. In IM Burnside (ed.), *Psychosocial nursing care of the aged*, 1st ed. (pp. 187-201). New York: McGraw-Hill.

Holtzen V. 1973. Short-term group work in a rehabilitation hospital. In IM Burnside (ed.), *Psychosocial nursing care of the aged*, 1st ed. (pp. 161-173). New York: McGraw-Hill.

Schutz WC. 1958. *FIRO: A three-dimensional theory of interpersonal behavior*. New York: Holt, Rinehart & Winston.

Tappen R, Touhy T. 1983. Group leader—Are you a controller? *J Gerontol Nurs* 9(1):34.

Van den Berg JH. 1955. *The phenomenological approach to psychiatry*. Springfield, IL: Thomas.

BIBLIOGRAPHY

Jones DC. 1975. Spatial proximity, interpersonal conflict, and friendship formation in the intermediate-care facility. *Gerontologist* 15(2):150-154.

Kuypers JA. 1972. Internal-external locus of control, ego functioning, and personality characteristics in old age. Part I. *Gerontologist* 12(2):168-173.

Kuypers JA, Bengston VL. 1973. Competence and social breakdown: A social-psychological view of aging. *Human Dev* 16(2):37-49.

Lowenthal MF, Haven C. 1968. Interaction and adaptation: Intimacy as a critical variable. *Am Soc Rev* 33(1):20-30.

Reid DW, Haas G, Hawkings D. 1977. Locus of desired control and positive self-concept of the elderly. *J Gerontol* 32(4):441-450.

Schutz W. 1961. On group composition. *J Abnormal Soc Psychol* 62:275-281.

RESOURCE

Joy of Communication (color, 18 minutes) 1975. This film, produced by Albert Saparoff, attempts to show how people of all ages communicate. It has no dialogue, only music. Dana Productions, Inc., 6249 Babcock Avenue, North Hollywood, CA 91606.

PART 3

Organizational Guidelines

Part 3 pulls together a variety of topics to provide some background on group work with the aged and to help launch the new practitioner. In the past, little systematic attention was paid to the ways in which levels of group work with the aged are similar and different, or to the specific differences between group work with the aged and group work with younger persons. That has changed; the literature in the field is increasing, and sophisticated studies are beginning to appear. The sheer number of old people is forcing all the disciplines to consider approaches for improving the quality of care and of life for their clients. The impact of OBRA '87 is also visible.

Chapter 7 discusses current needs and necessary training for mental health workers who deal with the aged in group settings. The projections of the number of mental health specialists needed to work with the aged population in the near future are staggering, and the need for group workers will continue to increase.

Contracts for group work, if they are initiated at all, are often poorly executed by new group leaders. Chapter 8 discusses the components of a contract and warns the reader of possible pitfalls to avoid during contract formation.

Chapter 9 focuses on group membership criteria, group settings, and group goals. Again, cautions are offered.

Chapter 10 explores a variety of problems in leadership and co-leadership commonly encountered in group work with older adults. Common group concerns and steps that can be taken to improve chances for a successful group are discussed.

CHAPTER 7

Education and Preparation for Group Work

Irene Burnside

KEY WORDS

- Chronicity
- Old-old
- Oldest-old
- Power resources
- Primary aging
- Secondary aging
- Primary prevention
- Secondary prevention
- Tertiary prevention

LEARNING OBJECTIVES

- Discuss the basic philosophy in education of mental health workers about care of older people.
- Define chronic illness.
- State two generalizations regarding chronic illness.
- Describe four power resources of an older person.
- Differentiate between primary and secondary aging.
- Define primary prevention.
- Define secondary prevention.
- Define tertiary prevention.
- List one example of group work for each of the three stages of prevention.

The question today is not whether "older people are no longer educable" but whether we, the mental health professionals, are.

JL RONCH, JS MAIZLER (1977, 283)

The first part of this chapter discusses education and preparation for group leaders. *Chronicity* is a concept with which group leaders need to be familiar to better understand their group members, so it is highlighted in this chapter. Because group leaders intervene across all three levels of prevention—primary, secondary, and tertiary—all three are discussed in the second part.

EDUCATION PHILOSOPHY

The basic philosophy behind the education of mental health workers at any level is to give life more meaning and to make death less fearsome for the aged. Thus, long-range training goals should be to keep the aged as physically, psychologically, spiritually, and socially healthy as possible and to maintain them as contributing members of society for as long as possible. Goals implicit in the educational objectives for mental health workers are:

- Giving expert care.
- Learning how to work with professionals from all disciplines: chaplains; physicians; sociologists;

occupational, recreational, and physical therapists; psychiatrists; psychologists; nurses; social workers; and staffs of community agencies.

- Assuming primary responsibility for a group of aged people.
- Instructing ancillary workers in group principles.

The wide range of educational requirements available to mental health professionals and ancillary workers reflects the different ways in which various instructors try to achieve these goals. Some or all of the following principal methods must be employed:

- Traditional classroom instruction.
- Field experience.
- Community teamwork experience—multidisciplinary.
- Case studies.
- Participation in research projects.

Volunteers need an initial orientation period and then a supervisor who will serve as a bridge between them and the appropriate agency or program. (See Chapter 28.) Paraprofessional technical assistants should be required to complete a basic program approved by the state department of education and/or the appropriate licensing board. At the college level, undergraduates should take some courses in group theory and practice as well as gerontology in an accredited professional school. Graduate courses should be available in teaching, administration, and/or implementation of group work or group therapy. At the postgraduate level, every student should have the opportunity to specialize in geropsychiatry. Beyond that, professionals need doctoral degrees for the highest level of expertise—that is, as authorities in the field and as administrators, professors of geropsychiatry in universities, and researchers.

Sites for Student Placement

Appropriate sites for students are general hospitals, extended care facilities (ECF), intermediate care facilities (ICF), family homes, day care centers, senior centers, retirement residences, public and private geriatric clinics, and universities. The training should be both multidisciplinary and unidisciplinary, but the emphasis should be on multidisciplines, because the health care of the aged involves intervention in multiple complex physical and mental health problems. The standards of training should be set by an accrediting body of the profession.

This brief survey of training requirements does not, of course, cover the special problems that inevitably arise. However, two should be emphasized here. First, the field is still young and requires teachers and researchers with open, inquiring minds and a willingness to try new methods, as well as the cooperation of many people from both private industry and the community. Second, training requirements must be flexible enough to meet the special needs of different types of groups of older people. Mental health workers should be able to communicate effectively with their clients and understand their customs, to empathize with the problems of the older persons, and to combine a sincere interest in their welfare with patience and tolerance.

One problem that confronts the prospective group leader is the wide variety of educational programs, which range from a two-year degree to a doctorate. In other words, who can do what in group work? The ability to lead groups of old people varies enormously and is based on the individual's knowledge of psychology, group theory, psychodynamics, and psychiatry and a background in gerontology and geriatrics. However, even with a satisfactory background, the leader may lack the motivation or the necessary supervision needed to begin a group. Sometimes one simply cannot find knowledgeable people to supervise.

Tappen and Touhy (1983) state that "people with little or no training often are used to lead groups of older adults. The use of untrained leaders frequently goes unnoted, as if there was no doubt about the appropriateness of this procedure" (p. 37). The need for professionals with psychosocial expertise, group leadership skills, and excellence in teaching will continue. There is a trend now toward teaching classes to students from a variety of disciplines; that trend is not likely to cease.

Helping Group Leaders Flourish

The education of the leader, the type of group to be led, and the special talents of the leader are all factors to be considered in the group leadership role. We have not yet sufficiently encouraged group leaders to flourish and develop their own style. Style in group leading is important. Some leaders have a flair for psychotherapy groups, some for music or art groups; others are abundantly patient with the regressed aged.

Instructors and persons in leadership positions who maintain an optimistic, warm attitude toward both students and older adults can also assist in the development of group leaders. A variety of co-leadership pairs should be encouraged, for they have much to learn from one another. The importance of people from multiple disciplines planning together in the care of the aged is best demonstrated in co-leadership (see Chapter 10), which is one way for leaders to share their multidisciplinary accomplishments. Students (and others too) need to keep detailed logs of their group meetings (or use videos or audiotapes) and obtain the critical feedback that is an excellent method of learning.

Instructors are remiss when they do not encourage students to submit reports of their accomplishments for publication. Often, students in graduate programs especially are very articulate and sophisticated practitioners. Many caring, innovative ideas and a great deal of knowledge come through in students' papers.

Because instructors become role models, they do need to maintain a clinical orientation. Their own interaction with aged clients and the ability to use real-life examples when teaching, in lieu of hypothetical cases, will endear them to students. And students do emulate the instructors.

Cautions for Beginning Leaders

Some of the secrets of successful group leadership are meticulous communication, careful scheduling, and attention to details. Students often create problems through lack of communication and consideration for the families of group members and the staff. For instance, they might come to an agency without goals and objectives. Poor scheduling and general disorganization lead to unnecessary demands on the staff and increase everyone's anxiety level and/or frustration.

One potentially serious problem is that it is not always possible for the group leader to limit or control what occurs in a group meeting. Difficult situations that new leaders need to be cautioned about include agitated members; hostile, belligerent members attacking other group members physically; sad sessions where crying may prevail; and discussion of suicide by a member. Nonprofessionals should be warned not to probe or encourage the strong feelings and emotions and should be reminded that they are doing group work, not group psychotherapy.

I have observed psychiatrists, psychologists, and social workers who challenge instructors who place students in a facility to do group work because they fear just that—they may be doing psychotherapy. The territorial turf may account for the reaction, but sometimes they seem to think that a student will unearth strong emotions and that the old people will go flying out of control. Although this may have been observed with younger groups, I have never heard new leaders of aged groups discuss such results, in spite of hearing many warnings. Old people are far less emotionally frail than is suggested by many professionals.

A related problem is both subtle and not-so-subtle sabotage by staff members in institutions or agencies. On the day of group meetings, the patients may be on pass, or they may be having an X-ray, or they may still be in bed. The cook may not know that coffee is needed. It may take time to break through the wall of resistance. However, resistance is not always the reason for the problem: Sometimes it is simply a brouhaha in the facility and a lack of organization and efficiency, or a lack of communication and organization on the part of the group leader.

A well-run facility can take group work in stride and encourage both the older members and the group leader in the endeavor. That cooperation and support have to come from the top. A supportive administrator and director of nurses will pass support down to the nurses' aides. But students usually have to prove themselves before there is much support from the staff in agencies. The doubting Thomases in facilities may not be sure what it is all about when a leader first begins a group. *Students doing group work—or any new group leader, for that matter—should have strong preceptor support.* Students may get discouraged with the group process and staff interpersonal relationships.

It is hoped that group leaders will have education in group process and the special biopsychosocial needs of older people. Because normal aging is succinctly covered in Chapter 2, Table 2–3, it will not be covered here, nor will pathological aging. The physical limitations of older people are discussed in Chapter 12.

Group Process

Leaders should know the fundamentals of group dynamics as well as the special skills needed for leading groups of older people. Berg and Landreth (1980, 51-60) provide some of the basic knowledge that also applies to group work with older people. Group dynamics may be different in an older group than a younger one, so modifications will be necessary. What comes to mind immediately are the increased physical limitations in older persons and the lower energy levels in the very old.

- Members need to know at the pregroup assessment when the group will begin and end.
- Leaders should plan ahead the goals they have for the group and share them with agency administrators.
- Leaders must plan well in advance whenever materials are needed for a group.
- Confidentiality is one of the basic ground rules of the group.
- Pregroup selection of members is most important.
- Heterogeneity is usually preferred over homogeneity.
- Each member needs to feel important and worthwhile.
- The leader must strive to help each member feel a sense of belonging and acceptance in the group.

It is helpful to become knowledgeable about how other disciplines lead groups of older persons so you can better relate to them. Also, there is a geropsychiatric international organization that offers research and insights into psychosocial care of older persons (see Resources).

CHRONICITY

Chronicity will be one of the stark contrasts for the group leader of older adults. The professional working with the aged must be able to work with both chronic physical and chronic mental conditions without excessive depression, frustration, hopelessness, or boredom.

Chronic disabling conditions by one definition are generally those lasting longer than three months (Metropolitan Life Foundation 1982). A more specific definition is the one by Miller (1992), "Chronic illness refers to an altered health state that will not be cured by a simple surgical procedure or a short course of medical therapy" (p. 4). The same author also presents two generalizations about chronic illness that are important for a group leader to keep in mind:

1. The person with a chronic illness experiences impaired functioning in more than one system—often multiple body-mind and spirit systems.
2. "The illness-related demands on the individual are never completely eliminated" (p. 4).

Sometimes slow progress or even sliding backwards in a group may be related to the above two generalizations. The group leader in any setting should be cognizant of these two factors, but especially when conducting groups in nursing homes and day care centers.

Lack of control is a pervasive aspect of chronic illness—from the etiology of the disease to negative experiences within the health care system (Miller 1992). Being a member of a group may help to empower an older person who is experiencing loss of control related to chronic illness. He or she also can learn in groups by observing how other members cope with the same or similar condition.

It is important to maximize a client's power resources to help the client cope with the chronic illness. Some of the old-old are lacking in power resources because of chronic illness. See Figure 7-1 for Miller's (1992) power resources.

The group members' unique coping strategies (CS) can be maximized in all areas through group experiences. Examples are presented in Table 7-1.

PREVENTIVE HEALTH CARE

According to Schroot (1988) "preventive health care is the central concept in the field of health and aging" (p. 18). The final goal of health psychology in aging is to modulate primary and secondary aging processes so that the vigorous years of life will be fully extended.

The same author states that primary aging is a steady decline in function even though the individual is in good health and disease free. Secondary aging is characterized by decline that is

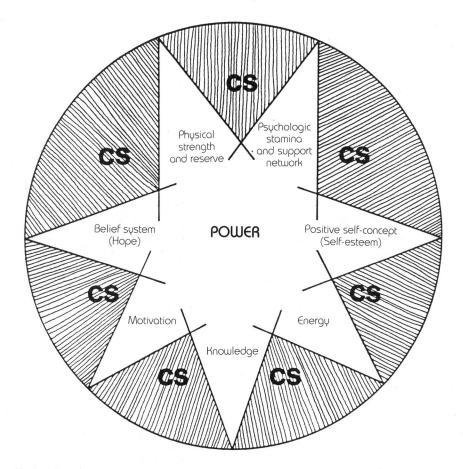

FIGURE 7-1 *Patient power resources*

SOURCE: Miller JF (1992, 8). Used with permission.

due to illness with age. It will be helpful to know the normal aging changes. Also, aging is an individual process, and the leader must take this into account when working with older persons.

The development of preventive health care programs for older persons has not received sufficient attention in the literature (Simson, Wilson, Hermalin & Hess 1983) and is an area of both concern and debate among health care professionals (Beaver & Miller 1992; Kennie 1984; Stults 1984). However, it has not yet been determined how much preventive activities affect the overall health of older people (Rubenstein, Josephson, Nichol-Seamons & Robbins 1984). Meta-analyses have

been published that indicate that some interventions are beneficial. One meta-analysis of 19 empirical studies (Gorey & Cryns 1991) reported that:

1. Overall group work was found to account for 42 percent of positive changes in clients; however, 81 percent appeared attributable to factors outside the control and intent of the group leader.
2. Groups are optimally effective for old persons who live alone and are moderately to severely depressed.
3. Client age is not a factor in the effectiveness of the group intervention.
4. The most effective format was small client groups with interventions of short duration.

TABLE 7-1 Miller's power resources

Physical strength and reserve

A 96-year-old woman residing in a nursing home began the group in a wheelchair, but began walking to group with help, and now comes on her own (Bowsher 1993, personal communication).

Psychologic stamina and support network

A reminiscence group is begun with isolated women in low-cost housing, many of whom are coping with chronic illness. They receive much support from one another and begin to call other members their "neighbors."

Positive self-concept (self-esteem)

A group of residents, all in wheelchairs, begin to meet in a resident council's group. As they are empowered, their self-esteem rises.

Energy

A group of six nonagenarians residing in a nursing home meet weekly. Low energy was observed initially. But as group progressed, they became more animated and saved their energy to attend group meetings.

Knowledge

A discussion group in a senior center forms to discuss special problems affecting older people with chronic illness (for example, heart problems, strokes).

Motivation

A group of poorly motivated older veterans in a Veterans Hospital join a small bingo group. The motivation to win becomes an important factor in getting them out of their rooms.

Belief system (hope)

A group meets weekly in an adult day care center. One member, who is losing her sight, receives great courage from talking to a blind member and feels more hopeful that she too can cope.

SOURCE: Based on Miller JF (1992, 8). Used with permission.

Another important finding of the meta-analysis was that the old-old (75+) and the young-old (55 to 64) had similar interventive effects. Therefore, such research argues against a therapeutic nihilism philosophy in the care of older people.

In another meta-analysis of 13 studies on the status of preventive care for older adults (Wilson, Simson & McCaughey 1983) both psychosocial and health-related interventions had a positive effect on the subjects. The only group modality mentioned was reality orientation, even though there were five psychosocial studies.

Group modalities as interventions for the aged can be categorized into primary preventive intervention, secondary interventions, and tertiary interventions. Beaver and Miller (1992) included group work as a modality for intervention in all three of the categories. Each will be discussed separately.

Primary Prevention

One annotated bibliography (Buckner, Tricket & Corse 1985) of primary prevention literature regarding mental health contained 1008 references. However, only 26 dealt with older adults, and of that number, only three were evaluated interventions.

Nickoley-Colquitt (1981) conducted a review of preventive group strategies with an aged population. She concluded:

1. Theoretical and methodological issues remain.
2. Unmet client needs are not clearly delineated.
3. Clarification of the preventive group approach is required to determine what leads to desired health outcomes.
4. Outcomes must be evaluated.

In primary preventive interventions, attempts are made to avert problems before they occur. One of the broadest mechanisms of primary prevention would be social policies to eliminate the problem at its source—for example, policies shaping income, health, and physical and social living arrangements (Simson et al. 1983). Primary preventions, of course, are preferable to secondary and tertiary interventions, because the goal is to prevent problems. If primary prevention is to be effective, the professional should know what causes dysfunction states (Beaver & Miller 1992). The same authors suggest that because we "may never have a comprehensive body of knowledge about the complexities and process of aging and old age . . . our efforts at prevention at the highest (primary) level will undoubtedly be based on what we currently know, no matter how imperfect that knowledge may be" (p. 87).

Examples of primary prevention groups could include: (1) groups focused on nutrition, exercise, or osteoporosis; (2) groups focused on preventing severe depression—for example, a group of newly widowed persons; and (3) a group for caregivers of persons with Alzheimer's, with the goal of helping them maintain their own health.

Siegel and Leifer (1983) conducted a staying-well group with 10 members in a senior citizens' center. The overall goal was to reduce stress. The leaders provided structured exercises adapted from the literature of mind-body unity.

It is important to note that the group experienced 60 percent attrition after the first meeting. The leaders listed possible reasons for the reduction in members:

1. Discomfort related to cohorts' sharing experiences in a group.
2. Problems in commitment because of health and transportation issues.
3. Depression symptoms were indicated in the general well-being schedule in several members.
4. Low self-esteem indicated by some in the first meeting claiming to have "nothing of interest to tell others."
5. Preference for other activities that were scheduled concurrently with the staying-well meetings.

These reasons are important to study, because this was a group of well aged persons living in the community, and because all five reasons can be issues for any group leader of older persons in any setting.

Secondary Prevention

Secondary prevention interventions are planned during the first signs of problems, and the focus is on early diagnosis and prompt treatment (Beaver & Miller 1992). This stage of prevention focuses on two areas: avoiding the occurrence of further breakdown in a situation and helping people to develop coping strategies that can help them avoid similar situations in the future (Fischer 1978).

Support groups implemented during this phase may help the convalescing older person and the family. While these are meant to be self-help groups, professional practitioners may present guest lectures (Beaver & Miller 1992). See Chapter 18 for further information on support groups.

Support groups that concentrate on a specific condition could be implemented—for example, arthritis, diabetes, chronic pain, cancer, Parkinson's and post-stroke. The group leader should have an in-depth knowledge of the disease and of some of the psychosocial complications the older people face.

Tertiary Prevention

Tertiary prevention has a preventive element because there is intense treatment or rehabilitation, and the aim is to control further disability. Deterioration in social functioning is to be prevented; the idea is to help the client make the best possible use of available resources (Parad 1965). In tertiary prevention, the goal is to limit disability.

Chronic depression is one of the major causes of mental impairment in older people (Beaver & Miller 1992). Another dysfunctional or impaired group is those with dementia. The group modality, while appropriate for both groups, requires skilled leadership. For example, depressed persons may be suicidal. There are three common types of dementia: Alzheimer's type, multi-infarct dementia, and dementia secondary to alcoholism. Groups may be implemented for each of these types of dementia. In the Alzheimer's type, the patients are in a downward spiral. However, the other two types of dementias may reach a plateau. The leader will need to be aware of the trajectory of diseases when conducting groups during tertiary prevention.

SUMMARY

This chapter discusses both the physical and mental health needs of older adults and their implications for group workers. The proportion of the population over 65 is continuing to grow. This increase will lead to an expanding list of needs and psychosocial problems, especially mental disorders.

Mental health workers should learn how to give expert care, work with members of all disciplines, assume primary responsibility for a group of older people, and instruct ancillary workers in group principles. Training methods include traditional classroom instruction, field experience, supervised group instruction, community teamwork experience, case studies, and participation in research projects.

The ability to lead groups of old people varies widely and is based on the individual's knowledge of psychology, group theory, psychodynamics, and psychiatry and a background in gerontology and geriatrics. Educational programs range from special courses to a doctorate. Group leaders should be encouraged to flourish and develop their own style. Co-leadership can be an important part of the process, for leaders can share their multidisciplinary accomplishments. See Chapter 10 for information on co-leadership.

New leaders should be warned not to probe or encourage strong feelings; they are doing group work, not psychotherapy. Meticulous communication, scheduling, and attention to detail are also important. Student leaders may encounter resistance from staff members or simply disorganization and inefficiency, but a well-run facility in which support for the new leader filters down from the top administrators can take group work in its stride. In any case, however, students or any group leader should have strong preceptor support.

Chronicity was highlighted because the leader will be challenged by chronic illness in many groups. Groups for primary, secondary, and tertiary prevention were also discussed as an important intervention.

EXERCISE 1

What have been the effects of OBRA '87 on implementation of groups in nursing homes? List as many effects as you can.

EXERCISE 2

Lack of knowledge about what other disciplines do regarding groups hampers our understanding. Make a list of all the disciplines you think might conduct groups with older people, and then write a succinct description of the types of groups you think they lead. Double-check your answers with a peer or colleague.

Example: Choose recreational therapists. Write your list; then read Chapter 27 and ascertain how close your perceptions were.

EXERCISE 3

It is a well-known fact that health care costs have escalated dramatically. Select an agency of your choice. Make an appointment with the director or administrator for an interview regarding the cost of running just one time-limited group in that particular agency. Write a reaction paragraph to the cost you were given. For example, was it higher or lower than you had expected? What ideas do you have about lowering the cost, if it seemed higher than you expected?

EXERCISE 4

Write one paragraph about a group you would implement for each type of prevention, primary, secondary, and tertiary. State why it would be appropriate at that level of intervention.

REFERENCES

Beaver ML, Miller DA. 1992. *Clinical social work practice with the elderly*, 2d ed. Belmont, CA: Wadsworth.

Berg RC, Landreth GL. 1980. *Group counseling: Fundamental concepts and procedures.* Muncie, IN: Accelerated Development.

Buckner JC, Tricket EJ, Corse J. 1985. *Primary prevention in mental health: An annotated bibliography*, DHHS Publication No. ADM 85-1405. Rockville, MD: National Institute of Mental Health.

Fischer J. 1978. *Effective casework practice.* New York: McGraw-Hill.

Gorey KM, Cryns AG. 1991. Group work as interventive modality with the older depressed client: A meta-analytic review. *J Gerontol Soc Work* 16(1/2):137-157.

Kennie DC. 1984 Health maintenance of the elderly. *J Am Geriatrics Soc* 32:317-323.

Metropolitan Life Foundation. 1982. *Statistical Bull* 63(1): 2-16.

Miller JF. 1992. *Coping with chronic illness: Overcoming powerlessness* (pp. 3-18). Philadelphia: F.A. Davis.

Nickoley-Colquitt S. 1981. Preventive group interventions for elderly clients: Are they effective? *Fam & Comm Hlth: J Hlth Prom & Mat.* 3(4):67-85.

Ronch JL, Maizler JS. 1977. Individual psychotherapy with the institutionalized aged. *Am J Orthopsych* 47(2): 283.

Rubenstein LI, Josephson KR, Nichol-Seamons M, Robbins AS. 1984. Comprehensive screening of well elderly adults: An analysis of a community program. *J Gerontol* 44:342-352.

Schroot JJF. 1988. Current perspectives on aging, health and behavior. In JJF Schroot, JE Birren, A Svanborg (eds.), *Health and aging* (pp. 3-24). New York: Springer.

Siegel E, Leifer A. 1983. A "staying well" group at a senior citizen center. In M Rosenbaum (ed.), *Handbook of short-term therapy groups* (pp. 229-246). New York: McGraw-Hill.

Simson S, Wilson LB, Hermalin J, Hess R. 1983. *Aging and prevention: New approaches for preventing health and mental health problems in older adults.* New York: Haworth.

Stults BM. 1984. Preventive health care for the elderly. *West J Med* 14(1):832-845.

Tappen R, Touhy T. 1983. Group leader—Are you a controller? *J Gerontol Nurs* 9(1):34.

Wilson LB, Simson S, McCaughey K. 1983. The status of preventive care for the aged: A meta-analysis. In *Aging and prevention: New approaches for preventing health and mental health problems in older adults* (pp. 23-38). New York: Haworth.

BIBLIOGRAPHY

Bok M. 1971. Some problems in milieu treatment of the chronic older mental patient. *Gerontologist* 2(1): 141-147.

Bourestom NC. 1970. Evaluation of mental health programs for the aged. *Int J Aging Human Dev* 1(3): 187-198.

Brink TL (ed). 1990. *Mental health in the nursing home.* New York: Haworth.

Brown DG, Glazer H, Higgins M. 1983. Group intervention. *Soc Work Health Care* 9:47-59.

Carey B. 1986. Social work groups with institutionalized Alzheimer's disease victims. *J Gerontol Soc Work* 9: 15-25.

Cohen PM. 1983. A group approach for working with families of the elderly. *Gerontologist* 23:248-250.

Coopersmith S. 1967. *The antecedents of self-esteem.* San Francisco: W.H. Freeman.

Corey MS, Corey G. 1992. *Groups: Process and practice*, 4th ed. Belmont, CA: Brooks/Cole.

Cowen EL. 1982. Primary prevention research: Barriers, needs and opportunities. *J Primary Prevention* 2: 131-137.

Evangelista A. 1986. Longer life brings more disease and disability. *The Connection.* San Francisco: American Society on Aging (July-August).

Flatten K, Wilhite B, Reyes-Watson E. 1987a. *Exercise activities for the elderly.* New York: Springer.

———. 1987b. *Recreation activities for the elderly.* New York: Springer.

Gray JAM. 1985. *Prevention of disease in the elderly.* London: Churchill Livingstone.

Haber D. 1983. Promoting mutual help groups among older persons. *Gerontologist* 33:251-253.

Hastings L. 1981. *Complete handbook of activities and recreational programs for nursing homes.* Englewood Cliffs, NJ: Prentice-Hall.

Horn BJ (ed.). 1990. *Facilitating self-care practices in the elderly.* New York: Haworth.

Macheath J. 1984. *Activity, health and fitness in old age.* New York: St. Martins.

Malnati RJ, Pastushak R. 1980. Conducting group practice with the aged. *Psychotherapy: Theory Res Pract* 17: 352-360.

Moerman C. 1988. Using group training methods to prepare students for group work with older adults. In BW Maclennan, S Saul, MB Weiner (eds.), *Group psychotherapies with the elderly* (pp. 269-327). Madison, CT: International Universities Press.

Parad HJ. 1965. Preventive casework problems and implications. In HJ Parad (ed.), *Crisis intervention: Selected readings* (pp. 284-298). New York: Family Service Association of America.

Rosen JC, Solomon LJ. 1985. *Prevention in health psychology*. Hanover, NH: University Press of New England.

Scharlach A. 1985. Social group work with institutionalized elders: A task-centered approach. *Soc Work with Groups* 8:33-47.

Stabler N. 1981. The use of groups in day care centers for older adults. *Soc Work with Groups* 4:49-57.

Stacey-Konnert C. 1983. Preventive interventions for older adults. *Generations* (Winter/Spring):77-78.

RESOURCES

Organizations

American Society of Aging, publisher of *Generations*, 833 Market Street, Room 511, San Francisco, CA 94103; phone: 415-882-2910.

Association for Gerontology in Higher Education, 1001 Connecticut Avenue, NW, Suite 410, Washington, DC 20036-5504.

Family & Community Health: The Journal of Health Promotion & Maintenance, Aspen Systems, 1600 Research Boulevard, Rockville, MD 20850.

Gerontology Society of America, publisher of *The Gerontologist* and the *Journal of Gerontology*, 1275 K Street NW, Suite 350, Washington, DC 20005-4006.

International Psychogeriatric Congress, Secretary, 3127 Greenleaf Avenue, Wilmette, IL 60091.

The National Council on Aging, 409 Third Street, SW, Washington, DC 20024.

Film

Seniors' Esteem Issues (30 minutes). A part of the *Journey into Self-Esteem* series, this film shows personal stories of older persons who are able to deal with life's changes through the maintenance of health self-esteem. J. Rowe, Filmmakers Library, New York, NY.

Video

Tai Chi (45 minutes). The art and exercise of Tai Chi are introduced in this video both through the experiences of seniors who have been involved with Tai Chi, and through an instructor who teaches some of the basic movements. Purchase: $89.95; rental: $55. Terra Nova Films, Inc., 9848 S. Winchester Avenue, Chicago, IL 60643; phone: 312-881-8491.

Audiotape

Aged to Perfection: Your Guide to Healthy Aging, 1990. A preventive program of the California Department of Mental Health by RW Lutz, RJ Pasick, KR Pelletier, and NL Klehr. This audiotape is a relaxation exercise.

CHAPTER 8

Group Goals and Contracts: Assessment and Planning

Irene Burnside

KEY WORDS
- Agreement
- Anxiety
- Confidentiality
- Group objectives
- Information
- Prejudging
- Verbal contract
- Written contract

LEARNING OBJECTIVES
- Define *contract*.
- List seven items of information to include in the contract.
- Discuss the importance of group objectives.
- State the importance of confidentiality to group work.
- Describe six secondary purposes of the screening interview.

This chapter offers students, instructors, health care workers, and volunteers a discussion of verbal and written contracts and of a variety of things a group leader should consider during the contract-making stage—for example, criteria for selecting members and procedures in handling such matters as anxiety and confidentiality.

VERBAL AND WRITTEN CONTRACTS

One important task of the group leader is the formation of a contract with each aged group member. This aspect of professional performance in group leadership is often ignored by beginners.

A *contract* is a "binding agreement between two or more persons or parties" (*Webster's* 1973).

"Contracting is essentially a process by which the necessary elements of the desired behavior are explicitly outlined in the form of a contact" (Steckel & Swain 1982, 33). Sometimes students confuse the words *contract* and *contact*. To make contact with a person is not the same as to contract with the person. A contact can be a casual "good morning" followed by the usually meaningless "How are you?" but a contract contains very specific information given to and, one hopes, received by the individual.

A contract is considered to be voluntary for both parties and is agreed to by both individuals. One can never simply assume that an aged individual is eager to be in a group, so the leader must move gently and never assertively in the initiation and completion of the contract. This is especially true of the frail and the institutionalized aged, who have little control over their lives. Tappen and Touhy (1983, 37) remind us that "group members frequently are selected on the basis of their ability to participate in a group (for example, mobility, hearing, social and cognitive functioning), but their desire to attend often is not considered." However, because many older adults in institutions have little opportunity to say no, they may refuse to enter into a contract agreement. The leader needs to consider if the older person is saying no and means yes or if he or she is saying no because this is one nonthreatening opportunity to do so. In either of these cases, the leader of the group should invite the individual to attend each meeting on a meeting-by-meeting basis. A personal invitation often works well. Respect for the client's wishes is important. It should also be remembered that too much explanation can sometimes rattle the potential group member, so that is a caution.

In group work, a contract is an agreement between the leader and a member regarding the group experience and should include a careful explanation of the objectives of the group. The aged person should be allowed to ask questions, especially if it is the member's first group experience. It is very important to give the potential member an opportunity to discuss the goals of the group as expressed in the original contract.

Contract information usually has to be repeated both in and out of the group for a variety of reasons. The leader cannot assume that a nod of the head means either understanding or compliance. It has been my experience that a nod of the head or even a verbal "yes" can mean "I am hard of hearing" or "Please go away and quit bothering me"—something I learned after some rather embarrassing or ludicrous situations in which the one-upmanship of the aged became very obvious. This one-upmanship of the confused aged is difficult for the professional to acknowledge. Regardless of how confused or disoriented a potential group member may seem, however, the leader is obliged to make an effort to establish a contract with the individual. One can never be sure how much of the message gets through, but that does not mean a concerted effort should not be made to communicate. This is especially true with the aged who are diagnosed as having an organic mental disorder.

A contract may be verbal or written. If one is working with forgetful, disoriented older persons, it is best to make both types of contract. Written

contracts can be referred to by the patients, by their families, and by the staff. M. Fatis and P. Konewko (1983) were writing about family contracts when they made this excellent point: "contracting procedures make use of productive language . . . (family members) are taught to avoid vague terms and to be precise in their decision-making" (p. 161). The contract should include the following information (Burnside 1976):

1. Time.
2. Place.
3. Duration of group sessions.
4. Lifetime of the group.
5. List of other members. (This information can be important because the presence of a peer or roommate on the list may serve as an incentive for a shy person to try the group.)
6. Purpose of the group.
7. Name of the leader.

In making the contract, the leader should keep the characteristics of the group members clearly in mind. (Group membership is discussed in detail in Chapter 9). Essentially, the group leader should consider the following information about the prospective member: age; physical and psychological problems; diagnosis; functional capacity; communication abilities; sex, race, and religion; amount of affect—depressed, sullen, giggly, and so forth; mobility; transportation; and living arrangements. Nursing care plans may be helpful as a source of some of this information. For example, a director of nurses in a Canadian nursing home keeps a small book entitled *Openers*, which contains a list of the interests, accomplishments, and talents of each resident. The lists give nurses' aides some leads for conversation during care. Such information would also be helpful to a group leader. These openers can then be placed on individual plastic-coated cards which can be inserted on a metal ring. The nurses' aide then gathers up the cards of her patients for care, or for a reality-orientation group. The aide then has possible topics to discuss or reminisce about with the resident.

Toseland (1990) offers an example of a group contract in Table 8-1. It is unique because the role of the leader is clearly stated, and the leader also signs the contract.

Goal setting must begin with the leader's statements regarding the purpose and function of the

TABLE 8-1 An example of a group contract

As a group member I agree to:	As the group leader I agree to:
1. Attend all group sessions.	1. Be prepared for each group meeting.
2. Arrive on time for each group session.	2. Begin and end all group sessions on time.
3. Keep the proceedings of each group meeting confidential.	3. Be respectful of each member's unique contribution to the group.
4. Participate fully in the group interaction.	4. Keep the proceedings of each meeting confidential.
5. Allow other members to finish a thought when they are speaking.	5. Help members to get the most out of their participation in the group.
6. Not dominate the group discussion.	
7. Pay for each group session in a timely fashion.	

Group Member's Signature _____ Group Leader's Signature _____

Date _____ Date _____

SOURCE: Toseland RW (1990, 68). Used with permission of New York University Press from *Group work with older adults* by Ronald W. Toseland. Copyright © New York University, 1990.

group (Toseland 1990). This is especially true for students doing group work in agencies. Preceptors need to insist that students be very clear in their minds about the type of group and what they hope to accomplish. It is helpful if goal formation is clarified so the leader can focus on three sets of interrelated goals:

1. Group-centered goals (proper functioning and maintenance of a group).
2. Shared goals (these goals focus on the needs of all members of the group).
3. Individual goals (such goals are focused on the particular needs of each group member) (Toseland 1990, 73).

A leader must help each member to fulfill expectations and to achieve his or her desired goals (Toseland 1990). Group experiences may be new to some members, and they might not know what to expect. But if a group does not provide fulfillment for them, they may drop out. Coffee, tea, and other refreshments are often strong reasons for some members to stay, especially those in long-term care facilities. There are other considerations about groups in long-term care. Toseland (1990) makes an important point when he suggests that it might be better not to start a patients' rights group in a nursing home if it is obvious that the administrator will ignore the concerns raised in the group meetings.

Goals for a group should be carefully balanced. Focusing exclusively on tasks or socioemotional

needs can cause the group to disband. Focusing on tasks can lead to undue competitiveness, conflict, and members relating only on an instrumental level. However, focusing only on the socioemotional needs of members can lead to displeasure, because the group cannot accomplish tasks efficiently (Toseland 1990).

The motivation to work on the goals changes during the life of the group. The leader can help the process by being positive and upbeat and by praising group members for their accomplishments; it is also important for the leader to state the obstacles individuals face (Toseland 1990).

It is well known that relationships with the aged begin on a one-to-one basis; this is also true in group work with the elderly. The vis-à-vis encounter is of great importance while establishing the contract. The time spent making the contract gives the group leader a chance to assess the individual both physically and psychologically. If the group is to be co-led, Irvin Yalom (1975) states that both leaders should meet with the potential member. This principle is especially important in egalitarian leadership. If there is to be a senior-junior or teacher-student co-leadership style, the individual carrying the responsibility for the group may choose to make the contract alone. Yalom does not speak favorably of co-leadership that is not egalitarian, but I would disagree with him in regard to group work with the aged. We desperately need to train people to replace present leaders and to train workers to take on new group leadership roles, so the apprentice approach may be a necessary means for training. Also, role modeling is viewed as an excellent mode of learning for many students.

GROUP MEMBER SELECTION

Assessment of the potential group member during the contract-making period is of crucial importance. It is better not to negotiate a contract if one has some doubts but rather just to visit with the older person for a while and secure more information.

A group leader should not take an individual into the group solely on someone else's advice—for example, the doctor, the family, the director of nurses. The leader should make the final decision about the appropriateness of the individual for a specific group. After several inappropriate decisions, students will learn how to make the correct ones. Judy Altholz (1975) gives an example. She was co-leading a group with a psychiatrist, and they had selected an uncontrollable member with bipolar disorder. The member proved to be more than both the co-leaders and the group could handle and had to be removed from the group. I once accepted into a group a woman whose behavior was upsetting to all of us. She was agitated, restless, and ruined our refreshment period by drinking the cream and eating the sugar on the serving tray; it was necessary to remove her from the group.

The size of the group should be carefully considered. Chapter 4 describes Maurice Linden's work (1953) with 40 to 51 regressed aged women on a geriatric ward; one wonders how he managed them all. Students often get carried away and feel that group work is like cooking potatoes—one more will not matter very much.

The frailties and physical status of the members should be carefully evaluated in considering a manageable group. If there are able, helpful, mobile members in the group, they will often be of great assistance to the leader. Also, if there are co-leaders, a larger group can be planned, because there will be one leader available to handle the extraneous occurrences such as observing the non-included, the silent members, or the nonverbal cues that might otherwise be missed. It is also helpful to have someone to assist with the transportation problems that inevitably arise in both hospital-based groups and those conducted on an outpatient basis. In outpatient or day care groups,

the receptionist or a volunteer is often most helpful with some of these logistics.

The leader should select a variety of persons, keeping in mind that two hard-of-hearing or three silent, withdrawn, depressed persons can make the work of a leader extremely difficult. If all group members are in wheelchairs, extra help will be needed. In an outpatient setting, the needs of the group members must be carefully analyzed. Subsequent poor attendance may be due to transportation difficulties that were not taken care of before the group began.

The group leader needs to be prepared to work hard, plan ahead, and change plans as group needs emerge in the meetings (Burnside 1971). Staff members and other individuals often view group work at an easy intervention, but group work with older adults requires energy, spontaneity, organization, and tenacity.

GROUP WORK EXPENSE AND PAYMENTS

Cost must be carefully considered at the time of the contract. Costs in terms of leadership, manpower, materials, supplies, refreshments, and staff time to assist in assembling group work can be an overhead expense for the leader—something I learned from my own experience. I once had a weekly group in a facility far from my home, which involved a fair amount of traveling. When gasoline was rationed during the energy crunch, I had to discontinue the group because I did not have the necessary fuel. Similarly, it is unfair for students to carry the costs of all props and materials used. Costs should be shared by the agency. Volunteers may wish to contribute, but it should be their own choice. In one group I led, the patients found out that I was furnishing the refreshments; they wanted to pay and would often share the expenses because they enjoyed the snacks that were served. Group psychotherapy in a private office and groups in an outpatient clinical setting would involve a cost to the aged person, but students usually work without pay.

GROUP GOALS AND ANXIETY

Group goals should be explicit in the beginning, even though they may change as the group evolves. Most new leaders and the group members need some structure to reduce anxiety. It is to be expected that a group of strangers meeting together for the first time will experience some anxiety.

Toseland (1990) reminds us that the beginning of a group can be a stressful time for those who have decided to participate. "Beginnings are characterized by caution and tentativeness as members attempt to find their place within the group while at the same time maintaining their own identities" (p. 69).

The goals of the group meetings may have to be restated frequently, since they are often unheard by anxious group members. Anxiety must be dealt with continually, first in the vis-à-vis encounter of the contract making and later in the group meetings. The new group leader should begin to look for cues to anxiety during the contract making; these may be cues the leader will observe in later group meetings. S.R. Slavson (1953, 386) stated:

> All groups evoke anxiety in all people. No person can be in a group without feeling anxious, even though the group may be one to which he is accustomed. The degree of anxiety is diminished with acquaintance and length of membership in it. However, no person feels as comfortable in a group as he does with one individual. An individual is seldom as threatening as a group, where anxiety is always present.

The leader may therefore see less anxiety in the initial interview for the contract than is later observed in the same individual during group meetings.

New leaders must also be prepared to deal with their own anxiety. Many of us who do group work with the elderly feel that we floundered when we began; we had no definite guidelines to follow and experienced high anxiety. Out of such floundering, however, came a sound rationale and an awareness of what to do and what not to do in group work.

CONFIDENTIALITY

Therapists agree that maintaining confidences is an essential component of group work and provides the member with "a sense of safety in the group" (Whitaker & Lieberman 1964). However, they do not agree on the means by which standards of confidentiality should be initiated and maintained. The crucial issue is whether the therapist should structure the situation by making a ground rule about confidences or should wait for an agreement to come from the group itself. According to Dorothy Whitaker and Morton Lieberman, "To be effective, a group solution or standard must emerge in response to the felt needs of the group" (p. 209). Yalom (1975) states that the rule about confidentiality can be raised by either the group or the leader and that a valuable discussion about trust, shame, fear of disclosure, and commitment to the group may arise when confidentiality is a matter of concern. In groups of older adults who cannot verbalize well or have problems being articulate, the leader may need to provide the direction and formulate the rule of confidentiality.

For new group workers, the structuring mentioned earlier in the chapter is applicable to confidentiality. Old people in institutions suffer from lack of privacy and often are afraid of punitive treatment by family or staff. For suspicious or paranoid persons, a ground rule of confidentiality stated by the group leader may offer some reassurance. In most cases, a group leader can announce in the contract that the group is to honor confidences. If problems arise later that need to be discussed with staff members or doctors (such as talk of suicide by a group member, a sudden change in mood, or a drastic change in behavior), the leader can request permission of the group member to discuss the matter with the staff or the doctor. Doing so can be seen as being an advocate for the older person in the group.

PREJUDGING THE MEMBER

New group leaders have a tendency to underestimate the potential of the individual members of a group in an institutionalized setting. Older persons living in the community are also often coping more creatively with their problems than health care workers realize. Underestimating the potential of a group member is more common than overestimating it.

SUMMARY

This chapter discusses contracts for group work with the elderly and suggests that the new group leader carefully consider group member selection, expenses and payments, anxiety, confidentiality, and prejudgment of members.

Initial interviews are needed to assess the potential group member and may lead to rejection of the individual for membership. The leader makes the final decision on whether a particular person is to be admitted to the group and should not be swayed by others.

A carefully made contract with each prospective group member is the first step initiating a new group. The contract can be either verbal or written (preferably both) and should include the following information: time, place, duration of group sessions, lifetime of the group, list of other members, purpose of the group, and name of the leader.

In making the contract, the leader should assess the prospective member both physically and psychologically and make as sure as possible that the member understands and agrees to the con-

tract. Size of the group, availability of assistance from both staff and group members, and financial arrangements must also be considered.

The initial contract meeting may give the leader a clue to the prospective member's anxiety level and effective methods for reducing it. Giving some structure to the group by carefully explaining group objectives early in the contract stage and throughout the life of the group may help to reduce anxiety in both new leaders and the group members.

Confidentiality in the group may be announced in a ground rule in the contract, or the leader may let the group decide. Protecting the confidences of the wary institutionalized aged is extremely important.

It is well to remember that we often underestimate the potential of aged group members; they may delightfully surprise us with their ability, talent, and performance in a group.

EXERCISE 1

1. Define *contract*.
2. List at least four important kinds of specific information that a leader should give to an older client while making a contract.
3. Suggest several steps a leader can take to reduce anxiety among group members.

EXERCISE 2

You have interviewed six older persons to make a contract for group work. The answers are two "maybes," one "I will think about it," and four "yes, I'll attend." List the three steps you would take next with the persons who answered "maybe" and "I will think about it." Give your rationale for each step.

EXERCISE 3

Design your own written contract based on information in this chapter. Ask two older persons to read it and critique it. What did they suggest to improve your contract?

EXERCISE 4

The agency in which you plan to conduct a group requests a detailed plan. Write goals, objectives, and evaluation methods, and enclose a contract.

REFERENCES

Altholz J. 1975. Group work with the elderly. Paper presented at conference entitled Successful Treatment of the Mentally Ill Elderly, Duke University, Durham, NC (May 22-23).

Burnside IM. 1971. Long-term group work with the hospitalized aged. Part I. *Gerontologist* 11(3):213-218.

————. 1976. Formation of a group. In IM Burnside (ed.), *Nursing and the aged*, 1st ed. (pp. 197-204). New York: McGraw-Hill.

Fatis M, Konewko P. 1983. Written contracts as adjuncts in family therapy. *Soc Work* 28(2):161-163.

Linden M. 1953. Group psychotherapy with institutionalized senile women: Study in gerontological human relations. *Int J Group Psychother* 3:150-170.

Slavson SR. 1953. Sources of counter-transference and group-induced anxiety. *Int J Group Psychother* 3:373-388.

Steckel SB, Swain MA. 1982. *Patient contracting*. Norwalk, CT: Appleton-Century-Crofts.

Tappen R, Touhy T. 1983. Group leader—Are you a controller? *J Gerontol Nurs* 9(1):34.

Toseland RW. 1990. *Group work with older adults*. New York: New York University Press.

Webster's New Collegiate Dictionary. 1973. HB Woolf, ed. Springfield, MA: Merriam Webster.

Whitaker DS, Lieberman MA. 1964. *Psychotherapy through group process*. New York: Atherton.

Yalom ID. 1975. *The theory and practice of group psychotherapy*, 2d ed. New York: Basic Books.

Compton B, Galaway B. 1979. *Social work processes*. Homewood, IL: Dorsey.

Croxton T. 1974. The therapeutic contract in social treatment. In P Glaser, et al. (eds.), *Individual change through small groups* (pp. 169-185). New York: Free Press.

DeResi W, Butz G. 1975. *Writing behavioral contracts*. Champaign, IL: Research Press.

Homme L, Csanyi M, Gonzales J, Rechs J. 1969. *How to see contingency contracting in the classroom*. Champaign, IL: Research Press.

Jensen DP. 1985. Patient contract. In GM Bulechek, JM McCloskey (eds.), *Nursing interventions: Treatments for nursing diagnosis* (pp. 92-98). Philadelphia: Saunders.

Maluccio W, Marlow W. 1974. The case for the contract. *Soc Work* 19:28-36.

Pincus A, Minahan A. 1973. *Social work practice: Model and method* (pp. 162-193). Itasca, IL: Peacock.

Seabury B. 1976. The contract: Uses, abuses, and limitations. *Soc Work* 21:16-21.

————. 1979. Negotiating sound contracts with clients. *Public Wel* (Spring):33-38.

Steckel SB. 1976. Utilization of reinforcement contracts to increase written evidence of the nursing assessment. *Nurs Res* 25:58-61.

Steckel SB, Swain MA. 1977. Contracting with patients to improve compliance. *Hospitals* 51:81-84.

————. 1980. Contracting with patient-selected reinforcers. *Am J Nurs* 80:1596-1599.

BIBLIOGRAPHY

Bristol MM, Sloane HN Jr. 1974. Effects of contingency contracting on study rate and test performance. *J Appl Behav Anal* 7:271-285.

CHAPTER 9

Membership Selection and Criteria

Irene Burnside

KEY WORDS

- Agitation
- Catastrophic reaction
- Catharsis
- Group setting
- Initial composition
- Intergenerational
- Life cycle
- Safety

LEARNING OBJECTIVES

- List 20 potential settings for group meetings.
- Describe four beneficial effects of intergenerational groups.
- Define *catastrophic reaction*.
- Discuss the types of persons to exclude from groups.
- State three factors to consider in regard to group size.
- Analyze the possible consequences of mixing demented and alert aged in a group.

By the crowd they have been broken, by the crowd shall they be healed.

L. CODY MARSH (1935, 392)

Old people comprise a fascinating, unique collection of individuals wherever they are, but what are the criteria for membership in a group? A student or a new group leader may approach the assignment of older people to groups with dismay, reluctance, trepidation, or any combination thereof. In this chapter, group settings, criteria for group membership, goals, and some cautions to consider are discussed.

SETTINGS FOR GROUP MEETINGS

The places where group meetings can be held vary widely. They include:

- Acute care hospitals.
- Board-and-care facilities.
- Churches.
- Community mental health centers.
- Day care centers.
- Domiciliary care by Veterans Administration.
- Foster homes.
- Hotel-apartment residences.

- Hotels in geriatric ghettos of cities.
- Industrial plants (for example, preretirement groups).
- Low-cost housing units.
- Mobile home units.
- Nonproprietary intermediate care facilities.
- Nonproprietary skilled nursing care facilities.
- Nutrition sites.
- Outpatient departments.
- Prisons.
- Private offices.
- Private residences.
- Proprietary intermediate care facilities.
- Proprietary skilled nursing care facilities.
- Recreation and park centers.
- Rehabilitation hospitals.
- Religious homes for retired persons.
- Retirement homes.
- School settings.
- Senior centers.
- State mental hospitals.
- Veterans Administration Hospitals.
- Volunteer centers.

The setting for group meetings can give some indication of the type and caliber of individual who will ultimately be available for group membership in that milieu. One can also make some assumptions about the age and physical condition of such individuals. For example, in nursing homes, one can expect to find very old people. I once did a demonstration group for a class at Prince Edward Island University and discovered later that the mean age of the six-member group was 87.3! Residents of skilled and intermediate care facilities can also be expected to be old and frail and to have multiple diagnoses. See Chapter 12 for suggestions for working with the physically impaired. However, at a senior center, there may be participants who retired early and are in quite stable health and are viewed as young-old.

Because health care providers' involvement with the aged population is so widespread, it is conceivable they could be doing group work in any of the above settings. The most likely settings, of course, are acute care hospitals, rehabilitation hospitals, skilled and intermediate nursing care facilities, outpatient departments, day care centers, and senior centers. It has been well documented that only 3 to 4 percent of those treated at community mental health centers are older persons, so group psychotherapy with the aged is still in its infancy.

GROUP MEMBER SELECTION

Irvin Yalom's (1985) and Robert Butler and Myrna Lewis's (1973) considerations for group membership are discussed here as they relate specifically to group work with older persons. Yalom, writing from the stance of a group psychotherapist, states:

> The fate of a group therapy patient and of a therapy group may, in large measure, be determined before the first group therapy session. Unless careful selection criteria are used, the majority of patients assigned to group therapy will terminate treatment discouraged and without benefit. Research on small groups...suggests that the initial composition of the group has a powerful influence on the ultimate outcome of the entire group (p. 156).

One aspect of group work with the aged that I learned about early is described by Yalom:

> Members are prone to terminate membership in a therapy group and are thereby poor candidates when the punishments or disadvantages of group membership outweigh the rewards or anticipated rewards. When speaking of punishments or disadvantages of group membership, I refer to the price the patient must pay for group membership. This includes an investment of time, money, energy, as well as a variety of dysphorias arising from the group experience, including anxiety, frustration, discouragement, and rejection (p. 173).

Corey and Corey (1992) described a combined group of older persons and adolescents. Michael Nakkula (1984), under the supervision of Joseph Morris at the University of Minnesota, designed a study in which two groups of junior high students and older nursing home residents met for eight sessions. The sessions are listed:

Session 1: Purpose of group explained by the leader. One member interviewed another; later each member introduced the member interviewed to the group.

Session 2: Members encouraged to look at their similarities and differences; then discussed them.

Session 3: Discussion of factors that lead to personal strengths and ultimately personal happiness. Asked to choose strengths they would like to possess that they saw in other age group.

Session 4: Photographs used so older group members could give their life perspectives. Photographs were of members in different stages of their lives.

Session 5: Discussed how young and old are depicted in the media; this was accomplished by sharing news articles.

Session 6: Messages in music explored; yesteryear's music compared with today's. Common themes elicited, and events in the world occurring at time of music identified.

Session 7: Ethnic backgrounds discussed; older members shared their heritage.

Session 8: Termination handled by dividing group into pairs to share what they had learned from each other. Exchanged names and addresses to keep in touch.

The posttest revealed the young group members were less biased toward older people than they were at pretesting. The older subjects reported increased self-esteem.

Butler and Lewis (1973), who conduct group psychotherapy with persons of various ages, feel that beneficial effects occur when different generations relate to one another in a group setting. These benefits include the ability to understand better the various developmental phases of the life cycle, the chance to act out family roles, the chance for the older adult to give support and advice to younger group members, and the opportunity for older members to review their values and experiences.

Butler and Lewis list these goals in the life-cycle approach to group therapy: the amelioration of suffering, the overcoming of disability, the chance for new experiences of self- fulfillment and intimacy, and the chance to verbalize emotions.

Many health professionals are employed in settings where elderly people do not have other age groups with whom to interact; some exceptions would be acute care hospitals, recreation and park settings, outpatient departments, and community mental health centers.

A neophyte group leader should probably exclude younger members from the first group led. The rationale is that the leader can focus on the problems of the aged, and exclusion of younger members should also decrease the number of variables for the leader to handle. One reason is that some new group leaders do not have a basic grounding in the developmental tasks of each age group. One beginning leader[1] compared her first group meeting to a birthday party for preschoolers

because of the brouhaha. The new leader should be quite knowledgeable about the eight stages of man (Erikson 1982; Hall 1983). And for leaders of all-women groups, I suggest an excellent review and critique by Hedva Lewittes entitled "Women's Development in Adulthood and Old Age" (1982) and "Group Work with Older Women" (Burnside 1989).

Personality Dynamics of Members

It is important to assess carefully the personality of the older person while negotiating the contract (See Chapter 8 for details on making a contract with each potential group member.) Group work requires the skillful selection of a variety of personalities. A well-balanced group should have both talkative and quiet persons, depressed and not-so-depressed persons. Mistrusting members need to be balanced with trusting persons. Hyperactive individuals can be offset by calm, serene individuals.

Members will take on various roles and tasks in a group. Making an assessment during contract negotiation is possible and important because the leader has an opportunity then to observe the patterns of behavior in each individual.

A "catastrophic reaction"[2] may occur when a person is overwhelmed by a task or an exercise that he or she cannot perform. It might cause the person to weep or blush or to become agitated, angry, or paranoid. The person may even strike out or get up and leave the situation. The best tactic for dealing with catastrophic reactions is, of course, prevention. When the interviewer or group leader perceives a slight increase in agitation or anxiety, the subject should be changed or the limelight removed from the group member. The leader can also avoid some catastrophic reactions by simplifying the task facing the individual and by assisting and helping the individual through the task. This is also a good role-model approach. The best information about preventing and handling catastrophic reactions is provided by Nancy Mace and Peter V. Rabins (1991) in their excellent book *The 36-Hour Day.*

---

[1] Hazel Mummah, personal communication, 1975.

[2] A reaction described by Kurt Goldstein (1942) that occurs when a brain-damaged individual cannot perform the tasks requested.

The leader should be aware that the members do not have to be at the same cognitive level, but that to mix very regressed, older individuals with alert and lucid persons is to court problems. The regressed individuals may be sent into a catastrophic reaction, since they will not be able to perform as well as some of the more alert members of the group. Also, the alert members may well perceive themselves to be slowed up and regressed if they are asked to attend such a group, and the experience could be harmful to their self-esteem.

Educational level alone cannot be used as an accurate tool for group selection. In one group in a skilled nursing facility, I observed a man with a third-grade education and another with a college degree. They got along famously and had the utmost respect for each other; in fact, when the group was terminated, the men asked to be roommates because the bond of friendship between them was so strong.

Mobile persons should be included with persons in wheelchairs if the group is in an institutional setting, especially if there is to be only one leader. There is the matter of proxemics to consider. A group consisting entirely of wheelchair patients is unwieldy—that is, the leader and the members cannot get close to one another in group meetings. Wheelchairs will also require a larger meeting room.

The leader often may have to assist in seating arrangements, especially with the physically frail or seriously impaired aged.

Persons to Exclude

From a brainstorming workshop on group work with the elderly (Altholz 1975) come these recommendations on people to exclude from a group.[3]

- Disturbed, active, wandering persons.
- Incontinent persons.
- Patients with a psychotic depression.
- Patients recommended solely by the staff.
- Individuals diagnosed as having bipolar disorder.
- Deaf persons.
- Hypochondriacal persons.

---

[3] I am grateful to Judy Altholz for helping to ferret out these recommendations from the group discussion.

Medical Problems

It is important that the group leader be aware of the medical problems of each person in the group. Patients with emphysema, for instance, may need medication before group meetings to enable them to participate more fully. Arthritic patients may need aspirin before meetings so that they are not uncomfortable; patients with recent hip fractures may also need medication. It would be wise for the leader to check the medications of the members. Sometimes overmedicated patients doze off in a group meeting, and their sleepiness has nothing to do with the quality of the meeting itself or with anxiety or withdrawal. New leaders may blame themselves for such behaviors. See Chapter 12 for further information on physical limitations in members.

Leaders also should be alert to the physical problems of group members. Edematous feet, for example, could be elevated during the group sessions to prevent severe stasis edema. Kidney problems are common in old age, and prostatitis or benign prostatic hypertrophy is a common problem in old men. Patients who have to urinate frequently may also need some special consideration in group meetings; for example, perhaps they should sit near the door, so they can easily go to the bathroom and come back into the group with a minimum of disturbance. Such individuals should also be advised to stop at the rest room enroute to the group meeting.

Number of Group Members

The number of people in the group is also a decision of the group leader. New leaders often have trouble deciding how many persons to include in a group. The number depends on such factors as who is available for group membership, the type of group (reality orientation and remotivation groups have different numbers of persons), whether there is a single leader or the group is co-led, available space (for example, wheelchair-bound persons require more physical space), whether it is an open or a closed group (an open group may allow for greater fluctuation of the membership and therefore would be a larger group), whether any members have a sensory loss, the degree of frailty of the members, and the past experience of the group leader. Reality orientation groups usually have four members (Acord 1975). There can be as many as fifteen in a remotivation group. If the leader chooses to work with cognitively impaired and regressed or very frail individuals, six is usually a workable number. See Chapter 11 for further discussion about leading groups of cognitively impaired members.

One of the difficulties encountered in institutions is that the people who are not asked to join the group are offended. Older people often become jealous of their roommates who go off to group meetings (or "classes," as many older persons describe them). Sometimes they request to be put on the waiting list. I recall a 90-year-old man, Mr. H., who approached me in the hall one day when I was on my way to a group meeting. "Excuse me," he said, "but I would sure like to join that group of old people who meet with you every Friday." He entered the group after another member died. Mr. H. had taken the initiative to join, was readily accepted by the group, and seemed to get a great deal of pleasure from the meetings. In fact, he insisted his daughter attend a meeting and meet "the friends"; he told her she would have to change her visiting hours because he had to go to his meeting on the afternoon she usually visited.

There are three salient points to be drawn from this man's experience: (1) A request for membership should be honored if at all possible. If older people take responsibility for their own lives, and are observant about their own milieu, they should be rewarded for such behavior. It also says something about the importance of group work if the residents discuss it among themselves. (2) The importance of the group meetings to the member must be considered. This man even had his family change their visiting hours! (3) Families may resent the group if it interferes with their own schedule, and some work may have to be done with members of the family if they express displeasure.

Toseland (1990) states that there is no optimum size for a group and that in larger groups there is less opportunity for the members to interact with each other. In smaller groups, there will be greater demands on each member to participate.

The same author recommends that support and therapy groups have from six to ten members. However, advocacy groups could benefit from larger numbers of members "because they can be used for their expertise and person power for selected projects and tasks" (p. 63).

Leaders will soon discover not only the types of groups they are most skilled at leading, but the optimum size of the groups as well.

SUGGESTIONS FOR THE NEW LEADER

The leader must decide whether to have an open or closed group. In open groups, members may come to meetings when they wish. (See Table 9-1.) The membership varies widely from meeting to meeting. Closed groups have a stable membership, and new members are usually added by a joint decision of leaders and members.

The leader also must decide on heterogeneity versus homogeneity in the group. Table 9-2 indicates the advantages and disadvantages of each.

A few hard-learned examples may serve as suggestions for the new leader. Including two or more persons of the same minority group in the membership will facilitate the group process. Once a student of mine included in her group a full-blooded native American and a white man who hated native Americans. The native American dropped the group within a few meetings. In the Hawaiian Islands, the melting-pot islands, I found that it is easier to include many ethnic groups because of greater tolerance for racial diversity and for different lifestyles there. In general, however, if a single minority person is included, he or she may drop out soon after the group has begun. Also, I have found that a lone man may not stay in an all-women's group.

Safety of Members

Another caution for the new leader concerns the unstable person who blows up frequently and is verbally or physically abusive. Just the verbal abusiveness can intimidate some group members. Even if obstreperous people behave well in the meetings, their reputations have probably preceded them, and group members will have heard enough hair-raising stories to be inclined to give such people a wide berth. Meetings can be strained if such an individual is included. New group leaders will eventually learn how to handle such a member. One of my group members, a tiny

TABLE 9-1 Open and closed groups

Open	Closed
Advantages	*Advantages*
•, Allows new resources and ideas to be brought to group. • Ensures sufficient participation over the life of the group. • Leader may find it more challenging than a closed group.	• Greater sense of cohesion. • Greater stability of roles and norms. • Passage through group steps is more orderly, predictable. • Fewer variables for a neophyte leader to attend to because of stability of membership. • Leader can effectively deal with absences and terminations because they are fewer.
Disadvantages	*Disadvantages*
• May become difficult to lead if many new members attend. Adding new members can be disruptive to the group. • New members do not know previous experiences in group. • Phases of group process are different because of changing membership. • Instability may result from leadership and membership changes. • Lack of cohesion. • Need to review ground rules with each new member. • Continuity between sessions is difficult to achieve. • Interventions made need closure within each session.	• When members drop out or are absent, group may become too small for effective interaction. • May become stale without ideas of new members. • Leader may become bored with the same members.

SOURCE: Based on Toseland RW (1990, 64-66) and Corey G, Corey M (1992, 87-88).

TABLE 9-2 Group composition

Heterogeneity	Homogeneity
Advantages	*Advantages*
• Different types of personality skills enliven group interaction. • Allows for intergenerational groups. • The variety of skills and problem-solving abilities in group can be educational for members and leader. • Members selected for diversity or expertise can enhance group movement.	• If members are confused, they may function better with others at similar level of cognition. • Peer groups of about the same age will remember the same historical events and may experience similar health problems. • Members share similar levels of social or communication skills, even physical problems.
Disadvantages	*Disadvantages*
• May be difficult for leader to deal with all the variables: age, culture, abilities, personalities. • May be difficult for leader to combine affluent members with those who have been poor. • Potential members who are ambulatory may refuse to be in groups with persons in wheelchairs.	• May increase work of leader, for example, group of very frail or group of confused elders. • Leader may get bored or impatient if group moves slowly.

SOURCE: Based on Toseland RW (1990, 64-66) and Corey G, Corey M (1992, 87-88).

95-year-old lady, was knocked off her chair by another resident during a violent outburst in the dining room before the group meeting (Burnside 1978). She was badly shaken up; although not physically hurt, she was thoroughly frightened and avoided the other woman thereafter.

It is the responsibility of the leader to provide for the safety of the members and to protect the frail members of the group. Some of the aged are truly frail and can be taken advantage of by stronger group members, by other residents, and unfortunately, by the staff.

Agitated Members

Agitation should not be confused with the initial anxiety group members experience when they first enter a group. Agitation is observable outside group meetings as well as within the group.

Initial anxiety is often seen in the resident who leaves the group. This problem is fairly common, and the leader will soon learn the most effective intervention for keeping the member in the group. Initial anxiety is also seen in chain-smoking, rapid talking, monopolization of the group, and nervous mannerisms of the extremities. Others handle anxiety by staring out the window or at the floor and avoiding eye contact with others, especially the group leader.

Confinement in a small circle at the group meetings seems to increase anxiety, especially in the early meetings. Because of the sensory defects usually apparent, however, the group has to be seated close together. It may take a while for group members to adjust to such physical closeness, and they may pull back from the circle. Usually if they have hearing or vision problems, they will prefer to be in a small circle so they do not miss anything.

Agitated members can be very disruptive, so the leader should carefully investigate agitated potential group members. Is the agitation fairly constant, or is it vacillating and triggered by events or certain people? Is there medication that will decrease such behavior? Will group membership really be beneficial to this person? I once accepted a woman because the staff convinced me that group membership would help her. She disrupted the group so much that I finally had to remove her. Ideally, there would be a doctor available with whom the leader could discuss the severity of agitation evident in an individual and the medication regimen.

State Hospital Patients

One problem a group leader may face in a skilled nursing facility concerns discharged state hospital patients. In some states, particularly California, New York, and Illinois, there was a push years ago to get the aged out of the state hospitals and into the community. The community for many of these less physically able turned out to be nursing homes, or to use Carl Eisdorfer's (1975) descrip-

tion, "semi, demi, hemi hospitals." In the nursing homes, many of the state hospital discharges received different treatment from that of the average resident because they were immediately branded as state hospital refugees by both the personnel and the residents. For example, I remember that in one nursing home, six state hospital women were placed in one room at the far end of the facility. It was not long until some of the mobile, lusty men in the facility discovered them, and multiple problems ensued. I have heard roommates of state hospital patients shout, "Get her out of here; she is crazy; she came from the loony bin!"

Mixing former state hospital patients and nonstate hospital members in a group may create problems for a new leader. If such patients are combined in a group, the leader should be prepared to deal with the resentment, hostility, and rejection that is often shown to these poor, shuffled-about human beings.

Staff members are often afraid of ex-psychiatric patients. The anxiety of the staff may be lessened, and they may be more accepting of a person, when the leader shares with them the behavior observed in a group. Group behavior may be quite different from the usual behavior during the rest of the time in the institution. Staff members are often quite surprised at how well patients do in group settings. Labels such as *senile*, *violent*, *obstreperous*, and *suicidal* may be on a patient's chart, and the staff latches onto the label even though it is no longer accurate.

One man of 83 had spent 50 years in a state hospital; he was a burned-out schizophrenic, and harmless; yet the nurses' aides were terrified of him. Someone had read on his chart that he had been violent in his early years in the state hospital and had been put in a straitjacket. He had had ground privileges for years at the state hospital and had been used to being outdoors all day. He felt very confined in the nursing home, and he paced the halls with the nervous restlessness of animals in a zoo. Then he started urinating on some expensive artificial trees in the corridors, which greatly upset the owner. Old men who lived on farms or have been outdoors as much as this man had used trees and toilets interchangeably. Yet the staff had trouble understanding the difficult transition for this old man when he was sent to a skilled nursing facility miles from the state hospital.

Religious and Politically Interested Members

If very religious or very politically minded persons are accepted in the group, the leader must be prepared to deal with the desires of such members to convert other members—either religiously or politically. One colleague handled this problem by making a ground rule that religion and politics could not be discussed in the group psychotherapy meetings (Altholz 1975). In that way, the group meeting time could be spent on the problems of the clients.

Assessment

And finally, the importance of pregroup assessments must be underscored. In Chapter 11, I discuss in detail problems I encountered when I did not thoroughly assess the potential group members' ability to handle a group experience. A leader should not accept a client who will not be able to function appropriately in a group, or worse yet will be deleterious to the entire group. Chapter 8 discussed how crucial the assessment process is for both the leader and the group members.

In a slightly different vein, Toseland (1990) discusses the importance of a needs assessment. He suggests that practitioners collect information from others to validate their perceptions of existing unmet needs. Team meetings could be one avenue, or a survey made by the practitioner of the population she or he intends to serve. If larger programs are being considered, a survey of the time and resources in a community might yield a more accurate estimate of what is needed.

SUMMARY

This chapter discusses criteria for group membership, based on the writings of Yalom (1985) and Butler and Lewis (1973). Yalom urges careful selec-

tion to prevent early termination by members. Butler and Lewis list goals for intergenerational groups as assuaging suffering; handling disabilities; and providing an opportunity for self-realization, intimacy, and catharsis.

Settings for group meetings, which can range from acute care hospitals to prisons, may well indicate the competence and caliber of a potential group member. In selecting members, the group leader should strive for a balance by including a variety of personalities. The leader is cautioned not to be too cavalier in mixing alert and nonalert members, however, and to remember that educational level alone is not an accurate indicator of group potential. The leader must consider the number of minority members to be included and always provide a safe, nonthreatening milieu. Former state hospital patients placed in nursing homes create anxiety in residents and staff. Finally, the leader should be skilled in handling political or religious issues if very pious or politically minded individuals are included in the group.

Persons who should probably be excluded from groups are those who are agitated or deaf. Persons diagnosed as psychotic, manic-depressive, or hypochondriacal also should be excluded, except for psychotherapy groups. The new leader needs to be wary of any individual enthusiastically recommended by the staff. Medical problems need to be assessed because they may affect group participation.

The size of the group will depend on the level and type of the group and whether there are co-leaders, or open or closed groups. Open groups allow for fluctuation of membership from meeting to meeting. Closed groups have a stable membership and are probably easier for a new leader to manage.

EXERCISE 1

The following is a list of older persons described by the staff as potential members for a group you are planning. Carefully screen out those you would *not* include if you were leading your first group. Give your rationale for not accepting them into your group.

1. Mrs. Loquacious is 90 years old, very stubborn and controlling, and talks incessantly. It is impossible to stop her, and she irritates both residents and staff by bawling them out for not listening to her.
2. Mr. Deaf is 78 years old and extremely hard of hearing but often pretends he hears by nodding his head or saying yes. He refuses to wear a hearing aid.
3. Mrs. Depressed is 88 years old and is now withdrawn, listless, and confused. Her husband died a month ago. She says over and over, "What's the use of living?"
4. Mr. Alone is 79 years old, a loner, and has been a heavy drinker most of his life. He never married, never had a steady job, and was a drifter. He does not mingle with any residents in the long-term care facility.
5. Mrs. Obnoxious is a 68-year-old behavior problem. She is aggressive, noisy, and scares other residents. She pushed Miss Frail off her chair in the dining room recently. Mrs. O needs help.
6. Miss Frail is 95 years old and has outlived all her friends. She is petrified of Mrs. Obnoxious and avoids her. Miss Frail is very paranoid; she thinks that the government took her house and that the nurses are having affairs with her brother.
7. Mr. Flirt is blind and 86 years old. He used to drink heavily, chased women, and was not a very good father. He is getting increasingly depressed and withdrawn and refuses to get out of bed.
8. Miss Learned is a 75-year-old former school teacher, sweet but terribly confused. She is especially confused at night. She keeps talking about her mother coming to visit. (Mother has been dead 20 years.)
9. Mrs. Old is a centenarian, physically frail but mentally alert. She loves to reminisce. She has become the pet because of her sweet disposition and sharp wit.
10. Mr. Sly is 86 years old and pretends to be out of it, but he bedevils the staff by hiding wheelchairs and linens; then he pleads innocence. When things get very boring, he pulls the fire alarm, turns up the thermostat, or calls the police department at 2 A.M. to tell them that the staff is beating up the residents and they'd better come down.

EXERCISE 2

Describe four possible settings for group meetings, and for each, indicate how the setting determines the type of elderly who will be available.

EXERCISE 3

A staff member has approached you because of your interest in group work and wants you to consider some form of group work with wanderers. Can you think of any type of group activity you might try with these individuals?

EXERCISE 4

You have just begun a small group in a nursing home. After the second meeting, other residents are waiting to talk to you. They want to know why they are not in your group. What will you tell them?

REFERENCES

Acord L. 1975. Reality orientation. Paper presented at conference entitled Mental Health in Nursing Homes, San Antonio, TX (October).

Altholz J. 1975. Group work with the elderly. Paper presented at conference entitled Successful Treatment of the Mentally Ill Elderly, Duke University, Durham, NC (May 22-23).

Burnside IM. 1978. Eulogy for Ms. Hogue. *Am J Nurs* 78(4): 624-626.

————. 1989. Group work with older women: A modality to improve the quality of life. In JD Gardner, SO Mercer (eds.), *Women as they age: Opportunity and triumph* (pp. 265-290). New York: Haworth.

Butler RN, Lewis MI. 1973. *Aging and mental health.* St. Louis: Mosby.

Eisdorfer C. 1975. Speech given at conference entitled Successful Treatment of the Mentally Ill Elderly, Duke University, Durham, NC (May 22-23).

Erikson E. 1982. *The life cycle completed: A review.* New York: Norton.

Goldstein K. 1942. *Aftereffects of brain injuries in war and their evaluation.* New York: Grune & Stratton.

Hall E. 1983. A conversation with Erik Erikson. *Psychol Today* 17(6):22-30.

Lewittes H. 1982. Women's development in adulthood and old age. *Int J Mental Health* 11(1-2):115-131.

Mace NL, Rabins PV. 1991. *The 36-hour day,* 2d ed. Baltimore: Johns Hopkins University Press.

Nakkula MJ. 1984. Elderly and adolescence: A group approach to integrating the isolated. Unpublished master's project, University of Minnesota-Duluth.

Toseland RW. 1990. *Group work with older adults.* New York: New York University Press.

Yalom ID. 1985. *The theory and practice of group psychotherapy,* 3d ed. New York: Basic Books.

BIBLIOGRAPHY

Francis A, Clarkir, Marachi J. 1980. Selection criteria for outpatient group psychotherapy. *Hosp Comm Psych* 31(4): 245-250.

Shaw ME. 1981. Group composition. In *Group dynamics: The psychology of small group behavior* (Chapter 7). New York: McGraw-Hill.

RESOURCE

Intergenerational Group Model. Michael Nakkula, 30 Lake Avenue, Newton Centre, MA 02159.

CHAPTER 10

Leadership and Co-Leadership Issues

Irene Burnside

KEY WORDS
- Absenteeism
- Entrée
- Hostile member
- Monopolist
- Roadblocks
- Sabotage
- Sensory deficits
- Silent member

LEARNING OBJECTIVES
- Discuss entrée into an agency.
- List four techniques in group leadership.
- List six categories of problems that may occur in a group.
- Discuss depression in relation to the leader.
- Discuss absenteeism.
- Define *sabotage* as it relates to group leadership.
- List 10 ways a leader may be sabotaged in an agency.
- List five qualifications for a group leader.
- State 15 simple techniques to promote a stable group of older persons.

Experience is a wonderful thing; it enables you to recognize a mistake every time you make it.

ANONYMOUS

Leadership is defined by Toseland (1990) as "the process of guiding development of a group through all stages of its life, from planning to termination" (p. 46). Furthermore, it is a shared function that is comprised of a sequence of actions rather than a certain quality in one person. The group has a designated leader, but that leader helps the members to become indigenous leaders within the group. For example, the designated leader helps the group and the members to achieve the goals they want to accomplish. See Chapter 8 for a discussion of goals.

Practitioners must be careful that they do not let the facility for which they work subvert group member leadership abilities. Some capable older people have been undermined by ageism; they accept dependency roles that deny them leadership roles.

The problems in maintaining a group of older adults are varied and unique, and they differ from those of leading a group of younger persons. In this chapter, students, health care workers, instructors, and volunteers are alerted to some of the common problems a new leader may encounter.

One participant in a conference on group work with the aged wrote on the evaluation form, "Why do groups get started and fall apart when we need them, and how can we make them more lasting?" The purpose of this chapter is to answer those questions.

Leaders need to keep in mind the developmental tasks of the aged. These tasks are described by several authors (Duvall 1971; Erikson 1963, 1982; Hall 1983; Havighurst 1968). An awareness of these developmental tasks will help the leader understand the group members better. Knowledge of group theory and process needs to be underscored.

Irvin Yalom (1985) feels that the curative factors in group therapy are mediated not by the therapist but by the members, who provide the qualities of acceptance, support, and hope plus the experience of universality, interpersonal feedback, testing, and learning.

Maurice Linden (1956) feels that the leader can reinstate independence in the older person only when the leader steadily divests the authority and moves to an area of mutuality. If the leader does not follow this pattern, the older person becomes more blissfully dependent.

Louis Lowy (1967) discusses roadblocks in group practice with older people; the attitude of the leaders, who may have little belief in the creative potential of an older member; the difficulty leaders have in communicating their hopes and feelings; and leaders' overconcern about time—ignoring the timing and sense of time of older people.

Smith (1980), a nurse who began therapy groups with chronically ill patients in a state psychiatric hospital, describes in an interesting manner how she carved out her own group leadership style. Basically, she went through three stages in her personal quest for a style:

1. I am the leader, and this is the law.
2. We are all equal, and whatever happens happens.
3. The group is self-directing, but there are rules and guidelines. I am here if you need me.

Some of Smith's guidelines include the following: the size of the group must be ideally suited for the level of therapy intended; to avoid isolating group members, use one-of-a-kind membership selection; and the group can be homogeneous or heterogeneous in terms of diagnostic categories.

ENTREE INTO AN AGENCY

One of the first problems faced by the group leader is the need to gain entrance into an institution or agency. This may be difficult for both nursing students and volunteers. Often, credentials are simply not enough. It is easier now with the tremendous pressure to upgrade the care of the aged in this country, but I had a difficult time in 1986 when I wanted to begin group work in a skilled nursing facility. The director of nurses kept avoiding me; the administrator canceled appointments I made to see her. Finally, a doctor who was interested in groups being started wrote an order for six of his patients to be included in group work so that I could begin. He also spent precious time one afternoon going over his entire list of patients in the facility, letting me choose those I wanted to interview for the group. After the group began, I sent him a monthly report on all his patients. I also initially gave a short talk in an in-service class describing what I planned to do with this particular group, but the staff was not very interested in group work. They remained uninterested for several months, until they began to notice some changes in the group members.

The staff criticized me for my short skirts, the bright colors I wore, and my jewelry. My attire was not happenstance; I selected what appealed to the aged. I was reminded that nurses do not do group work and that group work belongs in the domain of social workers and psychologists. Struggling to be the type of group leader-nurse-professional person I wanted to be in the face of opposition was difficult, and I sought preceptor support. I found a psychiatric nursing faculty colleague willing to supervise me, but as she so candidly said, "I don't know a thing about group work with the elderly, but I will certainly be your sounding board." Because group work with older adults by nurses is still fairly new, it is important that beginning group leaders have that kind of support.

It is well to warn new group leaders that they may not be accepted by the staff until they prove themselves, especially in facilities where group work has not been part of treatment plans. As nurses carve new roles for themselves, they will need support. These roles include geriatric nurse practitioner, geriatric nurse clinician, geriatric researcher, teacher in multidisciplinary gerontology classes, and, of course, group leader of aged persons.

At the time I began group work, no activity programs were required in skilled nursing facilities. There were occasional bingo games and sing-alongs. The residents I met were so bored with their lives that they welcomed the chance to be involved in a group meeting. I believe that their boredom motivated them to continue in the group experience. They frequently discussed their boredom and said how much they looked forward to the next meeting.

MULTIPLE PROBLEMS OF OLDER ADULTS

The group leader must juggle multiple problems simultaneously. Although this can be true in all group work, it is especially true in work with the aged, who may have socioeconomic, physical, and mental problems simultaneously. Eric Pfeiffer (1975) said it so well in a statement applying to nurses as well as psychiatrists: "In aging, the patient drives you back to being a generalist."

The prevalent and multiple health problems of the aged are both physical and psychological. Dealing with visual and hearing impairments will be a challenge. The rate of visual impairments appears higher with increasing age. The hearing deficits are the most common type of impairment with 383 per 1000 of those 65 and over reporting some hearing loss; white men have significantly higher rates than women in all age groups (U.S. Department of Health and Human Services, 1993). Patients in institutions are often diagnosed as having five or six different problems. The leader will have to be aware of that fact constantly. Deterioration will be observed in members if the group continues over a substantial period. There will be vacillation between good and bad days, and the group experience may be very helpful in the maintenance of such persons. Often they become ill or have a crisis situation (Burnside 1970). I have seen patients in the group become very sick, stay in bed for a while, and eventually return to the group.

The secret seems to be in always including absent members; that is, the leader sees those people at their bedside and finds out why they are absent and what is happening. Also, the leader reports to sick members what happened in the group session. Some new group leaders, however, are unaccustomed to working with older clients and do not seek out absent group members. It is not usually the role of a group leader of adults, but one needs to remember that the aged are actually incapacitated on some days. And, of course, forgetfulness on the part of aged group members plays havoc with any group. (Forgetfulness on the part of the group leader delights the group members to no end.) Follow-up work is easy in an institution where one has a captive group; but if one is leading a group in a day care center, an outpatient clinic, or elsewhere in the community, the leader might have to make phone calls to absent members.

Once the group is rolling, the leader is in essence the glue that holds the group together. Groups fall apart when the leader is insensitive to the needs of the group members. (See Chapter 5 on the importance of inclusion in group work with senescent people.) Groups also fail if the leader is not conscientious about the group leadership role; that is, if the leader is late, absent, cancels meetings frequently, and so on. The aged soon sense when a leader is making every effort to keep the group intact; and when concern is shown for an absent member, they are well aware that the same type of concern will be shown for them if they break a hip, have an embolus, or are so incapacitated that they cannot attend the group.

One woman in a group was bedridden due to a pulmonary embolus. When I visited her, she expressed regret about missing the meetings but could not get out of bed even though she felt much better. I rolled her bed into the meeting room, and she visited with the group for a portion of the meeting.[1] She felt somewhat nauseated and did not want any coffee; she had ginger ale. There is something symbolic about sharing coffee and refreshments, but this area has not been fully studied in reference to working with older persons (Burnside 1970). When I visited absent patients at their bedsides, I also brought them the refreshments we were having that day. Such continual inclusion, whether or not the member attends meetings, is an important factor in the maintenance of a group and should be remembered by new leaders.

Another important way to maintain the group is for the leader to pay meticulous attention to the levels of discomfort or pain of the group members.

---

[1] I learned this from Diane Holland Puppolo, who included patients on gurneys in her group.

The leader must also learn to handle the sensory defects of the group members and how to maximize the vision, hearing, and understanding of each member in the group. Usually, sensory defects are not much of a problem in younger age groups. One way to minimize them is to pay close attention to the environment itself. Students can be sensitized to the problem of sensory deprivation with the use of experiential exercises (Hickey, Hultsch & Fatule 1975; Hultsch, Hickey & Rakowski 1975).

GROUP CONCERNS

There are several categories of problems that may arise in a group. The following list illustrates those common group concerns.[2]

1. Problems with co-therapist or co-therapy.
   a. Nonacceptance of co-leader by group.
   b. Leadership role of co-therapist.
2. Problems with individual patients in group—that is, managing individual problem members.
   a. The monopolist.
   b. The silent member.
   c. The hostile member.
3. Problems with the leadership role.
   a. Leader's degree of directiveness or activity.
   b. Leader's role in maintaining group—for example, problem of attendance.
   c. Leader's role in establishing trust and confidentiality.
4. Miscellaneous concerns.
   a. Problem of inclusion.
   b. Ground rules.

The new leader should consider which problems may have to be dealt with, especially in the initial meetings. A list of problems in rank order appears in Table 10-1; in a class of 27 students, these were the problems the students requested help with on their weekly group summaries.

Problems in Co-Leadership

Yalom states that there is little research regarding the effectiveness of co-leadership (Yalom 1985). Problems in co-leadership run the gamut from interpersonal squabbles to power struggles. (Table 10-2 lists co-leadership's advantages and disadvantages.) Preceptors can be most helpful in mediating some of these problems.

Special attention must be paid to the location of co-leaders in a group. Both the arrangement of the room and the seating arrangements play important roles in the success of a group meeting. The seating arrangement for the members must be carefully planned. They must be close so that they can see, hear, and touch one another. I once observed co-leaders trying to conduct a group of confused elderly in a day care center. They had placed sofas around a coffee table to form a large square. The leaders sat next to one another. Needless to say, the group meeting was chaotic.

Most older persons cannot be expected to plan how a room should be arranged; therefore, the leaders must plan *ahead* to have the chairs and tables in the best position. Figures 10-1 and 10-2 show a variety of seating arrangements. I find that the one shown in Figure 10-2c is the most successful positioning of clients and leaders.

Remember that although the leaders may be aware of the problems inherent in poor seating arrangements, an attempt should be made to include the members in planning. Tappen and Touhy (1983, 37) note, "Group members may be treated as if they were helpless or incapable of contributing meaningfully to the group process. The leader may tell the people where to sit or rearrange their wheelchairs after they have moved into the group circle." The caution here is that if it is necessary to move a member, the leader should explain the reason why. "Mrs. Jones, I am going to move your chair over beside me so that I can hear what you say better," or "Mrs. Anderson, I am going to move you over here so that the glare from that window will not be in your eyes, because I know that bright sunlight makes you uncomfortable."

Depression of the Leader

The new group leader should be warned that it is not uncommon to experience feelings of depression, and the leader should examine how this depression might be affecting the group. Is the leader more quiet and withdrawn? Is the leader aware of how depressing the frailties of members and all the people in wheelchairs or with canes and crutches can be? During this time, when some

---

[2]Reprinted from class entitled N217B–Graduate Psychiatric Nursing. University of California School of Nursing, San Francisco (January 1968).

TABLE 10-1 Problems experienced by new group leaders in rank order

Rank order of problems	Type of problem
1.	Monopolizers.
2.	Members forget about meetings.
3.	Absent members.
4.	Adding new members to group.
5.	Group members approaching leaders individually after meetings for further discussion.
6.	The use of the group summary form. What is the purpose of describing mood of group?
7.	Anxiety and/or depression of leaders.
8.	How to handle person who refuses to join group.
9.	How to handle situation when member does not wish to remember sad parts of the past.
10.	Members who leave group while it is still in progress.
11.	Dealing with deafness, loss of memory, poor speech, soft voices, and so on.
12.	Interventions for withdrawn members.
13.	The one-to-one by the leader that occurs in early meetings.
14.	Touching during crying; is it helpful?
15.	Leaders' worries about lessening self-confidence of members.
16.	How much discussion of past changes, such as death and moves, is helpful to members?
17.	Dealing with leaders' feelings about losing group members or when the group members say meetings are not useful for them.
18.	What to serve for a snack.
19.	Getting members to feel more relaxed with leaders.
20.	Whether to pursue reality testing in group in the face of massive denial.
21.	How does leader respond to flat affect in members.
22.	Group members' problems hit close to leaders' own problems.
23.	Lack of support from staff.
24.	Topics to reminisce about.
25.	How to use props.
26.	Leader needs more professionalism and objectivity.
27.	Seating arrangements—continue same? Change?
28.	Co-leaders' attitudes and beliefs that conflict with elderly members' attitudes and beliefs.
29.	Co-leader conflict about roles, styles of leadership, and so on.
30.	Closure of group meeting.
31.	How to include all members in topics being discussed.
32.	Topics to include in groups.
33.	Group members concerned about taping the meetings.
34.	Inclusion of staff in meetings. Pros and cons?
35.	Strategies for dialog when group member comments *after* meeting, "I want to be dead."
36.	Termination: How to plan so members do not feel abandoned. Feelings of leader about termination.
37.	Leader needs to be better organized.

SOURCE: Reprinted from class entitled Group Work with the Elderly, San Francisco State University, Fall semester, 1976.

TABLE 10-2 Co-leadership

Advantages	Disadvantages
• Greater sense of cohesion. • Assistance when working with frail older persons. • Assistance during demanding group activities. • Support during difficult group experiences. • Validation for one another regarding group dynamics and events in group. • Catalyst for professional development. • Another role model for effective communication and group participation. • An educational tool, especially for neophytes. • When one leader is on vacation or ill, group continuity is not lost. • With two leaders, larger group may be possible. • Can reduce burnout in a leader. • If intense emotions are expressed, one leader can interact with member while co-leader scans group for reactions. • If one leader is strongly affected by session, other leader can be a sounding board. • If counter-transference occurs with one leader, other leader may be better able to work with the member.	• Costlier than having just one leader. • Co-leaders may not work well together. • Co-leading is time consuming (need to debrief and spend time between meetings planning). • Difficult to establish egalitarian relationship. • Members may attempt to play one leader against the other. • Experienced leader may resent having to explain and teach a new leader, which slows the leader. • A junior leader may resent not having the status of the senior leader. • Co-leaders from different disciplines may have different perspectives about how to conduct the group, which may not be discussed or resolved. • Problems arise if co-leaders rarely meet with one another. • Competition and rivalry can occur. • If they do not build trust, co-leaders may not trust each other's interventions. • One leader may side with members against the other leader. • Co-leaders involved in an intimate relationship may use the group to solve relationship struggles.

SOURCE: Based on Toseland (1990, 57-58) and Corey and Corey (1992, 29-31).

of the enthusiasm of the leader is waning, strong peer support or preceptor support can be very helpful. Not all students will be able immediately to pinpoint their depression and may need some help from the instructor.

A student from Argentina studying in the United States wrote after her first group meeting:

My first experience was that of sadness and depression. I felt completely lost, strange. I thought, "This is not my place." I thought that my place should be with the older children and young people. I know that I've got to continue ahead but I don't know how to face these feelings (Kratzig 1976).

Another comment from a student was that "I was feeling *very depressed* about Mrs. B., and her expression of futility—and just the *whole* institutional setting in general! I felt depressed the whole weekend . . ." (Leudtke 1976).

In the first group of older people I led, I was struck with their sensitivity to me. I was an inexperienced group leader, and at that time my husband was dying. In one meeting, the group wanted to talk about death and dying, but because of my own pain, I shied away from the topic. The group had imme-

diately picked up on my reluctance. The logs I kept helped me to understand later. They waited until I was comfortable about bringing up the subject.

In another instance, a pregnant young leader was conducting a group of older persons. Their concern for her was obvious in each meeting, and they made concerted efforts to help her with the group-related tasks.

Problems in Attendance

Inpatient groups may or may not have problems with attendance. Once the group is off the ground, the aged residents are usually there and waiting. A good deal of their receptivity may be prompted by the emptiness and boredom of institutional life. As the atheist in a group once said to me when questioned about going to mass so regularly, "Sure I go. There's nothing better to do around here on Thursday afternoon."

The real problem with group work in institutions is handling the residents who are not in groups. They may request that they be put on a waiting list. Sometimes relatives ask on behalf of their family member for a place in the group. One

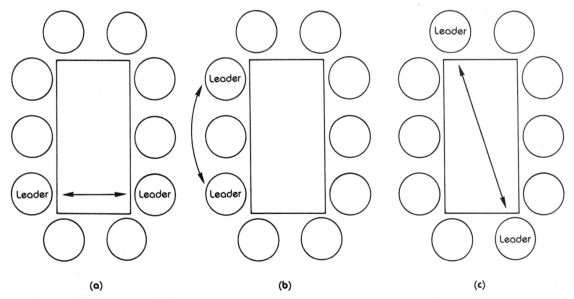

FIGURE 10-1 *Because of its length, a rectangular table can present seating problems—for example, the inability of group members to see or hear the leaders or others in the group. The leaders should position themselves with care. In diagram (a) the co-leaders are weighted at one end of the group and are unable to assist the four members at the opposite end of the table. In diagram (b) the co-leaders weight one side of the group; the arrangement also makes it difficult for the leaders to interact—they must look over the head of the member sitting between them. Diagram (c) shows the best seating arrangement for co-leaders if a long table must be used.*

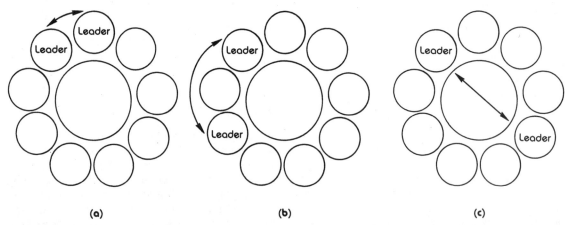

FIGURE 10-2 *In the seating arrangement using a round table shown in diagram (a), in which the co-leaders sit side by side, both authority figures are on one side of the table; the arrangement does not allow eye contact between the leaders or permit each of them to be close to two members. In the arrangement in diagram (b), the member seated between the co-leaders may feel overwhelmed, and eye contact between the leaders is limited. Diagram (c) shows the ideal seating arrangement for a round table. It offers eye contact, and each leader can assist the member on either side. This is important when the group contains frail, confused, disoriented members or aged persons with severe sensory losses. A round table is always preferable to a rectangular or square table.*

relative said, "I don't like to ask for special favors, but could my mother please be placed in one of the groups? I believe it would help her."[3] Such interest in groups may spur the administrator or the activity director to find more activities for the residents.

Most group leaders find that they have a stable membership with inpatient groups, but that is because they have concentrated on making a cohesive group. Outpatient groups are different. For example, in rainy weather, many of the group members may call in with transportation problems and/ or complaints of their arthritis. Older people are also afraid of falling during a rainy or snowy day.

Administrative Support for the Leader

Sometimes groups fail because of lack of interest and support by the administration. It is of paramount importance that the leader have support from two directions: (1) from the administrative staff of the agency where the group is to be held and (2) from a preceptor, supervisor, colleague, or whomever will be serving in that capacity.

The support of the administrator and the director of nurses is important, because they influence both staff and residents. The director of a senior center would influence the staff and the seniors coming to the group meeting. Lip service is not enough; there must be active encouragement and support by the people in top positions. The following list includes examples observed in which the administration made group leading easier for volunteers and students.

1.   One facility provided lunch for the volunteer group leader because the leader had a hectic schedule on that particular day and was skipping lunch to be at the group meeting on time.

2.   One interested administrator sat in on several group meetings so that she could observe the behavior of patients in the group setting (which may be quite different from usual behavior on the ward). However, if the administrator chooses to sit in on a meeting, the leader must realize that there may be some resentment from the members, there may be some concern about the authority figure

there, and there may be real reluctance to share. Confidentiality is one important factor to consider when there are observers.

3.   The same administrator always had a special goodbye cake for the group leader when she completed a group and left the facility.

4.   One director of nurses was very conscientious about having the patients ready in the room when the student arrived. She made a special effort to dress the patients neatly that day. The men came in white shirts and ties; the women had their hair done nicely. The message to both the staff and the residents of such concern for appearance was that "this is important for them; they must look their very best."

5.   In one facility, the nursing instructor who began a new group was provided with an assistant because of the multiple handicaps of the members.

6.   Photographers took pictures of group meetings and placed them on a bulletin board in the hallway, where the residents showed them to family members and friends.

7.   An in-service class or two devoted to group work or group dynamics also shows interest in the efforts of the leader.

8.   Training a co-leader who can take over the group when the student or volunteer leaves is also a way of maintaining the group. (It has been my experience that when the original leader leaves, patients will demand that the group be continued because it is meaningful to them, but that there is difficulty in finding someone to replace the leader.)

Sabotage

Sabotage is a negative term, but it is the word that keeps coming to mind when I think of the many barriers with which leaders have to struggle. There are numerous ways in which persons can sabotage the work of a leader and make it difficult to maintain the group.

1.   Constant criticism of the leader may occur—a put-down type of feedback implying that the group work is incorrect, foolish, or bothersome.

2.   Staff members may show no interest in the group, fail to report on the patients in the group, and ignore what is occurring in the group.

---

[3]Florence Patton, personal communication, 1975.

3. Patients are not ready for group meetings, they are brought in late, or the wrong patients are brought in and left.

4. Patients are sent home on pass, to X-ray, or to other areas on the day of the group meeting.

5. A negative approach regarding group meetings is used to the patient—for example, "You *don't* want to go to the group meeting today, do you?" (Hennessey 1976).

6. Patients are incompletely dressed when they do arrive—shoestrings not tied, one shoe missing, no lap robe (so bare knees are showing), no sweater (and the patient says she is chilled), no hearing aid or glasses or false teeth. The last do affect the ability to communicate.

7. There may be a reluctance to help the leader provide coffee, tea, fruit juice, or refreshments to enhance the group meetings. The kitchen staff may openly balk.

8. Lack of equipment can create problems—not enough cups for coffee, no paper napkins, no table available to do a group project, no record player for music, and so on.

9. There may be insufficient room space for the group.

10. The group may be shuffled around from area to area (which is not good for elderly patients; a minor translocation shock often occurs).

11. Patients may be taken out of a group meeting after it has begun, to go to X-ray, the dentist, and so on.

12. When no assistance with transporting patients is available, the group leader has all the responsibility. (This may happen both in the institution and in the community.)

13. Blame may be directed at the group for all that goes wrong with a patient. Such blame may stagger a new group leader; generally, the resident does not hear it because it is directed to the leader.

14. The facility may constantly assign different staff members to assist in transportation, and so forth. They do not know about the group and therefore have to be told what it is and why and where.

15. When patients become more assertive (which they often do after group experiences) and more demanding, the group may be blamed and seen as a disruptive force in the facility.

16. Staff members neglect to tell leaders important information—for example, when patients die, go AWOL, are critically ill, or have had a death in the family.

There are several steps a new leader can take to reduce sabotage by the staff.

1. Do not be defensive when criticized or given negative feedback.

2. Take care of your own feelings, such as depression, resentment, and frustration, by having a sounding board in a colleague, peer, or preceptor.

3. Gently remind the staff about the meeting in advance so that patients can be ready on time.

4. Write reminders to the patients to help them remember the meeting day, time, and place.

5. Develop a rapport with the nurses' aides who prepare patients for group meetings. Try to learn their names, praise them when patients look nice, and give them some feedback about how their patients are progressing in the group.

6. Explain what you are doing with the group to kitchen personnel so that they know the reason you need refreshments.

7. Make a contract with the director of nurses, the administrator, or the activity director, and state the type of equipment you will need from them.

8. Carefully plan the group experience so that you have adequate room space for all group members. Also, explain to management the difficulty when a group has to be moved so that they understand why the group should remain in the same location.

9. Conduct an in-service class and explain some of your expectations—for example, that patients will not be taken out of group meetings and that interruptions will be kept to a minimum.

10. Let the staff members know when you arrive and when you leave if you are not doing the group work as an employee of the facility.

LEADER QUALIFICATIONS

The qualifications for group leadership with the aged are very similar to those for working individually with the older client. General qualities that are important in the care of the aged are patience, flexibility, tenacity, compassion, gentleness, intelligence, and an astute ability to observe. Specific qualities to look for in group leaders include background in normal aging; background in the pathology of aging; experience in groups of any kind; tolerance for groups (as opposed to one-to-one relationships); ability to tolerate dependent relationships; ability to handle directness and criticism (old people can criticize par excellence); ability to handle one's own feelings regarding chronic illness, disabilities, depression, hostility, grief, and the various stages of dying; and organization in work.

In an excellent article on aspects of group leadership with the aged, Tappen and Touhy (1983) describe control and condescension in group work:

> Our particular concern here is that group work can extend and reinforce already-existing tendencies to control and be condescending toward older adults. It is important to be alert to these dangers and to conduct groups in such a way that these potentially negative effects are avoided and the most positive effects of group work can be achieved.

The reader will recall that cautions against control and disrespect were raised in Chapter 8, which discusses making contracts with older persons.

Marianne Corey (Corey & Corey 1992) feels that certain qualities are needed to work successfully as a counselor/leader with the elderly. The comprehensive list can be found in Table 10-3 and could be used as a checklist for new group leaders.

SUGGESTIONS FOR NEW GROUP LEADERS

The following suggestions should be helpful to new group leaders.

1. Explain to the staff what you are planning.

2. Include a variety of personalities to make group work easier. Try to balance the number of talkative and quiet members.

3. If there is only one leader, keep the group small—six to eight members.

4. Place members in a circle to maximize vision and hearing.

5. Ensure that the meeting place is well lighted and warm and that intercoms, glare from windows, and outside distractions are eliminated.

6. Provide a table if refreshments are to be served.

7. Always give individual attention at the beginning and end of the meeting.

8. In institutions, pay brief visits to the absent members at their bedsides; this is especially helpful in serious illnesses and crises and also encourages members to return to the group again.

9. Use names profusely.

10. Keep the rules few and simple.

11. Confine the purposes of the group to sensible goals that both leader and members can meet.

12. Capitalize on birthdays, holidays, current events, and so on. Themes can help—for example, nature, travel, books, and reminiscence. Dealing with sad themes is part of the leader's role.

13. Do not change meeting places or times too often; this has a tendency to rattle some members. Never be late for a meeting. If you anticipate being late, notify the members. Never fail to appear without an explanation or without providing a substitute leader. Do not make promises you cannot keep.

14. Make a contract with each person in the group (See Chapter 8 on contracts). Contracts are important; they alert the older person, particularly the confused, forgetful one, to the time and place of the meetings and give the leader a chance to assess that individual for confusion, disorientation, disabilities, and the like before taking him or her into the group. Do not depend on the staff for a list of potential group members. They may list, for various reasons, people difficult to handle in a group or people who cannot benefit at all from the group experience.

15. Recognize the importance of hellos and goodbyes to old people. They need to know the limits—how much time you will spend with them and where you are both physically and psychologically in the relationship. Handling this aspect of group work is an art. For example, a death may

TABLE 10-3 Personal characteristics of an effective leader

- Genuine respect for old people.
- A history of positive experiences with old people.
- A deep sense of caring for the elderly.
- A respect for the elderly person's cultural values.
- An understanding of the ways in which the individual's cultural background continues to influence present attitudes and behaviors.
- An ability and desire to learn from old people.
- An understanding of the biological aspects of aging.
- The conviction that the last years of life can be challenging.
- Patience, especially with repetition of stories.
- Knowledge of the special biological, psychological, and social needs of the aged.
- Sensitivity to the burdens and anxieties of old people.
- The ability to get old people to challenge many of the myths about old age.
- A healthy attitude regarding one's own eventual old age.
- An understanding of the developmental tasks of each period of life, from infancy to old age.
- An appreciation for the effects that one period of life has on other stages of development.
- A particular understanding of how one's ability to handle present life difficulties hinges on how well one deals with problems in earlier stages.
- A background in the pathology of aging.
- The ability to deal with extreme feelings of depression, hopelessness, grief, hostility, and despair.
- Personal characteristics such as humor, enthusiasm, patience, courage, endurance, hopefulness, tolerance, nondefensiveness, freedom from limiting prejudices, and a willingness to learn.
- An ability to be both gentle and challenging.
- The sensitivity to know when it is therapeutic to provide support and when to challenge.
- A working knowledge of the group process along with the special skills needed for group work with the elderly.

SOURCE: MS Corey and G Corey (1992, 422). Used with permission.

occur and a member will not be at the next group meeting. I have seen persons who felt guilty because they did not say a "neat, clean" goodbye to someone. But promising to come back when you never intend to is not a neat, clean goodbye.

16. Deal with all absences in the group. If a member has died, be sure to try to handle the death in the meeting. (I leave an empty chair in the meeting after the death so that if the members do not hear what I say, at least they can see what has happened.)

17. Recognize that touching and closeness— both leader-member closeness and member-member closeness—are of crucial importance.

18. Mix men and women when possible and alternate the group seating pattern.

19. Be meticulous in anticipating and meeting members' needs, since they cannot always verbalize them. Either say the words or allow the members to say what their needs are. Pain is one area to consider.

20. Use food and beverages to add surprise and ambience to meetings.

21. Recognize the importance of spontaneity and surprises. Do not let the surprise be, "Look, we are all moving to a new room today!" Jostling the group about is not helpful to the members.

Surprise should be within the structure of the group; but members who have dementia do poorly if moved about too much. Some of the surprises could be changing the food or beverages from week to week, adding an activity, occasionally having a guest leader take over the group, or changing the usual structure of the group.

22. Use the here and now. Talk about the weather, the seasons, or whatever to get started. The superficial is OK. You will also have to share things about yourself; the aged will not often let you out of that.

23. Work on self-image. Praise and compliment whenever possible, but be sincere. Do not have confrontation groups.

24. Arrange transportation to help members get to meetings.

25. Consider, when possible, the era and the geographical areas in which the members lived most of their lives and talk about them in the meetings.

26. Acknowledge your own feelings.

27. Do not mix individuals with dementia with alert patients; it creates problems. It is hard to keep all members interested, because situations may occur in which alert patients think that maybe they are really slipping.

It takes courage, stamina, creativity, and great patience to be a group leader, but there are results and rewards. The results may seem minuscule, but they are there. The rewards are an individual matter; what is rewarding for one group leader may not be so for another. As you continue to lead groups, you will discover your own style of leadership—one that is comfortable for you, therapeutic for the members, and always uniquely yours. When you have all that in tow, you can feel assured that you have arrived as a group leader with an aged clientele.

One would have to agree with Toseland (1990) that most leaders of groups of older persons combine different leadership models to help meet the needs of the group members in the most effective way. There is not one single practice model that is effective in all situations. The leader will need to be very flexible to provide tailor-made strategies for each situation. In fact, the methods used by the leader should reveal a comprehensive assessment of the group proposed. See Chapter 8 for more on assessments.

SUMMARY

The problems of maintaining a group of older persons are different from those encountered in other age groups. The problems of the aged may stagger the new leader, since they are multiple, complex, and sometimes recurring. Locating a receptive facility is usually the first hurdle. Sensory loss requires exquisite handling by the leader. Meticulous attention must also be given to psychosomatic complaints.

Conducting a group may present such problems as sabotage by the staff; nonacceptance of a co-leader; and monopolizing, mute, or hostile members. Trust, confidentiality, inclusion, and ground rules are also concerns. If absenteeism is a problem, the leader should consider possible reasons. Nursing home residents are usually so bored that they welcome a group experience.

Qualifications and abilities needed for group leadership with the aged include background in normal aging, background in the pathology of aging, experience in groups of any kind, tolerance for groups, ability to tolerate dependent relationships, ability to handle directness and criticism, ability to handle one's own feelings, and organization.

Suggestions for new leaders are given as guidelines to facilitate group movement, to decrease anxiety, and to promote learning from the aged themselves.

EXERCISE 1

A leader's role can be active or passive. Which is the more common stance in group leadership with the aged? State the reasons for your choice.

EXERCISE 2

Absenteeism is a common problem in groups of older persons and may be due to a variety of factors. Below is a sample form that you might use as a model. Make your own form and list as many reasons as you can that older people might not attend a group meeting. In the adjacent column, list interventions by the leader that might improve group attendance. Document if you have the sources for such information. The following is an example:

Reasons for absenteeism	Leader intervention
Example: Ill health	Leader visits resident at bedside (or phones home on day of meeting) and states that the member was missed at the group meeting; inquires about health problem. Uses active listening and is supportive and concerned.

EXERCISE 3

Obtain permission from the leader and a group of older persons to observe. Observe the leader's actions and interventions. List five actions observed and assess by filling in the following format:

Describe action/intervention	Effective or ineffective?	State why you think so

EXERCISE 4

This is an exercise in self-assessment. Because there are different types of leadership, list some of your own characteristics in group leading. Which ones would you like to improve?

REFERENCES

Burnside IM. 1970. Crisis intervention among hospitalized aged. *J Psychiatr Nurs* 8(2):17-20.

Corey MS, Corey G. 1992. *Groups: Process and practice* (pp. 399-430). Pacific Grove, CA: Brooks/Cole.

Duvall E. 1971. *Family development*, 4th ed. Philadelphia: Lippincott.

Erikson EH. 1963. *Childhood and society*, 2d ed. New York: Norton.

———. 1982. *The life cycle completed: A review.* New York: Norton.

Group Work with the Elderly. 1976. Class session, San Francisco State University. San Francisco (October 30).

Hall E. 1983. A conversation with Erik Erickson. *Psychol Today* 17(6):22-30.

Havighurst R. 1965. *Developmental tasks and education.* New York: McKay.

Hennessey MJ. 1976. Group work with economically independent aged. In IM Burnside (ed.), *Nursing and the aged*, 1st ed. (pp. 231-244). New York: McGraw-Hill.

Hickey T, Hultsch DL, Fatule B. 1975. Age effects in practitioner training for attitude change. Paper presented at Gerontological Society meeting, Louisville, KY (October 28).

Hultsch DL, Hickey T, Rakowski W. 1975. Adult learning in a meaningful context. Paper presented at Gerontological Society meeting, Louisville, KY (October 27).

Kratzig E. 1976. Student assignment for class entitled Group Work with the Elderly, San Francisco State University (October 7).

Leudtke M. 1976. Student assignment for class entitled Group Work with the Elderly, San Francisco State University (October 7).

Linden ME. 1956. Geriatrics. In SR Slavson (ed.), *The fields of group psychotherapy* (pp. 129-153). New York: Schocken Books.

Lowy L. 1967. Roadblocks in group work practice with older people: A framework for analysis. Part I. *Gerontologist* 7(2):109-113.

Pfeiffer E. 1975. Plenary speech given at conference entitled Successful Treatment of the Mentally Ill Elderly, Duke University, Durham, NC (May 22-23).

Smith LL. 1980. Finding your leadership style in groups. *Am J Nurs* 80(7):1301-1303.

Tappen R, Touhy T. 1983. Group leader—Are you a controller? *J Gerontol Nurs* 9(1):34.

Toseland RW. 1990. *Group work with older adults.* New York: New York University Press.

U.S. Department of Health and Human Services, National Center for Health Statistics. 1993. *Vital and health statistics: Health data on older Americans*, Series 3, No. 2. Washington, DC: U.S. Government Printing Office.

Yalom ID. 1985. *The theory and practice of group psychotherapy*, 3d ed. New York: Basic Books.

BIBLIOGRAPHY

Brost BE. 1970. The "active leader" in group therapy for chronic schizophrenic patients. *Perspect Psychiatr Care* 8(6):268-272.

Burnside IM. 1969. Group work among the aged. *Nurs Outlook* 17(June):68-71.

Chan DC. 1973. Using patients as group leaders in a VA hospital (program briefs). *Hosp Comm Psych* 24(8):531.

Folsom JC, Folsom GS. 1974. The real world. *Ment Hyg* 58 (Summer):29-33.

Forman M. 1971. The alienated resident and the alienating institution: A case for peer group intervention. *Soc Work* 16(2):47-54.

Levine B. 1980. Co-leadership approach to learning group work. *Soc Work with Groups* 3:35-38.

McLaughlin FE. 1971. Personality changes through alternate group leadership. *Nurs Res* 20(March-April): 123-130.

Puppolo D. 1980. Co-leadership with a group of stroke patients. In IM Burnside (ed.), *Psychosocial nursing care of the aged,* 2d ed. (pp. 253-270). New York: McGraw-Hill.

Racker H. 1953. A contribution to the problem of countertransference. *Int J Psycho-anal* 34(4):313-324.

———. 1957. The meanings and uses of countertransference. *Psychoanal Q* 26(3):303-357.

Sandler J. 1976. Countertransference and role-responsiveness. *Int Rev Psychoanal* 3(1):33-37.

RESOURCE

Social Work with Groups 3(4) 1985. This is a special issue on co-leadership.

PART 4

Clinical Modalities

Part 4 is the pragmatic section of the book; practitioners from a variety of disciplines explore implementing group work with older adults. This section should be of interest to readers from many disciplines, and families of regressed older persons may find it useful in their own efforts to improve care of their loved ones.

The projected increase of elderly persons in the population also means an increase in persons with dementia. Chapter 11, by Irene Burnside, looks at leadership struggles with mentally regressed groups of older people. Three groups are compared and contrasted: One group was conducted in a 287-bed locked facility; another in a 91-bed nursing home; and the third in a 68-bed, all-female locked facility. This chapter offers suggestions about selection of group members and how to use drawings to tap into long-term memories. In Chapter 12, Burnside describes some of the difficulties a leader may face when the group members are physically impaired and offers suggestions to help the members stay in the group and be as comfortable as possible.

Chapter 13 begins with a literature review of reality orientation by Elizabeth Williams, a gerontological nurse practitioner. The chapter concludes with practical suggestions gleaned from her experiences in a day care center and with long-term care.

In Chapter 14, Helen Dennis describes in detail a remotivation group she conducted in a state hospital. Although remotivation groups are now less frequently seen than other types of groups, they were one of the early types of group implemented with older adults.

Chapter 15, by Irene Burnside, is about reminiscence therapy groups and is based on clinical and research experience. While it is written from a nurse's perspective, the content should be helpful to anyone planning a reminiscence group.

James Birren and Donna Deutchman, in Chapter 16, spell out the important steps for leading a guided autobiography group, based on experiences with many groups.

Mary Jane Hennessey did not live to revise Chapter 17, but her words are as warm and instructive as when she first wrote them.

Support groups are the focus of Chapter 18, by Irene Burnside, who describes types of support and professional leadership in such groups.

Chapter 19, by Judith Altholz, a psychiatric social worker, is about group psychotherapy. She describes strategies for solving problems in that modality.

CHAPTER 11

Group Work with the Cognitively Impaired

Irene Burnside

KEY WORDS

- Alzheimer's disease
- Aphasia
- Delirium
- Dementia
- Flat affect
- Individualization
- Nonverbal communication
- Organic mental disorder
- Therapeutic nihilism
- We-ness

LEARNING OBJECTIVES

- Describe 10 ways to take care of one's self during work with older adults.
- Analyze four inappropriate group member selections.
- Discuss changes in behavior that might occur during the course of a group.
- Discuss individualization within the group setting.
- Expand on the staying-near phenomenon frequently observed in dementia.

Tell me, I'll forget. Show me, I may remember.
But involve me, and I'll understand.

ANCIENT CHINESE PROVERB

Although reports on a variety of aspects of caring for mentally impaired older adults in institutions have appeared in the literature,[1] the therapeutic nihilism prevalent among health professionals about treating the aged is especially blatant in

---

[1]For example, Brody et al. 1971; Brody et al. 1972; Brody et al. 1975; Feil 1982, 1983; Kleban & Brody 1972; Kleban, Brody & Lawton 1971; Kleban et al. 1975, 1976; Kobrynski 1975; Lee 1983; and Salter & Salter 1975.

regard to the mentally impaired aged. The word *senile* is used with great frequency by health care professionals, both in discussions about residents and on their charts. The patient whose diagnosis is dementia is often relegated to a back room (or the back ward in a state hospital), and little effort is made by staff members to prevent further slippage. The staff's ennui and lack of hope are soon picked up by family and friends, who sometimes cease even to correspond with and/or visit the patient.

Nurses' aides, in spite of their lack of knowledge and sophistication, are still the staff people most likely to offer support and hope to this group of aged people. The aides must patiently struggle against formidable odds; some of them do a remarkable job of relating to the mentally impaired.

But instilling hope is not an easy task, and a hopeful (but realistic) attitude toward the care of the regressed and mentally impaired aged is relatively rare. The book *Gramp* (Jury & Jury 1976) provides an outstanding example of caretaking and caring by a family. A filmstrip and cassette by the same authors is entitled *Gramp: A Man Ages and Dies.* This family's struggle with destructive behavior, incontinence, and loss of memory is a shining instance of the caring component of care.

Group work with mentally impaired older adults can be extremely difficult, but it can also be highly rewarding. This chapter offers students, instructors, and health care workers and administrators some cautions for the new leader and three examples of groups I led in institutions. Group A illustrates behavioral problems and membership selection; group B, individualization within a group; and group C, nonverbal communication. Each group contained six or seven members. (Group leading is much easier if the group is kept to about six persons, particularly if there are frail and/or disabled members in the group.) All met on a weekly basis except during the termination phase, when meetings were spaced further apart.

CAUTIONS FOR NEW GROUP LEADERS

Leading groups of regressed or mentally impaired older people requires intense involvement to combat low affect and lack of emotional response and to meet affectional needs of the members. The leader must grapple with superdependency, listlessness, apathy, low energy levels, and lack of information about the group members. The leader also needs to be comfortable with long silences in a group. Careful observation by the leader for any cues of increased awareness (verbal or nonverbal) helps pinpoint progress, but it is often slow, and observed changes may seem minuscule if the leader sets unrealistic goals. These problems help produce the anxiety or boredom that can overtake (and sometimes overwhelm) a leader about midway through the life of the group. Indeed, introducing crafts, projects, music, and exercises may be necessary to sustain the leader as well as the group.

New group leaders need reminding that to be effective they must take care of themselves. Some specific suggestions follow:

1.   Use a support system; have one person available on the staff to whom you can talk in confidence about your group experiences.

2.   Use staff meetings to explore feelings—not as a gripe session but as constructive catharsis with problem solving.

3.   Consider more frequent rest breaks (for example, go out for a brief walk and take deep breaths instead of taking the usual coffee break).

4.   Practice more spontaneity. Don't get so bogged down in routine that you become bored and indifferent.

5.   Assess your own reactions to the dependency and deterioration of the patients. Are the problems of the patients hitting too close to those of your own relatives, for example? Consider whether you are conducting the right group for you.

6.   Continued awareness of self is important. There are often subtle clues that you may overlook or ignore: slight pains, depressed feelings, physical fatigue, loss of interest in the job, resentment, a feeling of martyrdom.

7.   Plan careful, individualized programs within the group so that deteriorating patients have maximum support but continue to do as much for themselves as possible.

8.   If you are a staff member, suggest a monthly morale booster meeting. At each meeting, look at positive approaches to what is happening, find something to feel good about in your work, permit no negative input, and reward everyone with something different—a surprise. (Remember the psychological importance of beverages and food.)

9.   Discover new ways of being good to yourself, both on the job and off.

10.   Examine your own patterns of coping with discouragement, depression, dependency, and deterioration. What will you do about the patterns?

11.   Learn from one another. What people do you know who have unique and successful ways of taking care of themselves?

12.   Practice observing your members. How do they take care of themselves? The aged are our best teachers; borrow from their wisdom.

Leaders also have to be willing to try varied approaches. If one technique is a fiasco, they should abandon it and try another. Student leaders often get discouraged when their plans go awry, but problem solving is a learned leadership skill. I am reminded of the woman who called a local agency about a skunk under her home. They advised her to put a line of bread crumbs leading to the outside of the house. The next day she called to say that she had done so and now had two skunks under the house.

New solutions do have a way of backfiring, and the successful ones may even create new problems. If there is a change in a problem resident who has been a member of a group, the staff may think the group leader can perform minimiracles and then want to place obstreperous residents in the group to straighten them out. The leader should be very cautious about staff overenthusiasm about residents or clients. Such enthusiasm may mean that they want to hand over an especially difficult patient and then sit back and watch the leader struggle with behavior that they cannot handle or tolerate.

A series of classic experimental studies called the Hawthorne studies was conducted in the late 1920s and the early 1930s at the Hawthorne Plant of the Western Electric Company in Chicago. The *Hawthorne effect* is a term used to describe psychological reactions that occur in subjects and that tend to alter their responses. Subjects may change their behavior in an effort to please the researcher (Demsey & Demsey 1981).

Nonresearch group work can still create the Hawthorne effect—that is, heightened interest and unanticipated spin-offs. Curiosity is aroused when an outsider comes in and plans and prepares for the group. As a result, interest in the group members by the administrator and the staff often increases, and they begin to observe the members more closely. This curiosity and interest help group leaders to contact the staff while planning the group. The cook may be involved if refreshments are to be served. Receptionists and office personnel can provide a great deal of help. Indeed, maintenance men often helped me round up missing patients for groups B and C, since the men knew where the patients hid out.

The biggest spin-off I have observed is that friendships outside the group setting often become very significant, especially when the group is completed. I have gone back to visit later and have seen such friendships continue to grow.

GROUP A: BEHAVIORAL PROBLEMS AND MEMBERSHIP SELECTION

Group A met 30 minutes weekly for seven months. I led seven older women who were hospitalized in a 68-bed light mental (locked) facility situated in a quiet California neighborhood not far from a famous motion picture studio. The facility, once used to dry out overimbibing movie stars, was old and resembled a large, rambling house. No sign or name anywhere indicated that the house was an institution, as the neighbors objected strenuously.

Group A did not really get going until the seventh meeting. Staff members had suggested to me potential group members who they felt would benefit from a group experience. Selection of appropriate members for the group turned out to be a big problem. Five individuals had to be removed from the group soon after it was launched; each person was immediately replaced. Descriptions of the five individuals removed from the group follow. They were a colorful, albeit unmanageable, group and underline the danger of inadequate assessments of potential group members.

Inappropriate Group Selections

Mrs. A. Mrs. A, in her midsixties, was born in Warsaw. She rarely spoke, even in Polish. Though she seemed to understand English, her behavior left me doubting it much of the time. She attended five meetings and displayed unusually high anxiety. She frequently jumped up and left the room; when she did remain seated, she fidgeted and mumbled constantly. In the second meeting, with the leader's constant reminding, she was able to sit still, but she continued to disrupt the group by drinking the cream from the pitcher on the coffee serving tray, snatching the sugar when the cream pitcher was empty, and grabbing the refreshments before they could be served.

Improving social graces has always been one of the goals I try to incorporate into group work with regressed aged people, but there was absolutely no improvement with this woman. After the fifth meeting I decided to remove her. Her

TABLE 11-1 Members of Group A

Patient	Age	Marital status	Diagnosis	Ambulation	Strengths in group	Problems in group
Mrs. L. M.	71	Married	CAS,[1] schizophrenic, paranoid	Ambulatory	Gentleness	Dependency, crying spells, depression
Mrs. T.	85	Widow (from age 63)	CAS, paranoid	Ambulatory	Warmth, loving ways, quick to praise	Forgetfulness
Miss H.	95	Single (never married)	CAS, paranoid	Ambulatory	Toughness, sharpness, observation ability, articulate	Hallucinations
Mrs. V.	78	Married	OMD,[2] degenerative arthritis, CAS	Ambulatory	Sense of humor, warmth, spontaneity	Forgetfulness
Mrs. H.	72	Widow	Legally blind, congestive heart failure, epilepsy, CAS	Ambulatory	Sense of humor, articulate, courage, acceptance of blindness	Monopolization of group
Mrs. S. M.	79	Widow	CAS, manic-depressive	Ambulatory	Sharpness, helpfulness, appreciative	Bitterness, constant carping
Mrs. D. M.	78	Widow (at age 34)	CAS, reactive-depressive state	Ambulatory (with assistance)	Gratitude, articulate	Crying spells, depression

[1]Cerebral arteriosclerosis.
[2]Organic mental disorder.

behavior unnerved me so much at times that I focused on her instead of handling the entire group. This overindividualization wears the leader down and leaves the rest of the group resentful. It was soon clear that her disruptive behavior impeded the group's progress.

Someone once said, "You must look into people as well as at them." This was certainly true in this selection; I had not looked into Mrs. A. *The lesson Mrs. A taught me is to obtain adequate data about behavior (and observe for while if in doubt) before selecting a group member.*

Mrs. F. Mrs. F, in her mid-seventies, was religious—but more temperamental than religious most of the time. Her diagnosis was chronic brain syndrome with paranoia. Although she sat still, her tongue did not. She monopolized the conversation. She was constantly supercilious. She came to group meetings only sporadically but always with aloof, condescending behavior. By the seventh meeting, a close group was forming, but Mrs. F was not interested enough to attend, although she gave no specific reason. I did not encourage her to continue and finally terminated with her. *Mrs. F*

taught me that paranoid individuals can be very difficult at times to keep in a group and may intimidate both leader and group with their hostile ways.

Mrs. H. Mrs. H, age 72, attended only three meetings. She, too, felt the group was beneath her. Once after a meeting, she came up to me and said, "And how did you pick that motley crew?" In the second meeting, she flatly announced her dislike of men. I learned later from the staff that she was a long-time lesbian. Since I often touch aged individuals, I realized she already inhibited me in the group setting. I was disinclined to touch her; I thought she might misconstrue my touching as having sexual connotations. I had not experienced such a situation in group work before, nor did I wish to tackle such a problem when I was beginning a new group. My own anxiety has to level off in new groups; leaders must strive continually to lower their own anxiety in group work. I felt that my own reserve and inhibitions with this woman would ultimately influence my interactions with the entire group. Much to my relief, she voluntarily dropped the group after the third meeting. *Mrs. H* *taught me not to let the staff sway me in my selections and to double-check for missing information on a potential member.*

Mrs. M. Mrs. M, age 78, was a retired nurse. She was very hostile; her verbal abuse was sometimes matched by physically striking out at other residents. She usually hit patients when the staff could not see her, so that particular behavior was observed only if a staff member unexpectedly walked into the room. The staff thought she might benefit by joining the group. It soon became apparent that she wanted to attend meetings only at her whim. The nurse began setting strict limits with her at about the time the group was forming. Because of her quick and ill temper, hostile remarks, and the fear she engendered in other patients, I did not encourage her to continue attending meetings and finally terminated with her. Frail patients in groups need to be protected, and the group milieu should be safe and secure. There was a 95-year-old woman in this particular group, and I found myself frequently considering her frailty (Burnside 1978).

However, by the seventh meeting Mrs. M had heard that the coffee served in the meetings was hot and superb and that sweets were served with the coffee. She then decided she wanted to reenter the group. The director of nurses and I held the line and said no. She had had her chance; she could not come and go at her whim. *I learned from Mrs. M the effects an abusive person can have on a group. I also learned to be more protective of the very old and very frail members.*

Mrs. L. Mrs. L was 74 years old. She had been hospitalized for several years and spent most of her time in a wheelchair. She would not try to walk or talk. At the first meeting she stiffened her body and nearly slid out of the wheelchair. Her eyes became rather glassy, and she frothed a little at the mouth. I was not sure what was happening. The nurse helped me return Mrs. L to her room, adding that this was not uncommon behavior for her. She died suddenly two months after the trial group experience. *Mrs. L taught me to investigate physical problems in greater detail and to interrogate several staff members about a resident's life history, behavior, and physical complaints.*

These patients were simply too much of a challenge. However, one should not lose hope in working with even difficult old people. Janet Specht[2] once brought that home to me, and her perseverance in new approaches to the mentally impaired is commendable. These patients might have benefited from a one-to-one relationship with a student, an interested staff member, or a volunteer, or one of them might have been absorbed into an already established, stable group.

The Final Group Membership

The final group membership is shown in Table 11-1. The mean age of the group members was 79.7 years. Each individual in the group had a diagnosis of cerebral arteriosclerosis, and five of the women were diagnosed as having psychiatric problems. One resident had "delusional" for a diagnosis! It is not uncommon to find a symptom for a diagnosis in an older person's records.

There were several impressive things about this group. One was the lack of physical disabilities; there was a certain physical toughness about them, which I attributed to their many years of hard work. (Lack of education was also a characteristic of the group; most completed eighth grade only.) Another noticeable thing was the brevity of the diagnoses on the members' charts. There was no list of six or seven ailments, as is usually seen in an average older person's record. It is possible that the admitting doctors did not write down all the diagnoses or that complete physical histories were not done. It is also possible that the most fitting diagnosis was emphasized—that is, the one diagnosis that would gain fastest entrée into a locked facility and also pass the medical review team.

There were no aphasics in the group, no immobile persons, and no paralyzed persons. One woman, though legally blind, said one day, "I have ten eyes," and held up her 10 fingers to show the group. One reason for the lack of such impairments may be that to be admitted to this facility, most patients had to be able to care for themselves. Bedridden and wheelchair patients were not admitted.

One rather quick way a group leader can assess the sharpness of the members is to assign drawings.[3] Even if members follow short, simple instructions well, the leader can note problems, as

---

[2]Personal communication, 1976.

[3]I am grateful to Dr. Robert Katzman for his discussion about the use of clock drawings in assessment.

I did with Mrs. V as she struggled to draw, to spell, and to organize the sample assignments I gave (Figures 11-1 and 11-2).

Observed Changes

Improvements in social graces and/or behavior often make staff members more receptive to a resident. Behavioral changes in members of group A often followed a rewarding group experience. For example, Mrs. D. M. entered group A at the sixth meeting and was considered by the staff to be a problem patient. She refused to walk and had many psychosomatic complaints. She expressed guilt about her only child's suicide; her daughter had committed suicide while the woman was in a board-and-care home. Mrs. D. M. became so depressed and agitated that she was transferred to a

FIGURE 11-1 *Mrs. V, a member of group A, had extreme memory loss, was very aware of it, and struggled with it constantly. Asked to draw a memory, she drew a barn in South Dakota. Then she tried to write a description of it, and one can see what happened when she tried to organize the statement.*

FIGURE 11-2 *During a session when we reminisced about first toys, Mrs. V drew a tea set that she remembered from her childhood. Note in Table 11-1 that she had a severe memory problem, yet she drew the correct dishes for the tea. The strange object to the left of the creamer probably was the container for spoons, which was a common way to place spoons on a table in those days.*

locked facility. The director of nurses and I discussed the nursing care plan so that I could support the staff's therapeutic regimen during group meetings. Specifically, I would encourage her to walk, listen to but not encourage the psychosomatic complaints, offer her an opportunity to express guilt (and other feelings) in group meetings, and observe her degree of depression from week to week.

The staff and I were surprised at her rather sudden improvement. The day before Mother's Day, the group had weathered a stormy session. My small, inexpensive gifts for each member caused visible sadness, especially in Mrs. D. M. She took her gift, cried openly, and said, "I don't deserve it. I am not a fit mother. Plus I don't even have 10 cents to give anyone else a gift." I sat on the arm of her chair and put my arm around her. I served her tea, which she preferred to coffee. (Fixing a member's coffee or tea exactly as requested is one simple way to individualize care and is more important than the leader may realize.) We talked about the daughter's suicide and the mother's guilt. All of us acknowledged feelings we had had on Mother's Day. When the meeting was over, an aide and I helped her walk back to her room.

In the subsequent meeting, Mrs. D. M. was tearless, though obviously still depressed. I noticed that a staff member had shaved off the hairs on her chin. (That had been in the nursing care plan—she hated the hair on her face.) She apologized for not having combed her hair before coming to the meeting. This time she would not let me serve her tea and said that coffee was fine (if I would "just put a little cold water in it"). She did not mention her stomachache, as she had done many times in the previous meeting. I sat close to her but touched her arm or shoulder only occasionally.

During the sad expressions of loss during the Mother's day session, I suggested homework. Since coping with losses was a task the members were facing, they were to recall how they had coped with a particular loss in their lives and share with the group what had been helpful to them. It was during such sharing that we discovered that two members had lived very close to each other before their admission to the hospital. Such discoveries are important because they reveal information that helps members develop friendships outside the meetings. One should always capitalize on such serendipity when it occurs.

A similar incident occurred in group C; Mr. B and Mr. Z both spoke a French patois, so I encouraged them to converse in French. The talents of the aged so often go unnoticed, and group experiences do give the aged a chance to share talents, interests, and accomplishments.

Group A: A Summary

Several women in a light mental (locked) facility met weekly for seven months. We talked about things of interest to them, such as feelings about being a woman, clothes, teas, social affairs, and the "prisoner's life" they led (their description). Although we drew occasionally, mostly we talked. I always ended the group meetings with sweets and coffee.

After the weekly meetings were terminated, I often taught group work at the same facility. Some of the women were interviewed or participated in group demonstrations, and they did miss the regular meetings. Lack of staff and volunteers was the reason the meetings were not continued. I saw Mrs. H from time to time until she died, since she was the only one in the group without any relatives (Burnside 1978).

GROUP B: INDIVIDUALIZATION WITHIN A GROUP

Group B met weekly for six months in the small, cozy employees' dining room of a 91-bed extended care facility. (Group members are listed in Table 11-2). This group was launched in an unusual fashion. A biologist-researcher[4] suggested to me that there might be a relationship between testosterone levels and institutionalized depressed men. I met with an administrator and discussed plans for a group to study. Contracts were made, a group of six men was assembled, and testosterone assays were done. The Hawthorne effect in this instance was that elderly men not in the group would line up, expose an arm, and say, "I want to give my blood too!" However, since the biologist found that the levels were not unusually low, there was no reason to continue the group for the research project.

Because the group was under way, I did not feel that I could terminate it, especially after the

men had been so cooperative. The two least interested men were phased out of the group and replaced by two women.

The lack of affect, spontaneity, and motivation in the group forced me to try various methods: (1) topics were assigned to discuss, (2) reminiscence sessions were tried, and (3) simple art sessions were instituted, using chalk, crayons, and so forth. The last was the most successful of the three techniques I tried. Members were assigned a building, toy, pet, boyfriend, or girlfriend to draw—some thing or person out of their past (Figure 11-3). Only one art exercise was not successful, and now I understand why. Because I was still in a euphoric state from a trip to Africa, I asked the group members to draw an African animal. These people were never a wildly enthusiastic group at any time, but this day their enthusiasm hit a new low. In my eagerness, I had assigned something to meet my need, not theirs—a common (and often nontherapeutic) problem in leaders. Neither had I reckoned with asking them to draw the unfamiliar—after all, elephants and giraffes are usually at the very back of the average old person's memory file. And I was working with mentally impaired people besides!

Mr. D. M. The drawings in Figures 11-4a through 11-4d are from a series done by Mr. D. M. over a six-month period. Severe chronic brain syndrome was his diagnosis. His ability to compose a likeness, and neatly (Figure 11-4d), especially after the scribbling of his first drawing (Figure 11-4a), seemed remarkable, especially to a nonartist leader. As Sally Koslow (1976, 140) says, "Signs of therapeutic progress can be dishearteningly small—a patient whistling a tune, holding your hand, and this after months of work."

Mr. D. M. was easy to work with and was easily encouraged to draw. He was so quiet in the meetings that I wondered whether he understood. He smiled instead of answering me. (A way of conserving energy? A nonverbal way to handle unsure areas? A successful way to win over staff?)

Mr. D. M. attended the meetings consistently. He was also filmed by a CBS cameraman after the *Sex after Sixty* television show was filmed. One cameraman, taken by Mr. D. M.'s expression and eyes, had a cigarette with him on the patio. Shortly afterward, Mr. D. M. was transferred to another facility, and he died within two weeks.

---

[4]Caleb Finch, personal communication, 1974.

TABLE 11-2 Members of Group B

Patient	Former occupation	Age	Ambulation	Diagnosis	Visitors	Length of hospitalization	Restorative potential (by M.D.)	Strengths in group	Problems in group
Mr. D. M.	Automobile mechanic	75	Ambulatory	TBC (inactive),[1] malnutrition, dementia	None	2 years, 6 months	Fair	Sweet, gentle air, beautiful smile	Apathy, withdrawal, listlessness
Mr. G.	Railroad clerk	63	Ambulatory	Schizophrenic, simple type, marked deterioration	None	3 years, 6 months	Zero	Tried hard	Lack of social graces, sometimes inattentive
Mr. P.	Fisherman, construction worker	58	Ambulatory	CVA[2]	None	3 years	Poor	Sharp, improvement in self-care	Stubborn, cross, sometimes would not talk
Mrs. B.	Registered nurse	79	Ambulatory	Dementia secondary to Parkinson's (although she was extremely paranoid, not in diagnosis)	None	5 years, 8 months	Fair	Sharp, observing, enjoyed drawing	Hallucinating, high anxiety, would leave group abruptly, quiet
Mrs. M.	Journalist	90	Wheelchair	Dementia	Yes	2 years	Zero	Articulate	Anger at staff, monopolizing
Mr. D.	Gardener	88	Ambulatory	Dementia	Yes	2 years	Fair	Gentleness, obvious enjoyment of group, smile	Aphasic, difficulties in communication

[1]Tuberculosis.
[2]Cardiovascular accident.

Mr. S. Mr. S, the youngest member of the group, had suffered a stroke in his late sixties while on a construction job. He was sullen, morose, and withdrawn before joining the group. He often wheeled himself out of the meeting, but he always returned. He smiled, almost with disdain, when drawings were introduced, but he worked carefully on them. His left hand was paralyzed, so he placed a heavy ashtray on the paper to hold it still as he drew. The drawings in Figures 11-5 and 11-6 were done by Mr. S.

After several months, Mr. S began to loosen up and started combing his hair and wearing a clean shirt to meetings. After the group was completed, he went out AMA (against medical advice) and wheeled himself to the beach to live!

FIGURE 11-3 *Mrs. M drew a picture of her first toy, a doll.*

FIGURE 11-4a *Mr. D. M. scribbled intensely during the first drawing session but kept the scribbling contained in one area (unlike the member diagnosed as a burned-out schizophrenic, who scribbled all over the entire page). Mr. D. M. signed his own name with ease (and pride) on his drawings.*

FIGURE 11-4c *This drawing was Mr. D. M.'s response to a request to draw an old girlfriend or boyfriend. To identify the drawing, I printed in Mr. D. M.'s description, "Mary (16)" and "Las Vegas."*

FIGURE 11-4b *Houses were the theme for this group meeting. (House was the term used; home seemed a rather threatening word.) This drawing is of a house in Tucson, where Mr. D. M. lived for a short time as a young boy. Readers familiar with southwestern architecture will note that he captured the essence of his boyhood home. Often group members did successfully capture the essence in their crude sketches.*

FIGURE 11-4d *Mr. D. M. eventually drew a self-portrait. Contrast this with his drawing in Figure 11-4a, done early in the life of the group.*

Mrs. B. This 79-year-old woman suffered from Parkinson's disease and chronic brain syndrome. She also had severe paranoid ideation, which was not noted anywhere in her chart. She was very self-conscious about her crossed eye. She drew readily and with great concentration; she called the group "the drawing class." Her drawings are shown in Figures 11-7 and 11-8. Her anxiety in early meetings was manifested by jumping up suddenly and leaving. During the drawing sessions, she was able to concentrate intently on the drawings and did not leave the meetings.

The woman's decline over the span of the group can best be seen by comparing one of her first group drawings with one of her very last (Figures 11-9a and 11-9b).

Group B: A Summary

Group B had a rather unusual beginning. Members' problems included poststroke paralysis, aphasia, flat affects, and immobility of members. The most

FIGURE 11-5 *Mr. S drew one of his first remembered toys, a wagon; possibly it is what contemporary children might build using a box.*

FIGURE 11-6 *The subject for this drawing session was a pet. Note the bone Mr. S added for the dog. Mr. S also recalled the name of the dog, but later labeled the drawing "Dog" after another member said, "Oh, that's a billy goat."*

FIGURE 11-7 *When asked to draw her first remembered important building, Mrs. B drew a picture of a church.*

FIGURE 11-8 *One of the assignments in group B was for members to draw their first house. Mrs. B drew this house and windmill remembered from a childhood spent in foster homes in the Midwest.*

successful strategy was drawing and discussing the drawings. Perhaps the most significant aspect of this group was that it launched an entire group program in the facility, which later included current events groups, reminiscence groups by students, practice groups for students, and a group comprised only of residents over 90. That kind of ground breaking is one important aspect of the experimental groups described in this chapter.

FIGURE 11-9a *This is a drawing of a sailor Mrs. B dated in Seattle during World War I. Note her attention to detail—the tie, the chevrons on the sleeve. The buttons on the fly (as an old sailor will quickly notice) should probably have been positioned in the direction of an inverted U instead of as drawn by Mrs. B. Her drawing ability seemed to improve temporarily as the meetings continued, but three years later there was a noticeable deterioration in her work, as can be seen in Figure 11-9b.*

FIGURE 11-9b *This drawing by Mrs. B, a member of group B, was done during a group demonstration for a class three years after the original drawing (Figure 11-9a). Note the differences—a coolie hat instead of a sailor's cap, for example—and the deterioration in the interim.*

GROUP C: NONVERBAL COMMUNICATION IN A GROUP

The life of group C has been described in another article (Burnside 1973), in which the importance of touch as communication with the regressed aged is discussed. A colleague described group C (Table 11-3) as experiencing "nonverbal living."

The group of six met weekly for 30 to 60 minutes in a light mental (locked) facility in Gardena, California. The group was closed, and the group experience lasted for 14 months. Subsequently, every four to six months, I took my classes of students from the University of Southern California to the facility. I taught three-hour classes there and always used this same group for a class demonstration. Although the members could not recall my name, they remembered me. Mr. B called me "the doughnut lady," and Mrs. S. T. used to say as she hugged me, "God love you. I can't remember your name, but I'm sure glad you came!"

Eventually, during the demonstration classes, the group members turned into hams. Mrs. K would turn and wave to the students or blow them a kiss as she was wheeled out of the classroom by an aide. Mr. B and Mr. Z would smile as they conversed in a French patois to the class.

I still underestimate the ability of quite regressed older adults to perform well—even in stressful situations. Do not underestimate group members. These people brought home to me their strengths. Their ability to care, to receive and give affection, also became more obvious to me during the years I knew them.

TABLE 11-3 Members of Group C

Patient	Age	Marital status	Length of hospitalization	Diagnosis	Ambulation	Strengths in group	Problems in group
Mrs. K.	82	Widowed	1 year, 8 months	Dementia, fractured right hip with prosthesis, neurofibroma of scalp	Ambulatory and wheelchair	Affectionate ways, awareness, sense of humor	Aphasia, fidgeting, withdrawing by closing eyes
Mr. Z.	64	Divorced	2 years, 10 months	Dementia, arteriosclerosis, secondary polyneuritis, old TBC[1]	Ambulatory	Gentleness, kindly air, awareness	Inarticulate, listless, anxious at times
Mrs. S.	81	Single	5 months	Dementia	Ambulatory	Assisted leader, observed others in group, change gradual: increase in affect, increase in orientation	Forgetful
Mrs. S. T.	79	Widowed	1 year, 4 months	Dementia	Ambulatory, to wheelchair in thirteenth meeting	Sweetness, responsiveness, appreciative	Severe hearing loss, in wheelchair
Mr. B.	80	Single	10 months	Dementia, central nervous system lues (meningoencephalitic type), blindness, anemia	Wheelchair	Sense of humor, openness, courageous, uncomplaining gratitude, gave feedback to leader	Overweight, in wheelchair (hard to push chair), blind, heavy personal loss, speech impediment
Mr. K.	86	Single	8 months (died 2 weeks after eighth group meeting)	Dementia	Wheelchair	Independent, sense of humor, observant, slowly responded to increased interaction contacts with leader	Withdrawn, depressed, nearly mute, fiercely independent (I originally labeled it "stubbornness")
Mr. J. (replaced Mr. K.)	68			Fractured right hip, CAS,[2] dementia secondary to alcoholism	Ambulatory		

[1]Tuberculosis.
[2]Cerebral arteriosclerosis.
SOURCE: Revised from IM Burnside (1973). Touching is talking. *Am J Nurs* 73(12):2062.

The projects I tried with this group were many: exercises, music in the form of records, sheer socializing and discussing the refreshments and what they meant, slides of themselves (an absolute fiasco), bringing young people to group meetings. My 20-year-old daughter once went to a meeting with me. Because she had worked in a nursing home and on a back ward of a state hospital, she could relate to the group members with great ease. They also enjoyed the day my secretary played the banjo for them. But pervasive passivity was the outstanding feature of the total group.

Group C: A Summary

Nonverbal communication was an important component of the group leadership. Mrs. K especially had high affectional needs, which were obvious at the first group meeting (Burnside 1973). The use of touch with the mentally impaired would be a productive area of research, as well as the use of food, beverages, and music to maintain interest.

Students often describe the flat affect and/or apathy as a wall they cannot get through. That was my experience in group C. In fact, the slightly or overtly psychotic often make a far more interesting group to lead. Some of the illusions, delusions, and fantasies can be quite intriguing! *Gramp* is a fine example (Jury & Jury 1976).

It is amazing that in spite of some severe dementia, some persons retain their conversational ability, their interpersonal skills, and their fabulous sense of humor. In one day center, I was going to do a spontaneous demonstration group for a group of students. Since I remembered that one lady had been a star in a previous group, I was glad when she agreed to be a member. There was also a psychiatrist suffering from dementia yet with many of his social graces still intact, and others suffering from either the primary disease of Alzheimer's or a dementia secondary to Parkinson's, stroke, or alcoholism. This vignette will give the reader the reason why these sparkling people facilitate a group.

Mrs. A, a sprightly lady in her eighties, fooled most people during the first meeting because of her meticulous dress, her outgoing, friendly ways, and her humor. During the demonstration group, I was attempting to have members tap into the memories of long ago, which I thought would not be too threatening for them. I asked them to sit for a few minutes and think about something they remembered very clearly from their childhood. (It is so important to allow these thinking times. Not only does it help the members very much and give them a sense of slower pace, but it can also help the leader to assess what is happening in the group, what changes need to be made, and who has not had much of a chance to participate in the group.)

Suddenly Mrs. A became very excited and announced that she remembered something from when she was a little girl. She carefully and vividly told a story about following her brothers and their friend around until they were exasperated with her. Finally they went to the barn, and she traipsed along behind them. When they got to the haymow, they wanted to get rid of her, she said, and told her in emphatic terms to leave. She acknowledged that she was a pest, but she refused to budge. Then she said, "They sure did get rid of me all right." I asked her what had happened. With a big smile she said, "They peed on me." She absolutely broke the group up, and there was no doubt that even the most confused member of the group could enjoy her special brand of humor.

COMBINING ALERT AND REGRESSED MEMBERS IN A GROUP

Carroll and Gray (1983) found in their literature search that there is no empirical evidence for or against integration, and unfortunately it is a complex issue—more than just "should we?" or "shouldn't we?" (p. 20). They offer these thought-provoking questions:

1. What resident characteristics should be considered when planning integrated groups?
2. What types of activities are appropriate for integrated groups?
3. What special skills and techniques can be used by the leader of an integrated group?
4. How can large integrated groups be used effectively (pp. 26-28).

It is difficult to answer the question "Should one mix alert and confused individuals in the group?" A rule of thumb perhaps is not to mix the very confused with the very alert. If one is conscientious about making contracts before the group meetings, one can get a sense of the more alert, and sometimes haughty, members who will have no part of such a group meeting. It would be cruel to expose the demented person to insults, ridicule, and interactions that further lower self-esteem. And old persons are very up-front about their reactions and thoughts. They often speak out in the group; and while more often than not it is helpful and therapeutic, at times it can exclude some member. Older group members do not always "draw a circle that draws him in."

It is also important not to overload the group with so many confused members that there is no helper, no one vivacious enough to add spark to the group or to carry some of the understanding.

I have observed that confused individuals form pairs; when I have studied these pairings closely, I have found that the individuals quite often are of about the same level of confusion. In one group, a person with presenile dementia (a man who had just turned 60) and a woman with senile dementia (who was in her seventies) developed a warm and close relationship in spite of the fact that both were aphasic. Their kindness and devotion to one another was touching and also was encouraged by the staff. It is fortunate that the man's wife was quite understanding and felt that if she could no longer communicate with him, it was all to the good if there was someone else who could reach him. The group leader can also encourage such interactions by seating paired members next to one another in the group so that they can draw support and comfort from one another. Often they will walk to and from the group meetings together.

While a group leader may not encourage subgrouping in other types of groups, it becomes quite important in group work with the frail and demented older adults. It may be the subgrouping that keeps members in the group and gives them the courage to attend and to be a part of the larger group.

CAUTIONS

Students and new group leaders must assess the capabilities of prospective group members so that they do not overload the group with persons who either have the same diagnosis (for example, all depressed individuals) or are grossly impaired.

I have said elsewhere regarding sensory losses that it is easier to take no more than one blind person or one hard-of-hearing person. If the entire group is in wheelchairs, the burden on the group leader will be incredibly heavy—just transporting members back and forth to the meeting place will be an arduous and time-consuming task.

Regarding Alzheimer's disease, the leader should check potential members for apraxia (inability to distinguish and correctly use objects), because such people will have difficulty participating in any of the assigned tasks or crafts, and even during refreshment time. One man had to be helped each meeting simply to get the coffee cup to his mouth; he would wave it around in the air and yet be trying so hard to follow the leader's instructions.

It seems to be easier to draw in some of the withdrawn and quiet members than it is to curb the loquacious and noisy ones, at least for the student or the new group leader. One woman, who came to the group on her walker, sat at a separate table and refused to join the group in the early meetings. The student turned, addressed her, included her, and served her coffee as though she were participating in the group. It was difficult for the beginning student to do, but it helped the woman gain enough trust to move into the group gradually.

Arrangement in group meetings should follow some of these guidelines:

- Put the most alert, helpful person next to the disabled or anxious member.
- The leaders should sit between the two weakest (either physically or psychologically) members of the group.
- A hard-of-hearing person should have someone next to him or her who is willing to explain some of the group process. The same is true of a blind person.
- Two members who are always together and seem to have a close relationship should sit next to one another.
- If there are two minority persons (and one should never take just one into the group), they should be placed next to one another in the seating. This strategy and the one above help to increase the "we-ness" of the group.
- Check crafts carefully to ensure that they are safe. (After watching a woman grab the soufflé cup that was filled with white glue and try to drink its contents, the activity director changed the type of container used to hold the glue.)
- A very quiet area with no distractions should be used for group meetings. This is crucial for the demented, who can easily be overloaded.
- Push fluids in group meetings to prevent dehydration and increased confusional states. (See Chapter 12 for an elaboration of this basic concept).
- Be careful not to pressure group members because of the potential for a catastrophic reaction.
- Be aware of your own boredom and ennui. Group leadership with the aged can be a very draining experience; if you do not build in rewards for yourself, you may burn out.[5]

[5]The following vignette occurred in one long-term care facility: A nurses' aide became uninterested in her reality orientation group. She began to be late to work, and her absenteeism increased. It turned out that she had been assigned to five RO groups daily.

- Save the refreshments until the end of the group meeting. Confused older clients enjoy food and will often stay until they receive their share.
- If the group meeting is held on a ward that houses many demented persons, it is best to close, and if fire regulations will permit, lock the doors to the meeting area; otherwise wanderers and others may disrupt the meeting—especially if they see food or drinks.
- An easy, quick assignment to assess skills and literacy is a project that requires signing one's name or reading aloud briefly. The results will give you an idea of whom you should not put on the spot.
- Men in the group may balk at drawing or at arty crafts. It is best to have an alternate project that they can do. Not all men will view the tasks as kid's stuff, but those who do will be adamant about not participating.
- Be prepared for strange things to happen to your supplies, props, food, and so on. One woman put the plum blossom stem in her coffee. Another woman stirred her coffee with an orange crayon. Still another rolled her bingo card and placed it in her bedroom slipper. Another one colored her banana with a green felt-tipped pen. When things such as this occur, check to see if you have overloaded the group with materials or instructions, a common problem for many of us.
- A variety of approaches—use of exercises, music, reminiscence strategies, crafts, food—helps keep the group more interesting for both members and leaders.
- Do not expect to conduct insight groups or groups that are geared toward psychotherapy with the very confused.
- Analyze *all* nonverbal behavior for possible meanings. (This, of course, includes your own nonverbal behavior.)

GROUP SAFETY

Home safety for the person with Alzheimer's disease is a common concern. A group leader who has members with Alzheimer's disease should also be concerned about safety and carefully assess the environment for the group meetings before launching the group. Such a careful assessment could prevent problems occurring after the group has begun. Persons with Alzheimer's experience confusion and loss of judgment; therefore, the group leader needs to be extra cautious. Providing a safe, calm, secure environment is crucial for their well-being. There are three important principles to be remembered in regard to safety (Alzheimer's Disease Research Center n.d., 7).

1. Think prevention.
2. It is more effective to change the environment than it is to attempt to change most patient behaviors.
3. By minimizing danger you can maximize independence, because the member can experience increased security and mobility.

Table 11-4 presents a list of suggestions that promote safety in meetings.

REMINISCENCE

The use of reminiscence for the cognitively impaired is touted in the literature. It is an effective therapeutic intervention because reminiscence taps into long-term memory, which many of the cognitively impaired do retain. And, because there is no emphasis on short-term memory, it is a relatively nonthreatening activity and, of course, is not an expensive intervention, which must be considered in view of the cost-cutting so apparent in the health care system.

Reminiscence is effective because it can reinforce the identity as well as testify to what was significant and lasting in the older person's life, and compensate for a dull present (Charatan 1980). The "dull present" is particularly applicable to residents of nursing homes and board-and-care homes, especially if there is not a viable activity program. For frail and disabled older persons, discussing the past can be a substitute for active experience, and it is therapeutic because it validates the members' contributions in life (Sheridan n.d.).

Pleasant reminiscence is encouraged (which is one of the differences between reminiscence and the life review modality) as a cognitive-behavioral intervention for depression symptoms in clients with Alzheimer's disease (Teri & Gallagher-Thompson 1991). Depression may occur in the very early stages of Alzheimer's disease and should be treated.

Regarding the number of persons in a group, Maletta (1988) suggests three or four members and that they be at about the same cognitive level. It is very difficult to conduct groups in which there are alert and cognitively impaired members. Such groups require skilled and sophisticated leadership.

Themes and props also may be introduced by the leader. Props are particularly effective because they stimulate a variety of senses—for example, an orange can be touched, smelled, seen, and eaten. Themes that provide music are also quite effective

TABLE 11-4 Safety suggestions

- Due to the Alzheimer's patient's change in vision, use sheer draperies or perforated shades and blinds to diffuse sunlight and reduce glare.
- Hold evening meetings in rooms with indirect lighting, which reduces shadows that can be frightening and confusing.
- Use decals on sliding glass doors or windows so that they will not be mistaken for open spaces.
- Keep noise levels down. Turn off the intercom. Close windows and doors to reduce noise.
- Keep electrical and telephone cords around the edge of the room and out of traffic paths.
- Hide electrical outlets.
- Electric fans should not be used, or should be hidden from view if they are necessary.
- Radiators and other heating devices may be very hot to the touch. Check them out.
- Do not have meetings in a room with fish tanks. The combination of glass, water, electrical pumps, and potentially poisonous aquatic life could be harmful to the curious member with Alzheimer's disease.
- Floor surfaces should be level. Group members should not have to step up to another level of a room to get to the meeting place.
- Floor surface should have no design; large dark areas can appear to an Alzheimer's patient as a hole she or he might fall into.
- Floor surface should have a dull finish, not a wet look. Persons with Alzheimer's often interpret these surfaces as being wet and will refuse to walk on them.
- Remove scatter rugs.
- Interior designs need to be simple rather than busy in nature (i.e., plain wallpapers as opposed to paisley designs or those with patterns that might be interpreted as containing snakes or other such animals).
- Rooms with large bold prints or murals may cause confusing illusions.
- Remove or cover mirrors; some members may become confused or frightened.
- Do not use folding chairs or chairs with splayed-out legs; toes often catch in these types of chairs (see Figures 11-10 and 11-11).
- Use round tables instead of square or oblong ones to prevent injury if a member loses his or her balance and falls against a sharp corner.
- Keep the furniture in the same place in the room.
- Keep all trash cans covered or out of sight.
- Clutter can create confusion. Keep the meeting room clear.
- Lock all doors that lead to steps and exits.
- Place tape across the face of any door lock so that it will not engage.
- If possible, have the meeting room close to a bathroom.
- Provide visual clues or pictures for the bathroom and meeting room.
- If you meet outside, use outdoor furniture that is stable and has no sharp edges.
- Landscaping should ensure that there are no thorny or poisonous plants or bushes within reach of the members.
- Do not put refreshments in view until you are ready to serve; some members may eat them immediately.
- Be very careful with hot tea or coffee.
- Do not bring to meetings nonedible items such as artificial fruits and vegetables (one woman mistook small soaps for candy).
- For snacks, use dishes and table mats in contrasting colors for easier identification.
- Keep all condiments out of reach.
- You may want to learn the Heimlich maneuver in case of choking.
- Do not leave sharp knives unattended.
- Do not use knives, sharp fish hooks, and the like for props for reminiscence meetings.
- If you bring materials into the meeting room in plastic bags, keep the bags out of reach.
- Do not permit the members to smoke without supervision.
- Avoid having them watch violent or disturbing television programs; they may believe the story is real.
- If you have a box for them to freely rummage through or sort before or after meetings, it may keep them occupied. For example, they may enjoy scraps of fabric or old scenic postcards. When an Alzheimer's patient is bored or does not know what to do, safety problems can occur.
- Do not leave your keys lying around—it may symbolize departure, or they may be pocketed.
- Keep the group small and do not have outsiders come into the group until the group is cohesive.
- If a member wears a hearing aid, check batteries and functioning.
- If a member wears glasses, be sure they are clean.

SOURCE: Based on Alzheimer's Disease and Related Disorder Association, *Just the facts* (1990); Health, *Senior Highlights* (1992, 21); and *Home safety for the Alzheimer's patient* (n.d.).

FIGURE 11-10 *The chair to the left is the appropriate type to use for group work with the cognitively impaired.*

in eliciting enjoyable reminiscence. Members often remember words of the songs. In summary, reminiscence groups appear to have overtaken reality orientation groups (see Chapter 13), and remotivation groups have lost their popularity in recent years (see Chapter 14).

ACTIVITIES FOR PERSONS WITH ALZHEIMER'S DISEASE

In this chapter, I have described, in detail, activities I undertook with members who had a variety of diagnoses (see Tables 11-1, 11-2, and 11-3). Persons who have Alzheimer's may really challenge the group leader because of their limited concentration, inability to follow directions, and behavioral problems. The following steps may help a new group leader to introduce activities (ADRDA, "Activities" 1990).

1. Analyze the person's past activities and hobbies and try to match the abilities.
2. Build in structure.
3. Offer support.
4. Look for familiar and favorite pastimes.
5. Be flexible.
6. Emphasize involvement—help the person feel useful.
7. Focus on enjoyment, not achievement.
8. Be realistic.
9. Consider these specific activity areas to incorporate into group meetings:
    a. Painting, drawing, singing, working with clay.
    b. Exercise in a group.
    c. Music and dancing.
    d. Albums, pictures.
    e. Reading, such as poetry.
    f. Old movies (from 1930s or 1940s).

UNIVERSAL STRENGTHS

Lucero's (1993) list of universal strengths for persons with Alzheimer's disease should help in the planning of activities:

- They retain primary motor function (strength, dexterity, and motor control), but they may need to

FIGURE 11-11
This photograph depicts the importance of sturdy chairs with legs that are not splayed—the chairs have arms, which is important, but note the legs. The footstool by the blackboard has straight legs but is too low for older adults, has no arms, and no back support. Chapter 12 notes that it is important to pay attention to the space required for the accoutrements of older adults. The walkers and wheelchairs are typical of many settings.

PHOTO: Marianne Gontarz

break activities down into simple steps and may need help starting and stopping.

- They retain primary sensory function, and they experience sensations as pleasant, noxious, and so on.
- Their sense of rhythm and movement makes dancing, sawing, sanding, folding, and rocking appropriate activities.
- They can do things that are naturally repetitive but not boring such as kneading, sanding, turning, and pulling.
- They are emotional: They still experience positive and negative feelings, and they need outlets.
- They retain a sense of humor and react to the novel, the unusual, and the unexpected.

SUMMARY

This chapter includes descriptions of three nurse-led groups of mentally impaired aged. Cautions of such group work are discussed. Group leaders of regressed aged persons must remember to supplement and/or complement the individualized nursing care plans. The quality of life of aged people, whether in an institution or a day care center, can be greatly improved by membership in a group that meets regularly with a patient, empathic leader in a familiar, somewhat structured setting.

It was observed in all three groups that behavior does change and sometimes can improve rather suddenly and dramatically when the group process—for example, the "we-ness" of the group—is maximized. The leader's sensitivity, empathy, and dedication are of paramount importance. The leader should also be skillful in nonverbal communication. Normal behavior by a leader can be emulated by group members, and they will gain in confidence and trust with a leader who treats them with warmth and respect.

The difficulties of group work with regressed older adults include behavioral problems, passivity, short attention spans, superdependency, apathy, and minimal information on each member. Long silences are common. Minuscule changes observed in group members can be discouraging for impatient leaders. The ability to discard techniques that do not work and try new ones proves to be one of the challenges of work with this type of group, since so many approaches to problems simply do not work.

EXERCISE 1

When group therapy is begun, staff members often notice a decrease in problems of managing the group members, since they are stimulated to engage in more appropriate social behavior. However, the staff has to try to maintain that gain and may become very discouraged with such continued responsibility. Staff members may feel that much effort is expended for little observable gain, or they may feel burned out—tired of the job, the residents, and so on.

Consider ways that staff morale might be maintained or even improved during such discouraging times. Then list five suggestions for taking care of one's self, both as staff collectively and as staff members individually.

EXERCISE 2

Select one of the case histories from group A and write a one-page description of how you would have handled that person if you had been the group leader.

EXERCISE 3

View one of the films or videos in the resource list and write a critique.

REFERENCES

Alzheimer's Association/Greater Houston Chapter. 1992. Quoted in *Senior Highlights* (November):21 (San Diego).

Alzheimer's Disease Research Center. n.d. *Home-safety for the Alzheimer's patient*. San Diego, CA: University of California Press.

Brody EM, Kleban MH, Lawton MP, Levy R, Woldow A. 1972. Predicators of mortality in the mentally-impaired institutionalized aged. *J Chronic Dis* 25(12): 611-620.

Brody EM, Kleban MH, Lawton MP, Silverman H. 1971. Excess disabilities of mentally impaired aged: Impact of individual treatment. Part 1. *Gerontologist* 11(2): 124-133.

Brody EM, Kleban MH, Woldow A, Freeman L. 1975. Survival and death in the mentally-impaired aged. *J Chronic Dis* 28:389-399.

Burnside IM. 1973. Touching is talking. *Am J Nurs* 73(12):2060-2063.

——— . 1978. Eulogy for Ms. Hogue. *Am J Nurs* 78(4): 624-626.

Carroll K, Gray K. 1983. How to integrate the cognitively impaired in group activities. *Clin Gerontol* 1(4):19-30.

Charatan FB. 1980. Therapeutic supports for the patient with OBS. *Geriatrics* 35(9):100-102.

Demsey P, Demsey A. 1981. *The research process in nursing*. New York: Van Nostrand Reinhold.

Feil N. 1983. Group work with disoriented nursing home residents. In S Saul (ed.), *Group work with the frail elderly* (pp. 57-65). New York: Haworth.

Jury M, Jury D. 1976. *Gramp*. New York: Grossman.

Kleban MH, Brody EM. 1972. Prediction of improvement in mentally-impaired aged: Social worker ratings of personality. *J Gerontol* 27(1):69-76.

Kleban MH, Brody EM, Lawton MP. 1971. Personality traits in the mentally-impaired aged and their relationship to improvements in current functioning. Part 1. *Gerontologist* 11(2):134-140.

Kleban MH, Lawton MP, Brody EM, Moss M. 1975. Characteristics of mentally-impaired aged profiting from individualized treatment. *J Gerontol* 30(1):90-96.

——— . 1976. Behavioral observations of mentally-impaired aged: Those who decline and those who do not. *J Gerontol* 31(3):333-339.

Kobrynski B. 1975. The mentally-impaired elderly—Whose responsibility? *Gerontologist* 15(5):407-411.

Koslow SP. 1976. New, exciting direction in psychiatry: Dance/music/art therapy. *Mademoiselle* 82(1):106ff.

Lee J. 1983. The group: A chance at human connection for the mentally impaired older person. *Soc Work with Groups* 5(2):43-56.

Lucero M. 1993. Handout distributed at the Gerontological Nursing Conference, New Orleans, LA (February 26-27).

Maletta GJ. 1988. Management of behavior problems in elderly patients with Alzheimer's disease and other dementias. *Clin Geriatr Med* 4(4):719-747.

Salter C deL, Salter CA. 1975. Effects of an individualized activity program on elderly patients. Part 1. *Gerontologist* 15(5):404-406.

Sheridan C. n.d. Failure-free activities for the Alzheimer's patient. Oakland, CA: Cottage Books.

Teri L, Gallagher-Thompson DG. 1991. Cognitive-behavioral interventions for treatment of depression in Alzheimer's patients. *Gerontologist* 31(3):413-416.

BIBLIOGRAPHY

Abramson TA, Mendis KP. 1990. The organizational logistics of running a dementia group in a skilled nursing facility. In TL Brink (ed.), *Mental health in the nursing home* (pp. 111-132). New York: Haworth.

Allen C, Earhart C, Blue T. 1992. *Occupational therapy treatment goals for the physically and cognitively disabled*. Rockville, MD: Occupational Therapy Association.

Bartol M. 1979. Nonverbal communication in patients with Alzheimer's disease. *J Gerontol Nurs* 5(4):21-31.

Burnside IM. 1979. Alzheimer's disease—An overview. *J Gerontol Nurs* 5(4):14-20.

Davis JL. 1983. Support groups: A clinical intervention for families of the mentally impaired elderly. *J Gerontol Soc Work* 5:27-35.

Fernie B, Fernie G. 1990. Organizing group programs for cognitively impaired residents of nursing homes. In TL Brink (ed.), *Mental health in the nursing home* (pp. 111-122). New York: Haworth.

Fowler RS, Fordyce W. 1972. Adapting care for the brain-damaged patient. *Am J Nurs* 72(11):2056-2059.

Haycox JA. 1980. Late care of the demented patient. *New Engl J Med* 303:165-166.

Heacock P, Walton C, Beck C, Mercer S. 1991. Caring for the cognitively impaired: Reconceptualizing disability and rehabilitation. *J Gerontol Nurs* 17(3):22-26.

Manaster A. 1972. Therapy with the senile geriatric patient. *Int J Group Psychiatr* 22(2):250-257.

Mueller DJ, Atlas L. 1972. Resocialization of regressed elderly residents: A behavioral management approach. *J Gerontol* 27(3):390-392.

Wahl P. 1976. Psychosocial implications of disorientation in the elderly. *Nurs Clin North Am* 11(1):145-155.

Weisberg J. 1983. Raising the self-esteem of mentally impaired nursing home residents. *Soc Work* 28(2):163-164.

Yalom ID, Terrazas F. 1968. Group therapy for psychotic elderly patients. *Am J Nurs* 68(8):1690-1694.

RESOURCES

Programmed Instruction Unit

Mental Status Assessment (prepared by Stephen Cohen, Step-Design, Inc., New York, NY). A course that teaches how to assess a patient's mental status, provides a checklist for performing a mental status assessment, teaches interviewing procedures, and teaches how to increase the reliability of mental status assessments in your practice. Reprints are available from *American Journal of Nursing* Company, Educational Services Division, 555 West 57th Street, New York, NY 10019 (refer to product code P-48 1981).

Alzheimer's Disease Organizations

Alzheimer's Disease and Related Disorders Association (ADRDA), 360 North Michigan Avenue, Suite 601, Chicago, IL 60601. The Alzheimer's Disease Education and Referral (ADEAR) Center provides health professionals and the general public with information about Alzheimer's disease diagnosis, treatment, resources, and research. The Center also distributes printed information and maintains the Alzheimer's disease subfile of the Combined Health Information Database (CHID)—an outline bibliographic database. CHID contains references to health information and education resources, including brochures, audiovisuals, posters, newsletters, and other materials on Alzheimer's disease. Much of the material in the database is not referenced in any other computer system or print resource. CHID searches can be requested from the ADEAR Center staff. The services of the ADEAR Center are provided free of charge. Limited quantities of the following publications are available by calling or writing the ADEAR Center: *Alzheimer's Disease: Q&A, Alzheimer's Disease Centers Program, Differential Diagnosis of Dementing Diseases, Fact Sheet: Alzheimer's Disease Database, Special Report on Alzheimer's Disease,* and *ADEAR Center Brochure.* ADEAR Center, P.O. Box 8250, Silver Spring, MD 20907-8250; phone: 301-495-3311.

Films

The first two films listed here are available from Terra Nova Films, Inc., 9848 S. Winchester Avenue, Chicago, IL 60643; phone: 312-881-8491.

Designing the Physical Environment for Persons with Dementia (20 minutes, user's manual included). This program teaches how a carefully designed physical environment can offer support and help to compensate for deficits of persons with Alzheimer's disease or related disorders. It is meant to be helpful to designers and administrators responsible for design decisions and to families caring for persons with dementia. (Produced by the Institute of Gerontology at The University of Michigan.) Slides or videotape—purchase: $110; rental: $45.

Not Alone Anymore: Caring for Someone with Alzheimer's Disease (22 minutes). Designed for families, this video presents helpful down-to-earth information on how to care for someone who has Alzheimer's disease, and how to care for one's self while in the caregiver role. (Produced by Southern Illinois University School of Medicine.) Video—purchase: $195; rental: $55.

Detecting Dementia: Cognitive Assessment by the Home Health Care Professionals (20 minutes). This video provides training for the home health care professional on dementia and cognitive assessment, including detection and referral. Jewish Hospital, St. Louis, MO.

You Must Remember This (57 minutes). Filmed in Australia, this video interweaves the experiences of people who have Alzheimer's disease and their families with professionals who care for them. Filmmakers Library, New York, NY.

Peege (16 mm, color, 28 minutes), 1976. This classic film by Peege's grandson is an excellent example of eliciting long-term memories with a cognitively impaired older person. Phoenix Films, 743 Alexander Road, Princeton, NJ 08540; phone: 800-621-0379.

Gramp: A Man Ages and Dies (black-and-white filmstrip with cassette, 30 minutes). Based on the book *Gramp* by Dan and Mark Jury. Sunburst, P.O. Box 40, Pleasantville, NY 10570.

Activity Resources for Mentally Impaired Older Adults

Alzheimer's Association. 1987. *Adapting the adult day care environment for the demented older adult.* Springfield, IL: Illinois Department on Aging. (Available by calling 800-252-8966.)

———. 1991. *Steps to selecting activities for the person with Alzheimer's disease.* Chicago, IL: Alzheimer's Association.

Brancroft JH. 1952. *Games.* New York: Macmillan.

Beisgen BA. 1989. *Life enhancing activities for mentally impaired elders.* New York: Springer.

Caplow-Lindner E, Harpaz L, Samberg S. 1979. *Therapeutic dance/movement.* New York: Human Sciences Press.

DeBolt N, Kastner ME. 1989. *I'm in here: Strategies for one-to-one activities.* Torrington, WY: Lutheran Health Systems.

Flatten K, Wilhite B, Reyes-Watson E. 1988. *Recreation activities for the elderly.* New York: Springer.

Gwinnup PB. 1985. *Fragrance projects for sensory stimulation.* Buffalo, NY: Potentials Development for Health and Aging Services, Inc.

Hellen CR. 1992. *Alzheimer's disease: Activity focused care*. Boston: Andover Medical Books. Available from Butterworth-Heinemann, 80 Montvale Avenue, Stoneham, MA 02180 for $31.50, which includes shipping and handling.

Karras B. 1985. *Down memory lane*. Wheaton, MD: Circle Press.

Lake M. 1980. *Nursing home activities for the handicapped*. Springfield, IL: Thomas.

Lucas C. 1964. *Recreation in gerontology*. Springfield, IL: Thomas.

Mace NL. 1987. Principles of activities for persons with dementia. *Phys Occup Ther Geriatr* 5(3):13-27.

Merrill T. 1967. *Activity for the aged and infirm*. Springfield, IL: Thomas.

Sheridan CA. 1987. *Failure-free activities for the Alzheimer's patient: A guidebook for caregivers*. Oakland, CA: Cottage Books.

Teri L, Logsdon RD. 1991. Identifying pleasant activities for Alzheimer's disease patients: The pleasant events schedule-AD. *Gerontologist* 31:124-127.

Zgola JM. 1987. *Doing things: A guide to programming activities for persons with Alzheimer's disease and related disorders*. Baltimore: Johns Hopkins University Press.

CHAPTER 12

Group Work with the Physically Impaired

Irene Burnside

KEY WORDS

- Arthritis
- Chronicity
- Environment
- Hearing impairment
- Heart disease
- Mobility
- Old-old
- Oldest-old
- Quality of life
- Visual impairment
- Young-old

LEARNING OBJECTIVES

- Differentiate among young-old, old-old, and oldest-old.
- Discuss the importance of leader understanding of common physical limitations in older adults.
- List four limitations that may occur in older adults and one leader intervention for each.
- List four of the top ten chronic conditions for people over 65 years of age.
- List in rank order disability conditions of the oldest-old.
- Analyze two life style characteristics of the oldest-old versus younger elderly persons.

On a clear day you can see as far as you can look.

OCTOGENARIAN IN A GROUP

Acute conditions were once a predominant pattern of illness, but now chronic conditions are the more prevalent health problems for older people. More than four out of five people aged 65 and older have at least one chronic condition, and multiple conditions are commonplace among older people, especially older women (U.S. Senate, Special Committee on Aging 1991). Chronicity is discussed in Chapter 7.

However, the prevalence of chronic conditions will have a direct effect on the group and the leadership.

The group leader who chooses to work with older adults will have members who have chronic disease, physical illness, or some limitation. This will be true regardless of the setting in which the group is conducted. If the setting is the nursing home, the limitations will be even greater, and members often have multiple diagnoses. See Chapter 7 regarding chronicity and primary, secondary, and tertiary interventions.

This chapter is about some of the common physical impairments that may occur in older adult groups. These impairments have an effect on leadership, group attendance, and the group itself. They will be discussed in that order, and the chapter concludes with information about persons 85 and older (oldest-old) as group members.

LEADERSHIP

It can be overwhelming for a new leader of older adult groups to observe the many limitations of the group members. The first step in accepting the conditions is to be aware of them. The second step is to endeavor to understand some of the various conditions and how they limit the members. The third step is to analyze the possible effects they will have on leadership. The last step is to evaluate the effectiveness of the various interventions to ascertain those that appear to help members stay in the group, because attrition (especially in the early stages of the group) can decimate a group.

Acceptance of the Conditions

It is probably not wise to accept group members if the leader is really uncomfortable handling the existing condition. For example, a leader who has a close relative with Parkinson's disease may be constantly reminded of the relative, or compare the relative's disease progression to the members'. On the other hand, if the leader understands and accepts the effects of Parkinson's, he or she may have more empathy and may better understand how to intervene successfully.

Each leader must be introspective and be aware of biases. I have known health professionals who have great difficulty caring for alcoholics, because alcoholism exists in their own family. I recall how difficult it was for me to work with an old man who had dentures; he kept moving them about and clacking them; I was not very accepting about this particular behavior.

Understanding the Condition

There are many fine medical tomes to read that will help you to better understand the various conditions you will encounter. Being familiar with the common diseases and limitations will help the leader in several ways. Such basic knowledge should help in the formation of the group; for example, if you are leading the group alone, can

you handle transportation problems for those with limited mobility? Or the leadership problems inherent with the visually or hearing impaired? What about incontinence? What about shortness of breath and the individual's ability to carry on a conversation? Or a very low level of energy? Or a person prone to falling? Or a diabetic in the group? Any of these conditions will make more demands on the leaders, and you can glean some basic information by studying the members' charts (if they are in an institution) and through discussions with staff members. In nursing homes, nurses' aides can give much first-hand information because of their close daily contact. Your own observations during assessment are of the utmost importance. I have a rule of thumb related to gut-level feelings: When in doubt, leave him or her out. Chapter 11 explains the problems I encountered when I did not follow that advice. Common conditions in older adults can be found in Table 12-1.

ANALYZE POTENTIAL EFFECTS ON LEADERSHIP

The more physical illnesses a member has, the more a leader needs to take that into account. The awareness should occur during the pregroup assessment to help the leader decide what he or she can handle in the group. If you have some basic knowledge about the disease, illness, or limitation, it can help you ascertain what you need to plan for in your group meetings. Simple interventions for group leaders can be found in Table 12-2. If you are in doubt about any of them, check with the staff members in the facility. Sometimes the older adult may be very proud and independent and refuse or resent any special attention. Or the member may love the extra attention and soak it up. Or the member may be cunning and not admit to being a diabetic so that the sweets being served are not withheld. Or the member with some memory loss may go to great lengths to cover it up. For example, one member refused to write pre- and posttests because "my arthritis is so bad," but the next day played the piano. She handled her awareness of her failing memory by using a physical complaint. Physical complaints also are common reasons for not attending groups. And sometimes the complaints are vague indeed. Making contact with the person and listening intently helps, because sometimes there is something wrong in

TABLE 12-1 The top ten chronic conditions for people aged 65 and older (1989 data)

Condition	Rate per 1000 people
Arthritis	483.0
Hypertension	380.6
Hearing impairment	286.5
Heart disease	278.9
Cataracts	156.8
Deformity/orthopedic	155.2
Chronic sinusitis	153.4
Diabetes	88.2
Visual impairment	81.9
Varicose veins	78.1

SOURCE: U.S. Senate, Special Committee on Aging (1991, 113).

the group for that member. Exploration has revealed reasons like these:

- Feelings were hurt by a group member or the leader.
- The leader did not acknowledge the member's presence (see Chapter 6 for more details about the importance of inclusion).
- The member is waiting for someone (doctor, relative, etc.) or something (pain medicine has not been given).
- The person has been a loner, and the group is reaching cohesion. Now the member, who had not complained before, has physical ailments to prevent attendance.

There may be other reasons, of course. But the important point is that a physical complaint is safe, easy, and rarely questioned.

When a group is truly cohesive, it is another story. Members come with colds, fevers, and their aches and pains. Why? Simply because the group has great meaning for them. As one 86-year-old woman in a nursing home group said, "I'm just afraid I'll miss out on the gossip if I don't come." While enjoying gossip was not one of the leader's objectives, it was the group's. They either came a bit early or stayed a bit later for the juiciest gossip of the day, night, or week.

The primary functions of cohesiveness, according to Beeber and Schmitt (1986), are to support other important processes occurring in the group that will enhance members' self-esteem

through validation and affirmation. Perhaps the need for that validation and affirmation is the reason members do attend.

THE ENVIRONMENT

In Chapter 11, we offered suggestions for creating the safest possible environment. Many of those suggestions are applicable for the physically impaired, because "the environment can provide dysfunction. At the simplest level, it may produce hazards that lead to falls. At a more subtle level, it may require a level of effort that provides decompensation" (Kane, Ouslander & Abrass 1984, 12). The example is given of an older person who is short of breath and can manage in a ground-floor apartment, but not on the second floor.

The leader should assess the room in which meetings will be held and select the best possible room. Factors to consider are furniture, light, noise, accessibility—steps to climb, and temperature, to list a few.

The hearing and visually impaired must be considered, because the environment may well determine how well they can function in the group. See Table 12-2 for some of the possible strategies to consider.

Sensory losses of group members must be assessed prior to the group formation in order to plan the strategies. "Sensory deprivation requires an emphasis by the leader on stimulation well above visual and auditory threshold levels" (Lago & Hoffman 1977-78, 315).

LENGTH OF MEETINGS

It might be wise to plan shorter meetings with a group whose members have severe physical impairments; "because of the limited attention span, poor circulation, and other health considerations, sessions should be concise and short, at least initially" (Lago & Hoffman 1977–78, 315). The meetings can be increased in length gradually as the members are able to tolerate them both physically and psychologically. The best sign that the group is filling a need occurs when members begin to linger and stay to talk either with the leader or with other members.

TABLE 12-2 Interventions to consider with common conditions

Condition	May cause	Intervention
Arthritis	Pain	• Can member take pain medicine prior to group meeting? Discuss with member best solution for getting to and from group. You may need help transporting members.
	Immobility	• Do not hurry them.
Dizziness	Fall	• Prevent fall by having member rise slowly; assist if he or she appears unstable.
		• Use assistive device, if member has one.
		• Use rails or furniture to help with balance. (Be sure that furniture is safe to hold on to. Folding chairs are treacherous.)
		• Do not hurry members.
Hearing impairment	Communication problems, suspiciousness, isolation	• Speak at a slow rate.
		• Keep your voice at about the same volume throughout.
		• Do not drop your voice at the end of each sentence.
		• Always speak as clearly and accurately as possible.
		• Articulate consonants with special care.
		• Do not mumble.
		• Pronounce every name with care.
		• Change to a new subject at a slower rate, making sure that the person follows the change to the new subject. A key word or two at the beginning of a new topic is a good indicator.
		• Do not cover your mouth with your hand.
		• Do not speak too rapidly.
		• Address the listener directly. Do not turn your head away. Keep good eye contact.
		• Do not get irritated if you have to repeat. Try not to repeat the same word; if they do not understand, try a new word.
		• Touch them when talking to them.
		• Have good light on your face.
		• Women: Wear bright red lipstick to help them read your lips.
		• Men: Keep mustache trimmed to help them read your lips.
		• Describe what's happening in the group.
		• If a member wears a hearing aid, check that batteries are working.
		• Do not speak while standing behind group members.
Glaucoma, cataracts and visual impairments	Insecurity about environment, discomfort with glasses, night blindness; observers may believe the visually impaired person is confused	• Reduce glare. Do not hold meetings outside in bright sunlight.
		• Do not use glossy papers for group activities.
		• Be sure there is adequate but diffused lighting. Pull draperies or blinds over bright windows.
		• Do not schedule group meetings after dark.
		• Stairways must be well lit. Steps should be color coded at edges.
		• If a member wears glasses, be sure they are clean.
		• Encourage use of magnifying glasses.
		• Describe what is happening in the group.
		• Use large-print newspapers, books, magazines.
Deformity, orthopedic problems	Self-consciousness Transportation problems, use of accoutrements (canes, wheelchairs, etc.)	• Play down the deformity or problem. Offer assistance before actually doing anything.
		• Try to have transportation difficulties handled before group begins.
	Pain	• Request that members take medicine immediately before group.
	Unsteady gait	• Offer help as needed.
	Instability	• Offer help as needed; move slowly and do not rush them.
Hypertension and heart disease	Fatigue	• Do not call on members to perform if they are complaining of fatigue.
	Dizziness	• See above.
	Edema of feet	• Elevate feet on pillow or chair.
	Drug reactions (if on drugs)	• If a member seems different (begins to fall asleep, is very dizzy, etc.), report this to staff member.
		• A member may be on a low-cholesterol or no-salt diet; check if refreshments are served.
	Hypotension	• Change position slowly.
		• Avoid prolonged standing.

Continued

TABLE 12-2 *Continued*

	Hypotension	• Do not have meeting right after meals (postprandial hypotension occurs then). • Have a safe environment, good lighting, grab rails, no clutter on floor.
Diabetes	Member to be on special diet Diabetic retinopathy	• If serving refreshments, check with staff about what members may have. Do not plan food that would not be on special diets. • See intervention for visually impaired.
Parkinson's disease	Tremor Drooling Difficult speech Instability	• Table will help hide trembling hands. • Do not fill cups or glasses full. • Have tissues available to member. • Other members may understand better than leader; learn from them. • Offer help as needed.
Chronic obstructive pulmonary disease (COPD)	Shortness of breath, fatigue	• Do not expect member to speak a great deal in group. • Try to include member by asking questions that can be answered briefly in lieu of "Tell me about . . ." • Allow ample time to get to meeting room. • Suggest resting before group meetings. • Do not hurry the individual. • Ask if he or she needs help getting to and from meetings.

ACCOUTREMENTS OF AGING

Glasses and hearing aids are common accoutrements of aging. However, the group leader must anticipate that there will be crutches, walkers, canes, and wheelchairs as well. These items can be hazardous at times, and caution is advised. The latter will be discussed separately, because glasses and hearing problems are covered in Table 12-2.

Crutches are difficult to set in place. If they fall down, someone can trip over them. It is preferable to find a window sill or a table on which they can be placed. But remember, if they are placed too far from the user, he or she cannot ambulate until someone fetches them.

Likewise, wooden canes can fall down from a propped position. Because a cane can roll if stepped on, it can be extremely hazardous, as can be the user. I recall a belligerent old man who used his cane almost as a weapon. Once he grabbed an attendant around the neck when the attendant did something he did not like. I was supervigilant with him in group meetings after I learned this and made sure his cane was in a safe place during meetings.

The metal three-pronged type of cane remains upright. It is usually readily seen, and the individual keeps it close at hand.

Walkers on rollers are cumbersome. Like wheelchairs, they take up a great deal of space, especially when older adults want them kept close.

Wheelchairs require lots of space. If the person gets out of his or her wheelchair, be sure that the foot rests are up and out of the way and that the brakes are on when he or she is getting into or out of it. If you have a group of members all of whom are in wheelchairs, be sure you have adequate space in the meeting room to accommodate them.

All of these devices should be labeled with the person's name. If some are not, request help from agency staff to avoid confusion in the future. A real brouhaha can result when one person has another's belongings.

There also might be someone with a hook for a missing hand or an artificial limb. If she or he has had the prosthesis for a long time, she or he usually has adapted well. If it is fairly new, he or she may be self-conscious about it. The first inclination is to jump in and help the member, but it is better to wait and see how he or she manages. If it seems to be a struggle, ask gently if she or he wants some help. Always ask before you touch or do anything.

Keep in mind that your behavior is always being observed by group members. Your respect for efforts at independence will not be unnoticed. This is particularly important in the nursing home, where too much is done for them and "excessive disability" happens (Brody et al. 1971).

IMPACT OF DISEASE AND ILLNESS

The impact of disease and illnesses on the group leader's interventions has been noted in the suggested interventions in Table 12-2. However, there are two more effects of physical ailments: one on the group as a whole and one on members. The matter of group attendance was discussed earlier; sometimes physical complaints are given as a reason not to attend meetings. However, physical problems present an even bigger, more difficult problem for a group leader. The member has a doctor's appointment at the time the group is scheduled. Or an X-ray appointment. Or a dental appointment. Or a group member may be the caregiver for a parent. I recall having an 83-year-old in a group who went to the nursing home daily to feed the noon meal to her 103-year-old mother! It was necessary for her to rest a bit before she came to the group meeting. So physical problems in the member can play havoc with attendance.

The special needs necessitate special care— "for example, scheduling groups during times when members are most alert, providing a comfortable physical environment with adequate access to bathroom and other facilities and being sensitive to the sensory deficits or other physical limitations of members" (Capuzzi, Gross & Friel 1990, 47).

THE OLDEST-OLD

Bould, Sanborn, and Reif (1989) differentiate among the various age groups of older people instead of lumping them all together. *Oldest-old* refers to those who are 85 and older; *old-old* means those who are 75 and older; and *young-old* are those 65 to 74. The oldest-old who have aged successfully are not independent; rather, the characteristics of their life style are interdependence, reciprocity, and helping networks. The interdependence allows activity and contact with friends, which have been long considered important to successful aging. These latter are strong reasons for implementing groups with this age group.

"The health of the oldest old is the central concern underlying all other issues" (Bould, Sanborn & Reif 1989, 51), and that is why group leaders of that age group must be sensitive to their health issues. See Table 12-3 for the health problems in those 85 and older.

Those aged 85 and older have a rapid increase in functional disability as a result of chronic health conditions. The average nursing home resident is an 80-year-old white widow with several chronic conditions. Older women are twice as likely as older

TABLE 12-3 The most common chronic disabling conditions of the oldest-old

Condition	Common types
Bone and joint problems	• Osteoarthritis or degenerative joint disease. Osteoarthritis may be a key factor in falls. • Osteoporosis, thinning of bones. It causes pain and restricts mobility. Fractures can occur.
Cardiovascular disease	• Heart disease • Stroke • Arteriosclerosis (hardening of the arteries)
Vision problems	• Cataracts • Glaucoma • Macular degeneration
Cognitive impairment	• Dementia—Alzheimer's type • Secondary dementia
Depression and mental illness	• Reactive depression • Paranoia
High risk for disability	• Drug intoxication • Falls • Urinary incontinence

SOURCE: Based on Bould, Sanborn & Reif, 1989.

men to reside in a nursing home (U.S. Senate, Special Committee on Aging 1991). Therefore, a group leader in a nursing home should expect frailty, the oldest-old, and a group likely to be composed of all women. Table 12-4 should help the group leader better understand health in the oldest-old.

Quality of Life

The leader should be prepared to accept gifts, no matter how small, from the oldest-old. The ability to give gifts is important to the oldest-old. "Elderly people have a need to be needed; they will give as much to you—or more—than you give to them. Little gifts brought to you should be graciously accepted" (Huelskoetter, Murray & Zentner 1985, 231). This is important for a group leader to understand. A member of a nursing home group saved a banana from his breakfast tray to give me. Receive gifts graciously and quietly, because you do not want other group members to feel they should give you a gift also. Of course, there may be a policy in

TABLE 12-4 Health and the oldest-old

- Both acute and chronic diseases often go untreated in the very old, because they do not report symptoms to health providers.
- Common diseases of the oldest-old may have nonspecific symptoms, such as urinary incontinence, dizziness, acute confusion, refusal to eat or drink, weight loss, and failure to thrive (Besdine 1985, Table 22-5).
- The oldest-old are likely to have more than one chronic condition (Bould, Sanborn & Reif 1989).
- Most common disability conditions: bone and joint problems, osteoarthritis, degenerative joint diseases; osteoporosis; cardiovascular disease; vision problems; cognitive impairment.
- Other chronic disorders: depression and mental illness, drug intoxication, falls, urinary incontinence.
- Less disability for oldest-old: cancer, diabetes, and emphysema.
- The most likely causes of intractable disability are arthritis and Alzheimer's disease.
- Life styles are not characterized by independence, but rather by interdependence, reciprocity, and helping networks.
- The number of people 85 and older will reach 5.16 million by the year 2000.
- "An 85-year-old is two-and-one-half times more likely to enter a nursing home than a 75-year-old" (Cohen, Tell & Wallack 1986, 790).
- For the oldest-old, limited resources in one area will often mean limited resources in other areas as well.
- Among the oldest-old, women greatly outnumber men in institutions; the ratio is 4 to 1 (Sirrocco 1985).
- Over half of those 85 and older report limitations in walking.
- Of those aged 85 and older, 54 percent need the help of another person in order to handle daily living.

the agency about gifts, and you should know the position.

The classic article on group work with the oldest-old is Shere's (1964). Her two major goals were to "revitalize social drives" and "to induce group formation and resocialization among the hospital residents" (p. 140).

Kuhn (1987) described nursing home residents with multiple illnesses and suggested that residents "could experience better quality of life if there were an on-going therapeutic group..." (p. 27).

SUMMARY

This chapter provides the leader with some perspectives about group leadership with physically impaired older adults. Consideration of the physical difficulties of members will help the leader to implement a holistic approach to the leadership. Because there are common physical limitations and chronic diseases in older adults, suggestions for interventions are presented. The importance of preparing the environment, length of meetings, and accoutrements of aging are discussed. A discussion about health in the oldest-old is offered to help group leaders in the nursing home setting. The chapter ends with a brief discussion on quality of life.

EXERCISE 1

Interview a 65-year-old regarding health problems; then interview a 90- or 95-year-old using the same interview questions. What differences did you note?

EXERCISE 2

Mobility is a problem for older adults, especially the oldest-old. Write a list of strategies a group leader might devise to help get these persons to group meetings.

EXERCISE 3

Assess a room used for group meetings with older adults (church, nursing home, day care center, senior center, etc.). List all the potential hazards or problems for older people that you observe.

EXERCISE 4

Interview a group leader who is conducting groups with older adults. Ask what physical problems or disabilities the leader has observed in the group. What difficulties did they create for the group leader?

EXERCISE 5

You have selected members for your group. What physical limitations have you assessed? You plan to serve coffee, tea, and snacks to the group. What precautions will you take that are directly related to the limitations in the group?

REFERENCES

Beeber LS, Schmitt MH. 1986. Cohesiveness in groups: A concept in search of a definition. *Adv Nurs Sci* 8(2):1-11.

Bould S, Sanborn B, Reif L. 1989. *Eighty-five plus: The oldest old*. Belmont, CA: Wadsworth.

Brody EM, Kleban MH, Lawton MP, Silverman HA. 1971. Excess disabilities of mentally impaired aged: Impact of individualized treatment. Part 1. *Gerontologist* 11:124-133.

Capuzzi D, Gross D, Friel SE. 1990. Group work with elders. *Generations* (American Society on Aging) Winter:43-48.

Huelskoetter M, Murray R, Zentner J. 1985. Group work in nursing. In R Murray, J Zentner (eds.), *Nursing concepts for health promotion*, 3d ed. (pp. 202-235). Englewood Cliffs, NJ: Prentice-Hall.

Kane RL, Ouslander JG, Abrass IB. 1984. *Essentials of clinical geriatrics*. New York: McGraw-Hill.

Kuhn JK. 1987. Group work with the elderly: An effective intervention. *Nurs Homes* 36(4):27-28.

Lago D, Hoffman S. 1977-78. Structured group interaction: An intervention strategy for the continued development of elderly populations. *Int J Aging Hum Dev* 8(4): 311-324.

Shere ES. 1964. Group therapy with the very old. In R Kastenbaum (ed.), *New thoughts on old age* (pp. 139-160). New York: Springer.

Sirrocco A. 1985. An overview of the 1982 National Master Facility Inventory of Nursing and Related Care Homes. *Advance data*. National Center for Health Statistics (September 20).

U.S. Senate, Special Committee on Aging. 1991. *Aging America: Trends and projections*. Washington, DC: U.S. Government Printing Office.

BIBLIOGRAPHY

Abrams WB, Berkow R. 1990. *The Merck manual of geriatrics*. Rahway, NJ: Merck & Company.

Eliopoulos C. 1990. *Caring for the elderly in diverse care settings*. Philadelphia: Lippincott.

Hogstel MO. 1981. *Nursing care of the older adult*. New York: Wiley.

Miller CA. 1990. *Nursing care of older adults: Theory and practice*. Glenview, IL: Scott, Foresman/Little, Brown Higher Education.

Poggi RG, Berland DI. 1985. The therapists' reaction to the elderly. *Gerontologist* 25(5):508-513.

RESOURCES

General

AARP Books/Scott, Foresman, 1865 Miner Street, Des Plaines, IL 60018; phone: 800-238-2300—*Osteoporosis: The silent thief.*

American Heart Association, National Center, 7320 Greenville Avenue, Dallas, TX 75231; phone: 214-750-5397.

Arthritis Foundation, Box 19000, Atlanta, GA 30326; phone: 404-266-0795—*Understanding arthritis: The arthritis helpbook.*

National Arthritis and Musculoskeletal and Skin Diseases Information Clearinghouse, Box AMS, Bethesda, MD 20892; phone: 301-468-3235—*Osteoporosis: Cause, treatment, prevention,* Pub. No. 86-2226.

National Heart, Lung, and Blood Institute, National High Blood Pressure Education Program, U.S. Department of Health and Human Services, National Institutes of Health, Building 31, Bethesda, MD 20892; phone: 301-496-4236.

Visual Impairment

American Foundation for the Blind, 15 West 16th Street, New York, NY 10011; phone: 212-620-2000—A nonprofit organization that provides information and sells aids and appliances; a catalog of products is available.

American Bank Stationery, 7501 Pulaski Highway, Baltimore, MD 21237; phone: 301-866-1900. Produces checks in large print and Braille.

American Humane Society, P.O. Box 1266, Denver, CO 80201. Trains seeing eye dogs.

Bible Alliance, P.O. Box 1549, Bradenton, FL 33506; phone: 813-748-3031. Provides cassettes of Bible messages or the Bible free of charge; certification of need from physician or vision professional is required.

The Lighthouse, New York Association for the Blind, 111 East 59th Street, New York, NY 10022; phone: 212-355-2200. Provides information and some products.

Hearing Impairment

Alexander Graham Bell Association for the Deaf, 1537 35th Street, NW, Washington, DC 20007.

National Association of the Deaf, 814 Thayer Avenue, Silver Spring, MD 20910. Distributes information.

National Association of Hearing and Speech Agencies, 919 18th Street, NW, Washington, DC 20006: Distributes information.

The National Hearing Aid Society, 20361 Middlebelt Road, Livonia, MI 48152; phone: 313-478-2610. Distributes information.

CHAPTER 13

Reality Orientation Groups

Elizabeth M. Williams

KEY WORDS

- Confusion
- Reality orientation
- Reality testing
- Reality therapy

LEARNING OBJECTIVES

- Define confusion in the aged.
- Outline the historical development of reality orientation as a modality.
- Distinguish among reality orientation, reality therapy, and reality testing.
- Compare and contrast positive and negative findings of reality orientation research.
- Identify the major flaws in reality orientation research.
- Describe at least three factors that are important to keep in mind with reality orientation.
- State for whom reality orientation should be implemented and why.
- Plan how reality orientation can be incorporated into an existing therapeutic program.

Reality orientation (RO) has been credited as the first psychiatric technique to bring older confused people back to reality (Schwenk 1979). This chapter will explore the historical development of and research findings on RO and show how RO is used in a geropsychiatric day care center.

The reality orientation process is thought to help alleviate or in some cases stop memory deterioration through continual stimulation and repetitive orienting activities in one-to-one contacts or in groups (Letcher, Peterson & Scarbrough 1974). The concept is viewed as preventive, remedial, or both (Taulbee 1978). RO has been suggested for older adults who experience *confusion,* defined as disorientation to person, time, place, or thing

(Taulbee 1986), in any number of care settings: acute care hospitals, convalescent homes, day care centers, foster care homes, nursing homes, psychiatric day care centers, psychiatric hospitals, senior centers, and even in their homes (Brockett 1981; Burnside 1970; Colthart 1974; McDonald et al. 1971; Mulcahy & Rosa 1981; Taulbee 1978).

DEFINITIONS

Reality orientation, reality therapy, and *reality testing* are three terms that are often used interchangeably. Sometimes these terms confuse the beginning student, who mistakenly thinks that all three are the same process. *Reality therapy* is a specific treatment modality developed by a psychiatrist, Glasser (1965). It is a confrontive therapy designed to assist individuals in assuming responsibility for themselves and in facing up to the reality of their life situations (Silverstone 1976). Glasser worked with juvenile delinquents in the early part of his career as he firmed up the concepts for reality therapy.

Reality testing is done by all disciplines and is a necessary part of working with demented or delirious individuals in any setting. Reality testing is the process of giving information about the environment, events, or one's perception of a situation, which may differ from that of the confused person. Confused persons may misidentify people or objects. Some of this misidentification may be related to sensory losses. The caregiver should provide steady reality testing to alleviate the skewing of reality, the environment, and events (Burnside 1978). As an example, a caregiver working with a person who is hallucinating would say to the person, "I know you hear voices, but I do not hear them."

Reality orientation is a specific treatment modality that usually occurs in a group setting but is also done on a one-to-one basis.

HISTORY OF REALITY ORIENTATION

The development of RO occurred as a three-step process. In 1959, while at the Topeka, Kansas, Veterans Administration Hospital, Dr. James Folsom developed a pilot project to rehabilitate elderly geropsychiatric patients. Nursing assistants, who gave total care, were encouraged to initiate activities for the patients and to assist the patients in becoming more responsible for their own care. The approach succeeded. The patients were able to assume some of their care, began conversing with one another, and took part in different activities on and off the nursing unit. The new approach also influenced the staff's attitude; staff members were more interested in their patients as individuals and more enthusiastic about their jobs (Folsom 1968).

The initial guidelines for RO grew out of an attitude therapy program implemented by Folsom while he was at the Mental Health Institute in Mt. Pleasant, Iowa. According to Folsom, the expectation of participation in one's recovery was communicated to the new patient on admission to the pilot research unit. The specific guidelines developed by Folsom (1968) for the staff were:

(1) a calm environment; (2) a set routine; (3) clear responses to patient's questions, and the same types of questions should be asked of the patient; (4) talk clearly to the patient, not necessarily loud; (5) direct patients around by clear directions, if need be guide them to and from their destinations; (6) remind them of the date, time, etc.; (7) don't let them stay confused by allowing them to ramble in their speech, actions, etc.; (8) be firm, if necessary; (9) be sincere; (10) make requests of patient in a calm manner, implying patient will comply; and (11) be consistent (p. 299).

Patients were awakened by caregivers calling their names; the persons awakening them would introduce themselves. Calendars were given to patients who had difficulty with time orientation, and they were assisted in marking off the day. Folsom states that after one year, 57 percent of the patients returned to their prehospital adjustment, and some were able to leave the hospital.

The final stage of RO development occurred in 1965 at Tuscaloosa, Alabama, Veterans Administration Hospital; the program designed at Tuscaloosa by Folsom and Lucille Taulbee is the model for all RO programs used today. By that time, the process had been identified as consisting of three parts: basic classroom instruction, advanced classroom instruction, and 24-hour follow-through (Folsom 1968; Taulbee & Folsom 1966).

The basic class met twice daily for half an hour, and the advanced class met once a day five days a week. The class was held at the same time daily, and as much as possible the same personnel participated to give consistency. A specific attitude—active, passive, or matter of fact—was employed consistently with each patient. The use of an RO board with the name of the facility; month, day, and year; and other pertinent information was part of the basic class. Simple activities and games were part of the advanced class. The process started in the classroom was carried over through the 24-hour period following the class by all personnel coming into contact with the confused person. Folsom (1968) states that 24-hour orientation used in conjunction with the structured classroom experience improved the orientation of the majority of the patients.

Robert A. Mitchell, nursing assistant at the Tuscaloosa Veterans Hospital, made the following comment about RO: "Keep in mind that it may not be the actual activity or project that the patient is doing, but more likely the social interaction with others that helps him return to reality as his self-confidence and dignity are restored" (Folsom 1968, 302). Lee (1976) and Taulbee (1976) stress a similar point. Folsom's premise is that if you "behave as though you expect him [the patient] to participate in his own recovery . . . and that he will be able to get his life back into shape again . . .," RO will work (Freese 1978, 152).

REVIEW OF THE LITERATURE

Literature reviews of reality orientation by Schwenk (1979), Powell-Procter and Miller (1982), Burton (1982), and Gropper-Katz (1987) note that most of the research on RO lacks scientific validity because few of the studies were conducted under experimental conditions. Schwenk states that more than half of the studies fail to spell out the study participants' degree and source of confusion and the length of time participants were confused. The research did not control the age groups studied; that is, not all subjects were over 60, and the young-old (60–70) were studied along with the old-old (over 85). Ratings by caregivers were noted to lack validity because of the increased attention given by staff to disoriented older adults in an RO project (Harris & Ivory 1976). Length of time studied is another factor that lacks reliability—RO was studied for many different time spans.

Powell-Procter and Miller (1982) criticized inadequate sample size, questioned the significance of measurement tools for orientation, and noted the inability of research to validate that reality orientation was the cause of effects observed. Burton (1982) determined that research lacked uniformity in identifiable patient target groups and data-collection tools utilized and that there is a paucity of research on 24-hour orientation. Gropper-Katz's (1987) review of five studies noted that most:

- Were descriptive;
- Lacked or had poorly defined theoretical frameworks;
- Focused on reality orientation, not on defining or categorizing confusion;
- Lacked definitive target population identification;

- Did not guard patient rights.
- Had data-collection tools that were not specific for reversible or irreversible confusion;
- Lacked documented modes of therapy that would be best for either form of confusion; and that
- Research into transcultural and staff effect on reality orientation was nil.

A total of 30 research studies on RO were located in the literature. Of that number, 10 demonstrate inconclusive or negative effects of RO therapy (Akerlund & Norberg 1986; Barnes 1974; Hogstel 1979; Johnson 1980; MacDonald & Settin 1978; Parker & Somers 1983; Voelkel 1978; Winkler, as reported by Whitehead 1978; Zepelin & Wade 1975; Zepelin, Wolfe & Kleinplatz 1981). The remaining studies conclude that RO is effective (Bailey, Browne, Gable & Holden 1986; Brook, Degun & Mather 1975; Browne & Ritter 1972; Citrin & Dixon 1977; Folsom 1968; Hanley, McGuire & Boyd 1981; Harris & Ivory 1976; Lehman 1974; Letcher, Peterson & Scarbrough 1974; Merchant & Saxby 1981; Mulcahy & Rosa 1981; Nodhurft & Sweeney 1982; Salter & Salter 1975; Seaman & Roth 1989; Settle 1975; Stephens 1969; Taulbee & Folsom 1966; Trotter 1972).

All of the studies that are inconclusive or that demonstrate RO to be ineffective were controlled experimental studies (Schwenk 1979); only one of them had control validity problems (Winkler, as reported by Whitehead 1978). Eleven of the studies indicating RO to be an effective method were controlled experimental studies; six of these studies had severe methodological problems (Browne & Ritter 1972; Letcher, Peterson & Scarbrough 1974; Mulcahy & Rosa 1981; Nodhurft & Sweeney 1982; Salter & Salter 1975; Seaman & Roth 1989); the remaining studies that indicate RO to be effective are anecdotal in nature.

Barnes's (1974), Zepelin and Wade's (1975), and Hogstel's (1979) experimental data indicate no significant statistical changes in orientation for the experimental groups. Barnes notes small changes in the behavior of the experimental participants, but these changes were not tested for in the study. The anecdotal notes indicate that the participants were more cooperative and more interested in their surroundings. Voelkel (1978) notes that those in the experimental group who were moderately confused seemed to improve most in orientation and behavior, even though the statistical data did not bear this out.

Zepelin, Wolfe, and Kleinplatz (1981) demonstrated that after a one-year program of 24-hour RO and supplemental therapy, the experimental study participants exhibited an increase in belligerent behavior and a decrease in social responsiveness. The authors write that the experimental group had slightly higher mental status scores initially (although the difference was not significant) but that these scores decreased during the final six months of the study.

MacDonald and Settin (1978), Voelkel (1978), Johnson (1980), and Winkler (as reported by Whitehead 1978) compared and contrasted an RO class with a sheltered workshop, a resocialization group, an activity program, and an operant approach, respectively. Those participants in treatment modalities other than an RO class improved more in sociability and alertness than those in an RO class only.

MacDonald and Settin (1978) indicate that performing a meaningful task in a sheltered workshop program is more beneficial for life satisfaction than RO. The one very large drawback to the validity of this study's findings and application in regard to the aged is that the age range of the study participants was 34 through 74. Also, there are questions as to the level of confusion of the study participants (Schwenk 1979).

Participants in Voelkel's (1978) and MacDonald and Settin's (1978) RO groups expressed negative feelings about reading the RO board and about the value of the class itself. Sessions were called "boring."

The main failure of Winkler's (as reported by Whitehead 1978) study is that RO classroom participants received only three hours a week of reinforcement, while those participants in the operant conditioning group received constant 24-hour positive reinforcement from the staff.

Parker and Somers (1983) reported inconclusive results as to the utilization of 24-hour reality orientation techniques on a geropsychiatric ward. Participants were tested for pre- and postward environmental changes and implementation of 24-hour orientation. The inconclusive findings may be due to the short time element between pre- and post-data collection, which was two weeks. A program needs to be in place for several months to effect any significant changes.

The studies that demonstrate RO therapy to be positive note less confusion and disorientation;

more interest in surroundings; a decrease in resistive, combative, striking-out behavior; more pride in self-care; and an increase in socialization of the study participants (Browne & Ritter 1972; Folsom 1968; Mulcahy & Rosa 1981; Salter & Salter 1975; Taulbee & Folsom 1966).

Browne and Ritter (1972) demonstrated that an RO classroom with 24-hour follow-up assisted nine older chronic schizophrenic men to improve in behavior, orientation, and activities of daily living. Mulcahy and Rosa (1981) wrote a care plan for confusion and took the RO board to the bedside in an acute care hospital to use with older confused patients. The sample was very small, five, but the authors were positive about the progress noted in two patients they were able to study for three weeks. One patient became more interested in feeding himself, and the other showed more interest in self-care.

Letcher, Peterson, and Scarbrough (1974) state that the more self-sufficient the individual is at the onset of RO therapy, the more likely improvement is to occur. The researchers suggest that RO should be instituted at the first sign of confusion, especially after a stroke, surgery, or personal losses that affect the stress response. They advocate RO techniques as a preventive measure to assist the individual in adapting to a new institution or situation.

Salter and Salter (1975) found that a total rehabilitative program consisting of an RO class, 24-hour RO, retraining in activities-of-daily-living skills, and recreational activities were very effective in decreasing confusion and disorientation. A study by Loew and Silverstone (1971) found similar improvement in persons over 80 years of age in a nursing home when the staff was sensitized to the kinds of psychological and social needs the aged have. The program consisted of changes in the environment to provide cues to assist in orientation (for example, color-coded doors) and activities such as music therapy, a sheltered workshop program, religious services, and a volunteer visiting program. Reality orientation per se is not mentioned in the study—but the study is worth noting because the technique incorporates RO concepts.

Hogstel (1979) and Salter and Salter (1977) report that if RO is discontinued or not used consistently, the participants will slip back into a confused state and become more regressed. Salter and Salter (1977) indicate that the process can be reversed if RO is reinstated. Salter and Salter suggest that patients receive individual and group therapy in a day care program after discharge.

Erickson et al. (1978) describe a two-and-a-half-year-old RO program on the Rehabilitation Medicine Service of the Seattle Veterans Administration Hospital. Weekly records kept on 127 patients revealed that 75 percent did not show changes in level of orientation during hospitalization. Seventeen percent showed improvement in terms of confusion and disorientation. Two patients declined, four vacillated from one level to another, and four died. Three of the four who died showed a decline in mental status before their deaths.

Hanley, McGuire, and Boyd's (1981) experimental trials of two reality orientation approaches with persons with dementia from a psychogeriatric hospital ward and a residential home indicated positive results on cognition and behavior. Two approaches for the research were used: a reality orientation class and an individual-to-individual direct orientation training about the spatial layout of the environment. Staff were specifically trained for the reality orientation class. Results indicated that verbal orientation scores improved, especially for the persons in the residential home. The degree of dementia did not emerge as a significant variable. The unit training brought about change in ward orientation and behavior, but not in verbal orientation. The cost factor of a reality orientation class versus 24-hour orientation was higher, but researchers determined that the class should be retained because of the positive impact on participants.

Nodhurft and Sweeney's (1982) controlled experimental study reports significant positive results. There was no increase in participation in activities of daily living, but more interest was felt to be evident. A 1987 study by Baines, Saxby, and Ehlert indicated after an eight-week study of confused older adults that those who received reality orientation showed greater improvement than those who did not (Jenkinson 1992).

Bailey, Browne, Gable, and Holden (1986) conducted an experimental study of a 24-hour reality orientation program on a long-stay geriatric ward. The study is unique in that it was a multidisciplinary endeavor. Even though the statistical results were not significant for cognitive and behavioral changes, it is important that the test patients did not deteriorate during the study period, but showed improvement in communication skills. The results are not statistically significant, but hint that reality orientation may be important in maintaining a person with dementia at a particular level of functioning, and that return to previous vitality is probably unrealistic.

Seaman and Roth (1989) describe a two-pronged controlled study at a long-term psychiatric institution. Staff received extensive training and clinical supervision during the study period. The program consisted of two groups: lower (modified reality orientation–remotivation group) and upper (socialization group). Results of testing indicated an improvement in the patients' social competence, personal neatness, irritability, and psychosis. There was no statistical evidence of orientation improvement, even though anecdotal notes of staff reported that residents were more aware of their surroundings and responded more appropriately. Members of each group were able to be placed in higher functioning programs.

Akerlund and Norberg (1986) describe a change from a reality orientation class setting to a psychodynamic group process. The study is mentioned because the mental health nurse who conducted the group expressed burnout and boredom and questioned the effectiveness of the group. The participants appeared bored, and they were unable to learn and carry learning over to the ward. Staff felt that patients had a sense of failure with their inability to learn. A psychodynamic group was initiated in which members were encouraged to introduce topics of interest. It was observed that the participants became more active in conversing with each other and functioned at higher cognitive and emotional levels. The study points out the need to reevaluate daily classroom orientation after a period of time to determine the effectiveness of reality orientation classes; it also underscores the inability of participants to continue in a program above their cognitive level.

IMPACT ON STAFF ATTITUDES

Holden (1979), a clinical psychologist in the United Kingdom, describes three groups of individuals: The people in Group 1 were the most deteriorated; those in Group 2 were confused and withdrawn; those in Group 3 were mildly confused. Group 1 had a ratio of three clients to one therapist and was conducted in the traditional reality orientation format. Group 2 was apparently more of a reminiscence group. Group 3 combined cooking sessions, reminiscence therapy, theater and drama therapy, and so forth, with the therapists acting as "guides, encouraging, assisting and advising." Holden does not state what therapeutic results were obtained in the three groups.

Four articles specifically discuss the positive results RO technique has on the attitude of staff toward confused older adults (Hanley, McGuire & Boyd 1981; Reorientation stimulates . . . 1975; Seaman & Roth 1989; Smith & Barker 1972). The change in staff attitude is attributed to the positive changes noted in the patients' behavior or orientation. Citrin and Dixon (1977) suggest that RO may help the caregivers because the process teaches staff how to communicate better with confused older adults. Other studies previously mentioned also state that RO is beneficial for the staff.

Langston (1981) writes that the lack of empirical evidence as to the effectiveness of RO may be related to the format in which RO is currently conceptualized. She does not support the abandonment of the technique but urges a reassessment of RO as it relates to learning theory with positive reinforcement of desired behaviors (behavior modification).

Hanley, McGuire, and Boyd (1981) found that staff interaction was the main influencing factor on the success of 24-hour reality orientation and improved resident behaviors. Bailey, Browne, Gable, and Holden (1986) stress the importance of interdisciplinary staff involvement in the planning and implementation of a 24-hour reality orientation program. The researchers noted increased appreciation by the nursing staff of individual patient likes and dislikes, interests, skills, and abilities. Seaman and Roth (1989) report that unit staff recognized improvement in patient awareness of environment and thought patients responded more appropriately. Leaders of the classroom groups noted that the unit staff carried over the concepts on the unit.

McMahon (1988) states that critiques of reality orientation studies indicate that positive outcomes occur because of more individualized attention by the nursing staff. McMahon argues that studies demonstrate little or no lasting effect of reality orientation interventions on confused older adults. He stresses that reality orientation techniques require more direct interaction between nurse and patient and that therefore the patient receives more individualized care. McMahon suggests, as a baseline nursing intervention for all confused older adults, that 24-hour reality orientation be used as one approach. The technique is individualized, and individualized care is the basis of nursing theory.

Powell-Procter and Miller (1992) state that nurses would take more interest in their patients, gain job satisfaction, and "operate units in a less institutionalized way" if 24-hour reality orientation were employed. Jenkinson (1992) notes that research does not demonstrate that classroom or 24-hour reality orientation is effective alone, but that they are effective as a combination and are more effective if the participants' relatives and caregivers are included, and if programs are run over long periods. Those with early stages of dementia appeared to respond more favorably. The added attention by staff may be the reason for improvement. Holden and Woods (1982) indicate that research is needed on the effects of reality orientation on staff or the staff's effect on reality orientation. I have found no articles on this subject.

Wolanin and Phillips (1977, 1981), Hussian (1981), and Reisberg (1981) do not advocate RO therapy alone but favor a more total approach through environmental cues, behavior therapy, teaching activities-of-daily-living skills, or cognitive training by mnemonic devices. These authors believe that these activities can serve the confused person in different situations and aid the elder to care for himself or herself better than RO therapy alone can do. Hussian suggests that the materials and tasks in the classroom need to be upgraded; the participants should not graduate to an advanced RO group or a remotivation, resocialization, or attitude therapy group. Fisk (1981, 91) writes that a "well run recreational program will be more useful to the demented patient than the most sophisticated psychiatric care."

Gubrium and Ksander (1975), Butler and Lewis (1977), Hellebrant (1978), and Reisberg (1981) have reservations about forcing all confused older adults to face reality. Butler and Lewis suggest that dementia is a positive defense mechanism against painful realities. Gubrium and Ksander note that *reality*, as defined by the RO board, has been forced on confused group members by aides who are rigid and not sensitive to older adults' needs. An example given by the authors demonstrates their point: If, in response to a question about the weather, a confused person answered that it was sunny, the aide would point to the RO board, which read "raining," and direct the patient to respond that way, when indeed the patient was voicing reality based on what he had seen through a window—sunshine.

Tappan and Touhy (1983) remind us that the design of some group modalities for older adults is very highly structured and very controlling; they cite reality orientation and remotivation groups as two examples. These are certainly highly structured group modalities. The writers feel that the focus on one topic or theme may suppress the real concerns of individuals who need to discuss issues, the airing of which the leader would encourage in group work with younger adults. The danger of patronization of older group members by the leader is also pointed out in this article.

Another writer (Schwenk 1979) feels that the repetitive aspects of orientation to time, person, and place may be quite boring, useless, and devoid of meaning to the older person who has a serious cognitive impairment.

Morton and Bleathman (1988) discuss the frustration of nurses when they endlessly reorient residents who are unable to remember, especially those whose intellectual decline has so deteriorated that reorientation fails. They feel that continued use of reality orientation may be damaging to the patient when it constantly reminds him or her that he or she can no longer remember. The authors propose validation therapy for those who are no longer able to reap benefits from reality orientation.

It must be noted that all the literature cited stresses one very important point—kind, human contact that builds trust does more than all other therapies combined to relieve confusion. *The mechanical repetition of information will not reorient* (Taulbee 1976).

Wahl (1976) states that day care is the most effective means of maintaining orientation for those confused older adults who live in the community. Day care programs do incorporate RO theory into the daily program (Ansak 1975; Kalish et al. 1975).

RO IN AN ADULT DAY CARE CENTER: A CASE STUDY

Some years ago I was a geriatric nurse practitioner (GNP) in a geropsychiatric adult day care center, the Senior Socialization Center of Catholic Social Service in San Jose, California. The center had been in operation for nine years. The staff included the project director, a psychiatric social worker, the program coordinator, an occupational therapist, a part-time social worker, a driver, a secretary, and myself, a GNP.

The program employed the principles of RO; however, the overall therapeutic approach was eclectic. We utilized the concepts of remotivation, resocialization, recreational therapy, and various psychiatric therapies in planning our total rehabilitative milieu program. Our main objective was to prevent mental breakdown and deterioration through the various activities and through work with the client and the family. We wanted to maintain the clients in their community, in their own homes, and with their families, or in a retirement complex or a residential care facility and prevent premature institutionalization.

The clients who attended the day care center were the aged with mental and/or physical diagnoses: senile dementia (we had a few diagnosed with Alzheimer's disease), strokes with varying degrees of physical handicaps and/or aphasia, hypertension, diabetes, obesity, and so on. Many of the clients had long-standing histories of mental illness (that is, depression, schizophrenia, bipolar disorder, or paranoia). Not all of those with mental or physical health problems are confused, but a large number of our clients were.

Usual Props

The center used the usual RO props: the RO board, a calendar, and a clock. The RO board was large and movable. One of the participants was usually responsible for changing the date daily. The calendar was on heavy-duty cardboard, and the numbers and month could be changed as necessary. The spaces for the date were large enough so that the main activity for the day could be posted. A copy of each month's calendar was given to each of the clients.

Name tags on three-by-five-inch cards in large print were worn by all staff and clients. Clients and staff were called by their first names. The name of our program was above the entrance to the center. On the door were labeled photographs of all the staff and volunteers.

Program Format

The activities changed daily, but we followed a specific schedule every day. This was a helpful way to provide orientation and a sense of continuity for the clients. (See Table 13-1.)

TABLE 13-1 Suggestions for reality orientation

Activities

The following have been used for both individual and group reality orientation:

- Bird feeders.
- Cooking.
- Current events.
- Discussion groups.
- Exercises in chairs or wheelchairs.
- Flashcards.
- Games that stimulate verbalization (dominoes, hangman).
- Group gardening.
- Guest speakers on safety, health issues, and so on.
- History.
- Large puzzles.
- Music and dancing.
- Outings to museums, movies, and parks.
- Parties specific to the season or occasion.
- Pets.
- Photo albums.
- Picture taking.
- Record player, videos, TV, pictures, maps, posters, newsletter.
- Reminiscence.
- Rummage sales.
- Sensory testing: smells, touch, vision, hearing.
- Walks.

Props for reality orientation classes

- Any item mentioned under Activities.
- Blackboards.
- Felt boards.
- Flip charts.
- Reality orientation board can be made of any material that allows information to be changed easily.

Environmental changes

Some changes commonly made to physical environments:

- Creation of areas in which older adults can wander safely, with alarmed doors, sensors on shoes.
- Change to furniture that makes institution more homelike; arrangements to promote socialization.
- Expansion or building of rooms large enough to conduct activities or groups.
- Large clocks and calendars with large numbers.
- Large screen TVs, videos, record player, or musical instruments.
- Open visiting hours.
- Overhead speakers.
- Paint or decorate with appropriate wallpaper.

Therapeutic staff

- Teach staff how to assess what skills the confused person does or does not possess.
- Teach staff how to cue: Use verbal and nonverbal communication to get an idea across.
- Teach staff theory and techniques of reality orientation, especially communication with the confused person.

On arrival at the center, the clients were encouraged to socialize, have a cup of coffee, work on an individual project, listen to music, read, or discuss special problems with staff members. Those who were especially confused were engaged in simple concentration games. The period after lunch was spent in much the same way.

At 11 A.M., the occupational therapist gathered the clients in a circle for a basic RO exercise. We did not ask each client to read the RO board; the group as a whole was queried on the date, time, weather, next holiday, and so forth. If the person responding gave an incorrect answer, he or she was referred to the RO board. We had 18 to 21 participants daily. We had limited time, space, and staff, so a true RO was impractical. The very confused but socially adept aged mixed with the oriented clients. The oriented clients did not seem to be put off by the RO exercise. We informed new clients that this was a daily exercise for those who could not remember this information and that their intact memory was helpful in keeping those who were confused more oriented. We maintained a matter-of-fact attitude and at times a humorous one if clients poked fun at their own memory loss. After RO, the clients were led through simple chair exercises.

On completion of the exercises, the clients engaged in an activity designed to stimulate one of the five senses; revive old memories; instruct them in something new; or involve them in planning for an upcoming event, such as our annual vaudeville show, senior olympics, or a party. Cooking was a popular activity. Everyone got to put a finger in the pot—stir, measure, add—and with this many cooks we still did not ruin the soup! Anagrams, crossword puzzles, current events, painting, pottery, singing, horoscopes, talks about holidays, or guest speakers (from the police, Social Security, or the telephone company) were some of the planned activities. The OT and I led discussions on activities of daily living (ADL) or a health topic. Picnics and outings were popular events.

The Monday and Friday afternoon sessions were music, reminiscing, or special exercises led by an instructor from adult education. Group milieu therapy was on Tuesday and Thursday mornings and afternoons. (The large group was split into two smaller groups; one group had therapy while the other group was engaged in the day's activity.) The moderately confused were included in the therapy; only the very confused, those who were disruptive to the group process, and those who refused to be part of the therapy were excluded.

Another way orientation was maintained was the process by which the client was scheduled to attend the center. All clients came at least two days a week (if their physical and emotional health did not permit, then one day); they attended up to four days a week if they were experiencing great emotional or familial stress, confusion, paranoia, and so forth. The clients were scheduled for Monday/Thursday or Tuesday/Friday from about 10:30 A.M. to 2:15 P.M. The participants were called each scheduled day to ensure they were ready when the center's van or taxi arrived.

Depending on the client, our overall approach was active friendliness—these people received many hugs and kisses because they themselves were this way. For the less demonstrative participants we employed passive friendliness, ensuring that they also received positive reinforcement and touch when appropriate.

Families were provided needed respite by having the older person attend our program. Family members were encouraged to attend the family meetings held monthly, to share their frustrations but also to learn from other families how they coped with the older person in their lives.

The overall eclectic approach to clients at the center was very effective for the majority of the participants. It must be remembered that when dealing with groups of mixed diagnoses (dementias with varying degrees of cognitive loss, psychiatric disorders, and various physical health issues), each individual is at a different place emotionally, cognitively, and physically. An approach that is effective for one or more individuals will bore or insult others. Two approaches may be used: a matter-of-fact attitude or passive and active friendliness. For those who are bored or insulted by a technique, incorporating their expertise and retained skills to assist staff with those who do not have intact skills can be a positive motivator.

Those at the center who were more intact cognitively did assist the staff with the reality orientation exercise as well as being protective and watchful of those who were cognitively impaired. The cognitively intact do fear becoming like "them" and often need support from the staff. Even though they mixed with the cognitively impaired, they did not always socialize with them at meals or quiet times. I periodically provided programs on health conditions that affected mentation, and that did seem to alleviate some misunderstanding and fear about dementia. We did separate participants for some activities to preserve harmony and decrease frustration, anger, or other feelings toward those who were disruptive and unable to participate. Those with like problems seemed to recognize each other and seek each other's support.

Some family members received and sought extra attention from the staff because of an inability to cope with the participants' behavior. The center provided respite, allowing the caregivers time to spend on themselves. Alternative approaches were discussed for the caregivers to utilize at home to decrease frustration. I would connect some participants up with a Friendly Visitor or in-home support, which enabled many to remain at home longer than they would have without assistance. As health and mentation failed, the center staff offered alternatives to care already being provided and offered assistance in nursing home placement. It appeared that the length of time the participants remained in the program, receiving various therapies and health monitoring, improved or maintained cognitive functioning for a long time. They might have failed sooner without intervention.

To integrate reality orientation into any program, whether day care, nursing home, psychiatric ward, residential care, retirement home, or in the home setting, does take planning, coordination, and cooperation of all involved with the cognitively impaired. Preventing further deterioration must be the overall goal. The reader is encouraged to research the cited literature in the references and bibliography for the how-to and the pitfalls before embarking on a reality orientation program. The staff must be clear on how and when to use reality orientation, techniques of environmental change, prompters of orientation, therapeutic communication, and cause of confusion. Volunteers, family members, visitors, neighbors—anyone in contact with a confused person can benefit from some basic reality orientation instruction. Chances are, they can show you some techniques they have employed that are highly effective with the confused. Taulbee (1986) stresses the importance of determining whether confusion is functional or organic, correcting the cause, and determining if confusion is a defense mechanism.

Duffy, Lemming, and Bracey (1988), Taulbee (1976, 1978, 1986), Alfgren (1977), Folsom (1968), Langston (1981), and Wolanin and Phillips (1981) are all excellent resources to study for ideas about what seems to work best for reality orientation programs. The physical environment must be studied carefully for any age barriers to be a successful program. Many of the cited articles describe changes made within the environment. Be sure to include volunteers in a program to supplement professional staff—they tend to add a dimension of understanding and love that professionals may not.

SUMMARY

The reality orientation technique incorporated with other therapeutic approaches works well in diminishing the confusional state of the moderately confused older adult. As the literature demonstrates, however, RO is not a panacea. It succeeds only if the staff working with the aged person is committed and involved. An overall approach that includes other therapies and techniques; provision of a cheerful cue-filled environment; and activities that stimulate the senses, can be done successfully, and promote self-esteem are more effective than RO therapy alone.

Taulbee (1986) stresses that expanding the basic reality orientation program to include activities is important. She writes: "Correcting sensory deprivation may be one of the most fundamental responsibilities of any activity program. Reality orientation counteracts deprivation through daily activities, not through activities in special places at special times." The freedom to choose to participate in activities is important and promotes self-respect and dignity.

The one key to successful care of the older adult is providing caring human contact. Alfgren (1977, 88L) stresses an excellent point: "We must realize that not all patients will progress rapidly. Our attitude should be that patients are progressing as long as they're not regressing."

And isn't that the important point? Progress can't be measured solely by whether an older person is oriented in all three spheres—time, person, and place. It's the quality of the person's life that is really important. Reality orientation alone cannot improve the quality of life, but an overall eclectic approach can.

EXERCISE 1

Visit an adult day care center. Observe how reality orientation is used (or not used) and what environmental cues are employed to promote orientation. Describe other techniques that you think the center could use to improve orientation.

EXERCISE 2

Select a partner. Role play three examples of reality testing with a disoriented person.

EXERCISE 3

Study your facility and determine what is already in place that enhnces reality orientation. Is there something that can be added or changed to enhance the way the staff functons?

EXERCISE 4

Discuss with a psychiatric social worker or psychologist the possibility of implementing a reality orientation program in your facility. Determine how structured or unstructured the program will be. Should other treatment modalities be incorporated? Are there any other staff to train and incorporate into the training? Is there truly a need for a classroom program, or would a 24-hour program with supplemented modalities be best? Write a two-page report about your discussion.

REFERENCES

Akerlund BM, Norberg A. 1986. Group psychotherapy with demented patients. *Geriatric Nurs* 7(2):83-86.

Alfgren J. 1977. Reality orientation: Starting your own program. *Nurs* 7(4):88C-88L.

Ansak M. 1975. *On Lok senior health services manual.* San Francisco: On Lok.

Bailey E, Browne S, Gable R, Holden U. 1986. Twenty-four reality orientation: Changes for staff and patients. *J Adv Nurs* 11:145-152.

Baines S, Saxby P, Ehlert K. 1987. Reality orientation and reminiscence therapy: A controlled cross-over study of elderly confused people. *Br J Psychiatr* 151:222-231.

Barnes J. 1974. Effect of reality orientation classroom on memory loss, confusion, and disorientation in geriatric patients. *Gerontologist* 14(2):138-142.

Brockett R. 1981. The use of reality orientation in adult foster care homes: A rationale. *J Gerontol Soc Work* 3(3):3-13.

Brook P, Degun G, Mather M. 1975. Reality orientation: A therapy for psychogeriatric patients: A controlled study. *Br J Psychiatr* 127:42-45.

Browne L, Ritter J. 1972. Reality therapy for the geriatric psychiatric patient. *Perspect Psychiatr Care* 10(3):135-139.

Burnside IM. 1970. Clocks and calendars. *Am J Nurs* 70(1):117-119.

———. 1978. *Working with the elderly: Group process and techniques*, 1st ed. North Scituate, MA: Duxbury Press.

Burton M. 1982. Reality orientation for the elderly: A critique. *J Adv Nurs* 7: 427-433.

Butler R, Lewis M. 1977. *Aging and mental health: Positive psychosocial approaches*, 2d ed. St. Louis: Mosby.

Citrin R, Dixon D. 1977. Reality orientation: A milieu therapy used in an institution for the aged. *Gerontologist* 17 (1):39-43.

Colthart S. 1974. A mental health unit in a skilled nursing facility. *J Am Geriatrics Soc* 22(10):453-456.

Dietch JT, Hewett LJ, Jones F. 1989. Adverse effects of reality orientation. *J Am Geriatric Soc* 37(19):974-975.

Duffy H, Lemming D, Bracey R. 1988. Checking skills. *Nurs Times* 84(6):31-32.

Erickson R, English S, Halar E, Hibbert J. 1978. Employing reality orientation in a short term treatment setting. *ARN J* 3(6):18-21.

Fisk A. 1981. *A new look at senility: Its causes, diagnosis, treatment, and management.* Springfield, IL: Thomas.

Folsom J. 1968. Reality orientation for the elderly mental patient. *J Geriatric Psychiatr* 1(2):291-307.

Freese A. 1978. *The end of senility.* New York: Arbor House.

Glasser W. 1965. *Reality therapy: A new approach to psychiatry.* New York: Harper & Row.

Gropper-Katz E. 1987. Reality orientation research. *J Gerontol Nurs* 13(8):13-18.

Gubrium G, Ksander M. 1975. On multiple realities of reality orientation. *Gerontologist* 15(2):142-145.

Hanley IG, McGuire RJ, Boyd WD. 1981. Reality orientation and dementia: A controlled trial of two approaches. *Br J Psychiatr* 138:10-14.

Harris C, Ivory P. 1976. An outcome evaluation of reality orientation therapy with geriatric patients in a state mental hospital. *Gerontologist* 16(6):496-503.

Hellebrant F. 1978. Comment: The senile dement in our midst, a look at the other side of the coin. *Gerontologist* 18(1):67-70.

Hogstel M. 1979. Use of reality orientation with aging confused patients. *Nurs Res* 28(3):161-165.

Holden UP, Woods RT. 1982. *Reality orientation: Psychological approaches to the "confused" elderly.* Edinburgh: Churchill Livingstone.

Holden UP. 1979. Return to reality. *Nurs Mirror* 149(21): 26-29.

Hussian R. 1981. Psychotherapeutic intervention: Organic mental disorders. In R Hussian (ed.), *Geriatric psychology: A behavioral perspective* (pp. 123-151). New York: Van Nostrand Reinhold.

Jenkinson B. 1992. Does reality orientation work? *Nurs Times* 13(88):20.

Johnson C. 1980. Reality orientation in the nursing home: A test of effectiveness. Abstract in *The Gerontological Society of America, Thirty-third Annual Scientific Meeting Program*, Part 11, p. 132 (November).

Kalish R, Lurie E, Wexler R, Zawadski R. 1975. *On Lok senior health services: Evaluation of a success*. San Francisco: On Lok.

Langston N. 1981. Reality orientation and effective reinforcement. *J Gerontol Nurs* 7(4):224-227 .

Lee RE. 1976. Reality orientation: Restoring the senile to life. Parts 1 and 2. *J Pract Nurs* (January):34-35, (February):30-31.

Lehman E. 1974. Reality orientation. *Nurs* 3(3):61-62.

Letcher PB, Peterson LP, Scarbrough D. 1974. Reality orientation: A historical study of patient progress. *Hosp Comm Psych* 25:801-803.

Loew C, Silverstone B. 1971. A program of intensified stimulation and response facilitation for the senile aged. *Gerontologist* 1(11):341-347.

MacDonald M,Settin J. 1978. Reality orientation versus sheltered workshops as treatment for the institutionalized aging. *J Gerontol* 33(3):416-421.

McDonald R, Neulander A, Holod O, Holcomb N. 1971. Description of a non-residential psychogeriatric day care facility. Part 1. *Gerontologist* 11(4):322-327.

McMahon R. 1988. The "24-hour reality orientation" type of approach to the confused elderly: A minimum standard of care. *J Adv Nurs* 13:693-700.

Merchant M, Saxby P. 1981. Reality orientation—A way forward. *Nurs Times* 77(32):1442-1445.

Morton I, Bleathman C. 1988. Reality orientation: Does it matter whether it's Tuesday or Friday? *Nurs Times* 84(6): 25-27.

Mulcahy N, Rosa N. 1981. Reality orientation in a general hospital. *Geriatr Nurs* 2(4):264-268.

Nodhurft V, Sweeney N. 1982. Reality therapy for the institutionalized elderly. *J Gerontol Nurs* 8(7):396-401.

Parker C, Somers C. 1983. Reality orientation on a geropsychiatric unit. *Geriatr Nurs* (May-June):163-165.

Powell-Procter L, Miller E. 1992. Reality orientation: A critical appraisal. *Br J Psychiatr* 140: 457-463.

Reisberg B. 1981. *Brain failure: An introduction to current concepts of senility*. New York: Free Press.

Reorientation stimulates patients and staff. 1975. *Modern Health Care* 3(1):33-35.

Richter J. 1990. A need for social support: The chronically mentally ill institutionalized elderly. *J Gerontol Nurs* 16(8):32-35.

Salter C, Salter C. 1975. Effects of an individualized activity program on elderly patients. *Gerontologist* 15(4):404-406.

———. 1977. Regression among the elderly after an interruption in their therapeutic program. *Hosp Comm Psych* 28(2):101-105.

Schwenk M. 1979. Reality orientation for the institutionalized aged: Does it help? *Gerontologist* 19(4):373-377.

Seaman L, Roth L. 1989. Active treatment for long-term psychiatric patients. *Geriatr Nurs* 10(5):207-224.

Settle H. 1975. A pilot study in reality orientation for the confused elderly. *J Gerontol Nurs* 1(5):11-16.

Silverstone B. 1976. Beyond the one-to-one treatment relationship. In L Bellak, T Karasu (eds.), *Geriatric psychiatry: A handbook for psychiatrists and primary care physicians* (pp. 207-224). New York: Grune & Stratton.

Smith B, Barker H. 1972. Influence of reality orientation training program on the attitudes of trainees toward the elderly. Part 1. *Gerontologist* 12(3):262-264.

Stephens L (ed.). 1969. *Reality orientation*. Washington, DC: American Psychological Association, Hospital and Community Psychiatry Service.

Tappen R, Touhy T. 1983. Group leader—Are you a controller? *J Gerontol Nurs* 9(1):34.

Taulbee LR. 1986. Reality orientation and clinical practice. In IM Burnside (ed.), *Working with the elderly: Group process and techniques*, 2d ed. (pp. 177-186). Boston: Jones and Bartlett.

———. 1978. Reality orientation. A therapeutic group activity for elderly persons. In IM Burnside (ed.), *Working with the elderly: Group process and techniques*, 1st ed. (pp. 206-218). North Scituate, MA: Duxbury Press.

———. 1976. Reality orientation and the aged. In IM Burnside (ed.), *Nursing and the aged*, 1st ed. (pp. 245-254). New York: McGraw-Hill.

Taulbee LR, Folsom J. 1966. Reality orientation for geriatric patients. *Hosp Comm Psych* 17:133-135.

Trotter R. 1972. Reality orientation. *Science News* (December 23):411.

Voelkel D. 1978. A study of reality orientation and resocialization groups with confused elderly. *J Gerontol Nurs* 4(3):13-18.

Wahl P. 1976. Psychosocial implications of disorientation in the elderly. *Nurs Clin North Am* 11(1):145-155.

Whitehead A. 1978. The clinical psychologist's role in assessment and management. In A Issacs, F Post (eds.), *Studies in geriatric psychiatry* (pp. 153-168). New York: Wiley.

Wolanin M, Phillips L. 1977. The Cinderella effect, an administrative challenge. *Concern Care Aging* 3(3):8-12.

——. 1981. *Confusion: Prevention and cure.* St. Louis: Mosby.

Zepelin H, Wade S. 1975. A study of the effectiveness of reality orientation classes. Paper presented to the Twenty-eighth Annual Meeting of the Gerontological Society, Louisville, KY.

Zepelin H, Wolfe S, Kleinplatz F. 1981. Evaluation of a year long reality orientation program. *J Gerontol* 36(1):70-77.

BIBLIOGRAPHY

Barns E, Sack K, Shore H. 1973. Guidelines to treatment approaches: Modalities and methods for use with the aged. *Gerontologist* 13(4):513-527.

Charatan F. 1980. Therapeutic supports for the patient with OBS. *Geriatrics* 35(9):100-102.

Conlin J. 1981. A hotel or hospital? Applying the principles of reality orientation. *J Pract Nurs* 31(7):25-26, 51.

Conroy C. 1977. Reality orientation: Basic rehabilitation technique for patients suffering from memory loss and confusion. *Br J Occup Ther* 40(10):250-251.

Cornbleth T, Cornbleth C. 1979. Evaluation of effectiveness of reality orientation classes in a nursing home unit. *J Am Geriatr Soc* 27(11):522-524.

——. 1977. Reality orientation for the elderly. Washington, DC: American Psychological Association.

Day R. 1981. An integrative group approach to treating the dysfunctional elderly . . . reality orientation, remotivation therapy, and sensory training. *Nurs Homes* 30(5):38-40.

Downes JJ. 1987. Classroom reality orientation and the enhancement of orientation—a critical note. *Br J Clin Psych* 26:2.

Drummond L, Kirchhoff L, Scarbrough D. 1978. A practical guide to reality orientation: A treatment approach for confusion and disorientation. *Gerontologist* 18(6):568-573.

Ferm L. 1974. Behavioral activities in demented geriatric patients. *Gerontol Clin* 16(4):185-194.

Gillette E. 1979. Apathy versus reality orientation. *J Nurs Care* 12(4):24-25.

Godber C. 1976. The confused elderly. *Nurs Times* 72(28):vii-viii, x.

Greene J. 1979. Reality orientation with geropsychiatric patients. *Behav Res Ther* 17(6):615-618.

Hackley J. 1973. Reality orientation brings patients back from confusion and apathy. *Modern Nurs Home* 31(3):48-49.

Hahn K. 1980. Using twenty-four-hour reality orientation. *J Gerontol Nurs* 6(3):132-135.

Hanley I. 1986. Reality orientation in the care of the elderly patient with dementia—three case studies. In I Hanley, M Gilhooly (eds.), *Psychological therapies for the elderly* (pp. 65-79). New York: New York University Press.

Holden UP, Sinebruchow A. 1978. Reality orientation therapy: A study investigating the value of this therapy in the rehabilitation of elderly people. *Age and Ageing* 7: 83-90.

Holden UP, Woods RT. 1982. *Reality orientation: Psychological approaches to the confused elderly.* Edinburgh: Churchill Livingstone.

Holden UP, Woods R. 1988. *Reality orientation: Psychological approaches to the confused elderly,* 2d ed. Edinburgh: Churchill Livingstone.

Ireland M. 1972. Starting reality orientation and remotivation. *Nurs Homes* 21(4):10-12.

Kohut S, Kohut J, Fleishman J. 1987. *Reality orientation for the elderly,* 3d ed. Oradell, NJ: Medical Economics, Books Division.

Phillips D. 1973. Reality orientation. *Nurs Digest* 22(October-November):6-7.

Ratcliffe J. 1988. Worth a try. *Nurs Times* 84(6):29-30.

Robinson K. 1974. Therapeutic interaction: A means of crisis intervention with newly institutionalized elderly persons. *Nurs Clin North Am* 9(1):89-96.

Scarbrough D. 1974. Reality orientation: A new approach to an old problem. *Nurs* 4(11):12-13.

Shaw J. 1979. A literature review of treatment options for mentally disabled old people. *J Gerontol Nurs* 5(5):36-79.

Sherman E, Newman E. 1977-78. The meaning of cherished personal possessions for the elderly. *J Aging Human Dev* 8(2):181-91.

Stevens C. 1974. Breaking through cobwebs of confusion in the elderly. *Nurs* 4(8):41-48.

Sylvester K, Kohut J, Fleshma J. 1979. *Reality orientation for the elderly.* Oradell, NJ: Medical Economics, Books Division.

Trockman F. 1978. Caring for the confused or delirious patient. *Am J Nurs* 78(9):1495-1499.

Veterans Administration Hospital. 1974. *Guide for reality orientation.* Tuscaloosa, AL (April).

Weiler P, Rathbone-McCuan E. 1978. *Adult day care: Community work with the elderly.* New York: Springer.

Wershow HJ. 1977. Comment: Reality orientation for gerontologists: Some thoughts about senility. *Gerontologist* 17(4):297-302.

Woods RT. 1979. Reality orientation and staff attention: A controlled study. *Br J Psychiatr* 134:502-507.

RESOURCES
Films

Interacting with Older People (black-and-white; Part I, 30 minutes; Part II, 26 minutes) 1971. Using interchange format, these films identify techniques to promote interaction with older persons in terms of meeting psychosocial needs. They examine attitudes of hospital staff in dealing with older persons. Directions for Education in Nursing Via Technology, Wayne State University, c/o College of Lifelong Learning, Detroit, MI 48202.

Rescue from Isolation (color, 22 minutes) 1972. This film documents the problems experienced by the elderly who are socially isolated and the effects a psychogeriatric day hospital can have on decreasing isolation. Gerontological Film Collection, Media Library, North Texas State University, P.O. Box 12898, Denton, TX 76203.

Behavioral Manifestations in the Aging Patient (color, 16 minutes, author: Carl Eisdorfer, Ph.D., M.D.). Selected symptoms of common behavioral manifestations seen in the elderly within the nursing home setting are shown in this film. It stresses the importance of the staff in diagnosis and care of elderly patients and leads to a better understanding of the elderly and their problems. Free loan from Film Department, Sandoz Pharmaceuticals, East Hanover, NJ 07936. Also available from Association Film, 866 Third Avenue, New York, NY 10022.

A Time to Learn: Reality Orientation in the Nursing Home (16 mm, color, 28 minutes). Demonstrates some of the "how to" in implementing reality orientation, illustrated by scenes from three different nursing homes.

December Spring: 24-Hour Reality Orientation (16 mm, black-and-white, 29 minutes). Illustrates the application of 24-hour reality orientation, utilizing staff members and patients at the Tuscaloosa Veterans Administration Hospital.

Return to Reality (16 mm, color, 35 minutes). Introduces the concepts of reality orientation as they are used in the case of an elderly stroke patient by a team at the Veterans Administration Hospital in Tuscaloosa, Alabama.

Correspondence concerning rental or purchase of the preceding three films should be sent directly to National Audiovisual Center (NAC), General Services Administration, Order Section, Washington, DC 20409; phone: 202-763-1891.

Confronting Confusion (black-and-white, 24 minutes) 1977. This documentary filmed an elderly patient who withdrew into a fantasy world and became unmotivated and confused. Group leaders of an advanced reality ori-

entation group helped the patient to confront his fantasies and offered support. Improvement is shown in a variety of ways. An Electric Sunrise Film, distributed by Electric Sunrise, P.O. Box 11122, Piedmont Station, Oakland, CA 94611; phone: 415-655-2356.

Training Kits

This Way to Reality. This kit helps one understand reality orientation and how to implement it in long-term care facilities. It contains a guidebook including sections on introduction, planning, implementing, evaluating, training the staff, and training others. It also contains five sets of slides with accompanying audiocassettes that have audible and inaudible advance signals. Correspondence regarding purchase should be sent directly to National Audiovisual Center (NAC), General Services Administration, Order Section, Washington, DC 20409; phone: 202-763-1891.

Trainex Filmstrips (5) on "Reality Orientation." These filmstrips present the five sections on techniques that are developed in the *This Way to Reality* training kit. Available from Trainex Corporation, P.O. Box 116, Garden Grove, CA 92642.

Sources for Reality Orientation Boards

W. H. Collins Cabinets, Department N77, Route 1, Box 326, Cottondale, AL 35453. Board: $33.

Hillhaven, Inc., Printing Department, Department N77, P.O. Box 11222, Tacoma, WA 98411. Board $33; complete set of letters on cards an additional $9.

Raymco Products Inc., 212 South Blake, P.O. Box 248, Olathe, KS 66061. Model OC-32, self-contained, with a five-year supply of cards for days, months, years.

Instruction Manuals and Pamphlets

American Hospital Association. 1976. *This way to reality: Guide for developing a reality orientation program.*

Holden UP. *24-hour approach to the problems of confusion in elderly people* (pamphlet). Department of Psychology, Moorhaven Hospital, South Devon, England.

Ponsar W. 1973. *Policy and procedures manual: Reality orientation.* Tacoma, WA: Hillhaven.

CHAPTER 14

Remotivation Groups

Helen Dennis

KEY WORDS

- Behaviors
- Depression
- Life satisfaction
- Meaningful
- Remotivation
- Technique
- Therapy

LEARNING OBJECTIVES

- Define *remotivation therapy.*
- Describe the history of remotivation therapy.
- Define the goals of remotivation therapy.
- Describe the impact of remotivation therapy as reported in selected research studies.
- Explain the basic techniques for conducting remotivation therapy.
- Describe the characteristics that participants in a remotivation therapy program should have.
- Describe the content for a remotivation therapy program.
- Identify desirable behaviors elicited in group members by remotivation therapy.
- Describe ways in which the facilitator can reinforce these behaviors.

Remotivation therapy (RT) is a group technique for stimulating and revitalizing individuals who are no longer interested and involved in either the present or the future. This technique is essentially a structured program of discussion based on reality coupled with the use of objective materials to which individuals are encouraged to respond.

HISTORY AND GOALS

Remotivation therapy was originally designed to remotivate mentally ill patients. It has been used in mental hospitals and nursing homes for patients diagnosed as having mental disorders, physical disorders (Robinson n.d.), alcoholism, and depression (Donahue 1966).

Dorothy Smith originated the remotivation technique in her work as a hospital volunteer (Pullinger & Sholly n.d.) Subsequently, in 1956, she trained a large group at the Pennsylvania State Hospital (Long 1962). In response to increased interest from many hospitals, the American Psychiatric Association formed a Remotivation Advisory Committee. This committee, working with Smith, Kline and French Laboratories, established remotivation therapy programs throughout the country. By the end of 1967, 15,000 nurses and aides at 250 mental hospitals had participated in remotivation training programs (Robinson n.d.).

The following comments are by R. S. Garber (1965, 220):

> Remotivation is based on reality. A goal of the mental health professional is to help mentally ill persons recognize the realities we recognize. Through trust and communication, the professional attempts to restore a patient's ability to perceive people, things, and relationships for what they really are. A patient has sick and healthy roles. . . . Remotivation tells a patient that he is accepted as an individual . . . with specific features, with many roles, with unique traits that make him distinguishable from everyone else.

Garber also says that the older person has an objective existence to other people rather than an existence depending on what the individual thinks of the self. Remotivation creates a bridge between the individual's self-perception and the perception of others. Reminiscing about one's experiences with the concrete world and identifying and asserting one's experiences through interactions often strengthen the concept of reality. To accomplish this, the information and description of experiences must be concrete and specific.

The individual is strengthened by remotivation in two ways: (1) by being encouraged to describe the self concretely as a person with roles and specific social functions and (2) by being encouraged to speak accurately about past and present experiences. The individual also learns of roles to play that do not cause anxiety or create problems. Freedom, competence, dignity, and pleasure can be shared without revising or blocking every aspect of one's life. The smell, touch, and feeling of reality are recognizable and often give the individual a sense of meaningfulness from the past.

REVIEW OF THE RESEARCH LITERATURE

A preliminary report on remotivation therapy examined the effects of RT on chronic and acute hospitalized patients (Long 1962). Subjects were assigned randomly to one of six remotivation groups, three male and three female. A total of "nearly 1000" patients were involved in the study. The Solomon four-group design was used to con-

trol several of the variables. The experimental group was given a pretest, remotivation therapy, and a posttest. Control group 1 was given a pretest and posttest with no remotivation therapy. Control group 2 was given remotivation therapy and a posttest. Control group 3 was given only a posttest with no remotivation therapy. Attendants rated patients' behavior, which included response to meals, response to other patients, response to work, attention to dress, and speech. A two-by-two analysis of variance on the four posttests of behavior ratings indicated a significant difference between remotivation therapy and no remotivation therapy beyond a .01 level of significance. This analysis was performed only for chronic patients. Remotivation therapy patients were described as exhibiting a significantly higher level of behavior than patients who had no remotivation.

Bovey (1971), in a doctoral dissertation, investigated the effects of remotivation therapy on ward behavior, self-concept, and visual motor perceptions. The three groups were remotivation therapy with emphasis on patient-staff and patient-patient interaction; remotivation therapy with no emphasis on interaction, implemented by the staff reading to the patients; and a group that acted as a control and most likely received nothing. A pretest-posttest design with a six-week experimental period was used. Forty-five male and 45 female mental patients were selected randomly from a geriatric unit at a state hospital. Co-variant analysis, using pretreatment scores as the co-variant, suggested that remotivation therapy techniques were significantly more effective than reading in producing changes in self-concept. Remotivation and reading were significantly more effective than a no-treatment control group on all variables.

A trial of remotivation therapy versus conventional group therapy was conducted with 39 ambulatory, nondeaf geriatric patients (Birkett & Boltuch 1973). Patients were assigned randomly to remotivation therapy or group therapy. The researchers acted as co-therapists. The group therapy was intended as a placebo group, which took the form of psychoanalytically oriented therapy sessions. The subjects were treated for 12 weeks, receiving one hour of therapy per week. Personal relationships and group responses were tested before and after the therapy. Results on the two measures showed no significant group differences. However, group responses such as interest, awareness, participation, and comprehension did favor the remotivation group.

I conducted a study (1976) to evaluate the effectiveness of remotivation therapy with hospitalized geriatric patients. Twenty-three females and 14 males from two geriatric wards were assigned randomly to remotivation therapy, an extra-attention condition, and routine care. The routine care condition was dropped because of attrition. The remotivation and extra-attention condition consisted of 12 sessions, of 30 minutes to one hour, three times a week. The remotivation sessions were structured and based on a different topic for each session. The 12 topics were vacations, gardening, holidays, sports, rocks, pets, art, the sea, transportation, weather, hobbies, and animals and their by-products. In the less structured extra-attention condition, discussion topics included hospital activities, reasons for hospitalization, families, and past experiences. The routine care group received routine care and was not seen by the leader. Measurement of depression, life satisfaction, and behavioral ratings were completed after the treatment.

Contrary to the hypothesis, t test results indicated that subjects receiving remotivation therapy were significantly ($p > .02$) more depressed and less satisfied with life than the extra-attention group. No significant difference between the groups appeared in the behavioral ratings. One possible reason for the unexpected results is that remotivation therapy aroused feelings of conflict. Relating to meaningful and stimulating material could have stimulated the RT group to realize more fully their hospital situation. After completion of therapy, patients' control over their lives, day-to-day ritual, and prospects of release remained unchanged. Remotivation therapy may have caused the subjects to gain better contact with reality by realizing previous independence, interests, opportunities, and pleasures and by recognizing their absence during confinement. The realization of these differences could have been partially responsible for the increased depression and dissatisfaction in the remotivation group compared with the extra-attention group. If the conflict or dissonance analysis is correct, then the subjects were in a drive or motivational state. Remotivation therapy may be the first important step in motivating individuals to gain maximum benefit from subsequent therapeutic programs.

Linda Moody, Virginia Baron, and Grace Monk (1970) found patients alert and interested in life again as a result of remotivation therapy. The patients were involved in group interaction consisting of discussion topics geared to the group's past history and interests. An effort was made to involve the senses of touch, taste, and smell. Measures of life satisfaction revealed higher posttreatment scores. No tests of significance were performed, nor was a control group used. The authors advocated varied sensory stimuli and social interaction for maintenance of contact with reality.

HOW TO CONDUCT REMOTIVATION THERAPY

Initial Steps for Remotivation Therapy

Starting a new program in a facility with traditional and ongoing treatment techniques may be difficult for many reasons. Some of them are:

1. Changing methods or adapting to new ones may be threatening to some staff members.
2. Not understanding a new program may arouse suspicion and nonconstructive criticism.
3. Added responsibilities may be too much for an overworked and underpaid staff.

Some of these difficulties can be avoided by effectively communicating the nature and intent of the new program to all interested staff members. First, approval should be obtained in writing from the facility's director or chief administrator. Next, the director of nurses should fully understand and support the remotivation therapy program. The staff may be involved in conducting remotivation therapy, selecting individuals for the program, escorting individuals to the sessions, or keeping individuals available for remotivation. Staff members should be invited to attend a session to understand more fully the remotivation process. Information, experience, and understanding of the new program will increase the chances for acceptance and support.

Leading remotivation therapy does not require extensive training or degrees. Anyone sensitive to human needs could conduct remotivation therapy with training in the objective, technique, and process.

After the completion of the remotivation program, the leader may offer observations of individuals' responses to the therapeutic team. This new information will encourage a broader view of individual potentials.

Selection of Group Members

Ideally, group members should have some ability to interact with others and not be totally regressed. For the regressed person, therapy should start with reality orientation, followed by remotivation therapy and reminiscence therapy (Barnes, Sack & Shore 1973). However, few facilities for the elderly offer a series of therapies tailored to specific levels of a mental health continuum. If remotivation therapy is the only program available for the unmotivated person, criteria for selection include willingness to join the group, ability to hear and speak, and lack of preoccupation with hallucinations (Pullinger & Sholly n.d.; Dennis 1976). The group should consist of a maximum of 15 members (Robinson n.d.).

The remotivation leader has little need for information on diagnoses, prognoses, or histories. In fact, this type of information may influence the leader's expectation of individual participation and potential for change. As a remotivation leader, I found that not knowing about patient histories permitted me to strengthen my attitude of optimism. The group member in remotivation therapy has the chance to start anew and assume a different label from the one given by society or an institution. For example, a "mental patient" or "sick person" can become an "individual," "group member," or even a "student." Consequently, the remotivation leader must approach a group with the intention of offering new opportunities, change, and optimism with little or no reference to institutional or societal labels.

The ward staff is influential in persuading an individual to attend the first remotivation meeting. In some cases, the individual will attend if told to—rather than asked to—by the charge nurse. Invitations to join the group can range from "Please join us" to "I think it's important that you attend" to "Please attend." The same approach may not be effective for each person.

Content of Remotivation Therapy

According to the *Remotivation Techniques* manual (Robinson n.d.), remotivation therapy sessions are usually held once or twice a week for 12 sessions. I

found a more intensive schedule preferable—three times a week for four weeks. Sessions last from 30 minutes to one hour, depending on the attentiveness of the group (Robinson n.d.). Each remotivation session includes five basic steps (Robinson n.d.):

1. "Climate of acceptance" consists of introductions and getting acquainted (p. 7).
2. "Bridge to reality" encourages individuals to participate in reading an article aloud (p. 7).
3. "Sharing the world we live in" is topic development by means of questions, visual aids, and props (p. 8).
4. "An appreciation of the work of the world" prompts individuals to think about work in relation to themselves (p. 9).
5. "Climate of appreciation" is a time to express pleasure that the group has met and to plan the next meeting (p. 10).

From experience with geriatric patients in a state psychiatric facility, I found that steps 2 and 4 created little interest. For example, many subjects had poor vision or were unable to read. Consequently, I omitted the second step, bridge to reality. Also, topics that were not applicable to work in relation to the group were discussed in terms other than work. For example, the topics of rocks, holidays, hobbies, and vacations arouse interest in related visual aids and individual experiences, but work-related discussions did not. Consequently, step 4 was frequently omitted.

Each remotivation therapy session is based on a different topic. The topics are geared to appeal to diverse backgrounds, experiences, and interests and to appeal to as many senses as possible. Visual aids and appropriate objects are used to maintain a high level of attention, interest, and reaction.

The first few minutes of each session are devoted to greeting and establishing rapport. Comments on dress, hairstyle, or the leader's family are all part of establishing this beginning relationship. Reminiscing is encouraged as part of sharing experiences. Visual aids are passed from one person to another to encourage communication among group members.

The leader structures each therapy session to focus on nonpathological interests and behaviors. Discussion centers on those things that constitute the real world for the members. Topics dealing with individuals' problems and family relationships are avoided.

The group is told how many times they will meet. Halfway through the program, the leader prepares the group for termination. For example, the leader may state, "The seventh session has been completed, and the group will meet five more times." After the last meeting, the leader may arrange to visit with the group, although the formal therapy has ended.

AN EXAMPLE OF REMOTIVATION THERAPY

I became interested in remotivation therapy as a graduate student searching for a thesis topic. From personal involvement with several nursing homes, I was keenly aware of the desolate existence of most nursing home residents. Claims in a news magazine that reality orientation could deter or reverse the aging process aroused my curiosity. Subsequently, while reviewing the literature on reality orientation, I read about remotivation therapy.

The following description of group responses is a partial summary of the remotivation procedure I used at Metropolitan State Hospital in Norwalk, California. The remotivation group consisted of 12 geriatric patients hospitalized for an average of five years. The mean age of the group was 73.1 years. The group met three times a week for one month.

Session 1: Vacations

For the first session, I wrote each member's name on a card and placed it by the member's chair. I introduced myself and told the members something about my family and residence. The group was told that different topics of interest would be presented. To start the vacation topic, I took a heavy bucket of sand from person to person for each individual to feel. Then I asked the members where they would like to take a vacation. Previous vacation experiences were shared.

Group Response. The members were interested in my background and family. All except two appeared to enjoy feeling the sand. The group seemed cautious and reserved. One individual screamed throughout the session. Others shared some vacation experiences.

Session 2: Gardening

Gardening experiences and plant growth needs were discussed. The members each planted bean seeds in a cup with his or her name on it. Different green plants were passed around to look at, touch, and smell. A box of strawberries was distributed among the group for smelling and tasting. The meeting ended with reminiscences of preparing strawberries for pies and jams.

Group Response. The group seemed to enjoy planting seeds. They all smelled and touched the different plants. Experiences in growing flowers and vegetables and preparing fertilizer were shared. All except two members tasted the strawberries.

Session 3: Sports

I showed large, colorful posters of different sports, such as basketball, football, and baseball. Various sporting balls passed around included a basketball, golf ball, tennis ball, and softball, as well as a mitt. I bounced some of the balls to different persons, who bounced them back. Different sporting experiences were shared, as well as various sports individuals had tried. I also displayed pictures of sky-diving, ice hockey, and croquet. Several pieces of sporting equipment were passed around, such as a bar, a tennis racquet, and golf clubs.

Group Response. All the members held a piece of sporting equipment, and many told of experiences in that particular sport. Comments such as "when I used to caddy" or "when I played baseball" were made to the group.

Session 4: Rocks

Many different kinds, shapes, and sizes of natural rock, geodes, quartz, and granite were passed around and discussed in terms of shape, texture, temperature, and weight. Polished rock stimulated a discussion on the rock-polishing technique.

Group Response. A group member led a discussion on rock polishing. Everyone stated that the meeting devoted to rocks was their favorite one so far. Several said that certain rocks would make attractive jewelry.

Session 5: Pets

I displayed a covered cage housing a live rabbit, a procedure used by Hahn (1973). The group was asked to guess what was in the cage, given a few hints from me. The members were then asked to volunteer to feed the rabbit. After I showed different pictures of pets, I asked the members which pets they had owned or would like to own. Large paintings of rabbits and other animals were shown.

Group Response. Prior to session 5, one woman in the group had been very quiet. I subsequently discovered that she was considered mute. This "mute" woman spoke and guessed that the animal in the cage was a dog!

Session 6: Art

The group was shown examples of many art forms, such as sewing, painting, and sculpture. I displayed eight large tempera paintings completed by kindergarten children and asked each member to act as a judge for a children's art show. The group used clay for tactile stimulation and pleasure. Each one chose the color of clay he or she preferred. Puppets were shared as an art form.

Group Response. One individual responded by performing a puppet show for the group. All the members stated opinions on which picture should win first and second prizes and gave reasons for their choices.

Session 7: The Sea

The group compiled a list of sea-related items, which were listed on the blackboard. I displayed large colored pictures of different fish and asked the members which ones they had eaten or caught. A variety of seashells were passed around the group.

Group Response. Several group members shared sea-related experiences, such as visiting a marine museum and netting oysters in Louisiana.

Session 8: Transportation

I asked the members to name different forms of transportation, which I then wrote on the blackboard, to ascertain the most popular form of trans-portation from the group's experience. Models of a bus, a missile, a train, a submarine, and several types of planes were passed around the group. I then read a poem about transportation.

Group Response. All the members volunteered information about different forms of transportation. Many reminisced about experiences with riding a ferry, bicycle, bus, or train.

Session 9: Holidays

The group was asked to name holidays and the month of their occurrence and to associate colors with the different holidays. Holiday objects were shown, and the group matched the appropriate holidays with the objects.

Group Response. Several members talked about their ethnic backgrounds. One individual sang an Italian song; another described her Irish background. In general, however, the group was not very responsive to this topic.

Session 10: Weather

The members were asked to describe the weather on that meeting day. The composition and origin of rain and clouds were discussed. A blackboard demonstration of evaporation followed the discussion, as suggested by Pullinger and Sholly (n.d.). The session closed with a poem about rain and a newspaper weather report.

Group Response. Only a few members appeared interested and were responsive to the topic. Several members contributed information about evaporation.

Session 11: Hobbies

The group was asked to define the term *hobby*. Knitting, needlepoint, a matchbook collection, coins, stamps, Christmas balls, baseball cards, and newspaper headlines were passed around the group as examples of hobbies. Everyone talked about their hobbies. In discussing the collection of newspaper headlines, members were asked to recall what they were doing when President Kennedy was shot.

Group Response. All members recalled what they were doing when Kennedy was shot. The group accurately defined the term *hobby* and talked about their different hobbies. One member said that his hobby was shooting pool for money and that he would "love to play again." Two group members who had used wheelchairs to come to the sessions were no longer using them.

Session 12: Animals and Their By-Products

Two types of items were presented to the group: miniature models of animals and a variety of items made from animals. A lamb's-wool hat, perfume, glue, rabbit fur, milk, and salami were some of the by-products. The group's task was to guess the animals from which the by-products originated. The session ended with a snack of cheese, salami, crackers, and sweets.

Group Response. The group was successful in accurately relating the by-product to the animal. The snack was enjoyed and vigorously consumed. Several individuals stated how much they enjoyed attending the meetings.

EVALUATION AND REFERRAL

Little evaluative research on remotivation therapy has been published. Consequently, models of evaluation, areas for improvement, and personality characteristics most likely to change need investigation. To refine this therapeutic approach, the leader should specify desired behaviors and know how to reinforce them (Toepfer, Bicknell & Shaw 1974).

In retrospect, the behaviors I considered desirable during remotivation therapy were

1. Attentiveness to leader and others.
2. Participation in discussion.
3. Responsiveness to the material presented.
4. Appearance of enjoying the experience.
5. Realism in discussion.
6. Communication with others.

These behaviors were reinforced by attention and acceptance from me as well as from the group. In addition, the new role of group member, individual, or student may have been reinforcing for some individuals.

Remotivation therapy could function as the first important step in motivating individuals to gain maximum benefit from other therapeutic programs. For example, nursing home residents might benefit more from physical therapy if they were motivated to change. O'Neil (1966) believes that even a minimal response to remotivation therapy could indicate the need for other types of therapy.

It is very difficult to attribute progress or change exclusively to remotivation therapy. Many variables contribute to changes in mood, behavior, and attitude. The institutionalized individual is part of a complex physical and psychological environment, and remotivation therapy is a small part of the total milieu.

However, remotivation therapy does offer an opportunity to increase one's sense of reality, to practice healthy roles, and to realize a more objective self-image. A new awareness of one's potential for growth and the motivation to change are two significant achievements for the RT member. These goals are not an end but a beginning. Active physical and psychological rehabilitative programs, geared to individual needs, must follow. A life of dignity and fulfillment for the institutionalized older person is a realistic goal that must be met. Remotivation is just a beginning.

Few research or demonstration projects appear in the recent literature; however, two articles from the 1980s were located. Janssen and Giberson (1988) modified the steps of remotivation therapy to place emphasis on sensory stimulation for a group of cognitively impaired individuals. The themes were: gardening, wind, pets, bodies of water, canning fruits and vegetables, hobbies, transportation, and celebrations. Needler and Baer (1982), certified remotivation therapists, combined music, movement, and remotivation with regressed older adults in a long-term care facility. The treatment is offered on a daily basis "with the intent to maintain, stimulate, and reinvolve residents in activities of daily living" (p. 497). Each of the steps in remotivation therapy are presented with descriptions of how music and movement were incorporated into the steps.

It does appear that the principles of remotivation therapy have been incorporated into other therapeutic modalities. For example, the Baltzargarden Clinic outside Motola, Sweden, is using "modified reality training" (*Ageing International* 1992, 24) for patients with dementia to stimulate brain functions through the senses. Treatment includes particpating in routine daily activities such as shoveling snow, helping in the kitchen, painting garden furniture, feeding ducks, playing music, and singing (*Ageing International* 1992).

SUMMARY

Remotivation therapy is a step beyond the reality orientation group method described in Chapter 13. Like reality orientation, it is a very structured type of group meeting; the focus is on discussion of specific objects, and the individuals are encouraged to respond to the topic or prop of the meeting.

Aged people can be helped through remotivation therapy by sharing about themselves and their former roles and functions and by describing past and present experiences so that the past can become more meaningful.

Results of studies done on behavioral changes due to remotivation therapy were published as early as 1962. Later, Bovey (1971) demonstrated that remotivation groups produce changes in self-concept. Birkett and Boltuch (1973) found no significant group differences between a control group and a remotivation group. Dennis (1976) came up with a surprising result: The subjects who received remotivation therapy were significantly more depressed than the control group. One explanation is that interesting and stimulating material and increased interactions may have been a stark contrast to the patients' bleak existence and that they had become painfully aware of their present hospital existence.

Difficulties a remotivation leader may face in beginning such a program include staff concern about and reaction to change, suspicion and harmful criticism from staff members due to lack of understanding of the program, and staff inability to cope with the additional tasks to expedite such a therapy.

There should be no more than 15 in a group. Potential members should not be too mentally impaired and should be willing to join the group, be able to hear and speak, and not be prone to hallucinations. The five basic steps of each meeting are introductions, reading aloud, sharing time, considering the work world, and expressing appreciation and pleasure. Dennis (1976), in her work in a state hospital, found that patients did not eagerly participate in steps 2 and 4 and describes a variety of reasons in this chapter.

A diverse selection of topics is needed to appeal to and interest a wide range of patients. Possibilities are vacations, gardens, sports, rocks, pets, art, the sea, transportation, holidays, weather, hobbies, and animals and their by-products.

Behaviors to encourage are increased attention, participation in discussion, response to props, expression of pleasure, discussion of reality, and communication.

Remotivation therapy, although it does have drawbacks (for example, the structure is quite rigid), is a therapeutic technique that offers the opportunity to increase one's sense of reality, practice healthy roles, and realize a more objective self-image.

EXERCISE 1

Take a favorite theme that you would enjoy using with a group of elderly people and answer the following:

1. Why you chose this theme.
2. Number in your proposed group.
3. Average age of members.
4. Place where group will be conducted.
5. Theme of group meeting for that day.
6. What you will do as a leader to create interest.
7. Five other themes you would like to try in a remotivation group.

EXERCISE 2

You are a nursing home administrator and are considering remotivation groups in your facility. What are the pros and cons?

EXERCISE 3

Identify the specific outcome you want from your group participating in remotivation therapy. Define the success of your group.

REFERENCES

Ageing International. 1992. Institutional care: Swedish success in treating senile dementia stirs worldwide interest. 19(4):24 (no author).

Barnes EK, Sack A, Shore H. 1973. Guidelines to treatment approaches. *Gerontologist* 13(4):517-519.

Birkett D, Boltuch B. 1973. Remotivation therapy. *J Am Geriatr Soc* 21(8):368-371.

Bovey JS. 1971. The effect of intensive remotivation techniques on institutionalized geriatric mental patients. Doctoral dissertation, University of Texas. *DAI* 32:4201B-4202B; University Microfilms no. 72-4064.

Dennis H. 1976. Remotivation therapy for the elderly: A surprising outcome. Unpublished manuscript. Los Angeles.

Donahue HH. 1966. Expanding the program. *Hosp Comm Psych* 17(4):117-118.

Garber RS. 1965. A psychiatrist's view of remotivation. *Ment Hosp* 16(August):219-221.

Hahn J. 1973. Mrs. Richards, a rabbit, and remotivation. *Am J Nurs* 73(2):302-305.

Janssen JA, Giberson DL. 1988. Remotivation therapy. *J Gerontol Nurs* 14(6):31-34.

Long RS. 1962. Remotivation—Fact or artifact. *Ment Hosp Serv* 151:1-8.

Moody L, Baron V, Monk G. 1970. Moving the past into the present. *Am J Nurs* 70(11): 2353-2356.

Needler W, Baer MA. 1982. Movement, music and remotivation with the regressed elderly. *J Gerontol Nurs* 8(9):497-503.

O'Neil FJ. 1966. Involving the medical staff. *Hosp Comm Psych* 17(4):116-117.

Peter LJ. 1977. Peter's quotations: Ideas for our times. New York: Morrow.

Pullinger WF, Sholly EN. n.d. *Outline of a remotivation training course.* Philadelphia: American Psychiatric Association and Smith, Kline & French Laboratories Remotivation Project.

Robinson AM. n.d. *Remotivation techniques: A manual for use in nursing homes.* Philadelphia: American Psychiatric Association and Smith, Kline & French Laboratories Remotivation Project.

Toepfer CT, Bicknell AT, Shaw DO. 1974. Remotivation as behavior therapy. *Gerontologist* 14(5):451-453.

BIBLIOGRAPHY

Adams G. 1961. I didn't know the person in the next room, but . . . 1961. *Ment Hosp* 12(July):28.

Bechenstein N. 1966. Enhancing the gains: Remotivation, a first step to restoration. *Hosp Comm Psych* 7(April): 115-116.

Botwinick J. 1973. *Aging and behavior.* New York: Springer.

Brudno J, Seltzer J. 1968. Resocialization therapy through group process with senile patients in a geriatric hospital. *Gerontologist* 8(3):211-214.

Fields GJ. 1976. Senility and remotivation: Hope for the senile. *J Long-Term Care Adm* 4:1.

Frazier A. 1966. Developing a remotivation program. *Staff* 3(January-February):5.

Garber RS. 1965. Why does remotivation work? *Staff* 2(Summer):8.

Gershowitz SZ. 1982. Adding life to years: Remotivating elderly people in institutions. *Nurs Health Care* 3(3):141-145.

Greenfield DS. 1977. Remotivation therapy: A test of a major assumption of the treatment with domiciled geriatric veterans. Unpublished dissertation. *DAI* 36(6-B):2861-2862.

Huey K. 1977. A remotivation institute at Philadelphia State Hospital. *Hosp Comm Psych* 28(2):133-135.

Ireland M. 1972. Starting reality orientation and remotivation. *Nurs Homes* 21(4):10-11.

Kunkel S. 1970. Resocialization: A technique that combats loneliness. *Nurs Homes* 19(8):12-13.

Lyon GG. 1971. Stimulation through remotivation. *Am J Nurs* 71(5):982-986.

Mandel H. 1968. Renewed interest through remotivation. *Nurs Homes* 17(2):21ff.

Martin CH. 1967. Place of motivation techniques in cottage and ward life programs. *Ment Retard* 5(October):17-18.

McCormick E. 1962. New hope for darkened minds. *Today's Health* 40(March):44-45.

McFerrin ZH. 1967. Remotivation for family living. *Staff* 4(November-December):2.

Pullinger WF. 1958. Remotivation. *Ment Hosp* 9(January): 14-17.

———. 1960. Remotivation. *Am J Nurs* 60(May):682ff.

Sink SM. 1966. Remotivation: Toward reality for the aged. *Nurs Outlook* 14(8):27-28.

Stephens L. 1968a. How to start a remotivation program. *Staff* 5(January-February):6.

———. 1968b. Remotivation. *Staff* 5(May-June):20.

———. 1968c. Remotivation literature. *Staff* 5(September-October):11.

Stotsky B. 1972. Social and clinical issues in geriatric psychiatry. *Am J Psychiatr* 129(2):32-40.

Tabler M. 1965. Nature's therapy. *Staff* 2(Spring):9.

Tate PA. 1977. Rehabilitation and aging: The effect of remotivation therapy on activity level and life satisfaction with institutionalized elderly populations. Unpublished dissertation. *DAI* 36(6-B):2890.

Thompson DA. 1992. New direction. *Psychosoc Rehabil J* 15(3):105-109.

Thralow JU, Watson CG. 1974. Remotivation for geriatric patients using elementary school students. *Am J Occup Ther* 28(8):469-473.

Tilghman C. 1965. A remotivator considers the "five steps." *Staff* 2(Winter):4.

Traul H. 1964. Pipeline to remotivation. *Staff* 1(Spring):7.

Wallen V. 1970. Motivation therapy with the aging geriatric veteran patient. *Mil Med* 135(11):1007-1010.

Ward E, Jackson C, Camp T. 1973. Remotivation: A growing family of therapeutic techniques. *Hosp Comm Psych* 24(19):629-630.

Waters EB. 1984. Building on what you know: Techniques in individual and group counseling with people. *Counsel Psych* 12(2):63-74.

Wellman FE. 1984. Counseling with older persons: A review of outcome research. *Counsel Psych* 12(2):81-95.

Whalen L. 1960. Remotivation remodified. *Ment Hosp* 11(April):46-48.

Young LS. 1967. Remotivation helps community education. *Staff* 4(January-February):13.

RESOURCES

Organizations

National Remotivation Therapy Technique Organization. This organization distributes information lists and offers training at Philadelphia State Hospital and other centers throughout the country. Philadelphia State Hospital, 14000 Roosevelt Boulevard, Philadelphia, PA 19114; phone: 215-671-4939.

Training Aids

Basic Remotivation Training Course Outline (WF Pullinger, EN Sholly, Philadelphia: Philadelphia State Hospital, n.d.).

Advanced Remotivation Training Course Outline (WF Pullinger, C Young, Philadelphia: Philadelphia State Hospital, rev. ed., 1976).

Poems for Remotivation (WF Pullinger, Philadelphia: Philadelphia State Hospital, 1981).

Remotivation Kits

Remotivation Kit No. 240-1. For use in mental hospitals, this kit includes publications, instructional materials, and additional information.

Remotivation Kit No. 240. For use in nursing homes, this kit includes publications, instructional materials, and additional information.

For information regarding remotivation kits, write to American Psychiatric Association, Publications Services Division, 1700 18th Street, NW, Washington, DC 20009.

CHAPTER 15

Reminiscence Group Therapy

Irene Burnside

KEY WORDS

- Age appropriate
- Autobiography
- Culturally appropriate
- Flashbulb memory
- Gender appropriate
- Geographically appropriate
- Journaling
- Life review
- Long-term memory
- Props
- Recall
- Reminiscence
- Short-term memory
- Themes
- Triggers

LEARNING OBJECTIVES

- Define reminiscence.
- Differentiate between reminiscence and life review.
- List six types of reminiscence.
- Discuss the roots of reminiscence therapy.
- Describe three functions of reminiscence.
- Discuss short-term memory versus long-term memory as they apply to reminiscence therapy groups.
- Define *triggers*.
- Define *props*.
- List four props appropriate for older group members.
- Define *themes*.
- List 10 themes appropriate for a reminiscence group.

One of the reasons why old people make so many journeys into the past is to satisfy themselves that it is still there.

RONALD BLYTHE (1979, 38)

Reminiscence has come into its own in recent decades, and lay persons and professionals alike have been fascinated with the phenomenon. There is even an interesting magazine entitled *Reminisce,* which is published bimonthly. The astounding increase in the number of both anecdotal articles and research studies speaks to the increased interest in the concept of reminiscence (Haight 1991). Chapter 16, by Birren and Deutchman, describes guided autobiography groups, which also depend on the memory process. This chapter is about reminiscence groups and presents a literature review, an historical perspective, and a hefty section on clinical application.

LITERATURE REVIEW

A review of professional journals of several disciplines indicates that reminiscence is a common phenomenon of old age (Poulton & Strassberg

1986). The concept of reminiscence has been used as the basis for a therapeutic modality for both alert and confused older adults in the hospital and the community (Thornton & Brotchie 1987). Clinical reports indicate that reminiscence produces therapeutic outcomes in individuals and groups; however, many reports have not been substantiated by empirical evidence. The empirical research of reminiscence has lagged behind theory (Romaniuk 1981). Reports on the results of reminiscence therapy are conflicting (Thornton & Brotchie 1987). In the current literature, there is a lack of replication studies and also of qualitative studies.

DEFINITIONS OF REMINISCENCE AND LIFE REVIEW

A literature search indicates confusion regarding reminiscence and the life review, terms too often used interchangeably. Studies on group reminiscence rarely include operational definitions of reminiscence. One definition of *reminiscence* that does capture the essence is "A way of reliving, re-experiencing or savoring events of the past that are personally significant" (University of Michigan n.d.). The definition of *life review* most commonly quoted is from Butler's classic article (1963), "A naturally occurring, universal mental process characterized by the progressive return to consciousness of past experiences, and particularly, the resurgence of unresolved conflicts, simultaneously, and normally; these revived experiences and conflicts can be surveyed and reintegrated" (p. 66).

Webster and Young (1988) have well described life review as "a developmental process in which individuals reintegrate the past in terms of their present. The process of reintegration can be seen to have three process variables: (1) recall, (2) evaluation, and (3) synthesis" (p. 321). Only the variable recall is common to reminiscence therapy groups; if evaluation and/or synthesis occurs, it is done by the individual group member as a result of group discussions and not because the leader probed. Apparently, life review is usually accomplished in one-to-one interaction, because few articles detail the process in groups (Disch 1980; Georgemiller & Maloney 1984).

Currently, there is a debate about who conducts life review therapy. Professionals with psychiatric or psychological backgrounds suggest caution (Shute 1986). Birren and Deutchman (this text) state that the person should be a "seasoned professional therapist." Since life review is treatment and insight oriented, and often entails catharsis and working through old conflicts, it is probably best left in the hands of persons with some psychiatric or counseling training and experience (Schmidt 1993, personal communication). On the other hand, reminiscence group therapy is more growth oriented and enables members to find commonalities with one another and other members of their generation. They place themselves with their peers in a life-span perspective and compare their lives to other members' lives. They also gain a more supportive grasp of *then* and *now*. The sharing of their past lives indicates that they had trials and triumphs. Some members are more confident about the present grounded in obstacles they overcame.

Reminiscence groups could be led by supervised volunteers and paraprofessionals, although leadership may differ in groups with severely cognitively impaired members. Some goals and some kinds of populations require a high level of professional ability; Hogan (1982) taught volunteers to conduct reminiscence groups in nursing homes.

Reminiscence as a group modality competes with reality orientation, remotivation, validation therapy, and current events groups. Reminiscence techniques are easily incorporated into groups that have another focus; the use of memories is an adjunct to those groups: for example, art (Jungels 1991; Wolcott, 1978), bibliotherapy (O'Dell 1986), music (Hennessey 1986; Moore 1986), poetry (Koch 1977; Lyman & Edwards 1989), exercise or dance (Booth-Buehring 1986), and current events (Patton 1978). In the last type of group, current events and news may be compared to past events.

Tross and Blum (1988) state that life review psychotherapy consists of recalling one's past, absolving oneself of past guilt, stating positive personal values, and resolving intra- and interpersonal conflicts. That is a set of more comprehensive, in-depth goals than is found in the goals of the usual reminiscence group. In reminiscence groups, the recall often only involves bits and pieces of the past. Life review is regarded as a developmental task of later years (see Chapter 16). Reminiscence can hardly be called a developmental task because of its overall lack of specificity.That is not to say that themes for reminiscence could not be put in a developmental format. Regarding lack of specificity, Romaniuk (1981) stated, "reminiscence can be goal-directed or directionless, other or self-serving, broad or narrowly focused, significant or insignificant, entertaining or serious, public or private, etc." (p. 316).

TYPE OF REMINISCENCE

Researchers have identified a total of 29 types of reminiscence (Bliwise 1982; Coleman 1974; Fallot 1976; Lo Gerfo 1980-1981; McMahon & Rhudick 1964; Merriam 1989; Postema 1970; Walker 1984; Wong & Watt 1991). However, some types have been identified by more than one researcher, types overlap, or a type seems similar to another type with a different name. Table 15-1 portrays types of reminiscence as identified by researchers.

For example, overlap occurs in informative reminiscence (Bliwise 1982; Fallot 1976; Lo Gerfo 1980-1981; Walker 1984), simple reminiscence (Coleman 1974; Merriam 1989; Walker 1984), and life review (Coleman 1974; McMahon & Rhudick 1964; Postema 1970; Wong & Watt 1991). Only one researcher identified a type called "grief work reminiscence" (Walker 1984). It should be noted that three out of eight researchers included life review as one type of reminiscence, but some believe that the two concepts are not the same (Haight 1991; Burnside & Haight 1994; Merriam 1980).

At this writing, the most definitive and complete taxonomy of reminiscence is Wong and Watt (1991) and Watt and Wong (1991). They write that their taxonomy "incorporates all the major types of reminiscence in the literature and can accommodate all the available reminiscence data" (Wong & Watt 1991, 273). Wong and Watt's six types include integrative reminiscence (similar to Robert Butler's [1963] life review), instrumental reminiscence, transmissive reminiscence, escapist reminiscence, obsessive reminiscence, and narrative reminiscence. Watt and Wong (1991) state that it is not reminiscence per se that provides adaptive benefits, but that the benefits depend on the type of reminiscence. They state that each of the six types of reminiscence they described can be used for increasing the well-being of older people on an individual basis or in a group.

The reader may wonder why these types are important to the would-be reminiscence group leader. Knowledge of types of reminiscence could help the leader to:

TABLE 15-1 Typologies of reminiscence: 1964-1991

McMahon & Rhudick (1964)	• Storytelling • Material for life review • Defensive reminiscence
Coleman (1974)	• Simple reminiscence • Life review • Informative reminiscence
Fallot (1976)	• Affirming style • Negating style • Despairing style
Lo Gerfo (1980-1981)	• Informative reminiscence • Evaluative reminiscence • Obsessive reminiscence
Bliwise (1982)	• Flight from past reminiscence • Informative reminiscence • Ruminative reminiscence • Idealized reminiscence • Integrative reminiscence
Walker (1984)	• Simple reminiscence • Informative reminiscence • Life review • Grief work
Watt & Wong (1991)	• Integrative reminiscence • Instrumental reminiscence • Transmissive reminiscence • Escapist reminiscence • Obsessive reminiscence • Narrative reminiscence

- Appreciate the variance in the reminiscence process.
- Recognize the type of reminiscence he or she wishes to elicit.
- Recognize the type of reminiscence to discourage in groups.
- Identify the various types of reminiscence that occur during the group meetings.
- Incorporate a taxonomy of reminiscence into practice and further its refinement by basing group practice on research.
- Speed up the process of distinguishing between reminiscence therapy groups and life review therapy groups.

PURPOSES

Practitioners have given a variety of reasons for using reminiscence groups. Many reminiscence groups have been studied by nurse researchers for a variety of purposes: to reduce apathy and confusion (Wichita 1974), to alleviate depression (Cook 1988; Matteson 1984; Michelson 1981; Parsons

1986; Tourangeau 1988; Youssef 1990), to increase social interaction (Wilkinson 1978), to train lay persons in the leadership of reminiscence groups (Hogan 1982), to increase life satisfaction (Cook 1988; Moore 1985), to improve morale (King 1979), to increase self-esteem (Lappe 1987; Moore 1985), to tap into creativity (Bramlett 1990), to increase control over the environment (Baumann 1990; Tappen & Touhy 1986), and to measure ego integrity (Cook 1991). Other disciplines have implemented reminiscence as an intervention; examples are occupational therapists (Kiernat 1979), psychologists (Lowenthal & Mazzarro 1990; Poulton & Strassberg 1986), psychiatrists with other disciplines (Lesser, Lazarus, Frankel & Havasy 1981), and physicians (McMahon & Rhudick 1964). Social workers implement reminiscence groups for therapeutic reasons (Fielden 1990; Ingersoll & Goodman 1983; Kaminsky 1984; Orten, Allen & Cook 1989).

HISTORICAL PERSPECTIVES

Past writers described the negative views held about reminiscence. In fact, Pincus (1970), in an excellent article about reminiscence and social work practice, stated "Reminiscence is often squashed in our society as the babblings of the old" (p. 193). Hausman (1980) summed it up: "Reminiscence in the aged is frequently viewed as pathological—a wish to escape from the present, a loss of recent memory, or useless and repetitive rambling" (p. 31). No doubt, there are still lay people who believe that reminiscence is a sign of living in the past and should be discouraged. Also, they might find the content boring. Coleman (1986a) feels that there is a change in the attitude of gerontologists, who view it as a healthy activity rather than an unhealthy one.

Sometimes leaders fail to encourage the narrator to move on to more concrete details or greater depth, which might be beneficial to both speaker and hearers, and instead simply try to turn the reminiscer off. Group workers in the 1960s strongly emphasized the here and now and looked on excursions into the past as evasions of responsibility for present behavior (Schmidt 1993, personal communication).

The pejorative attitude about reminiscence can even be found in novels. The attitude was well expressed in a popular novel when a young clergyman thought, "Because Caleb was old, the young man had thought, of course, he would be garrulous and full of reminiscences, but he was wrong" (Craven 1974, 5).

EMPIRICAL STUDIES

The earliest empirical study in group work using reminiscence as an independent variable was the classic study by McMahon and Rhudick (1964). This study followed closely on the heels of the seminal work published by Robert Butler (1963), which did not address group reminiscence (Birren & Deutchman 1991). Butler described the phenomenon in terms of individual therapy based on his treatment of geropsychiatric clients. Only later did Lewis and Butler (1974) write about life review group therapy. Butler's (1963) and McMahon and Rhudick's (1964) articles provide the basis for many of the later studies about reminiscence group therapy.

Because of space constraints, it is not possible to include exhaustive descriptions of empirical studies on group reminiscence. However, a review of a few of the studies should help the reader better understand the evolution of reminiscence group therapy in the past three decades.

REMINISCENCE GROUP STUDIES

As stated above, the first empirical study of reminiscence group therapy was in 1964. McMahon and Rhudick described one group, the storytellers, who were old soldiers "recounting past exploits and experiences with obvious pleasure in a manner which is both entertaining and informative" (p. 297). McMahon and Rhudick (1964) were the first to pose a linkage between self-esteem and reminiscence: "The older person's knowledge of a bygone era provides him with an opportunity to enhance his self-esteem by contributing in a meaningful way to society" (p. 298). They observed that reminiscence was used to depreciate the present and to glorify the past. That is, if the reminiscer could see the past as being more important than the present, it might help her or him survive present circumstances better. Some believe that this is particularly true for nursing home residents.

In the 1970s there were anecdotal articles about reminiscence groups, especially by nurses who were beginning to implement groups. Two masters' theses (Wichita 1974; Wilkinson 1978) were the earliest studies located. Although reminiscence research studies appeared, they were not about reminiscence groups.

Although not about group reminiscence, one study offers interesting findings. Based on interviews with 377 people, whose ages ranged from 54 to 83 years, Rabbit and McInnis (1988) concluded that the age when earliest memory occurs is related not to current age but to intelligence. Those subjects with high IQ test scores remembered their first and second memories at an earlier age than did subjects with lower IQ test scores. It is to be noted that "The content of early memories was unrelated to age or intelligence" (p. 338). This may be useful information to group leaders who wish to elicit a first memory or earliest memory.

Rattenbury and Stones (1989), in a randomized study, compared the psychological well-being of aged nursing home residents who participated in reminiscence and current topics group discussion with a control group of residents. The members' happiness/depression, activity, mood, and function levels were measured before and after group interventions. The reminiscence intervention had a significant effect only on the happiness/ depression measure. However, both interventions were credited with positive changes when compared to the control group.

Fielden (1990) studied a reminiscence group intervention "as an adaptive tool for improving general psychological well-being, increasing life satisfaction and facilitating social interaction among residents of a warden-aided housing scheme" in the United Kingdom. This study showed that the intervention was effective in changing patterns of socialization, life satisfaction, and psychological well-being. The researcher made two important points. First, reminiscence is nonthreatening, because personal memories cannot be challenged and "everyone is an expert about their own past." Second, reminiscence reduces vulnerability because "reminiscing about the past self is personal but distanced in time and, therefore, not as apparently revealing of the present self" (p. 32).

Lowenthal and Marrazzo (1990) coined the word *milestoning* for their reminiscence therapy groups. The group members were mentally ill institutionalized older persons. They noted the following results:

1. Increased spontaneous and prompted verbalization.
2. Increased patient–patient interaction.
3. Continued patient–therapist interaction.
4. Increased receptiveness to listening to others (p. 271).

In developing their model, the researchers concluded:

1. Life review is not applicable to most mental hospital residents.
2. Dependent patients need a more structured and directed process than life review.
3. This group cannot and will not focus attention on questionnaires (either verbal or written).
4. This group usually lacks the curiosity and desire for group interaction reminiscence, necessitating the use of sensory stimulators (p. 271).

There has been a steady increase in studies about reminiscence group therapy in the past three decades, and one trend is that more studies are using community-based subjects (Bramlett 1990; Burnside 1990; Parsons 1986). While the benefits are highly touted, the negative results are less clear and rarely discussed in the literature. Cook (1988) did indicate that the theme of war in her protocol had elicited sad, unhappy memories; however, such sharing could have been cathartic for those reminiscers.

USES OF REMINISCENCE

Romaniuk and Romaniuk (1981) listed three uses of reminiscence in their findings. And although they were not studying groups, the uses are relevant for reminiscence group leaders: self-regard/ image enhancement, present problem solving, and existential self-understanding. Havighurst and Glasser (1972) might have disagreed with the problem-solving category, because in their classic article they stated that reminiscence was not used for problem solving. Five subscales on the functions of reminiscence that had the highest ratings in the Romaniuk and Romaniuk (1981) study can be extrapolated and used as a guideline to write goals for reminiscence groups:

1. Remembering pleasant events is enjoyable.
2. Remembering can lift spirits.
3. Remembering can entertain.
4. Remembering can further a description of self to others.
5. Remembering can identify what was better in the past.

REMINISCENCE AND CLINICAL PRACTICE

The practitioner implementing reminiscence groups is often not taken very seriously. It may appear to the casual observer that it is simply a fun-and-games technique and that just about anyone can do it. In reality, reminiscence groups require thoughtful planning and careful organization. It is helpful if the leader has an interest in history and in the developmental life span.

Coleman (1986a, 1986b), an expert in individual reminiscence, advises: Any helping person whether a professional or not should try to understand the older person's perspective, history, and circumstance before using reminiscence as a therapeutic intervention. He further recommends that the person implementing reminiscence should try to determine beforehand what the likely benefits might be. In bereavement support groups Huart and O'Donnell (1993) report that "the most enjoyable and poignant session is reminiscence therapy. Photographs, videos, music, artwork, and other memorabilia are brought in, shared, and laughed and cried over" (p. 74).

THEMES, PROPS, AND TRIGGERS

Themes

The lack of research about themes and protocols in reminiscence group therapy hampers our understanding of the effectiveness (or ineffectiveness) of themes. Themes may be selected using a life span approach, a shotgun list, or a list of firsts in members' lives (Burnside 1993).

The leader may need to be introspective and try to determine which themes are most comfortable for her or him to elicit. This is especially true if a selected theme bombs out. For example, in a group I led in Australia, the topic of Christmas fell flat, because most of the women had been so poor that they did not even celebrate the holiday. People who dislike pets or who never owned one do not share much in a group that discusses pets. A theme of children and grandchildren is usually not appropriate if group members are unmarried.

Weiss (1993) is one of the first writers to spell out the advantages of preselection of group themes and the reasons that it can be advantageous. See Table 15-2.

Props

Props are commonly associated with the theater or airplanes (Rodriguez 1990). In reminiscence groups, props are objects brought to the group by the leader or members with the intent of eliciting memories. Rodriguez (1990) further describes characteristics of props as age appropriate, culturally appropriate, gender appropriate, and geographically appropriate.

- *Age appropriate*—the prop will be familiar to a certain age cohort.
- *Culturally appropriate*—the prop will be known to members of certain ethnic groups.
- *Gender appropriate*—the prop will appeal to the gender of the group, or if there are both men and women in a group, it will elicit discussion from both sexes.
- *Geographically appropriate*—the prop pertains to the geographic region in which most of the group members live or lived.

Props require more work for the leader than themes do. Gathering props and keeping them intact may require more logistics than selecting a theme.

Props are often quite effective with persons with dementia. They are useful because they may appeal to more than one sense; for example, a piece of fruit appeals to the senses of sight, touch, smell, and taste. For the sensorily impaired, props also can elicit unexpected responses. I can still see my poodle sitting on the lap of a blind man in a group. The man had not petted a dog in the 10 years he had been in the nursing home. He held the poodle tightly, petting him and smiling all the while.

Old photographs are often effective props, but they should be large enough and clear enough so that all of the members can see them. Very old photographs may be highly treasured, and the leader will need to ensure that they are not lost or damaged. This is particularly true if the members have dementia. In one group, women mistakenly thought photographs were theirs, and some put the wrong photographs in their purses.

Shirley Hendrix (1992, personal communication) used props with nonagenarian women and

TABLE 15-2 Advantages of group themes and reasons for benefits

Advantage	Reason for benefit
Autonomy	Members are in control of interactions, even though a theme has been introduced.
Choice	Members can choose the direction of their sharing.
Commitment	Preselection of themes is intended to focus on the older person.
Continuity	Focus on one theme at a time may help the older member continue this as a leisure activity.
Depth	Holding the number of themes to one (or a few) allows for more detailed descriptions.
Increases confidence	Members are likely to select themes with which they are comfortable.
Provides structure	If themes are given to the members before the meeting, they may be more clear about what the meetings are about.
Reduces ambiguity	Older persons are not expected to discuss their entire lives (in contrast to a life review, which covers the life span).

SOURCE: Based on Weiss (1993, 42).

discovered that they did not seem truly interested in them—as though they had moved beyond them and were in an existential frame of mind instead. All the props chosen were apparently appropriate for the women and had been carefully selected.

Triggers are words or phrases or thoughts expressed by one member that help other members recall memories. One commonly hears "that reminds me of . . ." The purpose of selecting themes is to do just that. The best-laid plans of group leaders go awry, and themes do not always produce the desired results. Possible reasons for a theme not eliciting reminiscence could be:

- The theme is inappropriate for the age of the group members.
- There is something urgent to discuss that takes priority over the selected theme (for example, a natural disaster or an important news event).
- The theme is inappropriate because members do not have the knowledge or memories to reminisce about the theme.
- The theme is geographically inappropriate (for example, discussing cotton raising in a group in Seattle).
- The theme is inappropriate gender-wise (for example, men may not be wildly enthusiastic about discussing dolls).
- The leader may be tentative about the theme and may have trouble guiding the flow of reminiscence.

Newcomers group on an Alzheimer's unit was described by Carey and Hansen (1986). Ten sessions were held weekly for 30 to 45 minutes. Each session had a theme: hobbies, career, first dates, birthplace, and so on. "The groups were lighthearted and enjoy-

able. The emphasis was on interaction among participants" (p. 26). It is worth noting that people who had lived in the residence for years took an interest in the group, and the leaders did not exclude them from the group because they were not new residents.

FLASHBULB MEMORIES AND THE I'VE-NEVER-TOLD-ANYONE PHENOMENON
Flashbulb Memories

A flashbulb memory is one that causes instant recall in reminiscers. Perhaps the most common one is the assassination of President Kennedy. (See page 159 in Chapter 14.) However, memories associated with Charles Lindbergh's solo flight across the Atlantic are also powerful for persons who were young during that era. In a group of six women in a retirement home, three described in graphic detail attending a ticker-tape parade for Lindbergh. Two of the women had been at the New York parade and were surprised to learn that the other one had been there.

The I've-Never-Told-Anyone Phenomenon

One of the most poignant and powerful I've-never-told-anyone examples is described by Thorsheim and Roberts (1990). After a session of sharing, an older woman lingers on, approaches the leader, and shares the story of having been raped as a teenager and never having shared the incident.

While I've had persons state that they have never shared the information before in the one-to-one interaction, it also occurs in groups. A man in his seventies revealed a prank he pulled as a teenager, pushing a mule into the belfry of a small church in a rural area of the South. Perhaps the group climate reaches a high trust level when this occurs.

MEANING OF REMINISCENCE

I have often asked students or audiences to reminisce in a dyad situation. Then I have asked for brief descriptors of what the experience meant to them. The array of descriptors by three different groups is worth noting here and can be found in Table 15-3. As can be noted, not all memories are happy; some people recall sad memories. (I have wondered if they were concurrently experiencing a sad time in their life.) Many feel a connection to their childhood. It is my observation that only a few raise their hands when asked if they had shared a sad memory. A verse by an anonymous author expresses this emotional reaction to reminiscing.

> Come talk with me
>   of days gone by . . .
> Let's linger there awhile
> Some memories may make us cry
> But more will bring a smile.

If students can identify their own reactions and feelings that occur during or immediately after a reminiscence session, then perhaps they will better understand some of the meaning and importance reminiscence has for the older adult.

REMINISCENCE GROUPS AND THE ALERT

It is probably easiest for the neophyte group leader to begin a reminiscence group with alert older adults; it is not wise to try to mix the alert and the confused if one is leading a reminiscence group for the first time. See Chapter 11 on conducting groups with the cognitively impaired and that chapter's Resources for ideas for groups, especially the members with Alzheimer's disease.

REMINISCENCE GROUPS AND AFFLUENT OLDER PERSONS

I have given much thought to reminiscence with affluent older people. Probably I think about it because I have seldom felt successful with these people. In retrospect, some of the reasons appear to be:

- They frequently have the pejorative attitude about reminiscence that was described earlier in this chapter.
- They often have very busy schedules and cannot be bothered with either being a research subject or being involved in a weekly reminiscence group. They place much more importance on their golf, television programs, and social activities. They may travel a great deal and not be available for groups.
- Affluent older persons who oppose reminiscence will often state that they "live for the future." Their future orientation is so great that they adamantly oppose any discussions of the past.
- Intelligent and affluent older people often try to wrestle control of the group away from the leader. This may be especially true if they have been involved in groups in their professional lives (for example, teachers, physicians, social workers, nurses, psychologists, and so on).
- Intelligent affluent members also spend an inordinate amount of time in a group avoiding reminiscence and changing the focus or subject under discussion. One method is a constant interrogation of the leader about the purpose and meaning of the group—an indicator of the avoidance mechanism at work.

REMINISCENCE GROUPS WITH MEMBERS WHO HAVE MEMORY LOSS

Many years ago, I thought that it would not be possible to do reminiscence groups with older persons with memory loss, but I have changed my mind about that. The one thing that has remained constant, however, is that it is very hard work, and one should realize that one will have to expend a lot of time, thought, and energy to conducting groups with this special group of older people.

Adaptations will have to be made according to the severity of the memory loss. But even the most forgetful or aphasic individual can perceive the warmth and ambience of a group. And they will surprise you over and over again. Here is an example: A business executive, who was in his sixties

TABLE 15-3 Descriptors of an experiential exercise in group reminiscence

Graduate Social Worker Class[1]	First-year Students – MSW[2]	Conference Participants[3]	Conference Participants[4]
• Bonding	• Flowing	• Accomplishment	• Bonding
• Confident	• Funny	• Bonding	• Cathartic
• Expression of feelings	• Happy	• Closeness (to father)	• Nostalgic
• Feeling of connectedness	• Humorous	• Comfort	• Not alone
• Kinship to small child I was	• Insightful	• Excitement	• Reconnected to childhood
			• Safe
• Long-forgotten	• Intense	• Humor	• Self-satisfaction
• Remembering	• Intimacy	• Joy	• Sorrow
• Satisfying experience	• Laughter	• Peacefulness	• Warm
• Self-affirmation	• Melancholic	• Sadness, pain	
• Spills out gently—not invasive	• Rapport	• Security at the time the memory is being shared	
• Stimulus	• Touching	• Warmth	
	• Very enjoyable		
	• Wistful		

SOURCES:
[1]Professor Guy Shuttlesworth: Social Work 395D class at the University of Texas, Austin, Texas (1988).
[2]Professor Mary Gwynne Schmidt: Class at San Diego State University (1991).
[3]Conference at The Methodist Medical Center of Illinois, Department of Human Resource Development (1992).
[4]Conference at the San Diego Center on Aging, San Diego County Mental Health Department (1993).

and aphasic (Alzheimer's disease) was in a reminiscence group. He never spoke, but he smiled and appeared to enjoy himself. One day in the day care center, I taught a class on sexuality and noticed him sitting in the back. When I finished, he came up, patted me on the back and said "Good job"—the only words I ever heard him speak. Those are the small rewards one must find satisfaction in if one chooses to work with those with memory impairment.

The therapist must be active and draw the members out, set realistic goals, find the appropriate pace, and anticipate that there will be variable performances by the same member. That is true of the group as a whole too. One meeting will seem to go very well, and the next can bomb out.

Props that appeal to more than one sense are most effective. One day I brought shaving lotion for the men and cologne for the women—and how they enjoyed splashing themselves! I never had much success with photographs or pictures; however, there may have been more vision problems in the members than I realized.

CLINICAL PRACTICE

The following are suggestions for the implementation of reminiscence groups in clinical practice.

1.   There are kits available to use for reminiscence groups. I have never used one, but for a neophyte, they might prove to be useful and time-saving. The resources at the end of the chapter may be helpful in this regard. Martin (1993) wrote, "We have developed a reminiscence room decorated and furnished in the style of the 1940s. This area has stimulated a great deal of interest in patients, staff and visitors. It has proved to have a calming influence over the unsettled, confused elderly person and is an excellent communication stimulus" (See Resources).

2.   Reminiscence groups are usually easy to implement, and there is virtually no cost to any agency if the leader is a student or a volunteer. (Cost is involved if refreshments are served or props need to be purchased.)

3.   For some leaders, it is much less arduous than reality orientation, but if one chooses to work with confused and disoriented older adults, then it requires a great deal more skill, energy, and patience than working with alert elders.

4.   For me as an instructor, it has been the single most effective teaching strategy I have used to help reduce ageism in students. Older group members hook the student, so to speak.

5.   Using props can enhance the process and make reminiscence come alive. Props sometimes get

the families and/or the staff members involved. Sometimes the staff become interested; for example, a park ranger brought in leaves that the Indians had used for soap, and staff were interested in his sharing. Pets will bring staff and visitors to the group.

6. Health professionals in acute care hospitals should consider implementation of reminiscence because it "is a mechanism for avoiding or minimizing a present that is painful or empty from losses" (Carnevali & Patrick 1993, 256). The same authors reported that in New York, older persons who were discharged from hospitals and "who engaged in reminiscing tended to survive longer with fewer readmissions than those who focused on a bleak present and uncertain future" (p. 256).

7. Older persons can be superb teachers, and it can be rewarding to listen and learn from them. One has to be willing to accept the learner role and help them to feel comfortable in the teacher role.

8. With a knowledge base about the various types of reminiscence discussed earlier in the chapter, the leader will need to be aware of which types to encourage and which types to discourage.

9. New leaders often get hung up in trying to determine if the memories being shared are actually true. Unless the group member has Korsakoff's syndrome (a condition in which exaggeration and confabulation occur), the leader should rest easy, because "the past need not be accurate, but rather, it must be real and vivid" (Tobin 1991, 13).

10. One leader (Skoff 1992) asks group members to write short paragraphs of remembrances. Then she collects them, types them in large, bold type, places them in a booklet entitled "Remembrances," and gives one to each member (see Resources).

11. Rooms may be decorated for the purpose of encouraging reminiscence. See individual Resources.

12. One issue that may arise with the young group leader is countertransference. Sometimes the youthful leader is reluctant to intervene because "the person reminds me of my grandmother/grandfather and I feel I should be respectful." Or the group member may treat the leader as a grandchild, niece, or nephew.

13. Journaling is mentioned by Steffl in Chapter 30. Preserving memories allows them to be enjoyed again and again, in contrast to sharing memories verbally (Weiss 1993). Weiss's article lists reasons for documenting older persons' memories (p. 42), as shown in Table 15-4.

14. The benefits and rewards of listening to reminiscences are often ignored and should be noted here:

It has been stated than an open and interested recipient to the older person reminiscing can:
A. Gain knowledge and understanding about the older person and the period in which he or she has lived.
B. Build a bridge between past experiences and the present.
C. Establish a mutually satisfying relationship through the sharing of information and experiences.
D. Use a person's history as a therapeutic tool in building programming or establishing resources for others.
E. Have a context for gaining cues about the person's behavior in the present (University of Michigan n.d.).

15. Because many older people are seldom listened to, the best advice for new leaders is: "One can seldom listen his way into trouble" (Farnsworth 1972).

RESEARCH

Although Chapter 34 covers research issues with older subjects in detail, it is appropriate to include a few ideas here. First of all, it is not easy to conduct intervention studies. The discipline and adherence to research principles is one thing, but one also has to consider the needs of the older group members and agency demands. The matter of confidentiality is of utmost concern to the researcher and the group leader. Privacy can be a concern, because it may be difficult to find a room with doors or a time without interruptions by staff members. The researcher may be torn between the need to stay on track with the research and the need to reach out and spend more time with individuals who may be hurting because of the group experiences.

If one conducts pre- and posttests, one should allow extra time, especially with the frail aged (Bowsher, Bramlett, Burnside & Gueldner 1993). Taping sessions can help a student learn

TABLE 15-4 Reasons for documenting older persons' memories

Appealing to friends and family	• May provide comfort about the eventual loss of the older person.
Authenticity	• The actual words are available and are not second-hand accounts.
Authorship	• Can be a lofty experience.
Cues	• The recollections may actually continue the reminiscence process.
Expanded audience	• Memories are available to those who did not attend the original presentation.
Genealogy	• Those separated geographically can discover their roots.
	• Strengthens family ties.
Legacy	• Preserves the essence of the real person.
Tangibility	• Helps the older person feel productive.

more about techniques and will provide accurate data. Suspicious or paranoid individuals may balk, however. Choice of words is crucial. In Australia, I lost an entire group in an assisted living residence when I mentioned the use of a computer and stated that their identities would go in as numbers. The word *computer* absolutely turned them off, and all the women refused to be in a group.

Written records are important for students to share with a supervisor and also to help students pick up trends and changes over time and to determine if the leader's methods are working.

SUMMARY

This chapter has presented a brief literature review and historical perspective of reminiscence group therapy. Clinical application was discussed, and benefits for the listener were listed. Use of reminiscence groups with alert and confused older adults was discussed. Props and themes, important adjuncts to reminiscence groups, were presented. The leaders were cautioned about using themes and props, which are appropriate in these four areas: age, geographical location, gender, and culture.

EXERCISE 1

Interview an older person who has moderate memory loss. Endeavor to tap into long-term memory by using reminiscence techniques. What themes that you used were most successful in eliciting memories? What problems arose during the interview?

EXERCISE 2

Select three props, such as a washboard, a hat pin, an old iron, or an old coffee grinder, and share them with three old persons. Ask them to describe their memories about each of the props. Record the commonalities and the differences in the memories. Write in detail what you learned about the life style of each person from the discussion. Be sure to consider how the age of the individual affected the discussion.

EXERCISE 3

Close your eyes. Think about a memory that is important to you. Then analyze all the senses that are involved in this memory. Which sense do you think is the most important? Do the same exercise with an old person and compare and contrast your memory of the involved senses with those the older person described to you.

EXERCISE 4

Settle (1992) stated, "Memory can be intelligent, but recall is a sensuous thing" (p. 57). Do you agree or disagree? List reasons for your choice.

EXERCISE 5

In a brief paper, state definitions of reminiscence and life review and explicate the differences between reminiscence and life review in the definitions you have stated.

EXERCISE 6

Read Chapter 16, by Birren and Deutchman, and design a table that differentiates autobiography groups from reminiscence groups.

REFERENCES

Baumann MA. 1990. The effect of reminiscence group therapy on personal control of institutionalized elders. Unpublished master's thesis. Augusta, GA: Medical College of Georgia.

Birren JE, Deutchman DE. 1991. *Guiding autobiography groups for older adults: Exploring the fabric of life*. Baltimore: Johns Hopkins University Press.

Bliwise NG. 1982. Reminiscence: Presentations of the personal past in middle and late life. Unpublished doctoral dissertation. Chicago: The University of Chicago.

Blythe R. 1979. *The view in winter: Reflections on old age*. New York: Harcourt, Brace Jovanovich.

Booth-Buehring H. 1986. Dance/Movement therapy. In IM Burnside (ed.), *Working with the elderly: Group process and techniques*, 2d ed. (pp. 213-224). Boston: Jones and Bartlett.

Bowsher J, Bramlett M, Burnside IM, Gueldner SH. 1993. Methodological considerations in the study of frail elderly people. *J Adv Nurs* 18:873-879.

Bramlett MH. 1990. Power, creativity and reminiscence in the elderly. Unpublished dissertation. Augusta, GA: Medical College of Georgia.

Burnside IM. 1993. Themes in reminiscence groups with older women. *Int J Aging Human Dev* 37(3):177-189.

——— . 1990. The effect of reminiscence groups on fatigue, affect, and life satisfaction in older women. Unpublished dissertation. Austin, TX: School of Nursing, The University of Texas at Austin.

——— . 1994. Protocols for clinical practice: Reminiscence and life review. *Nurs Pract*. Accepted for publication.

Burnside I, Haight BK. 1992. Reminiscence and life review: Analyzing each concept. *J Adv Nurs* 17:855-862.

Butler R. 1963. The life review: An interpretation of reminiscence in the aged. *Psychiatry* (26):65-76.

Carey B, Hansen SS. 1986. Social work groups with institutionalized Alzheimer's victims. *J Gerontol Soc Work*—Special issue: Social work and Alzheimer's disease, 9(2):15-25.

Carnevali DL, Patrick M (eds.). 1993. *Nursing management for the elderly*, 3d ed. Philadelphia: Lippincott.

Coleman P. 1986a. Issues in the therapeutic use of reminiscence with elderly people. In I Hanley, M Gilhooley (eds.), *Psychological therapies for the elderly* (pp. 41-64). London: Croon Helm.

——— . 1986b. *Ageing and reminiscence processes: Social and clinical implications*. New York: Wiley.

——— . 1974. Measuring reminiscence characteristics from conversation as adaptive functions of old age. *Int J Aging Human Dev* 5(3):281-294.

Cook EA. 1991. The effects of reminiscence on psychological measures of ego integrity in elderly nursing home residents. *Arch Psychiatr Nurs* V(5):292-298.

——— . 1988. The effect of reminiscence group therapy on depressed institutionalized elders. Unpublished doctoral dissertation. Austin, TX: School of Nursing, The University of Texas at Austin.

Craven, M. 1974. *I heard the owl call my name*. London: Pan Books.

Disch R. 1988. *Twenty-five years of the life review: Theoretical and practical considerations*. New York: Haworth.

Fallot RD. 1976. The life story through reminiscence in later years. *DAI* (1977) 38:353B (University Microfilms, No. 77-14039).

Farnsworth D. 1972. Preparing for retirement. *Psychiatr Ann* 2(2):14-25.

Feil N, Wetzler M. 1979. An innovative method of working with the severely disoriented aged. *Am Health Care Assoc J* 5(3):41-44.

Fielden MA. 1990. Reminiscence as a therapeutic intervention with sheltered housing residents: A comparative study. *Br J Soc Work* 20:21-44.

Georgemiller R, Maloney HN. 1984. Group life review and denial of death. *Clin Gerontol* 2(4):37-49.

Haight BK. 1991. Reminiscing: The state of the art as a basis for practice. *Int J Aging Human Dev* 33(1):1-32.

Hausman CP. 1980. Life review therapy. *J Gerontol Soc Work* 3(2):31-37.

Havighurst RJ, Glasser R. 1972. An exploratory study of reminiscence. *J Gerontol* 27:243-253.

Hendrix S. 1992. Personal communication.

Hennessey MJ. 1986. Music therapy. In IM Burnside (ed.), *Working with the elderly: Group process and techniques*, 2d ed. (pp. 198-210). Boston: Jones and Bartlett.

Hogan J. 1982. The use of nonprofessional leaders in reminiscing groups for the institutionalized elderly. Unpublished master's thesis. San Jose, CA: Department of Nursing, San Jose State University.

Huart S, O'Donnell M. 1993. The road to recovery from grief and bereavement. *Caring* 12(11):71-75.

Ingersoll B, Goodman L. 1983. A reminiscence for institutionalized elderly. In M Rosenbaum (ed.), *Handbook of short-term therapy groups* (pp. 267-279). New York: McGraw-Hill.

Jungels G. 1991. "Looks like the starting of a house": Art therapy and the older adult. In N Weisberg, R Wilder (eds.), *Creative arts with older adults: A sourcebook* (pp. 201-209). New York: Human Sciences Press.

Kaminsky M. 1984. *The uses of reminiscence: New ways of working with older adults.* New York: Haworth.

Kiernat JM. 1979. The use of the life review activity. *Am J Occup Ther* 33(5):306-310.

King K. 1979. Reminiscing group experiences with aging people. Unpublished master's thesis. Salt Lake City: College of Nursing, University of Utah.

Koch K. 1977. *I never told anybody.* New York: Random House.

Lappe JM. 1987. Reminiscing: The life review therapy. *J Gerontol Nurs* 13:12-16.

Lesser J, Lazarus LW, Frankel R, Havasy S. 1981. Reminiscence group therapy with psychotic geriatric inpatients. *Gerontologist* 21(3):291-296.

Lewis MI, Butler RN. 1974. Life review therapy: Putting memories to work in individual and group therapy. *Geriatrics* 29(11):165-173.

Lo Gerfo M. 1980-81. Three ways of reminiscence in theory and practice. *Int J Aging Human Dev* 12:39-48.

Lowenthal RI, Marrazzo RA. 1990. Milestoning: Evoking memories for resocialization through group reminiscence. *Gerontologist* 30(2):269-272.

Lyman AJ, Edwards ME. 1989. Reminiscence poetry groups: Sheepherding—a Navajo cultural tie that binds. *Activities, Adaptation, & Aging* 13(4):1-8.

Martin J. 1993. Personal letter.

Matteson MA. 1984. Group reminiscing for the depressed institutionalized elderly. In IM Burnside, (ed.), *Working with the elderly: Group process and techniques*, 2d ed. (pp. 287-297). Boston: Jones and Bartlett.

McMahon AW, Rhudick PJ. 1964. Reminiscing: Adaptational significance in the aged. *Arch Gen Psychiatr* 10:292-298.

Merriam S. 1989. The structure of simple reminiscence. *Gerontologist* 29(6):761-767.

Michelson S. 1981. Reminiscence as a means of decreasing depression in the aged. Unpublished research paper. Boston: Boston University.

Moore EC. 1986. A music therapist's perspective. In IM Burnside (ed.), *Working with the elderly: Group process and techniques*, 2d ed. (pp. 426-439). Boston: Jones and Bartlett.

Moore MA. 1985. Effects of reminiscing and touch in group therapy on the self-esteem and morale of institutionalized elderly. Unpublished master's thesis. San Jose, CA: Department of Nursing, San Jose State University.

O'Dell L. 1986. A bibliotherapist's perspective. In IM Burnside (ed.), *Working with the elderly: Group process and techniques*, 2d ed. (pp. 410-425). Boston: Jones and Bartlett.

Orten JD, Allen M, Cook J. 1989. Reminiscence groups with confused nursing center residents: An experimental study. *Soc Work Health Care* 14(1):73-86.

Parsons C. 1986. Group reminiscence therapy and levels of depression in the elderly. *Nurs Pract* 11:68-70.

Patton F. 1978. The administrator as group leader: A current events discussion group. In IM Burnside (ed.), *Working with the elderly: Group process and techniques,* 1st ed. (pp. 311-319). North Scituate, MA: Duxbury Press.

Pincus A. 1970. Reminiscence in aging and its implications for social work practice. *Soc Work* 15(4):42-51.

Postema LJ. 1970. Reminiscing, time orientation, and self-concept in aged men. *DAI* 31:6880-B (University Microfilms No. 12-21, 332).

Poulton JL, Strassberg DS. 1986. The therapeutic use of reminiscence. *Int J Group Psychiatr* 36:381-397.

Rabbit P, McInnis L. 1988. Do clever old people have earlier and richer first memories? *Psych Aging* 3(4):338-341.

Rattenbury C, Stones MJ. 1989. A controlled evaluation of reminiscence and current topics discussion groups in a nursing home context. *Gerontologist* 29(6):768-771.

Rodriguez A. 1990. A descriptive study of selected props used to elicit memories in elders. Unpublished master's thesis. Austin, TX: School of Nursing, The University of Texas at Austin.

Romaniuk, M. 1981. Reminiscence and the second half of life. *Exp Aging Res* 7(3):315-316.

Romaniuk M, Romaniuk JG. 1981. Looking back: An analysis of reminiscence functions and triggers. *Exp Aging Res* 7(4):477-489.

Schmidt MG. 1993. Personal communication.

Settle ML. 1992. Recall is a sensuous thing. *Am Way* (October 15):57-58ff.

Shute GE. 1986. Life review: A cautionary note. *Clin Gerontol* 6(1):57-58.

Skoff H. 1992. Personal letter.

Tappen R, Touhy T. 1986. The effectiveness of reminiscence group work on mood levels of institutionalized older adults. Paper presented at the Gerontological Society of America Meeting, Chicago, IL (November 23).

Thornton S, Brotchie J. 1987. Reminiscence: A critical review of the empirical literature. *Br J Clin Psych* 2(26): 93-111.

Thorsheim H, Roberts B. 1990. Empowerment through storysharing: Communication and reciprocal support among older persons. In H Giles, N Copeland, J Wiemann (eds.), *Communication, health and the elderly*, Fulbright Colloquium Series No. 8. Manchester, England: Manchester University.

Tobin SS. 1991. *Personhood in advanced old age: Implications for practice* (pp. 13-14). New York: Springer.

Tourangeau A. 1988. Group reminiscence therapy as a nursing home intervention: An experimental study. *AARN Newsletter*, Part I, 44:17-18; Part II, 44:39-50.

Tross S, Blum J. 1988. A review of group therapy with the older adult: Practice and research. In B Maclennan, S Saul, M Weiner (eds.), *Group psychotherapies for the elderly* (pp. 3-29). Madison, CT: International Universities Press.

University of Michigan. n.d. Institute of Gerontology, APGO Session 3:#12, Ann Arbor.

University of Texas. 1989. Class: Social Work 395 D (October 24).

Walker LS. 1984. The relationship between reminiscing, health state, physical functioning, and depression in older adults. Doctoral dissertation. Washington, DC: The Catholic University of America (*DAI* No. DA8416061).

Watt LM, Wong PTP. 1991. A taxonomy of reminiscence and therapeutic implications. *J Gerontol Soc Work* 16(1/2): 37-57.

Webster JD, Young RA. 1988. Process variables of the life review: Counseling implications. *Int J Aging Human Dev* 26(4):315-323.

Weiss CR. 1993. Capture the moments: Preserving the memories of older adults. *JOPERD* 64(April):41-44.

Wichita C. 1974. Reminiscing as a therapy for apathetic and confused residents of nursing homes. Unpublished master's thesis. Tucson, AZ: University of Arizona.

Wilkinson CS. 1978. A descriptive study of increased social interaction through group reminiscing in institutionalized elderly. Unpublished master's thesis. New Orleans: School of Nursing, Tulane University.

Wolcott A. 1978. Art therapy: An experimental group. In IM Burnside (ed.), *Working with the elderly: Group process and techniques*, 1st ed. (pp. 294-309). North Scituate, MA: Duxbury Press.

Wong PTP, Watt LM. 1991. What types of reminiscence are associated with successful aging? *Psych Aging* 6(2): 272-279.

Youssef FA. 1990. The impact of group reminiscence counseling on a depressed elderly population. *Nurs Pract* 15(4):32-38.

BIBLIOGRAPHY

Beaver ML. 1991. Life review/reminiscent therapy. In PKH. Kim (ed.), *Serving the elderly: Skills for practice* (pp. 67-88). New York: Aldine de Gruyter.

Burnside IM. 1988. Reminiscence and other therapeutic modalities. In IM Burnside (ed.), *Nursing and the aged: A self-care approach,* 3d ed. (pp. 645-686). St. Louis: Mosby.

Hamilton DB. 1992. Reminiscence therapy. In GM Bulechek, JC McCloskey (eds.), Nursing interventions: Essential nursing treatment, 2d ed. (pp. 292-303). Philadelphia: Saunders.

Harwood KJ. 1989. The effects of an occupational therapy reminiscence group: A single case study. *Phys Occup Ther Geriatr* 7(4):43-57.

Head DM, Portnoy S, Woods RT. 1990. The impact of reminiscence groups in two different settings. *Int J Geriatr Psychiatr* 5:295-302.

Kastenbaum R. 1993. Mint, garlic, and the secret heart of time. *Gerontologist* 33(2):272-275.

Lieberman MA, Falk JM. 1971. The remembered past as a source of data for research on the life cycle. *Human Dev* 14(2):132-141.

Merriam SB. 1990. Reminiscence and life review: The potential for educational intervention. In RH Sherron, DB Lumsden (eds.), *Introduction to educational gerontology,* 3d ed. (pp. 41-58). Bristol, PA: Hemisphere Publishing.

Magee J. 1988. *A professional's guide to older adults life review*. Lexington, MA: D. C. Heath.

Martin J. 1989. Expanding reminiscence therapy with elderly mentally infirm patients. *Br J Occup Ther* 52(11):435-436.

Sacks O. 1985. Reminiscence. In *The man who mistook his wife for a hat* (pp. 125-142). London: Pan Books.

Sheridan C. 1991. *Reminiscence*. San Francisco: Elder-Press.

Sherman E. 1991. *Reminiscence and the self in old age.* New York: Springer.

Sherman E, Peak T. 1991. Patterns of reminiscence and the assessment of late life adjustment. *J Gerontol Soc Work* 16(1/2):59-74.

Smith GH. 1986. A comparison of the effects of three treatment interventions on cognitive functioning of Alzheimer patients. *Music Ther* 6A(1):41-56.

Thorsheim H, Roberts B. 1990. *Reminiscing together.* Minneapolis: CompCare Publishers.

Tobin SS. 1972. The earliest memory as data for research in aging. In DP Kent, R Kastenbaum, S Sherwood (eds.), *Research, planning, and action for the elderly: The power and potential of social science* (pp. 252-275). New York: Behavioral Publications.

Weiss C. 1989. Therapeutic recreation and reminiscing: The pursuit of elusive memory and the art of remembering. *Therap Rec J* 23(3):7-18.

Weiss C, Markve-Patch M, Thurn J. 1990. Meals, memories, and memoirs: A culinary odyssey. *Therap Rec J* 24(3): 10-22.

RESOURCES

Activity Products

Eldergames Inc. 1993. Catalog of activity programs that stimulate minds and memories: 11710 Hunters Lane Rockville, MD 20852; phone: 301-984-8336 or 800-637-2604.

Programs

Elders as Consultants: The Lifestories Program. A program encouraging older adults to share their life stories with others. The program seeks to increase the quality of life for people living in rural Minnesota communities. A program manual is available from CompCare Publications, 2415 Annapolis Lane, Northfield, MN 55057. For more information, contact Dr. Bruce Roberts or Dr. Howard Thorsheim, Department of Psychology, St. Olaf College; phone: 507-663-3142.

Monograph

Reminiscence: Finding Meaning in Memories. The program trains volunteers to use memory recall, communication, and visiting skills to help older adults get in touch with meaningful, significant past experiences and improve their feelings of self-worth. For more information, contact Betty Davis, Program Coordinator, Social Outreach and Support, American Association of Retired Persons, 601 E Street, NW, Washington, DC 20049; phone: 202-434-2260.

Magazine

Reminisce (P.O. Box 2916, Milwaukee, WI 53201-2916) is published bi-monthly. This magazine contains many ideas a leader could use to stimulate memories. Stories and excellent photographs about years gone by could serve as triggers for group meetings.

Individual Resources

Resource for a Reminiscence Room. Contact Jane Martin, Head Occupational Therapist, Ogwr Health Unit, Glanrhyd and Penyfar Hospitals, Brigend Mid Glamorgan CF31 4LN, UK.

Course on Reminiscence. Title: The Psychology of Reminiscence. For information, contact Kathy King, RN, PhD, 525 E. 4500, Suite F200, Salt Lake City, UT 84107.

Printing Group Members' Stories. Contact Helen Skoff, 7703 Chelton Road, Bethesda, MD 20814.

Music and Reminiscence

Moments to Remember contains 24 topics—some are songs from the past to use for reminiscence programs. Little or no preparation is needed. 8½" x 11", 114 pages (No. B54); price: $14. Order from: Eldergames, Inc., 11710 Hunters Lane, Rockville, MD 20852; phone: 301-984-8336 or 800-637-2604.

Senior Community Video Project, Inc. records life histories. Address: P.O. Box 29082, Portland, OR 97229; phone: 513-282-8634.

BiFolkal's Insights (91 Williamson Street, Madison, WI 53703) and *Scrapbook Pages* (Thistledown Products, P.O. Box 5583, Arlington, VA 22205) are especially devoted to reminiscence. The newsletters offer a forum for telling life stories and for triggering reminiscence among readers.

Circle Press (P.O. Box 74, Mt. Airy, MD 21771) offers a rich and varied collection of materials, e.g., video and audio cassettes, poetry, and games such as trivia quizzes.

GHI Media Products produces videos such as *Radio Days* that include clips from different periods of history that can be the focal point for a reminiscence activity; phone: 800-426-3812.

Potentials Development for Health and Aging Services, Inc. (775 Main Street, Buffalo, NY 14203; phone: 716-842-2658) offers games to share memories; *Sweet Memories* is designed to help older adults share memories.

Reminiscence: Finding Meaning in Memories (D13403) is a comprehensive kit based on the experience and knowledge gained through AARP's Reminiscence program. It includes a step-by-step guide designed to help individuals conduct a training on the techniques of reminiscence. Address: AARP, P.O. Box 51040, Station R, Washington, DC 20091.

Reminiscence: Reaching Back, Moving Forward (D13186) is a brochure that describes the benefits and techniques of reminiscence, including suggested questions and triggers to prompt memories, and a list of resources for reminiscence activities. Address: AARP Fulfillment, 601 E Street, NW, Washington, DC 20049.

Films: Oral Histories

Giants of Time (57 minutes). This film celebrates elders whose lives have already spanned two centuries, and are approaching their third. J. Rowe, Filmmakers Library, New York, NY.

Peege (color, 28 minutes) 1973. A grandson visits his grandmother in a nursing home. The film illustrates the significance of reminiscence through a flashback technique. Excellent teaching film. Director: Randal Kleiser. Distributor: Phoenix Films, 267 W. 25th Street, New York, NY 10016.

Minnie Remembers (color, 5 minutes) 1977. Originally written as a poem, this lovely film is about a lonely old woman and her silent reminiscence. Excellent teaching film.

The Hundred Penny Box (color, 18 minutes) 1975. Based on the book by Sharon Bell Mathis, this film is about a relationship between Michael and Aunt DW, and her attachment to an old wooden box in which she keeps a sack of 100 pennies. The story focuses on the significance of symbolic objects to older persons. Churchill Films, 662 N. Robertson Boulevard, Los Angeles, CA 90069.

Water from Another Time (16 mm, color, 29 minutes) 1982. Set in south central Indiana, the film shares the memories and artistic recollections of three older people. Through music, art, scrapbooks, and diaries, these people tell their stories. The film places high value on preserving expressions of the past, on the contribution of today's older persons, and on ingenuity and creativity. Reminiscence is portrayed as life enrichment. Kane-Lewis Productions, 1813 Cranberry Lane, Reston, VA 22091; phone: 703-264-0101. Also available from Terra Nova Films, 9848 S. Winchester Avenue, Chicago, IL 60643; phone: 312-881-8491.

CHAPTER 16

Guided Autobiography Groups

James E. Birren and Donna E. Deutchman

KEY WORDS

- Adaptation
- Autobiography
- Competence
- Developmental exchange
- Integration
- Legacy
- Life review
- Older adults
- Sensitization
- Thematic approach

LEARNING OBJECTIVES

- Understand the value of the autobiographical process, particularly as it benefits older adults.
- Distinguish *guided* autobiography from other forms of reminiscence.
- Design a guided autobiography group around a chosen purpose.
- Understand the importance of the group process in guided autobiography, and list ways to promote the developmental exchange.
- Learn methods for dealing with potentially disruptive group members.
- List themes that are most salient for autobiographical review, and describe the sensitization process.

Guided autobiography is designed to promote successful adaptation to old age and to assist persons in life transition to make positive choices. It combines individual and group experiences with autobiography, incorporating group interaction and leadership to sensitize people to recall the most salient issues of their lives and expand their private reflections. It requires the writing of two-page reminiscences or life stories on selected life themes, and reading these life stories and sharing thoughts about them in a mutually encouraging group, moderated by a group leader.

Guided autobiography creates an environment that provides the social support and mental stimulation for older adults to review their life stories and share them with others. Using strategies that ensure positive group experiences and sensitize group members to the significant themes of life, leaders can help older adults develop a heightened sense of self-awareness, social acceptance, and self-esteem. Through the process of guided autobiography, older adults can integrate their experiences and come to terms with their lives as they have been led. As a result, they become better prepared to meet changes and new demands with increased confidence and competence.

Everyone needs to feel important in some way, and older adults search for evidence that their lives have mattered, that there has been some purpose or impact on the world. From a human development viewpoint, there is little of greater importance to each of us as we age than gaining an insightful perspective on our own life story, to clarify, deepen, and find meaning in the accumulated experience of a lifetime (Butler 1963; Hall 1922; Myerhoff & Tufte 1975). Guided autobiography is an effective way to help older adults build greater understanding and self-worth.

In guided autobiography, participants typically write and share with the guided autobiography group nine separate two-page autobiographical life stories. Themes are chosen that elicit powerful recollections of experience and related feelings. A prototypical array of themes is as follows:

- The history of the major branching points in life.
- The history of the family.
- The history of career or major life work.
- The history of the role of money in life.
- The history of health and body image.
- The history of loves and hates.
- The history of sexual identity, sex roles, and sexual experiences.
- The history of experiences with death and ideas about dying.
- The history of aspirations and life goals and the meaning of life.

Additional themes may be added or used as replacements depending on the nature and major purpose of the specific autobiography group, particularly for groups brought together on the basis of similar history or current life crisis.

The typical guided autobiography group meets a minimum of 10 times for at least two hours each time. Meetings consist of the members' reading and discussing the theme assigned for that day's meeting and discussion of the theme that forms the writing assignment for the next meeting. Because the sharing of life stories at the group meetings stimulates further recall and interaction, each written story is restricted to about two pages. This allows enough time for each member to read his or her statement and allows the opportunity for group feedback. Also, the two-page limit is a device to get the participants to focus on key elements of their life stories.

BENEFITS OF GUIDED AUTOBIOGRAPHY

Guided autobiography is an efficient program for older adults to review their lives, using a proven series of themes and questions. The group leader uses these themes and sensitizing questions to create a road map, guiding persons interested in developing greater self-awareness toward recovering and integrating the memories and emotions most relevant to future decisions, the development of greater self-esteem, and the transmission of family history. Guided autobiography can make a positive difference in the quality of older adults' remaining years. Also, when it results in a written account, it can create an important legacy for others in the individual's family.

There is a rich literature base that grows out of research conducted to assess the consequences of life review, reminiscence, and the autobiographical process, a form of which is guided autobiography. This research has helped to clarify important outcomes and to highlight benefits for mature adults. The method of guided autobiography is designed to optimize these potential outcomes of life review. Table 16-1 summarizes some of this research.

Integration, Fulfillment, and a Sense of Competence

In keeping with the developmental theories of such scholars as Buhler, Erikson, and Levinson, later adulthood is viewed as a time for integration—resolution and acceptance of one's identity being key to mental and emotional well-being. Guided autobiography can play a vital role in this process. Research by psychologists such as Boylin, Gordon, and Nehrke (1976); Costa and Kastenbaum (1967); and Elbaz (1988) supports this view. A positive relationship has been found between the amount of reminiscence and the degree of ego integrity (or self-integration) achieved. *Reminiscence* is defined here as the process of recalling past events, a process on which the more structured guided autobiography is built. It is important to note that the relationship between reminiscence and ego integrity, and the positive outcome it implies for self-acceptance, is found even when memories of past experiences are painful or negative.

It is important to an older adult to be able to resolve old conflicts and feelings of ambivalence and to integrate his or her life as it is perceived to have been lived in relation to what was once possible or expected. The older adult must reconcile the past with present expectations and goals; this is particularly important in later life, since opportunities for altering the life course may be limited. Guided autobiography offers a chance for the older adult to reconcile the past and the legacy he or she

TABLE 16-1 Benefits of life review: An overview of research findings

Area of benefit	Focus of study/article	Authors
Acceptance of death	Dying persons	Georgemiller & Maloney 1984
Cognitive functioning	Older adults	Hughston & Merriam 1982
Communication	Health care facility occupants	Burnside 1988
Coping/adaptation	Health care facility occupants Sheltered housing residents	Burnside 1988 Coleman 1974
Depression relief	Demented older adults Older adults	Goldwasser, Auerbach & Harkins 1987 Magee 1988
Ego integrity	Older adult males	Boylin, Gordon & Nehrke 1976 Havighurst & Glasser 1972
Fulfillment	Older adults	Buhler & Massarik 1968
Future orientation	Older adults	Costa & Kastenbaum 1967
Increased sense of continuity	Older adults	Myerhoff & Tufte 1975
Integration	Older adults All ages	Butler 1983 Erikson 1963
Intergenerational connectedness	Older adults	Greene 1982 Myerhoff & Tufte 1975
Meaning in life	All ages Older adults	Birren & Hedlund 1987 Lewis & Butler 1974
Memory capacity	Older adults	Ebersole 1978
Mental adaptability	Nursing home residents	Berghorn & Schafer 1987
Reconciliation or resolution of past	Older adults Health care facility occupants	Birren & Hedlund 1987 Burnside 1988
Role clarity	Older adults	deVries, Deutchman & Birren 1994 Greene 1982
Self-disclosure	All ages	Birren & Hedlund 1987
Self-esteem	All ages Health care facility occupants Older adults	Allport 1942 Burnside 1988 Butler 1967 Ebersole 1978
Self-understanding	All ages Health care facility occupants Adults	Annis 1967 Burnside 1988 Hately 1985
Social integration	Older adults	Ebersole 1978
Spiritual well-being	Adults	Hately 1985

will leave behind, modify future plans, and reaffirm past and present values and goals, deriving a feeling of completeness, of fulfillment in life.

The guided autobiography process is not designed as a form of therapy. It is not actively directed toward the cure or amelioration of particular diseases or particular problems. Its therapeutic value is a by-product of that which occurs naturally and should only be purposefully harvested by the seasoned professional therapist.

In guided autobiography, older adults relive and recall a wide range of personal experiences. A feeling of significance is generally derived from reviewing the life course as a whole. In summing up the experiences of a lifetime, people are frequently surprised by their own ability and how much they have survived and transcended. Reactions of the group often support a person's perception and provide a sense that the ability to adjust or overcome the hardships of life is a formidable

FIGURE 16-1

This photograph portrays some of the guidelines offered in this chapter: (a) active listening by leader and members, (b) refreshments shared, (c) written accounts by members to share, and (d) use of a table. All of these factors are important to a guided autobiography group.

PHOTO: Marianne Gontarz

accomplishment. Insights of the group leader and other members can facilitate this process and smooth the road to greater understanding of the self. Renewed confidence in one's adaptive capacity and increased understanding of one's personal agenda often form the basis from which successful future choices can be made.

Related to the subject of planning is the perception of the role of chance in a person's life. Just as an inventory of successful strategies can provide increased confidence in one's ability to meet new demands, an understanding of how chance events have helped to shape the life course can have a freeing quality. Insight into the influencing factors that have been outside of our control can help focus attention on adaptive capacities and strength in the face of hardship.

Adaptation to Old Age

The ability to take inventory of the adaptive strategies used successfully over the life course is an important resource in late life as people are faced with many changes. Guided autobiography helps in coping with problems of old age as well as integrating early life experiences. As Kaminsky (1978) points out, it may:

(a) be enlisted in the service of denial, and in its defensive aspect help maintain self-esteem and allay anxiety provoked by physical and intellectual decline; (b) . . . lead to a reorganization of personality and a fuller acceptance of one's life cycle; (c) further interpersonal relationships and provide a means by which older people can share their knowledge of the past; and (d) help old people cope with grief and depression resulting from personal losses (p. 30).

If a person is able to affirm and accept the contents of life and the continuity of his or her identity, the late life task of integration is advanced. In addition to highlighting the capacity for adaptation, guided autobiography reveals ways in which a person has maintained continuity throughout life. This continuity, particularly as it concerns a person's belief system and related patterns of behavior, reaffirms and supports a coherent sense of self.

Reducing Isolation for the Older Adult

A problem facing older adults is often a diminishing social network of friends and relatives. The development of new late-life friendships and confidant relationships is often a by-product of participation in a guided autobiography group. These groups are ideally suited to this purpose, because they build social networks and develop relationships among group members. Enduring friendships are often created as a result of the group process.

For nursing home residents and others in institutional care, the move to the institution can symbolize separation from home and society. Newly institutionalized persons may further separate themselves due to depression, feelings of isolation, and fear of developing new emotional ties. The interactions afforded in guided autobiography groups have proven to have positive outcomes for such persons.

Since life review is a developmental task of the later years, older adults are likely to engage in some form of life review whether or not there is an opportunity to do so in a group. Yet the role of trusted listeners, or confidants, is particularly helpful at this point in life, since many older adults engage in an unsupported life review during periods of loss (such as a personal disability or loss of a spouse). Losses result in decreased life satisfaction and can lead to depression. A negative worldview, invoked by loss and depression, can elicit a preoccupation with exaggerated memories of defeat or failure. However, such distortion of a life may remain unidentified in the absence of persons with whom to share such thoughts. The support and perspective provided by the guided autobiography group and other confidants can assist people in viewing their losses from the perspective of the entire life span, helping the older adult to achieve a balanced view.

THE FAMILY CONTEXT

In reviewing life, models of role change and exchange emerge as the person reconstructs the history of evolving relationships with children, parents, and grandparents. Guided autobiography evokes memories of family episodes and can assist people in "assuming responsibility for their lives, evaluating themselves and kin with greater empathy, and using their insight for the benefit of younger generations" (Magee 1988, 17).

There are symbolic and emotional benefits that accrue to family members as a consequence of the guided autobiography process. The interpretation of life as it has been lived provides the older adult as well as younger generations with a perspective on the past. This expanded perspective

gives new shape to the current context and provides a basis for a confident approach to the future. Intergenerational contact afforded by sharing autobiographical writings can provide family members with bridges to historical times they may have not otherwise known or understood. Such connections can assist younger persons in synthesizing their own identities. Thus, older persons can represent living stories, their presence being a sign of tradition and transcendence. Sharing the family history provides a common ground, instilling a sense of belonging and continuity.

Understanding the continuity of the family can free the person by (1) exposing the roots of family successes, failures, conflicts, and hardships; (2) identifying similarities among family members, helping a person come to terms with family issues that, in the past, might have been viewed as a fault of another person or oneself; and (3) helping the person reconcile the anger or anxiety that are the residue of past events.

THE GUIDED AUTOBIOGRAPHY METHOD

A person can review his or her past from a variety of viewpoints: for example, recalling events as they happened chronologically in time, reviewing diaries, or focusing on specific facets of life or personality. We believe that exploring one's autobiography is most fruitful for older adults when done as part of a guided process that directs attention to major life themes. Guided autobiography is based on the conviction that certain themes elicit the most salient memories, are most relevant to the issues and needs of older adults, and therefore are best suited for use. The individual is guided along productive themes to make the search of personal history effective and efficient.

It is important to design and conduct the guided autobiography group according to your purposes and expertise. Nonprofessionals should keep in mind that they are offering an opportunity for older adults to explore their histories and begin to integrate their life stories—they are not offering group psychotherapy. With this in mind, nonprofessionals should be warned not to probe into the feelings and emotions of group members beyond those that emerge spontaneously from the participants and are shared easily. Group leaders also must protect their members by guarding against probing by other group members. However, group leaders should not discourage the expression of emotions that are a natural part of interpersonal sharing. Guided autobiography may bring to the surface many of the emotions of the past, and participants may laugh or cry as they tell their stories. Unless a group member is demonstrating signs of depression or is in emotional danger, a hands-off philosophy may be best—allowing emotions to emerge naturally, but not soliciting them. In over 16 years, we have not had a group member report becoming depressed or having adverse reactions as a result of the guided autobiography process. This may be related to the research finding that depressed persons are not likely to engage in reminiscence (Coleman 1974; McMahon & Rhudick 1967). However, should a person show signs of depression (for an excellent overview of such signs, see Bumagin and Hirn 1990), he or she should be referred immediately to a professional counselor.

Goals for the Group and Group Norms

It is important to develop group goals that encompass the purposes of conducting the guided autobiography. General group goals are:

- For members to get to know each other.
- To share life stories.
- To explore similarities and differences among the life experiences of group members.
- To share life strategies.
- To encourage the elaboration of each person's life story.
- To ensure confidentiality.

Other goals are derived from the purposes that determine the composition and nature of a specific group. For example, more specific goals might be adopted if guided autobiography is being used to begin to integrate group members into a new residential setting (e.g., nursing home life); to explore life strategies that might be applied to new demands or life transitions (e.g., widowhood, disability, or retirement); as part of later life education in senior centers; or to begin to come to terms with impending death.

Such group goals are in addition to the personal goals of the individual members. Personal goals may vary and be as different as the group members themselves. Regardless of each member's personal goals, however, it is important that the group's goals be identified and agreed on to ensure a spirit of camaraderie and sharing.

The group leader creates a subculture for the group, establishing the norms that govern its conduct and helping to guide the development of relationships among members. The leader must describe and, most important, *model* the game rules that govern group interactions, creating a nonjudgmental atmosphere of acceptance, empathy, and support. Group norms are established relatively early in the life of a group and are difficult to change later. Therefore, in advance of the first meeting, it is essential for you to carefully consider what norms should be developed in the group and to discuss these norms with potential group members prior to their joining the group.

Group members are often strangers before the first meeting, so the group leader serves as a transitional object, a home base from which relationships with others in the group can be explored and to which a person can return with trust and acceptance. An important function of the group leader is to maintain the stability of the group. The group leader plays an important role in facilitating the members' connecting with each other, promoting interaction, trust, and social bonding. This can be achieved by commenting about similarities among group members and facilitating interaction. It is important to remember, however, that the process may be slow, particularly with older adults who are facing new demands and may be experiencing crises in maintaining a sense of self-worth. Such adults may be slow to develop feelings of trust with other group members or may have a strong competing desire to be validated by the group leader. The group leader can best facilitate the process by making all members feel that they are equally important to the group and by focusing group members' attention on their own capacity to support and validate each other.

Group Design

Since groups of older adults, particularly those who are experiencing social isolation or the need to adjust to age-related declines, require time to sort through their memories and emotions, it is recommended that group size be kept small, about five to six members. Too many members will result in an unmanageable group. People may be cut short or not have an opportunity to read their life story or provide insight into the life story of others. Too few members may result in a group that does not have enough content, limiting your potential to draw similarities and contrasts. Most important, too few members at the beginning can result in dissolution of the group should one or two members become ill, travel, or choose to leave.

The nature of the guided autobiography group should be decided by the group leader, and members should be chosen to meet that purpose. Members will take on various roles and tasks in a group, so the leader may want to take into account backgrounds and personality types when combining people into a group. In addition, the leader should discuss with each member the importance of maintaining the stability of the group and should request a commitment to completing the process to the degree possible.

Although anyone *can* participate, group leaders should consider the effective functioning of the group when choosing members. Burnside (1986) suggests that the following be excluded from groups of this type:

- Disturbed, active, wandering persons.
- Patients with psychotic depression.
- People who do not participate on their own recognizance, for example, who are coerced by others to attend.
- Individuals diagnosed as having bipolar disorder.
- Persons who are unable to communicate effectively with other group members due to a physical or cognitive disability.
- Hypochondriacal persons.

To this list might be added persons with paranoid personality disorders and persons suffering from delusional states.

The prototypic group has been made up of individuals from a wide age range and diverse ethnic backgrounds and careers. Heterogeneity provides a rich experience that focuses attention on not only the differences among people but also the similarities and the universalities of emotion and experience. Other groups have consisted of cohorts, people of the same generation with a common connection in the history of a community or culture. This type of group can provide an opportunity for exchanging memories of shared events.

Common memories can stimulate further recall and provide the opportunity to view major life influences from the perspective of others. This type of group is particularly suited to the environment of a nursing home or senior center in that it promotes camaraderie and the opportunity for sentimental reminiscence. Individuals living in close association may initially be slow to divulge their life stories but will share as confidence in the group grows.

New members may be resistant or anxious about joining a group. Simple strategies can promote participation and enhance the group experience. For example, snacks have been found to increase attendance at most group meetings. After this is established, the group members may wish to rotate the responsibility for bringing snacks. This has proven to be an effective strategy for enhancing commitment to the group and for preventing member attrition, because members are brought back into the group when it is their turn to bring a snack. In addition to the enticement of snacks, opportunities can be created to show family photographs or to listen to music from the past as ways to attract and sustain participation. This also can help to prompt memories. Events and persons forgotten can be brought to mind by old photographs, and the emotions experienced can be heightened by such tangible stimulation.

During the time span of the guided autobiography group meetings, the leader may be called upon to deal with absenteeism, tardiness, and attrition. It may be necessary to intervene if a member frequently arrives late, is absent, or does not prepare a written statement to share with the group. Members may need to be reminded of their initial commitment, or it may be necessary to discuss the impact of inconsistent participation on the group process. It is useful at times to remind members of their important role in creating the group and how vital their full participation is to developing an atmosphere of mutual acceptance and sharing.

If a member has been absent, he or she should be asked to prepare the written autobiographical statement for the meeting that was missed and should be encouraged to briefly share this statement with other group members at the next meeting or upon his or her return. This is important because the guided autobiography process is a cumulative one that explores increasingly sensitive subject matter.

It is not recommended that new members be added after the second session, since this will disrupt the natural progression of the developmental exchange and the formation of a cohesive group. Should a new member be added, he or she should be asked to complete the previous life stories prior to entry into the group. The new member should summarize the content of these life stories at the first meeting he or she attends.

Meeting Times and Length

The guided autobiography group usually meets 10 times, including one meeting for each life story theme plus an introductory meeting. The process can be completed in an intensive experience of meeting every weekday for two weeks, or it can be extended over 10 weeks, meeting once a week, or any combination of times that is suitable for your purposes. Particularly in nursing homes and senior centers, group members may decide to continue to have meetings after the structured process is complete.

Each meeting should be scheduled for a minimum of two hours, since it must include both the sensitizing discussion of the next topic and the exchange of autobiographical statements. The individual reading time is typically 15 to 20 minutes. More than two hours will be needed if the group number increases beyond five or six, or if the process is part of a course that includes discussion of developmental issues. Sessions longer than two hours also have to schedule restroom and coffee breaks.

Meeting Content

At each meeting, approximately 20 minutes to a half hour should be devoted to discussion of the sensitizing questions that will guide the writing of the thematic life story for the next meeting. The group leader should distribute and read aloud a description of the topic and a sampling of the sensitizing questions (for a complete list of these sensitizing questions, see Birren and Deutchman 1991). The group leader might share some personal thoughts and experiences related to the topic as a way to initiate group discussion. In addition, he or she might ask the group some prompting questions derived from the sensitizing material. Discussion of the topic at this point should be kept brief and moderated by the group leader. The goal is to stimulate thinking and expand members' perspectives regarding how a topic might be approached. As necessary, members should be made aware of this goal and of the fact that they will have the opportunity to write about the topic and share their experiences at the next meeting.

Approximately one-and-one-half hours should be devoted to the reading of that day's life stories, allowing about 15 minutes for each person. This usually takes the form of 10 to 15 minutes of reading and 5 minutes of group interaction. The leader should moderate interactions to ensure that the group remains nonjudgmental and that each member has a turn of nearly equal length to tell his or her story.

The Importance of the Group

The exchange of life stories in a group is an important feature of the guided autobiography process. As each group member reads his or her thematic life story in the small group, intimate exchanges of her or his past with other persons reinforces and sustains the motivation to further review her or his life. This also provides the context for the development of new friendships and greater self-esteem. In addition, it is believed that the confidence and trust built in the small group experience enhance both recall and the ease of condensing experience on a written page.

A key feature of the guided autobiography process is the *developmental exchange*, the mutual sharing between members of where and how they grew up and personally important historical and emotional events. People involved in developmental exchange during the guided autobiography process move from tentatively and guardedly alluding to important features of their lives toward an increasingly open sharing of personal material. In the process, people implicitly take into account the affective importance of shared information. They trade personal information equivalent in affective value, though not necessarily similar in content. As time together increases and more of each life is shared, the developmental exchange leads to an increased willingness to self-disclose. Affective bonds are built among group members, and mutual respect and trust grow.

Increased confidence and trust among group members lead not only to greater willingness to share, but also to greater courage to explore. This exploration can lead to a clarity of one's identity and an understanding of the self that might otherwise not have been possible. The developmental exchange goes much like a poker game in which each player increases the ante on his or her turn. If a player does not want to proceed further, the last player's ante is simply met or the player passes and withdraws. By meeting the ante, the player remains part of the group but does not expand the emotional stake.

The group leader can promote the developmental exchange through the use of three primary strategies:

1. Link group members who have discussed similar stories by utilizing good listening skills and by alluding to connections between personal experiences.

2. Share your own thoughts or questions about what has just been said, thus demonstrating that you are not only hearing what they have to say, but also are genuinely interested in their life stories.

3. Use self-disclosure: It is recommended that the group leader facilitate interactions *between and among group members* as a primary role. This involves careful moderation of your own involvement in the group process of sharing life stories. When a group leader writes or shares excessive personal autobiographical statements, it may compete with his or her role as moderator and cause a feeling of inequality among members. However, it is important for members to feel that the group leader is an ally and to experience a sense of reciprocity. To accomplish this and to promote the developmental exchange, group leaders can engage in a limited use of self-disclosure by interjecting a *brief* personal vignette or sharing an emotion. It is best used when it is designed to highlight similarities between human experiences or universalities in human emotions. It is particularly important in situations in which a member feels alone or isolated in the group. It can be an effective antidote in instances in which group norms have been breached or privacy has been invaded.

Related to the developmental exchange, a benefit of sharing one's autobiography with a group is that cues to recall may arise from the discussion. Other people's experiences become reminders of feelings and events that have been set aside or forgotten. In addition, the distribution of attention among group members has the effect of reducing pressure on any one person and providing support in dealing with painful memories. One role of the group is to assist other members who become stuck at some painful point in the past, providing the stimulus to move on to new territory.

The Importance of the Written Form

Although the group experience holds rich potential and is a valuable component of the guided autobiography process, writing one's autobiographical statements is the basis of the process. The sensitization process that begins in the group is a first step in a person's journey into a review of the self and the personal past. Personal, private reflection and the motivation to delve deeply into the banks of the memory are summoned by the task of writing down one's recollections. In addition, the writing process itself is a stimulus to further recall. As thoughts are put on paper, rearranged, and read, related memories are elicited. In addition, by writing his or her thoughts down prior to sharing them with the group, a person can sift out what will be shared with the group, focusing on the experiences he or she perceives as most important. Without this opportunity, memories might ramble in a desultory manner, and the person's time to share with the group might be taken up by less productive recall. Similarly, a person has the opportunity to review his or her autobiographical statements on a particular life theme and determine what will and will not be shared with the group. This protects the individual's right to monitor the developmental exchange and not to share what he or she feels is too personal or painful.

Finally, without the written document, one would have difficulty reconstructing the flow of information in the group in order to expand later the autobiographical statement. It would also reduce both the potential of sharing one's autobiographical life stories with persons outside the group and the capacity of guided autobiography to help create a family legacy to pass on.

The Thematic Approach and the Use of Sensitizing Questions

The guided autobiography process is based on the conviction that there are certain common themes that provide the threads on which the fabric of human life is woven. The specific themes employed in guided autobiography are the result of many years of construction and refinement. These themes are described fully in Birren and Deutchman (1991) along with the sensitizing questions used to evoke memories and guide the participants in addressing the most meaningful, productive aspects of the themes. The themes and sensitizing questions have been chosen for four reasons. First, they are salient issues that underlie the life course. Second, review of one's life in this framework is believed to be beneficial in guiding the next steps and in transcending difficult transitions. Third, the thematic approach enhances the group process by providing a context in which common feelings and circumstances are explored collectively. Last, these themes represent life experiences and issues that are likely to be most relevant to individual development in other generations, thereby forming a meaningful legacy.

POTENTIAL OBSTACLES IN THE GUIDED AUTOBIOGRAPHY GROUP

Problems may arise in conducting guided autobiography groups. These can range from problems with a specific group member's behavior to lack of support from the institution. There are many ways to manage such problems, and the best will be based on the group leader's own judgment of the situation and personal style. It is important, however, to recognize the warning signs of such problems.

The Counterproductive Group Member

Problems with specific group members arise when someone in the group has poor interpersonal skills, suffers from a severe need for attention, or is misplaced in the group due to cognitive or emotional disability. Wherever possible, it is helpful for the group leader to meet individually with all group members prior to their entrance into the group. This will provide an opportunity to identify those who have personal styles that would be counterproductive to the group process and to limit or dissuade such members from entering the group prior to the first meeting. This can best be done by directing such persons to other groups or individual therapy, which might better meet their needs. The following is a list of some of the individuals who may appear in group meetings, and who require monitoring or action by the group leader.

The Monopolizer. This member presents himself or herself almost invariably to participate in group experiences. In need of great attention, and primarily motivated to be listened to, monopolizers consistently run over the time allotted for their stories and have a talent for drawing attention to their own lives even when the focus is on someone else's story. Monopolizers can seriously disrupt the guided autobiography group process, and they require attention from the group leader. This member may be very frustrating, and it is important to protect the group process. This can often be accomplished by offering the monopolizer an opportunity to meet with you once outside the group to discuss what she or he may do beyond the guided autobiography process to expand on her or his life story and share it with others, such as family members. Or it can be accomplished by validating the monopolizer's contribution to the group but firmly redirecting attention to other members. The group leader may also assign the monopolizer the last starting position in the group order for presenting his or her story. This should be used as a transient control until the monopolizer becomes a more regular member.

The Amateur Therapist. Amateur therapists feel that past experiences in therapy groups or their own insight has afforded them a unique ability to interpret other persons' lives and behavior. They may participate in the guided autobiography process based more on a desire to play therapist with others' stories than from a desire to review their own life story. Such a member may be particularly problematic if his or her insights tend to be evaluative judgments regarding the mental or emotional stability of other members. This kind of judgment often involves interpretation of another member's behavior or feelings as either normal or abnormal. To manage the amateur therapist in the group, it is necessary to emphasize strongly the group norm of nonjudgmentalism. In rare instances, it may be necessary to do so on an individual basis; however, wherever possible, it is best to avoid direct criticism of any member's behavior in the group and let the group process assert control. Subtle contradiction that pointedly reinforces nonjudgmental behavior can be used to protect a member being analyzed by the amateur therapist and to deter future analysis or judgment in favor of elaborating on the individual life stories.

The Nonparticipant.   The nonparticipant can take a number of forms, for the most part distinguished by degree of silence. Rarely, someone may join the group and insist that he or she would like to attend each meeting, but consistently forget or not have the time to write his or her autobiographical stories. Or he or she may refuse to share stories with the group. Such members are very disruptive to the group process and early on should be referred to a different kind of group experience. Other nonparticipating members may read their two-page autobiographical stories but withhold any amplifying personal or emotional information. This represents a challenge to the developmental exchange. In some instances, a person needs encouragement, a sign that his or her feelings are meaningful to the group and, especially, to the group leader. A simple question, such as "How did that make you feel?" can often release the tension surrounding the emotional expression. In other instances, a member may not feel comfortable openly expressing feelings despite your welcoming of such expression. As long as this person is not obstructing others, he or she is best left to harvest those aspects of the guided autobiography process with which he or she feels comfortable.

Ensuring Institutional Support

The success of the guided autobiography group depends in part on the commitment and support of the institution in which it is conducted. Particularly in sites such as nursing homes, the cooperation of the administrative staff and caregivers is essential to ensure that group members are able to attend each session and that there is positive reinforcement for continued participation. Without this support, group members may feel they are being forced to choose between activities or that their relationship with staff will be harmed by participation in the guided autobiography group.

In most cases, such support comes easily. Generally, families and personnel of senior care facilities are enthusiastic about the potential of guided autobiography and welcome the availability of such groups. In some instances, however, staff may be wary of new or outside persons. Key to engaging their support is enlisting the cooperation and support of the top administrator and, where applicable, the head of nursing. These people will greatly influence the degree of cooperation provided by direct care providers. Without such cooperation, difficulties may arise.

SUMMARY

This chapter has provided a brief guide to how effective guided autobiography groups can be conducted. Guided autobiography is an efficient way for older adults to review their lives by following a proven series of evocative themes and responding to questions designed to promote reflection. It provides an opportunity for older adults to strengthen their identities, increase their sense of competency, make new friendships, and create a legacy for their families.

There is a growing interest in autobiography, personal documents, and narratives of many sorts. This may reflect the fact that modern society gives little opportunity for personal exchanges during the work life. It also may reflect the transient atmosphere created by a society in which interpersonal relationships, jobs, and the structures of institutions are rapidly changing. Social change may make it difficult for older adults in particular to be able to integrate their lives and find durable meaning in their histories. In this context, guided autobiography has a place in raising the quality of life of the aged. The process is by no means fully explored in applications, and research will lead to further insights. Enough is known to encourage others to explore its use in helping the aged to find meaning in the way their lives have been led and to find companionship through sharing their stories.

EXERCISE 1

Following the themes and sensitizing questions in Birren and Deutchman (1991), write your own guided autobiography.

EXERCISE 2

Design a guided autobiography group by developing a list of potential members and group goals.

EXERCISE 3

Solicit members and conduct a guided autobiography group. Develop a questionnaire and evaluate the group's effectiveness after the tenth session.

REFERENCES

Allport G. 1942. *The use of personal documents in psychological science*, Bulletin 49. New York: Social Science Research Council.

Annis AP. 1967. The autobiography: Its uses and value in professional psychology. *J Counsel Psych* 14(1):9-17.

Berghorn FJ, Schafer DE. 1987. Reminiscence intervention in nursing homes: What and who changes? *Int J Aging Human Dev* 24(2):113-127.

Birren JE, Deutchman DE. 1991. *Guiding autobiography groups for older adults: Exploring the fabric of life.* Baltimore: Johns Hopkins University Press.

Birren JE, Hedlund B. 1987. Contributions of autobiography to developmental psychology. In N Eisenberg (ed.), *Contemporary topics in developmental psychology* (pp. 394-415). New York: Wiley.

Boylin W, Gordon SK, Nehrke MF. 1976. Reminiscing and ego integrity in institutionalized elderly males. *Gerontologist* 16: 118-124.

Buhler C, Massarik F. 1968. *The course of human life.* New York: Springer.

Bumagin VE, Hirn KF. 1990. *Helping the aging family: A guide for professionals.* Glenview, IL: Scott, Foresman.

Burnside IM. 1986. *Working with the elderly: Group process and techniques,* 2d ed. Boston: Jones and Bartlett.

———. 1988. *Nursing and the aged: A self-care approach,* 3d ed. St. Louis: Mosby.

Butler RN. 1963. The life review: An interpretation of reminiscence in old age. *Psychiatry, J Study Inter-Personal Processes* 26:65-76.

———. 1967. Studies of creative people and the creative process after middle life. In S Levin, RH Kahana (eds.), *Psychodynamic studies on aging.* New York: International Universities Press.

Coleman PG. 1974. The role of the past in adaptation to old age. Doctoral dissertation. London: University of London.

Costa PT, Kastenbaum R. 1967. Some aspects of memories and ambitions in centenarians. *J Genetic Psych* 100:3-16.

deVries B, Birren JE, Deutchman DE. 1990. Adult development through guided autobiography. *Family Relations* 39:3-7.

Ebersole PP. 1978. Establishing reminiscing groups. In IM Burnside (ed.), *Working with the elderly: Group process and techniques,* 1st ed. (pp. 236-254). North Scituate, MA: Duxbury.

Elbaz R. 1988. *The changing nature of the self: A critical study of the autobiographic discourse.* London: Croom Helm.

Erikson E. 1963. *Childhood and society.* New York: Norton.

Georgemiller R, Maloney HN. 1984. Group life review and denial of death. *Clin Gerontol* 2(4):37-49.

Goldwasser A, Auerbach SM, Harkins SW. 1987. Cognitive, affective, and behavioral effects of reminiscence group therapy on demented elderly. *Int J Aging Human Dev* 25(3):209-222.

Greene RR. 1982. Life review: A technique for clarifying family roles in adulthood. *Clin Gerontol* 1(2):59-67.

Hall GS. 1922. *Senescence, the last half of life.* New York: Appleton.

Hately BJ. 1985. Spiritual well-being through life histories. *J Religion & Aging* 1(2):63-71.

Havighurst RJ, Glaser R. 1972. An exploratory study of reminiscence. *J Gerontol* 27:245-253.

Hughston G, Merriam S. 1982. Reminiscence: A nonformal technique for improving cognitive functioning in the aged. *J Aging Human Dev* 15:139-149.

Kaminsky M. 1978. Pictures from the past: The use of reminiscence in casework with the elderly. *J Gerontol Soc Work* 1(1):19-29.

Levinson DJ et al. 1978. *The seasons of a man's life*. New York: Knopf.

Lewis MI, Butler R. 1974. Life-review therapy: Putting memories to work in individual and group psychotherapy. *Geriatrics* 29(11):165-169.

Magee JJ. 1988. *A professional's guide to older adult's life review*. Lexington, MA: Lexington Books.

McMahon AW, Rhudick PJ. 1967. Reminiscing in the aged: An adaptational response. In S Levin, RJ Kahana (eds.), *Psychodynamic studies on aging: Creativity, reminiscing and dying* (pp. 64-78). New York: International Universities Press.

Myerhoff BG, Tufte V. 1975. Life history as integration: Personal myth and aging. *Gerontologist* 15:541-543.

BIBLIOGRAPHY

Baird CR. 1957. The autobiography. *Ed Digest* 19:39-43.

Bertaux D. 1981. *Biography and society*. Berkeley, CA: Sage.

Bertaux D, Kohli M. 1984. The life story approach: A continental view. *Ann Rev Soc* 10:215-237.

Birren JE, Fisher LM, Deutchman DE. 1988. Older adult interest in personal history and autobiography: A survey of elderly college educated adults (unpublished manuscript). Los Angeles: University of Southern California.

Butler R, Lewis MI. 1982. *Aging and mental health*, 3d ed. St. Louis: Mosby.

Coleman PG. 1986. *Aging and reminiscence processes: Social and clinical implications*. New York: Wiley.

Cornwell J, Geering B. 1989. Biographical interviews with older people. *Oral History J* 1:36-43.

Frenkel E. 1936. Studies in biographical psychology. *Character & Personality* 5:1-34.

Gaston C. 1982. The use of personal documents in the study of adulthood. Paper presented at the Annual Meeting of the American Psychological Association. Washington, DC (August).

Geiger SN. 1986. Women's life histories: Method and content. *Signs* (Winter):334-351.

Greenwald A. 1980. The totalitarian ego: Fabrication and revision of personal history. *Am Psych* 35:603-618.

Kim SG. 1987. Black Americans' commitment to Communism: A case study based on fiction and autobiographies by Black Americans. Unpublished dissertation. Kansas City: University of Kansas. *DAI* 48:3415-6B.

Kohli M. 1982. Biographical research in German language area. Ad hoc group on the "Uses of autobiographical narratives," 10th World Congress of Sociology, Mexico City (August 16-21).

Lewis MI. 1973. The adaptive value of reminiscing in old age. *J Geriatric Psychiatr* 6:117-121.

Lieberman MA, Falk JM. 1971. The remembered past as a source of data for research on the life cycle. *Human Dev* 14:132-141.

Olney J. 1980. *Autobiography: Essays theoretical and critical*. Princeton, NJ: Princeton University Press.

Price C. 1983. Heritage: A program design for reminiscence. *Activities, Adaptation, & Aging* 3(3):47-53.

Progoff I. 1975. *At a journal workshop*. New York: Dialogue House Library.

Reedy MN, Birren JE. 1980. Life review through autobiography. Poster presented at Annual Meeting of the American Psychological Association, Montreal.

Riccio AC. 1958. The status of the autobiography. *Peabody J Ed* 36:33-36.

Rich SL. 1988. Mirror, mirror: An autobiographical study in creative process. Unpublished dissertation. New York: New York University. *DAI* 48:1766A.

Roos JP. 1985. Life stories of social changes: Four generations in Finland. *Int J Oral History* 6(3):179-190.

Runyan WM. 1984. *Life histories and psychobiography: Exploratories in theory and method*. New York: Oxford University Press.

Sarbin TR. 1986. *Narrative psychology: The storied nature of human conduct*. New York: Praeger.

Selling B. 1989. *Writing from within*. Claremont, CA: Hunter House.

Shaffer EE. 1954. The autobiography in secondary counseling. *Personnel & Guidance J* 32:395-398.

Sperbeck DJ, Whitbourne SK, Hoyer WJ. 1986. Age and openness to experience in autobiographical memory. *Exper Aging Res* 12(3):169-172.

Wachter PE. 1988. Current bibliography of life-writing. *Biography: An Interdisciplinary Q* 11(4):316-325.

Wrightsman LS. 1980. Personal documents as data in conceptualizing adult personality development. Presidential address to the Society of Personality and Social Psychology, American Psychological Association, Montreal.

CHAPTER 17

Music Groups

Mary Jane Hennessey

KEY WORDS

- Flexibility
- Group cohesiveness
- Listening
- Relaxation
- Responsiveness
- Stimulation
- Therapeutic
- Vibrations

LEARNING OBJECTIVES

- Define *music therapy*.
- List three ways music can be used in group work with older persons.
- State one example of a type of music that would be inappropriate to play for a depressed person.
- Explain the style of music that would be acceptable to begin work with a depressed person.
- List seven types of group modalities in which music could be used effectively.
- Describe how to choose music to enhance the reminiscence process.
- Describe the type of music preferred by a regressed elderly group.

The use of music in healing the body and mind dates back to antiquity (Carapetyan 1948; Licht 1946; Meinecke 1948). In modern times, music was used in hospitals as a soporific before World War II and was considered a morale builder. Musicians who played there were called music specialists and were often music teachers, school band leaders, or choral directors who believed that music is good for people (Gaston 1968). In 1944, Michigan State University established the first curriculum for training music therapists. The first academic course was taught in 1946 at the University of Kansas.

Alicia Ann Clair (1992) provided expert witness testimony to the Special Committee on Aging, U.S. Senate. She stated that the therapeutic uses of music have a long history; music therapy with older Americans is relatively new; music therapy with well aged is innovative. Music therapy with older Americans who are chronically ill is developing, and music therapy is very effective with persons who have dementia and their families. Furthermore, music therapy protocols have been developed with those in the early and through the late stages of dementia (pp. 1-2).

THERAPEUTIC USES OF MUSIC

Music therapy is defined as the controlled use of music in the treatment, rehabilitation, education, and training of adults and children suffering from physical, mental, and emotional disorders (Alvin 1966). Hanser (1988) examined findings of studies that used music as a stress reducer and concluded

FIGURES 17-1a, 17-1b *Music can be implemented in a wide array of groups. Consider limiting instruments to inexpensive and easy-to-use ones when you plan to play music in a group of older people.*

PHOTOS: Marianne Gontarz

that music does influence the psychological and physiological response to stress. Use of music in groups of older people is considered therapeutic and can enhance the day-to-day existence of the institutionalized aged. Three ways of using music in groups are listening to music, having music in the environment, and making music.

Listening is one of the important areas of concern in group work. The more disturbed individuals become, the less they listen to others. Through playing music in a group, such isolated individuals can be encouraged to listen and, in so doing, communicate in a nonverbal way that can be the beginning of responsiveness to their surroundings.

Old age in our culture, with the many losses incurred, seems to contain much sadness and disappointment. Depression, paranoia, and disorientation are found in most institutions, and music helps provide an atmosphere for catharsis or simply getting out in the open things that are bothering a client. Old people are also often afraid of the world around them. The group experience can help reduce their fears, and music can encourage people to be aware of their feelings and then express them in the safety of the group.

Physically, music can help people move with more freedom, and with physical improvement, confidence in oneself grows. The connection between physical and mental health has been demonstrated and is the basis for the concept of holistic medicine.

Music can be used to change moods, or it has strong powers of association. Care should be taken in the choice of music, because some stimulating music can produce higher levels of state anxiety, as well as physiological arousal and aggression when compared with sedative music (Buckwalter, Hartsock & Gaffney 1985). Although musicians tend to view music as a way to bring joy to people, there is a large repertoire of music filled with pathos that can help work out grief through tears. In treating cases of depression, for example, it is advisable not to expose the client to an onslaught of cheerful music, but to begin with slow, familiar, sad music such as Handel's Largo. If the goal of a group is to encourage people to be in touch with their feelings, the leader can without comment simply play some meaningful music before the group meeting starts, such as the plaintive spiritual "Sometimes I Feel Like a Motherless Child." The music will help the members focus on their feelings.

Another method for getting people in touch with their feelings involves relaxing deeply and letting the mind wander on the sounds of music. Deep relaxation and specific musical selections as a method used in therapy are described in detail by Helen Bonny and Louis Savary (1973). A modification of this method is included later in this chapter.

Finally, music can be used as a way to develop group cohesiveness.

> The aim of the music session during which live music is played, or if not live music, recorded music, is to integrate each member of the group and to build up a collective memory of feelings and facts which bind the members together, thus creating interpersonal relationships based on a common experience to focus general attention on a number of combined and auditory perceptions (Alvin 1966, 132).

One advantage of group cohesiveness is that the members feel they all share the same problems or at least attempt to understand them. Troubles seem easier to bear when people feel they are not alone. Ways in which music is useful for encouraging discussion and sharing in the group experience include identification with the feelings expressed in the music, associations that help related past experiences, and improvement in the perception of reality (by relaxing the individual and by stimulating free association of ideas, music tends to reveal hidden attitudes through the phenomenon of projection).

One way to begin working with music is to pay attention to your own music listening and draw up a list of selections that represent moods. Emil Guntheil and his colleagues (1952) describe music as fitting into six categories: (1) happy, gay, joyous, stimulating, triumphant; (2) agitated, restless, irritating; (3) nostalgic, sentimental, soothing, meditative, relaxing; (4) sad, melancholic, grieving, depressing, lonely; (5) prayerful, reverent; and (6) eerie, weird, grotesque. A second list could be created of selections tried in groups, with a description of the groups' reactions. If enough people worked in this way and a central clearinghouse were set up to receive these impressions and recheck them with other groups, gradually excellent guidelines could be published for health professionals to use in their work.

PHYSICAL EFFECTS OF MUSIC

The music therapist needs to be aware that music produces physical sensations in our bodies and can cause subtle physiological changes.

> Everyone to whom the succession of tones means anything responds by exhibiting very slight but characteristic changes of muscular tonicity. It is the listener and not the performer alone who creates the melody. In the act of response to the successive tones that strike upon the ear, he binds them together (Bingham 1968, 6).

Music also affects respiration, pulse, blood pressure, and galvanic skin response (Diserens & Fine 1939; Hyde 1968). For example, the Tchaikovsky *Symphonie Pathétique* depresses the cardiovascular system, and it is not recommended for individuals who are fatigued, depressed, or ill. However, the same symphony could be employed to subdue hilarity in individuals or crowds (Hyde 1968).

Music is sensation not only because it activates our hearing but also because it stimulates the entire body. Scientific studies have demonstrated that we are an assortment of constantly moving atomic and subatomic particles (Andrews 1966). The vibrations of sound hitting against the body, which is a loose collection of its own vibrating material, are rearranged in either a good or a harmful way. This accounts for the Iso principle in using music in therapy, which is defined as "like acting on like" and is a physical reality observed by orchestra players.

Imagine the feeling in the body of a musician sitting on the stage during a performance of the Verdi *Requiem,* who is caught between trumpets and the echo trumpets. The vibrations caused by trumpets are very strong; brass instruments create clear-cut sounds that shake up our atoms. When I experience this sound's changing my own energy system at performances, I am so energized that sleep is out of the question for many hours. Monotonous, soft, repetitive music has the opposite effect. Our bodies are lulled, soothed, and comforted; many people can fall asleep to it while sitting in a concert hall. On a different level, industrial noise or hard rock at a high volume can cause deafness by damaging the delicate structures of the ear. No part of the body escapes the effects of sound (Diserens & Fine 1939).

THE USE OF MUSIC IN GROUP WORK WITH INDEPENDENTLY FUNCTIONING OLDER PERSONS

Between 1977 and 1982, research on the effect of emotions on physical health proliferated. One example is *Music and the Brain* (Critchley & Henson 1977), which is concerned with the neurological effects of music due to the sensory nature of stimulation on the auditory system, somatic motor system, sensory system (including the skin), and memory. Elmer and Alyce Green, working at the Menninger Foundation in Kansas, have demonstrated through the use of sophisticated biofeedback equipment a psychophysiological principle that states:

Every change in the physiological state is accompanied by an appropriate change in the mental-emotional state, conscious or unconscious, and conversely, every change in the mental-emotional state, conscious or unconscious, is accompanied

by an appropriate change in the physiological state (Green & Green 1977).

From this theoretical base has developed the use of music to slow down physiological responses to induce a deeply relaxed state and to improve physical and mental health, as well as to motivate people to make better choices in life style.

Working with groups of independently functioning older persons, we have documented physical and behavioral changes that include decreased problems with insomnia, increased energy, and increased ability to walk farther and to perform flexibility exercises specifically designed for this age group. Combining stress management techniques that include discussions on the various stresses due to aging (Burnside 1971), nutritional information, flexibility exercises, and deep relaxation techniques has produced measurable health changes. Use of music to deepen the relaxation process has been an integral part of this program. Ostrander (Ostrander & Schroeder 1979) states that "the psycho-physical effects of different rhythms, time signatures and harmonic structures determine the usefulness of a composition for relaxed concentration." She recommends string music from the Baroque era with a metronome beat of 60 as being the most effective, and we have found this to be true.

If the discussion period has focused on sad material and the group morale is low, we have successfully used the concept of the Iso principle— that is, the concept of altering the mood with the music—by beginning with slow, sad music and gradually changing the rhythm and tone until a lighter, happier music is played. The use of music in groups for relaxing has increased in recent years, and we have included some resources for this reason. They are listed at the end of this chapter.

GROUPS FOR WHICH MUSIC IS APPROPRIATE

Music can be used in many different group modalities, including reality orientation groups, remotivation groups, reminiscence groups, socializing groups, sensory stimulation groups, preventive medicine groups, occupational therapy, physical therapy, recreational therapy, art therapy, and movement, exercise, and dance groups. The use of music in some of these is discussed in this section.

Reminiscence Groups

The most useful music selections for older adults are those that were popular between 1900 and 1920. The music we listen to and sing during our formative years becomes our music. The World War I years produced a wealth of music that is very poignant for many people in their eighties. Music also can be the central theme for discussion in a reminiscence group (Davis 1992). Patriotic selections, especially those traditionally played and sung on July 4, can also be very effective. Because they are sung with gusto and enthusiasm, such songs as "God Bless America," "The Battle Hymn of the Republic," and "Johnny Comes Marching Home" stimulate spontaneous and joyful reminiscing. One unusual approach is being employed by the staff of a senior citizens' center in Carmel, California: They are encouraging very old clients to tape their life histories using music to stimulate memories.

Socializing Groups

Music is an easy way to encourage social interaction, especially for an isolated person. It creates a nonthreatening environment. When new patients are admitted to geriatric institutions, they frequently react with feelings of hostility and/or depression, which can quickly show up in symptoms of advancing short-term memory loss. At this time, music can be used as a way to entice the patient to join a group designed for entertainment or for singing. Music that increases socializing includes dance rhythms, singable light music, and melodies familiar to the culture of the group.

Groups for Treating Short-Term Memory Loss

One of the most disturbing aspects of aging is the deterioration of mental acuity, with progressive short-term memory loss. Ira Altschuler (1959) writes, "The percentage of senile dements in our mental hospitals is high. A certain number of persons admitted to hospitals as senile dements are *not* demented. They are rejected persons whose families got tired of them and sent them to mental hospitals." Elias Cohen (1976) says, "The mentally impaired elderly are our most ubiquitous problem and we don't like to talk about them."

Although short-term memory loss may be due to organic brain disease, it often appears when an older adult is institutionalized. All too often, aged people are admitted to institutions because it is difficult for them to manage on their own and they have no other place to go. Robert Butler (1975) calls senility a myth. He states

> The notion that old people are senile . . . is widely accepted. . . . But anxiety and depression are also frequently lumped within the same category of senility even though they are treatable and often reversible. Old people, like young people, experience a full range of emotions, including anxiety, grief, depression and paranoid states (p. 9).

Butler lists other causes of so-called senility as drug tranquilization, malnutrition, unrecognized physical illness, and alcoholism.

My observation has been that if clients feel deserted and have not made the decision to enter the institution but have had the choice made for them, by either their families or social workers, they are apt quickly to show signs of diminishing mental functioning. The medical world has looked upon this trend as irreversible; only recently has it been shown that with consistent and daily stimulation and therapy, patients can be helped back toward reality (Hennessey 1976). Although specific techniques are now being used in the area of reality orientation, these can be supplemented by the use of music in groups.

For a year and a half, I worked with a small group of elderly women who were suffering from severe short-term memory loss. All came from good socioeconomic backgrounds; some had done graduate university work. Several of the women displayed acute anxiety when they experienced forgetfulness.

The group met in a central lounge with comfortable chairs and privacy. Assembling the group required two people, one to escort them and one to stay and hold their attention until all were present; otherwise they wandered about. The chairs were arranged in a circle, and I sat on the floor inside the circle looking up at them. For comfort, the group members were encouraged to take off their shoes if desired.

The first meeting began with a discussion of the difficulty in remembering things and people. I expressed my own difficulty in that area. We sometimes began group sessions with the exercise of recalling one another's names. Then I would talk about listening to music in a relaxed position, about how doing so would help us remember beautiful times and places and might even take us to new and exciting imaginary places if we let our minds go with the music. Bonny and Savary (1973) used this approach as an aid in psychotherapy and personal insight groups, and it seemed appropriate to try this method. (See the Resources at the end of the chapter for tapes by Bonny and Savary.)

Before beginning the music, we used a method that is described by Leslie LeCron (1964) to help relax our bodies; it consisted of paying attention to each part of the body in order from foot to head, tightening and then relaxing the muscles. I tried to keep the deaf women close to me to maximize their hearing during the group experience. The first time I experimented with this relaxation method, I was very apprehensive, feeling sure they would not cooperate, but I need not have worried.

I played quiet but interesting music (for example, the andantes from the Brahms symphonies), and each person was given an opportunity to talk about the experience. They all remembered where they had been and what they had seen in their imaginations; they enjoyed sharing this. A former Chicago school teacher who was never reconciled to life in a rural California community said, "I was going from floor to floor on an escalator in Marshall Field's looking at beautiful clothes." Another member said, "I was walking around in my grandmother's house looking at all the beautiful objects collected there. I haven't thought of this house for fifty years." And one woman recalled the gardens in which she had played as a child, saying she could smell the lilacs in bloom.

When the music concluded, the members expressed their approval or disapproval of the selection. They preferred symphonic or string music that was not too loud or percussive, although piano music such as Chopin's nocturnes was approved. No sudden sounds, but music building in emotional intensity was also preferred. Because of time limitations, I usually played only one movement; but if a longer selection was used, the members would be attentive throughout. This in itself was a positive change, because several of the members were pacers who had great difficulty sitting still and often moved from room to room. When music was played, they remained still and content and seemed reluctant to discontinue the session.

One important example of retention occurred. Although I was generally a regular group leader, one week I was absent. Upon my return six of the eight women remarked on my absence somewhat indignantly!

Movement and Music Groups

I have been working with a dancer and a musician to integrate singing and movement as one vehicle for giving group members a chance to express their feelings. Old people in institutions become very silent, and we have found that by adding sound to movement they are able to become much more lively and verbal.

We try to lessen the demarcation between moving and singing; when moving, members are encouraged to express the movement in a sound, and when singing, to accentuate the sound with movement. For example, when raising our arms, we take a deep breath and exhale without any sound. Then we exhale using any sound while focusing on very deep breathing. The leaders work as a team, moving back and forth from one dimension to the other, switching roles and reinforcing each other's suggestions for the deaf group members.

From these unstructured sounds, we gradually lead the group into singing simple songs unaccompanied except for clapping or using rhythm instruments played by the group, such as tambourines, drums, and wood blocks. At this point, some people spontaneously start to dance. We have found that this progression helps the group to lose feelings of self-consciousness and start moving more freely.

A group leader can easily add singing to the many ways of working with a group. Singing and dancing, if encouraged on a twice-weekly or daily basis, will raise the energy level of the group for other experiences. Chanting is another possibility. An ancient practice used through the ages to put people in touch with themselves and sometimes with another level of consciousness, chanting has become popular again in nonmusical groups. It is a good way to raise group energy and is a useful method for beginning a group. Laurel Keyes, in a book entitled *Toning: The Creative Power of the Voice* (1973), describes in detail ways in which the voice can be used.

Ambulatory Groups. We work separately with ambulatory people and wheelchair people. We begin our ambulatory group the same way each time. Structure is important because it increases cohesiveness if the same things are done together. We start with formal leadership and then encourage more spontaneous movement. Forming a circle large enough so that the members have room to swing their arms, we do a range of motion exercises in the sitting position. These include gentle, circular movement of all parts of the body but the hips. Having the member stand behind a sturdy chair and hold onto the back for support facilitates the hip motion. Care should be taken with members in this standing position, because the sense of balance is very poor in many older people and falls can occur. Head movements should be done in a sitting position with great care to prevent strain and/or dizziness.

After warm-up exercises, we work into sounds and music as already described. We dance with group members and encourage them to dance with one another. Hawaiian music, slow Beatles records, and excerpts from the classics that are dance tunes are all good. It is best to have music with a good beat but at a moderate pace.

One of the group members was a 90-year-old man who walked on crutches. Before joining the exercise program, which continued for six months, he often snoozed in his room. He did come to any music group, but he remained withdrawn. After he became involved in the music and movement group, his daughter told me one day that he was sharing his reminiscences with her as he had not done for many years. He also began to be more careful about his appearance. In the group sessions, he left his crutches in a corner and danced with me.

Wheelchair Groups.   One of the deprivations of the institutionalized aged—especially those in wheelchairs—is a lack of touch (Burnside 1973). The movement group is a natural opportunity to incorporate it. I hold members' hands and move with the music. Similarly, their feet can be helped to move to the music. I also hold the head and rotate it very gently, ending with some massage of the shoulders, which provides more physical contact and also increases circulation.

I also work with music as a form of nonverbal communication with very regressed wheelchair people, with good results. For example, Mrs. H was a wheelchair patient for many years. She often became very agitated, tore out her hair, and pulled at her clothes, but she was instantly calmed by the simplest musical performance, such as playing a tune on a recorder. Her son taped many favorite classical selections on cassettes, and the staff was asked to play these for her when she was upset. As long as the music was on, she was calm. The combination of personal contact (amateur musician playing or staff member starting her tape recorder) and the music helped her to sit more quietly through the long days.

Music also can help in cases of aphasia. A woman in her early sixties suffered a severe stroke, which resulted in hemiplegia and aphasia. Her husband, a professional musician, cared for her at home but could communicate only on a nonverbal level. One day he discovered that his wife could sing along with well-known tunes. He demonstrated this; it was startling to hear her enunciating clearly the words to "My Bonnie Lies over the Ocean." It was only one step away then to teach her to sing her requests to the familiar tunes; for example, "I want a drink of water" fits nicely to "It's a Long Way to Tipperary." Ruth Bright (1972) describes this phenomenon and suggests it as a means of communication for the aphasic. Staff members who are working with the patient on an hour-by-hour basis can use this method easily. Apparently the speech center in the brain is in a slightly different place from the center for singing.

MUSICAL INSTRUMENTS

Handbells are a beautiful way for people who have never played an instrument to make music. They are excellent for encouraging concentration, but unfortunately, they are very expensive. A church loaned me a set of handbells for six months, which I used as an adjunct to group work with people suffering from severe short-term memory loss. The activity was designed to help members concentrate in order to respond and ring the bells on cue. Although handbells require no special skills to ring, a musician is needed to give direction. Very regressed or forgetful people are satisfied with working with the melody line. For alert people, chords can be introduced. The members should choose the music, but a word of caution is needed here. Leaders should begin with simple melodies and supply the rhythm themselves.

SUMMARY

The healing properties of music have long been known, and music is an effective tool in group work with older adults. This chapter offers suggestions that can be used by a leader with a musical background or one who simply has an interest in music.

Music can help aged members increase their movements, but it is also important in setting or changing moods because of its strong powers of association. Music need not always be joyful and can even be successfully integrated into group meetings to facilitate tears and the expression of sad feelings. Another way to help older people in groups to get in touch with their feelings is by the use of relaxation exercises.

New group leaders might find it helpful to draw up a list of music that represents various moods of their own. The list could then be compared to the list of moods of music compiled by Guntheil et al. (1952): (1) happy, joyous; (2) agitated, restless; (3) nostalgic, sentimental; (4) sad, melancholic; (5) prayerful, reverent; and (6) eerie, grotesque. Another suggestion is to make a list of selections used in group work and collect data on the reaction of the group members.

One important use of music is to further group cohesion. Music helps encourage discussion and sharing among members. They can identify with the feelings expressed and relate to past experiences. Music may also improve the perception of reality.

Music is appropriate to include in many of the groups described in this book: reality orientation, remotivation, reminiscence, socializing. Gibbons (1988) states, "the role of music, music development, and music therapy is not clear. It can be defined only by careful research, integrated with competent practice, which are both based on sound theoretical constructs" (p. 39).

EXERCISE 1

This exercise is an introduction to how music helps people move their bodies.

1. Sit in a circle. Appoint a leader to begin simple exercises as described in the chapter. Try working for three minutes without music. Then add recorded rhythmic music—anything with a firm beat. Note any difference in the body's response to these exercises with music. Examples of appropriate music are Scott Joplin's piano rags and Hawaiian music.
2. To become more aware of the physiological changes due to music, first conduct a seminar discussion on the physical changes in the body due to music. Then listen to music that gets slower. Measure your pulse rate before and after. (An example of such music is the first movement of Beethoven's *Moonlight Sonata*.) Finally, listen to music that gets faster. Measure your pulse rate before and after. (A good selection to try is Ravel's *Bolero*.)

EXERCISE 2

This exercise focuses on unstructured use of the voice to raise group members' energy and increase nonverbal communication. The exercise requires that someone lead the group.

1. Begin with deep breathing, moving the air up slowly into the chest and holding it, and then release the air as slowly as possible.
2. Repeat, exhaling to the sound of "ahhhh." Mouths should be open wide, and members should be encouraged to make as much noise as possible.
3. Repeat, this time humming. Ask the group to feel where the hum is in the body—they may find it in the face, the throat, or the chest. When they find it, break the group into pairs and ask them to find each other's hum. Does it change with the note? (It will be in the face when the note is high on the scale and lower as the sound lowers.)
4. Discuss group members' reactions to the exercise.

EXERCISE 3

Develop a time line of music that older persons appreciate. Begin with 1900 and find one song for each decade.

EXERCISE 4

1. Interview several old people from different cultures to learn the music they would enjoy.
2. Select one culture and write a two-page description of the music they would probably like to listen to in a group.

EXERCISE 5

1. Even if you are not musical, plan a music group you would feel comfortable leading.
2. Describe in detail how you would incorporate music into your group.

REFERENCES

Altschuler IM. 1959. The value of music in geriatrics. In EH Schneider (ed.), *Music therapy*. Lawrence, KA: Allen Press.

Alvin J. 1966. *Music therapy*. New York: Humanities Press.

Andrews DH. 1966. *The symphony of life*. Lee's Summit, MO: Unity Books.

Bingham WV. 1968. Introduction to the effects of music. In M Schoen (ed.), *The effects of music*. Freeport, NY: Books for Libraries Press.

Bonny HL, Savary L. 1973. *Music and your mind: Listening with a new consciousness*. New York: Harper & Row.

Bright R. 1972. *Music in geriatric care*. New York: St. Martin's Press.

Buckwalter KC, Hartsock J, Gaffney J. 1985. Music therapy. In GM Bulecheck, JC McCloskey (eds.), *Nursing interventions: Treatments for nursing diagnoses* (pp. 58-74). Philadelphia: Saunders.

Burnside IM. 1971. Loneliness in old age. *Ment Hyg* 55(3): 391-397.

———. 1973. Touching is talking. *Am J Nurs* 73(December):2060-2063.

Butler RN. 1975. *Why survive? Being old in America*. New York: Harper & Row.

Carapetyan A. 1948. Music and medicine in the Renaissance and in the 17th and 18th centuries. In D Schullian (ed.), *Music and medicine*. New York: Schuman.

Clair AA. 1992. Forever young: Music and aging. *Hearing before the special committee on aging, U.S. Senate* (pp. 1-14), Serial No. 102-9. Washington, DC: U.S. Government Printing Office.

Cohen E. 1976. Implications for health and social services. Paper presented at Public Policy Forum, Western Gerontological Society meeting, San Diego, CA (March).

Critchley M, Henson RA. 1977. *Music and the brain*. Springfield, IL: Thomas.

Davis W. 1992. Music therapy and elderly populations. In WB Davis, KE Gfeller, MH Thaut (eds.), *An introduction to music therapy: Theory and practice* (pp. 133-163). St. Louis: MMB.

Diserens CM, Fine HA. 1939. *A psychology of music: The influence of music on behavior*. Cincinnati: Fine.

Gaston ET. 1968. *Music in therapy*. New York: Macmillan.

Gibbons, AC. 1988. A review of literature for music development/education and music therapy with the elderly. *Music Ther Perspec* 5:33-40.

Green E, Green A. 1977. *Beyond biofeedback*. New York: Dell.

Guntheil EA, Wright JT, Fisichelli UR, Paperte F, Capurso A. 1952. *Music and your emotions*. New York: Liveright.

Hanser SB. 1988. Controversy in music listening/stress reduction research. *Arts Psychother* 15:211-217.

Hennessey MJ. 1976. Music and group work with the aged. In IM Burnside (ed.), *Nursing and the aged*, 1st ed. New York: McGraw-Hill.

Hyde LM. 1968. Effects of music upon electrocardiograms and blood pressure. In M Schoen (ed.), *The effects of music*. Freeport, NY: Books for Libraries Press.

Keyes L. 1973. *Toning: The creative power of the voice*. Santa Monica, CA: DeVorss.

LeCron LM. 1964. *Self-hypnotism*. Englewood Cliffs, NJ: Prentice-Hall.

Licht S. 1946. *Music in medicine*. Boston: New England Conservatory of Music.

Meinecke B. 1948. Music and medicine in classical antiquity. In D Schullian (ed.), *Music and medicine*. New York: Schuman.

Ostrander S, Schroeder L, with Ostrander N. 1979. *Superlearning*. New York: Delacorte Press.

BIBLIOGRAPHY

Bright R. 1981. Music and the management of grief reactions. In IM Burnside (ed.), *Nursing and the aged*, 2d ed. (pp. 137-142). New York: McGraw-Hill.

Douglass D. 1978. *Happiness is music, music, music! Music activities for the aged*. Salem, OR: La Roux Enterprises.

Gilbert JP, Beal MR. 1982. Preferences of elderly individuals for selected music education experiences. *J Res Music Ed* 30:247-253.

Halpern S, Savary L. (1985). *Sound health: The music and sounds that make us whole*. New York: Harper & Row.

Karras B. 1987. Music and reminiscences for group and individuals. *Activities, Adaptation, & Aging* 10:79-81.

Kartman LL. 1977. The use of music as a program tool with regressed geriatric patients. *J Gerontol Nurs* 3(4):38-42.

Kartman LL. 1981. The power of music with patients in a nursing home. *Activities, Adaptation, & Aging* 1:9-17.

McCloskey, LJ. 1985. Music and the frail elderly. *Activities, Adaptation, & Aging* 7:73-75.

Millard KO, Smith JM. 1989. The influence of group singing therapy on the behavior of Alzheimer's disease patients. *J Music Ther* 26:58-70.

Olson BK. 1984. Player-piano music as therapy for the elderly. *J Music Ther* 21:35-45.

Plach T. 1981. *The creative use of music in group therapy*. Springfield, IL: Thomas.

Pullman L. 1982. Reaching the confused and withdrawn through music. *Aging* (333-334):7-11.

Riegler J. 1980. Comparison of a reality orientation program for geriatric patients with and without music. *J Music Ther* 17:26-33.

Rubin B. 1976. Handbells in therapy. *Music Ther* (Spring): 49-53.

Rudhyar D. 1982. *The magic of tone and the art of music*. Boulder, CO: Shambhala.

Smith GH. 1986. A comparison of the effects of three treatment interventions on cognitive functioning of Alzheimer Patients. *Music Ther* 6A(1):41-56.

Wolfe JR. 1983. The use of music in group sensory training programs for regressed geriatric patients. *Activities, Adaptation, & Aging* 3:49-62.

Wylie ME. 1990. A comparison of the effects of old familiar songs, antique objects, historical summaires, and general questions on the reminiscence of nursing home residents. *J Music Ther* 27:2-12.

RESOURCES

Associations

National Association for Music Therapy, 8455 Colesville Rd., Suite 930, Silver Spring, MD 20910; phone: 301-589-3300; FAX: 301-589-5175.

American Association of Music Therapy, Inc., P.O. Box 80012, Valley Forge, PA 19484; phone: 215-265-4006.

Lists of Suggested Musical Selections for Special Moods

Music and Your Mind: Listening with a New Consciousness. HL Bonny, L Savary. New York: Harper & Row, 1973.

Taped Music to Enhance the Relaxation Response

Emmett E. Miller, 945 Evelyn Street, Menlo Park, CA 94025.

Halpern Sounds, 1775 Old County Road, #9, Belmont, CA 94002.

Institute for Consciousness and Music, 31 Allegheny Avenue, Room 104, Towson, MD 21204 or (West Coast outlet) Third Life Center, 385 Bellevue Avenue, Oakland, CA 94610.

Songs in Large Print

Sing Along Senior Citizens. 1973. One hundred songs by Roy Grant. Springfield, IL: Thomas.

Chanting and Toning Guides

Gentle Living Publications, 2168 South Lafayette, Denver, CO 80210. Cassette available.

Toning: The Creative Use of the Voice. 1973. Paperback to complement tape. L. Keyes. Santa Monica, CA: DeVorss.

Price Lists and Descriptions

Children's Music Center, 5373 West Pico Blvd., Los Angeles, CA 90019.

Magnamusic-Baton, 6390 Delmar Blvd., St. Louis, MO 63130.

Music Education Group, Box 1501, Union, NM 07083.

Rhythm Band, P.O. Box 126, Fort Worth, TX 76101.

Handbell Music

Handbell Ringing: A Musical Introduction. (by Scott Parry). Available from Fisher, 62 Cooper Square, New York, NY 10003.

C. F. Peters Corporation, 373 Park Avenue South, New York, NY 10016.

Information on Orff Schulwerk Instruments

Joe Fioretti, 415½ Livermore Avenue, Livermore, CA 94550.

Overseas Information

The Council for Music in Hospitals, 340 Lower Road, Little Bookham, Surrey, KT 23 4EF, UK.

Newsletter/Miscellaneous

Eldersong, edited by B. Karras. A newsletter for those using music with seniors. Mt. Airy, MD: Eldersong Publications, Inc. Cost: $12/year; phone: 301-829-0533.

The Lost Chord. A book by music therapist Melanie Chavin that includes music games, sensory stimulation, and ideas to work effectively with those diagnosed with dementia. Subscription cost: $18/year. Eldergames, Inc., 11710 Hunters Lane, Rockville, MD 20852; phone: 301-984-8336 or 800-637-2604.

I Hear Memories. An audiocassette tape with 14 familiar sounds of yesteryear, a mystery sound game, and an 18-page accompanying book (TP601). Price: $16. Available from Eldergames, Inc.

Films

Antonia: A Portrait of the Woman. An affectionate portrait of Antonia Brico, the 73-year-old conductor of a community symphony orchestra in Denver. Phoenix Films Inc., 470 Park Avenue South, New York, NY 10016.

Close Harmony (16 mm or video, 30 minutes). A film about members of an intergenerational chorus made up of people from 9 to 90. (Award: CINE Golden Eagle.) Learning Corporation of America, 1350 Avenue of the Americas, New York, NY 10019.

Sunshine's on the Way (16 mm or video, 30 minutes). The story of a young girl who works part-time at a nursing home, where she encourages some of the residents to form a jazz group. This is an inspirational film. Available from Learning Corporation of America.

Cassette

Special Music for Special People (No. 85) by EC Lindner, L Harpaz, S Samberg. Available from Lindner-Harpaz, P.O. Box 993, Woodside, NY 11377.

A PROJECT GRANT FOR A BEST PRACTICE IN MUSIC THERAPY UTILIZING GROUP PERCUSSION STRATEGIES FOR PROMOTING VOLUNTEERISM

Abstract: Many music therapy strategies have been effectively used with older adults. Research on the rhythmic nature of human functioning indicates great potential for the use of group percussion strategies. The objective is to utilize new group strategies and techniques with the well elderly to help them maintain current levels of functioning through self-esteem, social involvement, and physical and mental activity. A best-practice manual for professional music therapists that delineates specific group percussion techniques and use of senior volunteers in community-based programs will be created and disseminated.

Approaches include (1) creating and testing a curriculum for developing group percussion skills appropriate to the learning styles and physical capabilities of older adults and (2) developing appropriate training materials to be used by music therapists to train them. Final products include a best-practice manual in music therapy for the well older adults and a brochure about training.

Relevant Problems: (1) The need for inexpensive interventions that help individuals age in place; (2) the need of active older adults for specific training for volunteerism, and (3) the need of communities to promote communication between generations.

Reasons for Choosing Group Percussion Strategies:

1. Response to rhythm is basic to human functioning, making percussion activities highly motivating.
2. Percussion activities are interesting to all people regardless of ethnic and cultural background, musical preferences, or age range, making them useful in creating multi-ethnic and multi-generational experiences.
3. They are based on a number of ethnic traditions, including African, South and Central American, Arabic, and Native American, which provides a sense of pride and cultural identity.
4. They can be done with little or no previous musical experience, making them easy for senior volunteers to learn and teach to others.
5. They are cost effective because they require minimal equipment or can use found or created instruments.

Contact Persons: For results of this project or additional information, please contact Dr. Barbara Reuer, Music Therapist, or Dr. Percil Stanford, Director of the University Center on Aging at San Diego State University; phone: 619-594-2814.

CHAPTER 18

Support and Self-Help Groups

Irene Burnside

KEY WORDS

- Common goal
- Depersonalization
- Empathy
- Explanation
- Morale building
- Mutual affirmation
- Positive reinforcement
- Psychological group
- Self-care
- Self-disclosure
- Self-help
- Sharing
- Support group
- Support network

LEARNING OBJECTIVES

- Define support.
- Define support group.
- Discuss the role of professionals in support groups.
- Compare and contrast support groups with those led by professionals.
- Discuss the conceptual framework of group process according to Bradford.
- List five help-giving activities that occur in support groups.
- Describe one successful support group.
- State five interventions a practitioner might introduce in sponsoring a support group.

This chapter is about a special type of group, the support group. Support groups have been in existence for a long time and have been particularly effective in the areas of mental health and alcoholism.

The continuing growth of support groups may be considered by some to indicate a failure of the helping professionals and/or social agencies to provide assistance with the problems of physical and mental health. Professionals have been active in the founding and the support of most groups. The members often seek professional assistance or counseling for their groups.

Professionals can either facilitate a support group or sponsor or consult with a group. Peer leaders, rather than professionals, may facilitate groups. Research reports indicate that peer leaders can also be as effective as professionals (Toseland 1990).

There are several roles professionals can play if they sponsor peer-led support groups: help peer leaders with material support (meeting place, supplies, etc.); serve as guest speakers; provide advice, consultation, or supervision; serve as brokers by referring individuals to the group; and plan the development of new self-help groups.

SPECIFIC GUIDELINES TO FACILITATE SUPPORT GROUPS

Toseland (1990) offers specific advice for facilitating a support group. Practitioners should focus on interventions that will help develop trust, empathy, and cohesion.

- Highlight thoughts, feelings, and experiences that members share.
- Praise members when they assist one another.
- Use the terms *we* and *us.*
- Begin or end meetings by listing the accomplishments of previous meetings.
- Make contact with each member.
- Invite members to contribute; listen attentively.
- Do not strip away defenses, confront, or probe.
- Help members show respect to each other.
- Amplify and highlight subdued responses.
- Agree on communication/interaction rules.
- Become thoroughly familiar with members' concerns and problems.
- Avoid giving advice until you really understand the situation.
- Avoid being judgmental or patronizing.
- Draw on previous experiences you have had with older persons who experienced similar problems.
- Help with the grieving process by redefining and replacing the roles that have been lost.
- In the middle phase of the group, have members consider ways to enhance their present coping abilities.
- In the termination phase, encourage more use of other resources and solidify support networks in the group. Encourage socialization before or after meetings.
- Have members show what it was like to have been in the support group.

Lieberman and Borman (1979) have edited a book that focuses on two types of groups: those designed to modify group members' behaviors or attitudes (for example, groups for alcoholics, gamblers, drug abusers) and groups formed to help members cope with particular life crises (major illness, aging, loss of spouse or child, for example).

DEFINITIONS

As a mode of intervention, a support group represents the merging of two theoretical perspectives: social support and small groups (Kinney, Mannetter & Carpenter 1992). Weiss (1975) defines social support as feeling sustained because needs are gratified, gaining knowledge, and being aware that others care about one.

Support groups help older persons cope with stress in their lives and can help them cope during some of the difficult life transitions (Toseland 1990). The same author lists selected characteristics of support groups for older persons (Toseland 1990, pp 100-101):

Goal   To help members cope with stressful life events.

Leadership   Facilitator of mutual support and mutual aid.

Focus   The shared concerns of the members.

Procedure   Informal operation of group.

Bond   Shared problems and common goals, based on a similar traumatic event.

Composition   Members who have had similar experiences.

Communication   Highly interactive, open, member-to-member, often with a high level of self-disclosure.

Benefits   Social contacts, social supports; members can share their wisdom; gives members a useful role in helping others.

A group may be defined in a variety of ways. A definition given by Cartwright and Zander (1960, 46) stresses two aspects of the group: goals and interrelationships. "A group is a collection of individuals sharing a common goal who have relationships to one another that make them interdependent to some significant degree.

To add to the selected characteristics stated above, Lieberman and Borman (1979) found that self-help groups have other characteristics in common:

- The members share a common condition, problem, heritage, or life experience.
- The groups are both self-regulating and self-governing and tend to emphasize peer cohesiveness rather than a formal structure of governance.
- The groups advocate self-reliance, and there is an emphasis on commitment and responsibility.
- The groups maintain a code of beliefs and practices.
- The members have a support network, usually a face-to-face or phone network. (Many groups publish a regular newsletter or bulletin).
- The members with the most experience provide guidance for the others.
- Group members provide empathy for one another.
- The groups provide specific help in handling the problems or conditions that exist for the members.

- The members have practical ways to handle the day-to-day difficulties they experience.

Another advantage of support groups is their cost effectiveness, according to Spiegel (1993). "You know, from the perspective of health care costs and implementation, group support is ridiculously inexpensive. It costs virtually nothing.... I can assure you that support groups are far easier to do and far less expensive than many things that we do in health care today" (p. 162).

EDUCATIONAL GROUPS

Kaplan and Fleisher (1981) recommend that information be provided in educational groups about the aging process and role losses. These authors also recommend that support groups would be helpful for middle-generation adults who are worried about the increasing demands of caretaking responsibilities. Many of them must make rather constant adjustments to handle everything on their schedules. A chance to discuss and share concerns with cohorts would help them by giving them ideas for coping and suggesting alternatives regarding their caretaking roles.

Kaplan and Fleisher (1981) also discuss coping groups. In these groups, older persons can discuss their feelings about the changes they have experienced in aging. Some of the topics that the authors suggest for selection by the members include feelings about widowhood, loss of the work role, loss of the social network provided by the work role, loneliness, shifting patterns of friendships, and disappointments (if, for example, their children have been unable to substitute for some of the losses they have experienced.) Such a group provides support for its members as they hear how their cohorts have coped and what survival strategies they have used.

TYPES OF SUPPORT GROUPS

Orville Kelly founded the group called Make Today Count for individuals who were faced with life-threatening illnesses. Simon Stephens, in England, established the Society of Compassionate Friends to aid bereaved parents. The first U.S. chapter began in the Miami area in 1972, and there are now more than 200 chapters in this country. These would be classified as stress, coping, and support

groups. They are only two of the many self-help organizations. The fact that they have spread rapidly and widely attests that they do respond to some need.

Some groups, such as Alcoholics Anonymous (AA), focus on behavior modification. AA was the original self-help group. It was begun in 1935 in the United States and currently has 28,000 chapters. It is impressive to watch self-help groups organize and grow; the members' understanding, empathy, and concern for one another cannot be underscored enough. Any helping professional who has called an AA member out of bed at 3:00 A.M. to come and listen to a patient can speak to the loyalty and true helping of such individuals.

Self-help groups usually arise spontaneously, and some are associated with already existing, structured organizations—for example, Stroke Clubs are under the aegis of the American Heart Association, and the Arthritis Foundation sponsors Arthritis Clubs.

Fuller and others (1979) briefly describe a supportive group for families of demented relatives. These groups were begun in a psychogeriatric unit in London. One group met at lunchtime for one hour every two weeks; another group was begun in the evening for relatives who had to work during the day. The latter group was attended mainly by patients' children or grandchildren. The common themes from the group described by Fuller and others included:

- Validation of the behavior of the family member by other group members who experience it.
- The cause of the dementia.
- Disorientation.
- Lack of recognition of spouse.
- Anger and resentment.
- Incontinence (not a major topic).
- Sexual problems.

Doris Weaver began support groups for teenagers and grandchildren of the demented in the Seattle-Tacoma area and report the need for such groups (Weaver 1982).

Sperry (1993, personal letter) described a support group based on the 12 steps of Alcoholics Anonymous programs. He and Carol Heckmann are "cofounders of Journey to Wholeness, a nonprofit corporation whose primary mission is to train nonpaid workers (volunteers) to facilitate support groups for the elderly and to provide these workers with a program for ongoing skill building and moral support." (See Resources.)

Occasionally one observes the development of dissension that is not resolved in the group and the formation of factions. The splinter group sometimes takes off in what is described by Kirschenbaum and Glaser (1978) as the "let's-form-a-new-organization" syndrome. The pitfall here, they say, is that when support groups "go off exploring in this direction, the majority never do it" (p. 54). In support groups of the self-help type, anger, smoldering resentments, or unacceptable rules and codes may be reasons for groups splintering—not unlike the divisions one sees in religious groups.

The literature reveals that one group theorist (Bradford 1978) believes that a group essentially re-forms every time it meets, because intervening events for each of the members, new expectations, pressures from sources outside the group, and subgroup cliques all help to provide a changed group from meeting to meeting. This phenomenon would seem to be applicable to Alzheimer's disease support groups, because of the many ups and downs that are experienced by members as their loved ones move through various stages of the disease and or show behavioral changes.

Bradford (1978) feels that a "psychological group" forms when:

1. Patterns of interaction are proven effective.
2. Differences in perceptions about tasks, communication, and procedures are clarified.
3. Relationships to other persons and groups are delineated.
4. Standards for participation are set.
5. Methods of work that elicit rather than inhibit contributions are established.
6. A respected plan for each person is secured.
7. Trust is established among members.

Groups for Widowed Persons

Another type of self-help group that has gained in importance is the widowhood groups. Like the Alzheimer's disease groups mentioned above, they have responded to a need felt by a particular group of people. They were begun by Phyllis Silverman in the 1960s (Silverman 1969, 1974; Silverman & Cooperband 1975).

The National Retired Teachers Association and the American Association of Retired Persons (NRTA-AARP) also have chapters of support groups for widowed people. The Widowed Persons Service (WPS) staff and volunteers organize, train, and offer consultation and materials to develop these programs. WPS goals in the community include:

- Volunteer outreach to the newly bereaved.
- Telephone referral and information assistance.
- Group meetings (to allow widowed persons to share both experience and concerns).
- Public education (problems of grief adjustment and services available for widowed persons).
- A resource directory (helps the widowed to locate available local services).

For further information on how to develop a WPS program in a community, contact the national office of NRTA-AARP. (See Resources section at the end of this chapter.)

These groups provide support, education, and social life for their members. A problem I observed in one group was that membership was open to those who were recently widowed as well as to those who had been widowed for 10 or more years. The needs and expectations of the group members were vastly different and conflict arose because of the difference in length of bereavement. The newly widowed needed to grieve, to ventilate, and to share their hurts in a safe milieu. Many were not ready for social activities or reaching out. The other members appeared to be well-adjusted to their loss (or losses), through the acute grief phase, and ready to socialize and/or change their lifestyles. It requires unusually sensitive and skillful leaders to meet the needs of both of these types of widowed persons.

Susan Huart and Mary O'Donnell (1993) recommend that the criteria for joining a bereavement support group is that the loss "should have occurred no less than six weeks and no more than 18 months beforehand" (p. 74). Group rules include the following: "confidentiality, no comparisons of whose loss is greater, listening to each other, no monopolizing of the group, and no confrontational behavior" (p. 74).

Lieberman and Borman (1981) report on the findings of a study of widows. Some of the findings are highlighted here:

- Informal social resources provided by one's social network do make a difference in the adjustment of a widow.

- Both the helping professions and researchers have been preoccupied with the early crisis phase of widowhood and not with long-term problems of transition. It appears that a widow's needs are both complex and changing.
- The problem of the widow's social isolation has been exaggerated. In a doctoral dissertation study, most widows had one or more significant individuals in their network whom they could turn to for emotional and instrumental support.
- As a widow moves from the early crisis and bereavement stage to the transition stage, she grows to rely more on persons similar to herself, namely, other widows and single friends.
- A key finding is the importance of *who* provides the support, rather than *what* is provided. In the crisis phase, it is the widow's mother; through the transition phase, it is the widow's single or widowed friends.
- In the early bereavement stage, how a widow sees the situation and who she thinks she can depend upon appear more important to her than real interactions and support. Her perceptions are more important than actuality.

Crouch (1990) advocates the use of the family diagram, or genogram, because it provides a framework that helps organize data about families. A *genogram* is a drawing or an elaboration of a family tree. "A genogram, more technically, is a clinical method of taking, storing, and processing information" (Herth 1989, 32). It also helps to broaden the older persons' views of themselves and their family origins and to view dynamics among family members in new ways. Crouch offers helpful suggestions for conducting widowhood groups in Table 18-1.

HELP-GIVING ACTIVITIES

Some of the important help-giving activities that occur in self-help groups are described by Levy (1979, 260-263). Empathy is one of the most important aspects of these help-giving activities. Mutual affirmation—that is, assuring one another that one is worthwhile and valuable—is another important aspect. Explanation—a better understanding of oneself or one's reactions to a situation—is a third. Morale-building rates high; group members often are able to reassure other members that the problems will eventually be worked out positively. Sharing past and present experiences and thoughts and feelings with other members is

helpful. Positive reinforcement, or applauding of behavior, by the group is highly rated among the help-giving activities. Self-disclosure—that is, the ability to relate personal thoughts or emotions that members would not normally tell other persons—is also an important part of the helpful group process. The ability to make goals and to check the progress made with the group is also helpful, according to the data provided by Levy.

Pender (1982) offers a list of general suggestions for enhancing support systems. Since support systems are so crucial to the maintenance and improvement of health, the list is included here.

- Increase frequency of contact with individuals with whom the client desires stronger personal ties.
- Build ties with individuals who share common life values.
- Participate in mutual goal-setting with significant others to achieve common directions in actions and efforts.
- Provide additional personal warmth, encouragement, and love to significant others.
- Support coping efforts of significant others in dealing with life experiences.
- Enhance personal identity and self-esteem of persons within support network.
- Provide increased intimacy to promote self-expression.
- Deal constructively with conflict between oneself and support-group members.
- Increase reciprocity and mutuality of interpersonal relationships.
- Offer assistance more frequently to individuals within personal social network, to show concern and promote trust.
- Increase personal capacity to accept emotional support and love.
- Seek counseling as needed to enhance marital adjustment.
- Make use of self-help groups or the extended family as a source of support.
- Make use of the nurse and other health professionals as community support resources.
- Make use of the church or religious affiliation as a source of emotional and spiritual support.
- Capitalize on ties to a number of social groups to expand horizons for new growth opportunities.

A MODEL

A group that is gaining in chapters, attendance, and interest is the Alzheimer's Disease and Related Disorders Association (ADRDA). With increasingly

TABLE 18-1 Dos and don'ts for conducting widowhood groups

Dos

1. Maintain a healthy respect for the elderly.

2. Realize that you cannot take a senior's pain away.

3. Listen carefully—without having your mind on something else or what you will say next.

4. Have a tolerance for the various reactions and behaviors you may see related to the death of a spouse.

5. Respect a person's position and attitudes toward family and friends.

6. Know there are many sides and versions to happenings in families.

7. Encourage free expression of thoughts and feelings.

8. Make widows and widowers active participants in the group.

9. Be patient if a widow cannot immediately express herself in the group. With time, she will.

10. Intervene if others become judgmental regarding a person's attitude or family situation.

11. Reassure widowed people that they are not losing their sanity in the grief process, where necessary.

12. Recognize the critical therapeutic value of presence, or being there. How could you just be there and not do for the grieving person?

13. Feel comfortable mentioning the dead person.

14. Use the word "died" instead of terms like "passed away." But allow seniors to use whatever terms are comfortable for them.

Don'ts

1. Don't expect a widow to be a certain place in the process of grieving on the basis of the time elapsed since the death.

2. Don't require widows to think differently about their families.

3. Don't let widows' situations overcome you. Often there are no easy answers to complex problems after death.

4. Don't impose your religious views on the elderly or criticize them for not having any.

5. Don't take away the hope for a person to come to better terms with a death.

6. Don't be afraid to give your view on a problem.

7. Don't force a widowed person to accept your way of thinking.

8. Don't force them to stay in the group when the time comes for them to go on to other endeavors.

9. Don't forget to be your thoughtful self with them.

SOURCE: LR Crouch (1990, 324). Used with permission.

more persons being diagnosed as having Alzheimer's disease, these chapters will undoubtedly continue to expand. Butler (1980, 167) states that Alzheimer's disease probably accounts for about 100,000 to 110,000 deaths per year. Some writers state that Alzheimer's disease may be responsible for two thirds of all dementia among older people (Dreyfus 1979). Those staggering figures speak to the need to support the relatives, because "the economic, social, and human costs of dementias, which already are staggering, will increase" (Hutton 1980, 149).

The ADRDA grew into a national health organization from support groups; chapters began across the country in response to the needs of Alzheimer's patients and their families. Families decided that local programs should be strengthened and supplemented by a national effort. A joint approach was needed, and in December 1979, the chapters united to form a national association.

Fundamental purposes are education, patient care, research, and advocacy. ADRDA's mission is to combat the disease by research to aid in diagnosis, improve treatment, identify the cause(s), and prevent the disease; education for medical professionals, to share information about the diagnosis, treatment, and management of patients; education and support systems for lay persons, to provide information and to cope with the practical details of daily living; and functioning as an advocate to inform government and social service agencies about the long-term custodial needs of the affected population.

The association began a public education and awareness campaign, first to destroy the myth that senility is a natural part of the aging process and also to ensure that people know that the organization exists and that help is available. The group was successful in having a week in November 1982 declared as "Alzheimer's Disease Public Awareness Week." In 1986, the House of Representatives considered a bill that placed special emphasis on the disease, especially in coordinating government-sponsored research on Alzheimer's disease and improving programs for care and treatment of Alzheimer's disease patients.

There is now an extensive body of knowledge regarding support groups for caregivers of persons with Alzheimer's disease, and the leaders are from many disciplines.

There has been a rapid growth in support groups in the ADRDA association nationwide.

There are well over 1000 support groups in the United States.

Edwards (1990) offers advice regarding support groups for caregivers of individuals with Alzheimer's disease:

- It is best not to invite persons who have Alzheimer's disease to support group meetings.
- There should be support group guidelines, especially regarding confidentiality. They should be concise and direct.
- The group should maintain autonomy and can avoid conflict by meeting in neutral sites such as schools.
- Facilitators should be knowledgeable about dementia, family dynamics, Alzheimer's disease, and group process skills.
- Co-facilitators can be advantageous; for example, if a group member becomes agitated and leaves the room, the second leader can attend to that individual's needs and the group can continue.

ASPECTS OF THE SELF-HELP HEALTH MOVEMENT

Katz and Levin (1980) offer some reasons for the growth of the self-help movement in the United States.

1. Medicine's depersonalization, overspecialization, and concentration on technology (leading to a general loss of confidence in it).

2. The health care system's embodiment of fragmented and episodic care rather than comprehensive and continuous care.

3. The changing nature of morbidity (chronic illness is now the most prevalent form of health problem).

4. The drive toward greater control of one's own life and destiny, represented in the United States by populist and anti-establishment movements. In the health field these have led to an empowering of consumers, in the belief that they can more positively discover and control the forces that affect their own health and risks of illness.

5. The greater understanding of the relationship between environment and illness and of stress-related disorders, physical and mental.

6. The emergence and popular appeal of alternative therapies ranging from diet, exercise, meditation, and other practices to modes of self-observation and self-treatment via such methods as biofeedback, imaging, and other techniques derived from clinical and scientific studies.

7. The vast expansion of self-help groups in the health field; these groups offer health information and specific instruction, provide social care and mutual aid to sufferers from a wide variety of illnesses and disorders, and give material and emotional support to their families. Katz and Bender (1976) estimate that self-help groups engage several million participants in the United States.

8. The development, in addition to all of the above, of a public consciousness about general health practice, that is, the importance of diet to avoid obesity, coronary artery disease, and other health problems; the hazards of cigarette smoking; the importance of physical activity, and so forth. There are some 15 million American joggers; a 25 percent replacement of animal fat by unsaturated fats has occurred in the U.S. diet in the past decade; and millions of copies of thousands of separate self-help books, pamphlets, and training programs have been sold to the public.

King (1980, 34) asks some questions about the self-help group concept. For example:

- What is the constraint versus the freedom in the group?
- What are the goals, and how are individual values and differences tolerated?
- Does the self-help group have to formally organize to survive?
- Structural effects of inner versus outer orientation—does the group become so homogeneous that it does not thrive and continue to grow?

SUMMARY

This chapter provides a brief overview of support groups; a few of the successful groups are described and one conceptual framework of a group process is discussed. A model of one of the newer self-help groups (ADRDA) is presented. The effectiveness of such groups in meeting the needs of their members surely indicates some of the shortcomings of groups convened and run by professionals. The voluntary aspects of such groups and the motivation, ingenuity, caring, the drive of their members are qualities to impress any of us.

EXERCISE 1

Attend a meeting of some type of support group. List five reasons why you think it is a successful group, and defend those reasons.[1]

EXERCISE 2

Attend a support group for families. List and explain four themes that you heard expressed by family members in the group meeting.[1]

EXERCISE 3

Select one support group that was started or aided by a professional. Study the history of the group, and write a two-page paper on the role the professional had in the formation of the group.

EXERCISE 4

Think about a time in your life when you would have appreciated a support group. Describe the group you would have liked to have had available.

---

[1]As a cautionary note, the student should be advised that it is important to check with the leader(s) of self-help groups before going unannounced to observe the meetings.

REFERENCES

Bradford L. 1978. Group formation and development. In LP Bradford (ed.), *Group development*, 2d ed. La Jolla, CA: University Associates.

Butler RN. 1980. Meeting the challenges of health care for the elderly. *J Allied Health* 9(3):6.

Cartwright D, Zander A (eds.). 1960. *Group dynamics: Research and theory*, 2d ed. Evanston, IL: Row, Peterson.

Crouch LR. 1990. Putting widowhood in perspective: A group approach utilizing family systems principles. In E Eliopoulos (ed.), *Caring for the elderly in diverse settings* (pp. 318-329). Philadelphia: Lippincott.

Dreyfus P. 1979. Understanding dementia: A closer look at Alzheimer's disease. *Consultant* 19(January):31-39.

Edwards M. 1990. Support groups for caregivers of Alzheimer's disease victims: The nurse's role. In C Eliopoulos (ed.), *Caring for the elderly in diverse settings* (pp. 290-307). Philadelphia: Lippincott.

Fuller J, Ward E, Evans A, Massam K, Gardner A. 1979. Dementia: Supportive groups for relatives. *Br Med J* 1(6179):1684-1685.

Herth KA. 1989. The root of it all: Genograms as a nursing assessment tool. *J Gerontol Nurs* 15(12):32-37.

Huart S, O'Donnell M. 1993. The road to recovery from grief and bereavement. *Caring* 12(11):71-75.

Kaplan B, Fleisher D. 1981. Loneliness and role loss. In *Occasional papers in mental health and aging*. Proceedings of the Focus on Mental Health and Aging Conference, University of Utah Gerontology program, Salt Lake City, UT.

Katz AH, Bender EI. 1976. *The strength in us: Self-help groups in the modern world*, 36. New York: Franklin-Watts.

Katz AH, Levin LS. 1980. Self-care is not a solipsistic trap: A reply to critics. *Int J Health Serv* 10(2):329-336.

Katzman R. 1976. The prevalence and malignancy of Alzheimer's disease. *Arch Neurol* 33(4):217-218.

King C. 1980. The self-help/self-care concept. *Nurs Pract* 5(3):34-35, 46.

Kinney C, Mannetter R, Carpenter MA. 1992. Support groups. In GM Bulechek, JC McCloskey (eds.), *Nursing interventions: Essential nursing treatments* (pp. 326-339). Philadelphia: Saunders.

Kirschenbaum H, Glaser B. 1978. *Developing support groups*. La Jolla, CA: University Associates.

Levy LH. 1979. Process and activities in groups. In M Lieberman, L Borman (eds.), *Self-help groups for coping with crisis* (pp. 234-271). San Francisco: Jossey-Bass.

Lieberman M, Borman L. 1979. *Self-help groups for coping with crisis: Origins, members, processes and impact*. San Francisco: Jossey-Bass.

———. 1981. Who help widows: The role of kith and kin. *National Reporter* 4(8):2.

Pender N. 1982. *Health promotion in nursing practice*. Norwalk, CT: Appleton-Century-Crofts.

Silverman P. 1969. The widow-to-widow program: An experiment in preventive intervention. *Ment Hyg* 53(3): 333-337.

———. 1974. *Helping each other in widowhood*. New York: Health Science.

Silverman P, Cooperband A. 1975. On widowhood: Mutual help and the elderly widow. *J Geriatr Psych* 8(1):9-27.

Sperry D. 1993. Personal letter.

Spiegel D. 1993. Therapeutic support groups. In B Moyers (ed.), *Healing and the mind* (pp. 157-170). New York: Doubleday.

Toseland RW. 1990. *Group work with older adults*. New York: New York University Press.

Weaver D. 1982. Tapping strength: A support group for children and grandchildren. *Generations* 8(1):45.

Weiss R. 1975. The provision of social relationships. In R Zick (ed.), *Doing unto others* (pp. 17-26). Englewood Cliffs, NJ: Prentice-Hall.

BIBLIOGRAPHY

Barnes RF, Raskin MA, Scott M. 1981. Problems of families caring for Alzheimer patients: Use of a support group. *J Am Geriatr Soc* 29(2):80-85.

Borkman T. 1976. Experiential knowledge: A new concept for the analysis of self-help groups. *Soc Serv Rev* 50:30.

Clipp EC, George LK. 1990. Caregiver needs and patterns of social support. *J Gerontol Soc Sci* 45:S102-S111.

Cook AS, Dworkin DS. 1992. *Helping the bereaved*. New York: Basic Books.

Cross L, London C, Barry C. 1981. Older women caring for disabled spouses: A model for supportive services. *Gerontologist* 21(5):464-470.

D'Afflitti J, Weitz G. 1974. Rehabilitating the stroke patient through patient-family groups. *Int J Group Psychother* 25(3):323-332.

Donnelly GF. 1980. Remember . . . you're not in this alone! *RN* (July):30-33.

Fengler A, Goodrich N. 1979. Wives of elderly disabled men: The hidden patients. *Gerontologist* 19(2):175-183.

Finlinson R. 1986. Self-help and family support groups. In I Hanley, M Gilhooly (eds.), *Psychosocial therapies for the elderly* (pp. 101-123). New York: New York Universities Press.

Foster Z, Mendel S. 1979. Mutual-help group for patients: Taking steps toward change. *Health Soc Work* 4(3): 83-97.

Gallo F. 1982. The effects of social support networks on the health of the elderly. *Soc Work Health Care* 8(2):65-74.

Getzel G. 1983. Group work with kin and friends caring for the elderly. In S Saul (ed.), *Group work with the frail elderly* (pp. 77-89). New York: Haworth.

Gordon T. 1977. *Leader effectiveness training*. New York: Peter Wyden.

Harris Z. 1981. Ten steps towards establishing a self-help group: A report from Montreal. *Canada's Ment Health* 29(1):16.

Hayter J. 1982. Helping families of patients with Alzheimer's disease. *J Gerontol Nurs* 8(2):81-86.

Haywood L, Taylor E. 1981. Strikes and support systems: What happened in Sudbury. *Canada's Ment Health* 29(1):18-19.

Katz A. 1970. Self-help organization and volunteer participation in social welfare. *Soc Work* 15(1):51-60.

———. 1979. Self-help health groups: Some clarification. *Soc Sci Med* 13(June):491-494.

Kilen E. 1979. Family discussion group meetings. *Am Health Care Assoc J* (Special report): January.

Knight B, Wollert RW, Levy LH. 1980. Self-help groups: The members' perspectives. *Am J Community Psych* 8(1): 53-65.

Levin L, Katz AH, Holst E. 1976. *Self-care: Lay initiatives in health*. New York: Prodist.

Lieberman M, Bond G. 1978. Self-help groups: Problems of measuring outcomes. *Small Group Behav* 9:221-242.

Lieberman M, Borman L. 1981. The impact of self-help groups in widows' mental health. *National Reporter* 4(7):64.

McCormack N. 1981. *Plain talk about mutual help groups*. Rockville, MD: National Institute of Mental Health.

Mann J. 1983. Behind the explosion in self-help groups. *U.S. News* 94(17):33-35.

Petty B, Moeller T, Cambell R. 1976. Support groups for elderly persons in the community. *Gerontologist* 16: 522-528.

Politser PP, Pattison EM. 1980. Social climates in community groups: Toward a taxonomy. *Community Ment Health J* 16(3):187-200.

Rogers J, Vachen M, Lyall W et al. 1980. A self-help program for widows as an independent community service. *Hosp Comm Psych* 31(12):844-847.

Rosenberg P. 1984. Support groups: A special therapeutic entity. *Small Group Behav* 15(2):173-186.

Sanford J. 1975. Tolerance of debility in elderly dependents by supporters at home; Its significance for hospital practice. *Br Med J* 3(5981):471-473.

U.S. Department of Health, Education, and Welfare. 1980. *A guide to medical self-care and self-help groups for the elderly*, NIH Publication No. 89-1687. Washington, DC (November).

Vachon MLS, Lyall W, Rogers J, et al. 1980. A controlled study of self-help intervention for widows. *Am J Psychiatr* 137(11):1380-1384.

Vattano A. 1972. Power to the people: Self-help groups. *Soc Work* 17(4):7-15.

Wolfelt AD. 1991. Toward an understanding of complicated grief: A comprehensive overview. *Am J Hospice and Palliative Care* 8(2):28-30.

Zola I. 1979. Helping one another: A speculative history of the self-help movement. *Arch Phys Med Rehabil* 60(1):452-456.

RESOURCES

Films

Beginning Again: Widower (30 minutes, color). Describes widowers aged 39 to 66 who show how they coped. Program could be used for support staff training workshops or inservice. Pre-view rates available: WHA Television Marketing Department, 821 University Avenue, Madison, WI 53706.

In Care Of: Families and Their Elders. Brookdale Center on Aging of Hunter College, 425 East 25th Street, New York, NY 10010.

Time to Care. New York State Office of Aging, 2 Empire State Plaza, Albany, New York 12233.

Organizations

National Association of Retired Persons—National Retired Teachers Association (AARP-NRTA). 1909 K Street NW, Washington, DC 20049.

The Self-Help Center, 1600 Dodge Avenue, Suite S-122, Evanston, IL 60201; phone: 312-328-0470.

Publications

Citizen Participation (newsmagazine). Civic Education Foundation, Lincoln Filene Center for Citizenship and Public Affairs, Tufts University, Medford, MA 02155.

Self-Help Reporter, c/o National Self-Help Clearinghouse, Graduate School and University Center/CUNY, 33 West 42nd Street, Room 1206A, New York, NY 10036.

Self-Help Groups

Alcoholism

Al-Anon Group Headquarters, P.O. Box 182, Madison Square Station, New York, NY 10010. Alcoholics Anonymous, 468 Park Avenue South, New York, NY 10017.

Alzheimer's Disease

Alzheimer's Disease and Related Disorders Association (ADRDA), 360 North Michigan Avenue, Chicago, IL 60601.

Arthritis

The Arthritis Foundation, 1212 Avenue of the Americas, New York, NY 10036.

Cancer

American Cancer Society, 777 Third Avenue, New York, NY 10017.

Cancer Care Inc. (CCI), of the National Cancer Foundation, One Park Avenue, New York, NY 10016; phone: 212-679-5700.

Cancer Patients Anonymous (CANPATANON), 1722 Ralph Avenue, Brooklyn, NY 11236; phone: 212-649-3481.

Make Today Count Inc., P.O. Box 303, Burlington, IA 52601; phone: 319-754-7266 or 754-8977.

National Cancer Foundation, One Park Avenue, New York, NY 10016; phone: 212-679-5700.

Reach to Recovery, c/o American Cancer Society, 777 Third Avenue, New York, NY 10017; phone: 212-371-2900.

Cardiac Disorders

American Heart Association, 7320 Greenville Avenue, Dallas, TX 75231.

The Mended Hearts Inc., 721 Huntington Avenue, Boston, MA 02115; phone: 617-732-5609.

Diabetes

American Diabetes Association Inc., 18 East 48th Street, New York, NY 10017.

Hearing

Alexander Graham Bell Association for the Deaf, 1537 35th Street NW, Washington, DC 20007.

American Humane Society, P.O. Box 1266, Denver, CO 80201 (trains seeing eye dogs).

American Organization for the Education of the Hearing Impaired, 1537 35th Street NW, Washington, DC 20007.

American Speech and Hearing Association, 9030 Old Georgetown Road, Washington, DC 20014.

The Better Hearing Institute, 1430 K Street N, Suite 600, Washington, DC 20005; phone: 800-424-8576.

Junior National Association for the Deaf, Gallaudet College, Washington, DC 20002.

National Association of the Deaf, 814 Thayer Avenue, Silver Spring, MD 20910.

National Association of Hearing and Speech Agencies, 919 18th Street NW, Washington, DC 20006.

The National Hearing Aid Society, 20361 Middlebelt Road, Livonia, MI 48152; phone: 313-478-2610.

Life Crisis

Widow to Widow, 25 Huntington Avenue, Boston, MA 02115; phone: 617-661-6180.

Lung/Breathing Disorders

American Lung Association, 1720 Broadway, New York, NY 10019.

Emphysema Anonymous Inc., P.O. Box 66, Fort Meyers, FL 33902; phone: 813-344-4266.

Mental Health

National Association for Mental Health, 1800 North Kent Street, Rosslyn, VA 22208; phone: 703-528-6405.

Measurements of Social Support

Brandt PA, Weinert C. 1981. The PRQ—A social support measure. *Nurs Res* 30:277-280.

Broadhead WE, Gehlback SH, de Groy FV, Kaplan BH. 1988. The Duke-UNC Functional Social Support Questionnaire: Measurement of social support in family medicine patients. *Med Care* 26:709-723.

Norbeck J, Lindsey AM, Carrier VL. 1983. Further development of the Norbeck Social Support Questionnaire: Normative data and validity testing. *Nurs Res* 32:4-9.

Pearson J. 1987. The Interpersonal Network Questionnaire: A tool for social support network assessment. *Meas Eval Counsel Dev* 20:99-105.

Salisbury CL. 1986. Adaptation of the Questionnaire on Resources and Stress-Short Form. *Am J Ment Deficiency* 90:456-459.

Sarason IG, Levine MH, Basham RB, Sarason BR. 1983. Assessing social support: The Social Support Questionnaire. *J Pers Soc Psychol* 44:127-139.

Siegert RJ, Patten MD, Walkey FH. 1987. Development of a Brief Social Support Questionnaire. *New Zealand J Psych* 16:79-83.

Weinert C. 1987. A social support measure: PRQ85. *Nurs Res* 36:273-277.

Source Books

Madera EJ, Meese A. 1986. *The self-help source book: Finding and forming mutual and self-help groups.* Denville, NJ: Self-help Clearinghouse.

Powell TJ. 1987. *Self-help organizations and professional practice.* Silver Spring, MD: National Association of Social Workers, Appendix 2.

Manuals

Caregivers' Support Group Facilitator's Manual. Department of Veterans Affairs, Central Office, Social Work Service (122), 810 Vermont Avenue NW, Washington, DC 20420.

Montgomery R (ed.). 1985. *Helping families help.* Seattle, WA: University of Washington Press.

Practical Help Guide for Course Leader. New York State Office on Aging, 2 Empire State Plaza, Albany, NY 12233.

Support Groups (Twelve Steps)

Journey to Wholeness. David Sperry, Program Director, 121 20th Avenue SW, New Brighton, MN 55112; phone: 612-636-4269.

CHAPTER 19

Group Psychotherapy

Judith A. S. Altholz

KEY WORDS

- Anger
- Caring skills
- Countertransference
- Group composition
- Group psychotherapy
- Management skills
- Meaning attribution skills
- Self-psychology
- Transference

LEARNING OBJECTIVES

- Define *group psychotherapy*.
- Identify three purposes of group psychotherapy with older adults.
- Discuss six criteria for group member selection.
- Discuss the role of leadership in group psychotherapy with the aged, identify three roles the leader(s) may choose to take, and give reasons for each choice.
- Discuss six benefits group psychotherapy may have for the aged.
- Identify five practical considerations that must be taken into account when leading group psychotherapy with the aged.

Many older people share the same fears, questions, and concerns, and too often they suffer these feelings silently, in isolation. One hears the aged refer to themselves as "odd" or "crazy" for experiencing what professionals consider reasonable problems of old age. Group psychotherapy offers older people an opportunity to see that they are not crazy, that many of their problems are not unique to them but are common problems of the aged. The realization by group members of the universality of their problems reduces their feelings of incompetence and inadequacy. This chapter is about group psychotherapy and assumes the reader has a background in psychodynamics.

According to Milton Berger (1968), *group psychotherapy* refers to all regularly scheduled, voluntarily attended meetings of acknowledged clients (patients) with an acknowledged trained leader (therapist) for the purpose of expressing, eliciting, accepting, and working through various aspects of the client's functioning and developing the client's healthier and more satisfying potentials. The group provides a "beneficial, controlled life experience within a group setting by the establishment of relationships with the leader, on interaction with group members, or both, together with some clarification of one's motives and those of others in the interaction" (Goldfarb 1972, 114).

REVIEW OF THE LITERATURE

The first report of group psychotherapy with the aged was published by Silver in 1950. Three years later, Susan Kubie and Gertrude Landau (1953) published a book that, although it describes experiences in group work in a recreation center for the aged, did much to bring the potential of group therapy to the attention of professionals. Maurice Linden's work (1953, 1954, 1955) with older women in a state hospital resulted in articles that have become classic readings, particularly on the significance of transference and dual leadership in group work with the aged. An article by Meerloo (1955) began to describe the adaptation of psychotherapeutic techniques necessary in working with older adults in groups.

In the 1960s, reports on group work with the aged became more common. Wilma Klein, Eda LeShan, and Sylvia Furman published a book entitled *Promoting Mental Health of Older People through Group Methods* (1965). *Social Group Work with Older People* (National Association of Social Workers 1963) contains examples of the group work done in the early sixties and includes not only clinical reports of groups but also some theoretical analysis of group therapy as a method of treating the aged. The works of Louis Lowy (1962, 1967) and of Tine, Hastings, and Deutschberger (1960) provided excellent frameworks for analysis of group therapy. Clinical reports of groups became available, including those of Barton (1962); Feil (1967); Liederman and Green (1965); Liederman, Green, and Liederman (1967); and Zimberg (1969).

Since 1970, the amount of literature on group work with the aged has increased markedly. The works of Irene Burnside (1970), Robert Butler (1974), and Myrna Lewis (1974) have contributed significantly to the understanding and use of group therapy. The literature shows that group therapy is an effective technique with most problems of the aged in almost any setting (Altholz 1973; Burnside 1970; Butler 1974; Cohen 1973; Conrad 1974; Lewis 1974; Rosin 1975; Tross & Blum 1988; Waters 1984).

Tross and Blum's (1988) review of the practice and research literature gives an excellent overview of the directions group therapy with older adults has taken over the years. The review

points out the development of different models within group therapy. These models are conceptualized by the authors as insight-oriented group therapy and supportive group therapy, each with subcategories. Leszcz (1990) examines what he sees as the three models of group therapy with the aged that have emerged as more experience has been gained in the area—psychodynamic, developmental, and cognitive-behavioral. Given the differing needs of the older participants, particularly the depressed aged, he calls for an integrated approach that combines all three models. Schmid and Rouslin (1992) describe a different type of integrated approach—the combining of cognitive-educational approaches with medical issues and medication, and the combining of aged persons and their caregivers.

Clearly the field of group therapy with the aged has expanded in many exciting directions, particularly in the past several decades. An area not fully explored in the literature concerns the techniques of evaluating group therapy with the aged; some work has been reported (Kaplan 1959; Liederman, Green & Liederman 1967; Lowy 1967; Tine, Hastings & Deutschberger 1960; Frey, Kelbley, Durham & James 1992; Sullivan, Coffey & Greenstein 1987), but more needs to be done, especially concerning delineation of variables and methods of evaluation as well as comparison of group and individual methodologies.

COMMON PROBLEMS

Group psychotherapy with the aged is a difficult therapeutic technique to employ because expressing personal problems in a group and trying to solve them through the group is alien to most older people. They are often slow to develop into a group and group continuity is threatened by such practical considerations as lack of transportation for members, high absentee rates, and unwillingness of members to discuss issues appropriate to a psychotherapy group, resulting in discouragement for the leader. Careful planning, however, can avoid many common problems in group psychotherapy with the aged.

Five areas to consider before a group is begun are purposes for group therapy, group composition, group goals, leadership, and practical considerations.

Purposes of Group Therapy

It is not enough to wish to begin group psycho-therapy simply because it seems to be a technique that may relieve the burden of seemingly endless and fruitless individual therapy. It is acceptable, however, to use this mode of therapy to save time and use professional personnel more appropriately. Therapeutically sound reasons for using group therapy can be determined by examining the aged client population. Is there a significant number of clients, for example, who have difficulty relating to friends and family and who would benefit from the responses of group interaction? If a number of clients are suffering crises of aging and it is be-lieved that their sense of isolation would decrease through the universalization of problems, group therapy is indicated.

Kohut's work on self-psychology (1977) has made valuable contributions in conceptualizing the purposes of group psychotherapy with older persons. As pointed out by Leszcz, Feigenbaum, Sadavoy, and Robinson (1985), and Leszcz (1990), group therapy can provide a vehicle for the rein-forcement of the individual's sense of self in the face of the narcissistic injuries of aging. In addi-tion, the loss of self objects—those relationships that sustain and complete the individual's sense of self—can be compensated for in the group by other members and by the therapist(s). Self-psychology not only helps us determine who might benefit from group psychotherapy but also gives us a framework for understanding the neces-sary attempts to protect and/or stabilize a sense of self, thus providing some insight into some of the more problematic behaviors in a group—for exam-ple, monopolization, grandiosity, and hostile with-drawal.

Group Composition

It is extremely important to remember that simply because people are old does not mean they can be put together with the expectation that old age alone will provide a sufficient binding force to enable a therapeutically sound group to develop. Each member of a group must be selected for rea-sons besides old age. Some groups are limited to new retirees (Wolfe & Wolfe 1975), others to peo-ple of extreme old age or groups such as veter-ans (Sullivan, Coffey & Greenstein 1987) or

discharged psychiatric patients (Schmid & Rouslin 1992).

Some therapists, notably Robert Butler and Myrna Lewis (1977), favor making a group as het-erogeneous as possible in terms of age, mixing per-sons from age 15 to age 80 and older. These therapists feel that age integration reduces the sense of isolation of the older members of the group, enabling them to "review and renew their own experiences and values" (p. 271). Such un-qualified age integration, however, is not necessar-ily the most desirable group format. Older people have few peer-group opportunities, and a group composed solely of persons over 60 fosters a feel-ing of the worth of being old, exposing members to alternative solutions developed by other older adults to commonly shared problems.

Sex is a criterion for group selection. Mixed male and female groups are preferable, because they foster appropriate sex role interactions and provide reality-oriented occasions for (re)learning more satisfying techniques of socialization. One should have particular reasons for assembling a group of all one sex—for example, isolated male nursing home residents (Frey et al. 1992; Leszcz et al. 1985). The sex of members will be deter-mined by and will help determine group goals.

The physical problems of potential members are also a criterion for selection. Certain physical problems bear on the practical considerations of group work with the aged. The room in which the group is held, for example, must be equipped with doors wide enough to admit wheelchairs if any member is not ambulatory. If members must walk upstairs, all must be capable of doing so. Physical problems of some members may interfere with their participation in a group or may be upsetting to other members. For example, a woman who had had cancer, necessitating the removal of part of her jawbone, met the criteria for admission to a group, but her inability to pronounce words plainly interfered with communication with other members, many of whom were hard of hearing. Also, her drastically altered appearance upset many of the others.[1] This woman left the group due to

---

[1]*Author's note*: For a thought-provoking study of profession-als' reaction to deformity and the aged, the reader is referred to R. P. Preston, *The Dilemmas of Care: Social and Nursing Adaptions to the Deformed, the Disabled, and the Aged.* 1979. Elsevier, New York.

relocation, but if she had not, her inability to participate and her effect on the group would have made it necessary to ask her to leave.

The use of a psychiatric diagnosis as a criterion for member selection has important implications for group development. If all members chosen have a diagnosis of withdrawn depression, for example, a danger exists that the group will not develop, since the members may not have the energy or ability to verbalize. However, we have found it effective to make a group homogeneous regarding a diagnosis of depression, but heterogeneous in other respects such as the amount of affect shown; the coping mechanisms used to deal with depression; and differences in background, education, income, current living situation, and social resources (Yalom 1975).

If group members are chosen on the basis of a mixture of diagnoses or if diagnosis is not a criterion for selection, the leader must exercise care in mixing those with no evidence of brain impairment and those with obvious impairment. Such a combination is often very threatening to those with no impairment, whose fears of becoming "senile" or "losing their minds" are represented by the impaired members of the group. The anxiety of the nonimpaired members often reaches a level that can only be dealt with by their leaving the group.

The most obvious criterion in selecting members for group psychotherapy is their ability to communicate, which means not only the ability to talk but also the ability to verbalize thoughts and feelings. Although some members may benefit simply by attending sessions, the therapeutic worth of a group rests on the interactions of the members. A leader's goals for the group must reflect the members' ability to communicate.

Certain persons should be excluded from a group—for example, those with severe hearing impairments and those with speech difficulties. In one group, an 82-year-old man who was almost totally deaf but who met most of the other criteria for selection wished very much to attend and was admitted. His hearing impairment prevented him from interacting with other members of the group. Not only did he feel isolated, but the other members felt tense and anxious when he attended because their attempts to include him in the normal flow of conversation were rarely successful. However, if the hearing impairment is not severe, accommodations can be made to include the hearing-impaired person. Hittner and Bornstein (1990) have written an excellent article on integrating the late-onset hearing-impaired older adult in a group therapy setting.

Uncontrolled psychotics should be excluded. Not only are they often difficult to handle in groups, but their presence disturbs other members, most of whom are uncomfortable with and afraid of mental illness. Some leaders feel that people who are hypochondriacal should also be excluded (Yalom 1975). However, such persons do not necessarily interfere with a group of older people. Other members often listen sympathetically to the recitation of symptoms, viewing them as part of the normal illnesses and discomforts they all experience. Such uncritical acceptance of the hypochondriac's problems tends to reduce that member's need to rely upon illness, allowing the hypochondriac to move into discussion of other issues.

Group Goals

When the reasons for starting a group and the composition of the group have been defined, the therapeutic goals of the group must be defined. Goals must be determined for individual members of the group and for the group as a whole. These goals must be made clear to the members, since many will have trouble understanding even the general goals for group therapy, let alone the specific ones for this group. If the leader is unsure of the group's goals, it is certain that the members will also be unclear and may see no need to participate.

Leadership

The number of leaders needed is dependent upon the size of the group and the goals for the group. Two leaders are usually preferable. Given the features common to many older adults—mild hearing and memory impairment, the importance of touch, and the topics of death, loneliness, and chronic illness often discussed in the group—it is very difficult for one person to sustain the enthusiasm and the energy, both physical and mental, necessary to lead a group. It is not possible, I believe, for one person to lead a psychotherapy group of more than ten aged persons effectively, and it is preferable to have two leaders whenever there are more than six persons. (See Altholz and Burnside, 1963 under Resources.)

The profession of each leader is also important. If it is decided, for example, that group therapy will replace individual therapy and many group members are on medications, at least one leader must be familiar with the purposes, side effects, and dosages of the drugs. These questions will be raised frequently, and often the leader can turn to someone else for help in this area.

The leaders must determine between themselves what role (or roles) they will fulfill in the group. Although these may change later, distinct roles should be chosen before the group begins. The leaders can be passive, functioning as listeners and targets for the ventilation of members' feelings, or they may be active, assuming the roles of teacher, facilitator, questioner, comforter, and moderator (Goldfarb 1972). Most often, the leader will fill a combination of roles, active at some times, passive at others.

In addition, there are certain leadership skills that appear to be particularly helpful with older adults. Some of these, according to Horton and Linden (1982), are management skills (physical and verbal control of the group environment), caring skills, and meaning attribution skills (helping members gain insight into their actions and relationships to the group).

How the group leaders are perceived by the members can become an important therapeutic tool. In addition to possessing the general qualities appropriate for a group leader, such as intrapsychic awareness (particularly of countertransference), flexibility, and tolerance for ambiguity (Maclennan 1975), leaders of psychotherapy groups for the aged should be selected for the qualities and roles they may represent to the group members (Linden 1954). I found, for example, that although an older leader represented both the wisdom and experience of age, a young co-leader symbolized the idealism and energy of youth. Butler and Lewis (1977, 272) believe that male and female therapists have the advantage of providing "both a psychodynamic and sociological orientation for a group, as well as opportunities for transference." In addition, they may represent the social reality of sex roles, serving as models for behavior outside the group. Leszcz et al. (1985) also point out the importance of the male-female therapy team in modeling family reenactment and stimulating engagement of the isolated older adult. (See Chapter 4 about Linden's cotherapy). Thus, although often ignored, using the potential of dual leadership fully can enhance the benefits of group therapy.

Practical Considerations

Practical considerations include providing transportation to and from the group as well as facilities that accommodate any physical impairments members have. Similarly, a decision must be made on the length of the session based on the energy levels of members. Group members may have frequent absences, which must be dealt with to preserve group continuity, yet allowances must be made for legitimate illness. An assistant to the group leader, someone who is able to coordinate absences, transportation, and so forth, is invaluable, because the amount of time required to coordinate arrangements may negate any time saved by employing group therapy.

GROUP PSYCHOTHERAPY: A PERSONAL STUDY

Major Goals

Describing a psychotherapy group I led that lasted more than two years will illustrate some of the unique qualities of group psychotherapy with the aged. This group functioned while I was affiliated with the Older American Resources and Services Program (OARS), sponsored by the Duke University Center for the Study of Aging and Human Development. The group began as part of the OARS outpatient clinic program of mental health care for elderly patients in the community. The group had three major purposes: (1) a socialization experience providing the opportunity to belong to a group at a time when group and other contacts are diminished, (2) exposure to alternative problem solutions developed by other older people, and (3) treatment of larger groups of people with limited personnel and time.

Size of the Group

The group membership varied from four to nine, although 15 persons were members for different periods. The average attendance was five persons, both male and female. The mean age of the men was 68.9 years and of the women 66.9 years. All the members had been in individual treatment with the staff of the clinic, two remained in individual treatment while in the group, and members could be seen individually in certain crises. All members chosen shared a diagnosis of depression, but the group was heterogeneous in background, current living arrangement, and defense mechanisms used in coping with current problems. The three foci of the therapy were the resolution of individual problems in adapting to growing older, improvement of reality testing, and social interaction.

Dual Leadership

Two leaders were chosen for the group—a psychiatrist and a social worker. This dual leadership functioned according to Linden's (1954) concept of social precept, wherein the therapists represent a marriage of complementary interests, the shared authority of an ideal parental team, and the social reality of the roles of the sexes. Many of the members had difficulty in social relationships and used the therapists as models for interaction outside the group. Experience showed that the members' relationships with the older male therapist "peer" and the younger female therapist "daughter" encouraged learning and experimenting with different and more satisfying ways of relating to friends and family. The leader(s) also must be prepared to deal with transferences. (See Figure 19-1.)

Contracts

I noted earlier that the concept of group therapy is alien to many older people. Consequently, in the beginning, members were often confused about the arrangements and purposes of the group. Much of this confusion can be dissipated at the beginning of the group by establishing a verbal and/or written contract. The leaders had met individually with each potential member before the first group session to explain the purposes of the group, to obtain a commitment for attendance, and to set individual goals. The general contract was designed by the group within the first three sessions, which were held weekly for one hour. Although regular attendance was stressed, if the leaders were apprised of absences due to illness or bad weather, the member was not charged for the session. Transportation was supplied when needed. The members decided to have an open-ended group and accept new members of the leaders' choice. The group was long term, with no stated termination date. (See Chapter 8 for further discussion of contracts.)

Group Participation

We found 10 minutes at least were needed for the members to warm up and begin to talk to one another. To encourage interaction, the members

FIGURE 19-1 Transference: *She reminds them of a granddaughter.* Counter-transference: *They remind the group worker of beloved grandparents. Both came prepared to like each other.*
PHOTO: Marianne Gontarz

were asked to enter the group room as soon as they arrived at the clinic. Here they carried on general discussion and were ready to begin focusing by the time the therapists arrived.

The session usually began with a member raising a topic for discussion spontaneously or by a leader asking the members individually what happened to them in the past week. The leaders took an active part in the group by serving as sympathetic authorities, providing information on community resources, and stimulating discussion, particularly in sensitive areas in which the members usually did not volunteer to relate their experiences. As Yalom (1975, 103) notes, "At times it is very helpful for the therapist to share some past and current real-life problem to afford a model for identification through his capacity to come through such a problem period constructively." The group encouraged all members to contribute to the discussion. However, no group pressure was exerted on members who benefited simply by attending weekly sessions even without regular verbal participation. The leaders summarized each session in the last five minutes, reemphasizing important points that had been discussed.

Mutual Support of Members

All members saw themselves as important parts of the group, and a high degree of cohesiveness was evident (Yalom 1975). Cohesiveness displayed itself early in the life of the group; by the third session, concern was expressed for those absent. By the eighth session, those present asked for an accounting of the missing members before the meeting could begin! This attitude of concern was not surprising. Since all older people have suffered many losses, the members present feared an absent member might be seriously ill or even dead.

With a single exception, no members had been in group therapy before, and such a group was indeed frightening. Consequently, during the first four or five sessions members sought the protection of the therapists, whom they saw as authorities who defined group limits, behavior, and goals. Within eight months, however, long-time members took responsibility for defining group behavior to new members. The members themselves reinforced acceptance of the patient role and self-disclosure. They also reinforced group goals whenever a member attempted to ignore these goals to avoid discussing a sensitive area.

Members encouraged one another to discuss problems by conveying group understanding and by assurances that no problem would be seen as an embarrassment. Indeed, members were quick to note, "We're all here because we're going through it too." The members also supported one another in reinforcing individual strengths and assets. Sometimes they brought some of their handiwork, for example, and all samples were accepted in this positive, encouraging manner, no matter what the quality. Similarly, statements made by members were accepted in a positive, encouraging way. The concerns of each member were understood by all to be important, no matter how trivial they seemed. All aches and pains, symptoms that might be ridiculed by a professional, were taken seriously and dealt with sympathetically (Hulicka 1963).

Members of this group showed much less intermember hostility than the leaders had anticipated. Although members did indeed confront one another, they did so in indirect, nonhostile, and supportive language. It appeared that the common burden of aging increased the sense of vulnerability and created sufficient empathy among members to minimize antagonism. Possibly many hostile feelings that may have been present were ventilated on topics external to member relationships, such as inflation and poor medical care for the aged. In her article on group therapy in a home for the aged, Feil (1967) noted the same phenomenon. Criticism and hostility in the group were often couched in humorous and subtle terms, which actually were more effective than direct attack. As Yalom (1975, 264) states, "Members can . . . profit from conflict providing its intensity does not exceed their tolerance. . . ." The members of this group determined their own tolerance and never exceeded it, even when urged to do so by the therapists.

Several common themes emerged in group discussion. The discovery of shared problems boosted self-esteem and fostered group identification. Common problems and concerns expressed frequently by members included depression and its manifestations (including suicide), development of new roles as aging persons, and difficulties in social relationships. The most common concern was loss: of the work role, of dignity, of physical and intellectual capacity, of family and friends, and eventually of one's own life.

The members dealt with a number of losses within the group, including the death of one member and the severe stroke of another. These events occurred within two months of each other. The leaders feared the group ego could not cope with a second loss so soon after the first, but this was not true. The ability of older people to adapt to stresses in their lives, as Butler (1974) notes, is remarkable. The ego strength of the aged to cope with crises is often overlooked by those who wish to place them in a fragile and dependent role and to emphasize mental illness rather than mental health. However, as one group member commented, with agreement by all, he was glad to belong to a group like this one because it was easier to face sad events with people he felt close to and with whom he could talk openly about his own fears of illness and death.

LIMITATIONS OF GROUP PSYCHOTHERAPY

Group psychotherapy cannot be a remedy for all the problems of the aged. A large group of older adults needs attention that group therapy cannot provide. Group psychotherapy cannot help individuals use community resources nor can it coordinate those resources. Many older people need environmental manipulation, including home services or placement, which can be effected only on an individual basis. However, group psychotherapy can be an effective mode of treatment with the aged. Simply knowing that a group exists exclusively for them increases the sense of self-worth among older persons. Through interaction with peers, group therapy helps specifically to develop a realistic self-image and provides social opportunities.

Our society provides few peer group opportunities for the aged. They can no longer relate to their work group, friends may have moved away or died, and those activities in which they may have participated as younger and middle-aged persons—such as civic and service activities—may no longer be relevant because of a loss of interest, age-appropriateness, or difficulties in remaining an active member of the group (Lowy 1962). Only rarely can older people meet together in a group to discuss their feelings, concerns, and difficulties. Group psychotherapy offers the chance to discuss common problems and the alternative solutions discovered by other older people. It can also offer an answer to the question many older people ask

themselves: "Now that I am old, what kind of a person am I supposed to be?"

Looking at life in terms of developmental stages, it is clear that for every age group except old age there exists a societally accepted set of expectations for behavior and achievement. However, these expectations cease with retirement, and then it becomes difficult to identify role expectations for older persons. There are some limited role definitions, such as grandparent, but that role is hardly adequate for the 24 hours a day of the 20-odd years many people live after they retire. What contributions, if any, are the aged to make to society? How are old people supposed to act and what are they to talk about? How are they to relate to those persons around them, both younger and older? And perhaps most important, how are they to feel about themselves? The persons who can most appropriately help define a role for the aged are the aged themselves.

SUMMARY

This chapter discusses common problems in group psychotherapy with older adults. The foremost difficulty in such a therapeutic strategy is that group sharing and group solutions are alien to most older people. Areas that must be thought through before the group begins are the purpose of group therapy, group composition, group goals, leadership, and practical considerations.

Group therapy saves time and uses professional personnel more appropriately than individual therapy. The group composition is important because it is not enough to put people in a group just because they are old; there must be other reasons. Criteria for group selection might include sex, physical problems, psychiatric problems, and communication ability. The group goals must be therapeutic. Also, the leader must not be unsure of the goals, for that uncertainty will be reflected in the members' participation. Leadership will depend on the size and goals of the group. Co-leaders must decide between them what role (or roles) they intend to fulfill in the group. Practical considerations include transportation problems, the length of the sessions, and absenteeism.

A personal study was used to describe group psychotherapy co-led by a female social worker and a male psychiatrist. Common themes that emerged from the group included discovery of shared problems and increased self-esteem. Common problems were depression and its symptoms, suicidal ideation, and taking on new roles as aging persons. The most common concern was loss—of the work role, dignity, physical and intellectual capacity, family, friends, and one's own life. Illness and death occurring within the group experience were handled well by the group members.

The self-worth of older persons can be increased considerably by their merely knowing that a group exists just for them. They develop a more realistic self-image and increase their social opportunities through group membership. Group psychotherapy also offers the older person an opportunity to discuss, define, experiment with, and adopt a satisfying and appropriate role in society.

EXERCISE 1

Behavioral problems in groups run the gamut from monopolization to muteness, from paranoia to easy permissiveness. Select one behavior of an aged member in a group you have led or observed and analyze it in a page or two. Include the following points and discuss theory whenever appropriate.

1. Patient's age, diagnosis (or diagnoses), and behavioral problem.
2. Rationale for selecting this patient's behavior to analyze.
3. Behavioral change to be achieved.
4. Reasons the change is desirable.
5. Therapeutic technique to be used.
6. Criteria for evaluating the degree to which change is achieved.

EXERCISE 2

Review other chapters in this book about group work and delineate how group psychotherapy is different from reality orientation groups, remotivation groups, reminiscence groups, and self-help groups. Consider these components in your answer: types of leaders, group composition, group goals, and leadership goals.

EXERCISE 3

One of the most common criteria for exclusion of older persons from group psychotherapy is hearing impairment. However, the percentage of hearing impairment in the population over 65 is estimated between 25 percent and 40 percent. As long as the hearing impairment is not severe, more appropriate than exclusion may be modification of the physical environment of the group and the development of group techniques that will accommodate the hearing-impaired participant. Consider these two areas:

1. The group environment.
2. Group techniques.

For each area, list and describe at least three modifications that would enable hearing-impaired persons to participate in the group. In making your list, consider physical space, verbal and nonverbal techniques, and group process issues such as participation rules and modeling.

EXERCISE 4

An area lacking in the group therapy research is the evaluation of group psychotherapy with older persons. One reason for this may be that since psychotherapy is seen as an open-ended and fluid process based on psychodynamic principles, there are frequently no clearly stated criteria for evaluation. In this age of accountability, however, we are called on more and more to evaluate the effectiveness of our work.

Choose either a group you have led or observed or the group described in this chapter, list four areas/issues/goals that the group appears to address and that could be evaluated—for example, self-esteem and interpersonal connectedness. For each of these four areas, give a one- to two-paragraph description of the methods you might use to evaluate that area. These methods could include scales, behavioral checklists, or any other measurable method. Be creative in determining ways to evaluate that still take into account the unique nature of the group.

REFERENCES

Altholz J. 1973. Group therapy with elderly patients. In *Alternatives to institutional care for older Americans: Practice and planning*. Durham, NC: Duke University.

Barton MG. 1962. Group counseling with older patients. *Gerontologist* 2(1):51-56.

Berger M. 1968. Similarities and differences between group psychotherapy and short-term group process experiences—Clinical impressions. *J Group Psychoanal Process* 1(1):11-29.

Burnside IM. 1970. Loss: A constant theme in group work with the aged. *Hosp Comm Psych* 21(6):173-177.

Butler R. 1974. Successful aging and the role of the life review. *J Am Geriatr Soc* 22(12):529-535.

Butler R, Lewis M. 1977. *Aging and mental health: Positive psychosocial approaches*, 2d ed. St. Louis: Mosby.

Cohen MG. 1973. Alternatives to institutional care of the aged. *Soc Casework* 54(8):447-452.

Conrad W. 1974. A group therapy program with older adults in a high-risk neighborhood setting. *Int J Group Psychother* 24(3):358-360.

Feil N. 1967. Group therapy in a home for the aged. *Gerontologist* 7(3):192-195.

Frey E, Kelbley J, Durham L, James J. 1992. Enhancing the self-esteem of selected male nursing home residents. *Gerontologist* 32(4):522-557.

Goldfarb A. 1972. Group therapy with the old and the aged. In H Kaplan, B Sadock (eds.), *Group treatment of mental illness*. New York: Aronson.

Hittner A, Bornstein H. 1990. Group counseling with older adults: Coping with late-onset hearing impairment. *J Ment Health Counsel* 12(3):332-341.

Horton A, Linden M. 1982. Geriatric group psychotherapy. In AM Horton (ed.), *Mental health intervention for the aged* (pp. 51-66). New York: Praeger.

Hulicka I. 1963. Participation in group conferences by geriatric patients. *Gerontologist* 3(1):10-13.

Kaplan J. 1959. Evaluation techniques for older groups. *Am J Occup Ther* 13(5):222-225.

Klein W, LeShan E, Furman S. 1965. *Promoting mental health of older people through group methods*. New York: Mental Health Materials Center.

Kohut H. 1977. *The restoration of the self*. Madison, CT: International Universities Press.

Kubie S, Landau G. 1953. *Group work with the aged*. Madison, CT: International Universities Press.

Leszcz M. 1990. Towards an integrated model of group psychotherapy with the elderly. *Int J Group Psychother* 40(4):379-399.

Leszcz M, Feigenbaum E, Sadavoy J, Robinson A. 1985. A men's group: Psychotherapy of elderly men. *Int J Group Psychother* 35(2):177-196.

Lewis M. 1974. Life-review therapy: Putting memories to work in individual and group psychotherapy. *Geriatrics* 29(11):165-173.

Liederman PC, Green R. 1965. Geriatric outpatient group therapy. *Compreh Psychiatry* 6(1):51-60.

Liederman PC, Green R, Liederman V. 1967. Outpatient group therapy with geriatric patients. *Geriatrics* 22(1):148-153.

Linden M. 1953. Group psychotherapy with institutionalized senile women: Studies in gerontologic human relations. *Int J Group Psychother* 3:150-170.

———. 1954. Significance of dual leadership in gerontological group psychotherapy: Studies in gerontological human relations III. *Int J Group Psychother* 4:262-273.

———. 1955. Transference in gerontological group psychotherapy: Studies in gerontological human relations IV. *Int J Group Psychother* 5:61-79.

Lowy L. 1962. The group in social work with the aged. *Soc Work* 7(4):43-50.

———. 1967. Roadblocks in group work practice with older people—Framework for analysis. *Gerontologist* 7(2):109-113.

Maclennan B. 1975. The personalities of group leaders: Implications for selection and training. *Int J Group Psychother* 25(2):177-183.

Meerloo JAM. 1955. Transference and resistance in geriatric psychotherapy. *Psychoanal Rev* 42(January):72-82.

National Association of Social Workers. 1963. *Social group work with older people*. New York: NASW.

Rosin A. 1975. Group discussions: A therapeutic tool in a chronic diseases hospital. *Geriatrics* 30(August):45-49.

Schmid A, Rouslin M. 1992. Integrative outpatient group therapy for discharged elderly psychiatric patients. *Gerontologist* 27(4):434-436.

Silver A. 1950. Group psychotherapy with senile psychiatric patients. *Geriatrics* 5(May-June):147-150.

Sullivan EM, Coffey JF, Greenstein RA. 1987. Treatment outcome in a group geropsychiatry program for veterans. *Gerontologist* 27(4):434-439.

Tine S, Hastings K, Deutschberger P. 1960. Generic and specific in social group work practice with the aging. In *Social work with groups*. New York: NASW.

Tross S, Blum J. 1988. A review of group therapy with the older adult: Practice and research. In B Maclennan, S Saul, M Weiner (eds.), *Group psychotherapy for the elderly* (pp. 3-29). Madison CT: International Universities Press.

Waters E. 1984. Building on what you know: Techniques for individual and group counseling with older people. *Counsel Psych* 12(2):64-74.

Wolfe B, Wolfe G. 1975. Exploring retirement in a small group. *Soc Work* 29(6):481-484.

Yalom ID. 1975. *The theory and practice of group psychotherapy*, 2d ed. New York: Basic Books.

Zimberg S. 1969. Outpatient geriatric psychiatry in an urban ghetto with nonprofessional workers. *Am J Psychiatr* 125(12):1697-1702.

BIBLIOGRAPHY

Greene RR. 1986. Countertransference issues in social work with the aged. *J Gerontol Soc Work* 9(3):79-88.

Maclennan B, Saul S, Weiner MB. 1988. *Group psychotherapies for the elderly*. Madison, CT: International Universities Press.

Solomon K, Zinke MR. 1991. Group psychotherapy with the depressed elderly. *J Gerontol Soc Work* 17(1/2): 47-57.

Yost EB, Beutler LE, Corbishley MA, Allaender JR. 1986. *Group cognitive therapy: A treatment approach for depressed older adults*. New York: Pergamon.

RESOURCE

Altholz J, Burnside IM. 1976. How to use group psychotherapy. In audiocassette series: *Successful treatment of the elderly mentally ill*. New York: Wyeth Laboratories.

PART 5
Settings for Group Work

The focus of Part 5 is on settings where group work with older people occurs. In Chapter 20, Florence Safford draws on her long experience as chief social worker at a large home for the aged. She describes groups in residential long-term care and ways to make them work well for residents and their families.

The second chapter in this part, by Janet Black, James Kelly, and Susan Rice—all social workers—is an innovative model for groups in retirement communities. The chapter has a double theme because it also offers a teaching model known as the *parallel process* for use with college students.

Jean Duchesneau, a gerontological nurse practitioner, traces the emergence of day care centers in the United States and then describes the role of groups in that setting in Chapter 22.

In Chapter 23, Janet Black, Sally Friedlob, and James Kelly describe the implementation of groups in board-and-care facilities.

Part 5 closes with Chapter 24, which deals with groups in acute-care settings. Its author, Elissa Brown, is a clinical nurse specialist and has conducted groups with geropsychiatric patients on inpatient wards. She offers examples from those group leadership experiences.

CHAPTER 20

Group Work in Long-Term Care Facilities

Florence Safford

KEY WORDS

- Autonomy
- Buddy system
- Control
- Floor groups
- High-level demand
- Learned helplessness
- Orientation group
- Parliamentary procedures
- Person-in-situation
- Preadmission group
- Psychoeducational programs
- Relocation shock
- Remembrance group
- Resident councils
- Therapeutic community

LEARNING OBJECTIVES

- Describe the particular value of group work in the nursing home for residents, families, and staff.
- Identify 12 categories of group services useful in long-term care facilities.
- Describe four types of support groups suitable for long-term care institutions.
- List benefits from groups in general; identify groups that may improve social skills and self-image and encourage reminiscence.
- Explain how family training programs, family support groups, and family councils differ and how they are similar.

For a variety of reasons, many older adults spend their last years in long-term care facilities. These facilities include nursing homes and congregate living facilities, large and small. Some are elegant showplaces, some are comfortable and caring, others are deplorable containers. Entry into any of these facilities may have included the older person in the decision-making process, following therapeutic preadmission assessment and counseling, or placement may have been arranged for a reluctant or mentally impaired person. Creating and operating programs to promote the psychosocial well-being of each unique resident in such a diverse range of facilities is a formidable professional challenge.

Whatever the type and quality of the facility, whatever the trajectory of the admission process, the move into a long-term care facility, generally representing the last transition of a long life, is often traumatic for the older person and his or her family (Brody 1974; Tobin & Lieberman 1976). Ironically, although the move is into a group living situation, the older person and the anxious family often feel alone with their troubles, unprepared for the changed environment. The use of group approaches to help the aged and their families to learn new roles in their new world; to help in adjustment to new routines, new people, and the demands of countless other psychological, social, and physical changes, has been amply documented (Berman-Rossi 1990; Hartford 1980; Lowy 1991; Miller & Solomon 1980; Saul 1988; Shore 1972).

This chapter presents a selection of groups appropriate in long-term care facilities, with the goal of providing the best quality of life possible for residents in an environment that welcomes their families and values staff morale. If this sounds overly optimistic, from my perspective as a gerontological social worker and educator for over 40 years, it is the least we can do.

Specialists in gerontological practice vary in their stance toward work with this population, some emphasizing the inherent strengths of people who have survived to advanced old age, others sensitizing us to the vulnerability of the frail and dependent who are depleted by multiple losses and problems. Experience with the aged dispels these generalizations—our work in nursing homes and congregate living facilities will be with independent, relatively healthy, well-adjusted elders as well as with physically and/or mentally impaired, fragile, lonely, and helpless elders.

The perspective adopted for this chapter emphasizes the need for accurate assessment of the aged individual in the context of his or her history and social network, along with an ongoing evaluation of the environmental context. This ecological perspective of the person-in-situation (Germain & Gitterman 1980) is accompanied by an eclectic approach to group methods, insuring a range of individualized program options. Working with groups of older adults calls for specialized knowledge and skill. It also calls for courage to stretch our capabilities, to venture into new territories fraught with risk, in order to offer an opportunity to aged residents for restitution, renewed development, a sense of accomplishment, and restored identity.

The groups to be presented will vary according to the size and nature of the facility and will be organized as follows: preadmission, for residents and family; orientation, for residents and family; floor or unit groups; resident councils; activity groups; educational programs; special groups (ther-

apy, roommates, support); family training programs; family support; and family councils. All of the groups to be presented will involve work with feelings, socialization, and increased competency.

PREADMISSION GROUPS

If facilities are large enough to have a group of prospective applicants waiting for vacancies to occur after they have been formally screened for admission, offer them the opportunity to visit the facility with their families. First, it makes the welcoming statement that the facility is reaching out to residents and family and establishes a beginning relationship. The preadmission group can mitigate the anxiety that generally accompanies this transition by providing information about the facility, preparing them for admission procedures, and providing them the opportunity to meet others in the same situation, which is often the basis for relating after admission. The group serves the purpose of preparatory socialization to the facility while providing a mutual aid format for participants who are struggling with similar issues. While a sense of loss is still the usual reaction to this transitional crisis, the comfort derived from peer support cannot be replicated (Solomon 1982). The staff member who runs the preadmission group must be thoroughly experienced in the facility and must communicate understanding and genuine empathy to the prospective resident and family. Particular attention to refreshments and the amenities of the environment are significant in reducing anxiety levels.

ORIENTATION GROUPS

Upon admission, orientation groups can be very helpful in lessening relocation shock for the older adult. Moving to a new home is one of life's major stressors, and it is especially stressful for the aged entering the totally foreign world of institutional care, when their homeostatic systems are weakened by the process of aging, their senses are diminished, and their support systems appear fragile or nonexistent. A hospitable environment with warm concern expressed by staff is essential to counter the panic and chaos of the moving process. Many facilities arrange for a buddy system, a welcoming committee or a volunteer resident who escorts the new resident to meals and programs for the first few days (Brody 1974).

Admission also is experienced as a crisis for family members, who generally view this transition as a time to grieve the changes in their loved one that have necessitated the move. Emotions are turbulent during admission and can be addressed during orientation meetings, preferably by combining residents (if cognitively intact) and family members (Lowy 1991; Solomon 1982). These meetings for new residents and family members, in addition to individual orientation, are a practical way for the facility to introduce staff. The meetings also impart and reinforce information about policies and procedures to several residents and relatives simultaneously, saving staff time and providing an opportunity for establishing new acquaintances. This helps older adults to overcome feelings of abandonment, rejection, or alienation. Such groups are a first step in describing and clarifying role expectations, the range of services offered, and the degree of choice available. Orientation groups can serve as a link between families and staff, setting the stage for a partnership in the optimal care of the elder (Dobrof & Litwak 1977). For new residents, groups can familiarize them with the positive aspects of institutional care in the company of peers, serving to balance the possible feelings of anonymity created by complex formal organization. As with preadmission groups, a warm atmosphere is important, emphasizing a caring as well as a more secure environment.

The amount of time a resident needs to adjust to a new facility varies and depends on the complexity of the institution, the past experiences of the resident and family, and the person's physical and mental status. At least two orientation meetings should be planned, and written material that describes the facility and clarifies policies, procedures, rights, and responsibilities should be provided. Meetings should be offered at a time when families can join the residents; for example, a weekend day just before or after lunch may be the optimum to maximize residents' participation and include family members who may not be able to come during the week because of work.

The orientation group can lead to the formation of an ongoing family group, an invaluable support for those relatives who must deal with their continuing concerns about the fluctuating needs of their relatives in the less-than-perfect milieu of the institution.

FLOOR GROUPS

An important strategy to facilitate a sense of belonging is the development of groups organized on the basis of the unit where the resident lives. The purpose of the group is to help residents connect with one another, to share concerns about their living environment—their room, floor lounge, their treatment—and to foster a sense of community (Lowy 1991). In psychiatric facilities, the use of a community meeting for all floors or sections is an integral part of what is termed the *therapeutic community.* These meetings generally include all staff working on the unit and serve the purpose of improving communication as well as promoting self-government.

An early contributor to knowledge about groups in institutions stressed that one of the functions of groups is to bring staff and residents together and suggested that one task of the social worker is to redefine staff and resident roles to ensure more active collaboration. Furthermore, group meetings should lead to feedback and evaluation from resident to resident, resident to staff, staff to resident, and staff to staff (Euster 1971).

In nursing homes, however, residents have often been reluctant to express criticism directly to staff, such as nurses or aides, for fear of retaliation; therefore, floor groups are usually run by a social worker who may separately discuss residents' concerns with other staff members. Although this format denies the residents the opportunity to overcome their diffidence and encourages dependency, in some instances it may be the only way to encourage continued participation in the group.

Many very old individuals have not had experience with a participatory problem-solving process. Some may have a poor self-image, may be distrustful, or may have physical problems that act as barriers to group interventions such as hearing impairment, incontinence, or mobility difficulties. To overcome these obstacles, individual counseling is sometimes prerequisite to interventions involving group activities (Cox 1988).

Miller and Solomon (1980) have also described the difficulty in establishing a floor unit group for the purpose of discussing residents' problems in living in the institution. Although many residents had individually voiced their complaints to the social worker, when meeting as a group they were unwilling to share their views and instead apologized for the institution, saying that things were not so bad and everyone did their best. The worker recognized that although these residents lived on the same floor, they did not know each other well enough to openly voice criticisms. This is categorized by the authors as a "high-level demand" for group involvement, requiring mutually helpful behaviors and recognition of interdependency. This can seem threatening to vulnerable elders. It was suggested that the group be replaced by special-interest groups that demand less intimate interactions and do not require members to risk exposing their thoughts or feelings. This was welcomed by the residents, who were able to develop more trusting relationships while participating in "low-level demand" activity groups. After two months of participation at that level, they were able to reorganize the floor group and gradually began to work on improving the quality-of-life issues.

This case reflects the eclectic nature of group practice in the institution as well as the trial-and-error approach that must often be used because of the unpredictable nature of the group experience.

Another practice example illustrates a marvelously creative model that integrates several methods to provide a therapeutic milieu. A video/drama group was started in a Veterans Administration nursing home in the format of a news show, with a resident anchorman announcing unit news and group members improvising serious and humorous skits on issues of concern to life on the unit. The videotape was shown at the community meeting and was so successful in increasing resident participation that it became a regular part of the program.

At the same time, a remembrance group was started for residents and staff to share feelings about residents who had died. This group was held immediately after the community meeting because the residents were already gathered. As the programs grew, the staff recognized that by scheduling the groups in sequence, they had created a dynamic that increased participation in the next group. Therefore, a half-hour exercise group was scheduled before the community meeting and an art therapy group after. This unusual model is detailed in an article that includes a case example showing the humorous characters developed in the video skits. They have become an ongoing theme in the facility, like a soap opera, and have created an environment of intimacy among staff and residents (Johnson, Agresti, Jacob & Nies 1990).

Despite the obvious challenges in establishing such groups, including the usual effort required to get the support of all levels of staff for a new program, once instituted, these groups can serve multiple purposes. A floor group accomplishes several things: It encourages residents and staff on the unit to meet regularly, provides a supportive environment to ventilate problems of unit living, provides a channel of communication between residents and staff, and offers residents an opportunity to demonstrate leadership. New residents can be more easily integrated into the unit environment through introduction at floor meetings. Floor meetings can lead to the formation of a resident council, if one does not exist, or can provide representation at the council if one is already extant.

RESIDENT COUNCILS

The value of resident councils as a democratic means to provide a formal role for residents in influencing the organization of their lives has been long recognized (Newmark 1963; Shore 1964). Model programs are primarily suited for cognitively intact residents and can serve as a formal unit of the facility system that seeks input from the residents about those aspects of decisions that directly affect the quality of their lives. The council also is seen as a logical structure through which residents and staff can channel information about institutional concerns.

An active resident council, with democratically elected members, can be the focal point for resident input on all aspects of institutional life. For example, each living unit of the facility can form a subcommittee to air their concerns and grievances and send a representative to bring these issues to the council for action. In addition to discussing problems with the administration, the council can form committees to survey residents' preferences and make recommendations for activity programs, variations in menus, and the like. It is an ideal mechanism to demonstrate respect for residents' autonomy, through which they can obtain some measure of control over their lives—a commodity in short supply in institutions.

As Shore cautioned in 1964, to work effectively and creatively with a resident council, the administration and staff must genuinely believe in the value of the council and subscribe to the democratic process. The work is time consuming and requires staff commitment to engage and sustain the residents in their efforts (Getzel 1982). The council should be democratically elected after reaching out to the entire resident population, and the council should elect its own officers. The staff member working with the council should act as consultant or advisor and not as a representative of the administration.

The staff consultant can assist in two important ways: by writing bylaws with the residents and by being the liaison with the administration and other staff to arrange for the time and place of council meetings and regular meetings with the administration. Residents generally need staff support to get minutes typed. Sometimes staff post them on residents' bulletin boards. An important spinoff from the council can be a newsletter or newspaper for the residents, which is an effective way of communicating matters of personal interest to the community. A council and a newspaper provide many significant new roles for residents, whose self-image is often diminished by institutional identification and who can enjoy new prestige, power, and recognition through service on the council or newspaper.

In order to help residents run the council in a fair and orderly manner, the staff member needs to be able to train them in the use of parliamentary procedure, and a copy of Robert's Rules of Order should be made available as a reference (Robert 1971).

These parliamentary procedures help council members conduct better meetings. For nursing home residents, it would be advisable to have alternates elected for each position, because of health concerns or attrition, and perhaps a co-chairperson to share the responsibility. Because Robert's rules serve as guides to running meetings smoothly, it may be preferable to be relaxed in their interpretation with aged members, who may not be comfortable being held too strictly to the order. On the other hand, it should not be assumed that the residents are unable to learn these rules—most important is their interest and motivation.

When resident or patient councils are developed in nursing homes, the members may find it difficult to decide on bylaws. In such cases, the staff assigned to work with the group might suggest a structure to start with, which members can modify as the group develops (Toseland 1990). Furthermore, if elections have not been successful in marshaling sufficient resident participation, the worker can encourage some residents to assume the roles of officers for a specified time until greater interest is generated, more leaders are identified, and elections can be held again. These strategies stress the value of resident control while compensating for the reality of diminished energy and initiative. These are examples of "doing with" the residents, rather than "doing for" (Silverstone & Burack-Weiss 1983).

COMMON PROBLEMS

Until leadership is developed so that the residents or patients can run their own meetings, the staff assigned (social worker or activity leader) may lead the group. Some common problems in running council meetings have been identified by Conger and Moore (1984, 97-98), who provide the following prototypes of members' roles and practical suggested strategies:

- The authoritarian member thinks his or her own ideas are best and does not recognize or fully accept information from other members. Suggest getting some other opinions. Ask this person to summarize for the group.
- The professor or show-off is overly talkative, monopolizes, or constantly teaches during the meeting. He or she often has the right answer, but keeps others out. Limit this person's time. Cut across the talk with a summarizing statement and direct a question to another team member, indicating that the meeting is a cooperative effort.
- The obstinate member will not budge or change decisions. He or she is not helpful and is indifferent toward other members and their opinions. Be tactful and try to get others to see the point. If the time is short, say frankly that it is necessary to go on with the meeting.
- The side-conversationalist constantly carries on small discussions with other members. The conversation may be related to the topic, but it is always distracting to the meeting. Pause and let others listen; it could be pertinent. Call the resident by name and ask directly if there is something to be added. Suggest that comments be saved until the appropriate time.

• The latecomer never gets there on time and disrupts the meeting by trying to find a seat, by asking the wrong questions, and by trying to find out what has been going on before his or her arrival. Indicate the pressure of time. Following the meeting, find out in private why the patient is always late and how to ensure prompt arrival in the future.

Toseland (1990) also offers practice principles to avoid counterproductive confrontations by coaching residents about their methods of discussing complaints with key personnel, such as dietary supervisors. He suggests counseling residents to present grievances in respectful and courteous terms, and he postulates the role of the group worker as mediator, to clarify communications and stress commonalities of interest, leading to negotiated solutions. Toseland also teaches practitioners how to advocate for residents with administrators, who often see councils as disturbing the status quo. He highlights a strategy that points out the responsibility and commitment to resident involvement in a nonthreatening manner, while delineating the potential benefits of such collaboration. From my own practice in a geriatric facility, I agree with this approach, which also can be described as old-fashioned tact.

Workers must avoid overidentification with aged residents and be empathetic to staff as well. They must understand emotions and defenses masked by an authoritative management style that reflects fear of authentic resident participation. In fact, many residents do complain freely, some unreasonably, which reflects their own unmet emotional needs. It is not unreasonable for staff to fear an increase in inappropriate complaints with an empowered council. The empathic worker can demonstrate understanding of these issues to the staff while helping residents deal realistically with legitimate concerns.

Inherent issues in council development are the hesitancy of residents to complain because of fear of retaliation and the reality that even when grievances are aired, there is no transfer of power (Devitt & Checkoway 1982; Getzel 1982; McDermott 1989; Miller & Solomon 1980). Despite its potential to empower the residents with a systemic voice in decision making, the function as permitted in day-to-day operations is often illusory. Officers of councils are often described as compliant, having been co-opted by the administration to serve the goals of the organization rather than the goals of the residents.

Since the passage of the Omnibus Budget Reconciliation Act (OBRA) and its revision in 1989, administrators of long-term care facilities are required to recognize the rights of residents and families to organize and participate in resident groups (such as councils) and must provide space and a designated member of the staff to assist. In addition, when such a group exists, "The facility must listen to the views and act upon the grievances and recommendations of residents and families concerning proposed policy and operational decisions affecting resident care and life in the facility" (OBRA '87, Compliance Checklist, *Federal Register* 1989).

With the support of these regulations, workers in long-term care facilities should be able to get more cooperation from reluctant administrators and staff. Getzel (1982) emphasizes the importance of preparatory work with administration and staff, ensuring their recognition of the reciprocal value of effective councils for both the residents and the institution. She cautions the council's worker to be a realistic mediator who helps residents understand the limits to meeting their requests while helping the administration to share some decision making. As mediator, she points out that patients *and* staff need one another and that administrators should be included in problem deliberations as advisors, not as adversaries.

When the resident council becomes experienced, it can authentically become the channel of communication, the collective voice of the residents, and the negotiator for changes. Administrators should meet on a regular basis with the officers, preventing problems from becoming big issues and easing the introduction of new procedures.

As nursing homes admit residents who are sicker mentally and physically, it will be more of a challenge to help residents organize into councils. An emphasis on the medical needs of aged patients can be translated into treating them as disabled or *unable*, promoting "learned helplessness" (Seligman & Elder 1986) or sick role behavior. A practice philosophy is required that identifies remaining competence and modifies the environment so that it enhances the resident's ability rather than diminishing it (Berman-Rossi 1990), by believing in the value of a resident council to promote autonomy for the group, in the benefits of improved self-image and identity for participants, and in the solidarity achieved by even small gains in affecting life in the institution.

ACTIVITY GROUPS

Recreation and activity groups are traditionally basic to all programs in institutions. (See Figure 20-1.) This is generally the domain of recreation therapists, although creative programming can be carried out by activity aides and volunteers as well. Activities can cover as broad a range of interests as are represented by the residents and the skills of the staff, such as arts and crafts, discussion groups, special event parties, dancing, music appreciation, sing-alongs, and so on. Special needs may be addressed through a card-playing club, a men's club, ethnic group clubs, and the like. Whatever the focus of the activity, it serves the purpose of stimulation, promotes socialization, and provides new roles for residents, in addition to continuation of former roles of significance. Equally important is the opportunity afforded for reminiscence, which enables older adults to recall selected meaningful aspects of their lives which develops a new identity based on what they were. Watt and Wong (1991) describe a taxonomy of reminiscence and call attention to the different functions of such forms as integrative, instrumental (problem-solving), and transmissive (history-sharing) reminiscence.

Because of the unique needs of each resident, an array of activity choices is required. I remember one resident who, despite considerable choices, could not be satisfied and languished alone in his room. His social worker diagnosed terminal boredom. This, of course, was a sign of depression, which required treatment before the resident was able to participate in activity programs. An eclectic approach includes the use of individual counseling and group counseling along with physical and psychiatric treatment (if indicated) in order to help residents find the activities that will bring current meaning to their lives.

EDUCATIONAL PROGRAMS

Although these are sometimes included as activities, they can have a particularly therapeutic effect with the older adult. Offering lectures and stimulating educational opportunities makes the statement that learning has a lifelong value and that the aged can grow through learning, just like other age groups. For many very old people who had to leave school early in order to work, formal learning experiences are treasured and are truly developmental opportunities.

FIGURE 20-1 *An exercise group is fun, keeps joints flexible, and allows residents to play an active role in their own wellness program.*

PHOTO: Marianne Gontarz

Some educational programs are brought into institutions by continuing education units of colleges or high schools. Some require regular attendance by the residents and result in some certification. As with activities, the range of educational programs is limitless. They provide a significant group experience for older adults, who can test out and develop new relationships while sharing a mutually rewarding experience.

SPECIAL GROUPS

Although all of the previously mentioned groups can be therapeutic in overcoming loneliness and feelings of unhappiness about being in an institution, for some residents special groups are required to deal with their problems.

Therapy Groups

Therapy groups address specific problems, such as depression, extreme reactions to stressors, or the inability to form new relationships or use other programs offered by the facility. These groups require skilled therapists who are trained in psychotherapy; they are beyond the scope of this chapter. All workers should have the assessment skills, however, to identify these problems and to refer and counsel such residents into acceptance of the specialized treatment groups. See Chapter 19 for further discussion of group psychotherapy.

Roommate Meetings

Workers in long-term care facilities must sometimes improvise or try out new approaches to meet special needs. One of my first experiences with group work, over 25 years ago, was a response to the ongoing, unrelenting problem we had at the Isabella Geriatric Center with roommates who were unhappy with each other.

Sharing a room with a stranger is perceived as an assault to one's individuality when it is forced as a condition for admission to a long-term care facility. At our facility, we had a mix of private and semiprivate rooms, and newcomers to the institution were assigned to shared rooms while waiting their turn for a private room (which usually took about six months). This period seemed interminable to those who were waiting, and the social work department was constantly besieged by residents pleading for private rooms. Individual counseling, joint counseling with roommates, and family counseling were all tried, as well as room changes when feasible. Despite all efforts, the problems continued, demanding a considerable amount of staff time.

I decided to try a group approach, inviting all 20 residents who shared rooms to come to a meeting to discuss their problems as roommates. Each resident received a personal invitation requesting that he or she come to a meeting for the purpose of "talking about the experience of sharing a room, sharing suggestions with one another about how to resolve some of the problems which arise, and how to make life in the home more enjoyable."

The personal invitation, which reinforced their identities as individuals, not as roommates, encouraged attendance. Everyone came, except one resident who sent word that she would be delayed in the clinic.

The room was arranged with chairs in a circle, although 20 residents required a very large circle. The first remarkable thing that happened was that most residents came to the meeting with their roommates, although they had been invited separately, and that each chose a seat next to his or her roommate. I started the meeting with some welcoming remarks and a brief summary of why the meeting had been arranged. Each resident was introduced to the group and was asked to tell a little about his or her background and what he or she hoped for from the home. This was an important icebreaker; it also served the purpose of expanding potential acquaintances for the members, decreasing the unchosen symbiosis with the roommate.

When we came to the business at hand, all were reluctant to start when I asked for someone to tell the group something about their experience in sharing a room. After a long pause, the resident whose roommate was in the clinic began, and in a tone of desperation told that she had an impossible roommate—she was hard of hearing and played the TV too loud and too long; she was very sloppy and left her belongings scattered all over the room; she ate snacks in the room, leaving crumbs that would surely attract roaches; finally, and worst, she never remembered to flush the toilet and sometimes the room smelled to high heaven! When she recited this litany of complaints, other members murmured to one another and nodded supportively. Just as she finished, the missing roommate walked in, and the room fell silent with embarrassment. I greeted her by name, and she took the only empty chair, which was opposite her roommate.

Although I also felt uncomfortable with this situation, I decided to handle it matter-of-factly. I told Mrs. X that I was sorry she had missed the beginning of the meeting and getting to know something about all of her neighbors. I told the group that Mrs. X was widowed for the past 20 years, she was born in England, she had no family here, and she was a retired secretary. She came to the home because her hearing problem and health problems were making her feel isolated, and she came for protective care. I then proceeded to tell Mrs. X that everyone would speak about their experiences as roommates, and that her roommate had just finished telling the group about some of the problems she had in sharing a room with her. I repeated the litany verbatim. When I finished, there was a long pause. Mrs. X leaned forward in the circle and shaking her finger at her roommate, said very loudly and with her strong British accent, "You're a lovely woman, Mary, and I'm going to do everything in my power to adjust to you."

After that response, the atmosphere became more relaxed, and I asked if any members of the group had any comments or suggestions. The rest of two hours was lively with interaction and a problem-solving approach, with helpful and not so helpful suggestions, recriminations against the difficult partners, and plaudits for the good roommates. Overall, the theme was support by the group for what they were going through as pairs. At the end of the meeting, considerable appreciation was expressed to the group leader, along with the general statement that they felt it was a very good meeting. Indeed, the social workers and other staff noted that there was considerable reduction in complaints and tension. This was planned as a time-limited intervention and was not repeated until six months later with a new group of roommates. It is an example of how a group method can be effective even as a single experience and is offered as encouragement to professionals inexperienced with the group approach. Although the meeting is challenging, if genuine empathy is conveyed, the group can enthusiastically work on problem solving while providing the kind of support that is only possible from peers.

Coyle and Getzel (1979) developed a different model, a roommate clinic that offers two groups for 10 weekly meetings with roommates divided into separate groups. Their previous experiences with groups that included both roommates were unsuccessful, and at times such groups *increased* animosity. By bringing together residents who shared the same situations, but without their own roommates present, these practitioners found there was more progress in solving problems, and a strong social network outside the group was an additional benefit.

These contrasting experiences with group work with roommates illustrate the unpredictability of our efforts and the need to try a variety of models.

Support Groups

This special type of mutual aid group has emerged as one of the most effective in helping people cope with losses and transitional and personal crises, such as widowhood, disability, chronic or terminal illnesses, relocation, and so on. The increasing use of such groups is related to changes in the social structure that have led to less availability of support from traditional family networks. In long-term care institutions, support groups can provide the comfort and understanding that may be available only among others who are in the same boat or who have already gone through the problem and survived (veterans).

If the facility has a number of residents who are dealing with similar traumatic events, the support group can be organized as an open-ended model, with members entering as the need arises and leaving if and when they feel they are coping adequately. For example, if there are always some residents who are dealing with problems related to dementia in the family (of a spouse, sibling, or friend), an ongoing support group could be organized on a biweekly or monthly basis that would provide empathy, knowledge, and shared strategies for coping.

In the case of a problem that is not as common in the facility, such as adjusting to the effects of a stroke or cancer, a time-limited support group might be formed, such as a semiweekly or weekly group to meet for one or two months, which would also provide empathy, knowledge, and personal methods of coping.

Cohesion often develops quickly in support groups, because members feel that they have much in common; psychological closeness is often achieved more quickly than in other groups (Toseland 1990). The worker leading support groups can facilitate group interaction by planning for the kinds of obstacles that frequently arise, such as the member who tries to dominate the discussions or the distractions caused by side-conversationalists. The worker helps to avoid these situations by discussing expectations for the group in preliminary interviews when selecting members and by developing ground rules with members during the first session. With some groups, it is helpful to repeat these agreed-on rules at the beginning of each session to ensure broad interaction.

As with all older groups that focus on self-disclosure and discussion, the worker assumes a directive role in facilitating member to member interaction. Toseland (1990, 108) recommends some of the following practitioner behaviors: acknowledging and praising members who respond empathically to each other; pointing out and highlighting shared thoughts, feelings, and themes; making connections among members' statements; asking members to respond to a particular question in a group go-round; and suggesting that members speak directly to each other rather than through the leader. See Chapter 19, p. 204.

It is also important for the worker to be prepared substantively with the information needed for an educator role in relation to shared problems. If necessary, the worker should invite other staff to provide technical information that is vital to reduce anxiety and dispel possible misconceptions about the problems with which the group is dealing.

TRAINING PROGRAMS FOR FAMILIES

If a facility values the maintenance of family ties with the relative in a long-term care facility, it must articulate this with an environment that is supportive of family efforts and with programs that encourage appropriate family participation (Dobrof & Litwak 1977; Montgomery 1983). The author's development of such a psychoeducational group for families is discussed in Chapter 28.

Family Support Groups

An interesting, innovative group program that combines family members and the cognitively impaired older adult was developed in a geriatric facility (Saul 1988). The purpose was to demonstrate to caregivers methods to improve communication and ways of working with their relatives. Patients were seated in an inner circle, with caregivers seating themselves in an outer circle. After 12 sessions, the group formed one large semicircle, with one family member explaining that he wanted to join the inner circle because the group was therapeutic for him too. The process of the group included exercises to encourage discussion, reality orientation, and problem solving for the patients at their own level. Including the family in this model provided a learning as well as a therapeutic experience.

In addition to support groups for relatives of the mentally impaired, institutional staff may observe that some family members are dealing with common problems that might be eased by a support group. For example, if several residents have had strokes or amputations, their relatives might benefit from the formation of a support group. This could be especially applicable in long-term care facilities that have a rehabilitation program and admit residents directly from hospital-based care. In some instances, it might be therapeutic to form a rehabilitation support group for families *and* residents. The focus, similar to that of training programs, would be to provide knowledge about the condition, skills for remediation as far as possible, an opportunity to talk out the feelings related to the condition, and an opportunity to air frustrations about life in an institution. Such support groups, as part of a range of therapeutic programs, impart a message from the long-term care facility that the family's needs are understood. Short-term therapy groups have also been successful as the starting point for helping families form support networks while learning to be more comfortable with the facility (Brubaker & Schiefer 1987).

Family Councils

Although there is increasing recognition of the family council as a means of formalizing interactions between the institution and the families of the residents, there is often an undercurrent of irritation at having to deal with what may be perceived as a grievance committee. Now that family councils are mandated by law (OBRA regulations), administrators are required to provide space and staff assistance to families who wish to organize as councils, but this is not accomplished easily. Many administrators personify the old joke about the owner of a large manufacturing plant who complains to an associate, "I know how important the union is. Without it, the workers would still be in a sweat shop, toiling fourteen hours a day for a few dollars of pay. But frankly, in *my* business it's a ruination!"

Some administrators sincerely believe that they know best how to run their facilities and feel uncomfortable with authentic inclusion of a family council. Staff who serve as advocates for families in developing an effective council must work with all levels of administration throughout the institution to clarify the roles of family members and to demonstrate how families can learn to work as a group and with the organization, with the shared goal of improved care for the residents (Horsman & Echtenacher 1981). This requires training for family members on how to work with staff: They need to respect work schedules and understand the pressures caused by too few hands, too much paperwork, and the difficulties of caring for frail elders. They also need help in documenting and prioritizing problems so they can be addressed more efficiently by the staff.

Family councils can benefit from training in parliamentary procedures just as resident councils do. A smooth-running and well-informed council can be an invaluable aid in developing a partnership model of care. It can be the linkage mechanism that balances the shared functions of the formal organization (the institution) and the informal system (the family) (Dobrof & Litwak 1977). By meeting regularly with representatives or subcommittees of the council, key staff members can communicate more effectively and educate the family about the institution's efforts and problems. Simultaneously, staff time is saved by hearing of problems screened by a group of relatives rather than by individual discussions with upset relatives.

A regularly scheduled family council can become an easy way to take advantage of family energy, leading to a sense of ownership and pride in the facility and improved community relations (Conger & Moore 1984).

Palmer (1991) presents a family council model in which staff and a family member assume co-leadership. While reinforcing the benefits of a council, she also presents the pros and cons of such co-leadership. In addition, Palmer points out that most council members appreciated the support that was provided, although they were not interested in joining a support group. She found (p. 133) that "a structured, task oriented group, such as the family council, provided a way for families to become more involved with the facility, and experience the group support, without implying that they were having difficulty adjusting to the placement of a loved one."

Although councils will vary in their style and competence in relation to the skills and personalities of the family members who are involved, from my practice experience, it is a group method well worth investing in.

SUMMARY

More than twenty years ago, Donald Kent gave a keynote address on "The Group Worker and the Institutionalized Aged" (1970). He pointed out that in addition to a need for activities that counteract isolation, there is a very basic need for closure at the end of life, a need for summing up. This is why the role of life review becomes so important: to review past accomplishments and make an assessment of them. And this is done best in a group that validates the experiences presented, the positive as well as the disappointments.

Kent also stated: "A wide variety of therapeutic programs have been conducted in institutions, and the remarkable thing about all of them is that no matter what program you use, you get results." Although this practice wisdom may not meet current research standards, it is a timeless reminder that every effort should be made to increase the extent of group intervention in the institution.

Unfortunately, this ideal is difficult to accomplish in a system that does not always provide adequate staff resources to meet the basic needs of residents. Group work services are often expected to be developed as add-on work, which calls for more than the usual professional commitment. The value of group work services to residents and families must be demonstrated by commitment of staff in developing programs, offering these programs at times that will attract the family, and advocacy of administrators for adequate numbers of staff necessary to realize this goal.

EXERCISE 1

Discuss the development of a resident council. What are some of the barriers? What can the staff facilitator do to ensure the residents' right to a council, and what specifically can the staff do to improve council function?

EXERCISE 2

Role play a strategy for developing a series of groups in a long-term care facility. Consider issues of resources, including use of staff time. Players include a social worker, an administrator, and a nursing director.

EXERCISE 3

List three programs to enhance family participation in long-term care facilities. Specify the goals and expected outcome of each type of family program.

REFERENCES

Berman-Rossi T. 1990. Group work and older persons. In A Monk (ed.), *Handbook of gerontological services*, 2d ed. (pp. 141-167). New York: Columbia University Press.

Brody E. 1974. *A social work guide for long-term care facilities.* Rockville, MD: National Institute of Mental Health.

Brubaker E, Schiefer AW. 1987. Groups with families of elderly long-term care residents: Building support networks. *J Gerontol Soc Work* 10(1/2):167-176.

Conger SA, Moore KD. 1984. *Social work in the long-term care facility.* New York: Van Nostrand Reinhold.

Cox E. 1988. Empowerment of the low income elderly through group work. *Soc Work with Groups* 11(4): 111-125.

Coyle F, Getzel J. 1979. Helping the angry elderly: The roommate clinic. *J Gerontol Soc Work* 1(4):347-350.

Devitt M, Checkoway B. 1982. Participation in nursing home resident councils: Promise and practice. *Gerontologist* 22(1):49-53.

Dobrof R, Litwak E. 1977. *Maintenance of family ties of long-term care patients,* DHEW Pub. No. (ADM) 79-400. Washington, DC: U.S. Government Printing Office.

Euster G. 1971. A system of groups in institutions for the aged. *Soc Casework* 52(8):523-529.

Germain CB, Gitterman A. 1980. *The life model of social work practice.* New York: Columbia University Press.

Getzel J. 1982. Resident councils and social action. *J Gerontol Soc Work* 5(1/2):179-186.

Hartford ME. 1980. The use of group methods for work with the aged. In JE Birren, RB Sloan (eds.), *Handbook of mental health and aging* (pp. 806-826). Englewood Cliffs, NJ: Prentice-Hall.

Horsman MN, Echtenacher B. 1981. Working with the family council. *Am Health Care Assoc J* 7(4):20-22.

Johnson DR, Agresti A, Jacob MD, Nies K. 1990. Building a therapeutic community through specialized groups in a nursing home. *Clin Gerontol* 9(3/4):203-217.

Kent DP. 1970. The group worker and the institutionalized aged. *Proceedings of a conference: The significance of the group activity program for the institutionalized aged.* New York: Central Bureau for the Jewish Aged. Conference at the Young Men and Young Women's Hebrew Association (April 7-8).

Lowy L. 1991. *Social work with the aging,* 2d ed. Prospect Heights, IL: Waveland Press.

McDermott C. 1989. Empowering the elderly nursing home resident: The resident rights campaign. *Soc Work* 34(2):155-157.

Miller I, Solomon R. 1980. The development of group services for the elderly. *J Gerontol Soc Work* 2(3):241-258.

Montgomery RJV. 1983. Staff-family relations and institutional care policies. *J Gerontol Soc Work* 6(1):25-37.

Newmark L. 1963. Development of a residents' council. *Gerontologist* 3(1):22-25.

Omnibus Reconciliation Act of 1987. 1989. Compliance checklist for long-term care facilities. *Federal Register* 54(21): Paragraph 483.15, Section C, #6, p. 5363 (February 2).

Palmer DS. 1991. Co-leading a family council in a long-term care facility. *J Gerontol Soc Work* 16(3/4):121-134.

Robert HM. 1971. *Robert's rules of order—Revised.* New York: Morrow.

Saul S (ed.). 1987. *Group work with the frail elderly.* New York: Haworth.

———. 1988. Group therapy with confused and disoriented elderly people. In BW Maclennan, S Saul, MB Wiener (eds.), *Group psychotherapies for the elderly* (pp. 197-208). Madison, CT: International Universities Press.

Seligman ME, Elder G. 1986. Learned helplessness and life span development. In AB Sorenson, FE Weinert, LR Sherrod (eds.), *Human development and the life course: Multidisciplinary perspectives* (pp. 377-428). Hillsdale, NJ: Erlbaum.

Shore H. 1964. Try a resident's council. *Professional Nursing Home* (November). Reprinted in Shore H (1972), *Adventures in group living* (pp. 139-141). Dallas, TX: The Dallas Home for Jewish Aged.

Silverstone B, Burack-Weiss A. 1983. *Social work practice with the frail elderly.* Springfield, IL: Thomas.

Solomon R. 1982. Serving the families of the aged: The four crises. *J Gerontol Soc Work* 5(1/2):83-96.

Tobin S, Lieberman M. 1976. *Last home for the aged.* New York: New York University Press.

Toseland RW. 1990. *Group work with older adults.* New York: New York University Press.

Watt LM, Wong PTP. 1991. A taxonomy of reminiscence and therapeutic implications. *J Gerontol Soc Work* 16(1/2):37-58.

BIBLIOGRAPHY

Berger R. 1982. A problem-solving model for in-service training. *J Gerontol Soc Work* 4(3/4):21-26.

Blenkner M. 1965. Social work and family relationships in later life with some thoughts on filial maturity. In E

Shanas, G Strieb (eds.), *Social work and the structure of the family: Generational relations* (pp. 46-59). Englewood Cliffs: NJ, Prentice-Hall.

Cohen D, Eisdorfer C. 1986. *The loss of self.* New York: Norton.

Hooyman N, Lustbacer AW. 1986. *Taking care.* New York: Free Press.

Mace NL, Rabins PV. 1991. *The 36-hour day: A family guide to caring.* Baltimore: Johns Hopkins University Press.

Montgomery R. 1983. Staff-family relations and institutional care policies. *J Gerontol Soc Work* 6(1):25-38.

Moran JA, Gatz M. 1987. Group therapies for nursing home adults: The evaluation of two treatment approaches. *Gerontologist* 27(5):588-591.

Numerof RE. 1983. Building and maintaining bridges: Meeting the psychosocial needs of nursing home residents and their families. *Clin Gerontol* 1(4):53-67.

Safford F. 1980. A program for families of the mentally impaired elderly. *Gerontologist* 20(6):656-660.

———. 1987. *Caring for the mentally impaired elderly: A family guide.* New York: Henry Holt.

Shore H. 1972. *Adventures in group living.* Dallas, TX: The Dallas Home for Jewish Aged.

Silverstone B. 1977. *Establishing resident councils.* New York: Federation of Protestant Welfare Agencies.

Smyer MA, Cohen MD, Brannon D. 1990. *Mental health consultation in nursing homes.* New York: New York University Press.

Zastrow C. 1989. *Social work with groups,* 2d ed. Chicago: Nelson Hall.

CHAPTER 21

A Model of Group Work in Retirement Communities

Janet E. Black, James J. Kelly, and Susan Rice

KEY WORDS

- Elaborating skills
- Empowerment
- Explicit norms
- Implicit norms
- Nonviolent conflict
- Open-ended groups
- Role modeling
- Self-select
- Termination

LEARNING OBJECTIVES

- Define the concept of empowerment.
- Describe three skills needed by workers in the forming stages of a group.
- Describe one process of nonviolent direct communication.
- Describe two skills needed by workers in the performing phase of a group.
- Identify two ways to assist group members in dealing with termination issues.
- Describe two positive and negative consequences of open-ended groups.
- Describe the process involved in dealing with problem members of groups.
- Describe three important needs of residents living in retirement communities.

Group work can be important to provide supportive services to a retirement community. A review of the literature on groups for older persons (Capuzzi & Gross 1980; Myers, Podevant & Dean 1991) suggests that the many benefits include reduction of loneliness, isolation, and rejection,

conditions often associated with the process of aging in our culture. Why groups specifically within the retirement community setting? Data from the National Long-Term Care surveys and the National American Housing survey show (Tilson 1990) that those most at risk for future institutionalization include those who have high rates of functional disability, very old average age, and high prevalence of living alone—the same characteristics of most residents of retirement settings, and of those who self-selected the program described in this chapter. While it is true that social support

Acknowledgment: The authors would like to acknowledge the efforts and contributions of Bob Gooden, Marjorie Light, and Sunny Lindauer, who are residents of the retirement community we worked with, and who were instrumental in providing leadership for the program.

alone cannot prevent institutionalization, most people prefer to age in place as long as possible, and social support does slow down the negative emotional consequences that accompany greater physical frailty.

This chapter is divided into four parts. The first part describes a specific project using students at an urban college campus as group leaders for a series of weekly support groups in a nearby retirement community. This specific project utilizes group work in two ways—as a methodology for training students to work with groups of older people and as a support group for people living in the retirement community. In a sense, each of these purposes has individual goals and objectives at the same time as each is an integral part of the whole project. The second part describes the developmental group work issues that emerge, in parallel fashion in the classroom and in the retirement community. The third part discusses some of the structural issues in coordinating such a program. The last part briefly discusses some of the results of this program in terms of fulfilling its purposes.

DESCRIPTION OF THE PROJECT

In a large urban area on the West Coast is a retirement community of more than 9000 residents who desired independent living in a sheltered, gated community. The community is 30 years old, and when it first opened, the corporation marketing the community targeted active new or preretirees in their late fifties or early sixties. They were successful in their targeting, and the units quickly filled. They were sold as cooperatives, meaning that residents paid a price for the unit they lived in and then a monthly maintenance charge for the upkeep of the grounds. Prospective residents were required to have the entire purchase price (which excluded low-income persons), and were required to be capable of independent living. This history helps one to understand the present-day flavor of this community and the needs of group members within their own community settings.

At the present time, the community has aged, and the average age is 80 rather than 50. Clearly, they are a much frailer population than when they moved in, and they have different needs. Additionally, these residents, who were middle-class then, are now retired, and so, despite having an adequate

place to live, as a rule they have much lower incomes. These changes have been largely ignored by the developers of this community, who continue to target healthy, fiftyish people who are looking for an active place to retire—golf course, numerous activity clubs, churches, and so on. There is a medical clinic within the community, on a fee-for-service basis, but there continues to be the requirement that all residents be able to live independently. The reality is that many residents have part- or full-time homemakers, but there is no official sanctioning or brokerage of these services.

A program of weekly support and discussion groups began when a group of residents approached the nearby state university and said they would like to have some interaction with students and some assistance in setting up discussion/support groups that would be different from the usual activity groups offered in their community. The fulfillment of this request, on their terms, illustrates the belief that empowerment is one of the primary purposes of social work and is a method for practitioners helping clients to facilitate the interaction between them and their environments for purposes of problem solving (Parsons 1991). Empowerment is both a process and an outcome; and it occurs in an environment of interaction in which support, mutual aid, and validation for one's perceptions and experiences are received.

After discussion among the interested residents and key members of the faculty who possess expertise and interest in working with older adults, a program eventually emerged that was a partnership between residents and the Department of Social Work of the university, with assistance from other areas including the psychology department. The people responsible for the program were residents of the retirement community, including a president, vice-president, secretary, and treasurer. A university faculty member was the liaison, a role that included teaching a two-semester course in which students would attend class, learn about group work, and then lead (or co-lead) weekly groups in the community. The faculty member also provided supervision to the students regarding their weekly groups at the retirement community. Students were juniors or seniors and included majors in psychology, social work, gerontology, nursing, and anthropology. Some retirement community members needed support services but were unable to attend an out-of-home group or were not comfortable in a group setting; program elements were added for them, including weekly in-home visits with home-bound residents by students in the program. To provide additional socialization and stimulation opportunities, workshops and pot-luck dinners were arranged, involving all members of the support groups and the student leaders.

The program serves only a minute segment of this retirement community of 9000—approximately 60 people at any one time. They are a self-selected group and tend to be frailer, older, and less mobile than the general population. They tend to live either with a spouse or alone, suffer serious health handicaps, and want an opportunity to talk about the difficult situations they face.

Students also self-select this program, although they are interviewed by a faculty member before beginning their internship, to explain the program and assess their level of interest and potential. They are required to have an interest in working with older people, and in group work, but are not required to have any specific kinds of experiences. They need to be willing to commit to both semesters of the course and stay with the same group members (and individual home visitor) for the entire year. The faculty member working with the students and residents plays an extremely active role in the administration of the overall program, as well as the teaching and group work supervision aspects of it.

GROUP WORK ISSUES: STUDENTS AND RESIDENTS

A variety of models are used to describe stages of group development (Garland et al. 1976; Levine 1990; Sarri & Galinsky 1985; Tuckman 1965; Tuckman & Jensen 1977), but whatever language is used, a process emerges whereby members of a group change over time from an aggregate of people into an interactive, mutually dependent and mutually influenced unit. Tuckman's (1965) taxonomy of the forming, storming, norming, performing, and adjourning phases of group work enables students to analyze their groups in relation to their stage of development.

Early on, the point is made to the students in the classroom that they are struggling with the same stages of group development and the same crises that members of the retirement community are dealing with in their group settings. Modeling is used to demonstrate worker tasks; process analysis utilizing class discussion, case vignettes, and experiential exercises assists students in recognizing the patterns in both sets of groups.

Forming

In the forming stage of the classroom unit, students are anxious about the year ahead, their tasks, and their future relationships with both each other and the older group members. Middleman and Wood (1990) describe the initial tasks of the social work practitioner as including "helping the members gain a sense of each other and their groupness." Group members need to interact with each other so that they can own the group as they progress. There is discussion about their hope that the classroom group will become a mutual support group, just as they hope the community group will provide support to the residents. Gitterman (1989) lists a group of skills needed to create such a support system, including:

- Directing members' transactions to each other.
- Inviting members to build on each other's contributions.
- Reinforcing mutual support and assistance norms.
- Examining group sanctions.
- Encouraging collective action and activities.
- Clarifying members' tasks and role responsibilities.
- Structuring collective decision making.

As students learn that the classroom is also run along this model, they gain familiarity and comfort in the process they take to weekly groups in the retirement community. Delineating this parallel process and these skills very specifically allows the forming process to proceed as students clearly define their purpose in being together.

It is understood that most students begin group work with many fears (Ephross 1989), including a fear of harm (being harmed by the group or harming the members), a fear of not knowing what to do, fears about intimacy, and fears about differences between themselves and group members in terms of social class, educational level, race or ethnicity, age, or condition of handicap. Initial anxieties are expressed in questions such as "What will I say to the group members? What if I insult someone? What if someone starts to cry? What if no one talks?" An additional factor for students to consider is that they are most often placed as co-leaders in a group, and so they need to develop a relationship with another student to allow them to work with their client groups.

The older members are struggling with the same issues, although they voice their concerns in their own context: "What do I have in common with these people? What if nobody likes me? What if they make fun of my problems? What if I start to cry?" When the students come to this realization, it is an enormous relief to them, and it is the beginning of the transformation from the forming stage to the storming stage. They recognize their own commonality, their own purpose, and the tasks they will need to deal with. This recognition also helps them understand what they need to do in the initial stages of group development in the community, namely, to assist the residents to find their own commonality, purpose, and tasks. At every step, the processes occurring in the classroom are examined for their relevance for the community. For example, a programmatic exercise will conclude with a discussion about how the exercise could be adapted for use by their groups.

Another aspect of the forming stage has to do with knowing the parameters of the kind of group experience you are providing. Support groups are different from therapy groups, and it is important to honor the contract that is set up between members and leader. Nelson (1989) cautions workers who are dealing with older populations to avoid delving into problems that elicit stronger emotions than the group is prepared to deal with. On the other hand, the concept of support means that members are entitled to nag and complain, and the worker needs to listen, without allowing himself or herself to feel burdened with the responsibility to do something about every grievance that is aired. This balance between too much and too little requires an accurate assessment of how frail members are and not treating them as frailer than they really are!

Storming and Norming

One of the factors that makes a support/discussion group different from normal social intercourse is that the rules about what is socially appropriate vary. In real life, if someone says to an older person, "How are you feeling?" he or she knows that the correct answer is "Fine," regardless of the truth.

Sharing honest feelings, especially when they are painful or negative, quickly drives away the casual acquaintance. In a group setting, members need to learn that the rules are different, that honesty is appreciated and necessary for intimacy to grow. Honesty leads to conflict, and most people are uncomfortable with conflict. Members need to have the experience of seeing a conflict emerge, be openly dealt with, and resolved rather than denied or avoided. Because many people (students too) have their own issues with conflict, the storming stage of groups becomes crucial in furthering group development.

In a retirement community, people are anxious to be and to have good neighbors. They often are reluctant to cross the boundary from acquaintance to friend because of the risk that if the friendship does not work out, the neighborship will be strained. As people become frailer and more dependent on the good will of neighbors, the risk becomes more unacceptable. As a consequence, residents enter the groups with a fear of arguing or fighting, and they will try to smooth over any conflicts that occur. Leaders need to become comfortable with their own feelings about conflict, to encourage group members to do the same.

It is useful to teach students a model of nonviolent direct communication, which they then often teach the members of their groups. The model (Gambrill & Richey 1985; Looney 1991) involves seven specific components of directly expressing one's feelings in a way that lets the other person hear the concern, rather than being threatened by the disagreement. The steps include:

1. I feel (describe your feelings, using words that refer to feelings).
2. When (describe the specific behavior of concern).
3. Because (specify how the offensive behavior affects you).
4. I would prefer (describe what you want).
5. Because (describe how you would feel—be sure to use words that refer to feelings).
6. Then (the consequences for the other person changing).
7. What do you think? (ask for the other person's reaction).

In the classroom, students have the opportunity to practice this new way of communicating. Optimally, this process is facilitated by attempting to create an open, accepting environment where students can feel free to make mistakes and to learn and to disagree with each other and the instructor when issues come up that make them uncomfortable. For example, the major assignment in the course is a weekly journal kept by all students, which is a description of what they do with their groups, the processes they observe, and their own feelings. Students quickly learn that this is an enormous amount of work and is often emotionally painful. When the assignment is discussed in class, it is important for the instructor to allow criticism of the assignment, to hear students' concerns, and to be clear about his or her own purposes for changing or not changing in response to student pressures. When done successfully, this is clear role modeling for the student: how to behave with the group when your leadership is questioned. The distinction between being questioned and being threatened is an important one, and it has to do with the confidence of the leader in his or her strengths. For beginning students or social workers, this is complicated by the fact that they often do not feel much confidence in their roles, and yet they need to act as if they do in order to deal with conflict effectively. Levine (1990) calls this an *authority crisis*, in which power begins to be shared more equally by the leader and the members; Levine posits that it is necessary for further group development to occur.

It is important to be aware that norms of groups are often implicit rather than explicit. For example, it would be rare that a group leader would tell everyone where to sit, but after a few weeks, patterns emerge. If one person is consistently isolated or placed at the head of the table, then it might be important to point out the norms that have developed so that the group can discuss them and decide whether those norms are helping or hindering the development of the group. For example, if a person who is hard of hearing consistently sits with her or his worse ear toward the group, she or he lowers chances of fitting into the group.

Performing

When group members have come to some understanding of who they are and how they will work, their focus moves to the tasks that they have set for themselves. In a retirement community setting, the members are often struggling with creating adaptive responses to life changes. Scharlach

(1989) discusses a perspective of role theory that says that alterations must be made in the "preferences, values, role norms and behaviors that comprise one's social identity." Because, for older adults, life transitions often involve limitations that challenge their old identity and threaten their sense of well-being, roles need to be modified to be comfortable. Through focusing on life review (further information in Chapter 16), discussing similarities in shared experiences, and solving problems, members of the group become more competent at dealing with the multiple losses and changes that accompany old age.

The performance stage of group development has been characterized as the "work phase" (Shulman 1992). A number of specific worker skills are necessary for the completion of the tasks the group sets for itself. Some of these elaborating skills, which encourage intermember communications, include:

- Containment, in which the worker refrains from jumping in too quickly as members speak.
- Focused listening, which involves listening while keeping in mind the purpose of the group and the here-and-now mood of the group.
- Questioning, in which the member is assisted in his or her elaboration of the problem, situation, or conflict under discussion.
- Exploring silences, which helps the members understand the nature of silence—whether it is thoughtful, resistant, or helpless.
- Reaching from the general to the specific, which involves helping members to focus on details so that the result of the group discussion and interaction can be helpful to the group as a whole as well as to each individual member of the group.

All of these skills allow the group to grow together while giving each other mutual aid.

Adjourning

Termination is often the phase of group development that is dealt with least effectively because it arouses so many issues for group members and group leaders. Many authors (Rice 1985; Ross 1991; Toseland & Rivas 1984) say that termination needs to begin in the first minutes of the first sessions—that members need to understand that they are working within some time frame, toward some ultimate purpose.

In the classroom, as the year draws to a close, students struggle with what they have and have not accomplished and what they will do in the future. They learn that the retirement group members are struggling with the same issues: "Was it worth my time? Did the rewards outweigh the costs?" Just as some students decide that gerontology is not the field they want to pursue, some older residents decide they no longer want to attend a support/discussion group. It is important, as part of termination, to allow people to feel acceptance about their decisions; not to feel like a failure because they did not get what they originally expected from the experience. On the other hand, there generally is genuine sadness as an experience that gave joy is ending.

Students often struggle with not wanting to say goodbye. They make promises to continue visiting the members of their group that they will not be able to keep, because it is too difficult to deal with the pain of saying goodbye. They must deal with the feeling that they are abandoning their older members. If they are helped to explore those feelings in class, they are then able to go to the group settings and help their residents explore similar feelings. For the residents, who have the option of continuing with the group in the next academic year, the dilemma is a bit different—is it worth the trouble of getting emotionally involved with this person if we have to say goodbye. An honest and open confrontation of these issues allows all participants to have the sense of closure that is needed to retain the long-term benefits of the group process.

Most residents and students can relate to the example of thinking about a long-term relationship that ended abruptly because of death, divorce, or physical lack of proximity, without the chance to talk about what the relationship meant. What most people do is downplay the importance of the whole relationship, because it is easier than feeling that it wasn't worth enough to deal with the pain of separation. Compare that to a relationship in which goodbyes were said and participants had the chance to think together about what worked and what did not work. The loss is still painful, but the memories are more complete and can include the positive ones as well as the hurtful ones. If participants are to remember and benefit from their group experiences, they need to be able to discuss what they meant to them.

Students are asked to participate in termination exercises, which they usually then adapt for their groups. For example, in one class, each student was asked to write on an index card something she or he admired about each person in the class. Each person then received all of the index cards with her or his name on them and had a tangible piece of evidence of some strengths. One year, there was a student who was doing very poorly in the class, who had difficulty with his groups, and who alienated the other students. The authors felt some apprehension about this exercise, because there was concern about students getting back at this individual by being cruel in their statements. However, with clear directions that this exercise was not about what students liked or didn't like, but something they could admire about each person, their unanimous (and separate) feedback was that they admired this student's persistence in the face of so much difficulty. Certainly the recognition that the field of gerontology was not appropriate for this particular student was made easier by knowing that it did not make him bad.

Another helpful part of termination allows members to think in a nonjudgmental way about what they would do differently if they had it to do over again; this gives people the tools to benefit from every experience they have. At every phase of the group process, members and leaders are encouraged to examine what they are experiencing to ensure that they are benefiting from it to the maximum degree possible.

STRUCTURAL ISSUES: STUDENTS AND RESIDENTS

One of the distinctive characteristics of this program is that all of the groups are open ended. Although there is a core group of regulars who have been with the program since its inception, and stated their preference for long-term commitment to the group, the reality is that the membership is constantly changing. Members can get sick for months at a time, and when they return, the group has a different flavor and texture. Members bring visiting friends and relatives for one or two sessions and juggle their participation in the group with physicians' appointments and family occasions.

There are both positive and negative consequences of this type of group (Galinsky & Schopler

1987). Positive features include the added motivation and stimulation provided by members who are at different points in the growing process. New members can directly see the benefits of attendance through the enthusiasm of old members. Older members reaffirm their commitment to the group as they take on leadership roles. Open-ended groups are also less threatening than closed groups as members have the ability (and the right) to distance themselves when discussions get too heavy. They do not, in practice, utilize that ability very often, because the group becomes so important to them, but knowing they could use it is both a freeing and an empowering feeling. Additionally, issues of trust and confidentiality are more easily confronted and discussed, because the group more closely emulates real life, which has arrivals and departures.

There are negative aspects as well, including repetition of stories (which is sometimes a problem with groups of older people in any circumstances) and a general slowing down of the process of group development because of the addition of new members.

The student-workers need to be aware of these factors and deal with them as they affect group process. Although this is one area where the student learning group optimally does not parallel the community group, in some instances, there is at least one student who drops out or one who adds the course midway through the year. Through an examination of how this affects the learning group, workers are helped to understand the dynamics of open- and closed-ended groups in a dynamic way.

Because the groups are self-selected, there is less control over size than is sometimes desired. For example, one of the groups in our program had 16 to 18 members attending each meeting, yet the group adamantly opposed a split into two groups. On the other end of the continuum, a group of only six regular members often flounders because of absences; it struggles to have a purposeful discussion with two or three members and two leaders. Although the faculty liaison can influence the inclusion of new members into specific groups, using that influence should be balanced with the desire to keep the groups as empowered as possible. Because the group takes place in a community setting, members often know other members at least by sight or reputation and have clear preferences as

to whom they want to get to know better and whom they would choose to avoid.

Every group has certain difficult clients, who can be described as those whose behaviors in group present problems you do not know what to do with; they are the clients to whom you are not able to respond in a helpful or effective way (Friedman 1989). Examples of such people include the monopolizer, the silent group member, the withdrawn member, the restless or agitated member, and the unmotivated member. It seems helpful to include this in a discussion of structural factors rather than of developmental factors because it underscores the inevitability of these occurrences. Consequently, the leader is less tempted to simply expel the problem member from the group. An understanding of why people act in certain ways, and that they are often playing out concerns of the group as a whole, can facilitate the leader's interventions.

For example, why does a monopolizer monopolize? A common assumption is that he or she wants all the attention, yet the underlying feeling of that person is often that he or she does not deserve any attention. A discussion that helps people look at their motives for behavior, especially behavior that attracts negative attention, allows every member of the group to learn, and it avoids alienating the person whose behavior provides that learning.

RESULTS

The program has two major purposes—to train students to work with groups of older people and to be a support group for people within a retirement community. How effective is this program? The first purpose is easier to assess, because students are used to being asked about effectiveness. Student evaluations of this course are consistently high—usually the most positive of all of the courses taught by these authors. Students feel that the time and energy has been worth it, because they have learned, because their choices have become clearer to them, and because they have gotten on-the-job training. The comment that "this is the most useful course I've taken in my whole college career" is fairly common as we go through the process of termination in the classroom. Most students end this experience with much more certainty about their career choices—they are either sure they will do group work with seniors or they are sure they want to go into a different area. We feel that both of these attitudes demonstrate success, as the students now know, with a greater sense of reality, what career they are moving toward.

For seniors in the community, the results are more anecdotal but are even more unanimously positive. One woman who has been in the group for five years is fond of approaching strangers and saying, "You know, my own son doesn't know me anymore because of this program. I used to be a mouse who never said anything because I had such a low opinion of myself, and now I know I'm a terrific person—that's what I've learned in this group." We have seen a woman deteriorate physically and progress from walking to using a cane, then a walker, then a wheelchair—and yet she continues to attend group sessions. She attributes her ability to remain in an independent living situation primarily to the support of the friends she has made in her group. Perhaps independent living is not always the most desirable outcome, but for this woman, in this situation, living independently is defined as success. After a long-time member of the men's group died, his widow called to say that the group had been the most important event of her husband's week for the five years before his death, and that she was as grateful as he had been

for our existence. These testimonials are what makes the group a success: Numerous lives may not be changed dramatically, but individual lives are improved by individual definitions of what is important. This seems to be the epitome of social support: to enable people to fulfill their own goals of achievement.

SUMMARY

This chapter describes a program within a program—one that allows students to learn about group work with older adults and simultaneously provides continuing supportive group work services to a portion of the retired aged living in the community. It is important for leaders to understand the phases of group development and that different tasks are required of the leader in each phase. Modeling is demonstrated to be an important part of teaching leadership to students and empowerment to members. The parallels between the classroom and the community group are described with attention to the differences as well. We hope that this material can give the impetus to further community programming of support groups.

EXERCISE 1

Choose one of the following activities to try out in class or with an informal group of colleagues.

1. Take a package of fortune cookies and have each participant read one and discuss how it applies to her or him and how accurate it is.
2. Have the group break into pairs, and in each dyad, find two ways you are alike and two ways you are different from each other. When the group reconvenes, have one spokesperson discuss the findings.

Both of these exercises can be used in the forming stage of a group to help group members forge a common bond. After you have tried it out, choose one exercise and think of how you could adapt the rules to assist the group members in understanding the storming stage of group development.

EXERCISE 2

This exercise is a five-step process to nonviolent communication, which can be used to tell another person something that is upsetting you.

1. Describe the way you feel when something specific occurs that another person does.
2. Describe the consequences for you, what you do with those feelings.
3. Describe in clear behavioral terms what you would prefer that the other person do.
4. Describe the rewards (the new consequences) that would occur if the other person changed.
5. Ask for the other person's reaction.

For example: Older woman to adult daughter whom she sees too infrequently (according to her own perception): "When three weeks go by between visits from you, I feel lonely and abandoned. Then I start to feel that I haven't been a good mother, that you really don't care what happens to me. I would really like it if you could manage to visit at least once a week. If you did, I think when we did see each other, it would be more pleasant, because I wouldn't be so angry at you. What do you think about all that?"

Try out this process with another person. Notice your own feelings and your partner's responses. Discuss each of your reactions to conflict and the differences between handling it nonviolently (as above) and in more confrontational ways.

EXERCISE 3

Think of a relationship in which you never had the opportunity to say goodbye—someone who died unexpectedly, a friend who moved away without a discussion of your feelings for each other, a romantic relationship that went sour and was abruptly terminated by either of you. Write that person a letter in which you tell him or her the positive and negative feelings you had, the best and worst thing that you took away from that relationship, and what you would do differently if you had it to do over again. Does this exercise change the perception you have of this old relationship? How?

EXERCISE 4

Form a group of six or seven of your classmates who will meet four to six times during the course of your learning. Have each person take on the characteristic of an older person whom he or she will describe in a short written autobiographical sketch. Each week, one member will be the leader (playing himself or herself rather than the older character) and will have the responsibility of deciding how to focus the group and help members to interact with each other.

After each meeting, have a debriefing session in which you discuss:

1. As your older character, what did the leader do that especially worked or did not work for you?
2. As the leader, what member behaviors especially troubled you or made you lose your focus?
3. For both members and leaders, what were the most positive and negative aspects of this experience for you?

(NOTE: This exercise is described more fully in Rice 1988.)

REFERENCES

Breton M. 1985. Reaching and engaging people: Issues and practice principles. *Soc Work with Groups* 8(3):7-21.

Capuzzi D, Gross D. 1980. Group work with the elderly: An overview for counselors. *Personnel and Guidance J* 59(4):206-211.

Ephross P. 1989. Teaching group therapy within social work education. In KG Lewis (ed.), *Variations on teaching and supervising group therapy* (pp. 87-98). New York: Haworth.

Fisher R, Brown S. 1988. *Getting together: Building relationships as we negotiate.* New York: Houghton Mifflin.

Fisher R, Ury W, Patton B. 1991. *Getting to yes: Negotiating agreement without giving in,* 2d ed. Middlesex, England: Penguin.

Friedman W. 1989. *Practical group therapy: A guide for clinicians.* San Francisco: Jossey-Bass.

Galinsky M, Schopler J. 1987. Practitioner's views of assets and liabilities of open-ended groups. In J Lassner et al. (eds.), *Social group work: Competence and values in practice* (pp. 83-98). New York: Haworth.

————. 1989. The social work group. In J Shaffer, M Galinsky (eds.), *Models of group therapy*, 2d ed. (pp. 18-40). Englewood Cliffs, NJ: Prentice-Hall.

Gambrill E, Richey C. 1985. *Taking charge of your social life.* Belmont, CA: Wadsworth.

Garland J, Jones H, Kolodny R. 1976. A model of stages of group development in social work groups. In S Bernstein (ed.), *Explorations in group work* (pp. 17-71). Boston: Charles River Books.

Gitterman A. 1989. Building mutual support in groups. *Soc Work with Groups* 12(2):5-21.

Gitterman A, Shulman L, eds. 1986. *The mutual aid group and the life cycle.* Itasca, IL: Peacock.

Henry S. 1981. *Group skills in social work: A four-dimensional approach.* Itasca, IL: Peacock.

Johnson DW, Johnson FP. 1991. *Joining together: Group theory and group skills,* 4th ed. Englewood Cliffs, NJ: Prentice-Hall.

Levine B. 1990. *Group psychotherapy: Practice and development.* Prospect Heights, IL: Waveland Press.

Looney J. 1991. *Alternatives to Violence: A Reader and Workbook.* Akron, OH: Peace Grows.

Lowy L. 1982. Social group work with vulnerable older persons: A theoretical perspective. *Soc Work with Groups* 5:21-32.

Middleman R, Wood G. 1990. From social group work to social work with groups. *Soc Work with Groups* 13(3):3-20.

Myers J, Podevant J, Dean L. 1991. Groups for older persons and their caregivers: A review of the literature. *J Special Group Work* 16(3):197-205.

Nelson RC. 1989. Choice awareness: A group experience in a residential setting. *J Special Group Work* 14(3):158-169.

Parsons R. 1991. Empowerment: Purpose and practice principle in social work. *Soc Work with Groups* 14(2):7-21.

Rice S. 1985. The termination process as a beginning: The importance of the relationship between client and worker. Paper presented at National Association of Social Work Michigan Chapter Conference. Saginaw, MI.

————. 1988. Group Process: Its use as an educational tool in gerontology. *J Teach Soc Work* 2(1):63-71.

Ross S. 1991. The termination phase in groupwork: Tasks for the groupworker. *Groupwork* 4(1):57-70.

Sarri RC, Galinsky MJ. 1985. A conceptual framework for group development. In M Sundel, P Glasser, R Sarri, R Vinter (eds.), *Individual change through small groups* (pp. 70-86). New York: Free Press.

Scharlach A. 1989. Social group work with the elderly: A role theory perspective. *Soc Work with Groups* 12(3):33-46.

Shulman L. 1992. *The skills of helping individuals, families and groups,* 3d ed. Itasca, IL: Peacock.

Tilson D (ed.). 1990. *Aging in place: Supporting the frail elderly in residential environments.* Glenview, IL: Scott, Foresman.

Toseland RW. 1990. *Group work with older adults.* New York: New York University Press.

Toseland RW, Rivas RF. 1984. *An introduction to group work practice.* New York: Macmillan.

Tuckman BW. 1965. Developmental sequence in small groups. *Psychol Bull* 63:384-399.

Tuckman BW, Jenson MAC. 1977. Stages of small group development revisited. *Group Organ Studies* 2:419-427.

Vinter RD. 1985. Program activities: An analysis of their effects on participant behavior. In M Sundel, P Glasser, R Sarri, R Vinter (eds.), *Individual change through small groups* (pp. 226-236). New York: Free Press.

BIBLIOGRAPHY

Alissi A. 1980. *Perspectives on social group work practice: A book of readings.* New York: Free Press.

Burnside IM. 1970. Loss: A constant theme in group work with the aged. *Hosp Comm Psych* 21:173-177.

Corey (Schneider) M, Corey G. 1992. *Groups process and practice,* 4th ed. Pacific Grove, CA: Brooks/Cole.

Douglas T. 1991. *A handbook of common groupwork problems.* London/New York: Routledge.

Whittaker JK. 1985. Program activities: Their selection and use in a therapeutic milieu. In M. Sundel, P Glasser, R Sarri, R Vinter (eds.), *Individual change through small groups* (pp. 237-250). New York: Free Press.

CHAPTER 22

Groups in Day Care Centers

Jean Kittredge Duchesneau

KEY WORDS

- Adult day care
- Adult day health care
- Caregiver
- Community resources
- Inappropriate institutionalization
- Individual plan of care
- Social adult day care
- Support group
- Therapeutic activities

LEARNING OBJECTIVES

- Define adult day care.
- Differentiate the two models of adult day care.
- Identify five elements in an individual plan of care.
- Give an example of how a participant's needs can be met through participation in a group experience.
- Identify three ways a caregiver's needs are met in the group experience.
- Describe two community resources that enhance day care center programs.

Adult day care centers offer a special place for the daytime care of adults who need professional supervision but who do not need 24-hour institutional care. Centers offer fun, friendship, and acceptance to frail or disabled persons who might otherwise be isolated with their problems (Webb 1989, 1). Day care centers create a safe environment where participants can improve or maintain physical and cognitive skills, receive a nutritious meal, and participate in group experiences. The self-esteem of the participants is enhanced and they feel as though they are contributing to their community. Caregivers of the frail and disabled find the day care center a reliable resource for problem solving and a planned source of respite.

This chapter is about the history of day care centers and the many types of groups that are conducted in them. The focus also will be on those programs that primarily serve the older adult population.

HISTORY AND DEVELOPMENT OF ADULT DAY CARE

Day hospitalization programs for the mentally ill date from the 1920s in Europe (Padula 1983). However, the development of adult day care for the aged had a slow beginning in the United States. The U.S. psychiatric community in the 1940s established programs similar to those in Europe for patients at well-known centers, the Menninger Clinic (Wish 1980) and the Yale Psychiatric Clinic (McCuan & Elliott 1976-1977). The day hospital program is still popular today in the mental health community. Dr. Lionel Cosin followed the psychiatric model in developing the first British geriatric day hospital in 1950. It was designed to reduce inpatient hospital stays and used a multidisciplinary approach. In the 1960s, adult day care was introduced to the United States when Dr. Cosin established a program based on his British model at

Cherry State Hospital in Goldsboro, North Carolina (Padula 1983, 1-3).

The Medicare (Title XVIII) and Medicaid (Title XIX) programs of care for the aged and disabled enacted in the early 1960s focused on acute medical care. Nursing homes were the only form of insured long-term care, and reimbursement for their services was provided only in conjunction with hospitalization for an acute medical problem. In many cases, this led to inappropriate institutionalization of the elderly (Blum & Minkler 1980, 134). Inappropriate institutionalization also has a human cost. It was found that the quality of life for older adults who remained in the community and received care was better than for those who entered long-term care facilities (Billings 1982, 2).

By 1973, there were fewer than 15 adult day care programs in the United States (DHEW 1978). That same year, Congress amended Title XX of the Social Security Act and passed Title III of the Older Americans Act. These public policy changes were aimed at assisting persons to achieve or maintain autonomy and preventing or reducing inappropriate institutionalization through provision of community and home-based care alternatives (Blum & Minkler 1980, 135). A funding source was now available for such services as:

- Adult day care.
- Case management.
- Counseling.
- Foster care.
- Homemakers.
- Information and referral.
- Nutrition.
- Recreation.
- Transportation.

In a 1974 policy change, the Department of Health, Education, and Welfare (DHEW) decided to encourage alternatives to institutionalization and agreed to make Medicaid funds available to states for adult day care centers.

The number of adult day care programs has grown steadily. In 1978, 300 programs existed. Two years later, the number rose to 618 (DHEW 1980). Twelve hundred programs were in existence in 1986 (On Lok 1987). The latest estimate by the National Institute on Adult Daycare is 3000 programs nationwide.

FIGURE 22-1   *A new friend or an old friend remembered? Interaction with animals allows participants to express affection and share experiences they may have had with an animal of their own.*

PHOTO: Jean Duchesneau

DEFINING WHAT ADULT DAY CARE DOES

As adult day care developed, arriving at a definition of what it does has posed problems for researchers, practitioners, and legislators. Early researchers in the field attempted to characterize programs by using models (Levindale Geriatric Research Center 1974; Robins 1975; Weissert 1975). These models typically categorized programs as social models and medical models (Weissert 1975).

Regulatory and funding statutes also tried to approach definition by using models. Under Title XIX (Medicaid), participants must need active health care services (medical, nursing, or rehabilitative

FIGURE 22-2 *Group interaction builds a sense of community. Physical exercise is important in maintaining strength and mobility. Exercises can be adapted as needed taking participants' limitations into account.*

PHOTO: Jean Duchesneau

therapies). Title XX (Social Security Act) and Title III (Older Americans Act) do not have this requirement. Professionals in the field have struggled with the model approach. Most agree that programs are a blend of both the social and medical approaches, which allows programs to serve the diversity of needs presented by participants and respond to these needs creatively.

DEFINITION

In 1984, the National Institute on Adult Daycare (NIAD), a constituent unit of the National Council on the Aging, Inc., proposed the following definition as part of its national standards for providing adult day care:

> Adult day care is a community based group program designed to meet the needs of functionally impaired adults through an individual plan of care. It is a structured, comprehensive program that provides a variety of health, social and related services in a protected setting during any part of a day, but less than 24 hour care. Individuals who participate in adult day care attend on a planned basis during specified hours. Adult day care assists its participants to remain in the community, thus enabling families and other caregivers to continue caring for an impaired member at home (NIAD 1984, 20).

This definition distinguished adult day care from other forms of care that may have components of adult day care and that may serve similar populations (Goldston,1989, 4). It also allows adult day care to address adult populations that are not aged but could benefit from adult day care, such as those with degenerative neurological diseases, victims of head trauma, those with disease-related cognitive impairment, and the terminally ill.

PART OF A CONTINUUM OF CARE

There are those who would argue that the more layers the care delivery system has, the more fragmented the understanding of the various components becomes; services become duplicated and the cost of providing services increases. Others would argue that having a range of options from which to develop an individualistic support system is the preferred goal. Adult day care uniquely answers the complaints of the first argument and provides the benefits of the second.

Because adult day care programs offer a basic core of services, whether they lean toward the social or medical model, they are successful in providing the assessment, services, and support needed to meet their clients' needs. When the older adult

FIGURE 22-3 *A nutritious meal offers the opportunity for social interaction and reinforces appropriate eating skills. The staff can help participants with physical impairments learn to use adaptive equipment.*

PHOTO: Jean Duchesneau

and his or her family are faced with needing care and support in order to remain at home rather than living in a nursing home, they become champions of the day care concept. A major problem day care programs have encountered is educating the people they could and should serve about the value of their services and how adult day care can forestall the need for more intensive types of care.

When it is time to utilize other components of the continuum of care, adult day care programs can offer appropriate referral, assurance, and support to their participants and their families as they make caregiving decisions.

THE ADULT DAY CARE SETTING

Day care programs are developed by organizations endeavoring to meet the special needs of a specific group of people and their caregivers. They usually begin with limited resources with which to start a program. Therefore, it is not uncommon to find adult day care programs in diverse settings such as community centers, churches, or other spaces that can be used on a shared basis with other organizations. Very few programs, at least initially, have the resources to enjoy the luxury of a setting that is specifically designed for the purpose of housing an adult day care program.

Regardless of where the program is housed, the atmosphere of the setting should convey to the participants and their families both warmth and security. Change of any kind, particularly for those who are physically and/or mentally frail, is a barrier to participating in care alternatives. The more comfortable the participants and their families feel about the new environment and the staff who provide the care, the less uncomfortable they will feel about the change in routine.

Ideally, there should be enough space to work in large or small groups. If therapy is provided, separate space should be available to house the required equipment and meet any privacy needs of the participants. There should be a place where a client can go to be alone for a period of rest and quiet. Outdoor space is desirable for activities as well as just being outdoors when the weather is pleasant.

GROUPS: AN INTEGRAL PART OF PROGRAM STRUCTURE

The essence of working with older adults in the adult day care setting is the group process. The adult day care staff needs to have a thorough understanding of how to utilize group techniques to create a therapeutic program to meet participants' needs.

How group work is used to create a program in the day care setting begins with meeting the needs of the participant through the individual assessment process. The assessment, done by a trained professional staff person, should be documented and contain information about the participant's abilities in the following areas (Webb 1989, 160-161). They are listed in order of importance:

- Physical status, limitations, and goals.
- Mental status, limitations, and goals.
- Emotional status, limitations, and goals.
- Functional status (activities of daily living and instrumental activities of daily living).
- Nutritional status and limitations.
- Social history and support system.
- Personal strengths and positive aspects of the individual's present life.
- Current and past interests.
- Participant's personal goals.
- Family's or caregiver's expectations.

From this assessment, an individualized plan of care can be established for each participant to meet his or her goals and expectations. Because many participants may have similar needs, goals can be accomplished by using the group process. One way to tie the goals of participants to group formation is to link needs to related activities. (See Table 22-1.)

The table is only a beginning, which can be expanded on by the needs of a particular center's current participants and the creativity of the staff. While each day may have certain program elements that are routine, such as exercise, other elements should vary to make the program meet the participants' needs and for pleasure.

The activities offered need to reflect an adult theme. They need to be meaningful to the participants or useful for others. Childlike activities have no place in an adult day care program unless children are present. Families and the public will receive the wrong impression of the program's value if they perceive that the activities do not have a therapeutic purpose for the participants.

An example of how groups are formed and the varied needs of participants met through one group activity is illustrated by the following:

It was the Tuesday before Easter. Vases filled with bright yellow daffodils were on each of the tables in the kitchen area. Hands had been washed and aprons donned by the participants joining this morning's baking session.

The staff had premeasured muffin ingredients and made the yeast bread dough, but there was still a lot to do. Mamie and Kay chatted back and forth as they mixed the muffins. While most of the men chose to read the morning newspaper, Clarence had joined the women eager to make the bread dough bunnies. Even Marilyn, usually restless and withdrawn, was sitting calmly with the group, watching the progress Mamie and Kay were making with their mixing. There was talk of Easter and Passover traditions and the spring weather that was making the flowers and trees bud out.

Clarence decided that the bigger dough bunnies needed small companions and delicately formed the dough into smaller shapes.

When the mailman brought the day's mail, he lingered a few moments longer than usual, remarking on the delightful aroma. Even those who had chosen not to be part of the group were enticed to join in when it was time to scrape the bowls.

From the example, it is evident that the baking group on this particular morning allowed the participants to work on many of their individual needs and also share in a group experience. There were elements of sensory stimulation, physical exercise, emotional support, socialization, and creativity.

In theory, the use of the group process has measurable outcomes. When this technique is applied to group work in the day care setting, the measurable outcome is how well the group work helps the individual client reach the goals established in his or her individual plan of care.

It is only fair to point out that in the adult day care setting, participants also should be allowed time to enjoy solo activities, have quiet time, and work one-on-one with staff. An example is the participant who expressed an aversion to dogs and cats. When the group was to have pet visitation from the Humane Society, she was allowed to exclude herself from participation in the group experience and even from the area. The staff supported her feelings without pressure or prejudice. Another example is the gentleman who kept a journal. Each day after the noon meal, he was encouraged to write in his journal. On occasion he wanted to discuss the thoughts he was recording with a staff member. Accommodating individual preferences of a particular client is an important part of meeting the client's total needs.

TABLE 22-1 Participants' needs and related activities

Participants' need	Related activity
Emotional expression	• Art therapy • Peer discussion • Reminiscence group • Singing • Writing
Health promotion	• Group work with therapist • Health education groups • Speakers and demonstrations
Intellectual stimulation	• Crossword puzzles • Current events • Discussion group • Logic/reasoning games • Memory games
Physical exercise (Large-motor movements)	• Armchair exercise • Balloon volleyball • Bowling (adapted) • Dancing • Walking
Physical exercise (Small-motor movements)	• Board and card games • Cooking and baking • Crafts • Setting the table
Sensory stimulation	• Dancing • Gardening • Music • Pet visitation • Sensory stimulation games • Singing
Social stimulation	• Discussion groups • Intergenerational activity • Parties and special events • Remotivation therapy

SOURCE: Based on Webb 1989, 166-167.

The physical and mental ability of the participant mix may also determine how much supportive interaction is required from the staff. In forming a group where the participants function at a high physical and/or mental level, the members may be able to be more participatory in preparing the materials needed for a particular activity or not need to adapt the rules of a game. In many adult day care programs, there is a wide range of ability. While each participant should be encouraged to exercise their highest degree of ability, having groups that have mixed ability levels works to everyone's advantage. Those who function well feel they are helping and those less able stretch to do their best. One of the benefits of working with older adults in the adult day care setting is seeing the renewal of an individual's self-esteem. Many individuals have had recent experiences with loss of ability that have placed their self-worth in jeopardy. When they are able to help others, feel a sense of community, and regain or maintain skills, they can go forward with life.

There are other factors that influence how group work is applied to the adult day care setting. The size of the population served and the number and capability of the staff determine how group techniques are applied. In small social model programs, it may be to everyone's benefit to work as a single group, moving through the day on a structured schedule. Programs that serve a large number of clients or have a heavy emphasis on medical services may structure their schedules to allow groups to be formed to work on specific goals.

At Redwood Elderlink in Escondido, California, the adult day care program follows the social model structure and each day serves 15 to 20 participants over 60 years of age. It is a nonprofit program that grew out of a full-service retirement community's desire to serve seniors who lived in the community at large.

On a given day, the staff may work with participants who have one or more of the following medical conditions:

• Arthritis.
• Depression.
• Hearing impairment.
• Mild to moderate dementia (Alzheimer's type).
• Parkinson's disease.
• Stroke.
• Visual impairment.

The program accommodates participants who are in wheelchairs and/or use walkers or canes. It accepts participants who can feed themselves and do not require more than one person's assistance to transfer.

The center is open Monday through Friday and offers a full-day and half-day format to clients and their families. The noon meal is included in both formats as an important component of the program content. The activities surrounding the serving and eating of the meal are important in maintaining physical and social skills. It offers participants opportunities to learn to use adaptive equipment and engage in social communication, and it fosters a sense of community.

TABLE 22-2 Structure of a day in the Redwood Elderlink program

Time/Who	Purpose	Activity choice	Equipment/Supplies	Leader
9 AM/All	Social stimulation Intellectual stimulation Nutrition	Current event Group discussion Morning snack	Newspaper Day/date board Coffee and muffins	Center staff
10 AM/All	Large-motor stimulation	Exercise Walk	Chairs Bean bag weights Ball and balloon	Exercise therapist
11 AM/All or 2 groups	Memory stimulation Intellectual stimulation Fine-motor stimulation	Reminiscence group Cooking and baking	Library materials Ingredients and utensils	Center staff/Volunteer
11:45 AM	Prepare for lunch	Toileting and hand wash		
Noon	Nutrition	Lunch	Hot meal delivered to center from retirement home	Center staff
1 PM	Solo activities Rest period	Quiet time One-on-one	Background music Books and magazines Reclining chair	Center staff available
2 PM/All or 2 groups	Large-motor stimulation Fine-motor stimulation Intellectual stimulation Social stimulation Sensory stimulation	Craft class Music/singing Bingo and bowling Pet visitation	Craft materials Guest entertainers Appropriate equipment	Center staff/Volunteer Community resource person
3 PM/All	Nutrition	Afternoon snack	Juice and cookies	Center staff/Volunteer
3:45 PM/All	Individual reassurance	Prepare for leaving	Personal belongings Toileting	Center staff
4 PM	Participant departure			

The day is structured so that participants have a variety of opportunities to work on their particular needs through the group process. (See Table 22-2.) Because this program currently serves a small number of people and has a limited staff, the participants work as a single group moving through the day on a structured schedule. Each month a calendar is prepared so that participants and their families know what activities are planned and when special entertainment and events are scheduled.

Even with careful preparation, a day may not run smoothly for a variety of reasons, and adjustments are necessary to handle the unforeseen. On one occasion, the weather changed from sunny to dark and blustery due to thunderstorms. The participants became anxious and concerned about how they were going to get home. It took an all-out effort by the staff to keep them focused on the afternoon activity. The curtains were drawn and

bowling was substituted for the scheduled activity so that there was a lot of physical involvement and noise of our own making to drown out the thunder claps. By the time the participants were ready to leave, the storm was over.

Programs serving a small number of people become close knit. New clients need to be helped to integrate into the existing group. It is not uncommon to find one or two participants for whom the role of welcoming the new participant enhances their own goals.

Similarly, small groups more acutely feel the loss of someone who is no longer able to attend the program. It is important to allow the group to express their feelings when a loss occurs. If the person has become ill or requires more care, the group may wish to send a card or show support for the family. The death of a participant is the hardest loss, and the staff may wish to have a spiritual counselor speak to the group.

THE UNHERALDED GROUP: CAREGIVERS

The individual participant is rarely the seeker of services provided by adult day care centers. It is the caregiver who, often reluctantly, seeks the adult day care program as a source of respite from the physical and emotional burden of providing care.

Most day care centers offer some form of support and counseling for the caregivers, usually in the form of a group meeting. On a regular basis the group meets with a professional facilitator who is knowledgeable about older adults. Some centers will schedule several such meetings to accommodate the time constraints of the caregivers. Adult children who work may find an early morning or brown bag lunch meeting fits their work schedules better than an afternoon or evening meeting time. Similarly, spouses may find that it is more convenient to meet closer to the time they transport the participant to the center. (See Chapter 18 on support groups.)

Another consideration of caregiver group formation is the caregivers' emotional needs. Spouses, particularly men caring for women, may have very different concerns from those of adult children caring for parents. Since the purpose of group work with caregivers is to provide an appropriate setting for them to share experiences, gain insight, and find support for their roles, the makeup of these groups is particularly important. (See Table 22-3.)

The facilitator of meetings with caregivers needs to allow individuals to express their feelings and seek solutions from members of the group, but also has to have a carpetbag of resources to answer specific, technical concerns that are frequently expressed. Professionals—psychologists, financial planners, and attorneys—may be needed to bring peace of mind to caregivers with special problems.

ENHANCING PROGRAMS WITH COMMUNITY RESOURCES

Adult day care programs can stretch their staff and financial resources and add to program diversity by using community resources. In many communities, adult education programs and community colleges offer to provide instruction on various topics if the adult day care center will agree to be a community classroom. The adult day care participants look forward to visiting instructors who present special activities, and the adult day care program receives exposure as a community resource.

TABLE 22-3   Concerns expressed in caregiver support groups

Spouses
- Managing resources.
- Loss of conjugal fellowship.
- Assuming responsibility for personal care.
- Lack of freedom.
- Handling behavioral changes.

Adult children
- Reversal of the parent–child role.
- Juggling career and/or family schedules.
- Invasion of privacy.
- Guilt about not doing enough.
- Financial burden.

Other caregivers (relatives or friends)
- Unwanted responsibility.
- Lack of proper authority.
- Time commitment.

Volunteers who are willing to support the program with their time and talents offer extra support to participants and staff. By utilizing this type of support, staff can plan special activities such as an outing to a ball game or a picnic in a local park.

Youth organizations, such as Scout troops, are looking for experiences to interact with older adults to complete the requirements of a merit badge. In some cases, they are seeking an opportunity to talk with older people, but often they can prepare and present a special program.

As a rule of thumb, most adult day care programs strive to provide dignified experiences for clients at the lowest dollar cost. Through liaisons with groups that also have a desire to serve older adults and the community, all programs are winners.

SUMMARY

Whether the group work in the adult day care setting is formal or informal, it must preserve the dignity and quality of life for everyone. By choice, no one would volunteer to be a participant in such a program, for we all value our independence and autonomy. Programs of adult day care strive to restore and maintain the frail older person at his or her highest level of functioning, in the least restrictive environment, for as long as possible. They also seek to support the caregiver with the physical and emotional burden of caring for a loved one.

EXERCISE 1

Mr. M suffered a stroke six months ago, which left him partially paralyzed. He is mentally alert but has difficulty expressing himself. During his rehabilitation, he learned to dress, feed, and toilet himself and to walk with a quad cane. Since he has been at home, he demands that his wife attend to his needs and is losing much of his ability to care for himself.

Mr. M has been enrolled in the adult day care program because his wife is feeling exhausted and overwhelmed by his behavior.

1. Identify three needs to include in Mr. M's plan of care.
2. Suggest three group activities that would help Mr. M achieve his care goals.
3. Describe how you would support Mrs. M's situation.

EXERCISE 2

You are a program aide in an adult day care program. You have noticed that several of the participants have broken and rough fingernails. Your program director has given you permission to lead a nail grooming activity.

1. Briefly outline how you would organize this group activity.
2. Make a list of supplies you will need and their cost.
3. What other health promotion issues related to the hands can be discussed?
4. Name one community resource who might help you.

EXERCISE 3

Music is a favorite group activity among older adults. They love to listen to, sing with, and dance to melodies they remember from various periods in their lives. A volunteer is scheduled to play some oldies from the thirties. You wish to expand and enhance her visit.

1. Research the popular composers of the thirties and their best-loved songs.
2. What dance steps were popular in the thirties?
3. Name two ways music helps achieve participant care goals.

REFERENCES

Billings G. 1982. Alternatives to nursing home care: An update. *Aging* 11(2):325-326.

Blum SR, Minkler M. 1980. Toward a continuum of caring alternatives: Community based care for the elderly. *J Soc Issues* 36(2):133-152.

Department of Health, Education, and Welfare. 1978. *Directory of adult day care centers.* Washington, DC: Health Care Financing Administration (HCFA).

———. 1980. *Directory of adult day care centers.* Washington, DC: HCFA.

Goldston S. 1989. *Adult day care: A basic guide.* Owings Mills, MD: National Health Publishing.

Levindale Geriatric Research Center. 1974. *Preliminary analysis of select geriatric day care programs.* Washington, DC: DHEW.

McCuan E, Elliott M. 1976-77. Geriatric day care in theory and practice. *Soc Work Health Care* 2(2):153-170.

National Institute on Adult Daycare. 1984. *Standards for adult day care.* Washington, DC: National Council on the Aging, Inc. (NCA).

On Lok Senior Health Services. 1987. *Directory of adult day care in America.* Washington, DC: NCA.

Padula H. 1983. *Developing adult day care: An approach to maintaining independence for impaired older persons.* Washington, DC: NCA.

Robins E. 1975. Operational research in geriatric day care in the United States. Paper presented at the Tenth International Congress on Gerontology in Israel.

Webb LC. 1989. *Planning and managing adult day care: Pathways to success.* Owings Mills, MD: National Health Publishing.

Weissert W. 1975. *Adult day care in the United States. A transcentury report.* Washington, DC: DHEW.

Wish F. 1980. Day care: Its value for the older adult and his family. *J Jewish Communal Serv* 174-180.

BIBLIOGRAPHY

Burnside IM (ed.). 1980. *Psychosocial nursing care of the aged,* 2d ed. (pp. 145-159). New York: McGraw-Hill.

————. 1980. *Psychosocial nursing care of the aged,* 2d ed. (pp. 145-159). New York: McGraw-Hill.

1986. *Working with the elderly: Group process and techniques,* 2d ed. Boston: Jones and Bartlett.

Eliopoulos C. 1990. *Caring for the elderly in diverse care settings.* Philadelphia: Lippincott.

Hanley I, Gilhooly M. 1986. *Psychological therapies for the elderly* (pp. 80-100). New York: New York University Press.

Kaye LW, Kirwin PM. 1990. Adult day care services for the elderly and their families: Lessons from the Pennsylvania experience. *J Gerontol Soc Work* 15(3/4):167-179. (Special double issue on Health care of the aged: Needs, policies, and services.)

Standards and Guidelines for Adult Day Care. 1990. Washington D.C.: NCA.

RESOURCES

Sharing the Caring: Adult Day Care. A VHS video that educates the public about the concept of adult day care by highlighting its benefits to clients and to caregivers. Washington, DC: NCA; phone: 800-424-9046.

Respite Report. A publication of the Bowman Gray School of Medicine, Wake Forest University, highlighting adult day care and dementia care issues particularly as they relate to the "Partners in Caregiving: The Dementia Services Program" that is funded by the Robert Wood Johnson Foundation. Antonia Monk Reaves is the editor. Available from the Department of Psychiatry and Behavioral Medicine, Bowman Gray School of Medicine, Medical Center Blvd., Winston-Salem, NC 27157-1087; phone: 919-716-4941.

Annotated Bibliography on Adult Day Programs and Dementia Care. This publication is designed to serve as a reference guide to day center staff, caregivers, and experts in the field of aging. There are two main sectons: Section I—Adult Day Programs, Section II—Dementia Care. The bibliography is indexed by subject matter. To order, send $7.95 plus $2.00 for shipping and handling to: National Alzheimer's Association, Attn: Inquiries Processing, 919 N. Michigan Avenue, Suite 1000, Order No. PF 1052, Chicago, IL 60611; phone: 800-272-3900. Also available from NCA, Attn: Rose Russell, Department of Administrative Services, 409 Third Street, Second Floor, Washington, DC 20024; phone: 202-479-6957.

CHAPTER 23

Reminiscence Groups in Board-and-Care Homes

Janet E. Black, Sally A. Friedlob, and James J. Kelly

KEY WORDS

- Confidentiality
- Life skills
- Relationships
- Reminiscence agents
- Scanning
- Team

LEARNING OBJECTIVES

- Describe a comprehensive model program for treating older adults at a board-and-care facility.
- Explain the individual professional roles and their relationship to standard roles in a multidisciplinary team approach to treating aged clients in a care home.
- Explain the advantages and disadvantages of a large group in a board-and-care home.
- Define five agents of reminiscence.
- List five relevant activities that facilitate reminiscence in a care home and the rationale for their use.
- Explain three obstacles, problems, or management issues that could arise when undertaking a reminiscence program.

Maturity for every individual depends on previous sequential developmental phenomena (Erikson 1950), because during each period of human development there are unique presenting issues and opportunities. Daub (1983) states that through the

Acknowledgment: The authors would like to thank Jane Manning, registered dance therapist, for her clinical contributions to this project. George Saslow, M.D., served as an educator, role model, and group work consultant. Murray Brown, M.D.; Richard Chung, M.D.; Fran Kelly, O.T.R.; Norma Donigan, M.S.W.; Betsy Alkire; and Judith Coleman Maurella provided the necessary support to survive the system.

process of adaptation, the individual explores these issues and opportunities, solves problems, learns, and grows. When stress interrupts development, however, individuals may adapt by regressing or stagnating. For example, for an individual who had lived independently for the majority of his or her life, a move to a board-and-care facility can be a highly stressful life event. To cope with this stress, an individual may adapt by blending into the surroundings, thereby inhibiting growth and/or failing to maintain his or her current level of functioning.

Therefore, when working with individuals in a board-and-care setting, one needs a thorough understanding of the developmental processes and related phenomena. The worker can then assist clients in adaptation that encourages growth by providing experiences that foster more successful coping skills.

Individuals also undergo many physiological changes during the natural maturation process of aging. Among these is possible loss of cognitive functioning. Clients sometimes display diminution of recent recall and reduced speed in learning; they show difficulty in integrating sensory input and output; and at times they are confused.

Another major cognitive characteristic of the geriatric life stage is the ability to retrieve past memories with clarity and detail. Herein lies a major asset that can be the foundation for building structure and function in successful adaptation. The phenomenon of reminiscence is an essential element in the continuing development of the older adult and can be utilized as an effective means of intervention in board-and-care homes because it is the one element that cuts across all special problems of individuals in these homes (Butler 1963; Butler, Lewis & Sunderland 1991).

Although there has been recent debate about the homogeneity or heterogeneity of the aged in board and care, generally the placement includes individuals undergoing the normal aging processes and three categories of individuals with an additional variety of special problems. The first of these three categories is former mental patients, carrying a diagnosis of chronic schizophrenia, who have been confined in hospitals for a major part of their lives. These individuals have coped with stress by regressing to earlier developmental stages. They have deficits in their social/emotional development, cognitive functioning, and perceptual motor development. They are typically withdrawn, shy, and egocentric and have poor posture and poor fine coordination. They have difficulty learning new tasks by trial and error, abstracting a sequence of ideas, and visualizing covert imagery. Long after the schizophrenic symptoms have been in remission, they have retained regressed behaviors acquired during their years of institutionalization. The term *burned-out schizophrenic* has been used to describe members of this group.

Individuals with other mental disorders in remission are a second type of client. These clients cannot manage in an independent setting and need the support and structure a board-and-care offers. They, too, have social/emotional deficits, and often lowered cognitive functioning is involved. Typically, they have difficulty in forming interpersonal relationships and demonstrate poor problem-solving abilities.

Individuals with neurological and medical conditions constitute a third category of client. These clients are found less frequently because board-and-care settings require independence in ambulation, continence, and self-care. Because those with neurological conditions must meet these requirements, the neurological involvement is minimal. Generally, the neurological condition involves upper motor neurons. The lesion may be located in the brain due to cerebrovascular accident (stroke) or head injury; or lesions may be located in the extrapyramidal system due to Parkinson's disease. In either case, deficits in perception, problem solving, personality, behavior, proprioception, sensation, stereognosis, hearing, sight, coordination, and voluntary or involuntary motion may be present.

After reviewing the heterogeneous issues of clients residing in board-and-care facilities, we are struck by the need for intervention that facilitates growth and adaptation. We are struck also by the particular need for group treatment because of its potential for helping clients discover the "universality" of their thoughts, feelings, impulses, and desires—in short, for helping them learn that they are not so different as they had thought. Yalom (1975) identifies *universality* as a major curative factor.

Despite the individual problems and deficits, there is one homogeneous factor shared by all clients—that is, all are aging and therefore share the ability to reminisce with clarity and detail. Thus, reminiscence is the one element that cuts across all special issues. Regardless of their impairment, all individuals respond to familiar activities that draw on previously learned tasks and experiences.

Familiar activities employ well-known motor schemes and facilitate abstract imagery and conception of end results. Activities utilizing established learning skills increase self-confidence and self-esteem. Therefore, they promote pleasurable experiences that encourage trust. A major benefit of employing reminiscence for all clients is marked growth in social/emotional development (Birren & Deutchman 1991; Magee 1988). This aspect of human growth encompasses the 12 general categories of curative factors developed by Yalom (1975).

Reminiscence also has an impact on the naturally occurring process of life review, important for putting into perspective one's successes as well as one's unresolved conflicts during the geriatric life stage (Lewis & Butler 1974; Magee 1988). Life review is especially important for the individual in a board-and-care home, who often feels cast aside by society.

In discussing the utilization of reminiscence in group intervention, the literature defines specific group therapy procedures, but the groups described are verbal only; group members individually explore and then share their memories (Ebersole 1978; Myers, Podevant & Dean 1991; Zimpfer 1987). *However, the authors contend that the therapeutic technique of reminiscence can take many forms.* Some involve movement, visualization, cooking, art, music, task planning, and activities of daily living. These activities provide opportunities not only for life review but also for growth and adaptation in all areas of human development—physical, sensory, perceptual, cognitive, social, and emotional. These phenomena, according to Willard and Spackman (Hopkins & Smith 1980), are intricately interwoven, and issues, stresses, or gains that take place in one area will bring changes in another.

THE ADVANTAGE OF THE MULTIDISCIPLINARY TEAM

The multidisciplinary team approach to rehabilitation-program planning and implementation has a distinct advantage in the board-and-care setting. As previously discussed, agents of reminiscence can take many forms. During a two- to four-hour session, a team can employ several reminiscence agents so that growth in one area will influence growth in another area. As King (1970) states, often there is little the staff can do to decrease external stress; however, the staff can help clients enhance their adjusting resources. Furthermore, a variety of modalities facilitates the clients' motivation, attention span, and tolerance for sitting and group interaction.

Each team member can provide experience in his or her area of expertise. Ideally, the team members complement each other so that the blending of resources facilitates effective, methodical treatment planning. For example, the movement therapist can initiate the session by providing a group

experience that stimulates pleasure centers in the body. This pleasure stimulation is critical, because clients who have been sedentary and have had little sensory stimulation often fail to experience pleasurable body sensations, a lack that decreases risk-taking behaviors in perception, cognition, and social/emotional growth. Thus, movement facilitates experiences that increase trust, decrease anxiety, and encourage growth in integrating sensory and motor abilities. The occupational therapist can then introduce an activity that requires increased attention span, orientation, concentration, and tolerance to sitting. The occupational therapist also can promote maintenance of cognition stimulated during movement and can facilitate an increase in functional level by utilizing familiar simple problem-solving tasks that can be readily recalled and mastered. The social worker and the nurse can expand on the treatment process by assisting clients in integrating their group experience through verbalization.

A major advantage to a multidisciplinary team approach is that a large number of clients can be treated in a group setting. Although the current literature emphasizes small-group treatment, a large group can be treated effectively with a team approach. Such an approach can ensure the inclusion of all clients in each session, which is vital in working with this type of client. Thus, team members can serve as co-therapists who provide mutual support and assistance in facilitating and processing a session.

Furthermore, each team member can provide training for students in his or her respective field, and the participation of students provides several advantages. They bring enthusiasm, youth, and stimulation to board-and-care clients. They offer an opportunity to encourage clients to impart advice drawn from past experiences and assist in student training, which closes the generation gap and promotes mutual growth, especially in self-confidence and self-esteem. In addition, during group activities students can be paired with clients requiring individual attention outside of the group process. Thus, in a large group, one-on-one treatment can be provided. Another benefit in utilizing students is that students learn early in their training about resources offered by other disciplines, as well as about ways to work with other disciplines to provide more effective client treatment. See Chapters 7, 30, 31, and 32, which elaborate on teaching students.

Still another advantage of the team approach is that other services can be provided during group activities. For example, doctors and nurses can assess patients individually for medical and psychosocial needs during a session. Medical students also can be included in the group process, along with social work and occupational therapy students. In addition, young doctors must be oriented early in their training to be sensitive to these clients' total needs. This training still is often excluded from the medical model as well as the nursing model.

Volunteers can be another effective resource for the team. They can include individuals who would benefit equally from group process to meet their emotional and social needs. For example, community members such as senior citizens or young psychiatric clients who have been isolated can be extremely helpful. In addition to being sensitive and empathetic to clients, these individuals can meet their own needs to be altruistic and to give and receive nurturance. Because volunteers need guidance and structure, however, the team must take care to plan for sufficient volunteer guidance. See Chapter 28, which discusses volunteers.

DEVELOPMENT OF INTERPERSONAL RELATIONSHIPS

To initiate a program at a board-and-care facility, three essential interpersonal relationships must be carefully developed. These are the relationships between members of the multidisciplinary team, team members and the board-and-care personnel, and team members and the clients.

Relationships within the Team

Linden (1953) found that working with the aged in a process group is exhausting, because clients require constant stimulation and individual attention. He concluded that co-leadership in group work is essential. Furthermore, believing that productive intervention depends on cohesion between the leaders, he outlined 10 essential components contributing to effective communication (see Chapter 4). The authors confirm Linden's findings and believe that management of a large group particularly requires co-therapy. In addition, we found that a large group presents special leadership issues.

Staff must be experienced professionals with a strong background in group leadership and co-therapy. Co-leaders need to communicate on multiple levels. Concurrent with dual communications and client group processing, they must guide and supervise students, volunteers, and board-and-care personnel. The demands of the position include sharp attention to detail, including constant scanning of each individual; sensitivity to the environment at all times; and continual dynamic processing of the various interactions. Judgments about setting up interactions, intervening, facilitating, and integrating material as it develops are a minute-by-minute process. These qualifications are absolutely necessary if leaders are to undertake, without disaster, a large group of 20 to 30 clients in a board-and-care. See Chapter 10 for a description of the aspects of co-leadership.

Team members need to be flexible, open to new ideas, and willing to explore their own feelings and defenses. Although each person contributes knowledge unique to his or her profession, each must be open to sharing responsibilities. Often, skills overlap professional boundaries. Territoriality, which can be destructive to group cohesion, can have a negative impact on clients, who are generally sensitive to staff process issues, by producing anxiety and conflicting attitudes toward supportive figures. On the other hand, conflicts cannot be overlooked; denial does not preclude conflict, and the feelings emerge covertly or overtly. Either way, denial will be deleterious to the prime work of the team, namely, client adaptation.

Conflicts can be discussed during regularly scheduled staff meetings. Differences of opinion, however, also can be dealt with during a treatment session. Satir, Staehowiak, and Taschmann (1975) have found, in their work with families in therapy, that this method sets an effective model for clients. The staff pull their chairs into the middle of the group with the clients around them and discuss issues face-to-face until there is closure. Staff then return their chairs to the outer circle with the clients and continue with treatment. The authors have found this approach to be effective in group work with older adults. It affords an opportunity to: (1) build trust toward staff, because they are open; (2) recognize that staff are human, with human flaws and feelings, rather

FIGURE 23-1 *Cooking and preparation of food is an activity enjoyed by older men and women. Note the plastic containers, which are preferable to breakable ones; also they are light weight. The man on the left appears to be struggling to separate paper muffin liners. Having them separated ahead of time might reduce frustration and speed the process.*

PHOTO: Marianne Gontarz

than condescending, inexperienced young people who think they are in control; (3) avoid staff resentment, which might build through a session when feelings were not discussed and which would affect client treatment; (4) prevent splits between staff and clients; and (5) model methods for clients to express feelings.

The final opportunity is worth expanding. Many clients are resentful and angry toward family members, board-and-care personnel, and other clients. They may resent team members, who they feel are controlling their lives by requiring group participation. Many have been taught that anger is not a polite feeling to express; because they fear rejection if anger is expressed, they repress their feelings. Unexpressed anger perpetuates depression and physiological illness and can lead to decompensation. By dealing with conflict openly, staff model communication skills and demonstrate that they have neither died nor become ill, nor have they been offended by another's anger. They also demonstrate the possibility of growth and increased warmth in a relationship in which taboo subjects can be discussed. Again, this method can be utilized only in an atmosphere where a close working relationship has been established by highly skilled leaders.

Satir (1972) has likened effective teamwork to a dance in which the co-therapists move gracefully and rhythmically in step together. Therefore, they must seat themselves so that they can watch each other and pick up cues from facial expression, body gestures, and eye contact. Body language will help them to employ the skills and confirming judgments previously discussed.

Team Relationship with Board-and-Care Personnel

The relationship between the multidisciplinary team and the board-and-care personnel needs to be carefully cultivated. While board-and-care operators are receptive to improving the quality of their programs and thereby maintaining their certification status, they may be threatened by the overwhelming power they have assigned to a professional team. Often, they fear they will be under scrutiny by the team, who will recommend that their certification be suspended. This apprehension can be advantageous in assisting clients. Mere team presence encourages board-and-care operators to maintain and upgrade services provided for clients, utilize client monies earnestly, and interact with clients respectfully. On the other hand, the presence of team members can evoke resentment and resistance. Personnel may experience disruption in their regular routines and may displace their frustrations onto clients, thereby hindering the team's primary purpose.

Therefore, before initiating a client-centered group, the co-leaders must establish rapport with the board-and-care operators and personnel. Purposeful inclusion of personnel in treatment sessions, with verbal and/or written credit for their participation, is essential. Courtesies, such as assisting personnel with cleanup, also are important. In general, the team needs to be sensitive to the needs of the personnel. Existing creative programs and positive client involvement must be acknowledged. Nevertheless, personnel may view the team as condescending in usurping leadership roles. Some of the personnel may have been highly involved with clients over many years and may feel their efforts are being negated by the so-called experts.

In addition, personnel must deal with what they view as the insurmountable and draining issues of the aged on a 24-hour basis. Therefore, they may feel resentful toward team members entering the home one session per week with a full entourage of staff offering "ideal" advice. Of course, the personnel may feel gratitude, relief, hope, and stimulation by having additional support and assistance. The team, however, must be aware of the total perspective. Everyone needs the esteem derived from receiving credit for a job well done. As previously discussed, the results of recognition are reflected in client attitudes and care. Mutual exchange of ideas should be given mutual professional respect. Finally, the therapeutic relevance of maintaining this special relationship needs to be imparted to students, who can hinder the process if this training is omitted.

Relationship between Team and Clients

The importance of the relationship between the team members and the clients should be underscored. A well-functioning team with respect for one another does not pass unnoticed by clients.

A MODEL PROGRAM

Initiating the Program

Entering the Board-and-Care Home. Although in many cases one of the first problems faced by the group leader is the need to gain entrance into an institution (Burnside 1978), such was not the case in the following model, which includes a detailed description of the program and the way entry was facilitated.

In January 1975, the psychiatry service in a large medical center reorganized from a medical model to a community psychiatry model. Each inpatient ward became a mental health center serving clients living in a particular geographical catchment area in the community. Each center was to provide inpatient crisis treatment, establish a multipurpose satellite center for outpatient treatment, establish working relationships with and provide education about mental health from community members, and assist clients in utilizing the community's resources. One philosophical belief in initiating such a program was that the rapport established among the medical center, the community, and the clients on a more personal level would ultimately have a greater benefit for clients with mental health disabilities than traditional medical models. Staff could better assist clients in making a transition from the hospital to the community by providing services that helped clients remain in the community for longer periods of time with shorter rehospitalization periods. They could encourage clients to seek help before hospitalization became a necessity.

In the spring of 1977, the authors were actively involved in program development with the research team at the community satellite center. The satellite was housed in a progressive community church, which allowed use of its facilities as part of the church's commitment to community action programs. The postdoctorate social worker, Jim Kelly, was involved not only in expanding his clinical skills but also in serving as a consulting expert in the field of gerontology. The occupational therapist, Sally Friedlob, was co-developer and clinical coordinator for a life-skills training and research program designed to assist clients with psychosocial disabilities in reintegrating into the community and in developing evening resource programs at the satellite center. The older adults comprised a target population that the mental health center had not reached. To meet the needs of the aged, the authors decided to initiate an evening program once a week at the satellite center.

Because extensive groundwork had been laid by the authors and the community social work service, the board-and-care operators were receptive to the idea. The satellite center was chosen for the group work for specific reasons: (1) to involve the aged in a community experience, to decrease feelings of isolation and feelings that they were society's castoffs; (2) to utilize the satellite center for a variety of community programs, to obtain community acceptance and participation; (3) to connect the older adults with the existing state geriatric program housed within the church; (4) to involve some of the clients in a possible grandparent program with preschool children; (5) to increase motivation and functional capacity to each individual's fullest potential by providing the stimulation of a new environment; (6) to increase reality orientation by holding the group in a special room at the same time each week; and (7) to provide stimulation by enabling clients to experience a weekly ride in an automotive vehicle.

In the first two attempts to initiate the program at the satellite center, the clients failed to attend. Therefore, for the third session the authors decided to take the program to the facility. They found that failure to attend was due to poor communication between day and evening personnel, lack of personnel coverage, low personnel interest, transportation problems, and financial problems. The physical needs of many of the clients dictated that working in the board-and-care setting would be logistically preferable. In addition, a large number of clients could receive desperately needed services. Although half of the clients were not qualified for direct services at the medical center, the authors believed that they were justified in treating the entire population, because the community psychiatry model encourages exchanges in services and programs among a variety of agencies.

The population was mixed and included outpatients with chronic psychosocial disabilities, former state mental hospital residents, and older adults from the community who needed the structure provided by a facility. Upon seeing familiar clients who had actively participated in a resocialization program one-and-a-half years earlier, the occupational therapist was appalled by their appearances. They had regressed in social skills, they displayed retarded motor activity, they were emaciated and showed little affect, and their grooming and clothing were poorly kept. More of the board-and-care population were withdrawn and appeared depressed.

After interviewing clients, the authors found that few knew the names of people with whom

they were living. During mealtimes, clients rarely spoke to each other. Most sat isolated all day; some drank coffee and smoked cigarettes, watching television occasionally. Most slept much of the day and evening. Three full meals were served daily, and clients were given an evening snack. Although the rooms were bare, the facility was kept clean and neat. The authors concluded that a major contributing factor to the apparent depression of the clients was the lack of nurturance, interpersonal connections, and stimulation. The authors concluded that a reminiscence program would be the total intervention for reasons discussed earlier in this chapter.

Creative Staffing and Administrative Issues.
The authors decided to implement the program one evening per week for a three-hour period (6 P.M. to 9 P.M.) after the dinner hour, because this time frame avoided interfering with the responsibilities of the board-and-care personnel. The authors functioned as co-therapists and included in their team a highly experienced registered movement therapist, occupational therapy students, social work students, nursing students, and medical students. The students rotated through the program; the number of weeks of participation depended on their schedules. Older adults from the community volunteered to assist in programming.

A unique part of the program was that a group of young outpatients served as volunteers. These young adults, who had completed an intensive inpatient life skills training program (Friedlob 1982), had been discharged to their own apartments or to cooperative housing. They had increased their social skills during the training, but they required community follow-up in order to maintain treatment gains. Most were overly concerned with their own well-being—an egocentrism that inhibited their awareness of others and affected their social skills.

The young adults met with the multidisciplinary team for dinner before the board-and-care evening program, going out for dinner or rotating dinners at the outpatients' apartments. Everyone contributed money toward groceries, did the shopping, and assisted in cooking the meal. The group used the dinner hour to plan the board-and-care session and to purchase ingredients for the session's cooking activities.

Another unusual aspect was that some of the young adults living in the board-and-care home formed relationships with their peers and participated in the volunteer program. These outpatients formed friendships that they continued throughout the week. Some of the young adults formed relationships with older adults at the board-and-care home and worked individually with them during a session. These social interactions and the young people's sense of altruism decreased their self-conscious behaviors and their psychiatric symptoms by allowing them to be less concerned about their own psychological well-being and social adequacy.

The co-therapists served as role models, providing leadership in program development, clinical expertise, client and student education and supervision, liaison with the medical center's research team and administrative personnel, and liaison with the university faculty. The co-therapists also were responsible for coordinating programmatic needs with the board-and-care administration. Arrangements for space, refreshments, and equipment (such as pianos) were made. The team continually strove for a combined effort in setting goals, planning implementation, and communicating about health care and staffing issues. The team was able to manage the varied needs of 20 to 30 board-and-care clients for the reasons previously discussed (see the previous section, Advantage of the Multidisciplinary Team).

Implementing this program was beneficial to the medical center, the taxpayers, and to the board-and-care facility. The board-and-care home received free services from skilled professionals who would have been far too expensive for it to employ. Furthermore, the activity program contributed to the status of the home in maintaining its certification. The taxpayers saved money in that the cost per day of hospitalizing a client is more than that of maintaining a client in the community. The medical center paid only small stipends to students and no salary to volunteers. The occupational therapist was able to treat a large number of outpatients during the weekly sessions. The postdoctoral social worker and the movement therapists were paid a flat consultant fee by the psychiatry service, which saved tax money. In addition, because the occupational therapy department budget included funds for supplies—such as cooking ingredients, equipment, and other materials, which qualified as treatment requisites in training patients in living skills essential to maintain a particular living environment—the board-and-care residents received additional benefits.

Reminiscence Program Goals

The ultimate goal of the program was to enhance clients' adjustive resources and therein facilitate growth and adaptation. To fulfill this goal, nine objectives were identified. Reminiscence experiences were aimed at providing opportunities for:

- Reality orientation.
- Sensory stimulation.
- Socialization.
- Friendship networks.
- Capitalizing on retained strengths (physical, sensory, perceptual, cognitive, social, emotional).
- Retraining in lost skill areas.
- Building confidence in retained skill areas.
- Supporting independence (by allowing decision making and encouraging autonomy in carrying out tasks when feasible).
- Increasing self-esteem (through opportunities listed above).

Program Structure

A routine program structure is important in assisting older adults with retention of recent memories and reality orientation. When these individuals know exactly what to expect, their sense of physical security and their self-confidence to risk participation are increased. Furthermore, motivation can be encouraged if the routine provides a pleasurable experience. For the aged, pleasure can be derived simply by purposeful activity that has been mastered by repeated familiar rehearsals and/or experiences. Routine need not lead to boredom. *Creativity can be explored within a structured program.* The information summarized in Table 23-1 is an outline of the basic plan used in this program, the rationale for the sequencing of events, and examples of related creative activities that were incorporated into the familiar routines.

Large-Group Involvement. Burnside (1976) states that students often get carried away and feel that group work is like cooking potatoes—one more will not matter very much. Yalom (1975), Levine (1979), and others state that unless clients

TABLE 23-1 Outline of basic program plan, rationale for sequence, and associated activities

Regularly structured program	Rationale for programmatic sequencing	Example of creative activities
Opening greetings	Orient to a purposeful beginning. Orient to new individuals. Reinforce memory of familiar persons. Convey feelings of individual importance by remembering client's name. A name or nickname is extremely important for self-identification. Names have many meanings and implications. "This is who I am."	*Through movement:* Say your name and everyone will say your name and copy your movement. *Game:* New staff and students will go around the room and try to remember everyone's name and movement (with creative cueing when students stumble; it is important to remember everyone). Clients sometimes feel good if they can stump a student briefly.
Getting clients who have not attended because they are isolated in their rooms, outside, or sleeping	Everyone needs to feel that he or she is important enough to be remembered. Everyone likes to feel included in the group process rather than left on the fringes. Clients need to be included early in the session to reinforce participation and orientation to date, time, and place.	Other clients assisted in getting each other once relationship had been formed. Younger clients who played guitars serenaded older client to group. Familiar jokes and storytelling before joining the group can be instituted to motivate clients.
Movement therapy	Developmentally, movement emerges from other abilities. Movement is the plane on which primal learning must take place, and it is the cognitive level that must be integrated before higher thought processes can evolve (Levy 1974). Creates a warm atmosphere and pleasurable physical experiences. Decreases anxiety, to prepare the group for forthcoming activities. Increases interaction and trust among individuals through shared experiences without having to verbalize cognitively integrated experiences (at the early stage).	Movement geared to expressing aspects of a particular holiday. Movement that grows out of a client's spontaneous action or reaction.
Music therapy period: music (harmonica, percussion, brass) and movement	Music was often used in conjunction with movement. Music stimulates affect, mood, and expression of feelings. Music was generally a natural outgrowth of movement. Clients frequently broke out in song after moving or wanted to perform for others; for example, one man brought his harmonica to play; another a guitar. Singing familiar songs from a book printed in large type stimulated vision, hearing, and following a familiar sequence and helped task conceptualization. Promoted increased trust and camaraderie among individuals.	Individuals in movement spontaneously pantomiming piano playing from time to time sat at the piano and played familiar songs while the group moved. Percussion instruments were included in a sing-along. Instruments were spontaneously created from familiar objects such as wax paper and combs.
Task planning group	Clients are now ready to sit for a longer period, with increased attention span and receptivity to ideas. Familiar tasks involving decision making increase self-esteem and the feeling of autonomy. Tasks require negotiation, compromise, expression of feelings, and sharing of ideas.	Planning next week's treat or special program. Planning a group project and carrying it out; for example, making simple learning toys for the children at Head Start (using familiar pictures from magazines for flash card words). Planning homework activities, such as taking a walk with a friend.

TABLE 23-1 *Continued*

	High-level thought processes are now ready to evolve.	Planning utilization of the community's resources.
Life skills activity: cooking	By this time, clients need a break that reinforces participation. Response is positive to oral gratification. Cooking, which involves familiar simple problem-solving task follow-through, reinforces higher-level thought processes and can be an extremely pleasurable and beneficial venture.	
Verbal psychodynamic group	Part of closure requires integration of evening's experience through verbalization.	Formal reminiscence group initiated by social worker.
	Clients need to convey unexpressed thoughts and feelings.	
	Clients have been stimulated and need to calm down before retiring.	
Formal goodbye	Orient clients to time.	Goodbye songs—such as "Goodnight Irene" and "Goodbye, Farewell" song from *The Sound of Music*—can be sung at the door.
	A formal goodnight hug or handshake for each person reinforces personal worth and friendship.	
	Provides reassurance of closure for those worried that they will not see the staff again. Provides hope that "we will meet again" (during the early stage).	

are carefully selected, the majority of patients assigned to group therapy will terminate treatment discouraged and without benefits; the authors, in managing a large, unselected group, found quite the contrary.

The leaders of this group, however, were highly skilled and experienced, and they had the advantage of adequate support systems. A number of guidelines for managing a large group have already been discussed, but a few additional comments are necessary. First, clients are never to be treated like another potato. In undertaking the program, the leaders carefully considered the physical and emotional needs of each client. Furthermore, the co-leaders were responsible for ensuring that each client was actively acknowledged and included in each session.

The primary technique found to be relevant for this size group was scanning. The co-leaders observed each individual successively clockwise and then counterclockwise throughout the session. At any given moment, co-therapists were aware of the physical location, facial expressions, verbalizations, and so on, of a particular client. Periodically, while one co-leader or allied staff member directed an activity, the other co-leader(s) scanned the group, picking up behaviors that required intervention. For example, one client's left leg began quivering while he was standing with the group in group exercise. A co-therapist used eye contact and subtle hand signals to direct a student to assist the client, who was able to complete the activity from his chair.

To help with scanning and other activities, higher functioning clients and team members can be seated next to those who need assistance. Staff can be redirected as necessary. Staff members should be positioned so that they can clearly see each other. Following are three other strategies for large-group management.

Small Groups. With adequate staffing, the large group can be broken into smaller groups. One method utilized in the program was to assemble the entire group for a given activity in order to explain it, and then to break into smaller groups. Upon task completion, group members rejoined to share their small-group experiences briefly.

Leadership for each small group was carefully assessed, given the assets and limitations of team members. The small-group leader had to be able to give directions clearly and to handle group issues. For example, an occupational therapy student was able to manage an art group that stimulated remote recall and then discussed content and process issues. A volunteer outpatient was able to lead a small group successfully in a cooking activity, such as baking a stir-and-frost cake, while a student served as an assistant. This strategy increased the level of participation and the self-esteem for the volunteer.

Dyads. Dyads, or pairs, proved to be another constructive means of working with a large group. Clients who worked in pairs created new friendships that carried over to daily routines. One pair, for example, began to take the bus to the satellite center two times per week, where they interacted in a therapeutic social club and participated in the senior citizens' lunch program. Dyads were utilized in task activities, such as making a Christmas decoration. They were used to personalize a group activity. For example, the leader directed the group to turn to a neighbor and discuss what he or she thought about the current topic. In addition, dyads were used in training clients to ask for help, and sometimes a buddy system was instituted for the forthcoming week.

Individual Treatment. Clients were treated individually while the group was concurrently convening, because clients frequently had individual problems and needs. As they formed trusting relationships with team members, they expressed pent-up feelings that they had repressed due to fear and/or isolation. For example, one aged woman had been placed in the facility by the county after she had been hospitalized for a broken hip, because she needed supervised aftercare. She was worried about her house, belongings, and garden. She was so concerned that she rarely left her room and rarely attempted to exercise her hip, as directed, to increase strength. She needed someone to listen and to empathize with her. A medical student was assigned to work with her for 30 to 35 minutes a week. The session was not only of benefit to the woman, but benefited the student in expanding his medical training; he learned that the needs of an aged patient may far exceed the physical treatment required to heal a broken hip. He found that healing was also facilitated by attitude and motivation. These needs might not be apparent to a medical team without a holistic approach to treatment.

Frequently, clients relied on team members to divulge negative feelings toward the board-and-care personnel. This is a delicate subject and will be discussed in more detail (see section on Problems, Obstacles, and Management later in this chapter).

AGENTS OF REMINISCENCE

Movement Therapy

Movement-oriented activity has emerged as an adjunctive form of treatment in psychiatric rehabilitation (Levy 1974). Movement sessions were purposefully developed in this program, with a routine structure to increase reality orientation. Predictable activities served to reassure clients who felt unsteady and unsure of their movement abilities. These sessions were developed with designated times for large-group activities, dyads, and individual expression. The large group offered skills in coping with interactions similar to those needed to cope with a large group of people on a day-to-day basis. At times, interactions were facilitated to require less intimacy. For example, clients were directed to find a familiar way to move their arms. Beginning with a large group was comforting for clients who had difficulty tolerating intimacy. At other times, the large group became more personal. For example, clients were directed to form a circle, turn, and give the person in front of them a back rub.

Small-group activities, such as finding a familiar way to balance together, encouraged trust and warmth. Dyads promoted an increased opportunity for intimacy and interpersonal skills. An activity such as mirroring with another individual (one person pretends to be looking into a mirror; the other is the mirror image and copies the looker) promoted an exchange of eye contact, facial gestures, postures, and feelings and led to one-to-one discussions following the activity.

Individual activities encouraged autonomy and confidence. Some individual movement was integrated with the large-group activity. For example, during movement charades, a client showed off his or her expertise and abilities by pantomiming an activity he or she enjoyed while everyone guessed what she or he was doing. Each performance ended with group applause.

The movement sessions began and ended with a large-group activity. The final activity was to stand in a circle holding hands, find balance together, and finally let go in order to find one's own balance. This promoted trust and reinforced a sense of relatedness to others and to self. The basic group structure served to orient group members to time and also to life review—that is, there was a definite beginning, middle, and ending during each session.

Movement directives stimulated familiar body motions and encouraged discussion of accompanying memories. For example, when directed to "find a way you like to move your arms and we'll follow you," one woman began to do the crawl stroke. She then related to the group that she had been an avid swimmer when she was a young girl growing up in Sweden. Her memories stimulated and encouraged a very shy Mexican man, who rarely initiated conversation, to act out the crawl stroke and share that he too had enjoyed swimming in his youth.

Familiar movements that were coupled with similar music encouraged individuals to discuss spontaneously instruments they had liked to play. These instruments were provided during succeeding sessions and incorporated into the weekly routine. One man played the harmonica; three played the piano; one, the organ; and two, the guitar. These individuals were encouraged to take turns providing the background music during the movement sessions. The instruments contributed to reminiscence. For example, the organ music stirred up memories about music accompanying ice skaters. The "Skaters' Waltz" was played while people pretended to ice skate. The activity further stimulated a variety of related memories that the group discussed. Movement also promoted sensory input through tactile, visual, and auditory stimulation.

Music Therapy

Hennessey (1978) states that the healing properties of music have long been known, and music is an effective tool in group work with older adults. Clients were extremely responsive to music. A regularly scheduled group developed as an outgrowth of the movement group. Music increased motivation, pleasure, mental alertness, and animation. Furthermore, music proved to be an excellent agent of reminiscence.

Music from time periods such as the big band era evoked activity and discussion. For example, one man who was delusional stopped his grandiose talk and began to tell a story about an experience he had had at a USO dance and demonstrated several fancy steps he knew, including the fox trot and the rhumba. For an individual to break out in solo spontaneously and for the group to listen and then applaud loudly was not unusual during a music session. In following sessions, people might spontaneously call for a favorite singer or piano player, clapping and demanding an encore performance.

Folk songs encouraged group interaction and stirred up childhood memories. One man recalled chopping wood with his father on his farm in Missouri. His memories encouraged others to share stories and stimulated sharing traditions and folk songs from various cultures.

Music encouraged closure of the generation gap. Folk songs, for example, were universally appreciated. One regressed young man, who was gifted at playing the piano, favored rock music. He was pleased, however, by the opportunity to play standard tunes, such as "Sweet Georgia Brown," and slower contemporary songs, like the Beatles' "Do You Want to Know a Secret?" for the group. He was encouraged by the gratitude shown toward him by older clients, which was expressed through applause and sing-alongs. Clients who had been angry at him because of his "noisy music" began to accept him and relate to him. In addition, they were willing to give special time for him to play rock music on the guitar, and he was willing to adapt some of his favorite pieces to meet their needs.

Music brought out a variety of moods and often stimulated moods correlated with past events, encouraging clients to share feelings verbally with the group. Music was also spontaneously used during other activities to assist in integrating the experience. For example, at the end of an evening's session, the group convened at the door while the staff serenaded the clients with a goodbye song, and the clients responded through song and perhaps a farewell tune.

Art Therapy

Art was not regularly scheduled as part of the program, but it was periodically employed as a highly effective agent of reminiscence. Initially, group members would declare, "I can't draw." Staff emphasized, however, that artistic ability was not the purpose of the activity. Art was a means to an end; namely, it was used to facilitate large-group and/or small-group discussion. For example, one directive was to "choose a color that creates a feeling you had about a historical event that happened during your lifetime." Sometimes the colors were not included in the discussion but were used solely to facilitate memories. Other times, the use of color was tied into the discussion. Directing clients to draw symbolic figures or markings was incorporated in a similar way. The co-therapists facilitated the discussions and encouraged young staff members to learn from clients. For example, one could learn a great deal about historical events firsthand. During art sessions, clients often discovered that they had many things in common with each other. Three clients were surprised to learn that they had all grown up in the same town in Ohio. These discoveries encouraged alliances and interactions outside the sessions.

Occupational Therapy: The Developmental Task Group

The advantage of employing the developmental task group was that it not only promoted autonomy in performing simple problem-solving and decision-making skills but it also encouraged using these skills with others. Typically in this type of group, the end result is secondary to the developmental process. Fidler and Fiedler (1969) write that task accomplishment is not the purpose of the therapy group but, it is hoped, the means by which the purpose is accomplished. In working with older adults, however, the authors found that the end result was equally important. Clients needed to be able to conceptualize an end result and experience mastery in task completion.

To meet these needs, familiar tasks that drew on past memories, abilities, motor activities, and assets were presented. For example, one task was to plan, set up, and participate in an old-fashioned barbecue. The role of the co-therapists during this group activity was that of resource persons. Without assuming responsibility for the group, they facilitated group process and made learning possible. The development task group provided a means for:

- Increasing independence by encouraging clients to contribute ideas drawn from past experiences.

- Providing gratification and success.
- Fulfilling narcissistic needs for self-actualization while providing an opportunity for sharing in a cooperative venture.
- Promoting social interaction and generalizing experiences to the community.
- Providing repeated opportunities to perceive cause-and-effect relationships.
- Providing parallel play-work situations that encourage modeling and imitation.
- Providing opportunities for problem solving, carry through, and observable results.
- Increasing sitting tolerance and attention span.
- Increasing risk-taking behavior by increasing physical and psychological security.
- Increasing self-confidence and self-esteem.

Life Skills Training

Cooking Activities. Brown (1982) found that training in life skills should closely correlate with skills required in a particular living environment. This correlation reinforces retention of learned skills and encourages utilization and autonomy in skill application. Although board-and-care facilities do not allow clients in the kitchen (county health laws prohibit clients from handling foods in the kitchen), simple cooking activities using developed task group methods were planned and carried out in the dining area. The authors found that issues relating to foods were extremely meaningful. Food invokes a variety of very personal feelings and memories.

To enhance the many therapeutic aspects incurred by a cooking activity, an art therapy approach was utilized after one cooking session. The art paper was divided into thirds. In the first section, clients were directed to remember a particular meal shared with their families by diagramming where each person sat. Foods served at that meal were drawn in the second section. Colors, markings, and/or drawings depicting feelings during that particular meal were placed in the last section, encouraging life review. Clients talked about their own values, habits, and feelings and then compared these. For example, many found that their parents did not allow discussions during mealtime. For others, mealtime was the only time family members gathered to share stories, jokes, and daily happenings and to plan family events. The discussion assisted clients in integrating feelings about current mealtimes. Clients also compared food preferences, mourned current losses involving consumption of favorite foods, and planned the preparation of foods, such as old-fashioned ice cream sundaes.

Activities such as the above, coupled with pleasurable cooking experiences, promoted social interaction during eating and the generalization of socialization during daily meals. Upon arriving during one dinner hour, the authors were gratified to find clients chatting, sharing, and calling each other by name. In addition, the authors found a way around the county health laws in order to assist one middle-age client. The client was able to assist kitchen staff for minimal pay after the doctor wrote in the chart that assisting in the kitchen was essential in the client's rehabilitation. Thereafter, this client's role, image, self-esteem, and ability to take on responsibility and social skills improved.

Other Life Skills Activities. The evaluation of a number of clients showed individual living skills needs (Brown & Munford 1983). Training in communication, health care, hygiene, budgeting, community resources, and time management skills was initiated when necessary. For example, one man with a progressive neurological condition was beginning to have difficulty dressing himself. His motor activity was retarded, and he displayed tremors upon voluntary motion. Inability to care for himself would lead to either rehospitalization or transfer to a nursing home facility. The occupational therapy student was assigned to work individually with him for part of each session. The patient's goal was to maintain his level of independent functioning for as long as possible.

Life skills training was sometimes employed in the group setting. For example, during one developmental task group, the members filled out a weekly schedule balancing each day with work, rest, and play. They chose homework assignments, such as taking a walk to the market for a snack with a buddy. The group members reviewed task accomplishments, difficulties, and areas for growth during the following week's session.

Other Therapeutic Modalities

Children. Occasionally, team members and board-and-care personnel brought children to participate with clients. Clients became animated, laughing and smiling with the children. Children facilitated the loosening of defenses and encouraged displays of warmth. For example, one client's cultural background had customs about appropriate touching; thus, he rarely touched others and never hugged them. The client was able to respond positively to a child's touch. An 89-year-old man had difficulty communicating with others because of his poor vision and hearing. He actively engaged a small child throughout a movement session. He cooed and waved at her and played peek-a-boo. Children also stimulated clients' childhood memories, which were reviewed and processed during verbal sessions.

Pet-facilitated Group Therapy. Pets also provide meaningful experiences for the aging and chronically ill (Brickel 1986; Brickel & Brickel 1980). There is a large body of literature on the positive effects on health of elders who have pets. One older woman, who was confined to a wheelchair, was able to hide a cat in her room. (Some health laws prohibit live-in pets.) Although she was depressed about living in the care home, the maneuvering and secrecy involved in feeding and maintaining the cat were thrilling. She had difficulty relating with the other clients, so the cat became her one reliable living contact. She held it on her lap and petted and hugged it. When she began to trust team members who worked with her individually, she shared her mischievous undertaking with them. As other clients found out about the cat, they became cohorts and helped her with management, leading to her increased socialization and ultimately to her group participation. Pets, like children, stimulated childhood memories and other stories related to animals.

PROBLEMS, OBSTACLES, AND MANAGEMENT

Although the program described in this chapter was well planned, well coordinated, and adequately staffed, problems were encountered. Obstacles were expected because the authors were well aware that any program has its drawbacks. Problems were managed with team planning and strategies.

One major problem in maintaining the program was surviving the changing conditions. Because the home had three owners within a three-year period, relationships had to be established with each new administration; furthermore, the staff changed monthly and sometimes weekly. Often, the new evening personnel had not been oriented to the program and were overwhelmed when the team appeared with a full crew and program plan. Some of the new personnel were offended when team members requested that they maintain routines, such as serving coffee after the task group. Some served the coffee before the authors could explain the rationale and disrupted the program.

At first, the authors attempted to remedy this situation by calling the staff on the afternoon of the group. Communication between the day and evening personnel was poor, however. Therefore, the team decided one of them would orient the personnel on arrival while the other would initiate the program. Then personnel were included in the refreshment period and other festive events such as holiday parties. Personnel were encouraged to join the group at will. The team was conscientious about postgroup clean-up, especially in the dining room where uniformed personnel had already completed their evening work by setting up the dining room for the following morning. Sometimes the team judiciously decided to reset the tables.

Providing alcoholic beverages on special occasions is another concern. In our society, alcohol is a significant object; the ability to consume alcohol is a mark of maturity. General rules and restrictions imposed on the aged living in an institution, especially rules and restrictions about alcohol, promote low self-esteem and self-confidence about their ability to maintain their autonomy. At the Michael Reese Institute in Chicago, the geriatric program encourages the inpatients and staff to dress formally for dinner one night a week, and wine is served with dinner. As a result, self-image and hope for the future were observed to increase during the session. The authors also found a similar outcome when one beer was provided during barbecues and special holiday events. There are several precautions that need to be taken to prevent deleterious effects, however. Some board-and-care clients may be alcoholics, some may be on medications that cannot be ingested with alcohol, or some may have a low tolerance for alcoholic beverages. Therefore, knowing the medical history of each client is important.

Clients frequently wanted to place the authors in an omnipotent role. This was both a blessing and a curse and often evoked conflicting feelings. Clients experiencing a loss in dignity improved their future outlook because of the power they invested in the team to help them with their plight. Although the team was instrumental in alleviating some of the problems, the team had to be tactful in order to prevent possible punitive actions to clients by the board-and-care staff and possible termination of the program. Clients confided in the team, and sometimes team members felt torn about their alliances. For example, when the woman who was hiding a cat in her room confided in the team, the team had to decide whether the cat might create a health problem and had to determine other possible consequences of failing to report the animal to the owner. In the end, the authors decided that the benefits the woman derived from having the cat outweighed the possible problems and decided to overlook the situation.

Other issues were not as easy to overlook. For example, several clients accused personnel of misappropriating their funds. The team decided that the best way to deal with the situation was to report the issue to the medical center's community social work service, which was responsible for quality assurance in board-and-care settings. When the community social worker probed the situation, the operator called for a team conference and demonstrated that the clients were confused and had fabricated stories.

Confidentiality

The issue of confidentiality with clients is an important one. Whether clients were correct in their perception about a situation was not always as important as the thoughts and feelings they were able to express confidentially. Common themes were: loss of dignity, low self-esteem, helplessness, and lack of control. Some of their attitudes and behaviors were found to be defenses against their anger and underlying hurt. The single most important quality in helping clients cope is empathy. Empathy skills include listening, helping the client to express his or her feelings, and conveying feedback that the client has been understood (Hepworth & Larsen 1993).

SUMMARY

The therapeutic technique of reminiscence is an excellent treatment in the board-and-care setting, because reminiscence is a major cognitive characteristic of the geriatric life stage. Individuals with a wide range of problems and deficits can be included in such a treatment program. A major advantage of the therapeutic technique of reminiscence is that it can take many forms such as movement, cooking, art, music, and activities of daily living. These activities provide opportunities for life review and for growth and adaptation in all areas of human development. In undertaking a program at a board-and-care facility, employing a multidisciplinary team is preferable. This approach can be beneficial in that a large number of clients can be treated in a group setting by utilizing skilled co-leaders directing a variety of assistant leaders. The large group can be divided into small groups, dyads, and individual group treatment.

A team member can provide experiences in his or her area of expertise to complement and enhance experiences provided by other team members. Ideally, team members need to be flexible in sharing responsibilities, because territoriality can be destructive to group cohesion. There are three interpersonal relationships that must be carefully cultivated: between the multidisciplinary team members, the team members and the board-and-care personnel, and the team members and the clients. In addition, a multidisciplinary team is cost effective in that a variety of services can be provided to a large outpatient group. Creative staffing can assist in this process. There is a substantial cost benefit in maintaining clients in the community in comparison with the cost of hospitalization. We as clinicians are focused on quality-of-life issues; however, to be able to ensure support in improving quality of life, we must be accountable to administration.

The quality of life for the patients in the program described in this chapter was enhanced primarily in terms of social-skills gains. Clients who had initially appeared withdrawn, emaciated, and unkempt showed improved grooming, became animated and involved in activities, and formed relationships with others. Clients acknowledged each other by first name or last name for endearment. Conversations at mealtimes became spontaneous, one-on-one friendships formed, clients independently initiated trips to the satellite center by bus, and drinking in local taverns decreased. Two major changes were noticeable: Clients developed interpersonal relationships that continued without staff facilitation, and when the physical environment began to deteriorate in terms of upkeep, food, and finances, the interpersonal relationships and morale remained high.

EXERCISE 1

Work with one other classmate or a small group of your classmates. Lay out a box of crayons and paper. Each person is to recall an historical event in his or her lifetime. Each is to imagine where he or she was at the time, people with whom he or she was involved, and related objects and events. Each person is to imagine how he or she felt at the time, to choose a color to represent his or her feelings at the time, and to express the events and feelings on paper. Artistic ability is not required. Participants may wish simply to put a color or two or a symbolic figure on paper.

1. Allow time for each person to share his or her events.
2. After each person shares, other group members are to imagine how that person felt in one or two feeling words. The members each have a turn to tell the speaker their two words. The speaker responds by validating or invalidating the words.
3. Allow time for spontaneous interaction by members—for example, two members may have common themes.

EXERCISE 2

In a group, recall events in your life from childhood to the present. Associate pertinent songs that each event brings to mind.

You may wish to enhance this exercise by having each individual select one of her or his pertinent songs and lead the rest of the group in singing or talking about the song lyrics, melody, and the like.

EXERCISE 3

Work with a group of classmates. Make a circle. Each person is to think of an activity he or she has enjoyed performing. One person is to pantomime the activity while the rest of the group guesses what the person is doing.

EXERCISE 4

Work with a group of classmates. Select a happy memory that focuses around a particular holiday or special event Each member will share his or her happy memory with the group. This exercise provides opportunities for socialization among group members and sharing of positive memories and experiences, and encourages members to identify common events in their lives. This exercise also has the flexibility to be used with whatever holiday or special event is happening at the time.

REFERENCES

Birren JE, Deutchman D. 1991. *Guiding autobiography groups for older adults—Exploring the fabric of life.* Baltimore: Johns Hopkins University Press.

Brickel CM. 1986. Pet-facilitated therapies—A review of the literature and clinical implementation considerations. *Clin Gerontol* 5(3/4):309-322.

Brickel CM, Brickel GK. 1980. A review of the roles of pet animals in psychotherapy and with the elderly. *Int J Aging Human Dev* 12(2):119-128.

Brown MA. 1982. Maintenance and generalization issues in skills training with chronic schizophrenics. In JP Curran, PM Monti (eds.), *Social skills training* (pp. 90-116). New York: Guilford.

Brown MA, Munford A. 1983. Life skills training for chronic schizophrenics. *J Nervous Ment Dis* 171(8):466-470.

Burnside IM. 1976. Overview of group work with the aged. *J Gerontol Nurs* 2(6):14-17.

———. 1978. *Working with the elderly: Group process and techniques*, 1st ed. North Scituate, MA: Duxbury Press.

Butler R. 1963. The life review: An interpretation of reminiscence in the aged. *Psychiatry* 26(1):65-76.

Butler R, Lewis MI, Sunderland T. 1991. *Aging and mental health*, 4th ed. New York: Merrill.

Daub MM. 1983. The human development process. In HL Hopkins, HO Smith (eds.), *Willard and Spackman occupational therapy*, 6th ed. (pp. 29-81). Philadelphia: Lippincott.

Ebersole P. 1978. Establishing reminiscing groups. In IM Burnside (ed.), *Working with the elderly: Group process and techniques*, 1st ed. (pp. 236-254). North Scituate, MA: Duxbury Press.

Erikson E. 1950. *Childhood and society*. New York: Norton.

Fidler GS, Fiedler JW. 1969. *Occupational therapy*, 2d ed. New York: Macmillan.

Friedlob SA. 1982. The development of a life skills training program for chronic schizophrenic patients: Three case studies. Unpublished paper.

Hennessey MJ. 1978. Music and music therapy groups. In IM Burnside (ed.), *Working with the elderly: Group process and techniques*, 1st ed. (pp. 255-274). North Scituate, MA: Duxbury Press.

Hepworth DH, Larsen JA. 1993. *Direct social work practice—Theory and skills*. Pacific Grove, CA: Brooks/Cole.

Hopkins HL, Smith HO. 1980. *Willard and Spackman's occupational therapy*, 5th ed. Philadelphia: Lippincott.

King LJ. 1970. Perceptual motor training of the adult psychiatric patient. Paper presented to the Arizona Occupational Therapy Association (January 26).

Levine B. 1979. *Group psychotherapy—Practice and development*. Prospect Heights, IL: Waveland Press.

Levy L. 1974. Movement therapy for psychiatric patients. *Am J Occup Ther* 28(6):354-357.

Lewis MI, Butler RN. 1974. Life review: Putting memories to work in individual and group psychotherapy. *Geriatrics* 29(11):165-173 .

Linden M. 1953. Group psychotherapy with institutionalized senile women: Study in gerontological human relations. *Int J Group Psychother* 3:150-170.

Magee JJ. 1988. *A professional's guide to older adults' life review*. Lexington, MA: Lexington Books.

Myers JE, Podevant J, Dean L. 1991. Review of literature on groups for older persons. *J Special Group Work* 16(3): 197-205.

Satir VM. 1972. *Peoplemaking*. Palo Alto, CA: Science & Behavioral Books.

Satir VM, Staehowiak J, Taschmann HA. 1975. *Helping families to change*. New York: Aronson.

Yalom ID. 1975. *The theory and practice of group psychotherapy*, 2d ed. New York: Basic Books.

Zimpfer DG. 1987. Groups for the aging: Do they work? *J Special Group Work* 12:85-92.

BIBLIOGRAPHY

Burnside IM. 1990. Reminiscence: An independent nursing intervention for the elderly. *Issues Ment Health Nurs* 11:33-48.

Harris PB. 1979. Being old: A confrontation group with nursing home residents. *Health Soc Work* 4(1):152-166.

Nazami KH, Eckert JK, Kahana E, Lyon S. 1989. Psychological well-being of elderly board and care home residents. *Gerontologist* 29(4):511-516.

CHAPTER 24

Groups for Older Persons in Acute Care

Elissa Brown

KEY WORDS
- Catastrophic reaction
- Cohesion
- Communication
- Dementia
- Flexibility
- Patience

LEARNING OBJECTIVES
- Identify at least four types of groups appropriate for older persons in acute settings.
- Describe two considerations for groups of older persons in the following areas: size of group, length of group meeting, frequency of meetings.
- Discuss common problems regarding safety in groups of older persons.
- List four important qualities of the nurse who leads groups of older persons.
- Note at least two inclusion criteria and two exclusion criteria for groups of older persons in acute care.

Although groups are a common treatment modality in psychiatry, they are not often considered in other areas. However, as in psychiatry, they may be an effective, efficient means of treating patients in a variety of areas. This chapter focuses on groups of older persons in acute inpatient settings, especially acute geropsychiatry and acute psychiatry units.

On acute wards, where the focus is traditionally to attend to physical needs of patients, the patients' need for emotional support, socialization, improved coping skills, and improved cognitive function is often on the back burner (Sautter, Hearney & O'Neill 1991, 814). Yet nurses express concern about patients who complain of being bored, depressed, and frustrated and having nothing to

do. Even those patients who are not able to clearly articulate their thoughts, such as patients with dementia or aphasia, appear to be frustrated and bored. In light of the changing health care system, with shorter hospital stays, there is a need to review and better organize patient environments to meet their needs. True, nursing staff may believe there is no way to do any more than they are already doing. In many instances, nursing staffing seems to be at a bare minimum and could not realistically allow for much one-to-one contact, especially in a psychotherapeutic way; therefore groups may be the most efficient way to begin to meet patients' psychosocial needs.

Experience and a review of the literature have shown that groups can be effective and can improve the patient's quality of life, at least for some period of time. Quality of life for the aged and for patients with dementia continues to be studied.

LITERATURE REVIEW

Articles and books about groups of older persons cover a wide range of topics: types of groups, advantages, outcomes, and recommendations. There is very little in the literature on groups of older persons in acute care settings, or on groups that include dementia patients. Interestingly, the literature does date back, perhaps to the 1920s, when, for example, the use of psychodrama with older persons was discussed. (Krebs-Roubicek 1989, 1262). Various types of groups were described in the literature. Wolff (in Krebs-Roubicek 1989, 1263) suggested that there are advantages to groups: time economy, older persons are less afraid in groups, other group members, rather than a powerful group leader, can provide support, loneliness can be decreased due to feeling accepted by the group members, and members can feel identification with others. Group outcomes included increased emotional support, increased awareness, increased appropriate behavior, increased cognitive functioning along with some increased depression, cohesion, improved involvement in other ward activities, and improved sense of perceived control (Gilewski 1986, 285).

Overall, studies on groups of older persons show that "the most frequently reported benefits of group therapy are improved patient and staff morale and improved cognitive and behavioral functioning for patients" (Gilewski 1986, 291). Improved staff morale may be reflected in their positive comments: pleasure in seeing patients more active and less bored; feeling they have learned more about patients from information shared by group leaders; and observing actual improvement in some patients after participation in groups.

Groups also seem to decrease the negative effects of institutionalization (Gilewski 1986, 287). Pfeiffer (in Krebs-Roubicek 1989, 1263) discusses "learning from a model," a potentially useful concept, since groups can be viewed as safe settings for patients to model or try new behaviors.

There are, as noted, relatively few reports on groups with brain-impaired older persons. The problems with many studies were: the diagnoses (parameters) were not always clear (criteria for diagnoses have changed); there were variations in the types of group treatment, with little consistency in leadership style or process; lack of clear outcome measures; questions about study designs; and a lack of long-term follow-up. All of these factors make it difficult to generalize results. (Gilewski 1986, 289-290). Kohut's self-theory model, described in Gilewski (1986) and often used with individuals, claims that the brain-impaired individual is not in control of his/her thought processes and therefore uses primitive defenses, which may often fail. The therapist's role is supportive. Kohut's model can be applied to groups (Gilewski 1986, 293-294). Cognitive retraining, another method frequently used with individuals to help patients improve their thinking ability, also can be implemented in groups (Gilewski 1986, 294).

Further studies need to be done, with more specific outcome measures as well as follow-up components to determine the long-range effects of groups of older persons. Implications for practice include more groups in various settings, with clear purposes, and planning specific methods to measure their effectiveness.

TYPES OF GROUPS FOR ACUTE CARE SETTINGS

A variety of groups are appropriate for older persons on acute wards. Many of these are discussed in detail in this book. The following groups are briefly described to help in choosing the appropriate groups for acute care settings.

1. *Reminiscence groups* focus on assisting patients to recall memories and to "integrate this experience with their current circumstances" (Mazor 1982, 578). They may, at times, lead to feelings of depression, and they will require follow-up. Reminiscence groups can be conducted in many settings, including acute care. (See Chapters 15 and 23.)

2. *Current events groups*, with discussion of the latest news, can be nonthreatening and nondemanding, may require more direction from the leader(s), and can be stimulating for patients. This type of group also is conducive to many ward settings.

3. *Activity and crafts groups*, such as cooking groups and exercise groups, can help make the most of skills still retained by patients, develop new skills, share experiences, and give people a sense of worth (Burgess 1990, 1034). The leader needs to be aware of such possible problems as apraxia or an inability for some patients to coordinate their movements, and to compensate for this by providing easier, simpler tasks and/or assisting the patient. It would be valuable for an occupational therapist and/or a recreational therapist to be one of the co-leaders of such a group. This type of group may be difficult to conduct on an acute ward, due to the need for space and many supplies.

4. *Psychotherapy groups*, which may aim at more insight-oriented work for patients, would require more careful selection criteria for group members. The group members would need sufficient cognitive ability, self-awareness, and attention span to be able to participate for at least an hour in such a group. Psychotherapy groups should be led by staff with psychiatric nursing skills, such as a nurse prepared at the master's degree level or a qualified co-therapist from another discipline such as psychiatry, psychology, or psychiatric social work. Acute geropsychiatry or psychiatry areas would be settings most conducive for implementation of these groups.

5. *Reality orientation groups* have been helpful for some patients, but they seem to work best when combined with an overall unit program of reality orientation (Gerber et al. 1991, 844; Hanley, McGuire & Boyd 1981, 10). Such groups may lead to improved cognition (Hanley et al. 1981) and can be conducted in creative ways. Possible problems include discouragement when a patient fails memory training (Akerlund & Norberg 1986, 83; Gilewski 1986, 288). A variety of acute care settings can introduce this kind of group: geropsychiatry, psychiatry, medical and surgical wards, as well as long-term care. (See Chapter 13.)

6. *Remotivation groups* "stress stimulation of the senses," utilizing objects in the environment such as plants and animals (Janosik & Davies 1989, 382). This type of group is also possible for acute care. (See Chapter 14.)

7. *Music* may be the only stimulation to which some patients seem to relate; it is nondemanding. If there is equipment and space, this is a feasible group for acute care. (See Chapter 17.)

8. *Movement therapy and dance therapy* are stimulating, help maintain mobility, and improve balance and coordination.

Example: A colleague related the story of Jane, a 69-year-old woman with dementia and depression, on a geropsychiatry unit, who continually refused to go to the nurses' station to get her medication. In music therapy, the staff discovered that Jane would get up and dance and seemed to love the sounds. The staff had an idea: They waltzed her over to get her medications and she accepted them.

9. *Art therapy* draws on the patient's creative skills; it can be positively stimulating.

Example: One group of older patients, with a variety of diagnoses from dementia to depression, worked with two registered nurses and one recreational therapist co-leader to produce collages. The patients' first collage, which they worked on as a group for about four weeks, had dark colors and mostly still life pictures. Four months later, this ongoing outpatient group did another collage, which was in striking contrast to the first one. The second one was bright, had pictures of people engaged in various activities, and was described as more cheerful. The group was more cohesive and active at this point.

These groups work well in acute geropsychiatry and psychiatry wards and may work elsewhere if space is available.

10. *Drama therapy* (Mazor 1982) entails the use of reminiscence, problem solving, and social interaction "to create and resolve conflicts . . . [through] role playing. . . ." The hoped-for outcome is to restore dignity and storytelling ability of the aged.

Example: Mary, an 84-year-old woman who was eventually diagnosed with multi-infarct dementia, was on the geropsychiatry assessment and treatment unit to determine the etiology of her dementia and further evaluate her medical problems. She attended the morning geropsychiatry group and was often quiet, only responding when asked a question. One morning, as the group discussed hobbies and what they liked to do, Mary began to recite poetry. She was able, with dramatic vigor, to recite a wonderful poem, over five minutes long, which her "father had told her" probably 70 years before. The group members appeared amazed and applauded her. She smiled and thanked them. In subsequent meetings, they often asked Mary to tell them other stories or poems.

This group requires a skilled leader if role-playing and psychodrama techniques are used.

11. *Bibliotherapy* is usually used with more withdrawn, confused patients; it involves reading to patients (Beck, Rawlings & Williams 1988, 528).

> *Example:* Joe, a 77-year-old man with a probable dementia related to alcohol use and vascular disease, would sit much of the day on the geropsychiatry ward, pace at times, go outside to smoke, and, at times, talk to himself. He was generally left alone. In group, however, he responded to questions and even told some jokes that made him laugh, if no one else. He also had a brother who would visit early in the morning. He was invited to join the group, and he entertained the patients with a repertoire of jokes. This provided a change and the patient group enjoyed it.

This kind of group can be conducted in acute care settings, even in a ward—a six- or eight-bed room.

12. *Problem-solving groups* would be most appropriate for higher-functioning patients. The process involves an ability to define and work on problems. These groups can be done in an acute care setting and, depending on the patient population, will vary in style and level of expected outcomes.

13. *Other groups* that can be implemented in acute care settings are memory training, self-help groups, family groups, and support groups.

> *Example:* In a large Midwest hospital, where electroconvulsive therapy (ECT) was a regular, established form of treatment, the clinical nurse specialist in psychiatry and mental health conducted an educational support group for patients receiving ECT; they met prior to each treatment day.

Other kinds of support groups that may be feasible in an acute setting include cancer support groups, dialysis support groups, and coping groups whose members have chronic obstructive pulmonary disease (COPD). These groups can meet in a large room of four to eight patients in bed.

GETTING STARTED: INITIAL PLANNING

When planning to begin a group on an acute ward, several steps are suggested. First, the group leader or leaders need to schedule meetings with the nursing staff involved in caring for the patients.

Depending on the kind of acute care setting, the staff may have little experience with groups. Discussions would center around the purpose of the proposed group, communication about what happens in the group and prior to each group, the role of the nursing staff in relation to the group, and who would be directly involved in the group, both patients and staff.

Discussion also would occur with the interdisciplinary team around the same issues. Again, there may be a team whose members are not familiar with, interested in, or experienced in group work. When going through this process, the group leaders need to prepare for a variety of responses. When the morning geropsychiatry group was started by the clinical nurse specialist in psychiatry and mental health and a psychologist as the co-leaders, some of the professional staff expressed concern that such a group would not be good for patients with dementias, that they would never sit through such a group. They would be too stimulated and they would get more agitated, and it just would not work. This group is still going strong after eight years. Perhaps such a group will not work in some settings, but it may be worthwhile to try.

Preparation for a group will help to avoid some problems. The group leaders first decide on the type of group by doing a needs assessment. This may be done formally· or informally through discussions with staff, observation of the patients, and gathering knowledge about the patient population in general. Problems could occur if, for instance, the group leaders fail to do an accurate assessment and decide to lead a problem-solving group on a ward where most of the patients have moderate to severe memory loss and cognitive impairment. Most of these patients would have difficulty taking in new knowledge and processing it, let alone identifying problems, formulating solutions, and remembering details from one session to the next. Therefore, a structured problem-solving type of group would be destined to fail with such a population of older persons.

Decisions about whether to have an open or closed group will depend on the type of group, its purpose, the setting, the space, the patient population, the average length of stay, and the availability of staff to lead the group.

Which patients can participate will depend on the previously mentioned factors, as well as the group leaders' beliefs and preferences. There are varying viewpoints on this. The theorists and researchers recommend following traditional group principles, including stable membership. However, experiences may differ. The inpatient morning geropsychiatry group noted before was open to all 12 of the geropsychiatry patients and 3 to 5 of the 16 patients on the geriatric medicine section of the same ward, sometimes involving as many as 15 patients. The core number, however, remained at 10.

DISRUPTIVE GROUP MEMBERS

There are potential disruptive factors and issues to consider. *Safety must come first.* If there are patients who are volatile or tend to regularly provoke others, the group leaders must judge the wisdom of including these patients. This process may have to occur on a day-to-day basis. Thus, a key point in conducting an inpatient group is the need for flexibility and patience.

INCLUSION CRITERIA

Another step in planning a group is to decide inclusion and exclusion criteria. Inclusion criteria may be any or all of the following, and more: patient diagnosis, patient behavior, a specified length of time the patient should be on the ward prior to attending group, and referral or approval by the patient's primary care provider. Patients whom some group leaders recommend excluding are those who are deaf, incontinent, wanderers, psychotic, or hypochondriacal (Burnside 1986, 113, 116). Such patients were not excluded from the inpatient morning geropsychiatry group, and there were no significant problems with them attending the group meetings. However, the group leader was an experienced psychiatric nurse. In most acute nonpsychiatric settings, the exclusion criteria previously mentioned ought to be followed in order to minimize problems.

Again, flexibility is needed, and who is included or excluded may vary from day to day.

Example: Jack, a 74-year-old patient with depression, mild dementia, prostate cancer, and a rather explosive personality, usually attended the morning geropsychiatry group. However, there were a few times when the staff reported that he had been up all night, tried to punch another patient, and was threatening to hurt someone else. Prior to the group session, the group leader talked with Jack, who said he was not sure he could come to group. He was afraid he could not control his anger, particularly toward Jim, another patient whom he had threatened. There was mutual agreement that Jack would not attend group that day and that he would talk with his physician later.

EDUCATION AND TRAINING

Staff who lead groups in acute care settings need some formal basic training in group process and group principles, previously described in this book; and they require additional knowledge about groups. Group leaders need to become familiar with Yalom's curative factors in group work. These include altruism, cohesiveness, learning, guidance, catharsis, identification, insight, hope, and existential factors (Yalom 1983).

Training is important for group leaders. Even for those leaders who had been more accustomed to groups with younger, not cognitively impaired patients, who also stayed longer, there is a need to change expectations and hoped-for outcomes and to add some new techniques for groups with older persons.

TECHNIQUES FOR LEADING GROUPS

The qualities of a good leader, as mentioned in this book, are caring about older people, respecting older people, and possessing an ability and desire to learn from older people (Burnside 1986). Furthermore, the leader of a group in an acute care setting should understand the biological aspects of aging, be patient and sensitive, and be committed to communicating with the members of the health care team. A co-leader is recommended, particularly to assist with the group process and to do pre- and postgroup planning and review.

Specific leadership styles have been addressed elsewhere in this book. In a previous inpatient morning geropsychiatry group that I led, the style varied with the population but was generally democratic, enabling everyone to have a turn to speak, and directive (e.g., what would you like to talk about today?), while still allowing the patients to choose their own topics. Some of the studies have shown the benefit of allowing patients to choose their own topics, to give them a better sense of control (Manaster in Gilewski 1986). There will be times when the leader will be more directive, depending on the group composition. At other times, the leader may be able to sit back and let the group be more active. In the acute care setting, particularly in current times, patients may be on the ward for less than one week. This will necessitate group leaders setting daily goals, rather than doing long-term planning.

EVALUATING GROUP OUTCOMES

There are a variety of ways to evaluate the outcomes of a group. Informal ways include patient, family, and staff feedback about the patients, with specific reference to something that occurred in the group or was a direct result of something that occurred in the group. Tools can be used to measure behavior changes: pregroup and postgroup measures, either short-term measures (daily or more frequently) or long-range measures to determine more lasting effects. Factors that can be measured are depression, mental status, level of anxiety and agitation, social skills, involvement in activities, and general change in cognitive abilities. Videotapes also may be used and evaluated objectively, *with written consent* from the patient, conservator, or guardian. The sociogram or diagram of patterns of interaction is a simple, useful tool. This would be completed after each group session and evaluated over a period of time for trends, changes, individual improvement, and group process in general.

PLANNING WITH A CO-LEADER

Planning with a co-leader, from the beginning if possible, will be helpful. In many settings, and particularly in acute care areas, it may be difficult to find a consistent co-leader. The group may have to be planned by only one leader, using input from other staff and with a rotating co-leader. The co-leader may be a registered nurse, a student nurse or trainee from another discipline, or a staff member such as a social worker. The inpatient geropsychiatry morning group initially had two constant co-leaders, a clinical nurse specialist in psychiatry/mental health and a psychologist. After the psychologist left, a psychology trainee rotated as co-leader for a three-month period of time. For one

year, graduate student nurses rotated through for four months each, and then a psychiatry resident for six months. The leader has the responsibility for some training and supervision or review with the co-leader.

Additional supervision for leaders by an expert in groups is ideal but often not available. (See Chapters 10 and 31.) Peer review with other group leaders is recommended; group situations can be reviewed and the leaders can assist one another in improving their skills.

COMMUNICATION ABOUT THE GROUP AND TO THE GROUP

It is important to view the group in the context of the patient's entire treatment plan. In this light, communication in all directions is important so that group experiences and outcomes are therapeutic. A conscious effort must be made to gather data about patients before group meetings and to share information from group. This requires team knowledge of the group, with the nursing staff sharing relevant information with the group leaders prior to group, and group leaders sharing information immediately after the groups. Regular discussion in team meetings should include the patients' behaviors in groups and the response of patients, staff, and families to groups. Communication books or logs may be kept, as well as periodic summaries in patient records of their participation in groups. Such written communication works fairly well if the team members know where to find it. Team treatment plans also would reflect each patient's involvement and response to groups.

Mary, the poet and storyteller described before, was discussed in a team meeting. The team members were surprised that this woman, who roamed about in her wheelchair, mumbling and complaining at times, was able to tell such stories. It reminded the team members of the need to look for and capitalize on those skills people still have and to increase their respect for older persons.

Jack, who during one group began pounding his fists on the table in anger, had been very pleasant just before the group met. He was able to calm down, but the group leaders reported his behavior to the team. Jack was more closely observed, and the nursing staff discovered that he had threatened another patient earlier that morning for wandering into his room. He also had been up wandering most of the night. Because more than one type of group, with the same patient population, was occurring on the same day, the earlier geropsychiatry morning group leader also shared information about Jack's behavior with the leader of the group scheduled for the next hour. The group leaders discussed how they managed Jack's behavior and discovered that he might be getting mixed messages about how to vent his anger. The group leaders and the team were able to discuss this issue in a team meeting and arrive at a consistent approach to this patient.

When the morning geropsychiatry group first began on the acute care ward, an unanticipated problem was negative reaction to information shared by the group leaders. Both group leaders had many years of experience in leading groups, mainly in psychiatry. However, the majority of the staff on the acute ward had experience in long-term care but not in psychiatry or with groups. When the group leaders shared patients' feelings and complaints, which had been expressed in the group, the staff said the group leaders should not do such groups. The leaders had not realized that such information might be interpreted as negative and critical of staff. The staff, having no experience with such groups, took it personally. This occurrence opened up opportunities to clarify the purpose of groups, the process, the communication issues, and the need for better education about groups, and the need for staff to learn more about working together, as well as with patients.

SPECIAL CONSIDERATIONS: WORKING WITH PATIENTS WITH BRAIN IMPAIRMENT

As noted, there is little in the literature about group work with dementia patients, and even less about groups with mixed populations. It is especially important for group leaders working in acute care settings to know about the patients' conditions and what kinds of problems these patients may present for groups.

What is a dementia? A *dementia* is an acquired, persistent compromise in at least three of the following: memory, language, visuospatial skills, personality/mood, and cognition. Types of dementia include Alzheimer's disease, multi-infarct dementia, Pick's disease, Huntington's chorea, Parkinson's

dementia, normal pressure hydrocephalus (NPH), alcohol-related dementia, drug-induced dementia, Acquired Immune Deficiency Syndrome (AIDS) dementias, and syphilis dementia. Brief descriptions follow.

Alzheimer's disease used to be a diagnosis of exclusion; everything else was ruled out first, including delirium and other alternate diagnoses. Now probable Alzheimer's has an onset between the ages of 40 and 90 years; it is progressive, with memory and other problems in cognition evident. There are visuospatial and neuropsychological changes, but usually normal motor function, indifference, delusions (at times), agitation, and depressed mood. The course is between 6 and 12 years. These people have difficulty taking in new information, apraxia, and a decreasing ability to communicate.

Multi-infarct dementia involves a step-wise progression, with focal and neural deficits. The patient often has a history of vascular disease and hypertension, and neuroimaging shows ischemic white matter and indication of small strokes.

Pick's disease is often confused with Alzheimer's disease. There is a personality change: Patients become disinhibited, show poor judgment, and become aphasic. Imaging of the brain shows frontal atrophy.

Parkinson's dementia occurs in about 20 percent of Parkinson's patients. There is also a change in mood and personality and the more recognizable movement disorder.

Huntington's chorea is a movement disorder. A high percentage of patients develop a dementia.

Normal pressure hydrocephalus causes three main changes: decreased cognition, incontinence, and gait disturbance. A computerized tomography scan shows enlarged ventricles.

Alcohol-related dementia causes memory loss, difficulties with practical problem solving and judgment.

Drug-induced dementia is often reversible and must be ruled out. One sees geropsychiatric and geriatric patients who present themselves at a clinic with a list of the 22 different medications they are taking, from 4 different places and at least 4 different physicians.

Dementia of syphilis is often misdiagnosed. In the geropsychiatry unit mentioned, at least two cases of this disorder were discovered and treated, one with dramatic improvement.

Patients in the earlier stages of any of these dementias can attend and participate to some degree in groups. In fact, there have been patients in the geropsychiatry morning group with all of the dementias mentioned except Huntington's chorea. The group leaders and other members of the health care team on a ward would jointly decide which patients would not be included, for example, a patient with Huntington's chorea whose movement disorder was so severe that it would be difficult and disruptive for the group and the patient.

COMMUNICATION WITH PATIENTS WITH DEMENTIA

There are problems to be anticipated when patients with dementias are in any group. This is particularly true in what may be a short-term group, in an acute care setting. These problems include an inability to understand and/or communicate due to aphasia and word-finding problems (the patient cannot get the correct word and may get quite frustrated, and the group leader has to decide how long to wait or to fill in the blanks or correct answers). At the same time, the group leader(s) must be alert to the needs of other patients in the group and how dementia patients and their behavior affect everyone. See Tables 24-1 through 24-3. Group process follows the same format and phases as other groups noted in this book, in spite of the mix of problems and diagnoses of the patients.

In the geropsychiatry morning group, maintaining a heterogeneous population proved to be a positive experience for the patients, group leaders, and staff. Some of the opportunities presented by such a group, because there are patients who are more cognitively intact than others, include discussion of problems such as confusion, memory loss, and how people help themselves and others remember things; discussion of the need to be patient and to understand that some behaviors are not controllable by some patients; recognition that most patients were not deliberately walking into the wrong room or calling people by incorrect names.

Another opportunity was evident in the early days of the group. There were three patients with Alzheimer's disease, one depressed patient, one

TABLE 24-1 Problems by stages in Alzheimer's disease

Stage 1 (1-3 years): Word-finding problems, empty speech, mild anomia, difficulty listing, memory problems, cognition problems, speech often remains normal in tone and articulation; awareness of deficits may lead to anxiety, depression, frustration.

Stage 2 (2-10 years): Decreasing comprehension, anomia, severely impaired memory, fluent paraphasia, able to repeat, apraxia, agnosia, much difficulty conversing, may forget names of family members, may be increasingly agitated, violent behavior, disorientation to time and place, trouble with dressing, grooming, perseveration, agraphia.

Stage 3 (8-12 years, maybe sooner): All intellectual functions severely impaired, speech severely restricted, echolalia, mute, dysarthria, may become totally disoriented, even forget own name, global aphasia, decreased motor activity; eventually requires total care.

patient who had many somatic complaints, and one patient who had a poststroke depression. Ray, one of the patients with Alzheimer's, who rarely spoke in full sentences and who seemed confused most of the time, came to the rescue of Tom, the somaticizing patient, who had sat down on the floor complaining of weakness. Ray suddenly stood up, went over to Tom, helped him to stand, and brought him to the group leader. Ray was crying. For the group leaders, and later for the team with whom they shared this scene, it was the first time that they realized how sensitive some of the patients with severe dementias are and that staff need to be alert to this sensitivity. At least on some emotional level, these patients appear to experience pain and pleasure; many of the staff thought they could not. This ability to experience emotions and feelings has many implications for treatment, caring, and the study of quality of life for dementia patients.

MANAGEMENT OF DIFFICULT SITUATIONS IN GROUPS

A group of older patients on an acute ward is likely to be heterogeneous, including patients with a wide variety of diagnoses. In addition, there may be a wide variety of behavior problems. Patients who are disruptive in various ways or patients who yell almost constantly may have to be excluded from or later escorted out of the group. If left in the group, they may provoke others to become agitated, angry, anxious, and even more confused. Patients who tend to touch others should be seated in a place where they cannot reach other patients. In the geropsychiatry morning group, it has been useful to explain to the group members specific appropriate approaches to some patients, including which patients they should not touch or be too near. Patients who have some brain impairment may experience a catastrophic reaction, that is, become extremely upset and panicked when they cannot perform what is asked. A calm, reassuring, firm approach will help, as will allowing one of the group leaders to take the patient to another area and stay with him or her for a while. All these management issues require extra attention from the group leaders. Anticipation of such possible problems, based on observations and communication by staff, should be discussed beforehand by the group leaders. If the behaviors occur, they must be reviewed and plans made to better manage such occurrences next time.

Patients with sensory deficits require different strategies. As with any group, the group leaders have a responsibility to recognize such deficits and assist these patients directly. For example, seat them next to the leader, or suggest that another patient help them as needed.

As demonstrated in earlier examples, it is important to focus on patients' strengths. People, especially older persons who have suffered many real losses, may need help to focus on what they have left, not what is gone.

> *Example:* Kay, a 79-year-old woman with memory problems, confusion, and rheumatoid arthritis, no longer groomed herself very well. She often said that she was "no good," that she used to "really be something." Indeed, pictures brought in by the family showed that Kay had been very pretty, wore designer clothes, and was very bright and active. On the ward, she had to walk with the group leader to get to group, or she would not find her way. One day in group, when people were sharing what gave them pleasure, Kay said, "Singing." The group asked her to sing, and she did. She had a lovely voice. She seemed pleased with the group's response and periodically offered to sing in subsequent groups.

TABLE 24-2 Communication problems: Terminology in Alzheimer's disease

Anomia: word-finding disturbances, inability to name things.

Apraxia: Inability to carry out purposeful movement or command.

Impaired category or list generation: Difficulty when asked to list something; disruption of conceptual framework such as losing "robin" before "bird."

Confrontation naming: When an object is presented, the person is asked to name it.

Echolalia: involuntary repetition of words spoken by others.

Empty speech: Noninformative speech; words contribute nothing to content of the speech, for example, "and so on. . . ."

Deitic terms: "This," "That," "There," "Here"; cannot answer specifically.

Indefinite terms: "Things," "stuff," "something."

Neologisms: New words, makes up words.

Palilalia: Abnormal repetition of words and phrases.

Paraphasias: The misuse of words—literal paraphasias (nonwords that sound familiar), semantic paraphasias (real words that are related), verbal paraphasias (real words with no relation to the subject), verbal-phonological paraphasias (real words not semantically related but related phonologically, for example, "bear" for "hair").

Using Available Resources

There may be times when there is only one group leader present, and more help is needed in conducting the group. In the geropsychiatry morning group, when it was possible, other nursing staff sat in. This was always an open invitation. Other resources include pets. Luckily, a wonderful pet dog had been living on the ward for several years and often joined the group. This conveniently led into discussions about pets, animals, and being loved.

Patients are another good resource, if they want to do more, if they can, and if it is helpful in their treatment. Patients can assist with lower-functioning patients, pushing wheelchairs, directing patients to the group, helping with a patient who is hard of hearing, and helping with ward activities.

TABLE 24-3 Recommendations for groups of older persons with dementia

Goal: Avoid frustration and plan individualized approaches.

Assessment

- Check patient's sensory abilities: hearing, vision, and touch.
- Check patient's mental status and attention span.
- Assess for other factors affecting communication such as infection, movement disorder, or medication reactions.

General approaches

- Begin each interaction by saying your name and the patient's name.
- Use low tone and calm manner.
- Use short, simple sentences.
- Ask only one question at a time.
- Speak slowly and wait for response.
- Avoid arguing.
- Look at the person.
- Be patient and move slowly.
- Use smile and touch when appropriate.
- Recognize patient's sensitivity to nonverbal behavior and to feelings.
- Use other signals; point, touch, and demonstrate; teach the patient to do the same.
- Observe; check the patient regularly, since he or she may not be able to communicate pain or needs.
- Do not pretend to understand if you do not; work toward understanding.
- Follow through on what you say you will do.
- Note and report patient's unique communications and responses; share information with others.
- Use humor when appropriate.
- Use a handshake.
- Promote self-care.
- Assist, support, and educate the family and significant others.
- Modify the environment.
- Try various treatment modalities, such as groups, list learning, movement therapy, relaxation techniques, and supportive therapy.

Recommendations

- Limit the size of the group to three to eight members.
- Plan short group sessions, about 30 minutes.
- Meet more frequently, three times per week.
- Stimulation and stabilization must be related to the group setting.
- Have a stable group setting; meet at the same place every time.
- An open group is possible.
- The group leader should be active and emotionally warm.
- Emotionally important content must be seen in relation to the acute situation.
- Have clearly defined inclusion criteria.
- Plan a method to evaluate the group.
- Seat hard-of-hearing patients near someone who will help. (This may be the leader.)
- The leader sits near the neediest or weakest patient.
- Limit distractions, such as noises and other people walking into the room.
- The leader must be prepared with a variety of approaches and to analyze all nonverbal behavior, including his or her own (Krebs-Roubicek 1989, 1266; Burnside 1986).

SOURCE: Unpublished lecture given by Elissa Brown in 1987.

STARTING A GROUP

After preparing and gaining some knowledge and skills in group work, the group can begin. In the first group meeting, the leaders may find that flexibility is a key factor. Often, just getting the group together, which can take 15 minutes, or half of the planned time, is exhausting. This may require coming early and involving other team members. Experience in each session will help the group leader to plan for subsequent group meetings.

Phases of the Group: What to Expect

The group leader(s) may have to learn to expect the unexpected. Although the phases of groups for older persons on acute units may be similar to phases in any group, how the leader gets through the phases may be quite different.

- Introductions occur each time, since some patients are apt to have memory difficulties.
- Expect more silences, depending on the population.
- Find common threads and topics of common interest; this may take more work.
- Balance what goes on when there is a heterogeneous group by trying different techniques.
- Deal with the patient who monopolizes or the silent patient: It will require the leader to know enough about the patient to determine how much the patient can do.
- Avoid a catastrophic reaction or disruptive behavior by planning ahead; this requires good communication and staff sharing information with the group leaders.

When patients are to be discharged, discuss discharges in the group. Even though the patient stay may have been only a few days, it is another opportunity for patients to feel valued and for others to discuss separation or what it feels like to stay.

If the group is a closed group (i.e., there is a prescribed number of sessions and a prescribed purpose), then plans for the termination phase may begin earlier. In fact, termination could be a topic in the first meeting of a short-term group.

A Typical Unpredictable Geropsychiatry Morning Group

A typical geropsychiatry morning group session, or class, as many of the patients refer to group meetings, is described in the following example.

Example: Patients included three higher functioning males, two depressed, one with multi-infarct dementia. They are waiting by the group's table in the day room when the group leader arrives. Another male patient is receiving eye-drops, and the nurse says he will be along shortly. The group leader goes to the other group members' rooms to invite them to group. Three male patients get up from their beds and head toward the day room. A fourth patient, Maggie, with chronic obstructive pulmonary disease, says she just cannot make it (mornings are difficult for her). Another male patient is having ECT and says he is just going to wait for his treatment. A female patient is wandering, but she takes the group leader's arm when offered and goes with

her to the day room. Ten minutes after the leader arrives, group begins.

The goal of these group meetings is to help the patients get going in the morning with some stimulation, reality orientation, and socialization. The first questions are "How is everyone? Did you have a good weekend?" There is minimal response, other than nodding. Then the group leader asks each patient to introduce himself or herself and say the name of the person to his or her left as they go around the table. One new patient begins to talk, nonstop, and to insult just about everyone in the room. The group leader suggests this is not appropriate and quickly directs attention to the next patient. Discussion then centers on the day's activity schedule; some speak up about bingo, because they won last time. The group leader then asks what they would like to talk about. One patient says: "Nothing. I just want to go home. I think they've done all they can do to me. Where's my wife?"

Feelings and frustration become the theme of the group for the remaining time. However, the group leader has many options: each member, if he or she does not initiate discussion, can be asked either, "What makes you frustrated?" or "What do you do when you are frustrated?" or What helps you when you are frustrated?" or "Do others have the same feelings?" The group leader can talk about confusion and how frightening it is to be in a strange environment, opening another line of discussion.

These are some of the challenges of group work in acute care settings. One female patient who came to the group sat in the background and only responded when spoken to. During a team family meeting with her daughter, planning the patient's treatment, the patient was asked what she would agree to do. From out of the blue she said she liked the group. "I learn from it." Such are the rewards for the group leader.

SUMMARY

In this chapter, a variety of issues regarding groups for older persons in acute care settings are addressed. The types of groups that can be conducted in acute rather than long-term care or psychiatric settings are described. Initial planning for such groups is reviewed, as well as disruptive factors, education and training, and group techniques. Evaluation of groups, planning, and special considerations with a more acute population are also discussed. Ideas about management of difficult situations, starting a group, and case examples are included. Throughout the chapter, patience and flexibility are noted as essential qualities for group leaders. The groups for older persons that have been described may not work in every acute care setting. However, with the need for programs and activities for older patients, it can be worthwhile to try groups as a treatment modality.

EXERCISE 1

Role-play an inpatient group for older persons in an acute setting. Write descriptions of various roles that participants can play, and distribute these to each of the five to eight group members. Examples of roles:

- A 77-year-old male patient who suffered a stroke four years ago; he has paralysis of the right side and a negative attitude
- An 80-year-old female, hard of hearing, who was admitted two days ago because of dehydration and weight loss.
- A 69-year-old male with a history of depression and increasing suspiciousness; he retired six months ago. His wife needed a respite.

Assign a group leader and a co-leader. If enough people are available, assign two observers. Ask the leaders to conduct a group for 5 to 10 minutes. The leaders discuss how they felt; the patients discuss how they felt. All participate in a discussion of what they learned. Observers may choose to do sociograms, illustrating communication patterns.

EXERCISE 2

For self-awareness regarding leadership style, use the group format described above, but focus on leadership styles, giving each person an opportunity to lead and receive feedback from the group.

EXERCISE 3

Select a setting in which you can co-lead an inpatient group. Arrange for group discussion and review after the co-leadership experience. Keep a log and draw sociograms to illustrate communication patterns. Compare the early group sessions with later ones.

REFERENCES

Akerlund BM, Norberg B. 1986. Group psychotherapy with demented patients. *Geriatr Nurs* 7(2):83-84.

Beck CK, Rawlings RP, Williams SR. 1988. *Mental health—Psychiatric nursing, A holistic life-cycle approach.* St. Louis: Mosby.

Burgess AW. 1990. *Psychiatric nursing in the hospital and community*, 5th ed. (pp. 1034-1035). Norwalk, CT: Appleton & Lange.

Burnside IM. 1986. *Working with the elderly: Group process and techniques*, 2d ed. Boston: Jones and Bartlett.

Gerber GJ, Prince PN, Snider HG, et al. 1991. Group activity and cognitive improvement among patients with Alzheimer's disease. *Hosp Comm Psych* 42(8):843-844.

Gilewski M. 1986. Group therapy with cognitively impaired older adults. *Clin Gerontol* 5(3/4):281-296.

Hanley IG, McGuire RJ, Boyd WD. 1981. Reality orientation and dementia: A controlled trial of two approaches. *Br J Psychiatr* 138:10-14.

Janosik EH, Davies JL. 1989. *Psychiatric mental health nursing*, 2d ed. Boston: Jones and Bartlett.

Kohut H, as noted by Lazarus and Weinberg in Gilewski M. 1986. Group therapy with cognitively impaired older adults. *Clin Gerontol* 5(3/4):293-294.

Krebs-Roubicek EM. 1989. Group therapy with demented elderly. In *Alzheimer's disease and related disorders* (pp. 1261-1272). New York: Liss.

Manaster A, in Gilewski M. 1986. Group therapy with cognitively impaired older adults. *Clin Gerontol* 5(3/4): 285.

Mazor R. 1982. Drama therapy for the elderly in a day care center. *Hosp Comm Psych* 33(7):577-579.

Pfeiffer E, as quoted in Krebs-Roubicek EM. 1989. Group therapy with demented elderly. In *Alzheimer's disease and related disorders* (pp. 1261-1272). New York: Liss.

Sautter FJ, Hearney C, O'Neill P. 1991. A problem-solving approach to group psychotherapy in the inpatient milieu. *Hosp Comm Psych* 42(8):814-817.

Wolff K, as quoted in Krebs-Roubicek EM. 1989. Group therapy with demented elderly. In *Alzheimer's disease and related disorders* (pp. 1261-1272). New York: Liss.

Yalom ID. 1983. *Inpatient group therapy*. New York: Basic Books.

BIBLIOGRAPHY

Clark P. 1991. Ethical dimensions of quality of life in aging: Autonomy vs. collectivism in the United States and Canada. *Gerontologist* 31(5): 631-639.

Cox CL, Kaeser L, Montgomery AC, Marion LH. 1991. Quality of life nursing care: An experimental trial in long-term care. *J Gerontol Nurs* 17(4):6-11.

Cox BJ, Waller LL. 1991. *Bridging the communication gap with the elderly: Practical strategies for caregivers.* Chicago: American Hospital Publishing.

Dustin VS. 1989. Just as you are. *Good Housekeeping* (March):68-69.

Hunter S. 1992. Day care: Promoting quality of life for the elderly. *J Gerontol Nurs* 18(2):17-20.

Hurley AC, et al. 1992. Assessment of discomfort in advanced Alzheimer's patients. *Res Nurs Health* 15: 369-377.

Mazor R. 1982. Drama therapy for the elderly in a day care center. *Hosp Comm Psych* 33(7):577-579.

Minde R, et al. 1990. The ward milieu and its effect on the behaviour of psychogeriatric patients. *Can J Psych* 35(March):133-138.

Teri L, Logsdon R. 1991. Identifying pleasant activities for Alzheimer's disease patients: The Pleasant Events Schedule—AD. *Gerontologist* 31(1):127.

Wilson HS. 1990. Nursing the mind: Easing life for the Alzheimer's patient. *RN* (December):24-27.

PART 6
Multidisciplinary Perspectives

Because group work with older adults is now conducted with people from many disciplines, it is important to explore perspectives from these disciplines.

Mary Gwynne Schmidt leads off in Chapter 25 with perspectives of the social worker based on her years of teaching and clinical experience.

In Chapter 26, Irene Burnside portrays the nurse's perspective.

Chapter 27, by Karin Vecchione, who is both an occupational and a recreational therapist, presents the view of a recreational therapist and her contributions to group work with older adults.

A Social Worker's Perspective

Mary Gwynne Schmidt

KEY WORDS

- Advocacy
- Confidentiality
- Host agency
- Least contest
- Values and purpose

LEARNING OBJECTIVES

- Describe circumstances in the early and more recent history of social group work that have led social workers to believe they have a duty to advocate for their clients.
- Discuss how the values and purposes of social work have contributed to an approach especially suited for work with older persons and their families.
- Tell why it is important for social workers in nursing facilities to work closely with nursing staff when planning groups.
- List three issues the social group worker should take into account when intervening in response to group members' complaints about their families or the setting.
- Describe two typical instances in which the nurse's responsibility for safety and the social worker's concern for self-determination have contributed to tensions. What developments are easing this?

Social group work differs from other group work not in its knowledge base, which is shared, but in the values and purposes of social work that guide it. Sometimes these alienate social workers from their natural allies, and group services to the aged suffer.

After reviewing the circumstances that have given social work its character, this chapter will discuss misunderstandings that sometimes occur between professionals in host agencies and steps the social worker can take to avoid them. The chapter will close with some of the practical concerns that arise from the juxtaposition of social work values and the functioning of the aged.

THE SHAPING PAST

The social work approach to small groups acquired its character in three phases: first, as part of an undifferentiated group work movement; next, as a method within social work; and finally, as a cluster of skills and learnings disseminated throughout the profession. The range of persons it dealt with and the nature of its interventions broadened as it developed from a specialty in the second phase to part of the general repertoire in the third.

In the first phase, group work began as classes and clubs in settlement houses and youth-serving organizations. This matrix led to optimism about man's press to health and the growth-generating power of the group. It also caused the group to be viewed as a medium for socialization.

Engaged in teaching new ways to new Americans, the settlement houses dealt with normal people and therefore looked to growth and learning rather than remediation. This created some reluctance later to move into group therapy, which was seen as undemocratic.

Many of the persons coming to the settlement houses worked in factories, lived in tenements, and were deprived of many of the protections and advantages automatically extended to the middle class. Settlement-house workers advocated for the poor and encouraged them to campaign for themselves. This past is evident in social work's continuing strain of reformism. Social workers are taught the duty of advocacy and the strength of the group to help its members act on their own behalf.

The settlement house offered young people opportunities to make new friends, but beneath this was a more serious purpose—socialization. The intent was to teach these people how things were done in America so that they might succeed in their new land. The youth organizations and church groups also had an educative, character-building thrust.

In the second phase, social group work moved into the mainstream of social work proper and became one of its three major methods, along with casework and community organization.

The first phase took place in the last quarter of the nineteenth century and the early years of the twentieth, when young families were immigrating from Europe and young Americans were losing some of the traditional supports they had experienced in rural communities. The second phase began when the government took over relief-giving in the Great Depression and social workers broadened their function beyond investigating the poor. It ended when the American Association of Group Workers joined other social work organizations to form the National Association of Social Workers in 1955. Group work was professionalized and then moved into social work as a methodological specialization.

When Gertrude Wilson (1976, 31-32), one of the leaders of the second phase, looked back over half a century of social group work, she recalled that the leadership of the American Association of Group Workers had consisted chiefly of social workers, although only a few years earlier the group work section of the National Conference of Social Work had drawn members from adult education, physical education, the agricultural extension program, and the Children's Bureau as well. Thus, a narrowing had occurred as social group work became not a profession in its own right but a method. Ten years after its introduction at Case Western Reserve in 1927, group work was being taught in ten schools of social work. Students had to choose among casework, group work, and community organization; specialization reigned.

In the meantime, two things had happened to group work. First, under the influence of persons like Fritz Redl, who worked with severely disturbed boys, it had moved beyond the original growth and task groups to include remediation (Douglas 1979). Second, social work purposes had come to determine its direction.

The third phase saw the end of group work as a separate specialty and the merging of its skills and theory into generalist practice.

In 1961, four organizations concerned with older adults convened a seminar on "Social Group Work with Older People." In the foreword to the proceedings, Ollie Randall stated that it was appropriate that social casework came first in the series of seminars but right also that group work should follow, because group workers had been the first to make some of the adaptations in method required by older people (NASW 1980a, 3-4).

In the same year, William Schwartz (1979), a group worker, had pointed out that social work's new roles in institutional and therapeutic settings indicated that the unit of service should be determined by client need, not by agency or practitioner specialization.

Today Schwartz's vision is largely realized. The generalist is taught to work with individuals, families, groups, or communities as the occasion demands. Group interventions have become part of the training of every social worker.

A fourth phase is emerging in response to changing roles. There are both more requirements and also more sources of reimbursement for social services, including work with small groups. With the rise of private practice and with membership on interdisciplinary teams, more social workers are leading therapy groups. With the growth of mutual-support groups, more social workers are organizing and facilitating self-help groups. With social services mandated in nursing facilities, more are working with resident and family groups in settings providing long-term care. Finally, more are engaging in case management, whether as traditional social workers or as relatively distant coordinators and cost cutters.

In response, there are differences in preparation. Undergraduates are still being trained as generalists, but, in addition to a general background, graduate students are becoming more specialized. Students electing to work with individuals and families take courses that equip them to lead groups; those seeking careers in social administration generally receive some training in group process.

Social group work has emerged from its 100-year history with values like those of the other helping professions—essentially a belief in the uniqueness and worth of the individual and in each person's right to self-determination. In the case of social work, these values are undergirded by a set of assumptions growing out of the profession's past in the youth organization and settlement house, with its optimistic view of human nature and its commitment to fight injustice. The optimism about human nature may have been somewhat tempered by two decades of work in protective services. Nevertheless, enough of these assumptions remain to make social workers critical guests in host agencies.

SOCIAL WORK VALUES AND THE OLDER ADULT

Social work's values and its range fit it for work with older adults. The range is that of both clientele and intervention. Social workers' education equips them to serve this heterogeneous population: They can facilitate groups for the well aged, provide support for organizations of older persons engaged on their own behalf, and lead patient and family groups for the institutionalized and those in day care.

Older persons experiencing losses tend to have multiple needs. The generalist is prepared to work with the individual, family, group, institution, or community and therefore can move—as the ear-

lier group worker could not—from leading a relatives' group to following up the members' concerns about establishing eligibility or securing special resources. This capacity is useful when a nurse or physician wants to organize a group around an illness and needs a co-leader who will share responsibility for other kinds of follow-up.

Although members of all helping professions operate with an awareness of the client's social systems, it is safe to say that no other profession is so explicitly required by its mission to relate to them. This perspective is helpful when dealing with a population that includes persons who are disabled, dependent, or institutionalized.

Older persons often present with situational depressions or troubled role transitions. Emphasis on self-determination and client strengths combats learned helplessness—the apathetic, passive, depressed kinds of behavior that often ensue when aging persons discover that they have lost control over many aspects of their lives. Social workers are taught to engage the healthy residue in the personalities of even the severely disabled. They emphasize coping.

This approach is illustrated in one of the early accounts of group work with the aged. In their book about the Hodson Center in New York during World War II, Kubie and Landau (1953) tell how the professional social worker arrived at this prototypical old people's center and quickly developed modes of democratic leadership among these seemingly passive persons, who previously had been bossed by two or three aggressive members.

The focus on socialization is serviceable both for persons moving into a life stage for which there are few guidelines and also for individuals going into group living.

Irving Rosow (1974) has written movingly about the poor schooling society gives people for old age. The young are told clearly what is expected of them, but the old are left to stumble into old-age roles, learning only through criticism and rejection.

Rosow points out that younger authority figures engender a sense of role reversal that stimulates geriatric "difficultness" as a "desperate rearguard action to retain vestiges of dignity, control, and independence that are steadily slipping" (p. 140). Certainly this is true in long-term care settings, where administrators and nurses tend to be middle-aged or younger. Many institutions for the aged offer few inspiring role models from whom members might learn how to be self-respecting older persons.

Rosow says that the support of the peer group ordinarily maintains the morale of persons moving as cohorts into new situations, but it is hard for older adults to identify with occupants of a devalued status (pp. 141-143). He proposes apartheid of the old—insulated enclaves of their own where they might make their own rules and find status and comfort (pp. 155-170).

What this formulation contributes to everyday life is an awareness of the strong need for older persons, especially those moving into sheltered care, to participate in small groups, particularly small groups that would provide induction into the system for newcomers and also opportunities for peer leadership. The social work group offers this kind of help because it fosters membership initiative and action.

THE GUEST CONNECTION

If social work values and principles equip the practitioner for service to the aged, they contribute also to misunderstandings and conflict with the other professions. The more needful the client, the more likely the social worker is to be serving that person in a host agency—that is, in a hospital, a mental health facility, or a nursing home, settings where social work is not the dominant profession. The more vulnerable the clients, the more likely they and their families are to be harmed if they sense disharmony among members of the treatment team.

Interprofessional collaboration is needed in the community also, but the prototypical situation, illustrating the full potential for value clash, is found in the nursing home. In all special settings for the aged, there are different degrees of disability and different responding levels of care and control. The higher these are, the more important is team communication.

The social worker may find that it is relatively simple to organize a poetry, music, or reminiscence group for the residents of a home for the aged. It may be necessary only to check the monthly schedule, get clearance from the administrator, and pay attention to member interests and competing events. In the same home's nursing unit, arrangements will be more complex.

The social worker who attempts to organize a patient group without consulting the director of nursing is likely to arrive to find that group members have

been sent to the beauty parlor or packed off for naps. Equipment may have been tidied away, a troop of Brownie Scouts scheduled for a sing-along, and a competing activity slated for the meeting room.

Before viewing this as sabotage, the social worker would be well advised to look at the logistics of the setting and the condition of the patients. The work schedules of nursing personnel swing around a five-day week and there may be absences and substitutions. The charge nurse on duty when the group held its first meeting may not be there on the date of the second. Nurses' assistants may function on a tight schedule around a predictable patient routine. Other events are likely to be overlooked for forgotten, especially if they do not occur on a daily basis.

Patients tend to be very old, very frail, or both. Therefore, a group member may be in bed with the side rails up not because someone wanted to keep her out of the meeting but because she manifested mild confusion and seemed unwell.

Before beginning a group, have the fullest consultation with staff. Not only the director of nursing and the administrator but others, including the nurses' assistants, should have an opportunity to share views, suggest patients, and when feasible, participate in leadership itself. Some group members will go out with relatives just when your meeting is scheduled and others will remain in bed or be shunted off to the podiatrist, but these things will be less likely to happen if staff is included in group planning.

The moral is threefold: In these settings, every other activity is secondary to nursing care, the staff is often stretched thin, and nursing personnel must cope with accountabilities of their own. These factors lead to conflicts, even when the values held by the two professions are either the same or very similar.

INTERACTION WITH OTHER DISCIPLINES

The Social Work Code of Ethics contains six sections with 16 items, but two underlying values are universally recognized; related to them are two duties that may be problematic for interprofessional collaboration (NASW 1980b). The two values are (1) respect for the inherent dignity and worth of the individual and (2) respect for client self-determination. Related duties are confidentiality and advocacy.

Other disciplines also believe in the uniqueness and inherent dignity of the individual and in client self-determination; others also respect confidentiality and view themselves as patient advocates. Countervailing this is professional caution. Physicians think they could be sued for practically anything, and nurses have been taught that they are responsible for the physical safety of every patient. They also sense the social worker's view that she or he is the only one in the setting who really cares.

The safety/freedom tension between nurses and social workers should be eased by federal nursing-home reform amendments and state regulations that emphasize (as patients' rights) a greater sharing of responsibility with the resident and family (U.S. Social Security Act). A major irritant in the past has been what social workers viewed as the excess tying of patients by overly cautious nurses. Nurses have provided much of the leadership in the movement toward restraint-free care that has culminated in the new laws.

Respect for Dignity and Worth of Individual

The need to respect individual dignity and worth is spelled out for nurses also (Ness 1980). Because they deal with persons in situations conducive to regression—around the provision of physical care, such as feeding, toileting, putting to bed—nurses are likely to respond to the patient's need for a comforting parental figure. The same patient may present a more coping self to the social worker because much of the business they do together involves decision making and negotiation by the resident and therefore elicits a more mature level of behavior. Nurse and social worker are reacting to different patient expectations arising out of the different circumstances of service. If nurses responded as social workers do, the patient might perceive their behavior as distancing and cold.

The social worker is likely to be jarred by the nurses' assistant who addresses an aged patient as she might a small child ("Still dry, Rosie?"). Excellent nursing practice frowns on this too.

Respect for Client Self-determination

The nurse is also aware of the patient's need for autonomy (Conti 1980), but the social worker is likely to view the nurse as needlessly restrictive

and the nurse, to see the social worker as heedless of patient safety. The experienced social worker does not loosen soft ties, help a patient out of a wheelchair, or promise an outing without consulting a nurse. The patient who requests a cookie may be diabetic.

The nurse's education emphasizes responsibility for patient safety. This awareness rises whenever an insurance salesperson addresses the local nurses about malpractice—and not without cause. The very family that protests soft ties to restrain an unsteady patient may be the first to complain if that patient falls. Moreover, family members will address their complaints to the nurse even though it may have been the social worker who loosened the ties when the patient in the group requested it. As long as the physician and laity are ready to blame the nurse, they must let the nurse set the limits.

The social worker can deal with some of these tensions by helping families to come to terms with their own feelings about placement so that they can act responsibly and determine how much risk-taking they are willing to support for their mentally frail patient. This is an appropriate issue for a relatives' group.

Confidentiality

Today's nurse is well aware of the right to privacy, both through professional education and through patients' bills of rights (Dittmar 1989). Confidentiality falters when accountability comes in. The nurse is not supposed to withhold information from the physician, and in the case of the confused aged patient, she or he may accept a paying relative's right to know. When the social worker has an obligation to report (as in court-related or guardianship cases), the worker usually deals with confidentiality by indicating its limits to the client, but there are persons who are unlikely to grasp such explanations.

Within the group, confidentiality is the rule, and its violation checks another norm, openness. One advantage of co-leadership with a member of the nursing staff is that it makes visible the fact of sharing. In the same way, if a patient group wishes to discuss some aspect of service with administration, supporting them rather than taking over this task permits group members to decide for themselves how far they are willing to go.

Advocacy

Social workers are taught that they have a duty to advocate for the helpless and oppressed. As born-again activists, they often campaign for patients' councils, less medication, and more freedom even when it entails an element of risk. This elicits some unpopularity, especially when the young reformer approaches the task with overtones of moral elitism. What needs to be remembered is that every person working with the aged has an obligation to prevent abuse. If the social worker is not bent on going it alone, this ethical obligation of the others will secure allies in the effort.

Three issues should be considered: the definitions of the protagonists, the principle of *least contest*, and the interdependence of the individual and his social system.

First, definitions differ. For example, the social worker whose patients are dozing through group sessions may view medication as a chemical straitjacket employed by physicians for the convenience of nurses, especially if the worker was born too late to see the state of psychotic patients before psychotropic medications. The physician may counter the criticism by viewing the social worker as a troublemaking upstart. In addition, what the social worker defines as advocacy may be seen by the administrator as disloyalty to the home. Definitions influence interaction.

Second, the principle of least contest suggests beginning with inquiries and quiet negotiation before making negative assumptions about motivation. The physician may be unaware that he or she is medicating the patient into drowsiness and may be willing to reassess the medication in light of a changing situation. The principle of least contest is built on the premise that it is easier to escalate protest than to temper it after defensiveness has been aroused.

Finally, it is rarely in the client's interest to denigrate his or her social system. In attempting to make institutions and persons responsive to client needs, social workers must take care not to harm the client in the process of "rescue." Old persons cannot leave certain systems, such as the family, even if technically they are extruded by their placement and by the family's withdrawal. The individuals continue to see themselves in the context of the family and quite often are seen in that relationship by others. This is why most efforts to serve one at the cost of the other fail. The separation and alienation remain a running sore.

In the same way, the client and the long-term care setting need each other. Therefore, it is not an act of disloyalty to make a setting aware that it is failing its residents. Even the for-profit facility receives its legitimation because it delivers a service to the sick and the very old. If the setting provides good service to patients and their families, it will fulfill its social mission and be confirmed in its profit-earning one. If it falls far below standards, it will jeopardize both. To attack the home without first attempting to change it through ordinary channels is to misserve the clients. The oldest, frailest, and most vulnerable suffer transplantation with difficulty and generally are better served by improvement of conditions where they are.

This fulfills the purpose of social work, which is to "promote or restore a mutually beneficial interaction between individuals and society in order to improve the quality of life for everyone" (Special Group on Conceptual Frameworks 1981).

VALUES AND GROUP INTERVENTIONS WITH THE AGED: PRAGMATIC ISSUES

The aged include individuals as diverse as retired executives and working men, mental patients grown old, the organically impaired and the newly depressed, elderly priests and nuns, women and men, poor and middle-class blacks, the rural elderly, and downtown skid-row residents. Together they present age and cohort differences that test social work and invite thoughtful attention.

Self-determination and Reluctance to Participate

Gerontological social workers sometimes criticize acute care settings for failing to make a serious commitment to talking therapies for older adults, but they are caught in a dilemma of their own. How much should they press old persons in residential care to participate in the small groups they offer? Even in an age of patients' rights, there is a power differential between professional and resident that most social workers would be reluctant to invoke. This leaves them little leverage but relationship, which may work least with the withdrawn and the angry.

The problem is that those perceived by the professional to be most in need of group services are often the least willing to try them. This dilemma is illustrated by Alice C.

Among the 25 patients in the nursing wing of the home for the aged, there were alert patients who had cocooned themselves away from the disoriented persons around them. Some had special friends who came from the boarding unit or sustaining contacts outside, but a few seemed both lonely and self-isolated and in need of something more. Miss C's transfer from the boarding unit to the nursing wing via the hospital brought this into focus.

When Miss C, 92, returned from the hospital with a broken hip, she was restless and unhappy, caught between a desire to go back to the independence of her room in the boarding home and the fears that made her reluctant to give up the safety of the nursing unit. She accused the nurses of wanting to keep her a patient and at the same time always found a reason for not walking when they came to help her. I could not deal with this in a casework relationship because she had displaced on me much of her anger at the administrator, a woman my own age, although ordinarily she got along well with both of us. I felt she might get support from her peers.

I approached Miss C and four other patients who had good minds and poor health. They agreed to try a meeting. One man had multiple sclerosis and another, Parkinson's disease. An 85-year-old woman who had adjusted well to transfer was added for balance. A fifth candidate agreed to join us and then discovered a plan to go off-grounds with a relative.

On the day of the meeting, the patient with Parkinson's disease "forgot" and was moving rapidly toward his room when I persuaded him to give it a try. The others gathered with less protest. I again repeated that the purpose of the meeting was to give them, as persons with keen intellects, an opportunity to lend one another some company and support. I repeated my hope that they would decide to meet on a weekly basis. They were polite but cautiously noncommittal, except for the gentle 85-year-old, the one least in need of the program. She remarked that this might be nice.

I waited, occasionally bowling in items to an essentially silent group. Finally I commented that Dr. M, the patient with the multiple sclerosis, had recently tried acupuncture. The group's interest quickened. All eyes upon him, Dr. M smilingly described his experience while the others plied him with questions. For a little while they were truly a group, but they never agreed to meet again.

The following week, Dr. M was "too tired"; the patient with the Parkinson's disease stumped resolutely to his room with a "not today"; and Miss C was not speaking to me. Only the outgoing 85-year-old was willing—and she could hardly constitute a group by herself. Miss C could not tolerate any contact at all that might threaten her brittle defenses. Later, when she had resolved her ambivalence about staying, she readmitted me to her good graces, quite amazed that I could ever have imagined that she might have been angry. For the two men, isolation seemed a means of conserving their failing energies.

In this instance, I had had several indispensable ingredients: the separate goodwill of all the members except Miss C, who was temporarily at odds with me; the support of the administrator and the nursing staff, who shared my concern; and, as potential members, a small group of persons who had much in common. These persons had had little energy to invest in a relationship, and yet for a moment Dr. M had scintillated and his smiling peers had urged him on. The unanswered question was how much pressure to exert. During the remainder of my association with the home, I continued to look in vain for a group solution to this problem of the isolated alert patient.

In the same home, two other groups fared somewhat better. I continued an ongoing music group because it was an activity that the alert and less alert could enjoy together. After several years, it collapsed under my unwillingness to go on when the nurses' assistants plucked out the more passive, confused members and put them to bed. The earlier morning hour had had to be shifted, and the new time chosen by the nurses was unwelcome to their assistants because it interfered with their opportunity to "finish up."

A reality orientation group was designed to provide stimulation for the most disoriented members and education for a social work student. It ended with her field placement. Attendance at the music group had required only encouragement and a reminder. The reality orientation group had the support of the paraprofessional staff and the passive willingness of the participants. Rather than reviewing the days of the week, an early exercise for this group was teaching the members the names of the nurses' assistants, an activity both participants and nursing assistants viewed as relevant.

Two factors are important in securing initial participation: a good relationship with the social worker and a low level of threat. Even when the social worker is brought in only to lead groups, he or she would be well advised to spend time first getting acquainted with the clients, the setting, and the staff.

At a downtown nutrition site, an extremely anomic group of seniors attended a current events group, a humanities group, and a men's group designed for heavy drinkers. In each instance, the group was led by students who were well known to the members and well liked by them. The humanities group provided stimulus for reminiscence of a very structured sort. The men's group was run by a male student who quickly saw that the Alcoholics Anonymous formula was not appropriate for these clients. He chose instead to support the flicker of companionship and limited here-and-now sharing. It is worth noting that attendees at these three groups represented a fraction of all the persons who used the center. It was a small pool fed by a big sea. At no time was the need for group activities, as it might be judged by the professional, a determinant of participation.

When attendance is compulsory, nonparticipation takes special forms. Lesser and his associates (1981) describe the restless, disjunctive behavior of older psychotics in traditional group therapy. Most members were silent; some displayed pseudoconfusion; others addressed irrelevant questions to the physician co-leader. *When reminiscence therapy was substituted, the same patients became alert and receptive, making it apparent that the disturbed behavior was a method of dealing with the threat.*

Respect for the Individual and the Too-bland Group

Forman (1967) has called attention to the rejection implicit in offering the aged only recreational and leisure-time groups and in supporting the suppression of conflict. Lakin (1988) compared groups for older adults with those for young adults and scored the aged as higher on conflict because they made more references to differences among themselves. Nevertheless, he went on to comment that they "avoid strong overt reactions to other members" (p. 52) and noted that they tend to avoid emotional intensity. Altholz, in Chapter 19, finds their antagonisms muted and their confrontations indirect.

While supporting openness, one has to respect and accept this lower key. A student social worker attempted to support some expression of divergent viewpoints, especially as she became aware of the many undercurrents among the residents in the home for the aged. The 87-year-old peer leader took her aside finally and explained that they lived too close together to tolerate open conflict in the group.

While it is better for a group to police itself, the social worker may question whether extreme tolerance for the monopolist does not communicate the worker's low expectations and even a sort of disrespect for the group as a whole.

Confidentiality and Responsible Others

Aged participants are not likely to present material they would be unwilling to share, and the limits of confidentiality should be discussed (Appelbaum & Greer 1993). When information must be passed on, it is helpful to discuss with the client how it should be presented. This solution has less meaning when the client is limited or forgetful.

In sharing with the confused person's adult children, the group worker may need to act as a surrogate ego, telling what the client would be willing to have told if he or she were aware of the circumstances. By not gossiping about the aged individual, as adults sometimes do when discussing a small child, the social worker is modeling respect for the still-adult status of the failing parent, an important consideration when the adult children may be struggling with concerns about their own aging.

In long-term care settings, students are sometimes reluctant to include members of the patient care staff when they are leading a group. Their rationale is that the presence of these persons may be inhibiting for the patients, whereas, in fact, it may be inhibiting for the novice group leader. Exclusion seems to show a lack of trust, both of the staff members themselves and of the group members' ability to deal with them. If there is a troubled relationship, generally it is better to have it where you can observe it.

One reason for including other staff members is to encourage their constructive interest in group activity. If time is taken to discuss the group with them before and after meetings, a major reason for their exclusion—the tendency of some to suppress the expression of negative feelings—can be checked.

The student's orientation group described earlier had its ups and downs. One morning the student telephoned that she would be arriving too late to start the group and asked the field instructor to take over. When the student came, she found the members rehearsing the names of their favorite nurses' assistants and of the licensed vocational nurse (LVN) who was present. The student commented that the aides and the nurse had never come when she led the group. Further inquiry showed that she had never asked them. In this group, the traditional material of reorientation groups was abandoned in favor of information likely to secure the members better lives within the home. Learning the names of the nurses' assistants was a single example.

The reward came when the social worker arrived one afternoon and found the LVN, surrounded by a circle of the more regressed patients, talking with them and encouraging them to address one another.

Advocacy and the Vulnerable Client

When dealing with dependent populations, there are three questions the practitioner must consider before embarking on advocacy.

First, will your intervention leave the client vulnerable to reprisals? This is no reason for not acting, but it does dictate a carefully thought-out strategy.

Second, what kind of changes does the client want? When I administered the Philadelphia Geriatric Morale Scale to residents in two settings, one woman with a very low morale score nevertheless replied to the item that asked, "Where would you live if you could live where you wanted?" "Right here!" She saw the setting as the best arrangement available to her and would not have welcomed vigorous intervention. What she wanted was more respect from some of the nurses' assistants.

Third, what is the function of the complaint? Just as there are adult children who complain about the inconsiderate behavior of a parent but continue to reinforce it, there are older persons whose laments have a conversational quality. This does not mean that the complaints should not be taken seriously but only that they should be examined. Specificity is a clue, and so is willingness to act when fully supported. Either diffuseness or inaction indicates the need for deeper listening: You may not have heard what the client really said.

SUMMARY

From its early development in settlement houses and youth organizations, social group work gained its optimistic view of human nature, its duty to fight injustice, and its use of the group to help people learn new ways. Social group work was once a separate method within the profession; but today most social workers are prepared to intervene as needed with individuals, families, groups, or communities, a flexibility that fits them well for work with the older client.

If they are to serve the most vulnerable older adults well, social workers leading groups in host settings must communicate with members of other professions and must be sensitive to the situational factors that lead them to translate similar values somewhat differently.

The social worker in the group must deal with issues raised by the interface of social work values and the special characteristics and needs of the very old: self-determination and the reluctant participant, confidentiality and the need of family and caregivers to know, advocacy without damage to a dependent client's supporting systems, and the rights of the individual and the group.

EXERCISE 1

Interprofessional collaboration demands the ability to understand the feelings of the other. This exercise asks you to look at a situation in a nursing home from two points of view, that of the charge nurse and that of the social worker who comes once a week to lead a patient group.

1.   You are the nurse. Other members of the class will read aloud:

Physician: Nurse, I have to examine Mrs. Smith right now. I don't have all day. Please get her ready.

Administrator: Nurse, don't let that group stay in the room too long. We have to get it ready for the board meeting tonight.

Patient: Help me, help me, help me, help me. . . (continues monotonously)

Beautician: Mrs. Brown's daughter wants her shampooed today so that she can take her out tomorrow. I can't do it unless you get her out of that group now.

Podiatrist: Nurse, surely you don't expect me to wait until Mrs. Green gets out of that group. You should have her feet soaking now so that she'll be ready when I get to her.

Daughter: After all, I drove down to see Mother. Surely she doesn't have to be in that group today.

Social worker: Nurse, Mrs. Jones seems to have had an accident. Could you get the aide to do something about it?

Explain to the group how the nurse feels.

2.   You are the social worker. You have arrived to find that only two group members are ready. Mrs. Ellis has gone off with her daughter. Mrs. Green is soaking her feet, waiting for the podiatrist, who has several other patients lined up and won't get to her for another half hour. The nurse has asked you to cut your group short today because someone else wants to use the room. Mrs. Smith is with the doctor, who chose this hour for his monthly visit. One of the two group members who appeared to be ready just had an "accident." You don't know why the aides couldn't have taken her to the bathroom first.

Explain to the group how the social worker feels.

EXERCISE 2

After attending one session, Mrs. Black announces that she does not belong in the group: "Those people are crazy." Mr. Ellis says he is too tired today; he'll let you know next time. Mrs. Rogers, who is always an active participant when she comes but is forgetful, has already begun a nap. Miss Marion, whom you persuaded to try it once, has—and says she doesn't want to come again.

You respect the client's right to self-determination, but you feel that each of these persons needs the group activity, especially Mr. Ellis, who seems to be depressed and withdrawing. How strongly would you act to persuade each of them to attend? What would be the determining factor in each case?

EXERCISE 3

Observe for at least an hour any small group of adults who customarily meet together and includes both younger and older members. This does not have to be a treatment group but can be an instrumental group, such as a committee or board. Tally the disagreements or confrontations that occur and note which members are involved and whether they disagree in a manner that is essentially direct or indirect and friendly, pseudofriendly, or hostile. How do they use humor? Do disagreements occur more consistently between certain pairs? Afterwards, review your notes to see whether there was any difference in the way older and younger adults expressed disagreement. Briefly summarize your findings and describe one exchange you observed that illustrates your conclusion. (Remember to protect the identity of the individuals involved unless they are public officials in an open meeting.)

EXERCISE 4

Your home health agency has encouraged you to form a group for family caregivers in a rural area. These people are relatively isolated, and it is hoped that eventually they will become a self-help group, meeting independently. At the first meeting, you explained that the purpose of these meetings was to enable them to share feelings, experiences, and solutions with other caregivers. Because you are their social worker, however, they initially arrived with lists of things they wanted you to do, individual problems to be solved, agency help to be procured. In each instance, you turned them back to the group. You remained after the meeting to take care of their individual concerns.

By the third meeting, most of the members have grasped that the meeting hour is for things that they wish to share with the group. Mr. Plover has not. He listens absently as other members speak and then addresses you directly about the problem he is having with his wife, the letter he received from Social Security, and his bill from the druggist. Your "Later" does not work nor does your "I wonder if anyone in the group has had a similar experience?" He is disrupting the group's discussion. Other members are plainly irritated, and each time he interrupts, they look toward you. What do you do now?

EXERCISE 5

Select one of the participants in the dialogue below and double for that person—that is, after his or her lines have been read, say what you think that person is really feeling.

It is the weekly meeting of the residents' Sunshine Committee at Sunny Harbor, a home for the aged. Mr. Hook arrives late. The social worker sighs, but updates Mr. Hook.

Social worker: Mr. Jones died last night and Mrs. Meeks was just proposing—(turns to Mrs. Meeks).

Mrs. Meeks: I was just saying, I'll get a card of condolence for us to send to his wife.

Mr. Hook: Don't send her any condolences from me. It's the best break she ever got.

Mrs. Martin: Say nothing but good of the dead, Mr. Hook!

Mr. Hook: Fair enough. You certainly didn't have anything good to say about him when he was living. (Mrs. Martin sniffs.)

Social worker: I wonder how the rest of you feel about sending Mrs. Jones a card? (There is general assent, interspersed with glares at Mr. Hook. Then the committee chairperson, Mrs. Brown, continues.)

Mrs. Brown: Let's turn to the next order of business—

Mr. Hook: I'm not ready for the next order of business. I'm not finished with Mr. Jones.

Mrs. Brown: Your presence at this meeting, Mr. Hook, is not compulsory. If you have something else you would like to do—

Mr. Hook: But I enjoy these meetings. All this sunshine invites a little vinegar. (By now, everyone is glaring.)

EXERCISE 6

Mrs. Adams would like to attend the spring luncheon meeting of her church's women's group. In past years, members have made arrangements, well checked in advance, to pick her up at the nursing home. This year no one calls, possibly because her unsteadiness has been a source of concern. (She fell on the steps last year.) Mrs. Adams presents her problem in a moving manner to the student social worker, who agrees to help. Mrs. Adams is exultant. The student social worker is pleased at her pleasure. The charge nurse, only a little older than the student social worker, is outraged. She points out to Mrs. Adams that her physician has not okayed the trip and to the student social worker that she cannot transport Mrs. Adams in her car. She points out that Mrs. Adams has medical problems that the student social worker does not understand. Then she calls the physician, reminding him of Mrs. Adams's fall last year, the brittleness of her diabetes, and her tendency to eat everything in sight on these occasions. Mrs. Adams tells everyone the nurse is treating her like a prisoner. The student social worker is crushed but resentful.

Describe the incident as each party might—Mrs. Adams, the student social worker, and the nurse. Which professional values might the nurse and the social worker have invoked and which might they have agreed on? How could each have handled it better?

REFERENCES

Appelbaum PS, Greer A. 1993. Confidentiality in group therapy. *Hosp Group Psychiatr* 44(40):311-312.

Conti ML. 1980. Continuity of care for elderly discharged patients. In IM Burnside (ed.), *Psychosocial nursing care of the aged,* 2d ed. (pp. 101-113). New York: McGraw-Hill.

Dittmar S (ed.). 1989. *Rehabilitation nursing: Process and practice.* St. Louis: Mosby. (The appendix contains the American Nurses' Association Code for Nurses, p. 587.)

Douglas T. 1979. *Group process in social work.* New York: Wiley.

Forman M. 1967. Conflict, controversy, and confrontation in group work with older adults. *Soc Work* 12(2):80-85.

Kubie SH, Landau G. 1953. *Group work with the aged.* New York: International Universities Press.

Lakin M. 1988. Group therapies with the elderly: Issues and prospects. In BW Maclennan, S Saul, MB Weiner (eds.), *Group psychotherapies for the elderly* (pp. 43-55). Madison, CT: International Universities Press.

Lesser J, Lazarus LW, Frankel R, Havasy S. 1981. Reminiscence group therapy with psychotic geriatric inpatients. *Gerontologist* 21(3):191-196.

National Association of Social Workers (NASW). 1980a. *Social group work with older people.* Proceedings of seminar held at Lake Mohonk, New York in 1961. New York: Arno Press.

———. 1980b. The NASW code of ethics. *Soc Work* 25(3): 184-188.

Ness KM. 1980. The sick roles of the elderly. In IM Burnside (ed.), *Psychosocial nursing care of the aged,* 2d ed. (pp. 229-252). New York: McGraw-Hill.

Rosow I. 1974. *Socialization to old age.* Berkeley: University of California Press.

Schwartz W. 1979. The social worker in the group. In BR Compton, B Galaway (eds.), *Social work processes* (pp. 14-28). Homewood, IL: Dorsey.

Special Group on Conceptual Frameworks (SGCF). 1981. Publications Committee, NASW. *Soc Work* 26(1):6.

U.S. Social Security Act, Amendments Section 1819 and 1919 (OBRA '87). See also Department of Health and Human Services, Health Care Financing Administration. 1991. Medicare and Medicaid: Requirements for long-term care facilities. *Federal Register,* Section 483:48826-48865 (September 26).

Wilson G. 1976. From practice to theory: A personalized history. In RW Roberts, H Northern (eds.), *Theories of social work with groups* (pp. 1-44). New York: Columbia University Press.

BIBLIOGRAPHY

Balgopal PR, Vassil TV. 1983. *Groups in social work: An ecological perspective.* New York: Macmillan.

Bogdanoff M, Elbaum PL. 1978. Role lock: Dealing with monopolizers, mistrusters, isolates, helpful Hannahs, and other assorted characters in group psychotherapy. *Int J Group Psychother* 28(2):247-262.

Corey G, Corey MS, Callahan P, Russel JM. 1992. *Group techniques,* 2d ed. Pacific Grove, CA: Brooks/Cole.

Glassman U. 1991. The social work group and its distinct healing qualities in the health care setting. *Health Soc Work* 16(3):203-212.

Henry S. 1992. *Group skills in social work: A four-dimensional approach,* 2d ed. Pacific Grove, CA: Brooks/Cole.

Lieberman MA, Yalom I. 1992. Brief group psychotherapy for the spousally bereaved: A controlled study. *Int J Group Psychother* 42(1):117-132.

Maclennan BW, Saul S, Weiner MB. 1988. *Group psychotherapies for the elderly*. Madison, CT: International Universities Press.

Qualls SH, Czirr R. 1988. Geriatric health teams: Classifying models of professional and team functioning. *Gerontologist* 28(3):372-375.

Roberts RW, Northern H (eds.). 1976. *Theories of social work with groups*. New York: Columbia University Press.

Toseland RW. 1990. *Group work with older adults*. New York: New York University Press.

RESOURCES

Few papers on group work with the aged are to be found in the journals dealing with groups, such as the *International Journal of Group Psychotherapy* or *Social Work with Groups*. On the other hand, practice-oriented journals dealing with the elderly do have papers on group work from time to time. Among these are *The Journal of Gerontological Social Work* and *Clinical Gerontology*. *The Gerontologist* occasionally has papers about the use of groups.

CHAPTER 26

A Nurse's Perspective

Irene Burnside

<table>
<tr><td valign="top">

KEY WORDS

- Confabulation
- Conversation deprivation
- Reality orientation
- Reminiscence
- Remotivation
- Sensoristasis
- Sensory retraining
- Somatic preoccupation
- Verbosity

</td><td valign="top">

LEARNING OBJECTIVES

- Describe the historical growth of group work by nurses with aged clients.
- List seven group modalities for the aged in which nurses have excelled.
- List six other terms that may be used for reminiscence.
- Describe four therapeutic values of reminiscence.
- Analyze specific adaptations made by nurses in group therapy with the aged.
- Synthesize nurses' unique contributions to group work with the aged.

</td></tr>
</table>

Nurses deal with individuals who are experiencing or anticipating transition or who may be completing the act of transition (Meleis 1975).

Nurses leading groups also deal with their own transitions. Nurses have begun groups in a practical way, often out of their own curiosity and desire for knowledge and expertise. Sometimes when they too are in transition—for example, in school—nurses also observe in the aged needs that they feel could be met by a group experience. Still others are enrolled in master's programs and organize and study group process and modalities. There are now excellent master's theses and doctoral dissertations by nurses that focus on group work with older adults.

My own introduction to group work in the late 1960s was a difficult beginning, and I still am surprised to see the results that ensued. I had been offered a chance to do group work with older,

affluent residents in a retirement center called Leisure World. The staff physician needed someone to work with depressed elders. However, I decided not to work as a volunteer with older adults who could afford to pay. What helped me decide to do group work was a visit to an aged neighbor who had been placed in a nursing home after his leg had been amputated (Burnside 1969a). But when I decided to do groups in a nursing home, I was not prepared for the road ahead.

When I made the decision to conduct group work with aged nursing home residents, I found that I was not welcome there. I could not get an entrée. I was told that nurses did not do group work—that only social workers and psychologists did. A local physician who was interested in my conducting groups wrote orders for group work on the charts of those of his patients I had chosen as potentials for group work. Fortunately, as group leaders of the aged, nurses have come a long way since my own entrée!

I felt a great need for supervision in that initial group experience, because my group work had been with young adult schizophrenics. However, I faced problems in finding a preceptor knowledgeable about older adults. I was advised to seek out a psychiatrist at a large urban medical center whom I knew had published about the aged and had given frequent speeches. I told him I had been referred to him by the director of the hospital. When I stated my request, he snorted, "You've got to be kidding." The learning process that I subsequently used is best known as "flying by the seat of one's pants." I do not highly recommend that process, hence this book.

The first group moved me so much that I tried to capture that two-year experience by writing descriptive articles (Burnside 1969a, 1970a, 1970b, 1971). What I learned in that pragmatic experience has held me in good stead and aided me greatly in teaching students. However, it was not theoretical. I learned that later.

OVERVIEW

The following information is presented chronologically, to show the growth of group work done by nurses with older clients.

The first indication that nurses were doing group work appeared in the 1950s, and the name of one of the first group-leader nurses remains unknown to us. Truly a pioneer and an effective leader, she is the nurse co-leader described in the classic work by Linden (1953). See Chapter 4 for an elaboration of the co-leadership they provided geriatric women in a state hospital.

The first article I wrote about groups appeared in 1969, but in 1968 Terrazas co-authored an article with Yalom on group therapy for psychotic elders in a state hospital in California. See Chapter 5 for concepts from Yalom.

The first nurse-authored book to contain substantive material on group work with elders by nurses appeared in 1973 (Burnside 1973). Gillin (1973) described factors that affected process and content in older adult groups. Morrison (1973) described her master's level work in group therapy for older women who were high utilizers of clinic facilities. Blake (1973) had led a group in a large public institution for the aged. She based her work with demented individuals on ego psychol-

ogy. Holtzen (1973) worked with a group in a similar setting and recorded themes of depersonalization, lack of trust, isolation, and hopelessness in her observations. Stange (1973) creatively explored use of props, sensory stimulation, and social graces with aged women on the back ward of a state hospital. Holland (1973) co-led a group of stroke patients in a chronic disease rehabilitation hospital. Her co-leader was a social worker. Their styles of group leadership varied, and the author describes her approach as activity centered in contrast to the verbal style used by the social worker.

Everson and Mealey (1978) have written perhaps the most complete and best article for nurse instructors who are teaching nursing students to be group leaders with older adults. It is highly recommended for nurses supervising students doing group work. The article by Tappen and Touhy (1983) is also recommended.

Smith (1980) described her struggles in leadership with chronically ill, institutionalized psychiatric patients. Although this nurse-author did not focus specifically on aged persons, her points are applicable for other nurses planning to begin groups. Smith points out that "on first making a decision that a therapy group should be established, one automatically sets up a chain reaction of decision making. Initial decision involves choosing group members" (p. 1301). These statements sound deceptively easy, but new nurse group leaders should be warned of difficulties; if cooperation from the agency personnel where the group is being held is not forthcoming, it can be a stormy start. Another important part of beginning group therapy, Smith points out, is that one needs the experts: the supervisors, instructors, and theorists on group therapy.

The other essential point for a nurse group leader is that she or he must strive to achieve balance because "a group leader must give the direction where necessary, but must remember that a certain freedom gives the group its potential to grow" (Smith 1980, 1303). I would add that the leader must give herself or himself freedom so that she or he, as well as the group members, may grow in the experience. I tell my students to allow themselves floundering time in the beginning (See Chapter 10 on leadership.)

The importance of literature reviews is often unappreciated. A fine review by Nickoley-Colquitt (1981) has examined the effectiveness of preventive group interventions for older clients. She notes that during the past decade, group approaches emphasizing health promotion have emerged and points out that this is a shifting emphasis that parallels the preventive trend occurring in the health care system.

Nickoley-Colquitt reviewed 18 group interventions involving the family members of an aged population. In spite of the great variety in the groups examined, all groups had one focus in common: to provide group interventions for older adults or their family members who were experiencing common developmental or situational changes or stresses.

Nurses, because of their orientation to wellness (rather than illness) and prevention (rather than disease processes and diagnosis), are well qualified to conduct group work with frail or cognitively impaired older adults. Such groups often begin slowly, with exceedingly high anxiety in the members. Reducing anxiety, pain, and discomfort so that the members will remain in the group is the first task of the leader in the initial meetings. Prevention of catastrophic reactions is, of course, the hallmark of the leader of confused older adults.

Nurse-authors Janosik and Phipps (1982, 252) point out that "there is an erroneous impression among some health workers that group work is inappropriate for the elderly because they have little capacity for change or because the quality of life cannot be sustained during the sunset years." The slow beginning of nurses in conducting group work with older clients is probably related to our professional and personal problems with ageism and/or the aging process, rather than with the recently acquired role as group leader. In the beginning, psychiatric nurses also had to prove their ability to conduct therapy groups. So it has been with elders. At times I felt we were not taken very seriously, and this was probably because we've been locked into a traditional role for so long—that is, carrier of bedpans, pills, and charts.

Janosik and Phipps (1982, 258) write about problematic behaviors to anticipate in group work with older adults. The negative nature of the listed behaviors could discourage the neophyte leader, particularly since there is not a balancing list of behaviors that might enhance the group experience. The long list of problematic behaviors—callousness, compartmentalization, somatic preoccupation, verbosity, denial, confabulation, regression, selfishness, and repetitiousness—presents a negative view but should be a challenge to any leader! The leader needs to understand the behaviors of staff, leader, or members that may encourage or cause such problematic behaviors to continue. It is difficult to accept that the behaviors we see in elders may be influenced by our approaches and interactions.

It has been my experience that confabulation (making up answers) is related to the disease process; the leader must be very sensitive to that fact. In some groups, regression and selfishness are the coping strategies for imposed institutionalization. Verbosity is often due to a lack of intervention skills on the part of the leader, and I believe it is related to conversation deprivation. So many older adults have no one to listen to them; a group experience certainly provides multiple sounding boards. Somatic preoccupations, as pointed out so beautifully by Poston and Levine (1980), may well be attributable to the leader's neglecting to provide nurturance and care to the members. In my early work with groups, I found that somatic preoccupation was directly related to the initial anxiety of the group members. When the leader listened and empathized, the complaints decreased considerably during the life of the group. Also, because group leaders are nurses, older adults feel that they should discuss physical complaints with them. It is difficult for some older adults to view nurses in the role of group leader and realize that we listen to feelings and emotions as well as to physical complaints.

Nurses also are beginning to include chapters about group work with the aged in their textbooks (Furukawa & Shomaker 1982; Janosik & Phipps 1982; Murray, Huelskoetter & O'Driscoll 1980), which is a giant step forward.

GROUP MODALITIES

This section of the chapter treats group modalities in which nurses have excelled: reality orientation, remotivation, reminiscence, health-related groups, sensory retraining, music groups, and support groups.

Reality Orientation

A nurse helped to pioneer reality orientation (RO) groups when they began in Tuscaloosa, Alabama, in the 1960s (Taulbee & Folsom 1966). See Chapter 13, written by a nurse, for an in-depth discussion of reality orientation groups. Scarbrough, also a nurse, has continued to further and refine the area of reality orientation classes (Scarbrough 1974; Drummond, Kirkoff & Scarbrough 1978, 1979).

I have been impressed as I observe nurses' work with very withdrawn patients in a group. Lois Acord once demonstrated to my class how gentle persistence and genuine expectation could produce results. Nursing home personnel had never known one withdrawn man in the demonstration group to speak. They were sure he would simply sit in the group and stare at the floor as he always did; yet he spoke for the nurse leader in that group, as she gently and tenaciously persisted, expecting a response.

Hogstel (1979) studied the use of reality orientation with aging confused patients. Pretests and posttests showed no significant difference in degree of confusion in the control or the RO group. Hogstel's study is one of the few experimental studies about RO groups done by a nurse.

Remotivation Groups

Remotivation articles date back to 1960 (Pullinger 1960). The remotivation technique manual that has consistently been used by group workers was written by a nurse-editor (Robinson 1976). Hahn (1973), Miller (1975), and Lyon (1971) have also described their work with remotivation groups. Gray and Stevenson (1980) designed a study to compare a remotivation and a resocialization group in a research study. They noted that group therapy with confused aged nursing home residents resulted in positive behavioral changes. Interestingly, the staff of the facility was surprised at the ability of the subjects to socialize and enjoy one another. An orientation by the leaders helped facilitate transition of the groups to the routines of the ward.

Remotivation is a technique of simple group interaction that is very structured and follows five steps. See Chapter 14, by Dennis, for an explanation of this group modality. Moody, Baron, and Monk (1970) conducted a study of remotivation therapy while in a master's program. They point out that it requires much planning to prepare the sessions and the refreshments. The most difficult task for these nurses was assembling the group quickly to reduce weariness. Nurses usually are quite sensitive to the energy levels and the need for elders to conserve energy. The authors discuss reactivating

lifestyles, which is an important and frequently overlooked aspect of group work with elders.

Reminiscence Groups

Nurses have been publishing about reminiscence therapy since the 1970s (Hala 1975; Ebersole 1976). The conceptual framework of reminiscence has been thoroughly discussed in previous chapters, so it will not be repeated here. But reminiscence may also be referred to by other terms; these include oral history, life review, memories, life story, biography, and journals.

Nurses have taken to this particular modality of group work with the aged (Baker 1983, 1985; Blackman 1980; Haight & Burnside 1992; Lappe 1987; Osborn 1989; Parsons 1986; Tourangeau 1988; Youssef 1990).

We need to consider the therapeutic value of reminiscence. It can:

- Improve body image and self-esteem.
- Increase ability to communicate and express self.
- Emphasize the individuality of each reminiscer.
- Permit the aged to assume a teaching role.
- Promote and retain cultural beliefs, pride, family tradition, and meaningful moments in life.
- Be positive; it need not be negative.
- Serve as a means to cope with failing memory.
- Help adaptation to later years.
- Be a developmental task.
- Cause resurgence of dormant interests and/or hobbies.
- Be an excellent learning experience about history for the leader.

Nickoley-Colquitt (1981, 82) says about reminiscing:

> Reminiscing as a technique also fits into the element of helping to mobilize psychological resources and master emotional burdens. This may be helpful in meeting the need for a positive self-esteem and might be used in assisting individuals to identify previously used coping skills.

Seven common modes of group work nurses often incorporate into a reminiscence group can be seen in Figure 26-1; they are reality orientation, remotivation, music, resocialization, sensory stimulation, art, and poetry. Figure 26-2 shows how a variety of modalities can be incorporated into a group.

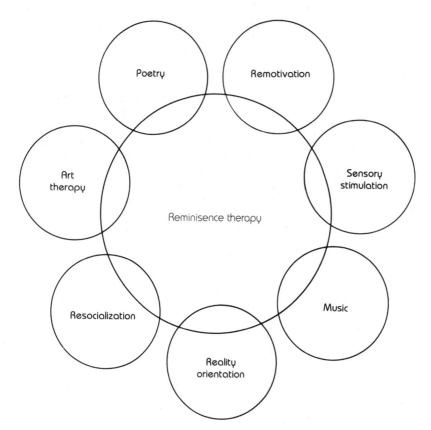

FIGURE 26-1 *Reminiscence therapy as an eclectic modality can incorporate a variety of group modalities.*

Health-related Groups

Besides the above three categories of groups, nurses also pioneered health-related groups (Heller 1970; Holland 1973; Holtzen 1973; Murphy 1969). These groups are perhaps a natural for a nurse to lead because of the nurse's interest in holistic health, prevention and alleviation of distress and pain, and the transitions that fall within the domain of nursing.

Because nurses must work with the accoutrements for the visually impaired and hearing impaired, they are sensitive to the assessment of sensory changes. Generally, nurses show exquisite sensitivity in handling sensory losses in the group setting. Nurses are accustomed to difficult patient situations, to complicated problems with a variety

of people, and to juggling many variables simultaneously in a situation. Mummah[1] once said, "Group work at times can be like a birthday party for a three-year-old."

Besides sensory changes, the group leader must also assess sensory overload or deprivation in members. Such conditions may occur in meetings and are most obvious in nursing home residents. The field of sensory alterations and sensoristasis (sensory balance) has long been of interest to nurses.

Sexuality, nutrition, disease processes (for example, cancer, arthritis, Alzheimer's disease), losses, depressive states, stress reduction, health

---

[1]Personal communication, 1975.

FIGURE 26-2 *A reminis-cence therapy group might include several modalities in one meeting or during the life of the group.*

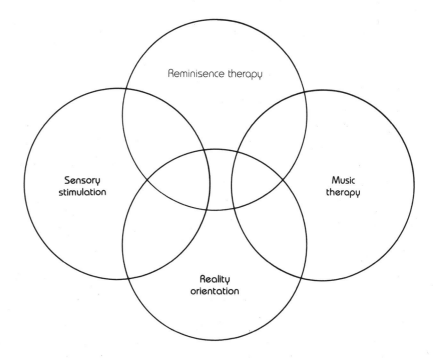

promotion, and relaxation are but a few of the topics of health to discuss. Much health teaching can be done within any of the modalities, however.

Sensory Retraining Groups

Scott and Crowhurst (1975), two Canadian nurses, conducted sensory retraining programs to put patients in touch with one another. Heidell (1972) also wrote about this group modality. The program combines activities that are designed to reawaken or maintain all of the senses: sight, sound, taste, smell, and touch.

One of my early articles (Burnside 1969b) was about the use of sensory stimulation with older adults in a nursing home. That group experience taught me the value of props, the importance of food and beverages, and the use of touch within a group.

Music Therapy Groups

Music therapy groups also have been implemented and refined by a nurse, M. J. Hennessey (1976a, 1976b, 1978). See Chapter 17 for her contributions

to this specialized group modality. Reminiscence therapy groups, as operationalized by nurses, often include the modalities seen in Figures 26-1 and 26-2, and one modality is music. King (1982, 24-25) writes, "Those with impaired hearing may be able to hear music better than speech, because music is rhythmically patterned and potentially familiar. Therefore, music offers the added benefit of sensory stimulation."

Nurses can and do combine their professional and personal talents and abilities in a unique fashion. Hennessey is one such role model; she was both a nurse group leader and a concert violinist. She described the meld of her music and nursing beautifully.

> In the past my life was split in two parts; I kept them carefully separated. I wore different clothes, worked with different people, and used different skills. Few of my musician friends were aware that I was a nurse, and my hospital associates did not know that my violin was a major part of my existence.
>
> When I discovered a way to combine work as a health professional and as a musician, it was as though I became a professionally whole person.

The dichotomy that had been defined by the nursing world began to disappear, and with the feelings of wholeness, the effectiveness of my work with groups increased.

This leads to the concept that many nurses could improve their skills if they were encouraged to be innovative and use all their talents. If love of music is one of these talents, a musician on the staff of nursing schools, whose work could be to introduce music into the healing environment, could be a help in further humanizing health care (Hennessey 1978, 37-38).

Support Groups

Nickoley (1978) studied the effects of supportive group intervention on the functional level of health and perception of control in aged women in the community. Leavitt (1978) studied the effects of a support group on adjustment to the changes of aging in older women living in the community. The support groups consisted of females, age range 65 to 83, whose mental functioning was intact but who were experiencing or had recently experienced some life-change events. Support group members lived in a senior citizen high-rise apartment house. The members met for one hour twice a week, and each session was followed by a half-hour socialization and refreshment period. Goals were to provide information, assist each other in getting greater control over self and environment, strengthen problem-solving skills, and improve interpersonal skills. Evaluation was done by pretest and posttest measures. Reported outcomes were observed but were not measurable. See Chapter 18.

Group Therapy for the Mentally Ill

Nurses conduct groups for older persons who have mental health problems (Abraham, Neundorfer & Currie 1992; Russell 1991; Waller & Griffin 1984). Group leaders recommend the use of the Beck Depression Inventory (Russell 1991) and the Hamilton Depression Inventory (Waller & Griffin 1984). In addition, Russell (1991) stated that the Social Anxiety Scale and Distress Scale would be useful and offered suggestions regarding her group leadership experience:

- Beware of transportation difficulties.
- Staff leadership styles may not coincide.

- Make clear the specific objectives and time structures in the beginning of the group.
- Obtain supervision very early—during the planning stage.

SPECIAL ASPECTS TO CONSIDER

Group Modality Selection

The selection of the appropriate group modality is crucial. Adaptations will have to be made in any modality the leader chooses. Because nursing deals with persons in transition, it might be well to assess group members using that dimension.

The common adaptations needed in group work with the aged should be based on the following:

1. Mutual determination of group goals and objectives by leader and members.
2. Assessment of and adaptation to losses, including:
   - Physical (most especially hearing, vision, and mobility).
   - Social (especially spouse and peers and pets).
   - Economic (home, income, personal belongings).
   - Status (job, respect), which may result in lowered self-esteem.
3. Attention to nutritional needs and fluid intake.
4. Attention to sensoristasis.
5. Skill and expertise of the leader.
6. Psychosocial needs of the aged.
7. Time and energy of the group leader.
8. Resources available:
   - Financial.
   - Support system.
   - Locations/space for group meetings.

The nurse will need to be skilled in assessment to select the right combination of members. See Chapter 8 for an in-depth discussion.

Refreshments

Poston and Levine (1980) have written a provocative article about their group therapy. The members came to a community-oriented psychiatric clinic for help with a depressive condition. The leader's first attempt at "a conversational group treatment with these patients was unsuccessful." That group never developed a sense of cohesion, splinter groups formed, and the patients said they felt worse than before the group experience "because they got upset listening to other patients' problems" (p. 159).

Based on what they had learned from the failure of the first group, Poston and Levine tried a second method of group treatment. A coffee lounge was prepared to "provide more direct gratification for these patients' needs" (p. 159), and refreshments were part of the group meeting. This is one of the rare instances in the literature in which leaders from a discipline other than nursing have approved of refreshments in group meetings. The willingness of nurses to be nurturing (even with nonnarcissistic patients) is one way that group work by nurses often differs from that of other disciplines.

Because most nurses are nurturing persons, they tend to use nurturing techniques in their group work with the aged. The literature notes group leaders of other disciplines also doing this. Poston and Levine (1980) describe nurturing behaviors, as do Friedlob, Black, and Kelly, who in Chapter 23 give an in-depth description of the use of fluids and food in groups.

The forms of refreshments served in groups vary from fluids to special types of snacks, pastries or cookies—and even popcorn! At first it might seem that these are party-only groups. Upon closer observation, a variety of rationales emerge for why nurses can successfully incorporate refreshments into their group work.

- Refreshments provide nurturing for those most in need—narcissistic patients, poorly nourished and/or dehydrated individuals, lonely or alienated members, sensorily deprived individuals.
- Food and drink also provide an easy method for improving social graces.
- The nurturing role allows the leader to assess appetite, coordination during eating, likes and dislikes in food, former lifestyles, and eating and drinking habits.
- The refreshments can create an element of surprise for those who complain of ennui.
- The nourishment itself (for example, popcorn) can be the theme for reality orientation, remotivation, and reminiscence groups.
- The nourishment can provide an educational theme for a meeting (for example, examining, discussing, and then eating papayas, mangoes, or pineapples).
- If the nourishment is prepared by the leader, it can provide a poignant moment (for example, a group member cried when I baked an angel food

cake for her birthday and our meeting. "It's been eighteen years since I have tasted angel food cake. It was at my granddaughter's birthday party.").
- The nourishment can serve as an instructional aid to a student leader. Questions to be asked include:
  - What do you serve diabetic members of the group?
  - How full do you fill the cups/glasses?
  - When and why do you use finger foods?
  - How do you intervene when a member colors the peeled banana green with the felt-tipped pen used to write the name tags?
  - Who will finance the cost of the nourishments?
  - What is the best type of glass or cup to use for your group?
  - Specifically how will you use the nourishment to improve activities-of-daily-living (ADL) skills or social graces?
  - Will you serve the refreshments?
  - Will you share the nourishment with the members?
  - When in the meeting will you offer the nourishment—before, midway, or after?
  - Who will clean up the mess that might occur?

One student in Lubbock, Texas, conducted a reminiscence group at a local nursing home and wrote, "To avoid the institutional look, I used table cloths, ceramic coffee mugs, brightly colored napkins, and patterned paper plates for all of our meetings. At each session at least one member of our group, man or woman, would comment on how attractive the table looked" (Slater 1982, 2).

Transferences

A new nurse may be accustomed to group dynamic class experiential groups or confrontation groups; the average oldster will not have such group experiences. They will often reenact the family group in the group life; transference may occur—for example, one member to the other, "You sound just like my brother used to," or older member to young leader, "You remind me of my granddaughter; she talks like that." A nurse with psychiatric background will be quick to recognize transferences within the group.

However, it always startled me when the transferences occurred in group; they tended to catch me off guard. One needs to be sensitive to the occurrence and also to analyze if we are treating group members like grandparents or great-aunts and great-uncles.

Students should have an experiential group experience to learn the basics of group process. Reminiscence groups of students should be a requirement before they themselves lead a reminiscence group.

Beginning students should be familiar with the early accounts of group work written by nurses.

EDUCATION

Everson and Mealey (1978) have written a fine article on baccalaureate student nurses as leaders of geriatric groups. That is one goal nurses need to work on in group work with the aged. The benefits for all are many when baccalaureate nurses' programs introduce such practicums. See Chapter 30 for elaborations of successful methods devised to teach baccalaureate nurses and Chapter 31 for supervision strategies.

I believe that the current master's and doctoral students graduating from nursing programs will be important health personnel who will improve the group techniques and methods favored by nurses. Nurses who conduct group work as the focus of their master's theses may be disappointed that their hypotheses do not reach significant levels, but the Hawthorne effect can be important in the real world. The Hawthorne effect takes the form of increased interest by the staff and sometimes relatives. It is a desired spin-off both for research and practicum.

Doctoral dissertations by nurses about group work with the aged are beginning to appear (Bramlett 1990; Burnside 1990; Cook 1988). As stated above, the doctoral programs offer us another rich source of nurses who can improve and refine group research methods and increase our understanding of people in transition. As nurses conceptualize preventive health behavior, they will also realize that group experiences are important health behaviors.

Nurses and social workers sometimes seem suspicious about what the other discipline does in group work with older adults. Even older persons are aware of the difference. La Monica and Schmidt (1986) noted that older clients in the community discriminated between the two disciplines and brought different concerns to each. The social work student who set up the student nurse's visits apologized for not providing interesting health problems. It turned out that even the well clients had plenty of questions for the nurses. Throughout this book, we stress the importance of working with other disciplines. With all the group work that needs to be done, squabbling over turfs seems unnecessary.

SUMMARY

Butler, Lewis, and Sunderland (1991, 421) state "nurses probably conduct more group work with older persons than do other professionals. Still, it seems we do very little in that area of the curriculum; for example, how many student nurses ever receive a group experience with elders?"

This chapter has delineated seven common nurse-led groups: reality orientation, remotivation, reminiscence, health-related, sensory retraining, music, and support groups. The increase in publications, theses, and chapters written by nurses in the past 20 years denotes the interest of nurses in group work with this specific age group. Evaluations of the group work are still highly subjective; nurses need to change that and move to a research posture. Evaluation of group work must be done by responsible clinicians who are able to judge the effectiveness of the group experience and the leaders objectively.

The overall goal for group work is to make the later years of life the very best that they can be instead of the very worst, as they now are for some elderly, especially the frail aged.

King (1982, 25) reminds us that "no therapeutic modality can fulfill the wants, hopes and needs of all clients." Yet there is no doubt that groups can change the quality of lives, including those of the leaders!

Regardless of what we write or expound, the true teachers are the aged group members. Sometimes I believe that they join our groups out of their great generosity and kindness, to please and help us. I find that a humbling experience.

EXERCISE 1

Read five nurse-written articles about group work with the aged. Are there commonalities in the techniques described by each of the authors? List two commonalities and discuss each.

EXERCISE 2

Choose Chapter 25 or 27. Compare and contrast the perspective of that writer with the nurse's perspective presented in this chapter.

EXERCISE 3

Interview a nurse who has conducted group work with older adults. What was her or his motivation to lead such a group?

EXERCISE 4

Select from the reference list and/or bibliography of this chapter two nurse-written articles that discuss the theory and practice of group work.

1. Critically read the selected articles.
2. List three concepts regarding groups that appear in the articles.
3. Write one intervention that a group leader might use for each of the three common concepts (problem areas) you identify. Defend your intervention.

REFERENCES

Abraham IL, Neundorfer NM, Currie LJ. 1992. The effects of cognitive group interventions on cognitive functioning and depressive symptomatology among nursing home residents. Research report. Nursing Research Conference, University of Virginia, Charlottesville (April 1-3).

Baker J. 1983. Combining touch and reminiscing in institutionalized elderly. Unpublished master's thesis. San Jose, CA: San Jose State University.

Baker NJ. 1985. Reminiscing in group therapy for self-worth. *J Gerontol Nurs* 11(7):21-24.

Blackman J. 1980. Group work in the community: Experiences with reminiscence. In IM Burnside (ed.), *Psychosocial nursing care of the aged*, 2d ed. (pp. 126-144). New York: McGraw-Hill.

Blake D. 1973. Group work with the institutionalized elderly. In IM Burnside (ed.), *Psychosocial nursing care of the aged*, 1st ed. (pp. 153-160). New York: McGraw-Hill.

Bramlett M. 1990. Power, creativity, and reminiscence in the elderly. Unpublished doctoral dissertation. Augusta, GA: Medical College of Georgia.

Burnside IM. 1969a. Group work among the aged. *Nurs Outlook* 17(6):68-72.

——— . 1969b. Sensory stimulation: An adjunct to group work with the disabled aged. *Ment Hyg* 53(3):381-388.

——— . 1970a. Group work with the aged: Selected literature. *Gerontologist* 10(3):241-246.

——— . 1970b. Loss: A constant theme in group work with the aged. *Hosp Comm Psych* 21(6):173-177.

——— . 1971. Long-term group work with hospitalized aged. *Gerontologist* 2(3):213-218.

——— . 1973. *Psychosocial nursing care of the aged.* New York: McGraw-Hill.

——— . 1990. The effect of reminiscence groups on fatigue, affect and life satisfaction in elderly women. Unpublished doctoral dissertation. Austin, TX: School of Nursing, The University of Texas at Austin.

Butler RN, Lewis MI, Sunderland T. 1991. *Aging and mental health: Positive psychosocial and biomedical approaches,* 4th ed. New York: Merrill.

Cook EA. 1988. The effect of reminiscence group therapy on depressed institutionalized elders. Unpublished doctoral dissertation. Austin, TX: School of Nursing, The University of Texas at Austin.

Drummond L, Kirkoff L, Scarbrough D. 1978. A practical guide to reality orientation: A treatment approach for confusion and disorientation. *Gerontologist* 18(6):568-573.

———. 1979. *Leading reality orientation classes: Basic and advanced.* Arlington Heights, IL: Intercraft Associates.

Ebersole P. 1976. Reminiscing and group psychotherapy with the aged. In IM Burnside (ed.), *Nursing and the aged,* 1st ed. (pp. 214-230). New York: McGraw-Hill.

Everson SJ, Mealey AR. 1978. Baccalaureate nursing students as leaders in geriatric groups. *J Nurs Educ* 17(7):17-26.

Furukawa C, Shomaker D. 1982. *Community health nursing and the aged.* Rockville, MD: Aspens.

Gillin L. 1973. Factors affecting process and content in older adult groups. In IM Burnside (ed.), *Psychosocial nursing care of the aged* (pp. 137-141). New York: McGraw-Hill.

Gray P, Stevenson J. 1980. Changes in verbal interaction among members of resocialization groups. *J Gerontol Nurs* 6(2):86-89.

Hahn J. 1973. Mrs. Richards, a rabbit, and remotivation. *Am J Nurs* 73(2):302-305.

Haight BK, Burnside IM. 1992. Reminiscence and life review: Conducting the processes. *J Gerontol Nurs* 18(2):39-42.

Hala M. 1975. Reminiscence group therapy project. *J Gerontol Nurs* 1(3):34-41.

Heidell B. 1972. Sensory training puts patients "in touch." *Modern Nurs Home* 28(June):40.

Heller V. 1970. Handicapped patients talk together. *Am J Nurs* 70(2):332-335.

Hennessey M. 1976a. Group work with economically independent aged. In IM Burnside (ed.), *Nursing and the aged,* 1st ed. (pp. 231-244). New York: McGraw-Hill.

———. 1976b. Music and group work with the aged. In IM Burnside (ed.), *Nursing and the aged,* 1st ed. (pp. 255-269). New York: McGraw-Hill.

———. 1978. Music and music therapy groups. In IM Burnside (ed.), *Working with the elderly: Group process and techniques,* 1st ed. (pp. 255-274). North Scituate, MA: Duxbury Press.

Hogstel M. 1979. Use of reality orientation with aging confused patients. *Nurs Res* 28(May-June):161-165.

Holland DL. 1973. Co-leadership with a group of stroke patients. In IM Burnside (ed.), *Psychosocial nursing care of the aged* (pp. 187-201). New York: McGraw-Hill.

Holtzen V. 1973. Short-term group work in a rehabilitation hospital. In IM Burnside (ed.), *Psychosocial nursing care of the aged* (pp. 161-173). New York: McGraw-Hill.

Janosik E, Phipps L. 1982. *Life cycle group work in nursing.* Monterey, CA: Wadsworth.

King K. 1982. Reminiscing psychotherapy with aging people. *J Psychiatr Nurs Ment Health Serv* 20(2):21-25.

La Monica G, Schmidt G. 1986. Teamwork training polishes students' home care skills. *Nurs Health Care* 7(8):45-54.

Lappe JM. 1987. Reminiscing: The life review therapy. *J Gerontol Nurs* 13(4):12-16.

Leavitt D. 1978. The effects of a support group on adjustment to the changes of aging in elderly women living in the community. Unpublished master's thesis. Rochester, NY: University of Rochester.

Linden M. 1953. Group psychotherapy with institutionalized senile women: Study in gerontologic human relations. *Int J Group Psychother* 3:150-170.

Lyon G. 1971. Stimulation through remotivation. *Am J Nurs* 71(5):982-986.

Meleis, A. 1975. Role insufficiency and role supplementation. *Nurs Res* 24:264-271.

Miller M. 1975. Remotivation therapy: A way to reach the confused elderly patient. *J Gerontol Nurs* 1(2):28-31.

Moody L, Baron V, Monk G. 1970. Moving the past into the present. *Am J Nurs* 70(11)2353-2356.

Morrison JM. 1973. Group therapy for high utilizers of clinic facilities. In IM Burnside (ed.), *Psychosocial nursing care of the aged* (pp. 142-150). New York: McGraw-Hill.

Murphy LN. 1969. A health discussion group for the elderly. In *ANA clinical conferences.* Atlanta, GA: Appleton-Century-Crofts.

Murray MR, Huelskoetter M, O'Driscoll D. 1980. Group work with the person in later maturity. In MR Murray, M Huelskoetter, D O'Driscoll (eds.), *The nursing process in later maturity.* Englewood Cliffs, NJ: Prentice-Hall.

Nickoley S. 1978. Promoting functional level of health and perception of control in elderly women in the community through supportive group intervention. Unpublished master's thesis. Rochester, NY: University of Rochester.

Nickoley-Colquitt S. 1981. Preventive group interventions for elderly clients: Are they effective? *Fam Comm Health: J Health Promo Maint* 3(4):66-85.

Osborn CL. 1989. Reminiscence: When past eases the present. *J Gerontol Nurs* 15(10):6-12.

Parsons CL. 1986. Group reminiscence therapy and levels of depression in the elderly. *Nurs Pract* 11(3):68-76.

Poston B, Levine M. 1980. A modified group treatment for elderly narcissistic patients. *Int J Group Psychother* 30(2):153-167.

Pullinger W. 1960. Remotivation. *Am J Nurs* 60(5):682ff.

Robinson A. 1976. *Remotivation techniques: A manual for use in nursing homes.* Philadelphia: American Psychiatric Association and Smith, Kline Laboratories.

Russell K. 1991. Group work with the elderly mentally ill. *Nurs* 4(10):25-31.

Scarbrough D. 1974. Reality orientation: A new approach to an old problem. *Nurs* 74(11):12-13.

Scott D, Crowhurst J. 1975. Reawakening senses in the elderly. *Canadian Nurs* 71(10):21-22.

Slater P. 1982. Group report. Unpublished paper. Lubbock, TX: Texas Tech University.

Smith LL. 1980. Find your leadership style in groups. *Am J Nurs* 80(7):1301-1303.

Stange A. 1973. Around the kitchen table: Group work on a back ward. In IM Burnside (ed.), *Psychosocial nursing care of the aged*, 1st ed. (pp. 174-186). New York: McGraw-Hill.

Taulbee L, Folsom J. 1966. Reality orientation for geriatric patients. *Hosp Comm Psych* 17(5):133-135.

Tourangeau A. 1988. Group reminiscence therapy as a nursing intervention: An experimental study. *AARN Newsletter* 44(8):17-18; 44(9):29-30.

Waller M, Griffin M. 1984. Group therapy for depressed elders. *Geriatr Nurs* 5(October):309-311.

Wichita C. 1974. Reminiscing as therapy for apathetic and confused residents of nursing homes. Unpublished master's thesis. Tucson, AZ: University of Arizona.

Yalom ID, Terrazas F. 1968. Group therapy for psychotic elderly patients. *Am J Nurs* 68(8):1691-1694.

Youssef FA. 1990. The impact of group reminiscence counseling on a depressed elderly population. *Nurs Pract* 15(4):32-38.

BIBLIOGRAPHY

Donahue EM. 1982. Preserving history through oral history reflections. *J Gerontol Nurs* 8(5):272-278.

Gillette E. 1979. Apathy vs. reality orientation. *J Nurs Care* 12 (April):24-25.

Gøtestam KG. 1980. Behavioral and dynamic psychotherapy with the elderly. In JE Birren, B Sloan (eds.), *Handbook on mental health and aging* (pp. 775-805). Englewood Cliffs, NJ: Prentice-Hall.

Hogan J. 1982. The use of volunteers as reminiscing group leaders. Unpublished master's thesis. San Jose, CA: San Jose State University.

Maney J, Edinberg M. 1976. Social competency groups: A training modality for the gerontological nurse practitioner. *J Gerontol Nurs* 2(6):31-33.

Mims FH. 1971. The need to evaluate group therapy. *Nurs Outlook* 19(12):776-778.

Sandel SL. 1978. Movement therapy with geriatric patients in a convalescent home. *Hosp Comm Psych* 29(November):738-741.

Shaw J. 1979. A literature review of treatment options for mentally disabled old people. *J Gerontol Nurs* 5(September-October):36-42.

Tappan R, Touhy T. 1983. Group leader—Are you a controller? *J Gerontol Nurs* 9(1):34.

RESOURCES

Film

Interacting with Older People (56 minutes, black-and-white, 16 mm). A two-part training film primarily for nurses. Discusses psychosocial needs of older adults and suggests techniques to use in interacting with them. Wayne State University A-V Center, 680 Putnam, Detroit, MI 48202.

Video

Reminiscence in Older Adults: A Group Demonstration. The group members live in a retirement home. Irene Burnside is the group leader; Sarah Gueldner is the discussant. Contact: Dr. Eula Aiken, Executive Director, Southern Council on Collegiate Education for Nursing, 592 Tenth Street, NW, Atlanta, GA 30318-5790. Cost: Approximately $50.

CHAPTER 27

A Recreational Therapist's Perspective

Karin Mueck Vecchione

Recreational therapy can be defined as the use of activity as an intervention to restore, remediate, or rehabilitate for the purpose of reducing or eliminating the effects of illness or disability. The U.S. Department of Labor describes recreational therapy as "the use of recreation services as a form of treatment—much as other health practitioners use surgery, drugs, nutrition, exercise, or psychotherapy" (U.S. Department of Labor 1992). Recreational therapy services are provided by trained, qualified recreational therapists. These services are not to be confused with general recreational activ-

ities, which are offered for the sake of enjoyment. However, many recreational therapists, particularly those working with older adults, also provide general recreational activities for the purpose of enhancing quality of life. This chapter will focus on the provision of group recreational services, and ways in which they can be modified to meet the needs of the aged.

HISTORICAL OVERVIEW OF RECREATIONAL THERAPY

Recreational therapy emerged in the 1940s, when the American Red Cross initiated recreational services to soldiers in hospitals and convalescent cen-

Acknowledgment: Special thanks to Dr. Nancy Butler, Craig Lakin, and Carolyn Johnson for their review of this chapter.

ters (Reynolds & O'Morrow 1985). Known as hospital recreation workers, these service providers offered diversional activities to the patients residing in these facilities. Currently, recreational therapists can be found in a variety of health care settings, including psychiatric facilities, rehabilitation hospitals, nursing homes, day treatment programs, substance abuse programs, pediatric hospitals, and chronic pain programs.

The National Bureau of Labor Statistics estimates there are 32,000 recreational therapists (also known as therapeutic recreation specialists) practicing in a wide variety of health care and community-based facilities (U.S. Department of Labor 1992). More than 170 universities provide higher education curricula in recreation therapy, ranging from the baccalaureate to the master's and doctorate levels. Certification is granted by the National Council for Therapeutic Recreation Certification, when educational criteria are met and a national competency examination, administered by the Educational Testing Service, is successfully completed.

REVIEW OF THE LITERATURE

Numerous studies concerning the benefits of recreational therapy have been conducted on various populations. In 1988, Temple University's Therapeutic Recreation Program was awarded a three-year grant by the Medical Sciences Division of the National Institute on Disability and Rehabilitation Research to examine the role recreational therapy has on medical outcomes. Results of these studies and others show that recreation therapy can and does impact positively on health and rehabilitation (Coyle, Kinney, Riley & Shank 1991).

Studies in the area of aging show that prescribed recreational involvement may yield many positive outcomes. A comprehensive research review conducted by Dr. Carol Riddick and Dr. Jean Keller (1991), for the Temple project, reveals investigation into several areas:

Cardiovascular Improvement. Riddick and Keller's research review found that involvement in recreational therapy can significantly influence blood pressure, pulse rate, skin temperature, general skeletal muscle tension, heart rate, cholesterol, glucose, and respiration rates. Activity interventions utilized in these studies include water aero-

bics (Green 1989; Keller 1991), plush pets (Francis & Munjas 1988), exercise/fitness programs (Morey et al. 1989), and aquarium watching (Cutler Riddick 1985).

Orthopedic Dysfunction. One study (Yoder, Nelson & Smith 1989) demonstrated that exercise with added purpose (such as stirring cookie batter) improved range of motion better than rote exercise, because there was a stronger tendency to repeat the motion more often. Exercise/fitness and water aerobics also demonstrated positive impact on flexibility, body fat, and weight (Buettner 1988; Morey et al. 1989; Green 1989; Keller 1991).

Senile Dementia. In their review of the literature, Riddick and Keller (1991) found numerous studies that examined the impact of recreational involvement on individuals with dementia. These studies found recreation to have a significant impact on cognition or life satisfaction when the following activities were engaged in: dance (Osgood, Meyers & Orchowsky 1990), music (Wolfe 1983; Norberg, Melin & Asplund 1986), plush pet/stuffed animals (Francis & Baly 1986; Banziger & Rousch 1983), reminiscence (Ferguson 1980), video game play (McGuire 1984), and a visitation program (Beck 1982).

Depression, Loneliness, and Life Satisfaction. In addition to the research cited above, there have been a number of studies examining the use of activity involvement with older adults and the impact that has on depression, loneliness, and life satisfaction. Adjustment problems pertaining to these three variables often cause rapid deterioration in older adults, primarily those residing in long-term care facilities. The research, however, demonstrates the positive impact that involvement in productive and meaningful activity can have on the quality of life of older adults.

A MANDATE FOR QUALITY OF LIFE

In 1987, Congress mandated a better quality of life for older adults in nursing homes by passing a nursing home reform law. Since the passage of this landmark legislation, known as the Omnibus Budget Reconciliation Act of 1987 (OBRA '87), strict regulations governing quality of care and quality of life in nursing homes have been implemented.

In its attempt to define quality of life, the Health Care Financing Administration (HCFA) focused on the following issues: self-determination (choice), dignity, participation in groups and activities, accommodation of needs, activity services, and social services. This new emphasis on the importance of meaningful and purposeful activity involvement has brought forth stronger awareness of the need for productivity and the impact this can have on life satisfaction (Medicaid & Medicare Regulations for Long Term Care Facilities 1992). Prior to this legislation, activity involvement, so commonly part of community-based facilities such as adult day care and senior centers, was often menial at best. Activities for adults in nursing homes have many times been limited to childish diversions such as coloring and birthday parties.

Since the adoption of these new regulations, recreation programs are beginning to take on a new life. Administrators are quickly realizing the positive benefits of an expanded program with a therapeutic emphasis. Activities are being adapted and modified to meet the functional abilities of residents. Activity options are being expanded to include diverse and adultlike opportunities, approaches are being incorporated into the plan of care, and residents are being empowered to make choices regarding their involvement in groups. Interdisciplinary cooperation is more prevalent among recreational therapists; nurses; social workers; and physical, occupational, and speech therapists. Group activities that are co-facilitated by two disciplines are more common, and stronger attention is being paid to the psychosocial status of the resident. Nursing home staff are working together as team members to assist residents in achieving their highest practicable level of functioning.

TYPES OF GROUPS UTILIZED BY RECREATIONAL THERAPISTS

Recreational therapists work within a variety of different group environments, depending on what they are trying to achieve with their clients. When significant goal-directed behavior is desired, one-on-one or small-group intervention using a specific activity might be utilized. When social or interpersonal outcomes are desired, small-group interventions might be implemented, and when

socialization, stimulation, and general enjoyment are sought, large groups might be conducted. The most commonly used interventions, however, are small groups of 5 to 10 participants.

CLASSIFICATIONS OF RECREATIONAL ACTIVITIES

In 1947, the World Health Organization adopted a multifaceted approach to the conceptualization of health, which includes physical, psychological, and social domains (Riddick & Keller 1991).

Recreational therapists classify activities similarly, utilizing four functional domains: social, psychological, physical, and cognitive. In this way, activities can be prescribed that have been predetermined to have the elements within them that will bring about the desired outcomes with the client. Most activities require the use of more than one domain and may be classified accordingly. Cognitive-motor activities, which include task-oriented activities, and psychosocial activities, which include interpersonal relations, are examples of these. Most activities can be placed into more than one domain and are often used to elicit a variety of outcomes with the client, such as many craft projects. In many instances, however, activities are classified according to their most significant area of impact. Examples of recreational activities within each functional domain that are commonly used with the aged can be found in Table 27-1.

ACTIVITY MODIFICATION AND ANALYSIS FOR SUCCESSFUL OUTCOMES

Modifying activities so that participants are able to successfully engage in them is critical to achieving positive outcomes for older adults. Activities that are too difficult, not challenging enough, or not reflective of the interests of the clients served will not be effective. The modification of an activity should occur before it is scheduled to take place. To modify an activity effectively, it is important to complete an activity analysis, which breaks it down into subcomponents for analysis of the functional skills and behaviors that are needed for successful participation. This way, adaptive equipment, supplies, room set-up, leadership style, environment,

TABLE 27-1 Examples of recreational activities within functional domains

Physical	Cognitive-motor
Exercise group	Cooking
Walking	Crafts
Dancing	Writing
Pedaling	Drawing
Bowling	Sewing
Horseshoes	Board games
Balloon/beachball volleyball	

Psychological	Psychosocial
Intergenerational events	Reminiscence/life review
Validation therapy	Sensory integration
Remotivation	Remotivation
Values clarification	Music
Therapeutic touch	Poetry
Art	

Cognitive	Social
Skill activities	Discussion groups
Board games	Special events
Current events	Parties
Reality orientation	Bingo
Crossword puzzles	Support groups
	Music

and other factors that will facilitate successful activity involvement by the client population can be prepared for.

Recreational therapists usually analyze activities for a variety of reasons (Peterson & Gunn 1984). These include:

- To determine the physical, cognitive, social, and emotional skills and/or behaviors needed for successful participation, in order to develop a better understanding of the complexity of the tasks involved.
- To determine the appropriateness of the activity for use in the manner planned and to confirm whether or not the activity contributes to the desired behavioral outcome.
- To determine the areas where modification will be required for individuals with functional limitations, and to evaluate where assistance with task segmentation and initiation might be warranted.
- To determine the leadership or instructional style most effective for the activity with this population. Are visual tools necessary? Do participants need to be seated in a certain manner to facilitate comprehension?

Activity analysis scrutinizes an activity to determine the skills it requires so that appropriate modification can take place. Checkers, for example, appears to be a relatively simple game. When examined more closely, however, one can see that numerous skills are required.

The social skills are:

- Cooperative behavior with another individual, as in taking turns and waiting for one's partner to make a move.
- Minimal necessary verbal interaction.

The physical skills are:

- Functional range of motion of one upper extremity and moderate control of fingers or hands.
- Good hand–eye coordination.
- Functional vision.

The cognitive skills are:

- The ability to understand and follow the rules of the game.
- The ability to strategize next moves, which requires higher levels of thinking and decision making.
- A high level of concentration.
- Accurate perception of space and spatial relations.

The emotional skill required is the ability to control emotions when winning or losing.

There are numerous activity analysis models; however, the one most commonly used is the Peterson and Gunn model (1984). This model, although somewhat extensive, is effective in determining the functional and behavioral skills necessary for any activity. (See Figure 27-1.)

MODIFYING ACTIVITIES

Once an activity has been analyzed for its functional and behavioral components, the required skills of the activity will need to be compared to the abilities of your clients. This means that a thorough functional assessment of each client needs to be completed. In nursing homes, this occurs with the Minimum Data Set (MDS), which is required by federal regulation. Most adult day centers also are required to conduct an individualized functional assessment of their participants.

Once it is determined how an activity needs to be modified for a specific group of clients,

FIGURE 27-1 *Activity Analysis Rating Form*

ACTIVITY:

PHYSICAL ASPECTS

1. What is the primary body position required?
   prone   kneeling   sitting   standing   other

2. What parts of the body are required?

   arms _____   neck _____

   hands _____   head _____

   legs _____   upper torso _____

   feet _____   lower torso _____

3. What types of movement does the activity require?

   bending _____   catching _____

   stretching _____   throwing _____

   standing _____   hitting _____

   walking _____   skipping _____

   reaching _____   hopping _____

   grasping _____   running _____

   punching _____

4. Coordination between parts and movements:

	1	2	3	4	5	
Much						Little

5. What are the primary senses required for the activity?

   Rate: 0 = not at all; 1 = rarely; 2 = occasionally; 3 = often

   touch _____

   taste _____

   sight _____

   hearing _____

   smell _____

6. Hand–Eye Coordination:

	1	2	3	4	5	
Much						Little

7. Strength:

	1	2	3	4	5	
Much						Little

FIGURE 27-1—*Continued*

8. Speed:

1	2	3	4	5
Much				None

9. Endurance:

1	2	3	4	5
Much				Little

10. Energy:

1	2	3	4	5
Much				Little

11. Flexibility:

1	2	3	4	5
Much				Little

12. Degree of cardiovascular activity involved:

1	2	3	4	5
Much				Little

SOCIAL ASPECTS

1. Interaction Pattern (check only one pattern):

_____ intraindividual: Action taking place within the mind or action involving the mind and a part of the body
   –requires no contact with another person or external object

_____ extraindividual: Action directed by a person toward an object
   –requires no contact with another person

_____ aggregate: Action directed by a person toward an object while in the company of other persons who are also directing action toward objects
   –action is not directed toward each other
   –no interaction between participants is required or necessary

_____ interindividual: Action of a competitive nature directed by one person toward another

_____ unilateral: Action of a competitive nature among three or more persons, one of whom is an antagonist or "it"
   –interaction is in simultaneous competitive relationship

_____ multilateral: Action of a competitive nature among three or more persons with no one person as an antagonist

_____ intragroup: Action of a cooperative nature by two or more persons intent upon reaching a mutual goal
   –action requires positive verbal or nonverbal interaction

_____ intergroup: Action of a competitive nature between two or more intragroups

2. How many participants does the activity require? _____

Continued

FIGURE 27-1—*Continued*

3. How closely spaced are the participants?

1	2	3	4	5

Close   Distant

4. Can everyone communicate with everyone else by nature of the activity?

Yes _____ No _____

5. Does the activity require cooperation or competition?

6. How much physical contact does the activity demand?

1	2	3	4	5

Much   Little

7. Does the activity promote sexual homogeneity or heterogeneity?

Explain: _____

8. How structured is the activity?

1	2	3	4	5

Highly   Freely

9. Noise Level:

1	2	3	4	5

High   Low

COGNITIVE ASPECTS

1. How many rules are there?

1	2	3	4	5

Many   Few

2. How complex are the rules that must be adhered to?

1	2	3	4	5

Complex   Simple

3. How much long-term memory is necessary?

1	2	3	4	5

Much   Little

4. How much immediate recall memory is necessary?

1	2	3	4	5

Much   Little

5. How much strategy does the activity require?

1	2	3	4	5

Much   Little

6. How much verbalization of thought process is required?

1	2	3	4	5

Much   Little

FIGURE 27-1—*Continued*

7. How much concentration is required?

1	2	3	4	5
Much				Little

8. How often are the following skills used?

   0 = never; 1 = rarely; 2 = occasionally; 3 = often

   Reading _____ Math _____
   Writing _____ Spelling _____

9. Intellectual skill required:

1	2	3	4	5
Much				Little

10. Complexity of scoring:

1	2	3	4	5
Very complex				Not complex

11. Rate the demands for the following identifications:

	Often				Never
Form and shape	1	2	3	4	5
Colors	1	2	3	4	5
Size	1	2	3	4	5
Tactile	1	2	3	4	5
Objects	1	2	3	4	5
Classes	1	2	3	4	5
Numbers	1	2	3	4	5
Nonverbal questions	1	2	3	4	5
Auditory symbols	1	2	3	4	5
Visual symbols	1	2	3	4	5
Concrete thinking	1	2	3	4	5
Abstract thinking	1	2	3	4	5
Body parts	1	2	3	4	5

12. Check directionality required:

   Left/right _____
   Up/down _____
   Around _____
   Over/under _____

Continued

FIGURE 27-1—*Continued*

Person/object _____

Person/person _____

Object/object _____

AFFECTIVE ASPECTS

1. Rate the opportunities for the expression of the following emotions during this activity:

	Often				Never
Joy	1	2	3	4	5
Guilt	1	2	3	4	5
Pain	1	2	3	4	5
Anger	1	2	3	4	5
Fear	1	2	3	4	5
Frustration	1	2	3	4	5

ADMINISTRATIVE ASPECTS

1. Leadership: specific activity-skill expertise _____
   general activity-skill ability _____
   supervisory _____
   none needed _____

2. Equipment: none required _____
   specific commercial product _____
   can be made _____

3. Facilities: none required _____
   specific natural environment _____
   specific man-made environment _____

4. Duration: set time _____
   natural end _____
   continuous _____

5. Participants: any number _____
   fixed number or multiple _____

SOURCE: Carol Ann Peterson/Scout Lee Gunn, *Therapeutic recreation program design: Principles and procedures,* 2e, © 1984, pp. 119-203. Reprinted by permission of Prentice Hall, Englewood Cliffs, New Jersey.

appropriate action should be taken to prepare for the modifications. Keep in mind, however, how clients may feel when being asked to perform the activity with the modifications. When modifications make an activity childlike or demeaning, attempt to find another way of modification, or consider another activity option.

Common activity modifications include the following (adapted from Carter, Van Andel & Robb 1985):

- Alter the rules of games, such as removing time limitations.
- Substitute lighter or softer equipment where heavy equipment would be prohibitive; for example, a beachball or balloon for volleyball.
- Bounce or roll balls instead of throwing them when working with someone who has impaired vision or poor hand–eye coordination.
- Encourage individuals to sit instead of stand.
- Change the color, size, or shape of items that are difficult to see or grasp.
- Change an activity that could place an individual on the spot and cause anxiety to a partner or team event.
- Decrease distances in horseshoes, bowling, bean bag toss, and the like.
- Modify equipment and/or use adapted equipment, such as attaching a string to a ball so it can be easily retrieved or using clamps to hold projects in place.
- Change the techniques required to complete the task, using two hands instead of one, for example.
- Provide more frequent rest periods.
- Use visual, verbal, and even tactile cues to explain and demonstrate activities.

LEVELS OF ACTIVITY INVOLVEMENT

There are various levels of activity involvement. Sometimes actual participation is limited or affected by functional limitations. Other times participation is affected by the level of interest in the activity. Planning programs of interest is a matter of knowing the past history and past life style of the individuals being planned for. It is important to involve clients in the program planning process. Participation in recreational activities will be higher if those you are planning for have input into what they will be asked to do.

Zgola (1987) addresses the grading of activities from the highest level of involvement to the

FIGURE 27-2 *Activity Grading Scale*

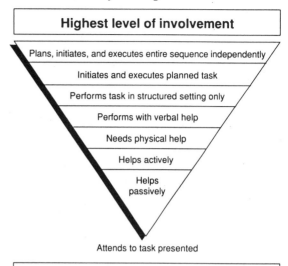

SOURCE: Zgola, Jitka M. *Doing things. A guide to programming activities for persons with Alzheimer's disease and related disorders.* The Johns Hopkins University Press, Baltimore/London, 1987, p. 35. Used with permission.

lowest. (See Figure 27-2.) Activities may be graded in a variety of ways. One effective way is to vary the degree of involvement by the client in planning, initiating, and executing a task (Zgola 1987). When you understand that activity participation can occur at a variety of different levels, it is easier to place individuals with functional limitations into groups, ensuring that each individual is enabled to be a successful participant of that activity. Tasks can be preassigned during group program planning, taking into consideration the functional abilities of the clients who will be involved in the activity. Careful preplanning ensures that clients are included to the maximal level possible and ensures that participants will have a positive experience in the activity.

An example of grading an activity would be baking bread. This task has numerous components: mixing ingredients, kneading the dough, rolling it out, and so on. Therefore, individuals can be assigned to complete the portion of the task that best matches their abilities. Some individuals will be able to plan and execute all the tasks independently, without any assistance, and may be responsible for making their own loaves. An individual with a physical disability, however, might need a structured setting with modified equipment to complete the task.

Individuals with cognitive impairment may require verbal or visual cues to complete even a portion of the task, such as rolling out the dough. An individual with multiple limitations might simply assist by holding the bowl in place while someone else kneads the dough. Clients with very limited functional skills might be present to enjoy the social setting, smell the fresh bread as it bakes, and enjoy the results. Such activities are especially successful with older adults, because they draw on life skills that are often no longer utilized but have played an important role in the life of the elder.

GROUP ACTIVITIES FOR CLIENTS WITH DEMENTIA

Developing group activities for individuals with Alzheimer's type dementia can prove to be a challenge unless the leader is prepared to deal with the behavioral issues and cognitive impairments that are often prevalent in this population. These include disruptive behaviors, such as yelling, wandering, rocking, and picking at things, as well as cognitive deficits in interpreting and following directions, short attention span, and inability to complete even simple tasks independently. Although the disease manifests itself differently in each individual, there are certain characteristics that are common. Understanding these behaviors and cognitive declines will assist the group leader in better planning for more successful activities.

Defining "Activity" for the Person with Dementia

Program goals change from a rehabilitative to a maintenance model when working with clients who have Alzheimer's type dementia. The objectives become restoring self-worth, enhancing quality of life, and providing a structure that encourages individuals to function at their highest level possible for as long as possible. For this reason, it is important to recognize the need for productivity and meaningful involvement. These needs are often better met if clients are engaged in routine work activ-

ity that was a significant part of their past life. This might include things like cooking, making a bed, washing dishes, sweeping, folding laundry, gardening, painting, wiping tables, cleaning a sink, and the like. These tasks are easily incorporated into the routine of a program, whether it be in an adult day center or in a nursing home. Often, though, staff must be trained to limit what they do for clients and to engage clients in tasks that usually are completed by staff themselves. This requires flexibility within the facility, since client involvement in work tasks of this nature often requires additional time.

The results of such a program, however, create a partnership approach in which clients are actively involved in their environment and as a result have a stronger sense of control over their surroundings. It is important that all of the staff (including the housekeeping and maintenance staff) in a facility, as well as the administration, subscribe to this philosophy if it is to be successful. In return, staff develop a stronger bond with clients and are more in tune to their needs.

Segmenting Tasks for Successful Completion

When working with clients who have Alzheimer's type dementia, particularly those in the middle to later stages, various modifications may be necessary for successful activity involvement. Segmenting or breaking down activity tasks into simple steps, for example, is imperative to successful participation. Activity analysis, mentioned earlier in this chapter, will assist with this process. For example, when leading an exercise group, use simple movements, repeat them slowly and often, establish eye contact with group participants—particularly those with hearing impairments—and give physical hands-on direction to those who are having difficulty initiating the task. Environmental factors, such as adequate lighting and reduced background noise, also are important to enhancing the successful integration of directions from the group leader.

Individuals with Alzheimer's type dementia often have difficulty initiating a task. It is as if they are stuck when trying to begin. This problem is often easily overcome by physically helping the individual to begin the task. An example would be wiping tables. If you were to direct or even demonstrate wiping the table to clients with dementia, there might be no response. However, by putting the sponges into their hands and beginning the motion for them, you will often help them get past the sticking point so that they are able to complete the task for themselves.

Activity Strategies That Are Successful

Although each client is different, there are some basic guidelines that may be utilized when choosing group activities for individuals with dementia. These include the following:

1. Use activities that are repetitive in nature. Tasks such as sandpapering, painting, wiping, folding, and washing consist of repetitive actions. These activities work much better than complex tasks that require numerous steps to complete.
2. Be aware of frustration levels. If you observe a client becoming frustrated, intervene immediately. Frustration often leads to catastrophic reactions, which can be prevented if group leaders are tuned in to their participants.
3. Do not introduce activities that require learning new skills. This includes things such as board games individuals have not played before. It is difficult for individuals with dementia to learn new tasks. What could have otherwise been a positive experience may end up a catastrophic reaction.
4. Utilize overlearned behaviors that no longer require cognitive effort. This includes things like playing the piano and typing. Oftentimes people with dementia are still able to engage in these activities.
5. Use music, movement, and rhythm. Experience tells us that individuals with dementia respond well to music and movement, such as dancing.
6. Do not overstimulate. Keep the environment limited to the stimuli required for the activity. Lots of background noise, people walking in and out of the room, intercom voices, and so forth, are disruptive, will diminish attention span, and may possibly cause a catastrophic reaction.
7. Use the individual's past history. Reminiscing about the past is often possible with clients who have dementia, since long-term memory stays intact the longest. Also use past history to give you clues about the present. If an individual had many children or taught school, for example, try an intergenerational activity.
8. When giving directions for an activity, use verbal and visual clues. If presenting a craft project, for example, make up samples for each phase of project completion to show the group.

GUIDELINES FOR PLANNING RECREATIONAL GROUPS

There are certain components that are inherent in good program planning and should be remembered when planning activities for the aged. These include:

1. Ascertain the past history and interests of the clients you are serving. If the individuals for whom you are planning group activities always disliked arts and crafts but actively participated in sports, then planning a craft program may not be the activity of choice.

2. Know the functional abilities of the individuals you are planning a program for. Recreational therapists differ from some other therapists because they utilize the strengths of the individuals they serve. Knowing the abilities of your clients will allow you to plan around their functional deficits. Adopt the attitude that each person can do whatever activity task you are offering as long as that activity is modified appropriately.

3. Freedom of choice during recreational activity is one of the most essential components of recreation. Remember that clients should be afforded the opportunity to make choices and not coerced into participation. Poor motivation can be a problem with institutionalized older adults and may require extra effort on the part of the group leader. However, learn when no means no.

4. Treat your clients with dignity, and remember that although they may have functional limitations, they can still successfully participate in most activities if they are appropriately modified. This takes advance planning and preparation, as well as thorough knowledge about the individuals and their strengths and weaknesses. Childlike activities are demeaning and not necessary. Some adult day care centers, for example, give participants dolls to comfort them. A better approach might be to have staff or volunteers bring in children. Complex activities can be broken down into subtasks and completed in steps. Keep activities meaningful and purposeful.

5. Always motivate clients to become involved. Tell people about upcoming events to

increase motivation. If an intercom system is available, use it to announce activities. One idea that has worked is to announce the daily news each morning, going over the day's events, the menu, birthdays, new staff and residents, and any other event that might be of interest. This can be done in any environment, including day centers.

6.   Be flexible. If an activity is not going well, shorten the length; if clients are responding, let it go longer and have it more often. One big mistake often made is that we become inflexible. Crafts are only held once a week because that's how it was originally scheduled, regardless of how many people truly enjoy participating. Remember that not all activities will work the first time around. If an activity is unsuccessful, evaluate why. Was it poor programming? Was it not within the area of interest of your clients? Was the activity not modified appropriately?

SUMMARY

Productivity and meaningful life experiences play an integral role in health and well-being that does not decrease with age. Recreational endeavors are ways to provide these opportunities, and when utilized as a part of the comprehensive plan of care, foster positive outcomes in the quality of life of the aged. The recent transition toward interdisciplinary service delivery requires the collaborative efforts of all care providers to function as a team. Integrating successful recreational opportunity into the team process is one effective way to enhance quality of life.

Health care providers of all types play an integral role in this area. Activities should not be limited to recreational group activities, but should include all of those life pursuits that provide individuals with a sense of purpose, meaning, and dignity. This responsibility does not fall on any one discipline alone, but rests on the shoulders of the entire interdisciplinary team. It is when these teams blend their services into an eclectic system of care that a holistic means of achieving quality is attained.

EXERCISE 1

This exercise will prepare you for activity analysis and modification. Choose an activity you personally enjoy. Write down the skills and behaviors *you think* are required to participate in this activity. Now locate the activity analysis tool in this chapter and complete it for the activity you have chosen. Compare your results. Now, write down two ways you could modify this activity for an older person:

- Who has left-sided paralysis.
- With moderate memory impairment.
- Who is depressed.

EXERCISE 2

This experiential exercise is designed to enhance your awareness of the need to modify activities to match the abilities of the population for which you are programming. Choose a simple recipe. Place all the ingredients and utensils required to prepare it on a counter. Blindfold yourself. Have someone read you the instructions; then complete the task. Try the same thing using only one hand, on which you are wearing an oven mitt. How might the activity have been modified to better allow for your participation?

REFERENCES

American Therapeutic Recreation Association. 1987. *Your invitation to join.* Hattiesburg, MS: ATRA.

Banziger G, Rousch S. 1983. Nursing homes for the birds: A control-relevant intervention with bird feeders. *Gerontologist* 23:527-531.

Beck P. 1982. The successful interventions in nursing homes: The therapeutic effects of cognitive activity. *Gerontologist* 22:378-383.

Buettner L. 1988. Utilizing development theory and adaptive equipment with regressed geriatric patients in therapeutic recreation. *Therap Rec J* 22 (3):72-79.

Carter MJ, Van Andel G, Robb G. 1985. *Therapeutic recreation, A practical approach.* St. Louis: Times Mirror/Mosby College Publishing.

Coyle C, Kinney WB, Riley B, Shank J. 1991. *Benefits of therapeutic recreation: A consensus view.* Ravensdale, WA: Idyll Arbor.

Cutler Riddick C. 1985. Health, aquariums, and the non-institutionalized elderly. In M Sussman (ed.), *Pets and the family* (pp. 163-173). New York: Haworth.

Ferguson J. 1980. *Reminiscence counseling to increase psychological well-being of elderly women in nursing home facilities.* Unpublished doctoral dissertation. Charleston: University of South Carolina.

Francis G, Baly A. 1986. Plush animals: Do they make a difference? *Geriatr Nurs* 7:140-142.

Francis G, Munjas B. 1988. Plush animals and the elderly. *J Appl Gerontol* 7:161-172.

Green J. 1989. Effects of a water aerobics program on the blood pressure, percentage of body fat, weight, and resting pulse rate of senior citizens. *J Appl Gerontol* 8(1):132-138.

Health Care Financing Administration. 1991. *Medicaid and Medicare regulations for long-term care facilities.* 42 Code of Federal Regulations, Part 483, Subpart B, Section 483.15—Quality of life (September 26).

Keller M. 1991. *The impact of a water aerobics program on older adults.* Unpublished manuscript.

McGuire F. 1984. Improving the quality of life for residents of long-term care facilities through video games. *Activities, Adaptation, & Aging* 6:1-8.

Morey M, Cowper P, Feussner J, DiPasquale R, Crowley G, Kitzman D, Sullivan R. 1989. Evaluation of a supervised exercise program in a geriatric population. *J Am Geriatrics Soc* 37:348-354.

Norberg A, Melin E, Asplund K. 1986. Reactions to music, touch and object presentation in the final stage of dementia: An exploratory study. *Int J Nurs Studies* 23:315-323.

Omnibus Budget Reconciliation Act of 1987 (OBRA). P.L. 100-203.

Osgood N, Meyers B, Orchowsky S. 1990. The impact of creative dance and movement training on the life satisfaction of older adults. *J Appl Gerontol* 9:255-265.

Peterson CA, Gunn SL. 1984. *Therapeutic recreation program design, principles and procedures.* Englewood Cliffs, NJ: Prentice-Hall.

Reynolds RP, O'Morrow GS. 1985. *Problems, issues and concepts in therapeutic recreation.* Englewood Cliffs, NJ: Prentice-Hall.

Riddick C, Keller J. 1991. The benefits of therapeutic recreation in gerontology. In CP Coyle, WB Kinney, B Riley, JW Shank (eds.), *Benefits of therapeutic recreation: A consensus view.* Ravensdale, WA: Idyll Arbor.

U.S. Department of Labor, Bureau of Labor Statistics. 1992. *Occupational Outlook Q* 36(1):20, 147-150.

Wolfe J. 1983. The use of music in a group sensory training program for regressed geriatric patients. *Activities, Adaptation, & Aging* 4(1):49-62.

Yoder R, Nelson D, Smith D. 1989. Added purpose versus rote exercise in female nursing home residents. *Am J Occup Ther* 43(9):581-586.

Zgola JM. 1987. *Doing things.* Baltimore: Johns Hopkins University Press.

BIBLIOGRAPHY

Bartol MA. 1979. Nonverbal communication in patients with Alzheimer's disease. *J Gerontol Nurs* 5(4):21-31.

Bedini L, Priode A. 1992. Expanding the recreation experience: A multistep approach to programming for long-term care facilities for older adults. *Ann Therap Rec* 3:1-9.

Blinn R. 1985. Effective one-to-one programming. *Activities, Adaptation, & Aging* 7(2):49.

Butler RN. 1963. The life review: An interpretation of reminiscence in the aged. *Psychiatry, J Study Interpersonal Processes* 26(1):65-76.

Carrauthers C, Sneegas J, Ashton-Shaeffer C. 1986. *Therapeutic recreation: Guidelines for activity services in long-term care.* Champaign, IL: University of Illinois at Urbana-Champaign.

Dwyer BJ (ed.). 1988. Recreational therapy and activities with elderly clients. *Focus Geriatr Care Rehabil* 1(10).

Flatten K, Wilhite B, Reyes-Watson L. 1988. *Recreation activities for the elderly.* New York: Springer.

Freeman S. 1987. *Activities and approaches for Alzheimer's.* The Whitfield Agency, 8560 C Kingston Pike, Suite 100, Knoxville, TN 37923.

Goodman M. 1983. "I came here to die": A look at the function of therapeutic recreation in nursing homes. *Therap Rec J* (3):14-19.

Greenblatt FS. 1988. *Therapeutic recreation for long-term care facilities.* New York: Human Sciences Press.

Gwyther L. 1985. *Care of Alzheimer's patients: A manual for nursing home staff.* Alzheimer's Disease & Related Disorders Association /AHCA.

Hurley O. 1988. *Safe therapeutic exercise for the frail elderly: An introduction.* Center for the Study of Aging, 706 Madison Avenue, Albany, NY 12208.

Molinari V, Reichlin RE. 1985. Life review reminiscence in the elderly: A review of the literature. *Int J Aging Human Dev* 20(2):81-90.

Paire JA, Karney RJ. 1984. The effectiveness of sensory stimulation for geropsychiatric inpatients. *Am J Occup Ther* 38(8):505-509.

Parent LH. 1978. Effects of low-stimulus environment on behavior. *Am J Occup Ther* 32(1):19-25.

Ross M, Burdick D. 1981. *Sensory integration: A training manual for therapists and teachers for regressed psychiatric and geriatric patient groups.* Slack, Inc., 6900 Grove Road, Thorofare, NJ 08086.

Weiss CR, Kronberg J. 1986. Upgrading therapeutic recreation service to severely disoriented elderly. *Therap Rec J* 20:32-42.

Wilhite B, Teaff JD. 1986. Nursing home recreation: An unchanged diet of bingo, birthdays, and Bible? *Parks and Rec* (August):38-63.

RESOURCES

Agencies

American Therapeutic Recreation Association, P.O. Box 15215, Hattiesburg, MS 39404-5215; phone: 800-553-0304.

National Council for Therapeutic Recreation Certification, P.O. Box 479, Thiells, NY 10984-0479; phone: 914-947-4346.

National Parks and Recreation Association, Leisure & Aging Branch, 2775 South Quincy Street, Suite 300, Arlington, VA 22206-2204; phone: 703-820-2204.

National Therapeutic Recreation Society, 2775 South Quincy Street, Suite 300, Arlington, VA 22206-2204; phone: 703-820-2204.

Clinical and Educational Issues

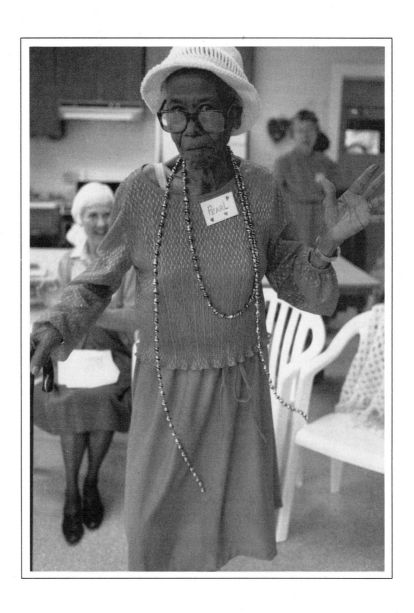

Part 7 contains five new chapters written for the third edition. Chapter 28, by social workers Florence Safford and Mary Gwynne Schmidt, describes these special groups: staff, volunteers, families, and residential groups. Chapter 29, by Joan Parry, focuses on single-group sessions for grieving older adults.

Bernita Steffl, who has taught many gerontological nursing students, shares her knowledge about curriculum and professional programs and emphasizes the need for clinical practice for students in Chapter 30.

Chapter 31, on consultation and supervision, by Irene Burnside, discusses some of the issues regarding consultation and preceptorship. The importance of preceptorship for a new group leader is described.

The ethical issues in group work are not commonly discussed in depth regarding groups and older persons—usually only confidentiality is covered. Mary Gwynne Schmidt, a social worker, spells out ethical concerns germane to group work with older persons in Chapter 32.

In Chapter 33, another little-discussed issue is covered by social workers Frederick Anderson and Roger Delgado: the importance of cultural issues in group work with older adults.

Chapter 34, by Joann Ivry and Florence Schwartz, is also about a subject rarely discussed in the literature: the issues surrounding research in group work with this population.

CHAPTER 28

Special Groups: Staff, Volunteers, Families, and Residential Groups

Florence Safford and Mary Gwynne Schmidt

KEY WORDS

- Community meetings/nursing facility
- Expressive groups
- Family groups
- In-service training
- Instrumental groups
- Psychoeducational groups
- Structure
- Volunteers

LEARNING OBJECTIVES

- List three agency or nursing-facility activities in which group process plays an important part.
- Describe how instrumental groups differ from expressive groups and give two examples of each.
- Give two reasons for introducing subgroup activities into a training group and two reasons for not doing so.
- Contrast the use of structure in training groups for volunteers and in insight-oriented treatment groups.
- Tell why the psychoeducational group is especially suited for working with the families of mentally impaired residents.
- Describe the function of the community meeting in a nursing facility.

This chapter deals with group process as a powerful dynamic in agencies and residential settings. The chapter discusses four situations in which attention to group process heightens effectiveness: (1) in-service training for staff, (2) programs for volunteers, (3) educational groups for families, and (4) community meetings for nursing home residents. Often these are not recognized as small-group activities, because their official purpose is educational or organizational and/or because the persons involved are not viewed as patients or clients.

As instrumental (or task) groups, they differ from expressive (or treatment) groups in purpose, structure, and emotional intensity. An example of an instrumental group is a work group with a defined purpose, understood role assignments and responsibilities, an agenda, and an emphasis on doing rather than feeling. An example of an expressive group is a therapy group marked by a degree of ambiguity that may conduce to anxiety and regression. In between these two polarities is a whole range of groups described in this book.

Because structure contributes to comfort and flexibility leads to creativity, many leaders of groups for the aged begin with structure and then ease up a bit as members make the group their own. This initially more-structured approach is supportive not only to aged participants but also to new leaders, who become better able to accept detours in the agenda as they gain more confidence. Reminiscence groups tend to be more structured than life review groups: Topics are announced, props are more likely to be employed, and participants are not encouraged to uncover feelings and memories that neither they nor their leaders are ready to deal with. Life review groups entail more probing and more risk taking by participants and leaders alike. The emotional level may become more intense. (See Chapter 15, Reminiscence Groups.)

If a member of a work crew bursts into tears on the job, something is wrong. If tears well into the eyes of participants in a bereavement group, this is entirely appropriate.

The four kinds of group situations described in this chapter move along a continuum of purpose, structure, and intensity of feeling. Goals in the in-service training of staff may include attitude change, and wise instructors will take staff members' feelings into account, but the purpose of such groups is to teach a process or technique or to impart other information needed for job performance. Even when experiential learning is employed, there must be points at which the instructor pulls together the learnings and prioritizes them. By organizing the information, the educator is helping the learner retain it. There are clear lines of authority in this teaching-learning situation. Attendance is rarely optional.

Volunteers are not employees. Training for them also has a how-to-do character. They would resent or be threatened by anything that smacked of treatment. They like organization in the educational process. Nevertheless, how they feel about the agency and its clientele, the educator, and one another is vital to ensuring their continuing engagement with the agency. They must receive emotional satisfaction.

Like volunteers, family members of residents and patients usually embrace the educational aspect of any program. At the same time, the real barriers to their support of their aging relatives are often emotional, and unless they can work through some of the feelings, any instrumental learning may be hobbled by pain, distress, and old hurts. These groups often exist near the border between education and treatment and sometimes tip over. The model of a program for families of residents with dementia described below takes into account their dual needs for emotional support and factual knowledge.

Finally, in institutional settings where people live so close to one another and yet, in so many ways, are isolated and lonely, there is a strong need to nurture community beyond shared recreation and shared meals. Above all, these very old people need to participate in a segment of group life in which they are responsible members, not patients with the recipient status that implies. The chapter will close with a description of a model for community meetings that was developed by the Live Oak Institute in Sobrante, California. Although that model evolved in a residential facility, it has been adapted for day care centers, senior centers, nutrition sites, and board-and-care facilities. The phrase "community meeting" in this chapter will refer to these residents' groups, not to neighborhood get-togethers in the wider community.

GROUP PROCESSES IN IN-SERVICE TRAINING

In-service classes do more than educate. They can improve staff morale, encourage peer discussions, and keep staff members in close touch with one another. The latter is especially important when they have little opportunity for daily contact but must build upon one another's work. This is as true in community agencies, where staff members may do much of their work alone in the field, as it is in nursing homes, where they work in shifts. Getting to know one another better prepares them for quick collaboration and substitution when either is required.

Because these are indeed small groups, certain roles are common: the expert, who is anxious to update the presenter; the yes-but-er, who takes issue with every point; the Scheherazade, who can provide a tale to illustrate—or challenge—every point; and the distractor, who comes in late, introduces irrelevancies, and otherwise impedes the process.

To a point, both the expert and the yes-but-er can be encouraged to expand their views further: They are often a reminder that the leader has been talking too long. If they are merely intrusive, the group itself will manifest impatience with them. When they are interrupting a sequence, they can be asked to wait. When the Scheherazade's tales are relevant, they can be powerful reinforcers of the instructor's point because they come from a member of the group. The late-entry distractor provides the speaker with a reason for recapitulating, which may be helpful for all. When the interruptions are disruptive, the speaker can be asked to tell the instructor afterwards or to prepare some written materials to share with the group.

Obstacles

Attendance may be compulsory, but attention is not. The leader may struggle against formidable odds if the very person who mandated the in-service training is less committed to its learning goals than to documenting that it took place at all.

This situation is best typified by the nursing facility that schedules two consecutive 30-minute sessions around the 3 P.M. change of shifts. The first session is attended by bone-weary nursing assistants, who drowse or watch the clock. Just when they have convinced the leader that she or he should consider another occupation, these weary workers leave and a new crew appears, wide awake and enthusiastic. Thirty minutes is not enough time to teach anything: Time for discussion and experiential learning is severely curtailed. The only solution lies in sharply limiting content. When time provision is inadequate, there often is equal inattention to the teaching environment. Confused residents may be permitted to wander in and out, participants may be called out to perform various tasks, and an intercom may break in at intervals.

The leader is further challenged when there are great educational disparities between participants, as when nursing assistants are included with licensed nurses. Generally, both groups are serving the same population, which does provide a common focus. The task is to make the content comprehensible to the less educated while acknowledging the expertise of the professionals.

The paraprofessionals are aided by frequent definition of terms and use of examples. The professionals can be engaged by invoking them as authorities and as helpers—and by reminding them privately that it is important for them to hear what their supervisees have been told so they can assist them with the material.

Often dedicated agency personnel are reluctant to waste time on staff meetings and in-service training because the needs of their clients seem more urgent. These are the very persons at risk of burnout. They need the intraagency support system and the larger perspective that training can provide. The instructor should never feel diffident about requiring their attendance but then must demonstrate that the content is relevant to their work.

Finally, there are many persons who experienced formal schooling as irrelevant to their daily lives, replete with putdowns, and boring as well. Androgogy (adult education) must relate to their real world better than the pedagogy of their youth (Knowles 1973). At the very least, no one should suffer humiliation during in-service training and no one should be set up for failure. Smith (1992) has tackled this disaffection by developing learning games for nursing assistants such as psychosocial bingo and lessons styled after the television game shows they watch.

Techniques

Seating communicates the expected level of participation: Classroom rows call for passive listening; circles and roundtables call for taking part.

Group process can be enlisted to promote active learning. Discussion changes attitudes, and simply viewing a videotape together stimulates discussion. Role plays within the larger circle elicit another level of involvement. For example, you can have one participant be the patient and two others play nursing assistants pushing her wheelchair and talking over her head. Afterwards all parties can discuss how they felt, and the group will make your point for you. Finally, breaking the large class into smaller groups or pairs for problem-solving exercises provides training in teamwork, builds group cohesion, and enables shy persons to speak up.

Only irrelevance and time constraints are barriers to this kind of learning. When they work well, these exercises always take longer than expected.

Because they foster fellowship, small-group approaches like these are even more important in work with volunteers. Their very flexibility makes it essential, however, that the leader develop a learning plan. See Table 28-1 for an outline useful for work with either staff or volunteers.

GROUP PROCESSES IN WORKING WITH VOLUNTEERS

Agencies and facilities serving the older adult benefit from the services of a broad range of volunteers who are often effectively recruited, managed, and retained in groups. Volunteering not only appeals to their altruism but offers them an expanded social network and an improved self-image through formal recognition.

Volunteers come in all ages. Aged volunteers are replacing the housewives who used to be the daytime volunteers. By 1990, 41 percent of volunteers were over 65 (Chambré 1993).

Engaging the older residents as volunteers in their own facilities and retirement communities makes sense. They should receive the same screening, training, supervision, and recognition as non-residents.

Hogan (1986) recommends a screening interview for volunteers and recommends getting two letters of reference. Her training program for volunteer group leaders includes reading assignments and films, participation in a reminiscence group, peer group discussion, and an evaluation.

Because they send volunteers into the homes of the dying, hospices have a great need for screening and also for bonding their volunteers into a strong, mutual-support group. Bonnie MacGregor, volunteer coordinator at a Doylestown, Pennsylvania, hospice, requires all would-be volunteers to take three weeks of bereavement training, followed by a second interview. At this point, some screen themselves out or are counseled into less stressful Doylestown hospital programs.

After the second interview, volunteers undergo intensive training designed not only to impart skills but to build relationships within the group. The most successful of these was a weekend retreat in a beautiful mountain setting. Staff members came and went, but volunteers and the coordinator remained overnight. Ms. MacGregor says no group has bonded more quickly nor has remained more faithful to the program.

TABLE 28-1 Lesson plan

Learning needs to be addressed: Why this lesson at this time?

Learners: Consider what you know about their learning style and how they are likely to feel about this content. Will it seem relevant to their goals and work?

Time and place:

  Goal(s): These can be more global than the objectives.

  Objectives: State these in specific, observable terms.

  Content: What you wish to cover.

  Method: This should include:

- *Modalities:* Lecturing, group discussion, experiential exercises, the case method, or any combination.
- *Strategy:* How you plan to get their attention, convey information, and help them retain it; how you intend to overcome attitudinal resistance to the content.
- *Sequencing:* How you plan to organize the material so they can integrate and retain it.

Material, equipment: Slides, overhead projector, handouts, chalk board, flip chart, and the like.

Measurement of goal achievement: Depending on the setting, this can be derived from quality improvement data, tests, charts, observation, questionnaires, and subsequent attendance figures. Stating your objectives in specific, observable terms makes measurement easier.

With tighter resources and overstretched staff, however, the away-from-home retreat was no longer possible, so for its next class the Doylestown hospice elected a Saturday–Sunday all-day retreat at a nearby children's day care center. The plants, animals, and bright colors promoted an easy informality that almost matched that of the predecessor training (MacGregor 1993).

The importance of training and supervision was illustrated in Project OASIS, which used older adults to provide mental-health counseling in nursing homes. Despite difficulties, 17 of the 18 aged volunteers were able to stay the course, supported by careful training, monthly in-service meetings, and weekly supervision (Crose, Duffy, Warren & Franklin 1987).

Throughout the education process, the volunteer coordinator will give a higher priority to creating a climate of acceptance and warmth than the staff developer, whose chief focus is skills acquisition. Volunteers also need skills, but their staying depends on their relations with people. Peer group support is equally important for a second group of persons, more burdened than volunteers, the families of the mentally impaired.

GROUP PROCESS IN TRAINING PROGRAMS FOR FAMILIES

The senior author of this chapter (Safford) developed a program at Isabella Geriatric Center to help families of residents deal with the devastating consequences of dementia. Its goal was to provide them with the nontechnical knowledge they needed about the causes and symptoms of mental impairment and the resources available, the skills they needed for responding to their relatives and for relating to the professional service system, and help with their emotional reactions. The program was organized as an educational opportunity on the assumption that many of these relatives would feel uncomfortable with a therapy format (Safford 1980).

In addition to families of Isabella residents, the group was opened to families caring for their relatives in the community. It was assumed that the community group and the nursing-home group could benefit from the same knowledge and that they would be mutually supportive through sharing experiences. This assumption proved correct. The community group learned about which factors led to the decision to place the relative in the institution, while members of the nursing home group were supported in their choice by the reminder of the ongoing nature of the problems in the community.

A two-hour intensive program was offered once a week for six weeks. The first hour covered didactic material; the second hour was open to questions and discussion of participants' experiences. The program drew 48 participants from a radius of 200 miles. Despite the large numbers, there was a great deal of participant interaction, and by the middle phase of the program, group cohesion was evident, with many participants sharing telephone numbers. This informal interaction was facilitated by the refreshments that were served before and after the meeting.

Careful attention was paid to the learning environment, with the goal of establishing a climate of informality and warmth. A multipurpose activity room was selected that was large enough for com-

fort but not so large that the participants would lose a sense of intimacy. The chairs were arranged in three concentric semicircles, filling the room but not overcrowding it.

Session One

A large number of participants arrived a half hour early and sat quietly, looking tense and not talking to one another. When a huge urn of coffee and platters of pastries were brought in, conversation started. The session began 20 minutes late to put the participants more at ease by allowing them to become acquainted. During the break, there was much animated interaction among the participants. The first session ended a half hour later than scheduled, and many participants remained to talk with their newly found peer group.

From the outset, the program was presented as a problem-solving model, with the goal of providing the tools needed for more rational, satisfactory family and institutional relations.

The heightened emotional level of the group was evidenced frequently by the urgency with which problems were presented for discussion and the tears with which experiences were shared. Although the format was educational, the program turned out to be at least as much a therapeutic experience.

As the knowledge component was developed, the participants were invited to raise questions or make comments based on their personal experiences, which were then used to reinforce the more abstract learning. A case example will illustrate the process.

The project director identified as a source of difficulties the need to acquire, without the benefit of role models, new role behaviors for which they had no prior experience. One married daughter in her fifties commented that when she brought her parents for their initial interview to Isabella Homes, she recalled having the same feelings as when she registered her children for kindergarten. She also recalled her feelings as she helped her mother dress: She was painfully aware of the difference in her emotions from when she had helped her own daughter dress. She said, with tears in her eyes, "I didn't want to be her mother—she had been a wonderful mother!"

The rest of the group nodded in agreement, most having experienced similar emotions at what seemed to be the strain of role reversals. The project director pointed out that it is not role reversal that takes place but the assumption of a new role, that of protective kin or helper. The psychological relationship between adult child and parent does not turn around because of the parents' impairment, although the incorrect concept of role reversal and second childhood is widely held.

The group was then introduced to the concept of filial maturity as the developmental task that confronted them (Blenkner 1965). This was explicated as the need to assume dependable role behavior, appropriate to the level of their kin's impairment.

The problems most frequently expressed centered around their difficulty during visits and their frustrations in seeking help from the staff. To deal with the first set of problems, the need to understand the nature of impairment and the meaning of their kin's behavior was emphasized. A factual presentation followed.

To deal with the second problem, the project director suggested that the group might form the nucleus of a family council, which could bring their shared concerns to the administrators of the home. There was immediate interest, and the project director undertook to discuss the mechanics of establishing such an organization with administration and report back at the second session. Because many participants had internalized the myth that families abandon their own, serving on a family council to counteract the guilt-producing myth emerged as an unanticipated goal of the program.

A common theme was the need to change the behavior of the mentally impaired, revealing lack of knowledge of the physiological disorder and a denial of the extent of the relative's impairment.

Because the litany of heartbreaking problems was beginning to sound like a soap opera, the project director made conscious use of humor to release some of the mounting emotion. Several amusing anecdotes provided welcome comic relief.

Groundwork for a Family Council

Before the second session, the project director talked with the administration about the relatives' interest in establishing a family council. The administration welcomed the plan as a means of demonstrating a responsive stance to criticisms

and an openness to suggestions. In addition, an active family council was viewed as a potential ally. Communication was to be established directly with the administration through elected representatives of the council.

Session Two

The difference in mood at the start of the second session was dramatic. There was already a sense of group cohesion, and animated discussion took place before the session began.

Picking up the common desire to change the behavior of their relatives, the project director suggested borrowing the Alcoholics Anonymous prayer: "Grant me the serenity to accept what cannot be changed, the courage to change what can be changed, and the wisdom to know the difference." This slogan was a psychological aid as the participants worked at the task of learning the nature of their relative's condition and at identifying when the condition might be ameliorated and when they had to accept irreversible decline. The participants' examples served as a springboard for clarification.

The second half of the session was devoted to role playing, in which several participants were to enact the problem of the family whose impaired older relative could no longer be maintained safely in the community but who refused to go into a nursing home. The goal was to give participants a chance to practice new skills and to experience more effective decision making, but role playing was a fiasco with this population, because they could not transcend their current roles to handle the problem situation. The project director was forced to drop role-play and teach directly. The report about the administration's cooperation in founding a family council was received enthusiastically. Some stayed afterward to work out plans for their new council.

Session Three

This session included another attempt at role playing, with a relative of a nursing home resident coming to the nurse with a long list of legitimate complaints of neglect. When the role-playing nurse responded to the complaints, "These things happen because your mother is so confused," the relative immediately retreated, saying, "I'm sorry I bothered you." When the project director tried to encourage other responses, a member of the group commented empathetically, "That's because nurses are so authoritarian that we're all intimidated by them."

This led to a fruitful discussion of the guilt-provoking behavior of many members of the staff in nursing homes and to the discussion of concrete methods relatives can use to present legitimate complaints. It was decided to drop other planned experiential techniques, because it was clear that this group was in need of more direct sources of information. Furthermore, it was evident that they were developing their new skills through interaction with their newly found reference group.

Sessions Four and Five

The most emotionally charged session was the fourth, when sexuality was discussed. There was absolute silence in the room as the project director discussed normal sexuality in old age and problems with the mentally impaired. Case examples were presented of behavior resulting from damage to the part of the brain that controls sexual impulses. Examples of problems in the nursing home, as well as in the community, elicited personal experiences that had been too painful for participants to discuss until that point. The suppressed embarrassment and outrage were released with evident relief, based on the newly acquired knowledge that unexpected sexual behavior can be part of the normal process of deterioration caused by dementia or related mental impairments.

Session five's discussion of value issues related to their conflicts seemed particularly stimulating to the participants. The values of independence, egalitarianism, responsibility, family security, and self-actualization were discussed, revealing how these values might conflict and lead to anger and then guilt. Analyzing situations to uncover the underlying values that dictate choices in everyday behavior was a new experience for most of the participants. These values were then related to the earlier discussion of filial maturity and the need to find a balance of shared function with the formal organizations equipped to care for the mentally impaired aged in modern society.

Session Six

The final session dealt with separation. Most participants expressed the wish that the program would continue. One stated almost angrily, "I'm sure you said the program was going to last ten weeks!" Another brought a bouquet of flowers. A community relative gave a contribution to the home. One took pictures of the group. The project director had to submerge a powerful impulse to continue the program.

The participant most interested in establishing a family council reported that the group had decided to hold their first meeting the very next Saturday in order not to lose their group identity and the impetus of their meetings. The session ended with a spirit of activism and optimism that they would as a group continue to manifest concern not only for their own mentally impaired relatives, but for all the residents of the home and for the aged in general.

We next tested 8- and 10-session programs. Each time participants asked for more sessions. The massive request for more time made it clear that the participants needed opportunities to talk out their feelings. As a result, a support group was formed and met on a monthly basis.

In the years since these programs and support groups were developed, the Association for Alzheimer's Disease and Related Disorders (ADRDA) was initiated. ADRDA now provides training and support for caregivers throughout the country. Families can be referred to local chapters or can benefit from some of the helpful books now available (Cohen & Eisdorfer 1986; Hooyman & Lustbader 1986; Mace & Rabins 1981; Safford 1987). Long-term care facilities still benefit through improved relations with residents' relatives when such programs are offered as an integral service. These programs are now called *psychoeducational*, because of the multiple benefits of knowledge, skills acquisition, and the opportunity for emotional release and repair.

Psychoeducational groups for adult children deal with an important component among the three that Abromovice (1988) identifies and describes in his psychosocial model of institutional care. These are the family, of which he sees the resident as a continuing part; the managed environment of the nursing facility; and the community.

He would promote mainstreaming by bringing in volunteers and churches, lodges, and other groups and by taking residents out.

GROUP PROCESS IN THE COMMUNITY MEETING

Not all old persons, especially those who have been living in nursing facilities a long time, have living families or community groups to turn to. In their model of a regenerative community, developed by the Live Oak Institute and implemented at the Live Oak Living Center at Greenridge Heights, Debora and Barry Barkan (1993) attempt to foster a community within the institutional walls that will nourish the individuality of residents and offer them meaningful roles.

The Barkans and their partner, Stephen Hooker, took over a setting where residents were already socialized to institutional dependence. Their goal was to create a regenerative community that would support the individuality and potential of the elders who lived there. They developed a special ethos to counter the isolation and resignation of the residents and to help them see themselves in a context larger than their infirmity.

One of their major tools has been the daily community meeting, which provides a centerpiece for life within the facility. This section will describe those meetings and the memorial services, which also are critical components in the regenerative community approach.

Although similar in size to the big groups often conducted in psychiatric settings, the purpose of Live Oak's community meetings is quite different: It is not to cure individuals but to create a community in which they can thrive through a sense of membership in a group that relates to them as multidimensional individuals and not as patients. No one is put on the hot seat, as in psychiatric centers, and the group is not employed as a coercive instrument, as in the Synanon model of the 1960s.

The outline of the community meetings provided in Table 28-2 brings into focus several notable features:

1. *There is a predictable order of events.* The dependable sequence not only provides the security of structure but also enables residents to use that structure to meet their individual needs.

TABLE 28-2 Structure of the community meeting

Exercises: Sitting exercises:
- Help participants become more alert for the meeting.
- Increase health and well-being.

Welcoming: Participating staff members go around the circle, greeting each member:
- Provides an opportunity to connect with the elders before the meeting.
- Helps participants feel known and appreciated.
- Lets participants know the meeting will begin soon.
- Provides opportunity to introduce visitors and guests.

Opening song:
- Connects people to one another.
- Builds group spirit and joy.

Community news: Two kinds of announcements:
- Coming and past events in the life of the community.
- Life events for participants and their families and the planning and decision making that arise from them.

World news:
- Stimulates and challenges participants.
- Invites involvement in community affairs and current topics of national and world discussion.

Discussion of the day:
- Stimulates and challenges participants through talking, feeling, and thinking about a topic.
- Helps participants get to know each other.
- Provides a point of connection for future conversations.

Closing song:
- Lets people know the meeting is over.
- Gives everyone a good feeling for and connection to the group.

SOURCE: Debora and Barry Barkan, Live Oak Institute and the Live Oak Living Center at Greenridge Heights, 2150 Pyramid Drive, El Sobante, CA 94803; 501-222-1242. Used with permission.

They may wander in after the exercises or leave before the closing song. No one is required to attend, but staff tries to make the meeting so interesting and relevant to their lives that everyone will want to come.

2. *Life within the environment is highlighted, and residents are actively involved in making decisions* about events affecting their lives as members of the group (Community News).

3. *They are intellectually challenged and encouraged to view themselves as part of the greater world* and to respond to issues and events that they find relevant to them as a community (World News and Discussion of the Day).

4. *Individuality is recognized, but connectedness also is nurtured* (Welcoming and Community News).

5. *There is ongoing attention to cueing.* Participants in the group include the full spectrum of any nursing facility population, ranging from persons who are cognitively integrated to those suffering from Alzheimer's disease and other dementias. All have a right to be there and a part to play.

The underlying concept is that all residents, even those who are severely impaired, have a part of them that is well. By staff's relating to them at their highest level of functioning, the well part is nurtured and expanded.

The role of the leader is defined as that of a community developer. As managers, the Barkans and Hooker participate frequently, and all staff members are encouraged to drop by and make a contribution whenever possible.

The memorial service for members is notable because it addresses an aspect of nursing facility life more often dealt with by denial. Instead, the memorial service seeks to turn an occasion of loss into an affirmation of the worth of the individual and a reaffirmation of community. Table 28-3 illustrates the process.

The Live Oak approach fits the wellness model that offers an alternative to the medical model, with its emphasis on problems and pathology. It is consistent with the resident-centered position promulgated by the Nursing Home Reform Amendments, which call not only for more humane care but also for active rehabilitation that will enable each resident to achieve his or her highest potential (DHHS 1991). This is the goal of such a program.

SUMMARY

Group process has always been an important element in staff and volunteer training and in general meetings for families and residents. Today, it is more consciously employed to foster the educational and developmental goals of the sponsoring agency or institution. This chapter has illustrated general principles and specific differences involved in working with staff, volunteers, families, and the resident community.

TABLE 28-3 The Live Oak memorial service

Preparing the community: During community meetings, members have discussed the memorial services and what they feel is appropriate. When a death occurs, members of the resident's family and other residents and staff who knew him or her best are consulted about the content of the service. Always, these services affirm that each person's life is precious and that he or she will be remembered by the community.

Introduction: The community developer or a resident welcomes community members and speaks a little about the deceased. For example, "We are gathered today to remember Joe Fraser. He came to the Home six years ago. Originally he worked as a tailor in New York, where he . . ."

Shared remembrances: Residents, staff, and family members share their memories of Mr. Fraser. Some may wish to bring poems or other appropriate readings.

Reflection: The community developer and others talk about what the community learned from Mr. Fraser. Usually embedded in these reflections is a message related to the community ethos.

Prayers: The community developer and/or others offer appropriate prayers for Mr. Fraser and his transition.

Well wishing: The community developer blesses the community, wishing its members healing from what ails them, health and joy for family members, and peace for the world.

Singing is added as appropriate.

SOURCE: Debora and Barry Barkan, Live Oak Institute and the Live Oak Living Center at Greenridge Heights, 2150 Pyramid Drive, El Sobante, CA 94803; 501-222-1242. Used with permission.

EXERCISE 1

Plan an in-service class for a nursing facility staff using the following format: (1) goal, (2) objectives, (3) outline of content, (4) brief quiz on content, (5) reading list, (6) audiovisual or teaching aids, and (7) supply list. Tell how you might adapt this if you were planning the class for volunteers.

EXERCISE 2

Go to your local Alzheimer's association and ask permission to attend a family-support group, or call a nursing facility and ask to observe a family council meeting. Be sure to clear your attendance with members themselves as well as the sponsoring body. Do not take notes at the meeting, but afterward prepare a short report describing the extent to which the meeting was devoted to business and the exchange of information and to what degree to emotional catharsis and the expression of feeling.

REFERENCES

Abromovice B. 1988. *Long-term care administration*. New York: Haworth.

Barkan D, Barkan B. 1993. The nursing home as community. Presentation at the Annual Workshop of the Organization of Social Service Providers in Long-Term Care, San Diego (April 15).

Blenkner M. 1965. Social work and family relationships in later life with some thoughts on filial maturity. In E Shanes, G Streib (eds.), *Social structure and the family: Generational relations* (pp. 46-59). Englewood Cliffs, NJ: Prentice-Hall.

Chambré SM. 1993. Volunteerism by elders: Past trends and future prospects. *Gerontologist* 33(2):221-228.

Cohen D, Eisdorfer C. 1986. *The loss of self*. New York: Norton.

Crose R, Duffy M, Warren J, Franklin B. 1987. Project OASIS: Volunteer mental health paraprofessionals serving nursing home residents. *Gerontologist* 27(3): 359-362.

Hogan J. 1986. Use of volunteers as group leaders. In IM Burnside (ed.), *Working with the elderly: Group process and techniques*, 2d ed. (pp. 261-271). Boston: Jones and Bartlett.

Hooyman N, Lustbader W. 1986. *Taking care*. New York: Free Press.

Knowles M. 1973. *The adult learner: A neglected species*. Houston: Gulf Publishing.

Mace NL, Rabins PV. 1981. *The 36-hour day: A family guide to caring*. Baltimore: Johns Hopkins University Press.

MacGregor B. 1993. Personal communication (May 26).

Safford F. 1980. A program for families of the mentally impaired elderly. *Gerontologist* 20(6):656-660.

―――. 1987. *Caring for the mentally impaired elderly: A family guide*. New York: Henry Holt.

Smith JC. 1992. *Unlocking the secrets of the effective in-service: A resource manual*. Escondido, CA: Legal Beagle Press.

U.S. Department of Health and Human Services (DHHS), Health Care Financing Administration. 1991. Medicare and Medicaid; Requirements for long term care facilities. *Federal Register* 56(187):48826-48865 (OBRA '87).

BIBLIOGRAPHY

Dobrof R, Litwak E. 1977. *Maintenance of family ties of long-term care patients*, DHEW Publication No. (ADM)-79-400. Washington, DC: U.S. Government Printing Office.

Gutheil IA. 1985. Sensitizing nursing home staff to residents' psychosocial needs. *Clin Soc Work* 13(4):356-366.

Johnson DR, Agresti A, Jacob MC, Nies K. 1990. Building a therapeutic community through specialized groups in nursing homes. *Clin Gerontol* 9(3/4):203-217.

Montgomery R. 1983. Staff-family relations and institutional care policies. *J Gerontol Soc Work* 6(1):25-37.

Palmer DS. 1991. Co-leading a family council in a long-term care facility. *J Gerontol Soc Work* 16(3/4):121-134.

Smyer M, Brannon D, Cohn M. 1992. Improving nursing home care through training and job redesign. *Gerontologist* 32(3):327-333.

Spitzer WJ, Burke L. 1993. A critical-incident stress debriefing program for hospital-based health care personnel. *Health Soc Work* 18(2):149-156.

RESOURCES

Books

Unlocking the Secrets of the Effective In-Service: A Resource Manual, by Janice C. Smith, is listed among the references. This manual is addressed to inexperienced staff developers teaching nursing assistants. It comes with equipment for psychosocial bingo and other learning games. Psychosocial Consultants, 13506 Hike Lane, San Diego, CA 92129.

Also listed among the references are highly recommended guides for families of the mentally impaired: Cohen and Eisdorfer, *The loss of self*; Hooyman and Lustbader, *Taking care*; Mace and Rabins, *The 36-hour day*; and Safford, *Caring for the mentally impaired elderly*.

Films

Because Somebody Cares (16 mm or video, 27 minutes). This film shows several real-life vignettes of volunteers, young and old, as they visit older persons who are homebound or in nursing homes. It shows the friendships that grow when people of all ages reach out to each other. Produced by Terra Nova Films, Inc., directed by James Van den Bosch. Purchase: $465 (16 mm), $295 (video); rental: $55.

Nurse's Aides: Making a Difference (1/2" videocassette, 31 minutes, color) 1991. This film, highly praised by *The Gerontologist* reviewer, presents a panel consisting of three nursing assistants and an LPN discussing the management of behavior problems with accompanying vignettes. Producer and distributor: UT Southwestern ADRC Videos, Department of Gerontology and Geriatrics Services, P.O. Box 45567, Dallas, TX 75245. Purchase: $85.

Agencies

ACTION, the National Volunteer Agency, 806 Connecticut Avenue, NW, Washington, DC 20525; phone: 800-424-8867 or 202-634-9424. This is the federal umbrella agency that administers the Retired Senior Volunteer Program (RSVP) as well as Foster Grandparents and Senior Companions. RSVP is its largest program and recruits volunteers for community agencies.

American Association for Retired People (AARP), Talent Bank, 1909 K Street, NW, Washington, DC 20049. The AARP sponsors a number of programs for volunteers. Its Talent Bank identifies volunteers and refers them to agencies nationwide.

The United Way. Contact the local United Way office for referrals of would-be volunteers.

CHAPTER 29

Another Special Group: The Single-Session Grief Group

Joan K. Parry

KEY WORDS

- Anxiety
- Death
- Grief
- Instant network
- Loss
- Single-session group
- Skilled nursing facility

LEARNING OBJECTIVES

- Differentiate between sudden death and terminal illness.
- State the role of the single-session group to meet crisis needs.
- Describe a single-session group as a means of coping with loss.
- Describe how this group is a way to process one's own feelings of fear and lack of knowledge.
- Describe three ways of recruiting members for a single-session group.
- Identify four necessary preplanning steps to implement single-session grief groups in a skilled nursing facility.

The areas of death and dying often are only a peripheral concern of the nursing home team (Parry 1989). The death of a resident in a skilled nursing facility (SNF) often is ignored. Not only is it ignored, but sometimes the staff behaves as if the death had not occurred. The bed is neatly made, and the roommates are left to wonder and then to relate to the new resident who will fill the empty bed.

Groups are one way for residents to gain control of their environment. Dying older patients would do well in groups, as would family members of these dying patients. In groups, the helpless become the helpers, which can help aged patients

to move from a dependent role to a more interdependent role. It would seem an ethical imperative to recognize the impact of loss, grieving, and death on residents and staff in any facility that serves the geriatric population.

The fact of death is final and irreversible, but dying is a process, and change and growth can occur during the process for the dying person, the family, and the professional. When death is sudden, however, the process will not occur, and it usually makes it more difficult for survivors to cope. Because sudden death does not allow a process, the professional's interventions must be concentrated on the survivors (Parry 1989). It is even more important for survivors to have assistance in processing their abrupt grief and fears, reducing feelings of isolation, reducing feelings of being different or abnormal, and addressing their sense of emptiness.

This chapter describes a very special and unusual group modality to deal with sudden death—the single-session group.

DEATH IN A SKILLED NURSING FACILITY

When death is experienced in an institutional setting, such as an SNF, it tends to be a negative experience. For families, the death may reawaken the ambivalence and pain they felt when they placed their relative in the SNF. For residents, the death is both a preview and a taboo. If they ask about a dying resident, they receive an evasive answer. Perceiving the professional calm of their caregivers, they come to believe that staff will be indifferent to their deaths too. Some staff members become close to the residents and, when they are dealing with their own anticipatory or unresolved mourning, they find it difficult to meet the emotional needs of families, other residents, or even the dying person. None can turn to staff when staff members themselves have been schooled in avoidance.

The nursing home is associated with death. Once, nursing facilities sent many of their moribund patients to the hospital to die. Today, the hopelessly ill resident is often spared that journey, and the SNF must cope with its own burden of dying.

According to figures from the previous decade, the death rate in SNFs in the United States has risen from 6 percent in 1958 to 11.3 percent in 1977 (Parry 1989). More recently, the death rate in SNFs is as high as 20 percent (McGinnis 1990). Thus, as institutional settings such as SNFs have more and more residents dying in their facilities, a response is an ethical necessity.

Death and dying are rarely discussed among the staff in SNFs. The avoidance of dealing with death and dying issues has negative effects for both staff and residents. This has been borne out by a study in Florida (Haber, Tuttle & Rogers 1981) that states that despite the increased attention given to the topic of death, most nursing homes practice a covert approach to dying and death designed to prevent the emotional upset of residents by avoiding reminders of their mortality. A study sample of 86 residents and staff members from two nursing homes supported this finding, yet many expressed an interest in modifying the policy. A majority believed that others should be told about the death (Haber, Tuttle & Rogers 1981). Although the nursing home industry is a large employer, its personnel tend to be less well paid and more poorly trained than aides, LPNs, and RNs who work in hospitals or private practice.

The workers in SNFs come from various minority cultures that may deal with death in their own way. The multiple issues of varying cultures and death is very important (Parry 1990). Minority workers can use specific rituals in regard to death but feel constrained in the facility in which they work. If minority residents attended a single-session grief group, it is possible they could provide their own cultural set to the process. However, African-American older adults have a lower utilization of nursing home care than other groups (Stanford Geriatric Education Center #4 1990).

As of 1990, only 2 percent of Asian/Pacific Island elders were in nursing homes. But will that change for Asian/Pacific Island elders as traditional cultural values regarding care of the elders by their adult children weakens (Stanford Geriatric Education Center #3 1990)?

The large group of employees in SNFs, nurses and nurses' aides of all cultures, could benefit from courses that would teach about mainstream caring for the dying and, conversely, they could benefit by sharing their cultures. In fact, because of the large numbers of residents who die in nursing homes or experience the death of another resident in the home, such knowledge for staff becomes a major concern. Death education is important for professionals who work in SNFs also and would include an understanding of the complex tasks associated with grief resolution. "This is especially true for the elderly, who often, in addition to experiencing the loss of their lifetime mate, are experiencing other losses" (Herth 1990, 108). But if staff are unschooled in death education, they tend to avoid the issue. The result of avoidance behaviors by staff is to close channels of communication among family members, residents, staff, and professionals, and to reduce the options and ability of the professional to intervene in meaningful ways.

THE DEATH OF A RESIDENT: A CASE EXAMPLE

In one particular SNF of 160 residents with which this author is familiar, it was known that the sudden death of a resident had a powerful effect on surviving residents.[1] Janet was one of the more active, visible, and vital residents of an SNF in northern California, and she died suddenly on a Tuesday. Janet was 84 and died of a massive cerebrovascular accident. She had lived in the facility for 18 months; she was a widow with two children. The administrator of the SNF was apparently aware that the event of sudden death of a popular resident would create serious negative consequences in the facility. The response would require more than the regular Sunday morning memorial service. The event of sudden death can exacerbate other problems residents may have.

The administrator called the social worker, as a representative of the ombudsman's office. The administrator shared her concerns, and the social worker suggested a single-session group meeting for residents and staff willing to participate in discussing Janet's death. Such a group would serve residents who did not participate also because they would know it occurred and could feel that the persons who operate the institution cared about the residents. The worker then visited the units and talked with residents, who appeared to be upset by the loss of Janet. The social worker focused especially on Janet's roommate, Judith. As was discussed above, it is not uncommon for death to occur in an SNF with no mention to the surviving roommate about the death. The surviving roommate simply has a new roommate.

The social worker then visited many of the residents and suggested to each one who had been close to Janet that she or he participate in the group. The worker explained it would be a chance for all of them to say goodbye to Janet. The administrator invited all of the facility staff to attend, as well as Janet's family. Her family chose not to come, although they did not give a reason for their refusal.

---

[1]This group information was provided by Roberta Rosenthal, a supervisor at the Veterans Administration Hospital in San Francisco. She had been in the ombudsman's office in Santa Clara County.

Group work with older persons is a very useful way of helping residents to discuss and share their losses. Fear of death is reduced by making the resident feel he or she is not alone. One study (Keller, Sherry & Piotrowski 1984) indicated that older persons were just as anxious about death as their younger counterparts. Their anxiety was for death in general, however, with low anxiety related to their own deaths.

This single-session group would not only serve the residents by reducing their anxiety about Janet's death, but also would enable the SNF staff, the administrator, and the social worker to say goodbye to Janet. The single-session group helps to bring together people in crisis who otherwise would remain anxious, isolated, and hurting. Such a group can also serve to allay anxieties, provide comfort and sharing, and encourage the development of coping skills. The single-session grief group gives members an instant network for ongoing support (Holmes-Garrett 1989).

To deal with grief, it is important to provide support and help as soon as possible after the event has occurred. This death occurred on Tuesday, and the group was held on Friday. Acute grief is almost always present as the result of sudden death (Suszycki 1981). The administrator felt the need to respond rapidly, and the social worker was in agreement. Because Janet was such a visible resident in this facility, her death could not be ignored.

PLANNING THE SINGLE-SESSION GROUP FOR RESIDENTS AND STAFF

The preplanning of the group was done by the social worker and the administrator on Thursday. The social worker knew that frequently the single-session group provides worker, agency, and clients with their only possibility of engagement (Parry & Schwartz 1987). The members may be unable to benefit from one-to-one services but may be willing to attend a single-session group. The constraints of the agency, such as limited availability of staff social workers and inability to disturb work schedules, were in operation with this SNF. Therefore, this would be the only group session offered to residents.

The social worker and the administrator knew how important it was for the members of the group to have a clear understanding of the purpose of the group. In fact, clarity of purpose is essential in any group work endeavor. According to Frey (1966, 25), it is of the utmost importance that each member "know the purpose, agree to it, and share in it." The social worker and the administrator decided that the purposes of the group were to say goodbye to Janet, to provide an opportunity for the members to share memories of other losses or other deaths, and to express feelings about Janet's death. Another goal of the group would be to reduce anxieties about death for the members.

Although the single-session group offered to the residents and staff was open to all, 10 residents and four staff attended the group. However, it was felt that if the group was a positive experience for the group members, they could share their ideas and feelings with others who did not attend.

Prior to the group meeting, the administrator and the social worker met. They decided the social worker would be the primary facilitator of the process, although to open the group, the administrator would talk about the facility's sorrow over the loss of Janet and would assure the group that the meeting was sanctioned by the facility.

The worker requested that all group members sit in a circle and then introduced herself. This social worker came to the facility periodically. The worker met with only a few residents on her visits; therefore, she was not known to all the residents.

The administrator thanked them for coming and expressed her own sadness at the death of Janet. Then the worker articulated the purpose of the group and followed this by going around the circle and asking each person to state his or her name and how he or she was feeling, in one word. The worker felt that if all members spoke, it would relieve some tension. The worker said members could pass if they chose, but no one did. Some of the words were "sad," "lonely," "unhappy," and a couple of members said "fine."

The social worker set up two rules of the group: One person talks at a time, and things said remain in the group. The worker also stated that the purpose of the group was healing. The worker then gave the group background about Janet: her age, information about her bereaved family, and the length of time Janet had lived in the facility. The worker's goal was to review Janet's life in the facility and to help the members review their own past losses. The worker then opened the meeting for general discussion and sharing of memories about Janet. There was discussion about how to cope with loss. The majority of the members were widowed women who had experienced multiple losses. The most severe loss had been the loss of a spouse, although there was one group member who had lost a child. Some members talked about losses in business; some said Janet was out of her misery, suggesting their own feelings of misery. The theme was one of toughing it out. The staff talked about losing parents and how working in the facility meant seeing many deaths.

The group talked about what works and what does not work when coping with loss. Many of the members cried during the meeting, and this was accepted and encouraged. Open discussion increases the chance that widely shared concerns and values will be incorporated into the group content (Schopler, Galinsky & Alicke 1985). Also, because of the nature of the single-session group's immediacy, the primary attachment of members is to the group and its purpose (Parry & Schwartz 1987).

The group lasted about 75 minutes and ended with a minute of silence. Before the minute of silence, the worker requested an evaluation of the group by the members. Members' comments were positive. They said they liked getting together as a group and that it felt good that the leader had encouraged everyone to talk openly. They said that it didn't change anything, but it was nice to talk, and some members said the opportunity to acknowledge the loss reduced their own anxiety about Janet's sudden death. "The idea for a group must begin with the identification with the clients' unmet needs, a missing piece in the service which the group method may be able to meet" (Shulman 1984, 178).

This single-session grief group was very much a response to unmet needs. During subsequent visits to this facility, the worker was approached with questions about the group by residents who had not come to the group. A vibrant member of the community had been cut down without warning, and it said to the residents, "If it can happen to Janet, it can happen to me." The group provided a sense of "we-ness" and helped group members to feel they were not alone, that each of them was feeling upset and distraught about Janet's death. The sense of belonging and the all-in-the-same-boat phenomenon provides for the start of the healing process. In a single-session group to mourn the loss of a well-loved member, the sharing of feelings allows the recognition of grief and the work that needs to be done to resolve it.

SUMMARY

Because of the positive feedback the social worker received from all the group members, the social worker felt comfortable recommending to the administrator of the SNF that this type of group be utilized when needed. Another suggestion made was to start a class on death education for the staff.

Professionals in SNFs could incorporate this type of single-session group into their overall plan for their facility. It would seem that any death, whether lingering or sudden, could be attenuated with group services for residents and staff. This type of group, if utilized for every death in an SNF, would be beneficial for residents and staff in dealing with fear, anxiety, and the resolution of grief. (See Chapter 28 for a description of a memorial service conducted in another facility.)

EXERCISE 1

Single-session groups require preplanning. What steps would you take to set up a one-time grief group in the facility where you work? Consider the following points:

- Is it open to all members?
- What is the purpose of the group?
- Where will the group be held?
- How will you set up the room?
- Will you send a written notice or make individual visits to prospective members?
- How long will the group last?
- What do you hope to accomplish?

EXERCISE 2

Find two articles about other groups in skilled nursing facilities that discuss death and loss. With your classmates, develop a reading list that could help you plan a grief group in a facility where you work.

REFERENCES

Frey LA. 1966. *Use of groups in the health field*. New York: National Association of Social Workers.

Haber D, Tuttle J, Rogers M. 1981. Attitudes about death in the nursing home: A research note. *Death Educ* 5(1):25-28.

Herth K. 1990. Relationship of hope, coping styles, concurrent losses, and setting to grief resolution in the elderly widow(er). *Res Nurs Health* 13(2):109-117.

Holmes-Garrett C. 1989. The crisis of the forgotten family: A single-session group in the ICU waiting room. *Soc Work with Groups* 12(4):141-151.

Keller JW, Sherry D, Piotrowski C. 1984. Perspectives on death: A developmental study. *J Psychol* 116:137-142.

McGinnis P. 1990. Personal communication from the executive director of the California Advocates for Nursing Home Reform, San Francisco, CA (August 31).

Parry JK. 1989. *Social work theory and practice with the terminally ill*. New York: Haworth.

———. 1990. *Social work with the terminally ill: A transcultural perspective*. Springfield, IL: Thomas.

Parry JK, Schwartz FS. 1987. Single-session groups. Paper presented at the Ninth Annual Symposium for the Advancement of Social Work with Groups, Rutgers, NJ.

Schopler JH, Galinsky MJ, Alicke MD. 1985. Goals in social group work practice: Formulation, implementation, and evaluation. In M Sundel, P Glasser, R Sarri, R Vinter (eds.), *Individual change through small groups*, 2d ed. (pp. 140-158). New York: Free Press.

Shulman L. 1984. The skills of helping. Itasca, IL: Peacock.

Stanford Geriatric Education Center. 1990. *Aging and health: Asian/Pacific Island elders*, #3. Stanford, CA.

———. 1990. *Aging and health: Black American elders*, #4. Stanford, CA.

Suszycki LH. 1981. Intervention with the bereaved. In O Margolis, HC Raether, AH Rutscher, JB Powers, IB Seeland, R Debellis, DJ Cherico (eds.), *Acute grief: Counseling the bereaved* (pp. 45-52). New York: Columbia University Press.

BIBLIOGRAPHY

Bolton C, Camp DJ. 1989. The post-funeral ritual in bereavement counseling and grief work. *J Gerontol Soc Work* 13(3/4):49-59.

Gonda TA, Ruark JD. 1984. *Dying dignified*. Menlo Park, CA: Addison-Wesley.

Gubrium JF. 1975. Death worlds in a nursing home. *Urban Life* 4(3):317-338.

Norris FH, Murrell SA. 1987. Older adult family stress and adaptation before and after bereavement. *J Gerontol* 42(6):606-612.

Orten JD, Allen M, Cook J. 1989. Reminiscence groups with confused nursing center residents: An experimental study. *Soc Work Health Care* 14(1):73-86.

Sankar A. 1991. Ritual and dying: A cultural analysis of social support for caregivers. *Gerontologist* 2(1):43-50.

Wells PJ. 1993. Preparing for sudden death: Social work in the emergency room. *Soc Work* 38(3):339-342.

RESOURCES

The Best Kept Secret (27 minutes). This film or video documentary shows how families feel about nursing homes. *American Journal of Nursing* Company, Educational Services Division, 555 West 57th Street, New York, NY 10019-2961; phone: 212-582-8820.

Pitch of Grief (28 minutes). This film or video reviews the mourning process via a documentary featuring four bereaved persons. Fanlight Productions, 47 Halifax Street, Boston, MA 02130; phone: 617-524-0980.

CHAPTER 30

Group Work and Professional Programs

Bernita M. Steffl

KEY WORDS

- Barriers
- Concept
- Evaluation
- Objectives
- Realizations and insights
- Remotivation
- Rewards
- Settings
- Socialization
- Therapeutic

LEARNING OBJECTIVES

- Define *preparatory steps* for group work with older individuals.
- Plan and implement a group work experience with an older age group.
- Identify two possible pitfalls and barriers to professional group work with the aged.

Through group work students develop a profound and sincere respect for old people.
RICHARD GRANT (1982)

The increase in the aging population; the explosive escalation of community services and programs for the aging, such as the thousands of nutrition sites; and the growing number of long-term care facilities have created a need and opportunity for group services, treatment, and recreation. The resocialization of aged individuals who suffer physical and psychosocial losses and relocation provides a fertile opportunity for development and growth of group work with older individuals.

Since the first edition of this text was published, there has been extensive development of medical, nursing, social work, and multidisciplinary courses in gerontology with clinical components that lend themselves to group work with older age groups (Brower 1981; Ellison 1981; Carter & Galliano 1981). In discussion about courses with faculty in various parts of the country and in observing students in various service areas, I have noted a great deal of interest in and activity with groups. I also have had many requests for assistance specifically for group work with well older adults. However, I also have observed situations where I believe specific guidelines for working with the aged were sorely needed, not available, and not included in the course content, namely, for work with older persons with dementia, for example, Alzheimer's disease. Thus, we have a mandate to provide this. There are specific basic human needs; developmental tasks; special characteristics; and special topics, strategies, and techniques to be considered in curricula for group work with older persons.

Much responsibility for meeting some of these needs falls on the professional schools, especially those of nursing and social work. Gerontology is not given the same time and attention in nursing curricula as child growth and development. The same is true in social work and in medicine (Cassell 1972). Inroads are being made, and now we are clearly identifying gerontological content in the curricula. Basic human needs and developmental tasks of aging are considered from a biopsychosocial aspect, and students are provided practice opportunities to demonstrate application of theory. The developmental model is steadily gaining in curricula content, thanks to Erikson (1950), Butler and Lewis (1982), Kimmel (1974), and Barrett (1972).

This chapter presents content for preparing students to do group work within the older population.

STUDENTS AS GROUP WORKERS

The use of groups falls into three main categories: (1) for effect on participants, (2) for collective problem solving, and (3) for change in social situations or conditions outside the groups (Hartford 1972). Groups also are used for research and often as a major part of a clinical learning experience. Bellak and Karasu (1976) state that group interventions with the aged are a valuable source of therapeutic help and that they can range from the psychotherapeutic to task-oriented socialization groups. Butler and Lewis (1982) suggest that group therapy should be widely used in institutions and outpatient seminars for the aged and that volunteers as well as professionals and paraprofessionals have been trained to varying degrees of competence, but nurses probably conduct more group work with older persons than do other professionals.

Nurses work primarily in three types of groups: task-oriented groups, teaching groups, and supportive therapeutic groups (Clark 1987). Sometimes, even though the goal is to provide therapeutic support, the best approach may be through a task-oriented group, because some older persons shy away from any label that may suggest a need for emotional support.

Rationale for introducing group work with older adults into curricula is that it provides a contact for students that accomplishes several goals. First, it quickly teaches students whether they are doing what they want to do, or at least provides the practical experience necessary for a realistic career or specialty choice. Second, it gives an invaluable opportunity for students to test what they have been taught against reality. Finally, and equally important, it helps teach the unwritten content of any profession—the ethics and values that determine behavior and underlie responsibility in the profession (Cassell 1972, 255).

Students need assistance to relate group work experience to theoretical concepts. This is particularly true in the planning stages of their group work.

The Beginning Student

Because of changes in life style in our culture—for example, movement away from the extended family and longer life—older people have to depend more on groups outside the family for social interaction. Current trends suggest that future cohorts of older persons may belong to and participate more in voluntary associations (Cutler 1976). This is group participation in its broadest sense. A neophyte in group work might first be exposed to old people by visiting a facility such as a senior center. Such an indoctrination provides an opportunity to study well older adults before dealing with the sick or seriously disabled.

More Advanced Students

Students with more background, sophistication, and preparation in basic social science courses are better able to handle some of the multiple losses of the aged, grief work, and the increasing physical infirmities of group members. The possibilities and settings for group work increase for these students and could easily range from hospital geriatric wards, extended care facilities, and psychiatric settings to day care centers for older adults. A clinical component should be dovetailed with theory and practice, whether the student is in an elective course in gerontology or in a clinically geared course. Essential gerontological content can be applied to clinical practice by nurses, social workers, psychologists, counselors, occupational therapists, physical therapists, ministers, and paraprofessionals at various stages in the educational curriculum and in a variety of settings.

In the past, I encouraged an optional experience in gerontology during the senior course in community health nursing. There are four or five students each semester who are interested enough to spend eight weeks in a community setting such as a day care center for older persons, a storefront senior center, and centers established primarily for Title III nutrition programs. There is unlimited opportunity for group work in such settings. Most students have been able to try out several levels of group work. They were surprised at the interest and hunger for knowledge about health problems. The old people themselves like to lecture or teach and share when they are given the opportunity. Many have not had much formal education, so positive feedback about their knowledge and skills from professionals is important to them and is also a way to increase sagging self-esteem.

Two Examples of Student-led Groups

Example 1. A paraprofessional health worker in a day care center attended a continuing educational extension course; her wealth of experience in family life and interest in her job made my teaching a joy. She began a reminiscence group at a day care center. Because it was difficult for her to use the university library, I made an effort to furnish her with literature and opportunity to share experiences of other students. Within several weeks she developed goals and started a reminiscence group with six Spanish-speaking old people. The entire group work was conducted in Spanish!

The following quote is from the student's report after the session:

> At least no one fell asleep during the sessions, and each contributed something of himself that enabled the others in the group to appreciate their common background of being Mexican, of being able to speak to each other in the language they consider their mother tongue, and of being able to look back on some of the hardships that they

had endured and had been able to survive. Just as we left the lounge, Mr. M quoted an old Mexican proverb that expressed their ideas on living. *"Vivir es triumfar."* "To live is to triumph." Looking back over his 87 years, because he still lives as fully as he is able, for Mr. M, life is a triumph (Montoya 1976, 10).

Several months later, the coordinator of the day care center reported that the reminiscence group was going well and that the staff was learning much more about their clients!

Example 2. Three students conducted an exercise program for a group of 10 to 15 senior citizens in a low-cost high-rise housing facility. The students rotated the leadership for half-hour sessions. After six weeks, the students felt that they had stimulated and motivated several of the members to add more physical activity to their daily routine.

Such an experience offers students a chance to assess older individuals physically as well as psychosocially. For example, the students became aware of the cumulative deficits resulting from a hearing loss. One distinguished man in the group was often criticized by the members. He was willing and able, but he was never in step because he could not hear the instructions or the cadence. He was always at $1/2$ time when the group was at $3/4$ time. The women in the group got very angry with him.

The students also had to learn to let old people give. The members took up a collection for the students on the last day of the group meetings. Many professionals have long been taught that it is not professional to accept gifts, but such a philosophy bogs down in work with the aged.

PREPARING FOR GROUP WORK WITH PERSONS WITH DEMENTIA

The incidence of dementia, particularly Alzheimer's disease, is increasing rapidly. The current estimate for the United States is four million cases. As a result, many long-term care facilities are adding special dementia units, and freestanding facilities specifically for Alzheimer's disease victims are emerging (Alzheimer's Association 1993). Because most of these persons eventually need constant surveillance and almost one-to-one care, there is a real challenge for implementing group activity whenever possible. These older adults generally respond well to group activities that include some stimulation for physical movement (music, dance, exercise, and activities with touch and gentle human guidance). See Table 30-1 for realizations that facilitate meaningful communication with persons with dementia such as Alzheimer's disease.

STEPS IN PREPARING STUDENTS FOR GROUP WORK

Evaluating Students' Background Knowledge

Students are expected to learn principles and techniques of group work, such as levels of groups, theories of group interaction, group roles, and group rules. They also learn therapeutic communication skills and interviewing techniques. This content is usually taught early in the curriculum, and students are encouraged to analyze and use these skills and techniques in group discussions and group conferences for their own learning. In spite of exposure to theory and experience, however, one cannot assume that the student is ready to lead a group, so assess your students' knowledge and skills in group work and help the students prepare accordingly. Asking the following questions helps students prepare and plan for a positive group experience:

- Can you identify and define your group?
- What are your objectives? Are they client centered?
- Have you assessed the mechanics, such as place, space, equipment, dates, time, accessibility and availability, and so on?
- Have you included agency and clients in your plans?
- Do you plan to do this alone? Will you need help?
- What about continuity after you move on?
- What kinds of records or documentation will you keep?
- How will you evaluate the effectiveness of your group?

Because a great deal of group work with the aged involves interviewing, it is necessary to assess students' skills in this area (see Burnside 1980). In any group work or communication with older adults, one should automatically assess distance,

both physical and psychological; assess hearing—older persons usually hear better from one ear than from the other; and assess comprehension.

Students sometimes need considerable coaching and reinforcement to assess and maintain the above. I find it helpful to role play with the students and demonstrate distances by (for example, the placement of chairs), sitting at the same height level, facing the interviewee, eye contact, and speaking slowly and waiting for answers.

Documentation

Documentation cannot be overemphasized! There must be a plan and preferably a prearranged format for documentation and completion after each session. See Table 30-2 for considerations when documenting group performance and progress.

Choosing the Type of Group and Group Members

Students generally need help in determining the level of group they want to lead and how to select the members. Students may desire a socializing group that ends up being a therapy session or vice versa. Does it matter if this happens? It is important that students do not get in over their heads. It is also important that student and teacher have well-stated objectives and evaluate according to the objectives. Whether the objectives were met is not as important as knowing if they were achieved and understanding what happened if they were not.

It is also necessary for students to develop well-defined criteria for group member selection. Help will be needed to consider age, sex, ethnicity, educational background, disabilities, diagnoses, and the number of persons to include. For example, a group of four to six persons with physical handicaps may be more realistic than six to eight because of the time involved in seating, the mobility problems, and so forth.

Groups have to have momentum and vitality to maintain continuity and reduce absenteeism and dropouts. Selection of members is critical. Butler and Lewis (1982) argue for heterogeneity. It is also helpful to combine a female-male team as leaders (Linden 1954).

Since many older individuals hunger for knowledge and seek learning opportunities by attending discussion groups, faculty and students

TABLE 30-1 Realizations and insights: Successful interactions with persons who have Alzheimer's disease

Communication

- Touch is the *first* form of communication a human being experiences; often it is the last to which an Alzheimer's patient is capable of responding.
- Good communication skills are the same in *any* interaction with *anyone*.
- Communication with persons with Alzheimer's is raw and open, with none of the social masks to which we have become accustomed.

Music

- Music can break through barriers of words and create an alternate way of communicating and socially interacting.
- Moods can be dramatically affected by music; it may carefully and sensitively be used to manage difficult behavior.
- It is important to present an opportunity to make noise, which most of the time must be discouraged in institutional care for the good of all concerned. Singing, dancing, and clapping hands provide good outlets for frustration.

Psychosocial needs

- The psychosocial needs of the person with Alzheimer's disease are the same as in any population, but they must be addressed in new ways with new communication forms.
- People with Alzheimer's disease need as many opportunities for options and choices as possible, allowing independence and control. Adequate staffing could provide this type of environment.
- Significant moments between patient and caregiver sustain the relationship; even if the memory of them is lost, the feeling may remain.
- It is important to note that although much emphasis has been placed on *reality orientation*, some higher-functioning people need *reality distraction* to cope with the pain and sorrow associated with the confusion and loss of self that attend Alzheimer's disease.
- People with Alzheimer's disease must be treated in accordance with their unique personality types, keeping in mind that some are conservative and staid and others are liberal and outgoing.
- Persons with Alzheimer's need a respite from grim seriousness and welcome humor as a vehicle to free the spirit.

Environment

- Environment is critically important—calm, quiet settings provide comfort.
- Problem behavior is aggravated by noise, too much stimulation, and too little stimulation.
- Minimize difficulties and smooth confusion whenever possible.

Caregiver hints

- Respond; don't react.
- Be gently directive; it provides security.
- People working with patients with Alzheimer's should be carefully selected, based on their potential for working with this population.
- Love, enthusiasm, and positive energy are the most effective tools when dealing with persons who have Alzheimer's disease.
- It must be remembered that the patient with Alzheimer's literally lives in the moment. The caregiver must live in a new reality, not that of the normal world. The question becomes, "Whose reality is it, anyway?"
- Burnout is avoided when the caregiver allows the affected person to give something in return. This exchange nurtures the caregiver and gives dignity to the patient.
- People with Alzheimer's disease often are capable of much more than is expected of them. When they are put in a particular social setting, appropriate behavior is sometimes automatic.
- The things that apply to human well-being at any level of mental and physical status still apply (i.e., the needs for love, self-esteem, acceptance, social interaction, physical contact, laughter, tears, joy, and individuality).
- It is important to look past the illness and address the wellness and the unique person who is still present—even on the most limited level. If life is to have any meaning, reason, or dignity amid the devastation caused by this condition, there must be a celebration of the person who remains—not a lament for the person who no longer exists.

SOURCE: Joan Denemark Valenti, Communication Specialist, 4144 West Stella Lane, Phoenix, AZ 85019. Used with permission.

TABLE 30-2 Considerations in documenting group performance

- Group composition and number present
- Topic covered—was it relevant?
- Individual participation
- Development of cohesiveness
- High points, low points
- Problems encountered
- Closure and plans for next meeting

might consider some specific preparation listed in William Hill's *Learning through Discussion* (1969), such as Fawcett's guide for leaders and members of discussion groups. This guide is more than a how-to manual; it includes roles, skills, and a list of criteria for learning-through-discussion groups.

Group Setting and Mechanics

Students need continual reminding and assistance to choose an adequate setting in terms of space; light; accessibility; and safety of tables and chairs, armrests, and work space. For example, older people often feel more comfortable if they can sit with their legs under a table and have the table top to lean on and put things on. Teenagers or college students may prefer pillows on the floor or a casual living room atmosphere for their group meetings.

Choosing Settings for Group Work with Older Persons

Choosing and finding a facility and groups for student experience is not difficult but takes considerable time and expertise in communication. Agency personnel are usually pleased to have students and welcome group activity for their clients, but it is absolutely necessary to have a clear understanding about logistics and responsibilities, such as who will be responsible for assembling the group if members are handicapped, and so on. Plans made by telephone should be followed up in writing, and plans for ongoing communication should be firmly established before group meetings begin. See Table 30-3 for suggested settings for group experiences with older persons.

A current trend is group education among older persons for writing and documenting per-

sonal family history and personal experiences (Hobus 1992; Supiano 1991). Journal writing and documenting oral histories have become increasingly popular recently, because they not only provide a meaningful activity and therapeutic exercise for older persons, but also provide a legacy for families. There is a trend to teach these in groups and in formal classes. Supiano (1991) has described writing at life's closure and has observed that it reveals an awareness of life's end, contentment with life lived, and peace. Smith (1993) states that "the developmental tasks the aged must master include those that are spiritual in nature. The spirit, like the body and mind, needs nourishment, education and training to develop. Journaling seems to promote the rendering of meaning from experiences even though not consciously intended." (For more specific information and guidelines, see resources listed at end of chapter and those in Chapter 16.)

Planning, Announcements, Dates, and Directions

I saw a student completely devastated after six weeks of group work when all the plans for her classes with a group of senior citizens in the community failed because, on the big day for her, the seniors did not show up. She did not follow up the telephone communications with specific written information on date, time, and place. Repetition is important not only because old people forget but because they are busy. Sometimes we forget that they have lived a long time and sat through lots of useless information. They may be quite choosy about what they want to hear or do. Accurate, written communications should be combined with verbal plans.

Group Interaction and Response

It is helpful to go over topics and expected responses with students. Doing so offers an excellent opportunity to demonstrate to the student group leader how to learn more about gerontology and relate learning to the literature and research. One way is for the student to make a continuing biopsychosocial assessment during group interaction. For example, the student needs to note the types of losses existing in group members. Do these losses fit with textbook descriptions? Body

TABLE 30-3 Settings for group work

Place	Activity	Leaders
Nursing homes/ skilled care	Opportunities for group work are limited. Patients are too ill and immobile. Prohibitive because of risks. Often too costly in staff time needed to assist in assembling groups. Focus is usually on socialization.	Activity director RN Occupational therapist Physical therapist Social worker
Residential/personal care facilities	Many opportunities for health education and recreational group activities. Usually organized and managed by activity director. Focus is usually on socialization, health education, exercise, and crafts.	Activity director Occupational therapist Physical therapist RN Resident Social worker
Day care center	Great opportunity for group work in health promotion. Most clients are handicapped but mobile with assistance. Focus on socialization, health promotion, nutrition, exercise, current events.	Activity director RN Social worker
Senior center	Many opportunities, but clients are quite selective about what they will attend. Focus is on noon meal, socialization, health promotion, and fieldtrips.	Activity director Other seniors Professionals from the community
Retirement complexes	Many group activities are available. Focus is on recreation, fieldtrips, crafts, and health promotion activities.	Social director Occupational therapist RN
Seniors in community at large	Travel tours, Elderhostel. Swimming, golf, spectator sports. Credit and noncredit courses at colleges and universities. Focus on lectures and activities responding to special interests and hobbies for older persons.	Professional agencies Educators Guest lecturers Senior group leaders

language and other nonverbal communications are important. Regarding verbal communication, can the student hear what the patient did not say?

Two students planned a series of reminiscence group sessions for eight to 10 older persons (late seventies and eighties) in a church-sponsored guest house for the aged. Because this was in Canada in a Scottish-French-Irish community, the group meetings were to begin with afternoon tea. A great deal of planning was done, and the students were excited and eager to start the first session. It turned out to be a big disappointment. Nothing went well except the tea! The report (Holder & Tilford 1974) went like this:

Students: These people have lived through so much and most are very sharp, but when we started our reminiscing it fell flat. We got no response.
Instructor: How did you begin?
Students: We asked the group this—"There have been many changes in the past fifty years. what has been most exciting or important to you?"

The students were then quizzed further about their ideas on why this might have happened, and eventually I suggested that perhaps because they were dealing with thought processes of persons in their eighties (keeping in mind that there is a slowing in registration and retrieval), it may have been quite difficult on the spur of the moment to sift through 50 years! I suggested that they try again—but pose a single question, such as "What do you think about man going to the moon?" or "What do you think about the long hair styles for young men these days?" When they did try again, they had a good response. This is one example of carefully relating theory to practice.

Students will need help in termination and dealing with separation anxiety. Because there is such a need for maintaining socialization among the aged, instructors should insist on building in plans for the group to carry on for a reasonable length of time. When this is not possible, it is important to begin plans for termination in the beginning by setting a specific number of meetings and in the last two or three sessions, discuss termination and separation.

Dealing with Problems

Students will need help and feedback in dealing with problems common to all groups, such as handling a manipulator, a distractor, a silent member, a monopolizer, or an overly anxious member.

It is also helpful to prepare students for the special problems of the aged and their behavior in relation to loneliness, depression, and sensory deprivation. Students should be well prepared to deal with tears, withdrawal, anger, and very candid opinions. Old people can afford to be outspoken. They have less to lose.

Rewards and Evaluation

Together with problems usually come positive feedback and satisfaction if the student's goals are realistic. The student leader must have clearly stated objectives, and it is up to the instructor to help the student develop realistic ones. Most leaders want to accomplish too much too fast. Even if groups fail, I believe that the process of trying provides activity for the client and usually an unforgettable learning experience for the student. However, this viewpoint may need to be suggested to the student.

Instructor Guidelines

No matter where in the curriculum, at what level or in what kind of course, elective or required, the following reminders usually work well:

- Be flexible about the setting.
- Be flexible about the type of clinical experience you will accept for student experience.
- Encourage creativity and remember to reinforce positively when you observe it.
- Allow the right to fail by giving support and constructive criticism if something does not work.
- Foster independent behavior and study, but be available for frequent individual conferences and for giving guidance and suggestions.
- Encourage unique and different activities, but expect students to share with the class and validate what they do.
- Insist on documented theory.

- Examine your own attitudes and values regarding the aged and your knowledge level in gerontology.
- Examine your own commitment and willingness to invest in planning, arranging, and evaluating the clinical aspects of the group experience (Steffl 1973).

Richard Grant, who has for several years used group work with older adults as a clinical experience for students in psychiatric nursing, states: "Above all, the students develop a profound and sincere respect for old people. Kids get in touch with their own heritage. A typical remark from a student is, 'I talk to my grandmother different now'" (Grant 1982).

Experiential Teaching and Learning in Groups

Experiential exercises are especially useful in helping students understand and develop empathy—that is, getting oneself under the skin and into the feelings of the client. (It is important always to help students differentiate between empathy and sympathy. *Sympathy* is feeling sorry for and *empathy* is feeling with.) Experiential exercises can be individually and creatively designed to fit the setting, situation, and group using art, music, dance, or exercises. Impact and/or success is directly dependent upon the preparation, skill, and comfort of the teacher or leader. Because experiential work deals with affect and exposure of self, it is imperative that the participants be prepared in a supportive manner for cohesiveness and self-actualization.

Students and participants should always be allowed the option of not participating. Those who resist or seem uncomfortable may try the exercise themselves later when they have grown and/or are in different circumstances.

RESEARCH

Group work and group therapy are more widely used in community and institutional settings for older adults than is generally realized or reflected in professional and scientific literature.

Dennis (1976) used group work to examine the effects of remotivation therapy on acute and chronic hospitalized psychiatric patients. Voelkel (1978) reported a comparative study that demonstrated greater improvement among moderately to severely mentally impaired residents of a nursing home who experienced a resocialization group than among those in reality orientation groups. Maney and Edinberg (1976) explored the potential of using social competency groups in senior citizen centers where the participant can improve self-maintenance skills.

One reason for the wide use of groups is necessity: It is economical and therapists (and other professionals) are not very interested in working with older individuals (Butler & Lewis 1982). A problem that tends to exist when working with students is maintaining continuity of a group over a long period of time for evaluation and research.

EDUCATIONAL BARRIERS TO PROVIDING CLINICAL PRACTICE

In addition to the scramble for time in the overloaded curriculum of most professional programs, negative attitudes toward old people still prevail. The problems of when, where, and how to place this content in the curriculum have been compounded by the many transitions in education for the helping professions, such as:

- It is a problem to meld separate courses into the integrated curriculum where there is insufficient time for everything.
- There are not enough educators with a broad background in gerontology.
- Gerontology is not a pure science. It is a body of knowledge that cuts across and draws from many disciplines; therefore, disciplines need to communicate and work together. This is not easy when everyone guards his or her own turf.
- Developmental tasks of aging are only recently being defined and added to theoretical content in human development.

Instructors become discouraged and impatient when they visualize experience for students in agencies or institutions and then discover the limitations around which they must plan and negotiate—for example, limited number of students to be accommodated at one time, times of day and days available in the agency, amount of reporting and recording required, cumbersome policies and procedures to reach the patient or client, amount of time for instructor and student orientation, limited assistance from staff due to staffing or financial problems, and traveling time and expense to supervise students.

SUMMARY

Group work with the aged provides a valuable way for students to meet a variety of educational objectives at all learning levels. There is opportunity to gain knowledge, test skills, test and practice observational skills, evaluate assessment skills, analyze and relate theory to practice and synthesize theory and practice with research, learn about oneself, develop a relationship with a preceptor, and develop a leadership and co-leadership role. Clinical practice involving groups of clients and staff fosters empirical research.

In the past few years, educators' interest in gerontology has grown considerably. Presently there are interesting and creative experiences for students to be developed, tried, and evaluated. As Brearly (1975, 79) says, "One positive thing that can be said about the use of group situations with elderly clients is that there is considerable scope for experiment." A cadre of gerontologists from both education and service fields is visible at national meetings; professional publications are increasing. Publications are also emerging from the ranks of students who have had opportunities for independent and creative experiences in group work with older individuals.

EXERCISE 1

If a video camera and viewing material are available, videotape a short session with several older persons and evaluate your interviewing techniques in terms of Irene Burnside's "Interviewing the Aged" (1980). If no videotape is available, select a partner, and write an evaluation of each other's interviewing techniques.

EXERCISE 2

Select a current newspaper article appropriate for one mode of group work with the elderly, such as a current events discussion in a day care center. List:

1. Four objectives that are teacher centered.
2. Four objectives that are participant centered.
3. Rationale for selection of the article.
4. Preparations you would have to make before the meeting and things you would do during the meeting to accomplish your objectives.
5. Criteria for evaluating your group leading.
6. What you learned by doing this exercise. (If you can, carry out an actual experience.)

EXERCISE 3

Life review helps persons to know who they are, what they have accomplished, and what they still want to do and can do, and helps prepare for demise. (Life review is not the same as general reminiscence, although some of the above may occur in reminiscing.) Methods:

1. Write it—autobiography, diary, or journal.
2. Tell it—tape recorder, interview.
3. Draw it—below is a line divided into time-segments, which you are asked to consider as representing your life.

   Birth 10 15 20 25 30 35 40 45 50 55 60 70 80 90 100

EXERCISE 4

"The Peanut" is a topic for reminiscence and stimulating memory and humor.

1. Bring peanuts in the shell for the group.
2. As you shell and eat the peanuts, discuss the following:
   - Where and how do peanuts grow?
   - Kinds of peanuts.
   - Early memories about peanuts—at movies, circus; peanut butter.
   - Likes, dislikes; salted or unsalted.
   - Jokes about peanuts; nickname "Peanut"; cartoon.
3. Evaluate participation and acknowledge and reinforce comments from the group.

REFERENCES

Alzheimer's Disease and Related Diseases Association, Inc. 1993. *Newsletter* 13(1) (919 North Michigan Avenue, Chicago, IL 60611-1676).

Barrett JH. 1972. *Gerontological psychology*. Springfield, IL: Thomas.

Bellak L, Karasu T. 1976. *Geriatric psychiatry*. New York: Grune & Stratton.

Brearly CP. 1975. *Social work, ageing and society* (p. 79). London: Routledge & Kegan Paul.

Brower HT. 1981. Groups and student teaching: Putting health education into practice. *J Gerontol Nurs* 7(8): 483-488.

Burnside IM. 1980. Interviewing the aged. In IM Burnside (ed.), *Psychosocial nursing care of the aged*, 2d ed. (pp. 5-18). New York: McGraw-Hill.

Butler RN, Lewis M. 1982. *Aging and mental health*, 3d ed. St. Louis: Mosby.

Carter C, Galliano D. 1981. Fear of loss and attachment. *J Gerontol Nurs* 7(6): 342-349.

Cassell EJ. 1972. On educational changes for the field of aging. Part 1. *Gerontologist* 12(3):251-256.

Clark CC. 1987. *The nurse as a group leader*, 2d ed. (pp. 4-5). New York: Springer.

Cutler SJ. 1976. Age profiles of membership in sixteen types of voluntary organizations. *J Gerontol* 31(3): 462-470.

Dennis H. 1976. Remotivation therapy for the elderly. *J Gerontol Nurs* 2(6):28-30.

Ellison KB. 1981. Working with the elderly in a life review group. *J Gerontol Nurs* 7(9):537-541.

Erikson E. 1950. *Childhood and society*, 2d ed. New York: Norton.

Grant R. 1982. Assistant professor of psychiatric nursing, College of Nursing, Arizona State University, Tempe. Personal communication (May 15).

Hartford ME. 1972. *Groups in social work: Application of small group theory and research to social work practice*. New York: Columbia University Press.

Hill WF. 1969. *Learning through discussion*. Beverly Hills, CA: Sage.

Holder M, Tilford L. 1974. Student reports on group work. School of Nursing, St. Francis Xavier University, Antigonish, Nova Scotia, Canada (July).

Hobus R. 1992. Literature: A dimension of nursing therapeutics. In JF Miller (ed.), *Coping with chronic illness: Overcoming powerlessness*, 2d ed. (pp. 342-343). Philadelphia: Davis.

Kimmel DC. 1974. *Adulthood and aging*. New York: Wiley.

Linden ME. 1954. The significance of dual leadership in gerontologic group psychotherapy. *Int J Group Psychother* 4:262-327.

Maney J, Edinberg MA. 1976. Social competency groups: A training and treatment modality for the gerontological nurse practitioners. *J Gerontol Nurs* 2(6):31-33.

Montoya D. 1976. Student report on group work in a day care center for the elderly. Tempe: Arizona State University (June).

Smith N. 1993. Journal writing for spiritual growth. Presentation for Center for Development of Resources for Older Adults Retreat at Mt. Claret Retreat Center, 4633 N. 54th Street, Phoenix, AZ 85018 (January 14).

Steffl B. 1973. Innovative clinical experiences in an elective course in gerontological nursing. Paper presented at National Gerontology Society Meeting, Miami (November 5-9).

Supiano KP. 1991. Writing at life's closure. *Clin Psychol* 11(2):43-46.

Voelkel D. 1978. A study of reality orientation and resocialization groups with confused elderly. *J Gerontol Nurs* 4(3):13-18.

BIBLIOGRAPHY

Cullen V. 1991. Van trips as activity for patients at John Douglas French Center for Alzheimer's Disease. Paper presented at Idea Exchange, American Society on Aging, New Orleans (March).

Developing curricula in aging. 1973. Proceedings of an International Workshop for Educators, Practitioners, and Consumers in the Field of Aging (April). Available from David Beattie, Ph.D., School of Social Work, University of Washington, Seattle.

Havighurst RJ. 1965. *Developmental tasks and education*. New York: McKay.

Hyman RT. 1974. *Ways of teaching*. Philadelphia: Lippincott.

Krathwohl DR, Bloom BS, Masiz BB. 1964. *Taxonomy of educational objectives: Handbook II—Affective domain*. New York: McKay.

Maddox GL. 1971. *The future of aging and the aged*. Atlanta, GA: Southern Newspaper Publishers Association Foundation.

Margolis FH. 1970. *Training by objectives: A participant-oriented approach*. Cambridge, MA: McBer Co., Sterling Institute.

U.S. Senate, Special Committee on Aging. 1971. *Research and training in aging*. Working paper. Washington, DC: U.S. Government Printing Office.

Yost EB, Beutler LE, Corbishley MA, Aliender JR. 1986. *Group cognitive therapy: A treatment approach for depressed older adults* (pp. 14-29). New York, NY: Pergamon.

RESOURCES

Module

Modular Gerontology Curriculum for Health Professionals. 1981. This book of modules would be helpful to a new instructor. The modules could easily be used independently of each other. Audiovisual aids, classroom activities, test questions, and annotated bibliographies are well done. There is no specific module on group work, however. The modules are suggested only to assist the instructor to present basic knowledge about aging. I Parham, J Teitelman, D Yancy, Gerontology Program, Medical College of Virginia/Virginia Commonwealth University, Richmond, Virginia.

Manual

Carlson R, Dewald D, Smith N, Vincent J, Weistart D. 1990. *Weaving the threads: A manual for fostering spiritual growth*. Published by Center D.O.A.R., 555 West Glendale Avenue, Phoenix, AZ 85021. Price: $16.

CHAPTER 31

Consultation and Supervision

Irene Burnside

KEY WORDS

- Directive
- Ego enhancement
- Feedback
- Preceptor
- Responsibility
- Self-esteem
- Supportive
- Understanding

LEARNING OBJECTIVES

- Discuss 10 ways in which group work with older adults may differ from that with other age groups.
- List four specific qualities of group work with older people as designated by Corey and Corey.
- Discuss three pitfalls for new group leaders.
- Explain the role of feedback given to students.
- Discuss four ways to increase self-esteem in the learner.
- Analyze one format for teaching group work.

This chapter is about consultation in the specific area of groups for older adults and supervision of students who are leading groups. Consultation is covered in the first part of the chapter, and the rest of the chapter is devoted to the preceptorship of students. The content about the latter is basic and intended for those who have never supervised students leading groups with older people.

CONSULTATION

The literature abounds with content on consultation (Bell & Nadler 1985; Block 1985; Steele 1982; von Schilling 1982); however, there is little in the literature that is germane to consultation with older adults (Duthie & Gambert 1983), and nothing was found about group work consultation. Therefore, basic general principles about consultation will provide the framework for this discus-

sion. It is interesting that *consultation*, as defined in the dictionary (*Webster's* 1985), uses the doctor as an example of the consultant: "Council, conference . . . a deliberation between physicians on a case or its treatments" (p. 282). Bell and Nadler (1985) define *consulting* as "the provision of information or help by a professional helper . . . to a help-needing person or system . . . in the context of a voluntary, temporary relationship which is mutually advantageous" (p. 1).

The Growing Need

Lippitt and Lippitt (1978) emphasize trends important for the consultant role: the rapid rate of technological changes and its effects; the awareness of underutilized, underdeveloped, and misused human resources—minority groups, women, children, the handicapped, the aged, the unemployed, and the uneducated; and the fact that the needs for help are growing faster than professionals are being prepared.

Characteristics of a Consultant

A consultant should have a stable personality, conceptual sophistication, good interpersonal skills, and a good sense of timing. Regarding the conceptual skills, Blake and Mouton (1983) spell out their theory spectrum for consultation. It begins with nontheoretical bases for action: trial and error, hunch and intuition, common sense, explanation, attitude, beliefs, and conventional wisdom. Then the spectrum moves to cognitive maps and conceptual systems, plans and planning. Finally, as a theoretical basis for action, they list theory expressed in testable hypotheses and principles that underlie human behavior. Group work with older adults has moved through that spectrum. The consultant should be knowledgeable about the theories and the underpinnings of groups. See Part 1 for some of the basic theories.

Often consultants are caught on the run, so to speak. That is, it is a one-shot deal, and one is asked to supply advice and information on short notice. Such instances could include a colleague requesting assistance regarding groups, or a director of nursing or an administrator asking for advice regarding groups, or problems with group leadership. Consultants may advise on group work curriculum continuum. Another example would be for a consultant to be asked to observe a group to help the leaders improve their skills. Two such examples are presented.

Example 1. A gerontologist with group work experience was conducting a seminar at a university. A young faculty member who was leading a group asked for some help in handling some of the behaviors in the group. She was especially frustrated by the monopolizing behavior of one of the men in the group. She requested that the consultant lead a portion of the group so she could sit back and observe. What she learned was that out of respect for the older adults, she hesitated to give feedback or intervene in behaviors such as monopolizing. When she compared her interventions to those of the consultant, she felt she had been too timid and too easy with them and had not provided the leadership they needed.

Example 2. An instructor was supervising a group of baccalaureate students in a day care center, all of whom were involved in leading groups. The director of the day care center called her aside to discuss a group-related problem. Two graduate students were co-leading their first group of elders and were enthusiastic about it. However, the members were less enthusiastic and wanted to quit the group, and she was not sure why. She asked the students if the instructor could sit in on their group to offer help and support them with suggestions that would help keep the group intact. Some of the problems observed were: The co-leaders sat next to one another so that the weaker members did not get support by having a leader by them; the group met in a lounge with huge, soft sofas and in a rectangle form, so that they could not see or hear one another well; several props were introduced at once, which confused some members and got conversation off the track; side conversation was common; a man who had had a stroke was put in the limelight to share—his face turned scarlet and he was unable to speak; the leaders kept probing for feelings, which made some of the members anxious and fidgety; and the lounge was noisy with people coming and going during the meeting. It was clear that the needs of some of the members were not being met, and they were attending to please the director of the day care center.

The above are simple examples. For larger jobs, there should be a contract, and a cardinal rule is to put everything in writing, even the smallest details. The reason for a contract is clarity, not reinforcement (Block 1985, 132).

Consultation is tricky. Either you are expected to solve all the problems (and then take the blame when they fail) or you are not taken very seriously and may be tolerated by some of the listeners only because someone above them in the hierarchy asked you to consult.

Because group work with the elderly is arduous, draining, and sometimes discouraging for the beginning group leader, considerable support is needed from a preceptor or supervisor. This chapter gives students, instructors, health care workers, and volunteers an understanding of the preceptor's responsibilities. Topics include the value of humor and feedback for students, pitfalls for new group leaders to avoid, anxiety and depression in new group leaders, how to increase self-esteem among new leaders, and some suggested formats for teaching group work.

DIFFERENCES BETWEEN OLDER ADULTS AND OTHER AGE GROUPS

The new leader working with the aged may have conducted other groups but will need help in discovering the ways in which group work with older adults is different. Some of the differences follow.

- Elderly people tend to be grateful and to express their appreciation to the leader in a variety of ways.
- The groups tend to be smaller—for example, four individuals for reality orientation or six members if the group is composed of disabled or regressed individuals. Most leaders recommend six to eight in a group; an exception is remotivation groups, which may have up to 15 persons.
- The pace of the group may be slower, and the goals will be more limited than in other groups.
- Losses of all kinds are a constant theme.
- The members will have physical, psychological, and socioeconomic problems to juggle.
- Sensory defects are frequent and sometimes severe.
- Physical ailments are many; a single member may have several.
- The physical environment of the meeting place is very important for the aged. Extreme temperatures, glare, noisy intercoms, and so on are generally poorly tolerated by older group members. (See Table 11-4 regarding the environment for cognitively impaired elders.)
- The leader may have to be very active, especially with groups of long-institutionalized people, and accept increased responsibility for group movement. Older people do not believe that joining a group will have any magical effects, so the leader must be willing to engage in one-to-one relationships within the group to get it off the ground.
- Although outside-the-group socializing and meetings are generally discouraged in most groups, such activities should be encouraged with the older group, because they may improve the members' enjoyment of life.
- Leaders are usually expected to share about themselves.
- Older people tend to conserve energy; therefore, anxiety may be more difficult to assess in groups of aged persons.

- Physical dependence needs may be very high because of the frailty of group members or the extreme age of some participants.
- Transportation to and from the group (whether it is an inpatient or an outpatient group) can create many problems.
- Evening meetings are generally not acceptable. The institutionalized patient is sent to bed early; the outpatient client is afraid to be out after dark.
- Groups should be planned around aged people's maximum-functioning portion of the day. If residents like to nap after lunch, that is not the best time for a group meeting.
- There may be a vast age difference between the leaders and the members.
- The subject of death and dying will come up frequently; death may occur within the group experience.
- Because of the poverty of many older people, those who could benefit from a group experience may not be able to afford it or have transportation available.
- Boredom and loneliness may be pervasive themes.
- Confrontation groups are usually not appropriate for most older adults; they need *ego enhancement*—a term used by James E. Birren (1973)—rather than confrontation.

In sum, group work with older people is more directive, less confrontive, more supportive, and more an ongoing function of teaching members ways of expressing themselves and listening to others (Corey & Corey 1977). Other differences include the prevalence of specific themes, such as losses and social isolation; some older people are more difficult to reach; attention spans may be short because of physical or psychological difficulties; group members may be on medications that affect mental sharpness; they may forget to attend sessions; regular attendance is difficult to maintain; group members need support and encouragement; and they have a great need to be listened to and understood (Corey & Corey 1992).

TASKS OF THE PRECEPTOR

The preceptor has several obligations to a student, the most important of which is to reduce a new leader's anxiety so that he or she can function reasonably well from the beginning. The preceptor will also need to help the new leader to be cognizant of the differences in group work with the older population and to make the necessary adaptations.

It has been my experience that when a student and I are having difficulties in the instructor-student relationship, the student is also having difficulty in the agency or with the group. Therefore, the supervisor must take the responsibility for improving a stormy relationship with the student and try to work through the difficulties. Doing so frees the student's psychic energies for the group experience.

Humor and Understanding

The use of humor helps both students doing group work and student-instructor conferences. Often we become so grim and determined in our work with the aged that we fail to see the joy and wit around us. Sometimes it takes an old person to teach the value of joy and humor.

In my first year of teaching, I had a maverick student who was going to change nurses, doctors, and agencies. She bulldozed her way along and wondered why there was such chaos in her wake. One day when I was trying to help her realign her ideals with realism, she flared up: "Irene, you sound just like my mother!" Too weary for further explanation, I asked her if she would change it to "grandmother" because at the moment my arthritis was bothering me. She laughed suddenly, and our heretofore stormy relationship seemed to change for the better.

Students often hear their peers comment, "How dull," "How depressing," or "How do you stand it?" It becomes tiring after a while continually to defend one's interest in the aged; until society's attitudes are turned around, these comments will probably persist. But students do need to find some rewards for themselves as they work with older adults, and preceptors can give feedback to help the students find pleasure in group work.

As students begin to see traits they admire and respect in old people and find that the aged are very human, they begin to appreciate their group work and their relationships with older adults. Not infrequently, students develop close relationships with aged clients and keep in touch long after studenthood has passed.

On one occasion, I attended a student's wedding, which was held in a lovely park. The terrain was a bit rough, so during the reception I said to the 90-year-old grandmother of the bride, "Could I get you another glass of champagne?" She looked me squarely in the eye and said, "What's the matter, don't you think I can get it by myself?" (I did not know she was leaving for Greece the next day.) When students begin to experience similar incidents and see the strengths, flair, and uniqueness of so many older adults, they often become staunch advocates of the aged client.

Identifying Pitfalls for Beginning Group Leaders

Preceptors bear the responsibility of discouraging students without the appropriate background who may take on the role of psychotherapist. The instructor should be alert for such a stance in a student and watch for too much probing of group members, constant confrontations with members about behavior or statements made in meetings, and a desire to push in especially painful areas—for example, grief, losses, or uncomfortable discussion areas such as sexuality. Although it seems to be true that aged persons reveal only what they wish to, a new leader may affront them or aggressively challenge them, and the members may subsequently refuse to participate in the group.

The preceptor also has to watch for occasions when new leaders' needs are usurping group needs. For example, a leader's need to help may end in infantilizing older people. Other leaders may give free rein to their curiosity and want the older person to reveal all while they sit back and share nothing. In the reverse situation, leaders use the group setting to vent their own problems and anxieties. It is not easy to teach the balance needed; students learn it as they make mistakes in group.

Feedback to Students

Feedback is crucial in teaching. One reason the preceptor should give feedback to students is that the instructor becomes a role model for students, who can then begin to give feedback to the older adults in their care. Many older persons suffer from lack of feedback, especially those who live alone. A second reason is that students do flourish with feedback. Students gain self-confidence with prompt, positive, and constructive feedback from a preceptor. There is no substitute for actual group leading.

Students should receive both positive and negative feedback on their performance with groups. How much of each should be given is up to the supervisor. Some students require a lot of stroking; others need to be restrained because they come on too strongly. Skillful observation of each student is required to find out the mode of supervision that will maximize the student's potential. Every effort should be made to prevent failures, which foster discouragement and depression in a student leader. The instructor should bring out the best in each student. Some students have had so much negative feedback that they do not know what their best is.

It is advisable to always present the positive comments first in the conferences or written evaluations. If you put the negative comments first, the student usually will not pay attention to the positive feedback that comes later.

Recognizing Anxiety in the New Group Leader

The instructor must also be on the alert for anxiety in a new group leader. As previously stated, the supervisor must help students understand their anxiety. Beginners often fear failure or are not sure what they can accomplish in the group (Burnside 1969). If a student has never been in an extended care facility before and the group meetings are to be held there, the student may have horrified initial reactions to everything from the smell of the place to the behavior of the personnel. When students are indignant and their complaints seem unending, they can often be reminded that they are forgetting the aged persons, that they are spending so much of their time and energy grumbling or coping with the staff that they have little energy left for creative work with the old people. This sort of behavior in a student may be one form of resistance. A student may hold back, as though stalling long enough will prevent having to go through the group experience. Procrastination is a common way for beginning group leaders to handle their anxiety. However, the instructor must also take responsibility when things are not going well. For example, if one gives vague, poor, incomplete instructions, the student can really get muddled trying to figure out what the assignment is or what the instructor expects.

Asking students what would help the most in their state of apprehension can bring a variety of requests—for example, just a desire to talk, to go for a cup of coffee, to go for a walk, to cry for a while. The preceptor should try to respond to any such requests; launching a new leader well into group work is important.

Preventing Depression in the New Leader

Other reactions a preceptor may view in a group leader include depression and low self-esteem. Students beginning group work may become depressed for a variety of reasons. Former students have discussed some of these reasons with me.

1. The student's lack of experience and knowledge may cause depression.

2. The deplorable living conditions of the aged where the student may be placed can be a factor.

3. The attitudes and behavior of staff and doctors toward the patients may depress a student.

4. Similarly, the attitude and behavior of the staff toward the student may cause depression.

5. As stated earlier, students may focus on aging relatives. A visit to parents and/or grandparents can suddenly make students aware of the aging process in their own relatives. As one nurse said, "I get goose bumps when I think of how my mother has aged." Another time I met a colleague in an air terminal; she looked wan and drawn. "I've just returned from seeing my folks in Boston; I can't believe how they have gone downhill," she said sadly, and readily acknowledged her depression.

6. Deaths that occur in the agency (but outside the group) can cause depression and sometimes guilt. For example, one student placed in a senior citizen residence was battling with an older social worker, soon ready to retire, over what seemed to me like inconsequential issues. I asked the student to write process records on her interactions with the social worker. The analysis of her own communication and behavior patterns brought about some change in the student. But

the real change occurred when the student discovered that the social worker had terminal cancer and had chosen to work until she could no longer cope physically with the job. The depression and the guilt of the student in this particular case had nothing to do with the older people at the senior center. But it had to be dealt with in supervision.

7.   Young students often get depressed because of slow results or not meeting their goals (which often are too high in the first place). Beginners have to be helped to get a more realistic view of what they and the group can accomplish in the allotted time.

8.   Grade-hungry students, when they do not get the grade they had hoped for in the group work experience, often get depressed.

9.   Termination of the group experience and the relationship with the instructor can cause depressed feelings, especially if the student terminates both at the same time. Supervisors must be able to handle their terminations well and to guide students through the group termination experience. Role-modeling behavior is important here; students will model their terminations with the aged after the way that preceptors handle their terminations with the students. Role modeling is still one of the most effective teaching strategies. (Barbara Sene's 1969 article on termination behavior is recommended.)

Increasing the Student's Self-esteem

Guiding new group leaders often requires pumping up deflated egos. Many students have low self-esteem and do not have a realistic idea of their assets and liabilities. If they have never led a group before, it takes a while for them to view themselves in the role of group leader.

Anxiety, lack of experience in group work, and fear of failure blend to make a new leader's trepidation blatant. Positive rewards in the way of immediate feedback (either verbally or on written assignments) on student accomplishments seem to help students quickly.

Availability of the supervisor is also important, especially in the beginning of the group experience. The dependency needs of the new leader usually diminish rapidly if the anxiety, depression, or lack of self-esteem are met with effective interventions by the supervisor and if sincere feedback, both constructive and corrective, is given very soon after each group meeting.

To provide effective interventions and feedback, the supervisor should attend student-led group meetings occasionally as an observer. According to Irvin Yalom (1985, 377):

> Group therapy supervision is generally more taxing than individual therapy supervision. Mastering the cast of characters, a formidable task in itself, is facilitated if the supervisor observes the group periodically or at least once. The student's written or verbal summary of the session often fails to capture the emotional flavor of the group, and ongoing audio or preferably videotapes are invaluable supervision aids.

It has been helpful for me as a preceptor to be an observer once or twice while a student is leading a group. One student leading her first group was having trouble with a man in his seventies who would interject statements with a sexual connotation that always brought the group and the leader to a sudden halt. The leader was so concerned about it that I decided to observe one group meeting. The group was going smoothly; the residents were reminiscing; and the old man blurted out, "No matter how much you shake it, the last drop always ends up in your pants." Everything skidded to a stop, and two of the quiet, genteel women in the group stared at him incredulously, as though they were mentally playing the remark through again to make sure they had heard it right. During another meeting, an 80-year-old woman said during a lull, "You know, Irene, no man has a decent orgasm until he is twenty-five years old." She startled me, but all the men in the group became noticeably more alert.

It has been my observation that young students may be comfortable discussing sexuality with their peers and/or the preceptor, but they can squirm noticeably when the subject of sexuality comes up in their group leadership. Sometimes they have to look at their own behavior. Are they overreacting? Are they unusually curious? Are they showing signs of disgust?

Although the student wanted to change the man's behavior in the group, she failed to realize how much he kept everyone in that group on their toes. If she had gotten him to stop making such remarks, perhaps the listening and alertness of all the group members would have diminished. Students bent on changing behaviors need to understand and discuss thoroughly their rationale for such changes. Moreover, group members often decide what behaviors they cannot tolerate in one another; that is the ideal way for changes to occur in group work.

Increasing Knowledge Base

The preceptor must help the student to increase knowledge in two areas: the aging process and group process. An excellent overview by Jean Hayter (1983) about necessary modifications in the environment of older persons is highly recommended for beginning group leaders. The author gives practical suggestions regarding deficits in vision, hearing, taste, smell, and touch. Territoriality is also discussed. Chapter 11 offers detailed suggestions for creating the environment for group work with cognitively impaired older adults.

For a student who is weak in group dynamics and process and is in need of remedial reading, I recommend Madelyn Nordmark and Anne W. Rohweder's book (1975, 395-398) and, of course, all of Yalom's books (1970, 1983, 1985).

Stressing Individualization

It goes without saying that individualization is a very important consideration in work with the older adult. Tappen and Touhy (1983) remind us that "flexibility, consideration of individual interests, and a wide range of choices" are needed. It is important for the preceptor to convey this understanding to students. Most of all, the preceptor should individualize the learning techniques with the student and be the role model. One might say that individualization begins at home, because teachers often fail to operationalize with students the content they are endeavoring to teach. (See Chapter 2 for more on individualization.)

Assisting Student Analysis

Preceptors play a critical role in assisting students to analyze and evaluate the group process in their practicum experiences. Because many refinements and changes may have to be made due to the age, abilities, disabilities, and losses of older adults, the student will need to know group dynamics. It is

by knowing and understanding the basics of group dynamics and theory that the student can better understand what must be changed and why. The student will also need to know that the outcomes for groups of aged persons might differ from those for groups of other ages. Students who expect unrealistic outcomes of their groups are bound to be disappointed when they evaluate the accomplishments of their group.

Tappen and Touhy (1983, 38) state that

> Evaluation of the effectiveness of group work with the older adult is usually based on relevant but global measures of change such as morale, life satisfaction, mental status, or ability to carry out activities of daily living. Communication skills, learning, ability to relate to others, resolution of problems, development of insight, and other more specific outcomes are measured less often. . . . In order to promote positive outcomes, group leaders need to be aware of the way in which their actions affect the group.

Outcomes should also be studied in relationship to the skill, expertise, and education of the leader. The practice continues of allowing untrained personnel to lead a group of frail elderly. These leaders must have some basic communication skills and some understanding of group dynamics. Their own attitudes about aging also should be examined since our attitudes ultimately shape our behaviors toward the older individual.

SUGGESTED FORMATS FOR TEACHING GROUP WORK

Students provide information about group meetings to the instructor in the following ways:

- Process recordings—typed from audiotapes or by playing the audiotape to the instructor.
- Logs written immediately after each meeting.
- A video of the group meetings.
- Discussion of meetings (the above methods are preferred to this).

It is useful to have a few structured formats when teaching group work. The following checklist may be helpful for both preceptor and student.

1. Number of individuals in the group.
2. Length of meetings.

3. Number of meetings each week; duration in months.
4. Days of the week meetings will be held.
5. Number of men and women in the group (if group is not mixed, give rationale).
6. Age range.
7. Disabilities that will be accepted.
8. Whether confidentiality will be a ground rule stated by the leader.
9. Whether the group will have a single leader or co-leaders.
10. The theoretical framework(s) to be used.
11. The special problems of the proposed group, to include:
    a. Attention span.
    b. Communication or speech difficulties.
    c. Diet regimens.
    d. Ex-alcoholics.
    e. Ex-drug addicts.
    f. Hearing problems.
    g. Impending death.
    h. Incontinence.
    i. Lack of social graces.
    j. Loss of spouse.
    k. Losses, such as economic or home.
    l. Mental health problems, such as withdrawal, loneliness.
    m. Physical health problems.
    n. Vision problems.
    o. Transportation problems.
    p. Whether plans have been made for transportation.
12. Whether support or supervision will be given and by whom.
13. Arrangements for pay (if the beginner is not on a volunteer or student basis).
14. Responsibilities for charting and reporting to the staff and doctor.
15. Philosophy and rules of the agency that will influence the group leader and/or the group.
16. Plans for terminating the group.
17. Props, supplies, and materials that may be needed for the group.
18. Who will pay for supplies.
19. If plans are made to record sessions on a tape recorder or to take photographs, from whom permission has been obtained. (Administrator's permission is required plus that of the patient or relative or conservator if the patient cannot sign for himself or herself.)
20. Plans for individuals who cannot handle group membership.

Preceptors bear the responsibility for double-checking the list to see that the items have been covered. In teaching, it is helpful if students give a rationale (and there may be several) for their choices. Giving reasons will help them think through the group experience more carefully.

If the instructor prefers not to use tapes or process records, using the list format in Exercise 2 can expedite reporting for the student and reading by the preceptor.

Agencies usually require goals and objectives written by the student. Writing objectives can be quite difficult for some students.

SUMMARY

This chapter deals briefly with consultation and the delicate, sometimes difficult task of preceptorship. The reader will note that both the reference list and the bibliography are quite short, indicating the need for more literature about the topic.

A preceptor should have a strong background in group work to be able to advise, instruct, and motivate the beginning group worker. Tasks of the supervisor include reducing students' anxiety, preventing depression, and raising their low self-esteem. Another responsibility is helping them distinguish the differences between group work with the aged and work with other groups. The preceptor also should advise students of the level of group they are qualified to handle and prevent them from assuming the posture of psychotherapists by probing, confronting, or pushing for insight into such areas as grief, losses, and sexuality. The instructor also will have to be alert to the problem of students' needs displacing group needs. In all these tasks, humor and prompt feedback to the students are extremely important. For preceptors, group therapy supervision is draining—more so than supervising one-to-one relationships.

This chapter also provides a detailed checklist to help both supervisors and new group leaders handle the group experience. Bernita Steffl (1973) gives recommendations for instructors of gerontological nursing who are supervising clinical experiences. She also discusses professional curricula for group work with the elderly in Chapter 30.

EXERCISE 1

Write a one-page description of the leader's role in a group of older persons. How does the role differ from that of a group leader of persons who are adolescents, young adults, or middle aged?

EXERCISE 2

Collecting accurate, meaningful data is important in analyzing the effectiveness of group work. The following format can be used by either group leaders or observers. If you are an observer, you should keep in mind that your presence will alter the group process. You should also confer with the group leader to determine what the goals for that meeting were before you answer the questions on the list. If you are currently leading a group, thoughtfully analyze what happened. Ask your instructor or supervisor to read your answers and give you feedback. The last step is to analyze the feedback from your instructor or supervisor. Was it helpful? If so, why? If it was not helpful, consider why not.

Before the Group Meeting

1. List attendance in the group.
2. Draw the seating arrangement of the group members. Describe any noticeable activity such as moving chairs, changing places, leaving the group, sitting on the periphery, and so on.
3. What was the group mood when you walked in? Were there any noticeable feelings in individuals? Were there any unusual events prior to the meeting, such as a death, an accident, a fire, an upset ward routine?

During the Group Meeting

1. List a few of the outstanding themes of the group meeting. If the mood of the group was related to the themes, explain.
2. Write one-paragraph descriptions of the mood activity of the members and of the leader.
3. Illustrate with:
    a. One intervention that was goal directed. List the goal and your rationale for your intervention and evaluate its success.
    b. One verbal or nonverbal intervention that was unsatisfactory. Explain why you think it was unsatisfactory and why a correction is desirable.

After the Meeting

1. Did anything unusual occur immediately following the group meeting?

Future Meetings

1. List proposed future interventions and the rationale for each.
2. List questions or problems with which you would like assistance.

EXERCISE 3

Get permission from your group to videotape a meeting. Then play it back to them. What are their reactions? Pretend you are a consultant, what will you recommend in future group meetings?

EXERCISE 4

Using a format based on those in *Group Protocols* (Gibson 1990), design a protocol for your favorite type of group for older adults.

REFERENCES

Bell C, Nadler L (eds.). 1985. *Clients and consultants*, 2d ed. Houston, TX: Gulf Publishing.

Birren JE. 1973. Panel discussion at Aging: Issues and Concepts conference, North Hollywood, CA (January).

Blake RR, Mouton JS. 1968, 1983. *Corporate excellence through grid organization development*, 2d ed. (p. 283). Houston, TX: Gulf Publishing.

Block P. 1985. Contracting: A tool for client-consultant understanding. In C Bell, L Nadler (eds.), *Clients and consultants*, 2d ed. Houston, TX: Gulf Publishing.

Burnside IM. 1969. Group work among the aged. *Nurs Outlook* 17(June):68-72.

Corey G, Corey M. 1977. Groups for the elderly. In G Corey, M Corey (eds.), *Groups: Process and practice* (pp. 345-374). Monterey, CA: Brooks/Cole.

Corey MS, Corey G. 1992. *Groups: Process and practice*, 4th ed. Monterey, CA: Brooks/Cole.

Duthie E, Gambert S. 1983. Geriatrics consultation: Implications for teaching and clinical care. *Gerontol Geriatr Educ* 4(2):59-66.

Ford C. 1985. Developing a successful client-consultant relationship. In C Bell, L Nadler (eds.), *Clients and consultants*, 2d ed. Houston, TX: Gulf Publishing.

Gibson D. 1990. *Group protocols: A psychosocial compendium*. New York: Haworth.

Hayter J. 1983. Modifying the environment to help older persons. *Nurs Health Care* 4(5):265-269.

Lippitt G, Lippitt R. 1978. *The consulting process in action*. San Diego, CA: University Associates.

Nordmark M, Rohweder A. 1975. Small group behavior. In *Scientific foundation of nursing*, 3d ed. (pp. 395-398). Philadelphia: Lippincott.

Sene BS. 1969. "Termination" in the student-patient relationship. *Perspect Psych Care* 7(1):39-45.

Steele F. 1982. *The role of the internal consultant*. Boston: CBI Publishing.

Steffl BM. 1973. Innovative clinical experiences in an elective course in gerontological nursing. Paper presented at Gerontological Society meeting, Miami (November 5-9).

Tappen R, Touhy T. 1983. Group leader—Are you a controller? *J Gerontol Nurs* 9(1):34.

von Schilling K. 1982. The consultant role in multi-disciplinary team development. *Int Nurs* 29(3):73-75.

Webster's Ninth New Collegiate Dictionary. 1985. Springfield, MA: Merriam Webster.

Yalom ID. 1970. *The theory and practice of group psychotherapy*, 3d ed. New York: Basic Books.

———. 1983. *Inpatient group psychotherapy*. New York: Basic Books.

———. 1985. *The theory and practice of group psychotherapy*, 3d ed. New York: Basic Books.

BIBLIOGRAPHY

Corey G. 1981. *Theory and practice of group counseling*. Monterey, CA: Brooks/Cole.

Fisher A. 1980. *Small group decision making: Communication and the group process*, 2d ed. New York: McGraw-Hill.

Kottler J. 1983. *Pragmatic group leadership*. Monterey, CA: Brooks/Cole.

Panneton PE. 1979. Current and future needs in geriatric education. *Public Health Repts* 94(January/February): 73-79.

Rudestam K. 1982. *Experiential groups in theory and practice*. Monterey, CA: Brooks/Cole.

Sampson E, Marthas M. 1981. *Group process for the health professions*, 2d ed. New York: Wiley.

Sargent D. 1980. *Nontraditional therapy and counseling with the aging*. New York: Springer.

Shaw ME. 1981. *Group dynamics: The psychology of small group behavior*, 3d ed. New York: McGraw-Hill.

Siegel H. 1979. Baccalaureate education and gerontology. *J Nurs Educ* 18(September):4-6.

RESOURCE

Game

Into Aging (a simulation game). This game is described in book format and played with colorful "Life Event" cards. It could be used to help students experience some of the daily struggles of the aged. One game may be played by 5 to 15 players. By TL Hoffman, SD Reif; publisher: Charles B. Slack, Inc., 6900 Grove Road, Thorofare, NJ 08086; phone: 800-257-8290.

CHAPTER 32

Ethical Issues in Group Work

Mary Gwynne Schmidt

KEY WORDS

- Accountability
- Confidentiality
- Ethics
- Ethical dilemma
- Privacy
- Release form
- Self-determination
- Values

LEARNING OBJECTIVES

- List three ethical dilemmas commonly encountered in group work with older adults.
- Describe the relation of ethics to values.
- Systematically analyze one ethical dilemma.
- Name three factors that affect ethical issues in group work with older adults.

This chapter deals with ethical issues in group work with the aged. These issues exist in the overlap of two areas of concern, gerontology and group work, but neither alone provides a sufficient guide to the practitioner. The main focus in this chapter is on the ethical principles themselves and the values that underlie them, in regard to both group treatment and research.

Some of the complexity was illustrated when Appelbaum and Greer (1993), discussing confidentiality in groups, cited a study that revealed the belief of group therapists that members of therapy groups were at risk of breaches of confidentiality. Most of the therapists handled this concern by discussing the importance of confidentiality in the first session. Fewer than one third, however, explained to their group members that complete confidentiality could not be guaranteed. This failure to explain was Appelbaum and Greer's main concern.

With older adults, however, even the careful discussion of confidentiality and its limitations that Appelbaum and Greer recommend is not enough.

Because the anxiety of group members is often high in the first meeting, important information should be reviewed in subsequent meetings as well.

Transfer this problem of confidentiality to a geriatric setting, where some of the very persons who might benefit most from participation would either be put off by the explanation or have difficulty grasping it. Then go a step farther and imagine that you wished to tape a group for teaching or research purposes. Some participants would be unable to give consent because they had conservators or guardians, and at least a few of those who could consent on their own behalf would have families who would object even if they did not.

VALUES, ETHICS, AND ETHICAL DILEMMAS

Ethics—standards of desired behavior or moral imperatives—are grounded in values, which are what the society or some part of it judges to be good. Thus, the value may be the human worth of all individuals; the ethical precept would be to treat each person with respect.

As Blumenfield and Lowe (1987) point out, an ethical dilemma arises when "acting on one moral conviction means behaving contrary to another or when adhering to one value means abandoning another" (p. 48). Thus, group leaders feel discomfort when someone they believe would benefit from a group experience refuses to participate: Their duty to provide the best professional care runs athwart their belief in the individual's right to self-determination.

This ethical conflict is heightened when that person's need is very great and when he or she is a resident in an institutional setting. The power differential makes the group leader even more reluctant to press the person to participate, because in this society there also is a norm against coercing the more vulnerable. This is viewed as an abuse of power and is summed up succinctly as "Pick on somebody your size." It should be added that in nursing facilities today, that particular dilemma is resolved by the federal regulation supporting the resident's right to refuse treatment.

The ethical conflict is heightened also when a research protocol calls for a certain group size and one more participant is needed to make up the quota. Professional values support research as a means to improve the quality of services for all.

In dealing with the ethical dilemmas encountered in hospital discharge planning, Blumenfield and Lowe (1987) introduce an approach to dilemma resolution that could aid group leaders in the solution of their own ethical problems. They state that before the analytical process can begin, the professional must first identify the dilemma and the competing values that are creating it. Then she or he must examine the interplay of the *database* (patient factors such as strengths, supports, vulnerabilities, and options), the *value systems* of all concerned (the patient's, but also those of the family, peer group, culture, and the other professionals involved), and the *dimensions of decision making* (for whom, by whom, types of consents required, and criteria). The outcome, *action,* must be arrived at with awareness of the consequences and the impediments, including institutional constraints, to each possible course.

The Blumenfield-Lowe model provides a good framework for analyzing ethical issues in group

work, even though it was originally designed to resolve dilemmas in hospital discharge planning. When applying it in a gerotological context, the group leader should take into account not only the individual's ability to decide but also what he or she knows. There is a tendency to assume that everything that has been said has been heard and that all 80-year-old vocabularies have necessarily been updated. A better explanation to the individuals involved often places an impasse in a different light.

Ethical dilemmas will remain dilemmas still and not be easy to solve, but one of the beauties of the Blumenfield-Lowe model is that it calls not only for awareness of one's own values but also for sensitivity to the values of all the others concerned. Insensitivity to the values of other disciplines often leads to strong disagreement in a multidisciplinary setting (Qualls & Czirr 1988).

For example, a social worker and a nurse, acting as co-facilitators, might part with ill-concealed anger if the nurse rescued a tearful participant whom the social worker was encouraging to ventilate her grief. The social worker would tell sympathetic colleagues, "She had no respect at all for the woman's ability to tolerate strong emotion," while the nurse would report, "You could see the poor woman's blood pressure rising, but she let her go on and on." Obviously, the nurse would be valencing protection and the social worker, faith in the individual's ability to decide. Either position is defensible, but each co-facilitator should understand where her colleague is coming from.

Glassman (1991), writing within a monodisciplinary context, spells out values that many other practitioners would find generic to group work in general and their own professions in particular. She describes nine values as informing the norms (or ethical rules) in democratic groups and then mentions ways the leader can support them. (See Table 32-1.)

Each group develops its own rules and creates its own moral climate, but the leader plays a crucial role, and the group's norms must be ones he or she can live with. (This is not to say that the leader may not wince when a cantankerous member snarls at an intruder who seeks to join the group, "Get out! You don't belong here!") The good leader respects the strength of participants and refrains from rescuing needlessly, but the good leader also provides a floor of safety for all within the group.

TABLE 32-1 Nine values shared by democratic groups

- The inherent worth of the individual.
- Individuals' responsibility for one another.
- The right to belong and to be included.
- The right to be heard and to take part.
- The right to self-determination.
- The leader's accountability to the group.
- The right to freedom of speech and freedom of expression.
- Enrichment through difference.
- Freedom of choice.

SOURCE: Based on a list by Glassman (1991).

Common kinds of ethical dilemmas that may arise for leaders include:

1. *Leaders' duty to the group versus their duty to the individual.* When the life of the group itself is at risk, the leader first preserves the group but then attends to the needs of the individual, with individual treatment if necessary. There are persons who are toxic to a group and, unrestrained, they may disrupt it beyond the members' power of restoration. This is especially possible when the disruptive individuals have paranoid ideation or when brain injury takes away their brakes, when their perseveration, agitation, or regression is simply more than the group can stand.

Leaders will find these situations easier to deal with if they recall that any person with an unremitting need to break up a group is plainly unable to use that group in a healthy manner. The principle entailed is the good of the greatest number, but close behind it is the worth of each individual.

2. *Leaders' duty to provide democratic leadership versus their professional responsibility to intervene.* Professional responsibility includes the duty to warn and to inform. No caring leader can be expected to stand by while the group runs off a cliff. Within reasonable bounds, groups, like individuals, have a right to learn from their own mistakes. Having sounded a few discreet caveats, the leader may wish to simply watch. Faith in the ability of all individuals to learn and to grow and trust that all persons have good motives as

well as bad ones make this possible. Under extreme circumstances, however, the leader may elect to exercise her or his right to self-determination and not be a part of it.

Metaphorically speaking, groups, even those whose members are in wheelchairs, can turn into lynch mobs. Such destructive behavior is ultimately destructive to the group that practices it. For example, members may turn on the confused, disoriented individuals least able to defend themselves and say, "You don't belong here!" This raises questions, of course, about the group's composition. Persons should not be invited into groups in which they are likely to be scapegoated.

3. *Leaders' obligations as employees and team members versus their duty to provide good professional services to the group.* This writer once carefully selected members for a state hospital talking group, only to be asked by staff members if she minded their adding an extra patient. She stepped into the room only to find eight pairs of indignant eyes fixed on the most disruptive patient on the unit. In this instance, the writer rose to the challenge—since the group members had to live in a dormitory with this patient—and helped members learn how they set off the very behavior they deplored. Keeping the disruptive one in the group was necessary to the treatment, but the initial byplay was between the group leader and her playful teammates and had nothing whatever to do with the good of the group. Other situations might call for a quite different course of action.

There are times to say no, but they should be carefully weighed. Sometimes the problem is not a value conflict but a poverty of solutions.

4. *Leaders' obligation to ensure confidentiality versus their duty to protect patient welfare.* This may be particularly difficult for nurses, because their code of ethics and job sanctions emphasize so strongly the duty to protect (Dittmar 1989).

In necessarily restrictive settings, such as prisons, conflict between confidentiality and welfare is handled by spelling out the limits of confidentiality at the very start. The leader points out that there are certain things, such as criminal activity and potential violence, that must be reported.

Older adults in nursing facilities are unlikely to start a riot, but they have been known to take their own lives. A hierarchy of values does exist: An ultimate duty is to protect from grievous harm.

Suicide risk must be reported. Other concerns also may properly belong in the resident's record, such as alterations in behavior or mood that may reflect untoward responses to medication or changing health status.

Most events can be charted in ways that present the participant more or less as he or she would like to be seen. You can test whether you have done so by envisioning that person reading his or her own record, as, indeed, he or she has every right to do. Nevertheless, there will be some things that belong in the chart but that the person would rather you did not report. In these situations, there are two things you can do to preserve a remnant of trust: (1) report the facts but also record the client's own point of view, and (2) tell the participant that you must share your concern. The person's first intimation that you have mentioned her or his suicidal ideation should not be staff's removing scissors and razor.

More troublesome are those situations when the competence of a group member is being studied to determine whether a conservator is needed or when a decision has been made and evidence is being collected to make a case. Leaders, supplying information for these purposes, are haunted by the don't-squeal norms of youth and feel like betrayers. Here the course of action must be dictated by its consequences, assessed in terms of the member's ultimate need.

A final dilemma relates to research.

5. *Leaders' duty to the group versus their need to support research.* Group leaders' duty to adhere to research protocols may be severely tested when the protocols are rigid and leaders feel locked into them. They often believe they are being forced to sacrifice some of the spontaneity, creativity, and fluidity of response they pride themselves on achieving. At the same time, if research is to move beyond anecdotal evidence, it is necessary to test theory under standardized conditions, which means, for example, that a six-session group remains just that no matter what crisis members are experiencing.

Unfortunately, human behavior does not come in standard units, nor does distress wait outside the door. When a group member announces that she has just learned that her grandson has AIDS, she needs the group's support, not a prescheduled session on memories of life on the farm.

Legal and Technical Considerations

Some decisions are taken out of the group leader's hands due to overriding regulations. Laws and regulations can provide a protection, an impediment, or a cover. The Nursing Home Reform amendments illustrate all three. These have greatly benefited aged persons in residential care. They were needed because the rule of the market and the fear of litigation too often outweighed professional and personal ethics.

When Congress was unable to push a reluctant administration into taking active steps to protect the rights of residents, it forced the issue by spelling out those rights with a specificity unusual in the law. The Nursing Home Reform amendments (OBRA '87) and the regulations derived from them deal quite directly with the rights to privacy, to confidentiality, to be informed, to be free of abuse and exploitation, to receive treatment, and to refuse treatment (U.S. DHHS 1991; Public Law 100-293 1987). This was reinforced by the Patient Self-Determination Act (DHHS 1992). All of this is clearly in the residents' interest.

Privacy is extraordinarily difficult to obtain even when the group is conducted in the setting for which these regulations were intended, the nursing facility. Nursing facilities, modeled after hospitals, were designed less to promote privacy than to facilitate surveillance. Even settings designed for well older adults, senior centers and club houses in retirement communities, often lack meeting rooms with doors that shut. Nevertheless, the Nursing Home Reform amendments do recognize privacy as a goal.

For all the values the OBRA '87 regulations do support, there are times when caring professionals may experience them as an impediment. Such a time may be, for example, when they are trying to persuade a depressed resident to join an activities group and she remains resolutely in her room.

The regulations also can be a cover. When the same reclusive resident firmly refuses to participate in any rehabilitative or recreational activities, staff need only to chart clearly and frequently their earnest efforts made to persuade her to do so. Her refusal frees staff members of responsibility for her participation and deprives her of an opportunity to engage in an activity that might raise her spirits. On the other hand, few group leaders would go back to the old days when residents were herded into treatment groups, willing or not.

More important than any particular regulations is the shift in attitudes they compel: By giving even impaired residents the right to refuse, staff members are recognizing those residents as human beings with preferences and some capacity for sharing responsibility. This is liberating for all parties.

Varying from state to state, there are laws mandating health care professionals to report reasonable suspicion of events like elder abuse. Failure to report can lead to fines, jail sentences, and sometimes loss of license for the professional. If group members in a nursing facility said that a staff member struck or otherwise abused a resident, the group leader would have to see that this was reported to the proper authorities. Reporting is a sobering process because of the penalties for the proven offender, but these laws are an important tool for combating abuse and an expression of society's obligation to protect the frail and the helpless. Nevertheless, the immediate response of colleagues and administration may be less than enthusiastic.

CONSIDERATIONS RELATING TO AGE AND RESIDENTIAL FACTORS

The Issue of Research

Two kinds of research are involved. First, there is the monitoring necessary to determine whether group and leader are meeting their goals. This presents no problems and, indeed, is obedient to the principles of accountability and good practice. The group leader may or may not share these findings with the group, but is under no obligation to do so. The purpose of this monitoring is to serve group members better.

The second is research intended to improve practice in the field in general. Closely related to this is using the group for teaching purposes. Case material for the classroom and journal articles may be used freely as long as precautions are taken to protect the anonymity of participants. When audio- or videotaping is contemplated, releases must be secured, as they must be for any experimental research group. Sometimes the permission of human subjects committees also is required.

If the participants are community residents in senior centers or similar settings, they usually can sign their own releases. If they are in day care or nursing facilities and impaired, the consent needed may be that of a conservator, guardian, or responsible family member. Courtesy would dictate an explanation to the resident of what the tape is for and who will see or hear it. Even when the resident has full capacity and signs on his or her own account, however, program directors or administrators may fear that family members will be upset. The safest course is to explain the project to those family members also and to note in the record that you have done so.

The Conditions of Aging

Although most of the aged are healthy, active, and mentally alert, some are frail, unprotected, and functionally impaired. Persons dealing with them sometimes generalize one deficit from another, for example, assuming that those who do not hear very well do not think well either. Their very vulnerability imposes an increased responsibility on the group leader to see that all ethical standards are met.

Some very old persons who are otherwise quite alert process things more slowly. They also have bad days when things do not come as clearly: This is due to the frail body's inability to compensate for extra stress. The leader must take this into account, neither placing additional demands on them at these times nor rushing to conclusions about incapacity.

The group leader has both an opportunity and an obligation to help older persons achieve their full potential at each stage of life. Whenever possible, no one should be deprived of group services because of a lack of transportation; because of hearing or visual problems; or because of race, color, or ethnicity.

Some scapegoating in any human group seems inevitable, but no one should be scapegoated beyond bearing. The worker has an obligation to know who is brittle, to ease the entry of new members, to see that members are pleasantly challenged but not overwhelmed. Members also need to be protected against overexposure of their own frailties, whether these are the emotional lability of the stroke patient, the aggression of the bully, or the endless whine of the chronically discontented.

Because the very old sometimes are reluctant to try new things they might enjoy, because they fear demands on their waning energies, the group worker must gauge the difference between strong encouragement to participate and excessive pressure. This is true also of persons who are depressed. No one needs to remember this distinction between encouragement and coercion more than the group leader who is engaged in research.

and fail to examine the implications of their acts. All too often, grateful participants collude with them in what are really violations of their privacy, confidentiality, autonomy, and other values simply because group membership is so meaningful to them. The price of leadership is responsibility, and group leaders have a special obligation to be even more sensitive to participants' rights than the group members who trust them.

SUMMARY

Ethical violations in group work are less likely to occur because group leaders are unprincipled than because they take their own good will for granted

EXERCISE 1

The Music Group: Miss Brinkly, 89 years old, is hard of hearing, but you seat her right by the record player and there is every evidence she enjoys the group. The nursing assistants are eager to put the residents down for their naps and today, again, they have whisked Miss Brinkly off to bed. When you protest, they declare, "She can't hear anyway."

Miss Apley has little patience with people who talk when she is listening. Her command to you is curt, "If they can walk, tell them to get out. If they are in wheelchairs, push them out!" Mr. Seldon taps the time with his cane, and Miss Apley is glaring in his direction.

The following week, you arrive to find Miss Apley pacing in her wheelchair and several residents clustered outside the closed door of the meeting room. The group's meeting has been abruptly canceled: The administrator wants the room set up for the board meeting tonight. You'd like to continue this group because it's an activity the alert and the impaired can enjoy equally, but you feel your time is being wasted. You think you'll quit leading it.

Outline the ethical and value issues involved in each instance and tell what you would do.

EXERCISE 2

Mrs. Lambert comes to Wednesday group with bruises on both arms. Before group begins, you ask her what has happened. "I stumbled and bumped myself," she replies, but her roommate interposes, "Fran shook her because she was so slow." Mrs. Lambert shakes her head. "I fell," she says—although the location of the bruises makes this implausible. Fran is a nursing assistant. At this point the group begins to gather. "Fran," begins Mrs. Pugh, hearing the name, "Fran's mean." "Yes," says Mr. Addison, "But she shouldn't argue with her." You know Fran will lose her job if you tell the director of nursing.

Describe the ethical, legal, and interpersonal issues entailed in reporting the bruises as possible evidence of resident abuse.

EXERCISE 3

Describe an ethical dilemma you have encountered in working with older persons. Analyze it, using the Blumenfield-Lowe model. First outline the dilemma and ethical issues; then give database, values, and dimensions of decision making; and finally, action.

REFERENCES

Appelbaum PS, Greer A. 1993. Confidentiality in group therapy. *Hosp Comm Psych* 44(4):311-312.

Blumenfield S, Lowe JI. 1987. A template for analyzing ethical dilemmas in discharge planning. *Health Soc Work* 12(1):47-56.

Dittmar S (ed.). 1989. *Rehabilitation nursing: Process and application* (p. 587). St. Louis: Mosby.

Glassman U. 1991. The social work group and its distinct healing qualities in the health care setting. *Health Soc Work* 16(3):203-212.

Qualls SH, Czirr R. 1988. Geriatric health teams: Classifying models of professional and team functioning. *Gerontologist* 28(3):372-376.

U.S. Department of Health and Human Services (DHHS), Health Care Financing Administration. 1992. *Federal Register* 57(45):8194-8204 (March 6).

———. 1991. *Federal Register* 56(187):48826-48879 (September 26).

U.S. Public Law 100-203. 1987.

BIBLIOGRAPHY

Abrams R. 1988. Dementia research in the nursing home. *Hosp Comm Psych* 39(3):257-259.

Agich GJ. 1990. Reassessing autonomy in long-term care. *Hastings Ctr Rept* 20(6):12-17.

Collopy B, Boyle P, Jennings B. 1991. New directions in nursing home ethics. *Hastings Ctr Rept* (Special supplement) 21(2):1-16.

Donnelly S. 1988. Human selves, chronic illness, and the ethics of medicine. *Hastings Ctr Rept* 18(2):5-8.

Jennings B, Callahan D, Caplan AL. 1988. Ethical challenges of chronic illness. *Hastings Ctr Rept* (Special supplement) 18(1):1-16.

Kapp M. 1989. Medical empowerment of the elderly. *Hastings Ctr Rept* 19(4):5-7.

Perlman GL. 1988. Mastering the law of privileged communication: A guide for social workers. *Soc Work* 33(5):425-429.

Reamer FG. 1985. The emergence of bioethics in social work. *Health Soc Work* 10(4):271-281.

Wetle T. 1985. Ethical issues in long-term care. *J Geriatr Psychiatr* 18(1):63-73.

RESOURCE

Film

Elder Abuse: Five Case Studies (40-minute video). Directed by James Van den Bosch, this video presents five victims telling their stories. This does not focus on the ethical issues but instead emphasizes the women's feelings about the abuse and interventions to stop it. Terra Nova Films. Rental: $55; purchase: $335.

CHAPTER 33

Cross-Cultural Issues in Group Work

E. Frederick Anderson and Roger Delgado

KEY WORDS
- Acculturation
- Coping
- Dignity/dignidad
- Familism
- Friendly conversation/platica
- Heterogeneity/homogeneity
- Hispanic/Latino older adults
- Institutional racism
- Jim Crow/de jure segregation
- Trusting in mutual trust/confianza en confianza
- Utilization of services

LEARNING OBJECTIVES
- Show how understanding the historical and contemporary experiences of older African Americans and Hispanics can increase the effectiveness of group work with them.
- Explain what respect means among African-American and Hispanic older persons, pointing out similarities and differences.
- Discuss formal and informal modes of address and explain the implications of respect and disrespect based on historical antecedents.
- Describe three strategies for gaining initial rapport and recognition as a helping entity with Hispanic and African-American older adults.
- Identify the stages of the group process in which cultural sensitivity is most crucial.

The purpose of this chapter is to introduce group work strategies for direct practice with America's two largest minorities: African Americans and Hispanics. Because both groups are complex, such an undertaking in one chapter must be succinct but informative.

The hopes, aspirations, and historical background of African Americans and Latinos will be linked with effective approaches to working with them in groups. The authors hope that this exposure will encourage students and professionals alike to seek further information to enhance their abilities to gain rapport and work effectively with older individuals in both groups.

At the outset, it should be noted that African Americans and Latinos are heterogeneous groupings that are often viewed monolithically in the professional literature. Failure to acknowledge intraethnic and interethnic differences seriously impairs a group worker's ability to relate to the many themes that might emerge in a diverse group of older Americans.

For the sake of clarity, each population will be discussed in turn, with attention to demographics, socioeconomic stresses, and life experiences that, together with coping styles, may affect members' responses to group work. Particular approaches will be suggested.

AFRICAN-AMERICAN OLDER ADULTS

Demographic Characteristics

From the statistics on infant mortality and morbidity to the statistics on longevity and old age, African Americans are shown to be underserved and overrepresented among the impoverished and disenfranchised (National Urban League 1992). The trends are so strong and compelling that they make it difficult for professionals who are socially distant from African Americans to see anything in their heritage but social disorganization, chaos, and anomie. Nevertheless, blacks in the United States have exhibited remarkable resilience despite the institutional racism they have had to cope with. They have developed sources of informal support, turning first to family, church, and friends (Taylor & Chatters 1986) and only secondarily to formal sources. Government and agencies sometimes have been quick to seize upon this intragroup self-reliance as an excuse for underservice. Dilworth-Anderson (1992) has warned that the extended family itself is overstressed and pointed out that black grandparents themselves "remain central figures in the survival process" (p. 31). Childcare and eldercare are exchanged on a two-way street, but the extended family must live near to provide the frail aged with services (Taylor & Chatters 1991).

African-American older adults represent a formidable population despite the pervasive and unrelenting institutional racism. Lack of access to well-paying employment has been a problem for a large number of black Americans throughout their lives and limits their income in retirement. Racial effects extend beyond income, however. Kravits (1975) underlined this point by showing that poor blacks were less likely than low-income whites to have seen a dentist within the year. Waller (1991) declares that African Americans suffer more strokes, cancer, and diabetes than whites and attributes many of the poor outcomes to poverty and delayed care. Stanford, who deplores many black-white comparisons as suggesting that majority behavior is normative (Stanford & Yee 1991), nev-

ertheless concluded that the survival of so many to hardy old age was a tribute to their ability to cope (Stanford 1992). African Americans who reach 75 tend to outlive their white counterparts (Manton 1982). (This is referred to as the black-white crossover, because younger blacks are more at risk, while later their relative life expectancy increases.)

The National Urban League's annual report (1992), *The State of Black America: 1992*, underscores the fundamental changes occurring in the population distribution of other minority groups that may affect policy and services for blacks. Between 1980 and 1990, the U.S. population as a whole grew from 226.5 million to 248.7 million. While African Americans, now numbering nearly 30 million, expanded both in absolute numbers and as a percentage of the whole, Hispanics and Asians were increasing even more rapidly.

Based on 1990 census figures, African Americans over age 65 make up slightly more than 8 percent of black Americans, with older women outnumbering men by nearly three to two. These aged survivors have arrived at old age freighted with the experience of their own lives and that of the generations that preceded them.

Historical Antecedents

African Americans were brought to the United States as chattel, and that circumstance left deep psychological and social wounds for the nation that are still in the process of healing (Franklin 1974). Unrest in the cities suggests that those historical antecedents have resulted in institutional discrimination in jobs, education, family integrity, and myriad other areas that has only been simmering beneath the surface.

From their arrival in America, African Americans have been tenacious in the defense of the family and their reliance on the church. Even under slavery, some black men bought their own freedom first with their extra labors and then that of their families. Those who could not struggled to stay together.

McAdoo (1987) says the black family has suffered three blows. With the hardships of Reconstruction, many freedmen left the South, separating themselves from the support of their extended families. A second exodus took place during the Depression of the 1930s, when younger adults migrated to the cities for work, sometimes leaving children and old people behind. The third blow to the black family was the social and economic disintegration that has spread through the cities since the mid-1970s. McAdoo says there was family stability on the plantation, where 75 percent of slave families had both parents present. She points out that in the 1940s, 82 percent of black families had two parents in the home. The single-parent family became a serious problem only in the late 1960s. Many black grandparents are shoring up the family by parenting their grandchildren (Burton & Devries 1992; Minkler, Roe & Price 1992).

The other pillar beside the family has been the church, which has served a multitude of functions. As slaves, African Americans showed themselves to be ingenious in outwitting slavemasters in order to achieve some solidarity. One strategy they employed was to adopt the Protestant church as a shield for religious meeting and discussion. There was little opportunity for group discussion among slaves outside the cover of the church (Mays 1933; Jackson 1922). During Reconstruction, church membership provided many African Americans with their first experience of property management and their first opportunities for leadership. Today, especially for the older generation, the church continues as a source of both instrumental and social support (Taylor & Chatters 1986), and is "a natural for service provision" (Morrison 1991, 109).

Despite the resources of church and family, there are many sources of stress, and one continues to be black history. Jones (1989) has pointed out that some areas of experience are unique to black Americans, especially history and the impact of racism, and that these must be taken into account in our explanations.

Stresses and Coping by Older Blacks

Every black American who is 60 years old today grew up during the years when segregation was enforced by both custom and law (de jure). Jim Crow regulations meant sitting at the back of the bus, separate washrooms, and living in ill-kept parts of town. Most—and all in the South—attended segregated schools. Because they were poor, they paid few taxes, which was then used as an excuse for inferior social provision. For example, their teachers were paid less, because it was

rationalized, "it costs them less to live." Under Jim Crow, there were many assaults on their dignity. Titles such as Mr. or Mrs. were never applied to blacks in the white press, and it was common for a white man, wanting service, to address a middle-aged African American as "boy." The contrasts were very palpable and built into the very fabric of life.

The remarkable fact is that many African Americans went to college and became physicians, lawyers, and teachers while others, less fortunate, nevertheless tilled their own land or wrested a living as tenant farmers, raised families, and formed islands of social support. Writing almost 30 years ago, Billingsley (1968) pointed out that while the Caucasian family often did not welcome the aged and other kinspersons as permanent guests, the black family saw each additional member as an extra pair of hands.

Today still, the stresses surround health, mental health, housing, work, transportation, and concern for younger generations, and to buffer them there are the church and family networks (Taylor & Chatters 1986; Taylor & Chatters 1991; Walls 1992), but, as Lockery (1991) points out, these supports need supports too.

When aged African Americans attempt to articulate their pain and the group leader, through ignorance or embarrassment, does not acknowledge it, the African-American member may simply tune out of the group or participate dysfunctionally.

Most black elders have developed an inner radar that warns them when their interlocutors do not wish to listen to past racial slights. What these older African Americans have to give the group is infinite experience in coping, not only with racism but also with life.

During the assessment, the group leader needs to be aware of both black troubles and black strengths in order to gain rapport. The leader should not bring up these issues precipitously, but if members raise them during the initial phase of the group, he or she should be prepared to acknowledge them.

GROUP WORK PRACTICE TECHNIQUES: DEFINING GOALS AND ESTABLISHING RAPPORT

Understanding the reason for the formation of a group is critical to the success of that group's endeavors. Groups in churches and senior centers may be formed for the purposes of reducing isolation, aiding the bereaved, discussing health care and other current issues, resolving problems arising from life transitions, or providing mutual support and education.

A prospective leader should know that there are usually three phases associated with the formation, development, and tasks of a group that are of special importance when the participation of African-American older adults is sought.

Phase One: Group Formation

It is important for the leader to be familiar with several key words as they affect African Americans. Among these are *respect, pervasive institutional racism*, and *Jim Crow.*

Respect. In the remembered past, African Americans were called by their first names instead of their surnames to reinforce a subordinate status. The X used by Malcolm X and many in the Nation of Islam is a reminder to all that the last names of African Americans were taken from them and European names put in their place. Therefore, it is imperative that group members first address black individuals as Mr. or Mrs. Jones instead of as Fred or Marie. Although using first names may appear friendly and informal, it may be perceived by African Americans as disrespect. Older African Americans do not refer to each other on a first-name basis until they are given permission to do so or have known the other person for some time. It is better to start the group in a more formal manner.

Pervasive Institutional Racism. There are two forms of racism in this country: overt racism, which everyone can see, and covert racism, which is harder to identify unless you know the red flags. Group leaders who deal with the minority aged in general and with African Americans in particular need to be aware of both kinds of racism and their implications for working with diverse groups. The process of gaining rapport entails understanding the impact of *Jim Crow* on the lives of older African Americans.

Group leaders should use the beginning phase to allow themselves and the group to learn a bit more than usual about each participant. This will be an aid to planning with members the course

the group is to take. Of particular importance during this phase is listening and letting the group become a group over several sessions.

Phase Two: Topical Discussion, Intervention, or Treatment

In phase two, it is important for the group leader to integrate what he or she has learned during the first phase into his or her leadership style. The key words *religion, coping behaviors, homogeneity,* and *heterogeneity* are crucial here.

Religion. Many black leaders are church trained or at least were raised in Protestant denominations. Even those who are more secular must deal with black churches (Mays 1933). As any health care professional serving older black adults soon learns, the church can be a recruiting point and a source of infinite help. The outsider should be aware, however, that there are delicate politics and competition among them.

Many members of your small group may have strong spiritual beliefs that have helped them cope with life. Some of these beliefs may appear foreign to a generation that believes in moral relativism as opposed to moral absolutes of right and wrong. The leader must be prepared to accept views that may be at variance with his or her own.

Homogeneity and Heterogeneity. While there are many general statements that may be made about older African Americans, the most general statement that can be made is that they are not monolithic. They are quite heterogeneous in their outlook and experience. Each has overcome discrimination in his or her own manner. Therefore, the group leader should not be surprised to find that many of his or her African-American members, while appearing very liberal on certain topics, may be fiercely conservative on others. Intergroup and intragroup differences must be acknowledged in this phase to keep the group on track.

Some writers have noted that the African-American older adults who live in cities may be spatially compressed, but they are divided on the philosophy of life (Warren 1975). The group leader should not take the opinions of one person as the gospel truth about what is transpiring in African-American communities. Keeping in mind the vantage point of the speaker and that person's social class will often clarify his or her statements.

Group leaders should not be surprised by African-American older adults who appear ethnocentric in their views. Ethnocentrism (group centeredness) appears in many organizations from the Sons of Norway to the Daughters of the American Revolution. Within one's own set, this "nationalism" is commonly considered group loyalty. It varies in degrees. What the group leader should do is listen and observe where individuals in the group are on a continuum and then intervene with the knowledge that their views and realities do exist and must be addressed in the course of the group's discussion.

Phase Three: Ending Phase

Group leaders new to group dynamics often do an excellent job of initiating a group and facilitating it, but they have a hard time determining when it should be ended. When the group has achieved its goal, it should be either terminated or transformed into another entity that can provide its members new opportunities for further growth and development: It should not be continued when its purpose has been accomplished. When the group is to end, the leader must elicit from each member what it was about the group that made him or her participate and what change, if any, has occurred in outlook.

HISPANIC OLDER ADULTS

This section focuses on the relevance of group process and group techniques for addressing the counseling needs of Hispanic older adults. Before more directly addressing the task at hand, it is useful to ascertain who the Hispanic aged are. In this chapter, the terms *Hispanic* and *Latino* are used as generic labels. It is important, however, for the reader to understand that there continues to be a lack of consensus regarding the preferability of each term. Sue and Sue (1990) use the term *Hispanic* to encompass individuals living in the United States who come or are of ancestry from Mexico, Puerto Rico, Cuba, El Salvador, the Dominican Republic, and other Latin American countries. Materials published on Hispanic older adults, to date, have primarily focused on Mexican Americans and Puerto Ricans. The latter, as well

as other specific ethnic group labels, will be used as appropriate to the group being discussed.

Demographic Characteristics

Older Hispanics are the second-largest and most rapidly growing ethnic group in the United States. (See Table 33-1 for a breakdown by national origins.) According to the 1990 census, there were 1,161,283 Hispanics 65 or older in the United States. Of these, slightly less than 59 percent were women. These older Latino adults constituted 5 percent of the Hispanic population in the United States (figures derived from the 1990 census).

Sources of Stress

Older Hispanics face serious financial, health, and social problems. Hispanic older adults are substantially more likely than Americans in general to report serious financial problems. For health care practitioners, it is important to recognize that the well-being of aged Hispanics is tied closely to the underlying problems of poverty and poor health (Andrews, Lyons & Rowland 1992). Cubillos and Prieto (1987), in their demographic profile of Hispanic older adults, report that aged Hispanics are more likely than whites to suffer from chronic illness or disability, but are less likely to use formal long-term care services. They identify the need for the family, the government, community-based organizations, and the private sector to work collectively to better serve the Hispanic aged.

In a telephone survey of 2299 older Hispanics aged 65 and older (Andrews 1989), it was found that although some Hispanic Americans have prospered, a great many still face a daily struggle, living on limited incomes and coping with poor health. In this survey, it was found that nearly three quarters of aged Hispanics have fewer than eight years of education; four in 10 do not speak English; and despite having worked throughout their lifetimes, their jobs offer low pay and no pension or health insurance benefits. It was further found that the most serious problems among aged Hispanics are not having enough money to live on (41 percent); being anxious or worried (41 percent); having too many medical bills (32 percent); and having to depend too much on others (30 percent).

A national needs assessment study conducted by the National Association for Hispanic Elderly

TABLE 33-1 How many Hispanic Americans are there, and what are their origins?

Number	Country of origin
11.8 million	Mexico
2.3 million	Puerto Rico
1.0 million	Cuba
3.7 million	Other (Central or South American or other)
Total: 18.8 million	

SOURCE: Based on U.S. Bureau of Census, 1987.

(Sanchez 1992) found that older Hispanics reported mental health as their third most urgent need after general health and income. Some of the specific mental health problems cited included feelings of uselessness, dependency, and low self-worth; feelings of loneliness and isolation; problems in adjusting to U.S. culture; thoughts and fears of death; and problems in interpersonal relationships. In the same study it is recommended that programs designed to provide mental health services to ethnic minority elders consider the importance of cultural dynamics as a key to the provision of more effective services.

Utilization of Formal Human Services

One might expect that a group beset with a multitude of biopsychosocial stressors would utilize existing formal human services at a high rate. For a number of reasons, this has not been the case for older Hispanic adults. In a study that examined the use of formal helping networks (i.e., agency, counselor, psychologist, doctor, or priest) to meet the psychological needs of the Hispanic older adult (aged 55+ years), it was concluded that the Hispanic aged are in need of psychological services but underutilize them (Starrett, Todd & Decker 1989).

In a collection of articles about different aspects of aging in the Hispanic community, serious concern is expressed by Hispanic gerontologists because of the low utilization rate of human and health care services by Hispanic aged (Sotomayor & Curiel 1988). Miranda (1990) posits that the underutilization of services by Hispanic

older adults is due to a wide range of structural barriers inherent in the service delivery system, such as the lack of cultural sensitivity in the design and delivery of services and the fragmented nature of continuing care services in the Hispanic community.

The Hispanic Family as Informal Support

While some writers believe that the extended family has been and continues to be the most important institution for Hispanics (Sotomayor & Applewhite 1988), others posit that the weakness in the explanation that older Hispanics underutilize social services because they continue to have access to extended family support is that it does not consider the influence of urbanization on the extended family; romanticizes the reality of the barrio where families are, in actuality, poor, thereby limiting the feasibility of mutual economic support; does not acknowledge the differential responses from service providers in the dominant Anglo-American society to minority communities; and lets service providers off the hook of providing needed services to Mexican-American elders (Krajewski-Jaime 1990).

Although there are, in fact, many positive aspects to the expressive and instrumental support received by Hispanic elders from the family as a social support system when it is available, Arevalo (1989) points out that in many instances, Latino families have become acculturated and nuclear and do not feel that they should support their oldest members. Markides and Krause (1986), in a study of intergenerational support for older Mexican Americans in a three-generation sample of 1125 respondents, found that while older Mexican Americans were often engaged in strong helping networks with their children, not all intergenerational support exchanges were beneficial, as dependency often resulted in psychological distress.

Cox and Monk (1990), in their examination of experiences and support networks of black and Hispanic caregivers of family members with dementia, found that both formal and informal support networks were used interchangeably; however, they also found an increased use of formal supports when available, followed by a decreased use of informal supports such as family.

Group Work with Aged Hispanics

Burnside posits that group work is one form of treatment that is effective with older adults and that should be considered in prevention and maintenance aspects of the health care of older persons (see Chapter 7, p. 70). However, as with other counseling services that only recently have been made available to Hispanic elders, the use of group work is a novel experience. A review of the literature on the use of group work, group therapy, and self-help groups with Hispanic elders reveals modest but encouraging efforts. Gonzalez del Valle and Usher (1982) report on a pilot project and study involving the use of group therapy with aged Latino women; Latin cultural factors and their relevance for group therapy are identified.

Acosta and Yamamoto (1984), in their examination of the utility of group work practice for Hispanic Americans, particularly those who are primarily unacculturated and monolingual Spanish-speaking, found that the consideration of cultural factors in conducting group work is crucial for maximizing effectiveness along with the use of behavioral and experiential approaches. Miranda (1991), in an exploration of mental health status among Hispanic older adults and avenues for improving mental health services to this population, advocates the use of natural support networks or self-help groups.

Mayers and Souflee (1990-1991), in their discussion of two approaches that can be used by social service providers to link and strengthen the social support system of aging Mexican Americans, recommend the use of mutual aid, self-help, and informal network strategies. The model proposed delineates the various roles that human service professionals can play in Mexican-American support groups. Sanchez (1992), in a review of mental health issues affecting the aged Hispanic population, also recommends the use of lay groups and informal support networks within the community.

In summary, there is a dearth of written documentation regarding the use of group work and group therapy with Hispanic elders (see Chapter 30, p. 354). Thus, the practitioner with an interest and need to provide such services may be quite unclear about how to develop and provide effective services to Hispanic older adults within the context of a group. The following section attempts to provide the reader with a selective review of issues that may be considered in efforts to provide group work or group therapy to older Hispanics. It is assumed that the worker is already familiar with basic principles, processes, and techniques of group work or group therapy.

Culturally Relevant Issues

In recent years, there has been increased attention to cultural factors in the delivery of mental health services to ethnically diverse populations. What is still lacking, however, is material that addresses strategies for counseling specific ethnic groups. In the case of Hispanic older adults, such a need is especially acute. One of the ongoing challenges to the development of practice-related materials for working with Hispanics is the latter group's intergroup/intragroup heterogeneity and cultural diversity; thus, recommendations made here must be considered within such a cultural milieu.

Given the ethnic diversity of Latino elders, it is difficult to present a how-to approach for providing social group work to older adults of Mexican-American, Puerto Rican, Cuban, and other Latino ethnic backgrounds. The effort here is, therefore, to provide the reader with a selective list of potentially relevant issues for consideration and possible exploration when providing group work services to Latino elders.

Historical Experiences

In addressing the aging process in general and the effects of minority experiences on aging, Moore (1971) postulates that each minority group has a special history; the special history has been accompanied by discrimination; a subculture has developed; coping structures have developed; and rapid change is occurring. Woodruff and Birren (1983, 57-58) point out that

> The historical memory of each group has been unique. Conquest, prolonged conflict, and annexation are antecedents linking the history of the Native Americans and Mexicans; dehumanizing enslavement and its special institutional forms in America are unique to the blacks; varied immigration and migration patterns of the Asian and Hispanic peoples have resulted in a cycle of recruitment, exploitation, and exclusion.

Suffice it to say, it is important for human services professionals to explore with Hispanic aged clients any long-term significance of cumulative historical experiences as it relates to their ability and willingness to use services, especially when rendered by nonminority service providers.

Level of Acculturation

Acculturation is a complex interactional process involving both members of the cultural group undergoing change and members of the host culture. In a model proposed by Mendoza and Martinez (1981), it is suggested that efforts to understand sociocultural adjustment consider four propositions:

1. There are different patterns of acculturation (i.e., cultural resistance, defined as an active or passive resistance to alternate cultural norms, while maintaining native customs; cultural shift, defined as a substitution of native customs with alternate cultural norms; cultural incorporation, defined as an adaptation of customs from both native and alternative cultures; and cultural transmutation, defined as an alteration of native and alternate cultural practices to create a unique subcultural entity).
2. Acculturation is multidimensional and therefore not a construct that can be analyzed by a single measurement or necessarily generalized from a cluster of correlated variables.
3. Many acculturating individuals are multifaceted.
4. As a dynamic process, acculturation reflects not only changes that occur as a function of time and exposure to an alternate culture but also changes that are dictated by contextual factors.

Valle (1990), in a discussion of guidelines for cross-cultural curriculum design, presents an acculturation continuum that posits traditional (reflecting values, norms, language, customs of the culture of origin), bicultural (reflecting incorporation of both ranges), and assimilated (reflecting values, norms, etc., of the host society) levels of acculturation. Cuellar, Harris, and Jasso (1980), in efforts to conceptualize and operationalize level of acculturation, have developed an Acculturation Rating Scale for Mexican Americans (ARSMA). The scale is able to differentiate five distinct types of Mexican Americans based on level of acculturation: very Mexican, Mexican-oriented bicultural, true bicultural, Anglo-oriented bicultural, and very

Anglicized. The measurement of acculturation on ARSMA is based on the dimensions of language familiarity and usage, ethnic interaction, ethnic pride and identity, cultural heritage, and generational proximity.

Applewhite and Daley (1988) assert that human service professionals need to be aware of the rich diversity of peoples within the Hispanic aged population. They further add that

> Professionals need to locate or position individuals and groups they seek to serve within this broad Hispanic elderly population. Specific individuals and groups may to a large degree share many characteristics, life experiences, needs, and aspirations with other Hispanic elderly. At the same time, each individual and group will have unique "common sense knowledge" and distinct perspectives that must be considered if the professional is to understand fully the manner in which Hispanic elderly define, constitute, and order reality (1988, 4-5).

Some Suggestions for Working with Latino Older Adults

Counselors and other mental health professionals who work with Latino clients are strongly urged to recognize that many psychological and social factors within their culture influence the efficacy of the counseling experience. Level of acculturation determines the use of bilingual-bicultural or monolingual-monocultural group work interventions with Latinos. However, with Latino older adults, especially those who have not yet become highly acculturated, there are several cultural areas that need to be considered and addressed throughout the various stages of the helping process (i.e., establishing the relationship, problem identification and assessment, facilitating therapeutic change, evaluation, and termination). Because most clients who terminate counseling prematurely do so within the initial sessions, the primary focus of the present discussion will be on suggestions for establishing the relationship.

Preliminary Tasks. Because most older Latinos have not been through the experience of individual or group counseling, it is important for the worker to: (1) give a brief description of the purpose and objectives of the group; (2) explore the client's expectations and the reason for participation in the group; (3) clarify and resolve any existing conflict in purpose and expectations to enhance therapeutic goodness of fit; (4) discuss the principle of confidentiality as related to group process and content; (5) assess the existence of both intrapsychic and extrapsychic factors in the client's biopsychosocial problem situation; (6) determine the need for the possible utilization of other support systems, both formal and informal; and (7) discuss with the client the need for the use of specific interventions and projected duration of the intended social group work experience.

Respeto (Respect). Due to cultural socialization experiences, older Latinos expect to be treated with respect by all, but especially by younger human service professionals. This gives rise to one of the reasons why special care must be exercised in how the older client is addressed (i.e., with respect, as in Senor Garcia/Mr. Garcia; Senora Lopez/Mrs. Lopez). Correct pronunciation of the client's name is also important; needless to say, the ongoing mispronunciation of a client's name by the worker can be counterproductive to the establishment of client-worker rapport.

Dignidad (Dignity). Associated with respeto is the older individual Latino's belief that what makes a person good and respected is an inner dignity (dignidad). Thus, the worker who is able to acknowledge and show respect for the client's dignidad through both verbal and nonverbal actions is able to help reduce initial client resistance while also establishing trust and personal and professional credibility. Such rapport is especially essential since for some Latino older adults, the seeking of psychological-emotional support outside the family may seem tantamount to being disloyal and dishonoring the family's pride and dignity.

Verguenza (Shame). Latino elders may be especially vulnerable to experiencing verguenza or shame when they are compelled, even by extenuating circumstances, to resort to the use of professional counseling services for personal problems and/or when the family support system is unable, unwilling, or unavailable to serve as the helping resource. The discussion of personal problems within a therapeutic group context may, initially, give rise to the experiencing of verguenza by the

older Latino at both the individual and the family level.

Confianza en Confianza (Trusting in Mutual Trust). Velez (1980) posits that confianza en confianza (trusting in mutual trust), a term that denotes mutualistic generosity, intimacy, and personal investment in self and others, may be used by the helping professional as a resource for reducing resistance and building the client-worker relationship.

Platica (Friendly Conversation). One of the strategies recommended for facilitating communication with Hispanic Americans is the use of platica (social conversation), especially during the initial phase of an interview (Valle 1980). Such helper-initiated conversation can be used to enhance the expressive, and eventually the instrumental, aspects of the helping relationship. It may be particularly useful for platica to be personalized so that it relates to recent or current events and activities that might be of interest or relevant to both the client and the worker. In addition to serving as a warm-up for a group session, the use of platica can also communicate to the client that he or she is still a person. Platica can be useful even though the worker will not be able to engage every member of the group during any given group session. Engaging group members in platica also presents the group leader as a socially gracious host, something that has special meaning in Latino culture.

Familism within the Group

One of the major themes associated with Latinos is the importance of the family, both nuclear and extended (when available) as a valuable source of emotional support. One of the desirable outcomes of a group is that it function as a system for mutual aid. Schwartz (1961) defines a *social work group* as "an enterprise in mutual aid, an alliance of individuals who need each other, in varying degrees, to work on certain common problems. The important fact is that this is a helping system in which the clients need each other as well as the worker" (p. 19). It is conceivable that for Latino older adults, a well-functioning group may come to represent something akin to a surrogate family. Thus, in this sense, prior positive cultural socialization experiences with the family group as a valuable resource may enhance the older Latino client's ability to benefit from participation in a social work group. Among the curative factors in groups that Yalom (1978) identifies, one, altruism, would seem to have special relevance to the Latino elderly.

SUMMARY

The use of social group work with minority elders can be a method for quality service delivery. Admittedly, there are many different types of groups and settings for practice. However, regardless of the type of group, setting, or background of the service provider, it is imperative that the history of aged minority clients be acknowledged and explored as appropriate. It is also recommended that group facilitators make a sensitive and concerted effort to explore, understand, and utilize the cultural strengths of minority older adults.

Although it often is tempting to place people into categories, it is critical for human service providers to understand that there is a great deal of cultural diversity within and among groups of minority elders. Thus, while generalizations are helpful, the group worker still must determine the individual preferences of each member. Therapeutic strategies recommended in this chapter may be applicable to some African-American and some Hispanic older adults but not to others and certainly not to all minorities, although certain concerns, such as the desire for respect, are common to all (see Figure 33-1). Because there continues to be a dearth of empirical data and literature on how to serve older minority adults, the group leader's own cultural sensitivity and willingness to learn are important. As a final point, the importance of enhancing the multilevel empowerment of older minority clients at the individual, family, group, and broader levels cannot be overemphasized.

FIGURE 33-1 *Like African-American and Hispanic elders and many other older adults, these Asian Americans may consider group informality, like using first names, as disrespectful.*

PHOTO: Marianne Gontarz

EXERCISE 1

In a small group of four to seven participants, discuss the statement, "We are all human, and we all have some uniquenesses and differences. But being human, we have a lot in common." What are some of the differences and similarities among the people in your small group as reflected by ethnicity or race?

EXERCISE 2

In a small group, discuss what you think you know about African-American and Hispanic elders; conversely, discuss with members of your small group any gaps in your knowledge and how you might be able to acquire knowledge and skills for enhancing the provision of services to African-American and Hispanic older adults.

EXERCISE 3

Conduct an interview with a minority elder and explore areas of life satisfaction as well as past and current sources of psychosocial stress. How does the interviewee cope with stress (i.e., personal, informal, and formal resources used)? What types of services are needed to resolve the major stressors being experienced by your interviewee?

REFERENCES

Acosta FX, Yamamoto J. 1984. The utility of group work practice for Hispanic Americans. *Soc Work with Groups* 7(3):63-73 (Special Issue: Ethnicity in social group work practice).

Andrews JW. 1989. *Poverty and poor health among elderly Hispanic Americans*. Baltimore: Commonwealth Fund Commission on Elderly People Living Alone.

Andrews JW, Lyons B, Rowland D. 1992. Life satisfaction and peace of mind: A comparative analysis of elderly Hispanic and other elderly Americans. *Clin Gerontol* 11(3/4):21-42.

Applewhite SR, Daley JM. 1988. Cross-cultural understanding for social work practice with the Hispanic elderly. In SR Applewhite (ed.), *Hispanic elderly in transition: Theory, research, policy, and practice* (pp. 3-16). New York: Greenwood.

Arevalo R. 1989. The Latino elderly: Visions of the future. In R Arevalo, R Delgado (eds.), *California Sociologist: J Soc & Soc Work* 12(1):1-7 (Special Issue).

Billingsley A. 1968. *Black families in white America*. Englewood Cliffs, NJ: Prentice-Hall.

Burton L, Devries C. 1992. Challenges and rewards: African-American grandparents as surrogate parents. *Gerontologist* 17(3):51-54.

Cox C, Monk A. 1990. Minority caregivers of dementia victims: A comparison of black and Hispanic families. *J Appl Gerontol* 9(3):340-354.

Cubillos HL, Prieto MM. 1987. *Hispanic elderly: A demographic profile*. Washington, DC: National Council of La Raza, Policy Analysis Center.

Cuellar JB, Harris LC, Jasso R. 1980. An acculturation scale for Mexican-American normal and clinical populations. *Hispanic J Behav Sci* 2(3):199-218.

Dilworth-Anderson P. 1992. Extended kin networks in black families. *Generations* 17(3):29-32.

Franklin JH. 1974. *From slavery to freedom: A history of the Negro*. New York: Knopf.

Gonzalez del Valle A, Usher M. 1982. Group therapy with aged Latino women: A pilot project and study. *Clin Gerontol* 1(1):51-58.

Jackson JJ. 1922. *A compendium of historical facts of the early African Baptist churches*. Bellefontaine, OH: JJ Jackson.

Jones R. 1989. *Black adult development and aging*. Berkeley, CA: Cobb & Henry.

Krajewski-Jaime ER (ed.). 1990. *Empowering Mexican-American elderly: An ecological model to plan culturally sensitive services*. Special Issue: Monograph Series (No. 2). East Lansing, MI: Geriatric Education

Center of Michigan, Eastern Michigan University. [ED: City OK? EMU is in Ypsilanti ??]

Kravits J. 1975. A summary of findings. In R Andersen, J Kravits, OW Anderson (eds.), *Equity in health services: Empirical analyses in social policy* (pp. 257-264). Cambridge, MA: Ballinger.

Lockery SA. 1991. Caregiving among racial and ethnic minority elders: Family and social supports. *Generations* 15(4):58-62.

Manton KG. 1982. Temporal and age variation of United States Black/White cause-specific mortality differentials: A study of the recent changes in the relative health status of the United States black population. *Gerontologist* 22(2):170-179.

Markides KS, Krause N. 1986. Older Mexican Americans. *Generations* 10(4):31-34.

Mayers RS, Souflee F. 1990-91. Utilizing social support systems in the delivery of social services to Mexican-American elderly. *J Appl Soc Sci* 15(1):31-50 (Special Issue: Applications of social support and social network interventions in direct practice).

Mays BE. 1933. *The Negro's church*. New York: Russells.

McAdoo HP. 1987. Blacks. In A Minahan (ed-in-chief), *Encyclopedia of social work*, 18th ed. (pp. 194-206). Silver Spring, MD: National Association of Social Workers.

Mendoza RH, Martinez JL. 1981. The measurement of acculturation. In A Baron Jr. (ed.), *Explorations in Chicano psychology* (pp. 71-82). New York: Holt.

Minkler M, Roe KM, Price M. 1992. The physical and emotional health of grandmothers raising grandchildren in the crack cocaine epidemic. *Gerontologist* 32(6): 752-761.

Miranda M. 1990. Hispanic aging: An overview of issues and policy implications. In U.S. DHHS Pub. No. HRS-P-DV 90-4, *Minority aging: Essential Curricula content for selected health and allied health professions* (pp. 609-622). Washington, DC.

———. 1991. Mental health services and the Hispanic elderly. In M Sotomayor (ed.), *Empowering Hispanic families* (pp. 141-154). Milwaukee: Family Service of America.

Moore JW. 1971. Situational factors affecting minority aging. *Gerontologist* 11(1):88-93.

Morrison JD. 1991. The black church as a support system for black elderly. *J Gerontol Soc Work* 17(1/2):105-120.

National Urban League. 1992. *The state of black America: 1992*. Washington, DC: National Urban League.

Sanchez CD. 1992. Mental health issues: The elderly Hispanic. *J Geriatr Psychiatr* 25(1):69-84.

Schwartz W. 1961. The social worker in the group. In *New perspectives on services to groups: Theory, organization, and practice* (pp. 7-34). New York: National Association of Social Workers.

Sotomayor M, Applewhite SR. 1988. The Hispanic family and the extended multi-generational family. In SR Applewhite (ed.), *Hispanic elderly in transition: Theory, research, policy, and practice* (pp. 121-133). New York: Greenwood.

Sotomayor M, Curiel H (eds.). 1988. *Hispanic elderly: A cultural signature*. Edinburg, TX: Pan American University Press.

Stanford EP. 1992. *Beyond the graying of America: Who cares?* San Diego: San Diego State University Press.

Stanford EP, Yee DL. 1991. Gerontology and the relevance of diversity. *Generations* 15(4):11-14.

Starrett RA, Todd AM, Decker JT. 1989. The use of formal helping networks to meet the psychological needs of the Hispanic elderly. *Hispanic J Behav Sci* 11(3): 259-273.

Sue DW, Sue D. 1990. *Counseling the culturally different: Theory and practice*. New York: Wiley.

Taylor RJ, Chatters LM. 1986. Patterns of informal support to elderly black adults: Family, friends, and church members. *Soc Work* 31(6):432-438.

———. 1991. Extended family networks of older black adults. *J Gerontol: Soc Sci* 46(4):S210-217.

U.S. Bureau of the Census. 1987. *Current population reports*, Series P-20, No. 163. Washington, DC: U.S. Government Printing Office.

Valle R. 1980. Social mapping techniques. A preliminary guide for locating and linking to natural networks. In R Valle, W Vega (eds.), *Hispanic natural support systems* (pp. 113-121). Sacramento: State of California Department of Mental Health.

———. 1990. The Latino/Hispanic family and the elderly: Approaches to cross-cultural curriculum design in health professions. In U.S. DHHS Pub. No. HRS-P-DV 90-4, *Minority aging: Essential Curricula content for selected health and allied health professions* (pp. 433-452). Washington, DC.

Velez CG. 1980. Mexicano/Hispanic support systems and confianza: Theoretical issues of cultural adaptation. In R Valle, W Vega (eds.), *Hispanic natural support systems* (pp. 45-54). Sacramento: State of California Department of Mental Health.

Waller JB Jr. 1991. Health, policy, and aged minorities. In RF Young, EA Olson (eds.), *Health, illness, and disability in later life: Practice issues and interventions* (pp. 83-98). Newbury Park, CA: Sage.

Walls CT. 1992. The role of church and family support in the lives of older African Americans. *Generations* 17(3):33-36.

Warren D. 1975. *Black neighborhoods: An assessment of community power*. Ann Arbor: University of Michigan Press.

Woodruff DS, Birren JE. 1983. *Aging: Scientific perspective and social issues*. Pacific Grove, CA: Brooks/Cole.

Yalom ID. 1985. *The theory and practice of group psychotherapy*, 3d ed. New York: Basic Books.

BIBLIOGRAPHY

Anderson EF. 1980. Program innovation for new and meaningful roles for minority elderly persons. In EP Stanford (ed.), *Aging policy issues for the 1980s*. San Diego: Campanile Press.

Applewhite SR (ed.). 1988. *Hispanic elderly in transition: Theory, research, policy, and practice*. New York: Greenwood.

Barresi CM, Stull D (eds.). 1993. *Ethnic elderly and long-term care*. New York: Springer.

Gelfand DE, Barresi CM (eds.). 1987. *Ethnic dimensions of aging*. New York: Springer.

Jackson J. 1988. *The Black American elderly: Research on physical and psychological health*. New York: Springer.

Markides KS, Mindel CH. 1987. *Aging and ethnicity*. Newbury Park, CA: Sage.

Saleebey D (ed.). 1992. *The strengths perspective in social work practice*. New York: Longman.

Yip B, Stanford EP, Schoenrock SA (eds.). 1988. *Enhancing services to minority elderly*. San Diego: National Resource Center on Minority Aging Populations, University Center on Aging, College of Health and Human Services, San Diego State University.

RESOURCES

Old Black and Alive, 1984. National Black Caucus on the Aged. Through a series of interviews and visits with elderly Black persons in Georgia, the dignity, strength, and individuality of each person is dramatically underscored. This film offers an excellent opportunity to view concerns and perspectives of several black older persons. (Greene 1988, 220).

So Far from Home: Elderly Hispanics in the United States 1984. National Public Radio (140.82.09.15). Washington, DC (Greene 1988, 220).

CHAPTER 34

Research Issues in Group Work

Joann Ivry and Florence S. Schwartz

KEY WORDS

- Data collection
- Informed consent
- Practice-research analog
- Practice-research dichotomy
- Practitioner-researcher model
- Process recording
- Record of service
- Sample
- Standardized research scales
- Summary recording

LEARNING OBJECTIVES

- Identify two reasons for research in group services.
- List and describe two common recording or data collection methods.
- Develop two hypotheses (questions) relevant to your work with groups.
- Evaluate the process of a group session based on the record of services and summaries of recordings.

Group work practice has become an increasingly valued approach to meet the diverse needs of the burgeoning aged population. With the recognition that participation in groups is beneficial for older adults, group services have emerged as an important practice modality. Group workers were among the first human service professionals to organize systematic programs in response to the expanding needs of older people (Shore 1952). Various types of groups have evolved over recent decades to reduce loneliness, increase social interaction, offer support, promote cognitive functioning, foster self-esteem, and assist with age-related transitions.

Group services had their origins in programs designed to serve the well aged, focusing particularly on the use of leisure time. Group programs for senior adults proliferated in settlement houses and community centers where Golden Age clubs flourished. Following this initial focus, group services also developed in response to the needs of frail elders in the community and in institutional settings.

Group practitioners formally acknowledged the significance of the aging phenomenon with a special conference devoted to group practice with the aged. This conference was sponsored by the National Council on Aging, the National Association of Social Workers, and the Public Welfare Association. The conference deliberations resulted in the publication of *Social Group Work with Older People*, a major bibliographical reference for group work with older people (Lowy 1985, 10).

The White House Conference on Aging in 1971 ushered in a new phase in the growth of gerontology as a multidisciplinary field and was also a major impetus toward placing aging on the social and political agenda. Aging had become a serious issue for policymakers and practitioners, and in order to deliver effective service, social and health care professionals required information on the aging process, the needs of the aged, and the evaluation of service effectiveness. Toward the goal of disseminating critical information for professional use, new multidisciplinary journals joined *The Gerontologist* and the *Journal of Gerontology*, which were already in the field. Currently, multidisciplinary practice and research efforts are a reality in gerontology, and research on groups for the aged has and will continue to come from many disciplines, including medicine, psychology, nursing, and social work.

RESEARCH AND PRACTICE

Group services are entering a new phase of development in which it is no longer sufficient to rely on practice wisdom—that is, experience and intuition—to inform practice. The differential application of group services to a diverse aged population requires precise knowledge about the aged, the services that best meet their needs, and careful evaluation of the various group modalities that have evolved to serve them. Such knowledge is accumulated by the systematic acquisition and analysis of data. Through a combination of practice wisdom and a careful monitoring of practice approaches, group services can improve and become more effective.

Despite the assumption of the benefit of group practice and its inherent appeal to provide the elderly with "solace, companionship, and support" (Rose 1991, 180), there has been insufficient attention to the systematic evaluation of the effectiveness of group interventions. Evaluation is the "process of obtaining information about the effects of a single intervention or the effects of the total group experience" (Toseland & Rivas 1984, 303). Program evaluation is a specific domain of research that is goal or outcome oriented, designed to ascertain whether service objectives have been achieved (Smith 1990). Although there have been ever-increasing demands for accountability and for empirically validated practice, resistance to research, specifically program and practice evaluation, exists. A variety of obstacles have impeded the conduct of relevant research about social problems and practice interventions (National Institute of Mental Health 1991).

Moreover, an unfortunate dichotomy has been created between research and practice. Practitioners sometimes have a negative attitude toward research, and tend to perceive research and practice as incompatible. This view emerges from a tension that exists within professional education as to the extent to which practitioners should be trained to do research (Fraser, Jenson & Lewis 1993). The goal of practitioners is to become highly skilled professionals, and only secondarily and reluctantly to engage in monitoring and evaluating practice. Practitioners tend to find research methods esoteric and unapproachable (Gantt, Pinsky, Rock & Rosenberg 1990) and often view research with fear and suspicion (Cheetham 1992). However, the systematic monitoring of one's own practice, which builds upon "accumulated clinical experience" (Weissman, Epstein & Savage 1983, 263) can contribute to the improvement of one's own practice as well as to knowledge building.

Practitioners frequently consider research studies, especially empirical ones using quantitative methods, as irrelevant (Festinger, Turnbull & Moncher 1992). Practitioners believe that quantitative research, which relies on objective measures and statistical manipulations, cannot capture the rich complexity of practice and hence tend to disregard it. The fact that practitioners have limited direct experience in doing research further serves to reinforce resistance to it, and the most that educators have hoped for is that practitioners will become, at least, educated consumers of research.

A further barrier to research in practice is the institutional context in which the research is conducted. To engage in evaluation research in an agency setting is to become involved in the politics of the agency (Smith 1990). Research about practice cannot succeed without institutional support (Toseland & Rivas 1984). In this time of ever-changing service delivery systems and scarce resources, all of which contribute to mounting staff pressures, research is generally considered an unnecessary burden by agencies as well as by practitioners. Research requires considerable financial and professional resources, which agencies usually have little of and which are always at a premium. Furthermore, practitioners are reluctant to sacrifice precious service time reserved for clients in order to engage in research activities. Research is usually perceived as burdensome and time consuming, offering little return for the investment.

In spite of these obstacles, practitioners are encouraged to become practitioner-researchers (Toseland & Rivas 1984) so that they may "participate(s) in the discovery, testing, and reporting of more effective ways of helping clients" (Briar, as quoted by Weissman, Epstein & Savage 1983, 264). The challenge that faces research and practice is to make research interesting and accessible (Gantt, Pinsky, Rock & Rosenberg 1990) so that practitioners may become not only consumers of research but also evaluators of their own practice (NIMH 1991). Practitioners need to assume greater responsibility for the acquisition of practice knowledge (Weissman, Epstein & Savage 1983), as it is only through the evaluation of practice that it can be corrected and advanced. Systematic evaluation of group practice, including positive use of failure, may in the long run improve and strengthen the accuracy and effectiveness of group work practice.

PRACTITIONER-RESEARCHER MODEL

The differential application of group services to the growing, diverse aged population requires more precise knowledge of the effectiveness and benefits of various group modalities. A wealth of knowledge exists naturally within the rich, dynamic world of practice. The extraction of knowledge need not rest within the exclusive domain of professional researchers, but can become part of the "daily routine of practice" (Weinbach 1988, 38). An evolving trend has been to train and encourage practitioners to develop the means to monitor and assess their intervention methods and techniques regularly in order to become knowledgeable and better informed practitioners (Grinnell 1988; Powers, Meenaghan & Toomey 1985; Weissman, Epstein & Savage 1983). The practitioner-researcher model is one that incorporates comfort and familiarity with fundamental research methods so as to produce professionals who "augment their intuition by using research findings, concepts, methods, and skills to enhance their practices" (Grinnell & Siegel 1988, 14).

Practitioners generally consider research and practice as two separate endeavors without a common base or shared framework. Practice and research do share a similar intellectual orientation, however, which has been identified as the problem-solving process or the practice-research analog (Grinnell 1988). When practitioners approach a problem, they engage in an assessment/intervention process that includes the following steps:

1. Problem identification.
2. Collection of relevant information.
3. Interpretation of the information.
4. Understanding of the problem.
5. Formulation of the reasons for the problem.
6. Selection, implementation, and evaluation of an appropriate intervention.

The problem-solving process used by researchers (Grinnell 1988; Royce 1991; Smith 1990; Yegidis & Weinbach 1991) is analogous to the one used by practitioners and involves:

1. Problem identification.
2. Literature review.
3. Development of an hypothesis.
4. Selection of a research design.
5. Data collection.
6. Data analysis.
7. Conclusions and dissemination of results.

The goal of the problem-solving process, for practitioners as well as for researchers, is to gain information about social problems and the interventions designed to ameliorate them.

The practitioner-researcher is not usually expected to conduct experimental research using sophisticated designs, random samples, and control groups. In the first place, agencies generally will not provide practitioners with opportunities for elaborate research studies. Second, the use of control groups presents ethical dilemmas for practitioners, as it implies that control groups may not receive an intervention (Barker 1991; Weissman, Epstein & Savage 1983). Finally, single-subject designs, rather than experimental or quasiexperimental designs, are among the preferred designs developed to conduct practice-based research, as they serve "to bridge the gap between research and practice" (Royce 1991, 55).

The single-subject design is appropriate for small-scale research aimed at evaluating the effectiveness of group or individual interventions (Cetingok & Hirayama 1983; Nelson 1988). The single-subject design provides a framework for collecting data over time on a group or individuals and comparing "baseline data to data collected when an intervention is made" (Toseland & Rivas 1984, 316). Thus, single-subject designs provide for the collection of information about clients and services pre- and postintervention. The independent variable is the planned intervention and the dependent variable is the "behavior, feeling, affect or cognition that we hope will change in the desired direction as a result of our independent variable or treatment intervention" (Nelson 1988, 362).

In general, the practitioner-researcher model takes a broad view of research and proposes that knowledge for practice can be generated through a systematic review of the practitioner's usual activities. Such knowledge-building activities need not be costly, need not rely on complex research methodologies, and should not deprive clients of needed services.

PRACTITIONER-RESEARCHER MODEL FOR GROUP PRACTICE

Group work practitioners need to become familiar with the practitioner-researcher professional model, as they too have a responsibility to contribute to the development of knowledge to advance group work practice. Evaluation of group practice can contribute to knowledge of process and outcome and also can be used to obtain information needed to plan groups, monitor group membership, develop new groups, and test for service effectiveness (Toseland & Rivas 1984). Practitioners wish to understand, for example, why members do or do not attend group meetings, under what conditions interventions succeed or fail, and whether service goals and objectives are achieved. Evaluation of practice also can demonstrate the usefulness of specific group modalities, improve skills, and enable group workers to share their knowledge with others doing similar work.

Before engaging in collecting data, however, practitioners should decide what is the specific focus of the evaluation and what information needs to be collected to answer the questions or hypotheses posed by the study. Concepts need to be clearly defined and stated in terms that can be measured. For example, service effectiveness must be defined and criteria established by which effective service will be judged. (In other words, what is a successful or nonsuccessful intervention? What standard will be used to ascertain whether clients' affect or behavior has been affected by the group intervention?) Specifically, if a practitioner wishes to evaluate whether group members' expressions and feelings of depression were changed by the intervention, then depression must be defined so that it can be clearly evaluated before and after the intervention.

The research sample generally consists of the members of a group who have been informed in advance about the service to be offered and the research protocol. The sample participants are group members who have indicated their willingness to participate in the study by signing a consent form. The sample participants also should be assured of confidentiality and protection from physical and mental harm (Royce 1991). A professional code of ethics guides research on practice, as it guides clinical practice itself (Barker 1991).

RECORDKEEPING

For most group workers, the record is the key instrument for systematically collecting pertinent information. Records have been used in agencies to document information about clients and as a means to hold practitioners accountable for services performed. Generally, records include the reasons for service, the service process, and future service recommendations. Records also include professional observations, client information, and a description of group interactions. For some time, practitioners have been urged to "look to the record" (Kane 1974) to generate knowledge, as records provide an "empirical but nonquantitative approach to diagnostic assessment and treatment planning and evaluation" (Weissman, Epstein & Savage 1983, 269).

Records are a valuable, though underutilized, tool for gathering data. Monitoring or evaluating one's own practice may be accomplished by practitioners directly as most workers write or dictate information about group members, the group process, and services rendered directly into the record. The trend toward standardization of recordkeeping to facilitate computerization of data is rapidly becoming a reality of daily practice. Computerization of data may have a major impact on practice evaluation research, as it will make data collection less cumbersome and hence the research process more accessible to practitioners.

Nevertheless, practitioners often find recording troublesome and time consuming, complaining that recordkeeping is a burdensome task and too complicated to do well. Practitioners often lack time to record completely, and lack of clarity exists as to what should be included in records. Despite frustrations with recordkeeping, records are a standard and convenient vehicle for monitoring practice. A variety of recording instruments have been developed and demonstrate utility for group workers (Toseland & Rivas 1984). These include:

1. *Process recordings*, detailed step-by-step narratives of a group's development. Though time consuming, they provide rich detail and help the worker analyze interactions that occur during group sessions.

2. *Summary recordings*, a more focused and selective form of recording. They focus on critical incidents that occur in a group and are used to monitor a group's progress after each session.

Generally, workers prefer using summary recordings rather than process recordings to indicate what has transpired in group sessions, as the summary recordings are less time consuming to do and more focused. However, whether using process or summary recordings to monitor practice, it is preferable for the group worker to record information about the group soon after each session so that events and dynamic processes are remembered (Toseland & Rivas 1984, 310).

Other methods of recording include:

1. *Record of service*, which asks the group worker to identify the problem or theme that emerges as the main focus of group sessions. Workers are asked to monitor their practice with the group in relation to this particular theme or problem (Getzel, Kurland & Salmon 1987; Garfield and Irizarry 1971).

2. *Group prospectus*, a special tool to evaluate and explore difficulties in the formation of new groups. Practitioners often work with groups that do not get off the ground, terminate prematurely, experience poor attendance, or do not seem to meet members' needs. Often, this is the result of inadequate planning, and hence the group prospectus offers a focus for evaluating the process in the formation of new groups. It consists of seven steps: agency context, purpose, structure, pregroup contact, need, composition, and content (Kurland, Getzel & Salmon 1986).

In addition to workers' direct recording, an observer may be used to record information about the group process. Moreover, automated monitoring devices such as audio and videotape recorders can be an effective and "accurate and unedited" method of collecting information about groups (Toseland & Rivas 1984, 309). Clients can also participate in evaluating service effectiveness by reporting changes in behavior and affect directly to the practitioner or by completing questionnaires. However, client self-reporting may not be accurate or consistent (Toseland & Rivas 1984).

Service effectiveness also can be evaluated through the use of objective, standardized scales that measure specific affect or behavior such as depression, memory, social interaction, and activities of daily living (Greene 1988; Kane & Kane 1981; Toseland & Rivas 1984). Standardized instruments are considered the most valid and reliable means to gather data about service effectiveness and changes in client affect or behavior. Yet practitioners are disinclined to use such measures because they are unfamiliar with them and have not had the training to administer them properly.

CASE VIGNETTE

The opportunity for a novel group intervention is illustrated by the following case vignette. The group was formed for the purpose of reminiscence, using art appreciation as the organizing theme. The group worker used art content from the late-life styles of Matisse and the well-known late Rembrandt self-portraits to encourage discussion about age-related transitions. The group experience met two goals: It offered the members an opportunity for life review, and it provided them with intellectual stimulation as they admired and learned about great works of art.

The Art Appreciation Group[1] was formed for the purpose of using art as a therapeutic tool for both reminiscing and motivation with the elderly. The core group of between eight to ten men and women was culled from well elderly, whose average age is eighty-five years old. They reside in an "enriched housing" complex, which consists of private apartments and a communal dining room, as well as other services.

The group meets weekly to view slides of art masterpieces that have been selected for

---

[1]Overholser D. 1993. Student, Hunter College School of Social Work.

their relevance to the viewing members—specifically those which are emotive. Among the topics explored have been family portraits, work, and leisure, as well as examples from artists' lives that may have applicability. In the last instance, we discussed Matisse's cutouts, a development that emerged late in life when his eyesight prevented his usual artistic expression. Later still, when he could no longer use the scissors, he began tearing colored sheets of paper.

With the exception of one member who prefers a lecture format and displays impatience when others participate, the rest of the members have been able to contribute to the discussions by sharing relevant experiences from their own lives as well as their knowledge of the artist. Discussions have focused on shared losses and the importance of new experiences and continued avenues of learning. A relevant example is the case of Mr. G. Upon entering the group, Mr. G initially shared with me his almost total hearing loss, which he felt would prevent him from being part of the group. In subsequent meetings, Mr. G shared with the group the feelings of isolation which his hearing loss had precipitated. This in turn led other members to share similar feelings of loss and isolation.

A legally blind member particularly empathized with Mr. G and encouraged him to continue attending, as she felt he had interesting comments to make. This encouraged other members to share their feelings about the group and their feelings of isolation and personal inadequacy, even though the sources of discomfort varied. Having shared these feelings with each other seemed to have freed members to creatively consider ways in which they could use their strengths. Mr. G now spends time in the library weekly reading about artists' lives and the ways in which they compensated for their physical losses. He in turn shares this information with the group. Thus, in using an example such as Matisse, group members were able to share their losses, receive support and encouragement, and move forward using the strengths they still possess.

Using a single-subject design, the worker could systematically monitor this group's experience over time. Baseline data such as demographics, health status, behavior, and affect would be compiled at intake. Additionally, it is important to identify the purpose of the group and the method used to select the members. During the course of the intervention, data would be collected about attendance, content, interactions, and a detailed description of the intervention. After the intervention, data would be gathered to measure changes in members' affect and behavior. Careful analysis of the data could yield further or additional directions for treatment as well as better understanding of the level of participation of all the group members.

This vignette demonstrates the wealth of information about the aged and the variety of creative group interventions that are found in daily practice. Unfortunately, such material only sporadically becomes part of the literature on group services, as workers hesitate to present or publish their work. However, practitioners need to become aware of the research potential of their own routine activities. Monitoring and sharing with other professionals the rich data of daily practice is essential for the advancement of group work practice with the aged.

SUMMARY

Group services have emerged as a valued practice modality to serve the needs of a diverse aged population. A variety of group interventions have evolved, and are used by professionals from many disciplines in community and institutional settings. Despite preliminary evidence that suggests that group interventions are beneficial for the aged (Capuzzi, Gross & Friel 1990; Gorey & Cryns 1991), systematic studies have only begun to evaluate their impact.

Group work practitioners, in the course of their usual activities, have accumulated a wealth of information about the effectiveness of various group approaches with the aged. These practitioners have a role in the development of knowledge about group practice with the aged. As practitioners become acquainted and comfortable with the practitioner-researcher model, the potential for contributing to the knowledge base of practice increases substantially. Practitioners and researchers would agree that effective practice is predicated on knowledge and that to help the aged through groups means knowing why, how, and when groups are effective.

EXERCISE 1

Write a summary record of a group meeting. Analyze the major themes that emerge from discussion. How does this meeting reflect other concerns? What else do you need to know, and how would you go about finding out this data?

EXERCISE 2

Apply program evaluation techniques:

The Director of a local senior citizens center notices that the seniors come and eat their hot meal at midday but they do not relate well to one another on a personal or social level. The seniors seem socially isolated and leave the center quickly after they eat. You were hired as a group facilitator. For two months, you direct socialization groups. Your practice instincts tell you that group intervention is working. However, you want to find a more scientific way to determine if your practice is effective in increasing the socialization of your elderly clients. What do you do? (Smith 1990, 8)

REFERENCES

Barker RL. 1991. *The social work dictionary*, 2d. ed. (pp. 273-280). Silver Spring, MD: National Association of Social Workers.

Capuzzi D, Gross D, Friel SE. 1990. Recent trends in group work with elders. *Generations* 14(1):43-48.

Cetingok M, Hirayama H. 1983. Evaluating the effects of group work with the elderly: An experiment using a single-subject design. *Small Group Behav* 14(3):327-335.

Cheetham J. 1992. Evaluating social work effectiveness. *Res Soc Work Pract* (Special Issue) 2(3):265-287.

Festinger T, Turnbull J, Moncher MS. 1992. Training the clinical-researcher. *Res Soc Work Pract* 2(3):324-337.

Fraser MW, Jenson JM, Lewis FR. 1993. Research training in social work: The continuum is not a continuum. *J Soc Work Ed* 29(1):46-62.

Gantt A, Pinsky S, Rock B, Rosenberg E. 1990. Practice and research: An integrative approach. *J Teaching Soc Work* 4(1):129-143.

Garfield GP, Irizarry CR. 1971. The Record of Service: Describing social work practice. In W Schwartz, SR Zalba (eds.), *The practice of group work* (pp. 241-265). New York: Columbia University Press.

Getzel G, Kurland R, Salmon R. 1987. Teaching and learning the practice of social group work: Four curriculum tools. In J Lassner, K Powell, E Finnegan (eds.), *Social group work: Competence and values in practice* (pp. 35-50). New York: Haworth.

Gorey KM, Cryns AG. 1991. Group work as an intervention modality. *J Gerontol Soc Work* 16(1/2):137-157.

Greene RR. 1988. *Continuing education for gerontological careers*. Washington, DC: Council on Social Work Education.

Grinnell RM Jr. 1988. *Social work research and evaluation*, 3d ed. Itasca, IL: Peacock.

Grinnell RM Jr, Siegel DH. 1988. The place of research in social work. In RM Grinnell Jr, *Social work research and evaluation*, 3d ed. (pp. 9-24). Itasca, IL: Peacock.

Kane RA. 1974. Look to the record. *Soc Work* 19(4):412-419.

Kane RL, Kane RA. 1981. *Assessing the elderly: A practical guide to management*. Lexington, MA: Heath.

Kurland R, Getzel G, Salmon R. 1986. Sowing groups in fertile fields: Curriculum and other strategies to overcome resistance to new groups. In M Parnes (ed.), *Innovations in social groupwork: Feedback from practice to theory* (pp. 57-74). New York: Haworth.

Lowy L. 1985. *Social work with the aging: The challenge and promise of the later years*, 2d ed. New York: Longman.

National Institute of Mental Health. 1991. *Building social work knowledge for effective services and policies: A plan for research and development*. Austin, TX.

Nelson J. 1988. Single subject design. In RM Grinnell Jr., *Social work research and evaluation*, 3d ed. (pp. 362-399). Itasca, IL: Peacock.

Powers GT, Meenaghan TM, Toomey B. 1985. *Practice focused research: Integrating human service practice and research*. Englewood Cliffs, NJ: Prentice-Hall.

Rose SR. 1991. Small group processes and interventions with the elderly. In KHK Paul (ed.), *Serving the elderly:*

Skills for practice (pp. 167-186). New York: Aldine de Gruyter.

Royce D. 1991. *Research methods in social work.* Chicago: Nelson-Hall Publishers.

Shore H. 1952. Group work program development in homes for the aged. *Soc Serv Rev* 26(2):181-194.

Toseland R, Rivas RF. 1984. *An introduction to group work practice.* New York: Macmillan.

Smith MJ. 1990. *Program evaluation in human services.* New York: Springer.

Weinbach RW. 1988. Agency and professional contexts in research. In RM Grinnell Jr (ed.), *Social work research and evaluation,* 3d ed. (pp. 25-41). Itasca, IL: Peacock.

Weissman H, Epstein I, Savage A. 1983. *Agency-based social work: Neglected aspects of clinical practice* (pp. 262-299). Philadelphia: Temple University Press.

Yegidis BL, Weinbach RW. 1991. *Research methods for social workers.* New York: Longman.

BIBLIOGRAPHY

Anderson JD. 1986. Integrating research and practice in social work with groups. *Soc Work with Groups* 9(3): 11-124.

Feldman RA. 1986. Group work knowledge and research. In SD Rose, RA Feldman (eds.), Research in social group work. *Soc Work with Groups* 9(3):7-14.

Garvin CD. 1988. Group theory and research. In A Minahan (ed.), *Encyclopedia of social work,* 18th ed. (pp. 682-696). Washington, DC: National Association of Social Workers.

Gilchrist LD, Schinke SP. 1988. Research ethics. In RM Grinnell Jr, *Social work research and evaluation,* 3d ed. (pp. 65-79). Itasca, IL: Peacock.

Ginsberg R. 1986. The log: A creative and powerful teaching tool in social work education. *Soc Work with Groups* 8(4):95-105.

Ivry J. 1992. Teaching geriatric assessment. *J Gerontol Soc Work* 18(3/4):3-22.

Lindsey D, Kirk SA. 1992. The continuing crises in social work research: Conundrum or solvable problem? An essay review. *J Soc Work Ed* 28(3):370-382.

Robb SS, Stegman CE, Wolanin MO. 1986. No research versus research with compromised results: A study of validation therapy. *Nurs Res* 35(2):113-118.

Rose S, Feldman RA (eds.). 1986. Research in social group work. *Soc Work with Groups* (Special Issue) 9(3).

Rothman B, Fike D. 1987. To seize the moment: Opportunities in the CSWE standards for group work research. *Soc Work with Groups* 10(4):91-109.

Toseland R, Siporin M, Gazda GM, MacKensie K. 1986. When to recommend group treatment: A review of the clinical and research literature. *Int J Group Psychother* 36(2):171-201.

Weil M. 1984. Involvement of senior citizens in needs assessment and service planning. In FS Schwartz (ed.), *Voluntarism and social work practice: A growing collaboration.* Lanham, MD: University Press of America.

Weisman CB, Schwartz P. 1989. Worker expectations in groupwork with the frail elderly: Modifying the model for a better fit. *Soc Work with Groups* 12(3):47-55.

Yesavage JA, Brink TL, Rose TL, Adey M. 1983. The geriatric depression rating scale: Comparisons with other self-report and psychiatric rating scales. In T Cook, S Ferris, R Bartus (eds.), *Assessment in geriatric psychopharmacology* (pp. 153-167). New Canaan, CT: Mark Powley Associates.

Yordi CL, Chu AS, Ross KM, Wong SJ. 1982. Research and the frail elderly: Ethical and methodological issues in controlled experiments. *Gerontologist* 22(1):72-77.

Author Index

Subject Index

incapacitation, 94
mental problems, 12, 185
multiple problems, 94
   need for generalists, 94
physical problems, 12
Old-old, 135
Oldest-old, 8, 9, 131, 135 (def.),
   136 (table)
common disabling conditions,
   135
health of, 135, 136 (table)
Omnibus Budget Reconciliation
   Act of 1987 (OBRA '87), 3,
   5, 12
Outpatient clinic, 94, 99

Personhood, 8, 21 (def.)
Physical impairments, 130-138
arthritis, 131, 132, 135, 136
breathing, 131
diabetes, 131, 132, 136
hearing impairments, 131, 132,
   134
heart disease, 132, 135
incontinence, 131, 135, 136
pain, 94, 132
Parkinson's disease, 121, 131
pulmonary embolus, 94
visual impairments, 131, 134,
   135, 136
Poetry groups, 30
Population projections, 10
Preadmission screening and annual
   resident review (PASARR),
   12
Preceptors, 67, 93
Preventive health care, 68-69
Privacy, 49
Probing, 184
Professional programs, 353-361
students in (beginning,
   advanced), 353-354
Props, 103, 157-159, 168
Prostheses, 134
Prospective payments, 21
Diagnosis-Related Groups
   (DRGs), 21
to hospitals, 12
Psychotherapy groups, 32-33

Quality of life, 126, 136

Reality orientation groups, 27,
   139-152
case study, 145-148
conducted by nurses, 308-309
definition, 139
history of, 140
literature review of, 14
and props, 145, 146 (table)
Reality testing, 139-140
Reality therapy, 139-140
Recreation therapy, 318-332
activities
   analysis of, 322-327
   classification, 320
   modification, 321, 327-329
benefits, 319
definition, 318
history, 318-319
OBRA '87, effect of, 319-320
strategies, 329
Refreshments, 94, 123
and dehydration, 122
Reminiscence
and the cognitively impaired,
   123, 170
definition, 164, 180
differentiation from life review,
   164
documentation of, 17 (table)
flashbulb memories, 169
meaning of, 170
typologies of, 165 (table)
uses of, 167-169
Reminiscence therapy groups 29,
   163-178
and affluent members, 170
and alert members, 170
and clinical practice, 171-172
as conducted by nurses,
   309-310
descriptors of group experience
   in, 171 (table)
empirical studies, 166-167
literature review, 163, 166
props for, 168
purposes of, 165-166
and research, 172-173
themes in, 168, 169 (table)
Remotivation groups, 28, 139-152
case study, 157-159
as conducted by nurses, 309

evaluation of, 159
history of, 153
literature review of, 154-155
member selection, 156
props, 157-159
steps for conducting, 155-157
Research, 393-400
agency attitudes, 394
barriers
   institutional, 394
   practitioner resistance, 394,
     395
   resources, 394
   time, 394
benefits, 395, 396, 398
data collection, 396
evaluation of, 395
practitioner-researcher, models
   for, 395-396
quantitative versus qualitative,
   394
records as source, 396-397
   forms of recording, 397
single-subject design, 395-396
Retirement communities, 240-249
changing over time, 241
Road blocks in groups, 93
Roles
dependency, 93
leadership, 92

Sabotage (of group leaders), 99
reduction of, 100
Safety, 124
Scribotherapy, 30
Seating arrangments
of co-leaders, 44
of leaders, 95 (figures)
Self
assessment, 104, 110
awareness, 179
concept, 8, 21 (def.)
disclosure of, 187
esteem, 102, 179, 180
in later life, 16-17
perception of, 8, 21 (def.)
Sensory defects, 95, 122
Sensory deprivation, 95
Sensory stimulation, 123
Senior centers, 3-4
Sex differences, 10